My Generation

William Styron

COLLECTED NONFICTION

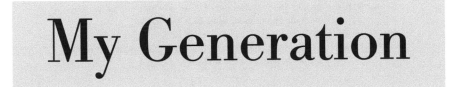

My Generation

Edited by James L. W. West III

Foreword by Tom Brokaw

RANDOM HOUSE

NEW YORK

Copyright © 2015 by Rose Styron
Foreword copyright © 2015 by Tom Brokaw

Published in the United States by Random House, an imprint and division of
Penguin Random House LLC, New York.

RANDOM HOUSE and the HOUSE colophon are registered trademarks
of Penguin Random House LLC.

Library of Congress Cataloging-in-Publication Data
Styron, William, 1925–2006, author.
[Essays. Selections]
My generation : collected nonfiction / William Styron ; edited by James L. W. West III.
pages cm
Includes index.
ISBN 978-0-8129-9705-7
eBook ISBN 978-0-8129-9706-4
I. West, James L. W., editor. II. Title.
PS3569.T9A6 2015
814'.54—dc23
2014038029

Printed in the United States of America on acid-free paper

www.atrandom.com

2 4 6 8 9 7 5 3 1

First Edition

Book design by Jo Anne Metsch

Foreword

TOM BROKAW

A few years ago I made a pilgrimage to Rowan Oak, the stately but deserted home of William Faulkner in Oxford, Mississippi, and wandered through the great man's library.

Even in midday light it was a dim, dusty room with no furniture, but the shelves were lined with books. By chance, one caught my eye: *Lie Down in Darkness*, the first novel by my friend Bill Styron of the Virginia Tidewater.

In his inscription which as I recall Bill addressed to "Mr. Faulkner," Styron introduced himself a young Southern writer and explained that this was his first novel.

It was thrilling just to hold the book and imagine the day Faulkner received it, smoking his pipe, turning it over, reading the inscription, perhaps carrying it into the room where I now stood.

That and more came back to me as I read Bill's account for *Life* magazine of Faulkner's death and funeral. It was Styron as reporter, gracefully moving through the "hot, sweaty languor bordering on desperation."

"People in Mississippi have learned to move gradually, almost timidly, in this climate," he wrote. "Black and white, they walk with both caution and deliberation."

And in this collection of nonfiction about his generation and time, Styron is deliberate but neither cautious nor timid.

He writes about his generation, the South, and race with a voice that is at once lyrical and unsparing. Bill, the grandson of a slave owner, describes himself as practically a brother to James Baldwin, the tiny, fiery African American who wrote with uncompromising passion about the long overdue need for racial equality.

As you might expect, there are several references to *The Confesions of Nat Turner,* Styron's initially successful novel based on the true story of a rebellious slave in the nineteenth century who led a revolt against slave owners.

It was scheduled to become, as they say, a major motion picture, but by then the black consciousness movement was in full voice and Styron was condemned as a "whitey," incapable of writing about a black hero.

Race is a continuing theme for this son of the South, as it has been for many white Southern writers, and Styron takes it north, into his adopted state of Connecticut, to the murder trial of a mentally challenged black man with a lifetime of poverty. His guilt was indisputable, but a death sentence— was that justice? Would it have been for a white defendant with the same limits?

Reading this evocative collection reminded me of the excitement I felt as a young man in the fifties, knowing that James Jones would be out with a new novel, or Truman Capote, James Dickey, Terry Southern, Nelson Algren, Philip Roth. They're all here, Styron's boon companions, and by extension ours as well.

It was a golden time in American literature, as this new generation took hold of social issues and made them the stuff of great books. They also were masters of the nonfiction form, as Styron is here.

Mailer's provocative essays on Vietnam. Capote on murder in Kansas. Roth on social issues. John Updike's peerless farewell to Ted Williams at Fenway. They made way for Joyce Carol Oates and Joan Didion, who moved gracefully between fiction and nonfiction.

In another nonfiction book, Bill wrote about his bout with depression, a haunting and yet instructive guide for others who were dealing with similar issues. Two of his closest friends were also struggling with depression. Art Buchwald and Mike Wallace often walked the beaches of Martha's Vineyard with Bill as a kind of three-man support group.

Art later complained, in his Buchwaldian way, "We all had depression, but Bill was the only one who made money out of it."

Styron was meant for the literary life and the people who occupy it. Here he pays tribute to their work and personalities. He also shares his affection for his life-mate, the indomitable Rose, and their four spirited children. Styron would be incomplete without them.

Thank you, Bill, for sharing.

Contents

Presidential

Reports

Literary

Antecedents

Friends and Contemporaries

Crusades, Complaints, Gripes

Bagatelles

Amours

In Closing

Editor's Note

My Generation includes all individual pieces of writing from William Styron's two previous collections of nonfiction: forty-four items from *This Quiet Dust* and fourteen from *Havanas in Camelot*. To these have been added thirty-three new items—essays, memoirs, op-eds, articles, eulogies, speeches—seven of them previously unpublished. The result is a comprehensive collection that covers a period of fifty years, from October 7, 1951, when Styron published an autobiographical note in the *New York Herald Tribune Book Review,* to August 19, 2001, when he delivered a tribute to Philip Roth at the MacDowell Colony. *My Generation* is not, however, an omnium gatherum. A full listing of Styron's published nonfiction is provided in the back matter of this book; his papers at Duke University contain additional items that have not yet seen print. Most of these writings will likely be included, some years hence, in a collected edition of Styron's works. For now, *My Generation* brings together his most important essays, reviews, and memoirs and demonstrates the high quality and wide range of his achievement in nonfiction.

This Quiet Dust, the only nonfiction collection that Styron published during his lifetime, exists in two editions. The first was published by Random House in 1982, the second by Vintage Books in 1993. For the Vintage edition Styron added six previously uncollected essays and substituted a later reminiscence of his friend James Jones for the memoir that he had included in the 1982 edition. Styron prepared a good deal of new writing for the edition of 1982: a "Note to the Reader"; separate introductions to three of the sections; and a further report on the fate of Benjamin Reid, the prisoner whose cause he had originally taken up in 1962. Of these materials only the report on Reid, called "Aftermath of 'Aftermath,'" is included here. The other pieces were prepared specifically for *This Quiet Dust* and belong with that volume, which remains in print. *Havanas in Camelot,* published in 2008, two years after Styron's death, is also still in print, as is *Darkness Visible,* Styron's memoir of depression, a separate work of nonfiction that is one of his great achievements.

Styron organized the items in *This Quiet Dust* into eleven sections. Following his example I have grouped the writings in *My Generation* into sixteen categories. Most of the items within each category are presented chronologically, by date of composition or publication, but I have departed from this practice occasionally to allow items to play against one another or to show the progress of Styron's thinking on a particular issue over time.

For previously collected items in *My Generation,* I have followed the texts from *This Quiet Dust* and *Havanas in Camelot.* For heretofore uncollected writings, I have used the texts of first periodical or newspaper appearances. When a manuscript or typescript version of an individual item survives in Styron's papers, I have checked the published text against that earlier text. Apart from a few typos, however, I have found no significant variations. Occasionally a magazine or newspaper was compelled to shorten a piece of writing for space; in these cases the longer version is published here. The texts of the previously unpublished items are taken from manuscripts or typescripts among Styron's papers. A citation giving date of publication or composition appears within brackets at the end of each item. Styron's annotations from *This Quiet Dust* have been preserved. I have added several editorial annotations, marked by my initials. A few other notes and citations appear in the back matter of the volume.

In the spring of 1989 Styron was invited to review Michael Shnayerson's biography of Irwin Shaw for *Vanity Fair*. Styron began writing the review and set down some two thousand words, intending to provide a full reminiscence of his friend, who had served as an early supporter and mentor. At this point Styron was informed by the editors at *Vanity Fair* that the magazine wanted only one thousand words. Styron recalibrated and produced a review of that length, much shorter on incident and detail. This review appeared in the August 1989 issue. For this volume, I have combined the original two-thousand-word beginning, previously unpublished, with an abbreviated version of the *Vanity Fair* text. The abbreviations eliminate repetitions; the juncture between the two versions is indicated by three asterisks. This portmanteau text appears in the section "Friends and Contemporaries." Manuscripts of both versions survive in Styron's papers at Duke, and the full *Vanity Fair* text is available online at the website of that magazine. The original two-thousand-word beginning appears in *My Generation* in its entirety.

Styron was primarily a novelist, but he took quite seriously his role as a public author and invested a good deal of effort and energy in the composition of his nonfiction. He was closely attuned to the issues and concerns of his time: as the years passed and he found himself unable to move forward with his fiction, he turned increasingly to the essay and op-ed forms to put his ideas on the record. He was also a good memoirist and found the form an agreeable one in which to write. During his last years he produced much excellent nonfiction, including "Nat Turner Revisited," "Prozac Days, Halcion Nights," "Auschwitz and Hiroshima," "A Case of the Great Pox," "Havanas in Camelot," and "A Wheel of Evil Come Full Circle." All of these pieces are included here, together with much other noteworthy writing from earlier in his career. It is my belief that he would have been pleased by the publication of this volume.

J.L.W.W. III
May 1, 2014

Apprenticeship

Autobiographical

I was born in Newport News, Va., in June of 1925, and after two and a half years in the Marines and a brief editorial job, I met Hiram Haydn, who encouraged me to start a novel, which I did. It took me three years to finish, writing steadily and living variously in Durham, N.C., Nyack, N.Y., and on West 88th Street. The process of writing the book was very painful. I wrote it in longhand on large yellow sheets, and some days, after three or four hours of pacing and thinking and listening to music, I managed to put down as much as forty or fifty words. Toward the end, though—last winter—the thing became clearer to me, and the Marine Corps was breathing down my neck again, so I began to write pretty fast; the final seventy or eighty pages, in fact, I wrote in less than three weeks.

I was called up last spring to the 8th Marines training at Camp Lejeune, N.C. Though I have now been returned to inactive duty, like all my fellow Marine reservists, who for the second time in ten years have had their families, jobs, and lives generally disrupted, I am pretty much in the dark about the future.

I would like to go to Europe, and to read a lot more than I've been doing lately. I would like to discover the moral and political roots of our trouble, and to learn why it has come about that young men, like my friends at Lejeune and, more particularly, in places like Korea, have to suffer so endlessly in our time. If I found out why all this has come about I'd be able to write intelligently and without so much of the self-conscious whimper that characterized a lot of the writing of the '20s, and consequently perhaps I'd be able to commemorate not a lost generation but a generation that never was even found, and work out, to my own satisfaction at least, a vision of hope for the future. But it will require more study and more thinking.

[*New York Herald Tribune Book Review,* October 7, 1951. Written for the publication of *Lie Down in Darkness,* by invitation from the newspaper.]

The Prevalence of Wonders

I hardly think that anyone in so short a space can do much justice to what he believes, and perhaps least of all should this be attempted by any writer, whose works, finally, should be sufficient expression of his credo. Lots of writers find themselves hopelessly baffled when it comes to dealing with ideas, and even though I suspect that this is a grave and lazy weakness, I nonetheless count myself among the group and, in a symposium of this sort, flounder about in a vague wonderland of notes and inconclusive jottings. But I was asked to write a "frank and honest statement of your feelings about your art, your country, and the world," so I will proceed, as frankly and as honestly as I can.

About my art: I know little of the mechanics of criticism and have been able to read only a very few critics, but I respect those people—critics and readers—who feel that the art of writing is valuable, since, like music or sailing or drinking beer, it is a pleasure, and since, at its best, it does something new to the heart. I for one would rather listen to music or go sailing, or drink beer while doing both, than talk about literature, but I am not averse to talking about it at all, just as lawyers talk about law and surgeons about surgery. And I take it quite seriously. I have no conscious illusions of myself as teacher or preacher; I do know that when I feel that I have been writing my

best I am aware of having gathered together some of the actualities of myself and my experience, projected these whole and breathing on the page,
and thereby have enjoyed some peculiar poetic fulfillment. This is a self-
indulgence; but I trust that it sometimes approaches art, a word which I'm
not ashamed to use from time to time, and I trust that it might also please
some reader, that person who, in my most avid self-indulgence, I am not so
ingenuous as ever really to forget. So I might say that I am not interested in
writing propaganda, but only in that sort of personal propaganda engendered by afternoons of vicious solitude and the weird, joyful yearning which
it pleases oneself to think, just for a couple of seconds, that Bach must have
felt. If out of all this, placed as vividly as I can place them in their moment
in time, there are people who emerge worthy of a few moments of someone's recollection, I am satisfied. Good people and bad people—bad enough
to justify the truth at every signpost in one's most awful nightmares, good
enough to satisfy every editor on *Time* magazine and so much the worse.

I would like to say something in regard to my feelings about America. I
have lived in France and Italy for something over a year now—not a long
time but long enough for me to feel well ahead in my postgraduate education. I have been here under a large handicap, though a handicap which, as
I will try to demonstrate, might have its redeeming qualities. This handicap
may be explained simply by the fact that I am one of those people who are
unable to enjoy a painting, a piece of sculpture, a work of architecture, or,
for that matter, practically any visually artistic representation. To suffer such
a lack while in Italy is somewhat like being let loose, while suffering from
ulcers, on one of those wonderful, large West Side delicatessens; yet, as
Clive Bell, to whom I have run for refuge as apologist, so sympathetically
points out in his essay called "The Aesthetic Hypothesis," there *are* people
congenitally incapable of such an experience, just as there are people born
without the sense of smell, and no more to be blamed than their equally
sensitive friends who can visualize in the aerial, clear abstractions of a Vivaldi
concerto, only horses galloping, nymphs and shepherds, or the first girl they
ever kissed.[1] So, deprived as I am in a place so rich in wonders as Rome of
the means to assimilate those wonders, I have been thrown a bit on my own
devices, so that my viewpoint, as an American living abroad, has probably
often been closer to Burbank and his Baedeker among the ruins of Venice
than any number of generations of comfortably adjusted artists.[2] Many people can feel the true rapture at the façade of Chartres, and these are no

doubt a step further toward an affection for France and its people than the aesthetically more limited who, attuned to the nightclubs of Montparnasse or escargots primarily, are outraged, stricken, and resentful when it dawns upon them that the French consider them jackasses. Not all art lovers, of course, are nice people. But a warm and tolerant feeling of brotherhood for man is, I believe, often measured by the extent of one's love for man's monuments and man's artifacts; and not a few American tourists, like myself, don't know a Piero from a peanut.°

I think this blindness of mine, though, has had its worthy effects, for if it has helped to keep me from understanding the more beautiful things about Europe it has also conspired with a sort of innate and provincial aloofness in my nature to make me much more conscious of my *modern* environment, and self-consciously aware of my emotions as an American within that environment. And thus at last, after more than a year, I think that I am as "adjusted" as I ever will be, having succumbed neither to the blandishments of exile nor to any illusions of a faultless America. There cannot be much dogma about nations when one lives in One World, eighteen hours from home, and for me now things are pretty well balanced.

The "U.S. Go Home" signs no longer offend me, since I have learned that they are the work of Communists and don't mean *me* but the American army encamped nearby. I have even come to the point where I can sympathize with the signs and ask myself: "Suppose New York were full of Swedish soldiers all mouthing orders for beer in an alien, thick, jaw-breaking tongue. Would I not want to scrawl 'Swedes go home!' on every available wall?" I have learned, too, that anti-Americanism is many different things: unjustified among the spoiled and snobbish Italian upper class, with whom it's currently in vogue, and among whom was the famous actress heard at a party recently to utter the most slanderous anti-American remarks, and enplane the next day, via TWA, for New York; justified when a Parisian reads about McCarthy in *Le Figaro,* or when our most widely read weekly editorializes upon France and compares it to a whore; nonexistent, finally, among most Italians whose happiest tradition has been an inability to be anti-anything and each of whom has a cousin in Brooklyn.

What I suppose I've really learned is the elderly truism that all of us can

---

° Piero della Francesca (ca. 1415–1492), Italian painter of the early Renaissance period.—J.W.

learn something from each other. That whereas our radios are better, no car from Detroit can match a fleet, shiny Alfa Romeo; that our planes work, crack up less often, and are generally on time, but that the dreadful snarl on Madison Avenue might be alleviated by a study of the marvelous Paris bus system; that, on the other hand, a bottle of Châteauneuf-du-Pape is ambrosia, indeed, but that there's still nothing like a Coca-Cola on a hot summer day, as every Frenchman knows but won't admit; that the man from Chicago gobbling hamburgers on the Champs-Élysées is undoubtedly a fool, but there is something wonderful to be said about his brother, the July tourist with his straw hat and his lurid tie and his camera, and his almost pathetic eagerness to find, in a strange land, some kind of dazzling and miraculous enlightenment: sometimes his manners are bad but he's making the effort at least, and one finds few French tourists outside of France; that our mass production is the world's finest: "Oh," says the American, "your Italian sports cars are great, but in the States everyone can own a car." "But Signore," is the reply, "here not everyone *wants* a car"; that our Park Avenue head-feelers are the very best: "But Signore, here we do not *need* psychoanalysis." It's simply a matter of balance.

One must end a credo on the word "endure," but I think we will do just that—Americans and Italians and Frenchmen, in spite of all those who threaten us momentary harm. Humans have become involved too much in life, and the wonders are too thick about us, to be daunted by a handful of madmen who always, somehow, fall. The hope of heaven has flowered so long among us that I just can't envision that hope blighted out in our time, or any other, for that matter; perhaps the miseries of our century will be recalled only as the work of a race of strange and troublous children, by the wise men in the aeons which come after us. Meanwhile, the writers keep on writing, and I should like to think that what we write will be worth remembering.

[*Nation,* May 2, 1953. This was Styron's contribution to a symposium on creativity. The other contributors were James Jones, Maude Hutchins, Leonard Bishop, Jefferson Young, and John H. Griffin.]

Moviegoer

For seven or eight months during my fourteenth year I kept a diary. This was in the late 1930s, when I was living in southern Virginia with my father and a male cousin a little older than I—my mother having died a year before. Because of the absence of my mother there was considerably less discipline in the household than there ordinarily might have been, and so the diary—which I still possess—is largely a chronicle of idleness. The only interruptions to appear amid the daily inertia are incidents of moviegoing. The diary now records the fact that hardly a day went by without my cousin and me attending a film, and on weekends we often went more than once. In the summertime, when we had no school, there was a period of ten days when we viewed a total of sixteen movies. Mercifully, it must be recorded, movies were very cheap during those years at the end of the Great Depression. My critical comments in the diary were invariably laconic: "Pretty good." "Not bad." "Really swell movie." I was fairly undemanding in my tastes. The purely negative remarks are almost nonexistent.

Among the several remarkable features about this orgy of moviegoing there is one that stands out notably: nowhere during this brief history is there even the slightest mention of my having read a book. As far as reading was concerned, I may as well have been an illiterate sharecropper in Alabama. So one might ask: how does a young boy, exposed so numbingly and monotonously to a single medium—the film—grow up to become a writer of fiction? The answer, I believe, may be less complicated than one might suppose. In the first place, I would like to think that, if my own experience forms an example, it does not mean the death of literacy or creativity if one is drenched in popular culture at an early age. This is not to argue in favor of such a witless exposure to movies as I have just described—only to say that the very young probably survive such exposure better than we imagine, and grow up to be readers and writers. More importantly, I think my experience demonstrates how, at least in the last fifty or sixty years, it has been virtually impossible for a writer of fiction to be immune to the influence of film on his work, or to fail to have movies impinge in an important way on his creative consciousness.

Yet I need to make an immediate qualification. I do not wish to argue matters of superiority in art forms. But although I cannot be entirely objective, I must say here that as admirable and as powerful a medium as the cinema is, it cannot achieve that complex synthesis of poetic, intellectual, and emotional impact that we find in the very finest novels. At their best, films are of course simply wonderful. A work like *Citizen Kane* or *The Treasure of the Sierra Madre* (by one of the greatest of directors, John Huston, who, interestingly enough, began his career as a writer) is each infinitely superior, in my opinion, to most novels aspiring to the status of literature. But neither of these estimable works attains for me the aesthetic intensity of, say, William Faulkner in a book like *The Sound and the Fury,* or comes close to the profound beauty and moral vision of the novel that, more than any other, determined my early course as a writer: *Madame Bovary.*

After saying this, however, I feel obliged to confess without apology to the enormous influence the cinema has had on my own writing. Here I am not speaking of films in any large sense contributing to my philosophical understanding of things; even the films of Ingmar Bergman and Luis Buñuel, both of whom I passionately admire, fail to achieve that synthesis I mentioned before. While a fine movie has changed my perceptions for days, a great novel has altered my way of thinking for life. No, what I am speaking of is technique, style, mood—the manner in which remembered episodes in films, certain attitudes and gestures on the part of actors, little directorial tricks, even echoes of dialogue have infiltrated my work.

I am not by nature a creature of the eye (in the sense that I respond acutely to painting or pictorial representation; I vibrate instead to music) but I'm certain that the influence of films has caused my work to be intensely visual. I clearly recollect much of the composition of my first novel, *Lie Down in Darkness,* which I finished when I was twenty-five. So many scenes from that book were set up in my mind as I might have set them up as a director. My authorial eye became a camera, and the page became a set or soundstage upon which my characters entered or exited and spoke their lines as if from a script. This is a dramatic technique that by no means necessarily diminishes the literary integrity of a novel; it is, as I say, a happy legacy of many years of moviegoing, and it has resonance still in my latest work, *Sophie's Choice.* For example, I wrote the scene toward the end of the film where Stingo ascends the stairs in the rooming house to view the dead bodies of Sophie and Nathan with such an overpowering sense of viewing it through the eyepiece of a movie camera that when I saw the episode recreated in the film I had a stunning sense of déjà vu, as if I myself had photographed the scene, directed it, rather than written it in a book.

Indeed, the film version of *Sophie's Choice* gives me an excellent opportunity to sum up my attitudes toward the relationship between literature and the cinema. Alan Pakula's production is, I think, a remarkably faithful adaptation of the novel, the kind of interpretation that every writer of novels ideally longs for but almost never receives. When I first saw the film it was a joy to note the smooth, almost seamless way the story unfolded in scrupulous fidelity to the way I had told it; there were no shortcuts, no distortions or evasions, and the sense of satisfaction I felt was augmented by the splendid photography, the subtle musical score, and, above all, the superb acting, especially Meryl Streep's glorious performance, which of course is already part of film history. What then, when it was all over, was the cause of my nagging uneasiness, the sense that something was missing?

Suddenly I realized that much that had been essential to the novel had been quietly eliminated, so much that I could scarcely catalog the vanished items: the important digression on racial conflict, the philosophical meditations on Auschwitz, the intense eroticism between Sophie and Nathan, the exploration of anti-Semitism in Poland, even certain characters I had considered crucial to the novel—these were but a few of the aspects which were gone. Yet in no sense did I feel betrayed. After calm reflection I understood the necessity for the absence of these components: many things had to go; otherwise a ten-hour film would have ensued. But more significantly, those elements which had been so carefully integrated into the novel, and which were so important both to its execution and to that sense of density and complicity which makes a novel the special organism it is, were those which most likely would have ruined the film had there been an attempt to include them.

Thus the film had to be not a visual replica of the novel—such was impossible—but a skeleton upon which was hung only the merest suggestion of the novel's flesh. For me it illustrated more graphically than anything the necessity for not expecting a film to perform a novel's work. The two art forms—basically so different—coexist but rarely achieve a coupling. At best, a film (like *Sophie's Choice*) can take on a felicitous resemblance, as in a fine translation of a poem from a difficult language. And that is no small achievement. But even the most satisfied moviemaker will say, if he is honest, that for the true experience one must return to that oldest source—the written word—and confront the original work.

[*Le Figaro*, May 7–8, 1983.]

Christchurch

In December of the second of my two years at Christchurch, there occurred an event which would decisively alter my life and the lives of my
friends here at school and indeed people everywhere. On that day—it
was a mild and golden and cloudless Sunday—I had taken illegal leave of
the campus and had gone on a gently beer-soaked automobile ride through
this incomparable Virginia countryside, which was beautifully forlorn and
wild-looking in those days. It was a wintry, leafless afternoon—very bright,
as I say—with no hint in it of menace. My companions on the ride that afternoon were a classmate named Bill Bowman and two girls from Urbanna,
who even at this late date shall remain nameless. Bowman, besides being a
year older than I was, was a native of New York City, and thus I trusted him
in sophisticated matters, such as beer. The beer we were drinking out of
brown bottles, purchased stealthily the day before at Cooks' Corners, was a
vile concoction called Atlantic, so crudely brewed that gobbets of yeast
floated in it like snowflakes. I earnestly hope it is no longer being manufactured. At any rate, our car and its occupants finally ended up down the road
in West Point, where, inhaling the sweet fumes of the paper mill's hydrogen
sulfide (intense and ripe even on the Sabbath), we dismounted at a seedy
little café for hamburgers. It was while we were in this dive, eating hamburgers and surreptitiously swilling the foul Atlantic, that the waitress came
to the table and announced the perplexing and rather horrible radio news.

I'll never forget her homely face, which was like a slab of pale pine with two small holes bored in it, nor her voice, which had all the sad languor of the upper Pamunkey River. "The Japanese," she said, "they done bombed Pearl Harbor." Her expression contained a certain real fear. "God help us," she went on, "it's so close. Imagine them gettin' all the way to South Carolina."

That woman's knowledge of geography was only a little less informed than our own, and the next day—as we sat in study hall listening to the radio and President Roosevelt's call for a declaration of war against the Axis powers—few of us sitting there could realize how irrevocably things would be changed—for us and the world—and how all of our lives thenceforth would be in one way or another determined by the existence of war.

I would not be so fatuous as to say that when I was here all was perfect bliss, that in this garden of earthly delights high above the Rappahannock a scuffed toe would not have uncovered a toad or two. But of all the schools I attended, including the three institutions of higher learning I went to subsequently in the South and North, only Christchurch ever commanded something more than mere respect—which is to say, my true and abiding affection. I think that much of the warmth and sweetness I felt and still feel for Christchurch has to do with the fact that when I was a student the place was very small and resembled a family—a sometimes tumultuous and quarrelsome, always nearly destitute but at the same time close-knit and loyal family. There were, I believe, only fifty-odd boys. We were poor. The school was poor. Many schools at the end of the Depression were poor, but the threadbare nature of Christchurch was almost Dickensian in its pathos. The library, for instance. At sixteen, I had a natural inclination for geography and I loved to pore over maps, but in the library there was only one geography book. It was not a *bad* atlas, had it been left undamaged, but it had been divested of Africa and all of Eastern Europe—something which to this day has produced significant gaps in my knowledge of the earth. The works of American literature stopped with Jack London—no Hemingway, no Fitzgerald, no Thomas Wolfe, no Theodore Dreiser; in compensation, we had that laudable work *Tom Sawyer,* but even this boy's classic palled upon perhaps the fifth reading. The *Encyclopaedia Britannica* was of such antique vintage that its information in the technological sphere alone ceased, I remember, with the invention of the telegraph and the diving bell. The pride of the entire library was a complete twenty-volume Shakespeare, but at least three volumes had been left out in the rain and the pages were stuck together, while someone else had stolen both *King Lear* and *Richard III*. Despite all this deprivation, I managed to get educated enough to pass on to college and acquit myself with at least passable honor. Our masters, good-natured and hideously underpaid drudges who possessed nonetheless high ideals and admirable patience, dispensed as much learning as was within their power. I still salute them in memory. When out of sheer exhaustion the teachers flagged and stumbled, the brotherly family-like nature of the school allowed us to teach each other. My classmate Tommy Peyton taught me all the trigonometry I ever knew. Langley Wood tutored me in chemistry, also about the girls in Richmond. It was in Jimmy Davenport's late-evening seminar that I learned how to beat the dealer at blackjack.

In later years, after leaving Christchurch and college, I became the good friend of several of those who had attended the great preparatory schools of New England. In all truth, it must be said that the potential for a good early education must have been somewhat larger at these richly endowed schools, with their splendid libraries and other resources, than it was at Christchurch; but I emphasize that word "potential" in the realization that at Christchurch, for those of us who had the determination—and most of us did—it was possible to overcome the handicaps and obtain an excellent preparation for college while in the process having a good time. Most of my friends who went to those venerable Northern institutions with names like Andover and St. Paul's did *not* seem to have a good time; so often their descriptions of school life are bleak, cold, impersonal, resembling a bearable but monotonous servitude rewarded later by glorious times at Princeton or Yale. At Christchurch I remember we worked as hard as anyone else to get our learning, but we also enjoyed ourselves. And I say that with memory uncontaminated by false nostalgia. Nothing warms my heart more than the recollection of those little sloops we sailed down on this matchless river. Certainly there are few schools in America that have proximity and access to a waterway of such magnificence. It mattered little to us that some of the boats were ancient and badly caulked and waterlogged and had been known with some frequency to sink sedately beneath the waves, even in the middle of a race; they were *our* boats and we loved them. Sailing, like the other sports, gave us ravenous appetites, and this leads to another obvious delight: the always tenderly prepared meals of Mr. Joseph Cameron, who of course is now an almost global legend. Could anything be more incongruous, more preposterous than the idea of any institution of learning where the food was consistently palatable and often superb? While my Ivy League friends still complain thinly and bitterly of soggy Swiss steaks and glutinous mashed potatoes, I recall cheese biscuits and pastries and delicately grilled fish, fresh from the river or the bay, which would have caused a French chef to salivate with envy. Christchurch may not have been in those days a well-heeled place, but it had a warm and golden ambience, and life was sweet, and we ate like kings.

[From Styron's commencement address at Christchurch School, May 24, 1974.]

William Blackburn

William Blackburn cared about writing and had an almost holy concern for the language. I realized this the first time out, with a brief theme in which we were required to describe a place—anyplace. In my two-page essay I chose a Tidewater river scene, the mudflats at low tide; attempting to grapple with the drab beauty of the view, groping for detail, I wrote of the fishnet stakes standing in the gray water, "looking stark and mute." A pretty conceit, I had thought, until the theme came back from Blackburn covered with red corrections, including the scathing comment on my attempt at imagery: "*Mute?* Did those stakes *ever* say anything?" This was my first encounter with something known among grammarians as "the pathetic fallacy."

A certain precision, you see, was what the professor was after and I was lucky to be made to toe the line early. Also, it was not a permissive era. Blackburn graded his themes with rigid unsentimentality. That theme of mine, I recall, received a D-minus, and through discreet inquiry I discovered that it was the lowest grade in the class (I think the highest was a C). Chastened, I began to regard Professor Blackburn with apprehension and awe, and both of these feelings were heightened by his redoubtable appearance and demeanor. A large, bulky, rather rumpled man (at least in dress), he tended to slump at his desk and to sag while walking; all this gave the impression of a man harboring great unhappiness, if not despair. Nor did he smile effortlessly. There was something distinctly cranky and dour about him, after so many teachers I had known with their Ipana smiles and dauntless cheer. He was ill at ease with strangers, including students, and this is why my first impression of Blackburn was one of remoteness and bearish gloom. Only a remarkably gentle South Carolina voice softened my initial feeling that he was filled with bone-hard melancholy and quiet desperation. For several weeks it seemed to me impossible that one could ever draw close—or be drawn close—to such a despondent, distant man.

But before too long my work got much better, and as it did I found myself able to strike through the Blackburnian mask. Possibly because I was so eager to meet his demanding standards, I sweated like a coolie over my essays, themes, and fledgling short stories until my splintered syntax and humpbacked prose achieved a measure of clarity and grace. Blackburn in turn warmed to my efforts—beginning to sprinkle the pages with such invigorating phrases as "Nice!" and "Fine touch!"—and before the term was half through I had begun to acquire a clutch of B's and A's. More importantly, I began to know Blackburn, the great-hearted, humane, tragicomical sufferer who dwelt behind the hulking and lugubrious façade. One day to my astonishment he invited me to lunch. We went to an East Durham restaurant. The beer was good, the food atrocious. He spoke to me very little of writing, or of my own efforts (which did not bother me, my A's were enough praise and this terrible lunch sufficient accolade), but much about reading. He asked me what I had read in my lifetime and was patient and understanding when I confessed to having read next to nothing. Most gently he then informed me that one could not become a writer without a great deal of reading. Read Thomas Mann and Proust, he said, the Russians, Conrad, Shakespeare, the Elizabethans. Perhaps, he added, I would like to sign up, next semester, for his course in Elizabethan literature. We were a little embarrassed and uneasy with each other. Occasionally there were blank silences as we munched on our ghastly wartime hot dogs. In the silences Blackburn would give a heaving sigh. All his life he was an expressive sigher. Then he would begin to rail, with marvelously droll venom, at the Duke University administration bigwigs, most of whom he regarded as Pecksniffs and Philistines. They were out to smother the Humanities, to destroy him and his modest writing class; they were Yahoos. He got superbly rancorous and eloquent; he had an actor's sense of timing and I laughed until I ached. Then he grew more serious again. To write one must read, he repeated, *read* . . .

Blackburn readily admitted that there was a great deal of logic in the accusation, so often leveled at "creative writing" courses, that no one could actually be taught to write English narrative prose. Why, then, did he persist? I think it must have been because, deep within him, despite all doubts (and no man had so many self-doubts) he realized what an extraordinarily fine teacher he was. He must have known that he possessed that subtle, ineffable, magnetically appealing quality—a kind of invisible rapture—which caused students to respond with like rapture to the fresh and wondrous new world he was trying to reveal to them. Later, when I got to know him well, he accused himself of sloth, but in reality he was the most profoundly conscientious of teachers; his comments on students' themes and stories were often remarkable extended essays in themselves. This matter of caring, and caring deeply, was of course one of the secrets of his excellence. But the caring took other forms: it extended to his very presence in the classroom— his remarkable course in Elizabethan poetry and prose, for instance, when, reading aloud from Spenser's *Epithalamion* with its ravishing praise, or the sonorous meditation on death of Sir Thomas Browne, his voice would become so infused with feeling that we would sit transfixed, and not a breath could be heard in the room. It would be too facile a description to call him a spell-binder, though he had in him much of the actor *manqué;* this very rare ability to make his students *feel,* to fall in love with a poem or poet, came from his own real depth of feeling and, perhaps, from his own unrequited love, for I am sure he was an unfulfilled writer or poet too. Whatever— from what mysterious wellspring there derived Blackburn's powerful and uncanny gift to mediate between a work of art and the young people who stood ready to receive it—he was unquestionably a glorious teacher. Populate a whole country and its institutions of learning with but a handful of Blackburns, and you will certainly have great institutions of learning, and perhaps a great country.

I deeply miss him, because ultimately he became more than a teacher to me. He became the reason why, after the war was over, I returned to Duke and why, too—although at this point the university and I were on mutually amicable terms—Duke acquired a meaning to me beyond the good times I enjoyed there and its simple power to grant me a bachelor's degree. Bill

Blackburn had become a close friend, a spiritual anchor, a man whose companionship was a joy and whose counsel was almost everything to one still
floundering at the edge of a chancy and rather terrifying career. It helped
immeasurably to have him tell me, at the age of twenty-one, that I could
become a writer—although I am still unable to say whether this advice was
more important than the fact that, without him, I should doubtless never
have known the music of John Milton, or rare Ben Jonson, or been set afire
by John Donne. In any case, he was for me the embodiment of those virtues
by which I am still able to value the school he served (despite bearish
grudges and droll upheavals) so long and so well. Surely over the years the
ultimate and shining honor gained by a university is the one bestowed upon
it by a man like William Blackburn and his love, requited and unrequited,
and his rapturous teaching.

[From *Duke Encounters*. Duke University Office of Publications, 1977.]

Almost a Rhodes Scholar

In the winter of 1947 it appeared that I was on my way to becoming a Rhodes scholar. During the period after World War II when I went back to continue my studies at Duke University, I had applied myself with considerable passion to what was then, as now, known—I think unhappily—as "creative writing," and it became about the only academic discipline in which there was descried that I had any talent at all. However, my promise was such that my late teacher, Professor William Blackburn—God bless him—determined that it might be a good idea to apply for a Rhodes scholarship on the basis of my writing ability. I was a graduating senior, an English major, impoverished, with nothing much looming on the horizon in the way of a livelihood after my midyear graduation a month or so hence. Professor Blackburn—who had himself been a Rhodes scholar—was, like most Rhodes scholars, an ardent Anglomaniac, and was able to beguile me with visions of all the delights that a year or two at Oxford might offer: studying Old Norse and Middle English in the damp and drafty rooms at Merton College—a place which, he said, one grew fond of; reading Keats and Hardy under the tutelage of Edmund Blunden; drinking sherry and eating scones, or picnicking on plovers' eggs and champagne, as the pale lads did in novels by Aldous Huxley; having one's own fag—whatever that meant; going *down* to London for weekends; enjoying summer vacations in Normandy or boating along the Rhine. Another attraction: one would be paid a reasonable stipend. Whatever its defects (and I could not see many), it mostly sounded perfectly wonderful, and so I was quite acquiescent when Professor Blackburn urged me to try out for the preliminary competition—that of the state of North Carolina, held in Chapel Hill. I was a little apprehensive; my grades had not really been outstanding throughout my academic career, and I had been under the impression that "Rhodes scholarship" and "outstanding" were virtually synonymous. No matter, said Professor Blackburn; the new policy of the Rhodes selections placed much less emphasis on scholarly achievement than previously; candidates were beginning to be chosen far more for their promise as creative talents, and therefore I stood a very good chance. Well, it turned out that he was right. I submitted the manuscripts of several short stories. To my astonishment, out of a field of more than twenty I was one of *two* students to win the competition from North Carolina. The field had been loaded with hotshots, too: straight-A scholars from Davidson and Chapel Hill, an accredited genius from Wake Forest, a magnificently proficient German linguist from Duke. What a heady and vainglorious triumph I felt—and what a victory it was for the creative spirit! I was so exhilarated that day when I heard the good news that many hours passed before sober reflection set in, and I began to wonder just how much of my success had been determined by the fact that Professor Blackburn, my beloved and idealistic mentor, had been chairman of the selection committee. Anyway . . .

The regional competition for the Southeastern states was held a few days later here in Atlanta—indeed, within the very bowels of this hotel where we are all meeting. I was twenty years old and the trip marked several "firsts" for me. The era of air travel, for instance, had not then really arrived in all of its dynamic and stupendous actuality; it was not yet really part of the matrix of our national existence. I had flown several times on military planes in the Marine Corps, but my trip to Atlanta from Durham was my first experience with a commercial aircraft. It was an Eastern DC-3, and I got slightly airsick, though my malaise may have been compounded by the truly visceral excitement which now agitated my every waking hour; I was racked with visions of Oxford in the mists of fall, of pubs and golden yards of foaming ale, of pretty Scottish lasses with that weather-rouged flush on their creamy cheeks, and of myself, winning my honors with a thrilling exegesis of *The Faerie Queene*. But then—Atlanta! Down through the clouds our plane made its descent. And here was an airport—imagine!—about the size of the

Greyhound bus station in Goldsboro, North Carolina, and then, a leisurely, halting taxi drive by way of a bumpy two-lane highway through a sleepy Southern city where Peachtree Street was thronged with Negro vendors and the air was still haunted by the ghosts of Sherman's departed legions, and finally, the Atlanta Biltmore, its lobby filled with potted palms, cuspidors and salesmen from as far away as Moultrie and Al-benny.

There was also something intangibly sinister about the place—something that troubled me even as I went through the check-in proceedings—until at last I realized what the problem was: behind nearly every potted palm, at every portal and exit, there lurked a uniformed fireman. I hope that my memory of this detail does not cast a shadow over the present assembly, but the fire alert was due to a terrible catastrophe that had struck Atlanta only a week before my arrival. In one of the worst fires in Atlanta history—and the greatest conflagration in Georgia since the burning of Atlanta in 1864—the Hotel Winecoff, only a few blocks away, had been destroyed, with the loss of over a hundred lives. The presence at the Biltmore of all this firefighting muscle caused me to seek for a striking metaphor, but I had to settle for the homely and rather imperfect one of the barn door being shut after the horse has run away; so many firemen *should* have allayed certain basic anxieties about nocturnal safety (I'm not exaggerating too much when I say that there seemed to be firemen enough around for one to spend the night with each and every guest), but their presence inexplicably made me *more* nervous, and that night I went to bed in a deep unease, worrying about my interview the next day, and waking hourly to the smell of imagined combustion.

The next day—the day of the interviews—was nearly interminable, lasting, I recall, from very early in the morning until eight or nine in the evening. During those long hours I had time to sit and fret miserably on one of the couches on the Biltmore mezzanine, to read, to chat with a few of my thirty or so competitors, and in doing so, to take stock of my chances. I felt profoundly intimidated. These young men comprised the intellectual elite—no, the super-elite—of all the colleges and universities of the Southeast; they possessed, I was certain, staggeringly high IQs, had burnt countless gallons of midnight oil to achieve scholastic mastery. They were, in short, the flower of their generation, and win or lose, I was proud to be counted among them. Hooray for Cecil Rhodes! Hooray for Oxford! I thought. The hours dragged on. Even in some of the darkest trials of my officer candidacy in the Marine Corps I did not suffer such suspense, such spasms of anxiety, such despair mixed with forlorn hope. How sweet it would be, I thought, munching on my ham-and-cheese sandwich, to row for old Balliol, to hit a wicket or swing whatever is swung at cricket for Oriel or All Souls. I thought of the Lake Country, Cornwall, Westminster Abbey. I can recall now nothing of my own interview, only that I seem to have acquitted myself with dignity and aplomb; I think it must have lasted half an hour or more. It was long past dark when, fatigued with the bone-stiffening fatigue that only such miserable waiting can induce, we sat and watched a committee member—himself quite haggard—emerge from the conference room and slowly read the names of the dozen winners. My name was not among them. The relief—no matter how painful the undergirding of disappointment—was immediate, almost blissful. And I felt some small twitch of solace—albeit solace mixed with puzzlement—when, after extending routine thanks to all, the committee member singled me out, requesting that I stay behind after the other candidates had dispersed. What on earth was this? I wondered, with a deft surge of hope. Was I to be given some secret, heretofore unrevealed and unannounced consolation prize? A watch? A Bible? A set of the *OED*?

I sat there alone for a long while on the nearly deserted, stale-smelling mezzanine, stranded in my bafflement. Finally only a single fireman shared my solitude. At last out of the conference room shambled the tired but friendly-looking chairman of the committee, a doctor of divinity who was also the distinguished chancellor of Vanderbilt University. His name was Harvie Branscomb. He was a good man. He extended his hand and offered his condolences, and then sat down beside me on the couch. As I may have known, he said, he had been a close friend of Bill Blackburn's when they both taught at Duke several years before; because of this connection it was all the more difficult for him, personally, to have had to pass me over.

"It was because of you that we took so long," he said in his fatherly, friendly voice. "We argued and argued about you for at least an hour. You see—your writing, those stories—they really were very impressive, we all thought, but—" He paused, then said, "We did want a creative person, but—" And then he halted.

"I appreciate what you tried to do," I said. "I'll always be grateful for that."

"I guess you know why we finally felt that we had to pass you over—"

"My grades—" I interrupted.

"Yes," he went on, "it's not that you just flunked physics. Even the Rhodes scholarship doesn't demand perfection. One or two of the winners today had rather—well, shaky areas in their academic records. It was—"

"You don't have to tell me," I put in.

The chancellor said, "Yes, to flunk physics not just once but *four* times in a row. And that final exam grade, the last semester: thirty-eight. We couldn't overlook that." He hesitated, then gave a rueful smile. "One of the committee members said that you seemed to demonstrate a 'pertinacity in the desire to fail.' We had to consider how such a trait might appear to the people at Oxford . . ."

I could say nothing. Finally, after a bit of a silence, the chancellor said, "You know, son, maybe this is really for the better. I mean, I was at Oxford over twenty-five years ago, and I've watched hundreds of Rhodes scholars come back to America and begin their careers and I'll be dogged if I can name a single writer—a single poet or playwright or short-story writer or novelist—that came out of the entire huge crowd. Oh, a lot of brilliant people and a lot of brilliant careers in many fields—but not a single writer worth the description. Funny thing, Oxford—it's a wonderful place for learning, the finest place of its kind in the world, and yet it has a way of tending to *channel* people, to fit them into a mold. If you really want to know the truth, I believe that if we had chosen you it may have been the end, once and for all, of your ambitions to be a writer. Most probably, you would have become a teacher—a doggone good teacher, you understand, but not a writer." He stopped and looked out over the deserted mezzanine with its potted palms and spittoons. "A *good* teacher, mind you," he insisted again, as if to stroke my bruised ego. "I'm sure you would have come back and begun teaching at Duke or the University of Virginia or Sewanee or someplace. It'd be a good life, you'd have been truly distinguished—but you surely wouldn't have become a writer."

The chancellor's eyes, glazed with a terrible tiredness, seemed to rest on a remote distance, and I have wondered recently when thinking of that moment, if in his touching and truly generous concern for me, he might have been brooding upon other possibilities in the theoretical career which my "pertinacity in a desire to fail" had caused him and his colleagues reluctantly to deny me: that is, for example, membership in the South Atlantic Modern Language Association, which, thirty-odd years later, in 1979, would bring me to this very hotel, ready for the familiar annuity of cerebral interplay, conventional tedium, painful politics, and the saving balm of various sorts of fellowship.

But the chancellor and I bade each other goodbye then, and I terminated my stay in Atlanta with another dubious "first." I had been since my early adolescence an imbiber of beer and beer alone; Budweiser had always seemed to be a beverage I could handle. But this night, on my way to the train station, I bought a bottle of Old Grand-Dad bourbon; it was, I remember precisely, a full half pint, which was a prodigious amount of booze for a young man of twenty—at least, I know, for me. I got gloriously drunk on the Southern Railway local that rattled its way all night up through the Carolinas, gazing out at the bleak, moon-drenched, wintry fields and happily pondering my deliverance. The chancellor, bless his soul, had really taken most of the curse off the bitter defeat I had initially felt there at the Biltmore. It really was better for me not to go to Oxford, I told myself, throwing in various Anglophobic injunctions: the food you wouldn't feed to a starving hound dog, the men were prancing homosexuals, the women all had foul breath, it was a moribund civilization. "Screw Oxford," I remember saying aloud, and "Up yours, Cecil Rhodes!" Next year, instead of shivering to death in some library carrel, instead of—and "Get this, old fellow!" I heard myself cackling—instead of writing a paper on the hexameters of Arthur Hugh Clough, that old Victorian nanny, I would be in New York, beginning my first novel. It was with this fantasy in mind that I slipped off into a bourbon-heavy slumber, sleeping past Durham and waking up with a stupefying headache in Norlina, practically on the Virginia border, feeling (despite this dislocation and my hangover) amazingly happy.

[Speech delivered to the South Atlantic Modern Language Association, Atlanta, Georgia, December 1979.]

A Case of the Great Pox

A mong the performances that helped make the movie *Casablanca* immortal was that of Claude Rains as the French police captain Louis Renault. Rains played the part with astringent urbanity and created a lasting model of the tough cop attractively humanized, Monsieur Nice Guy lurking behind the domineering swaggerer. I belong to the first of several generations that have fallen under the film's febrile romantic spell. By the late autumn of 1944 I had seen the film three times, and Rains seemed to me only slightly less crucial to its hypnotic unfolding than Bogart and Bergman. You may well imagine my amazement, then, when, in that wartime autumn, a veritable replica—the spitting image—of Claude Rains sat behind a desk in a doctor's office on the urological ward of the naval hospital at Parris Island, South Carolina. I stood at attention, looking down at him. A sign on the desk identified the doctor as "B. Klotz, Lieutenant Commander, Chief of Urology." I recall registering all sorts of impressions at once: the name Klotz, with its pathological overtone, and Klotz-Rains himself, duplicated—somewhat narcissistically, I thought—as he posed in prewar civvies in one of several framed photographs on the wall. The other photographs, completing a kind of triumvirate of authority, were of President Franklin D. Roosevelt and Admiral Ernest J. King, chief of naval operations. There was one notable difference between Klotz and Rains, aside from the doctor's white blouse instead of the gendarmerie kepi and tunic. It was that the actor, even when he was trying to be threatening, had a twinkly charm, a barely repressed bonhomie, while Klotz appeared merely threatening. I knew that this was not the beginning of a beautiful friendship. That morning, Klotz sat silent for a moment, then came directly to the point. No elegant British vocables. In a flat, mid-Atlantic accent, he said, "Your blood tests have been checked out, and they indicate that you have syphilis."

I remember my cheeks and the region around my mouth going numb, then beginning to tingle, as if my face had been dealt a brutal whack. Traumatic events powerfully focus the perceptions, leaving ancillary details embalmed forever in memory—in this case, the window just beyond Klotz's head, a frost-rimed pane through which I could see the vast asphalt parade ground swarming with platoon after platoon of Marine recruits like me (or like me until the day before, when I was sent to the hospital), performing the rigorous choreography of close-order drill. Dawn had not yet broken, and the men moved in and out of the light that fell in bright pools from the barracks. Most of the platoons were marching with rifles, a drill instructor tramping alongside and screaming orders that I couldn't hear but that, up close, would have sounded like those of a foul-mouthed and hysterical madman. Other platoons remained still, at ease, shrouded in cigarette smoke or exhaled breath or both; it was a bitterly cold November. Beyond the parade ground and its clumps of marines in green field jackets were rows of wooden barracks. And beyond the barracks lay the waters of Port Royal Sound, roiled by an icy wind. All these things registered in my mind clearly, but at the same time they seemed to coalesce around a single word, uttered by the voice of Klotz: *syphilis*.

"You will remain on this ward indefinitely for further observation," Klotz continued. There was an unmistakably antagonistic tone in his voice. Most doctors in my past—the few I'd had contact with, anyway—had been chummy, avuncular, and genuinely if sometimes clumsily sweet-mannered. Klotz was of another breed, and he caused my stomach to go into spasm. I thought, What a prick. Before dismissing me, he ordered me to report to the duty pharmacist's mate, who would instruct me about the series of regulations I'd be subject to while on the ward, a regime Klotz referred to as "the venereal protocol." He then told me to return to my bed, where I would wait until further notice. I was wearing a blue hospital robe, in the pocket of which I had thrust a copy of one of the first paperback anthologies ever published, a volume that had kept me company for at least two years—*The*

Pocket Book of Verse, compiled by an academic named M. Edmund Speare. My legs had an aqueous, flimsy feeling. I lurched back down the ward, still numb around the mouth, gripping the book with feverish desire, like a condemned Christian clutching a Testament.

I should say a word about the great pox, so named, in the sixteenth century, to distinguish the illness from smallpox. Although syphilis had been regarded, since the late fifteenth century, as a plague that would never in any real sense yield to the strategies of medical science, it had been dealt a sudden and mortal blow only a year or so before my diagnosis. It was one of medicine's most dramatic victories, like Jenner's discovery of a smallpox vaccine or Pasteur's defeat of rabies. The breakthrough took place soon after American researchers—building on the work of Sir Alexander Fleming, who had discovered penicillin, in the twenties, and Sir Howard Florey, who had developed a technique for producing the drug—found that a one-week course of the miraculous mold could wipe out all traces of early syphilis, and even certain late-stage manifestations of the illness. (Penicillin also had a devastating effect on the other major venereal scourge, gonorrhea, a single injection usually being sufficient to put it to rout.) Since mid-1943, the medical authorities of the American armed forces had ordered doctors in military hospitals around the globe to discontinue a syphilis treatment called arsphenamine therapy and to commence using penicillin as it became available. Arsphenamine—better known, variously, as Salvarsan, 606, or the magic bullet—was an arsenic-based compound developed in 1909 by the German bacteriologist Paul Ehrlich. He discovered that his new drug (the six hundred and sixth version proved successful) could knock out syphilis without killing the patient; it was a remarkable advance after several hundred years during which the principal nostrum was mercury, a substance that worked capriciously, when it worked at all, and was for the most part as dangerous as the disease itself.

Because the disease sprang from the dark act of sex, *syphilis* was not a word uttered casually in the Protestant environment of my Virginia boyhood; the word raised eyebrows around America even when it was discreetly murmured in *Dr. Ehrlich's Magic Bullet,* a 1940 movie starring Edward G. Robinson, who I thought was a pretty convincing healer after his parts as a ruthless mobster. *Dr. Ehrlich's Magic Bullet* didn't make much of an impression on me; I doubtless was too young. But even if I had been older I would probably not have realized that the movie failed to tell an essential truth. While the doctor's magic bullet was a vast improvement over the forlorn remedy of the past, his treatment was shown to be sadly insufficient; the drug rendered patients noncontagious, but it wasn't a very reliable cure, and the treatment required dozens of painful and costly injections over such a long period of time—often many months—that a great number of patients became discouraged, and were consequently prone to relapses. So the epidemic suffered a setback but was not halted. It would take Alexander Fleming's surefire bactericidal fungus to produce the real magic. And I was in the vanguard of those victims upon whom this benison would descend. Or so it seemed, until, with a gradual dawning that was sickening in itself, I began to suspect that health was not so readily at hand.

As a diagnosed syphilitic, I had good cause to think passionately about penicillin during the interminable hours and days I spent in the Clap Shack, as such wards were known throughout the Navy. But, from the first day following Dr. Klotz's announcement, I had the impression that I was a very special case. I was not an ordinary patient whose treatment would follow the uneventful trajectory toward cure, but one who had been hurled into an incomprehensible purgatory where neither treatment nor even the possibility of a cure was part of my ultimate destiny. And this hunch turned out to be correct. From the outset, I was convinced not only that I had acquired the most feared of sexually transmitted diseases but that I would at some point keel over from it, probably in an unspeakable cellular mud slide or convulsion of the nervous system. As an early-blooming hypochondriac, a reader besotted with *The Merck Manual,* I had a bit more medical savvy than most kids my age, and what my diagnosis actually portended made me clammy with dismay. I believed that I was beyond the reach of penicillin. I was sure that I was a goner, and that certainty never left me during the days that stretched into weeks of weirdly demoralizing confinement.

My bed was at the very end of the ward, and I had a view from two windows, at right angles to each other. From one window, I could see the sound, a shallow inlet of the Atlantic, on the edge of freezing; from the other, I had a glimpse of a row of barracks not far away and, between the barrack buildings, concrete laundry slabs, where marines bedeviled by the cold—I watched them shake and shiver—pounded at their near-frozen dungarees beneath sluiceways of water. What nasty little Schadenfreude I might have felt at their plight was dispelled by my own despair at having been separated from longtime buddies whom I'd gone to college with, officer candidates like me—or like the person I had been before the onset of an illness that, because of its carnal origin and the moral shame it entailed, would prevent me from even thinking of becoming a lieutenant in the United States Marine Corps.

Winkler, the hospital corpsman who had checked me onto the ward, returned to bring me these tidings. No way, he said, that you can get a marine commission if you've had VD. He had other awful news, too, most of it bearing on my health. After escorting me to my sack and telling me where to stow my seabag, he told me—in answer to my bewildered "Why the hell am I here?"—that my Kahn test was so high it had gone off the chart. "It looks to me," he said with maddening whimsy, "like you've got a case of the great pox." When I asked him what a Kahn test was, he replied with a counterquestion: Had I ever heard of a Wassermann reaction? I replied, Of course, every schoolboy knew about a Wassermann. A Kahn, Winkler explained, was almost the same as a Wassermann, only an improvement. It was a simpler blood test. And then, as I recalled the endless trips I'd made in past days to the regimental dispensary to verify the first routine test, and the vial after vial of blood extracted from my arm, I had a foreshadowing of the stern warrant that Dr. Klotz would serve up to me the following morning. I must have radiated terror, for I sensed a conscious effort by Winkler to make me feel better; his tactic was to try to cast me as one of the elite. At the moment, he told me, I was the only syphilitic on the ward. Most of the patients were guys with the clap. And when, despondently, I asked him why he thought victims of syphilis, as opposed to those with gonorrhea, were such rarities, he came back with a theory that in my case was so richly inconceivable that it caused me to laugh one of the last spontaneous laughs I would laugh for a long time. "You can catch the clap a lot easier than syphilis," he explained. "Syph you really have to work at to contract." He added, with a hint of admiration, "You must have been getting a new piece of ass every day."

After my interview with Klotz, which took place very early, before his regular morning rounds, I had a chance to sit next to my bed and take stock of my situation while the other patients slept. Winkler had explained the configuration of the ward. It was a warehouse of genitourinary complaints. On one side of the ward were a dozen beds occupied by clap patients. As a result of crowding in the clap section, I was lodged on the other side of the center aisle, at the end of a row of patients whose maladies were not vene-

real in origin. Most of these marines had kidney and bladder disorders, primarily infections; there was a boy who had suffered a serious blow to his
kidney during one of the savage internecine boxing matches that the drill
instructors, virtually all sadists, enjoyed promoting during morning exercises. There was an undescended testicle that Winkler said would never
have got past the first medical screening in the robust volunteer days, before
the draft allowed all sorts of misshapen characters into the Marine Corps.
The marine in the sack next to me, breathing softly, his face expressionless
in sleep's bland erasure, had just the day before been circumcised by Dr.
Klotz; the fellow had suffered from a constrictive condition of the foreskin
known as phimosis. Winkler's last task the previous night had been to swad-
dle the guy's groin in ice packs, lest nocturnal erections rip out the stitches—a
mishap that obviously could never happen to a Jew, said Winkler, who was
plainly New York Jewish, in a tone that was a touch self-satisfied. As for the
marines with the clap, Winkler pointed out that in most cases this was not
your standard garden-variety gonorrhea but an intractable chronic condition that usually came about as a result of the guys' refusing, out of shame or
fear—and often out of sheer indifference—to seek treatment, so that the
invasive gonococci began after time to wreak havoc in the prostate, or became lodged in the joints as an exquisitely painful form of arthritis. Marines
and sailors from up and down the Atlantic coast came to this ward for what
was possibly last-ditch therapy, since Klotz was known as the best doctor in
the Navy for handling such complications.

Later that first day, another hospital corpsman outlined to me the details
of the venereal protocol. VD patients were in certain respects strictly segregated, both from their fellow sufferers on the ward and from the hospital
population at large. Our robes were emblazoned with a large yellow V over
the breast. When we went to the head, we were expected to use specially
designated toilets and basins. Those of us who were ambulatory were to eat
at mess-hall tables reserved for our use. When we attended the twice-weekly
movies at the base recreation center, we would be escorted in a separate
group and then seated together in a section marked off by a yellow ribbon.
I remember absorbing this information with queasiness, and then asking the
corpsman why we were subject to such extraordinary precautions. While I
was not unaware of the perils of VD, I had no idea that we posed such a
threat. But as soon as I began to express my puzzlement, the corpsman
explained that syphilis and gonorrhea were contagious as hell. True, most

people got them only from sex, but one of those little microorganisms could infect through a tiny scratch. BUMED (as the Bureau of Medicine was called) was taking no chances; furthermore, he added with a knowing look, Dr. Klotz "had a kind of personal fixation." This was an enigmatic, faintly sinister statement that became less opaque as time passed and Klotz became the dominant presence in my life.

As the only patient with syphilis, I was spared the short-arm inspection that was the centerpiece of Dr. Klotz's early rounds that morning and every morning at the stroke of six. At that hour, a bell in the ward jangled and the overhead lights came on in an explosion. The bedridden on my side of the aisle remained in their sacks. But in the interval of a minute or so between the flood of light and the appearance of Dr. Klotz, the dozen clap patients in the opposite row all scrambled to their feet and stood at ragged attention. There was usually a certain amount of wisecracking among these guys, along with self-dramatizing groans and reciprocal "Fuck you's." Most of them were regulars, not effete college-bred recruits like me, and were five or ten years older than me. Their accents were about equally divided between Southern cracker and Northeastern working class. I soon understood that many of these die-hard cases had one thing in common: they were obsessive Romeos, fornicators of serene dedication whose commitment to sexual bliss was so wholehearted that they could keep up a flow of jokes even as the disease that such pleasure had cost them gnawed away at the inmost mucous membranes of the genitalia and tortured the joints of their wrists and knees.

I was amazed at this nonchalance, and also at their apparently incandescent libidos, especially since my own nineteen-year-old hormonal heat had plunged to absolute zero the instant Dr. Klotz confirmed the nature of my problem; the word *syphilis* had made the very notion of sex nauseating, as if I were beset by some erotic anorexia. But the members of the gonorrhea faction quieted down as soon as Winkler or one of the other corpsmen shouted, "Attention on deck!" and Klotz made his businesslike entrance through the swinging doors. It was important, Winkler had told me, that these bums be inspected as soon as they woke up, before heading to the urinals; from looking at the accumulated purulence called gleet, and checking the amount and consistency of the discharge, Klotz could determine how the treatment was proceeding. And so, accompanied by a litany—"Skin it back, squeeze it, milk it down"—intoned by the corpsman, Klotz would pass down the line of victims, making his evaluations. He didn't waste a word, and his manner was frostily judgmental, as if these rogues and whore-mongers were unworthy of even so much as a casual "Good morning." Nor was his manner with me any less reproachful. As I stood stiffly at attention, I was thankful only that I didn't have to submit my dick to such a degrading scrutiny at that hour of the morning. During each tour of the ward, Klotz would glare at me briefly, ask the corpsman about my daily Kahn test—it remained at the highest (and therefore the most alarming) level, day in and day out—and then pass on to the nonvenereal patients.

Early in the afternoon on that first day, however, Klotz did examine my penis. This was a procedure that I might ordinarily skip describing were it not for the monstrous effect that it had on my psychic balance, which had already been thrown badly out of whack. For it was Klotz's judgment regarding my penile history that helped crystallize my belief that I was doomed. I was summoned to his office, and, as I stood in front of him, he checked through my medical-record book and brusquely asked some routine questions. Any history of syphilis in my family? (What a question!) No, I lied. In the preceding weeks or months had I experienced any unusual rash or fever? I had not. Any swelling in the groin? No. Had I noticed any unusual growth on my penis? This would be a hard, painless ulcer, he said, called a chancre. I knew what a chancre was, everyone had heard about chancres (corpsmen were even known as "chancre mechanics"); but I had not seen one. During Klotz's interrogation, I held in view the eye-level portrait of a solemn, reso-lute Franklin D. Roosevelt, who kept looking back at me. I was grateful for the reassuring gaze of this surrogate father, my perennial president, the only one I had ever known, and I steadfastly stared back at him through most of Klotz's examination, which he carried out with cold, skeletal fingers.

He twisted my penis, not very gently, gave it an unnecessary squeeze or two, and turned it upside down. I recall thinking that, though it had known various attitudes, it had rarely been upside down. Then he bade me to look down, saying that he had discovered, on the underside, a scar. Chancres leave scars, he murmured, and this looked like a chancre scar. I glanced down and, indeed, discerned a scar. A tiny reddish outcropping. Since the chancre had been painless, he added, it had come and gone, without my ever noticing its presence, leaving only that small scar. He seemed to have put aside, at least for the moment, his customary distaste. He said that the chance of my having been infected by nonvenereal contact was astronomically remote. The toilet seat was a myth. Syphilis usually created distinct symptoms, he went on—first the chancre, then, later, the fever and the rash—but quite often these symptoms never appeared, or appeared so insubstantially that they went unnoticed. Klotz surprised me by saying something that, in the midst of his dispassionate exegesis, sounded almost poetic: "Syphilis is a cruel disease." And then, after a brief silence, during which I became aware that he was constructing an answer to the question that sheer fright kept me from asking, he declared, "What happens in the end is that syphilis invades the rest of the body." He paused and concluded, before dismissing me, "We're going to have to keep you here and figure out just how far it's advanced."

I went back to my bed at the end of the ward and, in the cold midday light, lay down. You weren't supposed to lie on a bed in daytime, but I did anyway. The hospital was a venerable wooden structure, warm, even overheated, but I felt nearly frozen, listening to the windows creaking and banging in the bluster of an Atlantic gale. The sex maniacs with the clap across the aisle were noisily trading lewd adventures, and I gradually sank into a stupor of disbelief, beyond the consoling power of even *The Pocket Book of Verse,* which had saved me in many a lesser crisis but was plainly beyond the scope of this one.

Its history "is unique among great diseases," the medical historian William Allen Pusey wrote, "in that it does not gradually emerge into the records of medicine as its character becomes recognized, but appears on the stage of history with a dramatic suddenness in keeping with the tragic reputation it has made; as a great plague sweeping within a few years over the known world."

This observation, made in the early part of the century, has an all too painful resonance today, and it might be worthwhile to compare syphilis with our present pandemic. Unlike AIDS, syphilis was not invariably fatal, despite its extremely high rate of mortality. This may have been its only saving grace, depending on whether death is viewed as a blessing preferable to the terrible and irreversible damage the disease is capable of inflicting on the body and the mind. After the introduction of Dr. Ehrlich's not-so-magic bullet, and especially after penicillin's knockout blow, syphilis lost much of its capacity to evoke universal dread. Still, for various reasons, it remained a horror, aside from the fact that no one wants to be infested by millions of

Treponema pallidum, the causative microbe, whose wriggling corkscrew can reach the bone marrow and spleen within forty-eight hours of infection, and produce a persistent malaise, rashes, ulcerous skin lesions, and other debilitating symptoms. For one thing, there was the stigma—and I mean the appalling stigma arising from anything at all suggesting misbehavior as we young people traversed the parched sexual landscape of the thirties and forties.

I've mentioned that the word itself was taboo. Among nice people, *syphilis* was uttered sotto voce if at all, and only occasionally found its way into print. *Social disease* and *vice disease* were the usual substitutes. When I was in grade school, the only time I recall the word's catching my eye was when I happened upon it in a medical pamphlet. I asked my teacher, a maiden lady of traditional reserve, what it meant. She instantly corrected my pronunciation, but her cheeks became flushed, and she didn't answer my question. Her silence made me guess at something wicked. And wicked it was in those prim years. For most of its existence in the Anglo-Saxon world, syphilis, as AIDS has often done, stained the people who contracted it with indelible disrepute.

But there was a far graver trouble: the sheer awfulness of the malady itself. Even after medical intervention, and treatment with penicillin, there could still be dire complications. No cure was absolutely foolproof. And my obsession—that syphilis had taken possession of my system and had commenced its inroads, penetrating tissues and organs, which thus had already suffered the first effects of dissolution—grew more fixed every day as I dragged myself through Dr. Klotz's venereal protocol. I wore my yellow V stoically, and soon got used to going to the mess hall and the movies in a segregated herd. I had plenty of time to brood about my condition, since there were no organized activities for patients on the ward. I kept wondering why I was not being treated. If penicillin could work its miracle, why was it not being used? It only aggravated my distress to think that the disease, for reasons beyond my understanding, had reached a stage where treatment was useless, and was merely waiting for some fatal resolution. I had to blot out thoughts like these. Mostly, I hung around the area near my bed, sitting on a camp stool and reading books and magazines from the small hospital library. I returned hesitantly to *The Pocket Book of Verse,* to Keats and A. E. Housman and Emily Dickinson and *The Rubáiyát of Omar Khayyám.*

Except during morning rounds, I never saw Dr. Klotz. My only actual duty was to bare my arm once a day for the Kahn test, which invariably showed the same results: "Off the chart," as Winkler had said. I grew friendly with Winkler, who seemed drawn to me, most likely because I'd been to college and he'd had two years at CCNY before Pearl Harbor. One of his generosities was a loan of a little red Motorola portable radio, which I kept tuned to the Savannah station and its news about the war. The bulletins added weight to the black and anxious mood that each afternoon crept over me—a mood that I would recognize only years later as the onset of a serious depression.

Just before I entered the hospital, marines had stormed ashore on a remote Pacific island called Peleliu and had met with "heavy Japanese resistance"—a common Pentagon euphemism to describe our troops' being slaughtered. What I heard on the radio was unsettling enough, but the news chiefly reminded me of the doubtfulness of my own future. For at least three years, I had lived with the bold and heady ambition of becoming a marine lieutenant; to lead troops into combat against the Japs had been an intoxicating dream. A sexually transmitted disease was not permissible for an officer candidate, Winkler had ruefully pointed out to me—not even if he was cured, so ugly was the moral blotch—and thus I began to realize that the microorganisms seething like termites within me were destroying my vision of honor and achievement as effectively as they were laying waste to my flesh. But this regret, wrenching as it was, I could somehow deal with. What was close to intolerable—beyond the disgrace, beyond the wreckage it would make of my military ambition—was the premonition, settling around me like a fog bank, of absolute physical ruin. A death-in-life, for example, like that of my Uncle Harold, whose case was a harrowing paradigm of the malady and the disaster it could inflict.

He was my mother's younger brother, and at twenty-seven, during the Great War, he had gone overseas as an infantry corporal in the Rainbow Division. During the Saint-Mihiel offensive, he had suffered a bad shrapnel wound in the leg and had been mustered out in 1918 to his hometown, in western Pennsylvania, where he married, had a son, and settled down to the life of a businessman. Sometime in the late twenties, he started to display odd behavioral symptoms: he woke at night in the grip of nightmares, and began to have terrifying hallucinations. He complained of anxiety and had almost daily episodes of feverish agitation, which caused him to speak of suicide. He told anyone who would listen that he was tormented by memo-

ries of the war, the agony of men and animals, the carnage. After he disappeared for a week and was finally found in a dingy Pittsburgh hotel room,
fifty miles away, his wife made him seek medical help. At a veterans-aid
clinic a diagnosis was made of extreme psychosis as a result of the violence
of war. The syndrome in those years was generally known as "shell shock."
My uncle was sent to the mental unit of the veterans hospital in Perry Point,
Maryland, and there he remained for the rest of his life.

I recall visiting Uncle Harold with my mother and father once when I
was a young boy, before the war. We were going to New York, and the visit
was planned as a side trip on our way from Virginia. I had never seen him,
except as a figure in photographs taken years earlier: a cheery kid with
prominent teeth, like my mother's, and flashing, exuberant eyes. I had been
fascinated by Uncle Harold, the war hero, and he had taken on for me an
almost mythic shape. My mother was devoted to him, and, as a sedulous
eavesdropper, I couldn't help but absorb all the captivating details of his
dramatic life: the flaming battle for Saint-Mihiel that killed more than four
thousand Americans, his letters describing the savagery of combat, his painful recovery in a convalescent facility behind the front, the breakdown in
Pennsylvania, his sad confinement. By the time we turned up at the veterans
hospital on a luminous June day, I was looking forward excitedly, though
with a touch of squirmy disquiet, to meeting my shell-shocked uncle. I don't
remember whether my parents prepared me for the encounter, but it was
certainly not like anything I might have imagined, and I think that they, too,
may not have been ready for such an apparition.

The male attendant who brought him outside to greet us on the lawn
seemed to feel the need to urge him along, as he tottered toward us in his
army-issue robe and slippers, with gentle but persistent prods to the back.
This probably made him look even more helpless and disoriented than he
actually was, but he was plainly a soul without a mooring. I was alarmed by
his shambling gait and his empty gaze; I couldn't reconcile the old face, so
bony and desiccated, and the balding skull and trembling hands with the
vivid boy of the pictures. Most awful to me was the moment when he me-
chanically embraced my mother and whispered, "Hello, Edith." It was the
name of their older sister.

We remained there on the hospital lawn for perhaps no more than an
hour, amid the debris of a messy picnic. Uncle Harold said almost nothing
as we sat on a bench, and the monosyllables my mother coaxed from him

had a softly gargled incoherence. I knew that this was a scene I couldn't continue to witness, and I turned away in misery from my uncle and his drowned, sweetly musing brown eyes, and from the sight of my mother clutching his palsied hand, squeezing it over and over in some hopeless attempt at comfort or connection.

I later learned the truth about Uncle Harold. My father did not tell me until several years after my mother died, when I was eighteen or so, and presumably old enough to absorb the dread secret that our kinsman had been suffering not from shell shock but from syphilis. My father was a candid and sophisticated man, but even he had an awkward time telling me the truth. After the shock wore off, the knowledge that my uncle was still alive—that, as was so often the case, the microbes, rather than quickly murdering their host, held him hostage while they continued their leisurely depredations—made me ache inside. The great pox could dwell in a body for decades. By the time he was sent to the veterans hospital he was most likely afflicted by late syphilis; according to my father, the disease was acquired after his marriage and the birth of his only child. There was never a hint that either my aunt or my cousin, a boy whom I spent many summers with, had been tainted by the illness. But who knew exactly when he had got it? Somehow the plague had entered him. It had been a quiet case, but viciously malignant, beyond reach of the magic bullet or any other medical stratagem, and at the time of our visit he was succumbing to forms of neurosyphilis that devastate the brain and the spinal cord. The spirochetes had wrought a vegetative madness.

I thought a lot about Uncle Harold during my stay on the ward. Especially at night, in the dark, with Winkler's little radio pressed against my ear, trying to distract myself with the Artie Shaw or Glenn Miller tunes I could capture from the ether, I'd have a moment of sudden, heart-stopping panic and my uncle would draw ineluctably near. I could sense him in his hospital robe, silent, standing somewhere close by among the sleeping marines, a stooped figure whose presence portended a future I dared not think about.

While on a trip through Europe in 1760, Giovanni Casanova, that tireless gadabout, cocksman, and celebrity hound, stopped at Ferney to pay a visit to Voltaire. There seems to be no record of the two superstars' talking about syphilis, but it would have been a fitting topic, given its perennial fashionableness, and if they had spoken of it their attitude, in all likelihood, would have had a mocking overtone. Voltaire never let the horrid nature of the illness obtrude upon his own lighthearted view of it—he wrote wittily about the great pox in *Candide*—and throughout Casanova's memoirs there are anecdotes about syphilis that the author plainly regards as excruciatingly funny. Making sport of it may have been the only way in which the offspring of the Enlightenment could come to grips with a pestilence that seemed as immutably fixed in history as war or famine. In a secular age, gags were appropriate for an inexplicable calamity that in olden times had been regarded as divine retribution. Previous centuries had seen people calling on God for help, and God had not answered.

The disease first swept like a hurricane over Europe during the period of Columbus's voyages (whether Columbus and his crew were responsible for importing syphilis from the West Indies is disputed by scholars, but it seems a strong possibility), and it took an exceptionally virulent form, often killing its victims in the secondary, or rash-and-fever, stage, which most people in later epochs (including me) weathered without harm. In its congenital mode, it was particularly disfiguring and malevolent, which increased the terror. No wonder that the Diet of Worms, the same assembly that condemned Martin Luther for heresy, issued a mandate declaring that the "evil pocks" was a scourge visited upon mankind for the sin of blasphemy.

But it was the doctrine of original sin, falling upon both Catholics and backslid Presbyterians like me, that made the sufferers of syphilis pay a special price in moral blame unknown to those who acquired other diseases. This was particularly true in the early Victorian era, when a return to faith, after a long time of frivolous impiety, was coupled with a return to the Pauline precept that the act of sex is an act of badness—absolute badness more often than not, exceeding all other abominations. This connection with sexuality gave syphilis, in a puritanical culture, its peculiar aura of degradation. As Susan Sontag has shown in *Illness as Metaphor,* her study of the mythology of disease, all the major illnesses have prompted a moralistic and punitive response, and have given rise to entire theoretical systems based on phony psychologizing. The bubonic plague implied widespread moral pollution; tuberculosis was the product of thwarted passion and blighted hopes, or sprang from "defective vitality, or vitality misspent"; out of emotional frustration or repression of feeling has come the curse of cancer, whose victims are also often demonically possessed. As I have discovered firsthand, mental disorders may be the worst, inviting suspicion of inborn feebleness.

In such views, the disease itself expresses the character of the victim. Syphilis, however, has suffered a different stigma, one that has been of a singularly repellent sort. It has reflected neither feebleness nor misspent vitality nor repression of feeling—only moral squalor. In recent years, AIDS has been similarly stigmatized, despite extensive enlightenment. But in square, churchgoing America at the time of my diagnosis, a syphilitic was regarded not as a sexual hobbyist whose pastime had got out of hand—in other words, with the ribald tolerance Voltaire would have brought to the circumstance— but as a degenerate, and a dangerously infectious one at that. Doctors are, of course, supposed to be free of such proscriptive attitudes, but there are always some who are as easily bent as anyone else by religion or ideology. Klotz was one of these, and while I'm sure that he was only doing his duty in tracking my history, his temper was chillingly adversarial. Also, he was, in my case, guilty of an act of omission that unalterably stamped him as a doctor who hated not the disease but its victims.

As the wintry days and nights in the hospital wore on, and the Kahn tests continued to show my blood serum swarming with spirochetes, and I worried myself into a deeper and deeper feeling of hopelessness, I brooded over my past sex life, which seemed to me a paltry one, at least numerically speaking. By what improbable mischance had I sealed my doom? Even in those repressed years of the Bible Belt South, to have had at nineteen only three partners, two of whom I'd met in boozy mayfly matings already dimming in memory, scarcely made me feel like a red-hot lover, much less the randy alley cat generally associated with the disease. Still, as Winkler pointed out, even though syphilis was not as widespread as the clap, all it took was one quick poke in the wrong partner's hole and a man could be done for. Whose hole, then, and when? The actual encounters were all so recent, and together so few, that I could easily let my mind pounce on each one, trying to figure out which specific grappling had permitted the *T. pallidum* to begin its infestation.

On a bright morning, as I sat on my camp stool plunged into one of these self-lacerating reveries, Winkler came up with a mournful look to say that he was sorry but my Kahn remained "highly reactive." Then he announced that Dr. Klotz—finally, after many days—wished to see me, to take my case history. Was I religious? Winkler asked. When I said that I wasn't but asked him why he wanted to know, the corpsman rolled his eyes, then declared,

"He's got a kind of narrow-minded view of things." He added, as he had once before, that it was all part of a "personal fixation."

As I look back on that time, I can see that Klotz, whatever the complexities of his motivation, had a need to squeeze the most out of the vindictive rage against syphilis already prevailing in the armed forces—one that mirrored the broader abhorrence in American society. While Klotz was doubtless not typical of navy doctors, or the medical profession in general, he was working well within the pious and cold-blooded restraints regarding sexually transmitted diseases that had prevailed in the navy for many years. During the First World War, President Wilson's secretary of the navy, Josephus Daniels, a godly North Carolinian if there ever was one, made history in a small way by banishing alcohol from officers' wardrooms and elsewhere on naval ships and bases, thereby bringing to an end an ancient and cherished custom. But at least this created no mortal danger. In his intolerance of carnality, Daniels ruled against a proposal that sailors and marines be given free access to condoms, and thus became responsible for unnumbered venereally related illnesses and deaths. Apart from his own belief, Klotz was obviously the inheritor of a tradition with a firm root in Southern Christian fundamentalism.

In presenting my case history to Klotz that morning, I had to describe my relations with a girl and two older women. Klotz referred to these as "exposures." While the doctor took notes, I told him that, almost exactly two years before, I had lost my virginity for two dollars in a walk-up hotel room in Charlotte, North Carolina. I was a college freshman, and the woman was about thirty-five. In answer to his question about whether I had used protection, I replied that I thought so but could not be sure, since I had drunk too much beer for clear memory. I then went on to the next exposure. (What I did not describe to Klotz was the interminable anxiousness of waiting in the dismal little hotel lobby while my anesthetized classmate, a raunchy dude from Mississippi, who had initiated our debauch, preceded me for what seemed hours with Verna Mae, which was what she called herself. Nor did I tell the doctor that my memory of Verna Mae was of an immensely sad and washed-out towhead in a stained slip and dirty pink slippers who raised a skinny arm and took my two dollars with such lassitude that I thought she might be ill; nor did I recount being nearly ill myself, from apprehension and a stomach-churning disbelief at the idea that what I'd awaited with anxious joy since the age of twelve was about to happen, something so unbearably momentous that I barely registered the words when, sliding the two bucks into her brassiere, she said in a countrified voice, "I sure hope you don't have to take as long as that friend of yours.")

The second exposure was a girl, age eighteen, a college sophomore I'll call Lisa Friedlaender. (It is a reflection on the aridity of sexual life in the forties—even, or, I should say, especially, on college campuses—that there was a gap of nearly a year and a half between Verna Mae and Lisa.) I told Klotz that I had met Lisa, who was from Kew Gardens, New York, at a college in Danville, Virginia, the previous spring. I was by then enrolled in the Marine V-12 program at Duke and had traveled up to Danville for a weekend. That weekend, we had had intercourse (a word that made me writhe but that Klotz encouraged), and we had had it many times after that, both protected and unprotected, on my weekend leaves in April and May. She went home to Kew Gardens for summer vacation, and when she returned to Danville we resumed intercourse, having weekend sex until I was sent here, to Parris Island. I was certain that Lisa was not the source of the disease, I went on, since I was only her second partner and she was from a proper middle-class Jewish background, where the acquiring of such an illness was unlikely. (I had often wondered how a proper middle-class Southern lad like me had come to deserve anyone as angelic as my ripe and lively Lisa, with her incontinent desires, which matched mine and were the real reason, though I didn't tell Klotz, for our frequent lack of protection: we were fucking so continuously and furiously that I ran out of condoms. My native WASP folklore, which tended to idealize asthenic, inaccessible blondes, had not prepared me for this dark and lusty creature; we began rolling around on a moonlit golf green within two hours of our first meeting. I didn't tell this to Klotz, either, though Klotz the moral inquisitor at one point tipped his hand by demanding, "Were you in love?" To this I had no reply, having a sense that such a question really implied a policy decision. What of course was impossible to make Klotz understand about love was that if you were not yet twenty, and were a marine eventually headed for the Pacific who shared with your brothers the conviction that you would never see twenty-one, or a girl, ever again, and if the delirium of joy you felt the first time Lisa Friedlaender's nipples sprang up beneath your fingertips was love, then you were probably in love.)

My last exposure was a woman named Jeanette. Age about forty. I told Klotz that I was with a fellow marine in Durham when we picked up old

Jeanette and a female friend at a barbecue joint one night during the past August. They were both employees of the Liggett & Myers factory, where they worked on an assembly line making cigarettes. I had intercourse with Jeanette only once, unprotected. (The subtext in the case was largely anaph-rodisiac amnesia. As with Verna Mae, the beer I had consumed made mem-ory a slide show of incoherent instants: a wobbling ramble through the dark, collapsing together on the cold ground of a Baptist churchyard, hard by a tombstone, and inhaling the sweet raw smell of tobacco in the frizzy hair of Jeanette, who had just come off the night shift. I remembered nothing of the act itself, but for some obscure reason, as my confession spilled forth, the recollection of the carton of Chesterfields she had given me left a taste of sadness.)

When I finished, Klotz fiddled with his notes for a moment, then said, "You betrayed the girl, didn't you?"

I nodded my miserable agreement but made no reply.

"Has it occurred to you that you might have infected her?"

Again I nodded, for the possibility of having passed on the contagion had lingered in my mind for days, jabbing me with fierce self-reproach.

"You probably were infected by the prostitute in Charlotte or the woman in Durham," the doctor said. "Syphilis is prevalent among lower-class South-ern white women. That's why it's dangerous to go roaming around in the wrong places if you can't practice abstinence."

I couldn't respond to this. Although I was smothered with regret, I felt no remorse and was not about to say that I was sorry.

"There's no way now of knowing which woman infected you. Suppose you just write a letter to that girl and tell her that she may have been ex-posed to syphilis. You should also tell her to get tested right away and have appropriate treatment."

I recall trying to retrieve, at that moment, some serene boyhood mem-ory, a foolish escapade, any innocent event that might let me float above this anguish, but Klotz was too quick to permit me the solace.

"Nature has a way of compensating for nearly every reckless thing we do," he said.

A day or two after my interview with Klotz, the hospital corpsmen began to place tacky Christmas ornaments up around the ward; they painted a silver NOEL on the glass of the door and hung a hideous plastic trumpet-tooting angel from the central light fixture. The same day, I noticed that my gums were beginning to bleed. There had been some irritation before, but I had ignored the tenderness. This was serious bleeding. It was not "pink tooth-brush," a symptom employed to help advertise Ipana, the hot toothpaste of the day. It was a slight but constant seepage of blood into my mouth, one that made me aware of the sweetish taste throughout the day and left a red stain on my handkerchief whenever I blotted it away. I could tell it was ag-gravated by smoking—but I kept steadily puffing. My gums had become raw and spongy, and that night the act of toothbrushing created a crimson cataract. I developed a feverish, cruddy feeling. I was terrified, but I kept my alarm to myself. The spirochetes were on the attack. There were count-less ways the disease could make itself known, and I calculated that this was just one of them. When I told Winkler about my new trouble, he seemed puzzled, but said I should pay a visit to the hospital dentist, who might at least be able to relieve some of my distress. The dental officer was a dour man, trapped in routine, who offered neither comfort nor explanation; he did, however, swab out my mouth with a florid and repulsive lotion called gentian violet, a vial of which he gave me for daily application. It was an absurdity, a flimsy barrier against the onrushing ruin.

Days passed in a kind of suspended monotony of fear. Meanwhile, the weight of hopelessness, bearing down on my shoulders with almost tactile gravity—I thought of a yoke in the animal, burdened-down sense—had be-come a daily presence; I felt a suffocating discomfort in my brain. Sitting on a camp stool next to my bed, remote from the other marines, I began to withdraw into the cocoon of myself. The sex-demented clap patients, jab-bering about cunt and pussy, magnified my despair. I lost my appetite. Out-side my window, marines marched in the distance on the asphalt drill field, exhaling clouds of frigid breath. The glittering white inlet of the ocean rolled endlessly eastward like Arctic tundra. At night, after lights-out, I began to prowl the ward, padding about in anxiety until, returning to the stool, I would sit and stare at the expanse of water, dim in the starlight, and seem-ingly frozen solid. What a blessed relief it would be, I thought, to lie down and be encased in that overcoat of ice, motionless, without sensation and, finally, without care, gazing up at the indifferent stars.

I had kept up a busy correspondence during my early Marine Corps days. Fat envelopes, lots of them with addresses in familiar handwriting, envelopes of various colors and lengths (some with a not-yet-stale hint of perfume), were gifts that guys in the service awaited with greedy suspense, like children at Christmastime. I kept my seabag stuffed with reread letters, and Lisa Friedlaender had written to me often at Parris Island. In that buttoned-up age, it was probably not all that common for letter-writing lovers to express their craziness in steamy strophes, but Lisa had a gifted hand. Her remembrances to me were generally graphic and sometimes astonishing; she was way ahead of her time. But those were letters I could not read any longer; the very packet, which I kept tied up with string, was cursed with a vile pathology. Nor, despite Klotz's order, could I bring myself to write to Lisa.

Instead, I addressed myself to another problem: that of maintaining my composure in the face of a final, insupportable outrage. One morning, Winkler brought me two letters—one from Lisa (I put it away, unread) and one from my stepmother. Only two years before, my father had married, for reasons I was never able to fathom, an ungainly, humorless, pleasure-shunning middle-aged spinster, and the antipathy we felt for each other had been almost as immediate as our differences were irreconcilable. She was an observant Christian, curiously illiberal for an Episcopalian, while I had proudly begun to announce my skepticism and my fealty to Camus, whose *Le Mythe de Sisyphe* I'd read laboriously but with happiness in French at Duke, and whose principles, when I outlined them to her, she deemed "diabolical." I thought her a prig; she considered me a libertine. She was a teetotaler; I drank—a lot. Once, frankly baiting her while a little crocked, I praised masturbation as a universal delight, and she denounced me to my father as a "pervert." (I *had* gone too far.) She was educated, intelligent, and that made her bigotry the more maddening. I preserved a chill truce with the woman because of my love for my misguided father. She was a teacher of nursing, actually quite a good one—even, in a way, distinguished (onetime district president of the Graduate Nurses Association)—and therein lay another contradiction: nurses, like doctors, were supposed to be free of the moralism that drove her to write a pious letter meant to make me writhe on the rack of my dereliction.

How appalled she and my father were, she wrote, at the terrible news. (I had sent them a letter in which I was disingenuous enough to say that I had been sidelined with "a little blood problem," an evasion she immediately scented.) The only serious blood problem I could have was one of the malignant diseases like leukemia, and I plainly didn't have that, given my remarks about feeling in such good health. She went on to predict, in her chilly, professional way, that in all likelihood I could be cured by the new antibiotics, *provided* the disease had not progressed too far into the CNS (central nervous system, she explained helpfully, adding that the damage could be fearful and irreversible). Shifting into the spiritual mode, she informed me that one could only pray that the illness had not yet been invasive. She had no intention of judging me, she announced (pointing out that there was, of course, a Higher Judge), but then she asked me to look back on my recent way of life and ponder whether my self-indulgent behavior had not led to this—the words remain ineffaceable to this day—"awful moment of truth." Finally, she hoped I would be reassured that, in spite of her disapproval of the conduct that had brought me to this condition, she cared for me very, very much.

In pondering these events of fifty years ago, I've never felt seriously betrayed by memory—most of the moments I've re-created are so fresh in my mind that they have the quality of instant replay—but I know that I've been slightly tricked from time to time, and I've had to adjust my account of these events. That memory could be a clever deceiver was neatly demonstrated, when I began finishing this chronicle, by my "Medical History"—a little manual, faintly mildewed, with pages the color of a faded jonquil—which surfaced among my Marine Corps mementos while I was searching for something else. This is the standard medical record that accompanies every marine throughout his career. While my lapses were minor, the "Medical History" showed me to be quite off the mark about certain matters of chronology. I could have sworn, for example, that I was still in the hospital until a few days before Christmas, when in fact I had been returned to duty by then; the awful Yuletide decorations I recalled must have adorned not the ward but my barracks, considerably later. Also, I have written of those apparently unceasing Kahn tests, a ritual that kept me tense with fear. It seems impossible to me now that I was not bled daily—as I awaited the results, I recall, I was nearly devoured by anxiety—but the "Medical History" shows that there were only five of these procedures in the course of a month. I'm fascinated by the fact that my tendentious memory lured me into exaggerating the number of times I experienced this torture.

But Dr. Klotz and his behavior have remained mysterious. The "Medical History" reveals only his routine notations and a final, meticulously clear signature. I think Klotz has compelled my attention (slightly this side of obsession) all these years because, to put it simply, he was frightening. He represented, in his bloodless and remote way, the authority figure that most people dread encountering but so often do meet face-to-face: the dehumanized doctor. In later years, I would come to know many exemplary physicians, but also more than one for whom my memory of Klotz provided a creepy prototype. I never fathomed Klotz's need to chasten those whom he conceived to be sexual hoodlums among all the miserable, unwell marines who showed up for his help. I wasn't alone among these miscreants. Was it religion (as Winkler had hinted) that gave him his hang-up, some narrow faith that had provided him with a view of sex that was as fastidious as it was harsh? Perhaps, as Winkler also suggested without contradiction, it wasn't religion so much as that "personal fixation." If that was true, it was a fixation animated by cruelty. Nothing else would account for his failure to tell me from the outset that there was a possibility that I didn't have syphilis at all.

Several days after I received the letter from my stepmother, I was summoned to the end of the ward by Winkler, who led me into the tiny office of Klotz's second-in-command. Everyone called him Chief. He was a chief pharmacist's mate named Moss, a sandy-haired, overweight Georgian with a smoker's hack, good-heartedness written all over him. As in the past, he put me quickly at ease. He was an old man by my standards, probably thirty-five or older. I had come to trust and respect most of the medical corpsmen, like Moss and Winkler, who held out to sick marines a kind of spontaneous sympathy beyond the capacity of the doctors, or at least of the doctors I knew. And the feeling I had for Moss was not so tepid as mere respect; it was more like awe, for the year before he had taken part in the bloody landing at Tarawa, that slaughterhouse beyond compare, and there he had risked his big ass to save the lives of more than one marine, winning a commendation in the process. Marines and sailors were traditionally hostile to each other, but one could only regard someone like Moss with admiration, or even love, as I think I did that day. A couple of times before, he'd come by my sack to chat, always cheery and plainly eager to calm my fear, a good ol' boy from Valdosta, a bearlike, rather untidy guy who plainly conceived medicine to be a tender enterprise not entirely bound by technology. He told me that Lieutenant Commander Klotz had departed on Christmas leave but had left him instructions about my case. My case, in fact, was contained in a file on Moss's desk, and he said he wanted to talk to me about it.

First off, I didn't have syphilis.

I recall thinking, despite my apostasy, of Revelation: "He that over-cometh shall inherit all things . . ."

"I had a talk on the phone with the chief dental officer," Moss said. "He told me what he told Dr. Klotz. Your Vincent's disease cleared up almost immediately. Just a couple of old-fashioned applications of gentian violet. Smile for me, boy."

I smiled widely, a big, shit-eating grin, and Moss heaved with laughter. "Damned if you don't look like a Ubangi. Gentian violet. That old standby. The man who could find a way to get the violet out of gentian violet would make him some money."

"Tell me something, Chief," I said as Moss motioned for me to sit down. "If I get the situation correctly, my Kahn test has gone to negative. Zero. If this is true, and I guess it is, what's the connection?"

"Let me ask you a question," said Moss. "Did you ever have this condition—it's also called trench mouth—anytime before?"

I reflected for an instant, then said, "Yes, I believe I did, come to think about it. Up at Duke. There were these marines for a while—I was one of them—complaining about this inflammation in the mouth, and bleeding. I had it badly for some time, then it seemed to go away. I didn't think about it anymore. There was talk about it being spread by the unclean water we used to wash our trays in the mess hall. So tell me, Chief, what's the connection?"

Moss patiently explained to me what appeared to be the reason for Klotz's misdiagnosis, and what in fact had been behind the entire fiasco. He said that Klotz, after receiving the dental report, had written in my record book, "Dentist discharged patient for his Vincent's." That morning, Moss, out of curiosity, had followed up on this notation, checking out various venereal-disease manuals and textbooks for further enlightenment, and had discovered that the principal causes for false serological positives in the Kahn test were leprosy and yaws. (Jesus, I thought, leprosy and yaws!) There was no chance of my having acquired either of those exotic, largely hot-climate diseases, Moss went on. Klotz must have ruled them out all along, convinced (or, I thought, wanting to be convinced) that I had syphilis in a more or less advanced form. Moss said that Vincent's disease was mentioned as a possible cause, but a rare one—so rare that Klotz must have discounted it. I learned from Moss that despite Vincent's preposterously gruesome official name—acute necrotizing ulcerative gingivitis—the inflammation of the mouth itself was relatively mild and easy to treat, often with a single application to the gums of the powerful bactericide gentian violet. One of the causative organisms in Vincent's was another busy little spirochete (Moss spelled it out: *Treponema vincentii*), and it had shown up in my blood tests. With me there had been a recurrence of symptoms. "It's a good thing you finally went to the dentist," Moss concluded, "or you might have been here forever."

As much as I felt a friend and ally in the Chief, I still hesitated to state my case against Klotz, upon whom my rage and loathing grew more grimly focused, if that was possible, at every item Moss disclosed. I didn't want to strain the rapport I had with Moss by attacking his superior—for all I knew, though only God would know why, he might hold Klotz in high esteem. At the same time, the evil suspicions that sprang to mind as Moss murmured his litany of details had actually begun to make me a little nauseated, taking the glow off my euphoria, and there was no way I could let the suspicions rest. I said, "You know, Chief, he wanted to find the worst things. I guess I was too intimidated to tell him I've had that little scar on my dick all my life." Then I said, "Anyway, what this means is that Dr. Klotz could have told me there was a possibility of a false positive. A possibility." I paused. "But he didn't do that."

"That's really right." Moss didn't wait an extra beat, uttering the words with a soft, rising inflection that had a distinct edge of contempt and carried its own conviction of wrongdoing. I knew then that he was on my side.

"He's read what you've read," I persisted. "He knew about Vincent's disease. He could have run me through that drill, couldn't he? But he didn't do that, either. He could have spared me a lot of misery. He could have given me some hope—"

"That's really right."

"What is this jerk's problem, Chief?"

Klotz was on leave. Within a few hours I would return to the barracks and the drill field, just another healthy recruit thrust back into the maw of the war machine. I would never see the Chief again. Under the circumstances, it would be safe for Moss to give voice to whatever innermost feelings he had toward Klotz. But Moss was too much the wise old salt, too professional, and, doubtless, too loyal to an honorable code to go that far. Still, I sensed a comradely affinity, and it was denunciation enough, a spiritual handclasp, when he squinted at me and said, "He was punishin' you, boy, punishin' you."

As I left the hospital that day, I looked forward to the ordeal that my phantom illness had interrupted. Mean corporals with taut shiny scalps and bulging eyes would be at me again, poking their swagger sticks into my solar plexus, ramming their knees up my butt, calling me a cocksucker and a motherfucking sack of shit, terrorizing me with threats and drenching me with spittle and hatred, making my quotidian world such a miasma of fright that each night I would crawl into my bed like an invalid seeking death, praying for resurrection in another life. After that, there was the bloody Pacific, where I would murder and perhaps be murdered. But those were horrors I could deal with; in that gray ward I'd nearly been broken by fears that were beyond imagining.

Late that afternoon, I trudged past the drill field in the waning light, packing my seabag on my shoulder, hefting a load that seemed pounds lighter than it had a month before. At the far end of the field, a platoon of marines was tramping across the asphalt, counting in cadence, a chorus of young voices over which one voice, the drill instructor's, soared in a high maniacal wail. In some undiscoverable distance, faint yet clear, a band played the "Colonel Bogey March," that jauntily sad evocation of warfare, its brassy harmonies mingling triumph and grief. The music made me walk along with a brisk step, and I felt it hurrying me toward a future where though suffering was a certainty, it wore a recognizable face.

I had just enough time for a stop at the PX, to stock up on cigarettes and candy bars. The candy was a clandestine indulgence I felt I owed myself, and couldn't resist. Nor could I resist, along with the Baby Ruths, buying a postcard showing a photograph of marines grinning insincerely as they performed calisthenics, and the caption "Greetings from Parris Island." Toward Christmas I addressed it to my stepmother, and scribbled:

Dear Old Girl,

My frantic, obsessive copulations produced not syphilis but trench mouth. (Escaped from the Clap Shack in time to celebrate the birth of our Lord and Savior.)

Much love, Bill

[*New Yorker,* September 18, 1995.]

The South

The Oldest America

George Washington, never so versatile and wide-ranging in his interests as Thomas Jefferson, was nonetheless a man of many parts who knew well how to employ his leisure time. Firmly implanted in the American mythology is Washington the solemn, taciturn soldier and statesman, the Rembrandt Peale portrait of the postage stamps; less well known is the pre-Revolutionary Virginia planter who was devoted equally to horse racing and the theater and who regularly traveled the hundred and fifty miles south from Mount Vernon across the somnolent Tidewater to Williamsburg—then the capital of the colony—where he placed bets on the horses by day, and by night attended performances of Shakespeare by troupes imported from London. If today one should wonder how that Tidewater countryside appeared to Washington's eyes, the answer is: much as it does now. For to a degree largely unmatched in America, the region resembles in topography its ancient, earliest configuration.

It is the oldest part of our country, and suffered its upheaval and exploitation not in the nineteenth century like New England nor in the present century like California, but decades before we became a nation. Recklessly overcultivated in tobacco for more than a century, the once-rich bottomlands and green fields became fallow and depleted, so that even by the time of Washington's later years the abandoned farms and pastures were becoming reclaimed by new growths of woodland—oak and ash and sycamore and scrub pine. Long before the invention of the steam locomotive, much of the region—especially in the northern reaches, in the area just south of the Potomac and bordering on Chesapeake Bay—had subsided into the lazy sleep of a depopulated backwater, lacking either industry or productive agriculture, and for this reason (somewhat rare in the pattern of American regional growth), the absence of factories and railroads and great superhighways left the landscape mercifully unmarked. For this reason, too, the Tidewater has retained, generally speaking, a unique, unspoiled loveliness. Of course, architectural styles have changed the face of the landscape; shopping centers and split-level houses, indistinguishable from those elsewhere in America, have set their imprint here and there upon the land, and one should not visit the Tidewater in the expectation that each small town will yield a glimpse of something resembling Colonial Williamsburg or a Christopher Wren church. Also, the sprawling industrial and military complex that has grown up around Norfolk and Hampton Roads does not represent the quality of the Tidewater of which I speak.

Nevertheless, the old mansions and the eighteenth-century courthouses and churches still exist, their weathered brick rising out of the countryside from behind a grove of oaks in the most pleasantly disarming way. Such great old manor houses as Westover and Brandon and Carter's Grove still reign in lordly and stunning elegance along the banks of the James (these are the homes that H. L. Mencken, in outrage over the encroachment of all that was hideous in American architecture, described as the most perfectly proportioned dwellings ever fashioned by man).

Yet beyond all these noble relics of the past, there is the landscape itself, sometimes unspectacular and ordinary (cornfields, pine woods, country stores) but more often possessing a sorrowing beauty—everywhere lovelier and more mellow and melancholy and fledged with green than the hard-clay country that dominates the higher elevations of the Upper South. All this has to do, of course, with the rivers, the noble waterways that indent the face of the Tidewater and give the region so much of its character, including, indeed, its very name. Rarely here is one more than a few miles from a great brackish tideland stream, like the Rappahannock or the York or the James (and these are monumental rivers, too, in breadth if not in length: the James at its mouth is nearly six miles across, one of the widest estuaries in America), so that what is specifically Southern becomes commingled with the waterborne, the maritime. Thus the vistas of the solitary stands of pinewoods and barren cornfields, the sawmill in a remote clearing, the sudden immaculate and simple beauty of a freshly painted clapboard Negro church in a sunny grove are combined with a sense of broad, flat reaches of tidal shallows, mighty river estuaries, fish stakes and oyster boats, inlets and coves and bays, wild sudden squalls blowing out of the Chesapeake, the serene magnificence of sunrise coming up over the mouth of the Rappahannock, blood-red through the milk of morning mists. This is a low, drowsing, placid topography, literally half drowned. From the exhausted land the people have turned to the water for sustenance—river and estuary and bay. There is an odd truth in the remark that every native of the Tidewater is a skilled boatman, even if he is a farmer.

I love the place-names of the Virginia Tidewater—that juxtaposition of the Indian and old England, which is more mellifluous and striking than any other place in America. The names of the counties alone are resonant with the past: Essex and Middlesex and York, Isle of Wight and Sussex, King William, Surry, Prince George, King and Queen. These are mingled with the ancestral names of the red men, who still exist in diminishing numbers, isolated on small reservations, where they make a modest living by fishing for the fat shad that still teem in the rivers bearing their tribal names: Pamunkey and Mattaponi, Chickahominy, Powhatan and Kecoughtan, Chuckatuck and Corotoman. Names like these have a lazy beauty, corresponding to the meandering pace of a bygone era.

Yet at the same time, no place of comparable area owns such an abundance of curiously or fancifully named hamlets and villages—Ark, Rescue, Ordinary, Naxera, Shadow, Zuni, Lively (the posted speed here is five miles an hour), Bumpass. These are often nothing more than a crossroads, a general store with a post office, and here one is most likely to hear the throaty, slurred Tidewater speech—beyond doubt the speech of the Father of His Country. Encapsulated in time and space, the natives of the remoter reaches of this part of Virginia still use the phonetic forms of a language spoken two and a half centuries ago by their ancestors, settlers from Devon and Dorset. Its quality cannot be fully savored unless heard, but it may be suggested by noting that in the Tidewater you never go out but "oot," and that "house" rhymes less directly with "mouse" than with "noose." Still occasionally heard is the "yar" sound, in which "garden" becomes "gyarden," "far" turns into "fyah," and that old family name of Carter, one of Virginia's most illustrious, is transmuted into "Cyatah." This locution was, in my childhood, largely the property of old ladies fragrant with lavender—usually Daughters of the Confederacy—and still hovers in my memory as the quintessential sound of Southern womanhood and good breeding. Alas, it is dying out and will soon be gone forever, absorbed into the flattened-out tonality of Basic American.

Neither the Tidewater nor the rest of Virginia is, of course, the Deep South, but the underlying quality of the region remains, ultimately, distinctly Southern, adumbrated by the memory of a tragic past. Some of the bloodiest battles of the Civil War were fought on this soil, the selfsame soil to which there was brought for the first time—at Jamestown, in 1619, in the form of a handful of African slaves—the institution that became, in large part, the basis for that awful conflict. The legacy still remains. A majority of the Tidewater counties is heavily populated by Negroes; in many counties Negroes outnumber whites in a ratio resembling parts of Alabama and Mississippi. Here, as elsewhere in the South (and the North), there are grievous inequities; it is not in order to minimize those inequities that I reflect on the fact that no part of the South where such a racial composition is found has been so free of friction or strife. The Ku Klux Klan has never found a welcome here; the reign of terror that swept the South in the 1920s and 1930s— the decades of blazing crosses and lynchings—would have been unthinkable in the Tidewater.

I suggest that over the reach of decades a certain way of life may produce attitudes—a sense of fair play, an abhorrence of violence, a respect for the dignity of men—that supersede all other considerations and come to dominate moral conduct. However strongly it may be argued that this is not enough, it remains a tradition to be reckoned with, and the Virginia Tidewater lays justifiable claim to such a heritage. The region possesses the shortcomings common to all places, but the land and its people have achieved a certain harmony. Perhaps more than in any other comparable part of America, men have learned to get along with one another. It would be a pleasant irony if the land where the American dilemma began—close by the shores of the tranquil and lovely James, with its memory of black chained cargoes— should by its way of life come to embody an answer to that same dilemma.

[*McCall's,* July 1968.]

The James

In the early 1940s, despite my mediocre record at Christchurch School, my father set about to find a place where I might consummate my higher education. My wretched grades at Christchurch—by that I mean I had, I recall, flunked trigonometry four times in a row—made a scholarship anywhere out of the question, and since my father was paying the ticket, he felt (with great justification, I now realize) that he could determine the school I was going to attend. Anyplace north of the Potomac was unthinkable, since although my father was not really an unreconstructed Southerner (having married my mother, a lady from Pennsylvania), he was born in North Carolina only twenty-odd years after the Civil War; until his dying day his own father, my grandfather, limped from a knee wound obtained at Chancellorsville, and thus his mistrust of Yankee education was abiding and considerable. He resolved, then, that I should enroll in a college either in his native state or in Virginia, which was mine. Any institution farther south he regarded as primitive, and totally unfit for a lad of my ancestry and upbringing.

He narrowed the choices down. The University of Virginia, the most obvious option, was immediately cast aside; its reputation in regard to alcohol was more horrendous then than it is now; there were freshmen there, he had heard on good authority, who had been apprehended wandering the streets of Charlottesville in the throes of *delirium tremens,* and since my father sensed my own incipient predilection for the bottle, he was not about to throw me into the lion's den. Then there was William & Mary. So close at hand to my hometown, William & Mary seemed another obvious choice. But the school was eliminated on the grounds of what he called intellectual vacuity—a condition which had prevailed there ever since the founding of Phi Beta Kappa in 1776. Likewise, Washington & Lee was rejected. He found the place effete and frivolous, lacking in depth of concern for the examined life, and with some reason: after a brief visit to Lexington, he was profoundly offended by the hundreds of uniform seersucker suits and white buckskin shoes. He called them "Lightweights!" Finally, then, my father and I traveled up here to Hampden-Sydney, whose Presbyterianism and strictures about alcohol my father regarded happily. I hope you will not take it as all loose flattery when I say that I was so totally beguiled by this serene and lovely campus (it remains so, I'm happy to say, to this very day) and by the splendid easygoingness of the place, and by so much else in the human sense that was wonderfully attractive, that I said to myself: This is where I want to be. My father, I could tell, was also not immune to the charms of the school, physical and otherwise; but he was even more of a pushover for honorifics (it was one of his venial sins), and when he was informed that this venerable institution had contributed, on a per capita basis, more biographic subjects to *Who's Who in America* than any college in the country, he had all but had me enrolled. But soon after this, fate intervened—fate in the form of those four consecutive F's at Christchurch. To my intense disappointment I was turned down, and so I went to another Presbyterian college— Davidson, in North Carolina, which inexplicably overlooked my academic shortcomings and gained the indifferent student that Hampden-Sydney had prudently shunned. I was not a good scholar at Davidson either.

A short time ago, while brooding on this melancholy tale, I was naturally led into thoughts of Virginia. Despite my longtime residence in the North, my native state still compels a strong hold on me. If it is true that an artist's world is largely determined by the experiences of the first two decades of his life, and this is a theory held by Sigmund Freud, Ernest Hemingway, and myself, then the Virginia which I so vividly and poignantly recall from my early years worked on me a lasting effect, made me in large measure the writer that I am. And so, as I cast about for a theme which might be appropriate to talk about, I hesitated, wondering if the simplicity of the idea that struck me might not, in its very simplicity, be inadequate. On the other hand, what I had in mind did seem to represent something profoundly important, even critical, in its significance not only for Virginia but for the future and the quality of all our lives.

I am speaking of a river, one that flows less than forty miles north of here. A nearby stream, the Appomattox, is its tributary, familiar to all of you. I am referring, of course, to the James. To the north, as it winds through Buckingham and Albemarle counties, and past the old plantation of Bremo in Fluvanna, the James is a modest and pleasant stream, a mere trickle of an unfledged watercourse meandering through the Piedmont. But down on the east bank of the lower Peninsula, where I was born and reared, the river is nearly six miles across at its widest, a vast and lonely expanse that makes up one of the broadest estuaries of any river in America. More than anything else, the James River was the absolute and dominating physical presence of my childhood and early youth. As I envision how a child growing up on the flanks of the Rockies or Sierras must ever afterward be enthralled to the memory of mountain peaks, or as I recollect how a writer like Willa Cather, brought up on the Nebraska prairies, was haunted for life by that majestically unending "sea of grass," so for me the sheer geographical fact of the James was central to my experience, so much a part of me that even now I wonder whether some of that salty-sweet water might not have entered my bloodstream. A good deal of this, of course, had to do with the omnipresent spell of the river's prodigious history. No river in America was ever compelled to carry such an onerous burden, and we little tykes were never allowed to forget it as we sat in our classrooms overlooking the sovereign waterway itself, informed by one schoolmarm after another that yonder—just there!—Captain John Smith sailed past on his momentous journey, while just there, too, in 1619, another ship lumbered upstream with a different cargo to make the James the mother-river of Negro slavery for the whole New World. And nearby were the great river mansions—Carter's Grove, Westover, Shirley—populated with ghosts of bygone centuries.

But if the James was the past, that past coexisted with the present—and what a vital present that was! Winter, summer, spring, and fall—the river was rarely out of my sight; its presence subtly intruded on all my other senses. When I woke up on spring mornings the first thing I smelled was the river's brackish odor on the wind, a rich mingling of salt and seaweed and tidal mud, of organic matter in benign dissolution. There was the music of

the river, too, diurnal sounds which wove themselves into the very fabric of
village life—the cry of gulls; waves thrusting, lapping; the flapping of sails as
they luffed at the pier; boat horns; and always the singsong voices of Negro
oystermen as they labored above their tongs. We swam in the river from
April until October; the water—partly fresh, partly oceanic—was faintly sa-
line on the tongue, and in July it was as warm as mother's milk, and just as
reassuring. The salinity, of course, accounted for the quality of the oysters;
cousins to the Lynnhaven variety, they were the size of small saucers and
utterly luscious to swallow; and then there were crabs. The crabs were not
simply abundant; they existed in such flabbergasting profusion as to seem
almost menacing. In midsummer we netted swarms of them with absurd
ease from the village pier, using hunks of gamy meat for bait. When I was
eleven or twelve I was a soft-shell-crab businessman; the delicious little
creatures were so numerous in the mudflats of low tide that I could fill a
market basket in less than an hour and then peddle these—layered with
fragrant seaweed—at the back doors of the village houses, where the ladies
grumbled at my exorbitant price: three cents apiece, an inflationary penny
more than the previous year. I loved this big, fecund, blowsy, beautiful,
erotic river. It was erotic, and I achieved with it a penultimate intimacy by
nearly drowning in it in my thirteenth year, when the little boat in which I
was learning to sail capsized and sank. Still, I loved the James, and in memory its summertime shores are tangled with all that piercing delight of
youthful romance; recollecting the moonlight in huge quicksilver oblongs
on those dark waters, and the drugstore perfume of gardenia, and boys' and
girls' voices. I no longer wonder why the river had such a lasting effect on
my spirit, becoming almost in itself a metaphor for the painful sweetness of
life and its mystery.

[Excerpted from a commencement address at Hampden-Sydney College, May 23,
1980.]

Children of a Brief Sunshine

If the accident of birth caused you to spend most of your early life, as I did, on what is known as the Virginia historic peninsula, you were apt to grow up with a ponderous sense of the American past. As a boy I was made constantly aware of the trinity of national shrines—Jamestown, Yorktown, and Williamsburg—which even then, in the 1930s, brought tourists flocking to that seventy-mile oblong of somnolent Tidewater lowland that juts southeastward from Richmond between two of the country's most venerable rivers, the York and the James. But at that age, proximity and familiarity breed, if not contempt, then a certain callow indifference, and I don't recall being at all thrilled by the greater part of my admittedly august surroundings.

Jamestown was merely a boring landing on the river, heavy with melancholy and ancient, illegible tombstones. Yorktown, for me, possessed no glamour, none of the allure of a world-class battleground on the order of Waterloo or Hastings, but was simply a river beach where we went to gorge ourselves on hot dogs and to swim in the soupy tidal water, thick with jellyfish. For some reason verging on the heretical, Colonial Williamsburg never captured my fancy; it seemed even then a place largely contrived and artificial, and it left me cold. But part of my spirit was always mysteriously drawn to the James River mansions. They spoke to me in a secret, exciting way that other landmarks could never speak, and I still consider them among the state's truly captivating attractions.

Westover and *Brandon*. *Shirley* and *Carter's Grove*. There are other fine Colonial structures in the Tidewater, but these four remain the exemplars of the noble species of dwelling that the early planters built on the banks of the James, creating, from native brick and timber, likenesses of the country houses of England they had left behind, but in each case, out of some quirky genius, imparting to the whole an individuality that remains arrestingly American. The mansions have of course undergone much restoration since the mid-eighteenth century, when they were built. (William Byrd's Westover, perhaps the most splendid of the group, was badly mutilated by fire during the Civil War.) But one of the remarkable things about these houses is the way they have escaped the look of having been prettified by the embalmer's hand. Although they are linked in spirit by their obviously Georgian origins, part of the charm of each lies in its almost defiant distinctiveness—Shirley, with its absence of wings, having a lofty solidity, in contrast, say, to the dignified horizontal expansiveness of Brandon and its rectangular wings attached to the center by connecting passageways. Each is unique, and a surprise.

There are perhaps few habitations anywhere that ever so successfully fused aesthetic delightfulness with unabashed commerce. The plantation houses were really the headquarters for complex business enterprises. Their situation on the river happened not primarily because of the ingratiating view, but because the James was the means whereby each estate's golden harvest of tobacco was shipped back to the insatiable pipe smokers and snuff dippers of England and the Continent. What strikes one, then, is that the homes—created by gentlemen for whom profit was a paramount concern—are so fastidious yet so sensuous in their elegance, so satisfying in terms of all those components that make up the nearly perfect human abode. And all of this took place on the breast of a raw and primitive continent whose often violent settlement had begun not many years before.

How easy the temptation must have been to erect something tacky and utilitarian and to make one's getaway; the banks of the waterways of the earth have been littered by exploiters' shameless eyesores. But Virginia planters like William Byrd and his fellow proprietors, entrepreneurial though they were, made up a rare breed whose sense of environment was subtle and demanding. We know from the records they left that they responded with passion to the music of Purcell and Lully, to the *Eclogues* and *Georgics* of Virgil; why should they not be determined that their surroundings be imbued with equal serenity and refinement?

Among other things, these fog-dampened Britons were plainly intoxicated with the flowering of Virginia's lush and sun-drenched countryside. And so what impressed me as a boy, perhaps unconsciously, impresses me now with logic and force; the harmonious connection between the mansions and their natural surroundings, each of them seeming to grow like an essential ornament in a landscape of huge, hovering shade trees, boxwood-and-rose-scented gardens, and a sumptuous lawn undulating to the river's edge. Two hundred and fifty years later this mingling of elements has a flowing integrity and authenticity. Also, humanity and wit.

Look for humanity and wit almost everywhere in one of the James River mansions. In the great downstairs hall, the visitor will see how two doors facing each other allowed guests to arrive from opposite directions: by way of a tree-lined carriage road or, for people coming by barge or boat, across the lawn from the bank of the river. In the solitude of that barely civilized wilderness, guests were welcomed and fussed over, and they came incessantly. Isolation made hospitality more than a ritual: It was part of a hungry need for communion, and the splendidly paneled rooms that give off the main hall saw manic activity: dancing and reading aloud; parlor games; music played on spinet and mandolin and harpsichord; gossip, flirtation, and seduction; card games; much drinking of local applejack and fine Bordeaux wine around fireplaces that were everywhere and fueled from inexhaustible sources of Tidewater timber. Early on, Virginia developed a serious cuisine. At tables in the big dining room, the food—usually supplied from outside cookhouses—was served to the household and to the endless stream of visitors in orgiastic plenty that still makes one marvel.

No time or place is without its woes and discomforts, and surely the planters often worked hard and were besieged by problems, but a nimbus of hedonism surrounds our vision of the James River mansions in their heyday. Both the inhabitants and the crowd of callers must have had a lot of fun. Set down as they were in a delectable backwater where their only excuse for being was to supply their countrymen with a mildly euphoric weed they extracted from the fat land with absurd ease, the planters were among the favored few in history for whom the circumstances of life had produced a vast amount of enjoyment and relatively little adversity. Although the

American Revolution would eventually produce friction and discontent, the proprietors appeared blissfully free of political anxieties. The pestilences that had decimated Jamestown had subsided. War—both European and domestic—was many comfortable miles away. The local Indians had been pacified years before. The low-church Episcopal God whom the planters sometimes worshipped was forgiving and tolerant of their voluptuous pleasures, leaving the burden of sin to be suffered by the Puritans, far north in icy New England. In the long and disorderly chronicle of the West, with its chiaroscuro of serenity and dark agony, they were children of a brief sunshine.

One discordant presence was usually forgotten, or overlooked, even then. As the present-day visitor looks out across the tidy beds of flowers bordered by boxwood and traversed by brick walls, his gaze may linger on the outbuildings (or the spot where they once stood), and they too will seem to fall symmetrically into place. These smaller buildings—servants' quarters, cookhouse, tannery, and smokehouse, carpenter's shop, all decently contrived and of honest and workmanlike construction—were, of course, the demesne of the black slaves, whose toil had been essential to the creation and success of the mansions, and continued to assure their perpetuation. The "people," as they were so often called, had been generally treated with care and kindness, so it is understandable that the planters suffered vexation over their common plight and cursed heaven for their predicament. However, not knowing what else to do, they allowed the problem to pass into the hands of later generations, who resolved the matter in one of the most murderous wars ever fought. Meanwhile, the beautiful mansions endured, and still endure.

[*Architectural Digest*, March 1984.]

Race and Slavery

This Quiet Dust

You mought be rich as cream
And drive you coach and four-horse team,
But you can't keep de world from moverin' round
Nor Nat Turner from gainin' ground.

And your name it mought be Caesar sure
And got you cannon can shoot a mile or more,
But you can't keep de world from moverin' round
Nor Nat Turner from gainin' ground.

—OLD-TIME NEGRO SONG

My native state of Virginia is, of course, more than ordinarily conscious of its past, even for the South. When I was learning my lessons in the mid-1930s at a grammar school on the banks of the James River, one of the required texts was a history of Virginia—a book I can recall far more vividly than any history of the United States or of Europe I studied at a later time. It was in this work that I first encountered the name Nat Turner. The reference to Nat was brief; as a matter of fact, I do not think it unlikely that it was the very brevity of the allusion—amounting almost to a quality of haste—which captured my attention and stung my curiosity. I can no longer quote the passage exactly, but I remember that it went something like this: "In 1831, a fanatical Negro slave named Nat Turner led a terrible insurrection in Southampton County, murdering many white people. The insurrection was immediately put down, and for their cruel deeds Nat Turner and most of the other Negroes involved in the rebellion were hanged." Give or take a few harsh adjectives, this was all the information on Nat Turner supplied by that forgotten historian, who hustled on to matters of greater consequence.

I must have first read this passage when I was ten or eleven years old. At that time my home was not far from Southampton County, where the rebellion took place, in a section of the Virginia Tidewater which is generally considered part of the Black Belt because of the predominance of Negroes in the population. (When I speak of the South and Southerners here, I speak of *this* South, where Deep South attitudes prevail; it would include parts of Maryland and East Texas.) My boyhood experience was the typically ambivalent one of most native Southerners, for whom the Negro is simultaneously taken for granted and as an object of unending concern. On the one hand, Negroes are simply a part of the landscape, an unexceptional feature of the local scenery, yet as central to its character as the pinewoods and sawmills and mule teams and sleepy river estuaries that give such color and tone to the Southern geography. Unnoticed by white people, the Negroes blend with the land and somehow melt and fade into it, so that only when one reflects upon their possible absence, some magical disappearance, does one realize how unimaginable this absence would be: it would be easier to visualize a South without trees, without *any* people, without life at all. Thus, at the same time, ignored by white people, Negroes impinge upon their collective subconscious to such a degree that it may be rightly said that they become the focus of an incessant preoccupation, somewhat like a monstrous, recurring dream populated by identical faces wearing expressions of inquietude and vague reproach. "Southern whites cannot walk, talk, sing, conceive of laws or justice, think of sex, love, the family, or freedom without responding to the presence of Negroes." The words are those of Ralph Ellison, and, of course, he is right.

Yet there are many Souths, and the experience of each Southerner is modified by the subtlest conditions of self and family and environment and God knows what else, and I have wondered if it has ever properly been taken into account how various this response to the presence of the Negroes can be. I cannot tell how typical my own awareness of Negroes was, for instance, as I grew up near my birthplace—a small seaside city about equally divided between black and white. My feelings seem to have been confused and blurred, tinged with sentimentality, colored by a great deal of folklore, and wobbling always between a patronizing affection, fostered by my elders, and downright hostility. Most importantly, my feelings were completely uninformed by that intimate knowledge of black people which Southerners claim as their special patent; indeed, they were based upon an almost total ignorance.

For one thing, from the standpoint of attitudes toward race, my upbring-ing was hardly unusual: it derived from the simple conviction that Negroes were in every respect inferior to white people and should be made to stay in their proper order in the scheme of things. At the same time, by certain Southern standards my family was enlightened: although my mother taught me firmly that the use of "lady" instead of "woman" in referring to a Negro female was quite improper, she writhed at the sight of the extremes of Negro poverty and would certainly have thrashed me had she ever heard me use the word "nigger." Yet outside the confines of family, in the lower-middle-class school world I inhabited every day, this was a word I commonly used. School segregation, which was an ordinary fact of life for me, is devastat-ingly effective in accomplishing something that it was only peripherally de-signed to do: it prevents the awareness even of the existence of another race. Thus, whatever hostility I bore toward the Negroes was based almost en-tirely upon hearsay.

And so the word "nigger," which like all my schoolmates I uttered so freely and so often, had even then an idle and listless ring. How could that dull epithet carry meaning and conviction when it was applied to a people so diligently isolated from us that they barely existed except as shadows which came daily to labor in the kitchen, to haul away garbage, to rake up leaves? An unremarked paradox of Southern life is that its racial animosity is really grounded not upon friction and propinquity, but upon an almost complete lack of contact. Surrounded by a sea of Negroes, I cannot recall more than once—and then briefly, when I was five or six—ever having played with a Negro child, or ever having spoken to a Negro, except in tri-fling talk with the cook, or in some forlorn and crippled conversation with a dotty old grandfather angling for hardshell crabs on a lonesome Sunday af-ternoon many years ago. Nor was I by any means uniquely sheltered. What-ever knowledge I gained in my youth about Negroes I gained from a distance, as if I had been watching actors in an all-black puppet show.

Such an experience has made me distrust any easy generalizations about the South, whether they are made by white sociologists or Negro playwrights, Southern politicians or Northern editors. I have come to understand at least as much about the Negro after having lived in the North. One of the most egregious of the Southern myths—one in this case propagated solely by Southerners—is that of the Southern white's boast that he "knows" the

Negro. Certainly in many rural areas of the South the cultural climate has been such as to allow a mutual understanding, and even a kind of intimacy, to spring up between the races, at least in some individual instances. But my own boyhood surroundings, which were semi-urban (I suppose suburban is the best description, though the green little village on the city's outskirts where I grew up was a far cry from Levittown), and which have become the youthful environment for vast numbers of Southerners, tended almost totally to preclude any contact between black and white, especially when that contact was so sedulously proscribed by law.

Yet if white Southerners cannot "know" the Negro, it is for this very reason that the entire sexual myth needs to be reexamined. Surely a certain amount of sexual tension between the races does continue to exist, and the Southern white man's fear of sexual aggression on the part of the Negro male is still too evident to be ignored. But the nature of the growth of the urban, modern South has been such as to impose ever more effective walls between the races. While it cannot be denied that slavery times produced an enormous amount of interbreeding (with all of its totalitarianism, this was a free-for-all atmosphere far less self-conscious about carnal mingling than the Jim Crow era which began in the 1890s) and while even now there must logically take place occasional sexual contacts between the races—especially in rural areas where a degree of casual familiarity has always obtained—the monolithic nature of segregation has raised such an effective barrier between whites and Negroes that it is impossible not to believe that theories involving a perpetual sexual "tension" have been badly inflated. Nor is it possible to feel that a desire to taste forbidden fruit has ever really caused this barrier to be breached. From the standpoint of the Negro, there is indifference or uncomplicated fear; from that of the white—segregation, the law, and, finally, indifference too. When I was growing up, the older boys might crack wan jokes about visiting the Negro whorehouse street (patronized entirely, I later discovered, by Negroes plus a few Scandinavian sailors), but to my knowledge none of them ever really went there. Like Negroes in general, Negro girls were to white men phantoms, shadows. To assume that anything more than a rare and sporadic intimacy on any level has existed in the modern South between whites and Negroes is simply to deny, with a truly willful contempt for logic, the monstrous effectiveness of that apartheid which has been the Southern way of life for almost three quarters of a century.

I have lingered on this matter only to try to underline a truth about Southern life which has been too often taken for granted, and which has therefore been overlooked or misinterpreted. Most Southern white people *cannot* know or touch black people and this is because of the deadly intimidation of a universal law. Certainly one feels the presence of this gulf even in the work of a writer as supremely knowledgeable about the South as William Faulkner, who confessed a hesitancy about attempting to "think Negro," and whose Negro characters, as marvelously portrayed as most of them are, seem nevertheless to be meticulously *observed* rather than *lived*. Thus, in *The Sound and the Fury*, Faulkner's magnificent Dilsey comes richly alive, yet in retrospect one feels this is a result of countless mornings, hours, days Faulkner had spent watching and listening to old Negro servants, and not because Dilsey herself is a being created from a sense of withinness: at the last moment Faulkner draws back, and it is no mere happenstance that Dilsey, alone among the four central figures from whose points of view the story is told, is seen from the outside rather than from that intensely "inner" vantage point, the interior monologue.

Innumerable white Southerners have grown up as free of knowledge of the Negro character and soul as a person whose background is rural Wisconsin or Maine. Yet, of course, there is a difference, and it is a profound one, defining the white Southerner's attitudes and causing him to be, for better or for worse, whatever it is he is to be. For the Negro is *there*. And he is there in a way he never is in the North, no matter how great his numbers. In the South he is a perpetual and immutable part of history itself, a piece of the vast fabric so integral and necessary that without him the fabric dissolves; his voice, his black or brown face passing on a city street, the sound of his cry rising from a wagonload of flowers, his numberless procession down dusty country roads, the neat white church he has built in some pine grove with its air of grace and benison and tranquillity, his silhouette behind a mule team far off in some spring field, the wail of his blues blaring from some jukebox in a backwoods roadhouse, the sad wet faces of nursemaids and cooks waiting in the evening at city bus stops in pouring rain—the Negro is always *there*.

No wonder then, as Ellison says, the white Southerner can do virtually nothing without responding to the presence of Negroes. No wonder the white man so often grows cranky, fanciful, freakish, loony, violent: how else respond to a paradox which requires, with the full majesty of law behind it, that he deny the very reality of a people whose multitude approaches and often exceeds his own; that he disclaim the existence of those whose human presence has marked every acre of the land, every hamlet and crossroad and city and town, and whose humanity, however inflexibly denied, is daily evidenced to him like a heartbeat in loyalty and wickedness, madness and hilarity and mayhem and pride and love? The Negro may feel that it is too late to be known, and that the desire to know him reeks of outrageous condescension. But to break down the old law, to come to *know* the Negro, has become the moral imperative of every white Southerner.

II

I suspect that my search for Nat Turner, my own private attempt as a novelist to re-create and bring alive that dim and prodigious black man, has been at least a partial fulfillment of this mandate, although the problem has long since resolved itself into an artistic one—which is as it should be. In the late 1940s, having finished college in North Carolina and come to New York, I found myself again haunted by that name I had first seen in the Virginia history textbook. I had learned something more of Southern history since then, and I had become fascinated by the subject of Negro slavery. One of the most striking aspects of the institution is the fact that in the two hundred and fifty years of its existence in America, it was singularly free of organized uprisings, plots, and rebellions. (It is curious that as recently as the late 1940s, scholarly insights were lagging, and I could only have suspected then what has since been made convincing by such historians as Frank Tannenbaum and Stanley Elkins:* that American Negro slavery, unique in its psychological oppressiveness—the worst the world has ever known—was simply so despotic and emasculating as to render organized revolt next to impossible.) There were three exceptions: a conspiracy by the slave Gabriel Prosser and his followers near Richmond in the year 1800, the plot betrayed, the conspirators hanged; a similar conspiracy in 1822, in Charleston, South Carolina, led by a free Negro named Denmark Vesey, who also was betrayed

---

* There are several references to Elkins in these essays. Elkins's work has undergone such severe revision by other historians as to make my own responses to his theories appear perhaps a bit simplistic. Nonetheless, his work remains important and most of his insights are still valid.—W.S. (1982)

before he could carry out his plans, and who was executed along with other members of the plot.

The last exception, of course, was Nat Turner, and he alone in the entire annals of American slavery—alone among all those "many thousand gone"—achieved a kind of triumph.

Even today, many otherwise well-informed people have never heard the name Nat Turner, and there are several plausible reasons for such an ignorance. One of these, of course, is that the study of our history—and not alone in the South—has been tendentious in the extreme and has often avoided even an allusion to a figure like Nat, who inconveniently disturbs our notion of a slave system which, though morally wrong, was conducted with such charity and restraint that any organized act of insurrectory and murderous violence would be unthinkable. But a general ignorance about Nat Turner is even more understandable in view of the fact that so little is left of the actual record. Southampton County, which even now is off the beaten track, was at that period the remotest backwater imaginable. The relativity of time allows us elastic definitions: 1831 was yesterday. Yet the year 1831, in the presidency of Andrew Jackson, lay in the very dawn of our modern history, three years before a railroad ever touched the soil of Virginia, a full fifteen years before the use of the telegraph. The rebellion itself was of such a cataclysmic nature as practically to guarantee confusion of the news, distortion, wild rumors, lies, and, finally, great areas of darkness and suppression; all of these have contributed to Nat's obscurity.

As for the contemporary documents themselves, only one survives: "The Confessions of Nat Turner," a brief pamphlet of some five thousand words, transcribed from Nat's lips as he awaited trial, by a somewhat enigmatic lawyer named Thomas Gray, who published the "Confessions" in Baltimore and then vanished from sight. There are several discrepancies in Gray's transcript but it was taken down in haste, and in all major respects it seems completely honest and reliable. Those few newspaper accounts of the time, from Richmond and Norfolk, are sketchy, remote, filled with conjecture, and are thus virtually worthless. The existing county court records of Southampton remain brief and unilluminating, dull lists, a dry catalogue of names in fading ink: the white people slain, the Negroes tried and transported south, or acquitted, or convicted and hanged.

Roughly seventy years after the rebellion (in 1900, which by coincidence was the year Virginia formally adopted its first Jim Crow laws), the single scholarly book ever to be written on the affair was published—*The South-ampton Insurrection,* by a Johns Hopkins Ph.D. candidate named William S. Drewry, who was an unreconstructed Virginian of decidedly pro-slavery leanings and a man so quaintly committed to the *ancien régime* that, in the midst of a description of the ghastliest part of the uprising, he was able to reflect that "slavery in Virginia was not such to arouse rebellion, but was an institution which nourished the strongest affection and piety in slave and owner, as well as moral qualities worthy of any age of civilization." For Drewry, Nat Turner was some sort of inexplicable aberration, like a man from Mars. Drewry was close enough to the event in time, however, to be able to interview quite a few of the survivors, and since he also possessed a bloodthirsty relish for detail, it was possible for him to reconstruct the chro-nology of the insurrection with what appears to be considerable accuracy. Drewry's book (it is of course long out of print) and Nat's "Confessions" re-main the only significant sources about the insurrection. Of Nat himself, his background and early years, very little can be known. This is not disadvanta-geous to a novelist, since it allows him to speculate—with a freedom not accorded the historian—upon all the intermingled miseries, ambitions, frustrations, hopes, rages, and desires which caused this extraordinary black man to rise up out of those early mists of our history and strike down his oppressors with a fury of retribution unequaled before or since.

He was born in 1800, which would have made him at the time of the insur-rection thirty-one years old—exactly the age of so many great revolutionar-ies at the decisive moment of their insurgency: Martin Luther,* Robespierre, Danton, Fidel Castro. Thomas Gray, in a footnote to the "Confessions," de-scribes him as having the "true Negro face" (an offhand way of forestalling an assumption that he might have possessed any white blood), and he adds that "for natural intelligence and quickness of apprehension he is surpassed by few men I have ever seen"—a lofty tribute indeed at that inflammatory instant, with antebellum racism at its most hysteric pitch. Although little is known for certain of Nat's childhood and youth, there can be no doubt that

---

* See Erik Erikson's *Young Man Luther* for a brilliant study of the development of the revolutionary impulse in a young man, and the relationship of this impulse to the father figure. Although it is best to be wary of any heavy psychoanalytical emphasis, one cannot help believing that Nat Turner's relationship with his father (or his surrogate father, his master) was tormented and complicated, like Luther's.—W.S. (1982)

he was very precocious and that he not only learned to read and write with ease—an illustrious achievement in itself, when learning to read and write was forbidden to Negroes by law—but at an early age acquired a knowledge of astronomy, and later on experimented in making paper and gunpowder. (The resemblance here to the knowledge of the ancient Chinese is almost too odd to be true, but I can find no reason to doubt it.)

The early decades of the nineteenth century were years of declining prosperity for the Virginia Tidewater, largely because of the ruination of the land through greedy cultivation of tobacco—a crop which had gradually disappeared from the region, causing the breakup of many of the big old plantations and the development of subsistence farming on small holdings. It was in these surroundings—a flat pastoral land of modest farms and even more modest homesteads, where it was rare to find a white man prosperous enough to own more than half a dozen Negroes, and where two or three slaves to a family was the general rule—that Nat was born and brought up, and in these surroundings he prepared himself for the apocalyptic role he was to play in history. Because of the failing economic conditions it was not remarkable that Nat was purchased and sold several times by various owners (in a sense, he was fortunate in not having been sold off to the deadly cotton and rice plantations of South Carolina and Georgia, which was the lot of many Virginia Negroes of the period); and although we do not know much about any of these masters, the evidence does not appear to be that Nat was ill-treated, and in fact one of these owners (Samuel Turner, brother of the man whose property Nat was born) developed so strong a paternal feeling for the boy and such regard for Nat's abilities that he took the fateful step of encouraging him in the beginnings of an education.

The atmosphere of the time and place was fundamentalist and devout to a passionate degree, and at some time during his twenties Nat, who had always been a godly person—"never owning a dollar, never uttering an oath, never drinking intoxicating liquors, and never committing a theft"—became a Baptist preacher. Compared to the Deep South, Virginia slave life was not so rigorous; Nat must have been given considerable latitude and found many opportunities to preach and exhort the Negroes. His gifts for preaching, for prophecy, and his own magnetism seem to have been so extraordinary that he grew into a rather celebrated figure among the Negroes of the county, his influence even extending to the whites, one of whom—a poor, half-cracked overseer named Brantley—he converted to the faith and baptized in a millpond in the sight of a multitude of the curious, both black and white. (After this no one would have anything to do with Brantley, and he left the county in disgrace.)

At about this time Nat began to withdraw into himself, fasting and praying, spending long hours in the woods or in the swamp, where he communed with the Spirit and where there came over him, urgently now, intimations that he was being prepared for some great purpose. His fanaticism grew in intensity, and during these lonely vigils in the forest he began to see apparitions:

> I saw white spirits and black spirits engaged in battle, and the sun was darkened; the thunder rolled in the heavens and blood flowed in streams. . . . I wondered greatly at these miracles, and prayed to be informed of a certainty of the meaning thereof; and shortly afterwards, while laboring in the fields, I discovered drops of blood on the corn as though it were dew from heaven. For as the blood of Christ had been shed on this earth, and had ascended to heaven for the salvation of sinners, it was now returning to earth again in the form of dew. . . . On the twelfth day of May, 1828, I heard a loud noise in the heavens, and the Spirit instantly appeared to me and said the Serpent was loosened, and Christ had laid down the yoke he had borne for the sins of men, and that I should take it on and fight against the Serpent, for the time was fast approaching when the first should be last and the last should be first. . . .

Like all revolutions, that of Nat Turner underwent many worrisome hesitations, false starts, procrastinations, delays (with appropriate irony, Independence Day 1830 had been one of the original dates selected, but Nat fell sick and the moment was put off again); finally, however, on the night of Sunday, August 21, 1831, Nat, together with five other Negroes in whom he had placed his confidence and trust, assembled in the woods near the home of his owner of the time, a carriage maker named Joseph Travis, and commenced to carry out a plan of total annihilation. The penultimate goal was the capture of the county seat, then called Jerusalem (a connotation certainly not lost on Nat, who, with the words of the prophets roaring in his ears, must have felt like Gideon himself before the extermination of the Midianites); there were guns and ammunition in Jerusalem, and with these captured it was then Nat's purpose to sweep thirty miles eastward, gathering black recruits on the way until the Great Dismal Swamp was reached—a snake-filled and gloomy fastness in which, Nat believed, with probable justification, only Negroes could survive and no white man's army could penetrate. The immediate objective, however, was the destruction of every white man, woman, and child on the ten-mile route to Jerusalem; no one was to be spared; tender infancy and feeble old age alike were to perish by the axe and the sword. The command, of course, was that of God Almighty, through the voice of His prophet Ezekiel: *Son of Man, prophesy and say, Thus saith the Lord; Say, a sword, a sword is sharpened, and also furbished: it is sharpened to make a sore slaughter. . . . Slay utterly old and young, both maids, and little children, and women. . . .* It was a scheme so wild and daring that it could only have been the product of the most wretched desperation and frustrate misery of soul; and of course it was doomed to catastrophe not only for whites but for Negroes—and for black men in ways which from the vantage point of history now seem almost unthinkable.

They did their job rapidly and with merciless and methodical determination. Beginning at the home of Travis—where five people, including a six-month-old infant, were slain in their beds—they marched from house to house on an eastward route, pillaging, murdering, sparing no one. Lacking guns—at least to begin with—they employed axes, hatchets, and swords as their tools of destruction, and swift decapitation was their usual method of dispatch. (It is interesting that the Negroes did not resort to torture, nor were they ever accused of rape. Nat's attitude toward sex was Christian and high-minded, and he had said: "We will not do to their women what they have done to ours.")

On through the first day they marched, across the hot August fields, gaining guns and ammunition, horses, and a number of willing recruits. That the insurrection was not purely racial but perhaps obscurely pre-Marxist may be seen in the fact that a number of dwellings belonging to poor white people were pointedly passed by. At midday on Monday their force had more than tripled, to the number of nineteen, and nearly thirty white people lay dead. By this time the alarm had been sounded throughout the county, and while the momentum of the insurgent band was considerable, many of the whites had fled in panic to the woods, and some of the farmers had begun to resist, setting up barricades from which they could fire back at Nat's forces. Furthermore, quite a few of the rebels had broken into the brandy cellars of the houses they had attacked and had gotten roaring drunk—an eventuality Nat had feared and had warned against. Nevertheless, the Negroes—augmented now by forty more volunteers—pressed on toward Jerusalem, continuing the attack into the next night and all through the following day, when at last obstinate resistance by the aroused whites and the appearance of a mounted force of militia troops (also, it must be suspected, continued attrition by the apple brandy) caused the rebels to be dispersed, only a mile or so from Jerusalem.

Almost every one of the Negroes was rounded up and brought to trial—a legalistic nicety characteristic of a time in which it was necessary for one to determine whether *his* slave, property, after all, worth eight or nine hundred dollars, was really guilty and deserving of the gallows. Nat disappeared immediately after the insurrection and hid in the woods for over two months, when near-starvation and the onset of autumnal cold drove him from his cave and forced him to surrender to a lone farmer with a shotgun. Then he, too, was brought to trial in Jerusalem—early in November 1831—for fomenting a rebellion in which sixty white people had perished.

The immediate consequences of the insurrection were exceedingly grim. The killing of so many white people was in itself an act of futility. It has never been determined with any accuracy how many black people, not connected with the rebellion, were slain at the hands of rampaging bands of white men who swarmed all over Southampton in the week following the uprising, seeking reprisal and vengeance. A contemporary estimate by a Richmond newspaper, which deplored this retaliation, put the number at close to two hundred Negroes, many of them free, and many of them tortured in ways unimaginably horrible. But even more important was the effect that Nat Turner's insurrection had upon the institution of slavery at large. News of the revolt spread among Southern whites with great speed: the impossible, the unspeakable had at last taken place after two hundred years of the ministrations of sweet old mammies and softly murmured "Yassuh's" and docile compliance—and a shock wave of anguish and terror ran through the entire South. If such a nightmarish calamity happened there, would it not happen *here*—here in Tennessee, in Augusta, in Vicksburg, in these bayous of Louisiana? Had Nat lived to see the consequences of his rebellion, surely it would have been for him the cruelest irony that his bold and desperate bid for liberty had caused only the most tyrannical new controls to be imposed upon Negroes everywhere—the establishment of patrols, further restrictions upon movement, education, assembly, and the beginning of other severe and crippling restraints which persisted throughout the slaveholding states until the Civil War. Virginia had been edging close to emancipation, and it seems reasonable to believe that the example of Nat's rebellion, stampeding many moderates in the legislature into a conviction that the Negroes could not be safely freed, was a decisive factor in the ultimate victory of the pro-slavery forces. Had Virginia, with its enormous prestige among the states, emancipated its slaves, the effect upon our history would be awesome to contemplate.

Nat brought cold, paralyzing fear to the South, a fear that never departed. If white men had sown the wind with chattel slavery, in Nat Turner they had reaped the whirlwind for white and black alike.

Nat was executed, along with sixteen other Negroes who had figured large in the insurrection. Most of the others were transported south, to the steaming fields of rice and cotton. On November 11, 1831, Nat was hanged from a live-oak tree in the town square of Jerusalem. He went to his death with great dignity and courage. "The bodies of those executed," wrote Drewry, "with one exception, were buried in a decent and becoming manner. That of Nat Turner was delivered to the doctors, who skinned it and made grease of the flesh."

III

Not long ago, in the spring of the year, when I was visiting my family in Virginia, I decided to go down for the day to Southampton County, which is a drive of an hour or so by car from the town where I was born and raised. Nat Turner was of course the reason for this trip, although I had nothing particular or urgent in mind. What research it was possible to do on the event I had long since done. The Southampton court records, I had already been reliably informed, would prove unrewarding. It was not a question, then, of digging out more facts, but simply a matter of wanting to savor the mood and atmosphere of a landscape I had not seen for quite a few years, since the times when as a boy I used to pass through Southampton on the way to my father's family home in North Carolina. I thought also that there might be a chance of visiting some of the historic sites connected with the insurrection, and even of retracing part of the route of the uprising through the help of one of those handsomely produced guidebooks for which the Association for the Preservation of Virginia Antiquities is famous—guides indispensable for a trip to such Old Dominion shrines as Jamestown and Appomattox and Monticello. I became even more eager to go when one of my in-laws put me in touch by telephone with a cousin of his. This man, whom I shall call Dan Seward, lived near Franklin, the main town of Southampton, and he assured me in those broad cheery Southern tones which are like a warm embrace— and which, after long years in the chill North, are to me always so familiar, reminiscent, and therefore so unsettling, sweet, and curiously painful—that he would like nothing better than to aid me in my exploration in whatever way he could.

Dan Seward is a farmer and prosperous grower of peanuts in a prosperous agricultural region where the peanut is the unquestioned monarch. A combination of sandy loam soil and a long growing season has made Southampton ideal for the cultivation of peanuts; over 30,000 acres are planted annually, and the crop is processed and marketed in Franklin—a thriving little town of 7,000 people—or in Suffolk and Portsmouth, where it is rendered into Planters cooking oil and stock feed and Skippy peanut butter. There are other moneymaking crops—corn and soybeans and cotton. The county is at the northernmost edge of the Cotton Belt, and thirty years ago cotton was a major source of income. Cotton has declined in importance but the average yield per acre is still among the highest in the South, and the single gin left in the county in the little village of Drewryville processes each year several thousand bales, which are trucked to market down in North Carolina. Lumbering is also very profitable, owing mainly to an abundance of the loblolly pines valuable in the production of craft wood pulp; and the Union Bag–Camp Paper Company's plant on the Blackwater River in Franklin is a huge enterprise employing over 1,600 people. But it is peanuts—the harvested vines in autumn piled up mile after mile in dumpy brown stacks like hay—that have brought money to Southampton, and a sheen of prosperity that can be seen in the freshly painted farmhouses along the monotonously flat state highway which leads into Franklin, and the new-model Dodges and Buicks parked slantwise against the curb of some crossroads hamlet, and the gaudy, eye-catching signs that advise the wisdom of a bank savings account for all those surplus funds.

The county has very much the look of the New South about it, with its airport and its shiny new motels, its insistent billboards advertising space for industrial sites, the sprinkling of housing developments with television antennas gleaming from every rooftop, its supermarkets and shopping centers and its flavor of go-getting commercialism. This is the New South, where agriculture still prevails but has joined in a vigorous union with industry, so that even the peanut when it goes to market is ground up in some rumbling engine of commerce and becomes metamorphosed into wood stain or soap or cattle feed. The Negroes, too, have partaken of this abundance—some of it, at least—for they own television sets also, and if not new-model Buicks (the Southern white man's strictures against Negro ostentation remain intimidating), then decent late-model used Fords; while in the streets of Franklin the Negro women shopping seemed on the day of my visit very proud and well-dressed compared to the shabby, stooped figures I recalled from the Depression years when I was a boy. It would certainly appear that Negroes deserve some of this abundance, if only because they make up so large a part of the workforce. Since Nat Turner's day the balance of population in Southampton—almost 60 percent Negro—has hardly altered by a hair.

"I don't know anywhere that a Negro is treated better than around here," Mr. Seward was saying to the three of us, on the spring morning I visited him with my wife and my father. "You take your average person from up North, he just doesn't *know* the Negro like we do. Now, for instance, I have a Negro who's worked for me for years, name of Ernest. He knows if he breaks his arm—like he did a while ago, fell off a tractor—he knows he can come to me and I'll see that he's taken care of, hospital expenses and all, and I'll take care of him and his family while he's unable to work, right on down the line. I don't ask him to pay back a cent, either, that's for sure. We have a wonderful relationship, that Negro and myself. By God, I'd die for that Negro and he knows it, and he'd do the same for me. But Ernest doesn't want to sit down at my table, here in this house, and have supper with me— and he wouldn't want me in *his* house. And Ernest's got kids like I do, and he doesn't want them to go to school with my Bobby, any more than Bobby wants to go to school with *his* kids. It works both ways. People up North don't seem to be able to understand a simple fact like that."

Mr. Seward was a solidly fleshed, somewhat rangy, big-shouldered man in his early forties with an open, cheerful manner which surely did nothing to betray the friendliness with which he had spoken on the telephone. He had greeted us—total strangers, really—with an animation and uncomplicated good will that would have shamed an Eskimo; and for a moment I realized that after years amid the granite outcroppings of New England, I had forgotten that this *was* the passionate, generous, outgoing nature of the South, no artificial display but a social gesture as natural as breathing.

Mr. Seward had just finished rebuilding his farmhouse on the outskirts of town, and he had shown us around with a pride I found understandable: there was a sparkling electric kitchen worthy of an advertisement in *Life* magazine, some handsome modern furniture, and several downstairs rooms paneled beautifully in the prodigal and lustrous hardwood of the region. It was altogether a fine, tasteful house, resembling more one of the prettier medium-priced homes in the Long Island suburbs than the house one might contemplate for a Tidewater farmer. Upstairs, we had inspected his son Bobby's room, a kid's room with books like *Pinocchio* and *The Black Arrow* and *The Swiss Family Robinson,* and here there was a huge paper banner spread across one entire wall with the crayon inscription: *"Two . . . four . . . six . . . eight! We Don't Want to Integrate!"* It was a sign which so overwhelmingly dominated the room that it could not help provoking comment, and it was this that eventually had led to Mr. Seward's reflections about *knowing* Negroes.

There might have been something vaguely defensive in his remarks but not a trace of hostility. His tone was matter-of-fact and good-natured, and he pronounced the word "Negro" as *"nigra,"* which most Southerners do with utter naturalness while intending no disrespect whatsoever, in fact quite the opposite—the mean epithet, of course, is "nigger." I had the feeling that Mr. Seward had begun amiably to regard us as sympathetic but ill-informed outsiders, non-Southern, despite his knowledge of my Tidewater background and my father's own accent, which is thick as grits. Moreover, the fact that I had admitted to having lived in the North for fifteen years caused me, I fear, to appear alien in his eyes, *déraciné,* especially when my acculturation to Northern ways has made me adopt the long "e" and say "Negro." The racial misery, at any rate, is within inches of driving us mad: how can I explain that

with all my silent disagreement with Mr. Seward's paternalism, I knew that
when he said, "By God, I'd die for that Negro," he meant it?

Perhaps I should not have been surprised that Mr. Seward seemed to
know very little about Nat Turner. When we got around to the subject, it
developed that he had always thought that the insurrection occurred way
back in the eighteenth century. Affably, he described seeing in his boyhood
the "Hanging Tree," the live oak from which Nat had been hanged in Courtland (Jerusalem had undergone this change of name after the Civil War),
and which had died and been cut down some thirty years ago; as for any
other landmarks, he regretted that he did not know of a single one. No, so
far as he knew, there just wasn't anything.

For me, it was the beginning of disappointments which grew with every
hour. Had I *really* been so ingenuous as to believe that I would unearth
some shrine, some home preserved after the manner of Colonial Williamsburg, a relic of the insurrection at whose portal I would discover a lady in
billowing satin and crinoline who for fifty cents would shepherd me about
the rooms with a gentle drawl indicating the spot where a good mistress fell
at the hands of the murderous darky? The native Virginian, despite himself,
is cursed with a suffocating sense of history, and I do not think it impossible
that I actually suspected some such monument. Nevertheless, confident
that there would be something to look at, I took heart when Mr. Seward
suggested that after lunch we all drive over to Courtland, ten miles to the
west. He had already spoken to a friend of his, the sheriff of the county, who
knew all the obscure byways and odd corners of Southampton, mainly because of his endless search for illegal stills; if there was a solitary person alive
who might be able to locate some landmark or could help retrace part of
Nat Turner's march, it was the sheriff. This gave me hope. For I had brought
along Drewry's book and its map, which showed the general route of the
uprising, marking the houses by name. In the sixty years since Drewry, there
would have been many changes in the landscape. But with this map ori-
ented against the sheriff's detailed county map, I should easily be able to
pick up the trail and thus experience, however briefly, a sense of the light
and shadow that played over that scene of slaughter and retribution a hundred and thirty-four years ago.

Yet it was as if Nat Turner had never existed, and as the day lengthened
and afternoon wore on, and as we searched Nat's part of the county—five of

us now, riding in the sheriff's car with its huge star emblazoned on the doors, and its radio blatting out hoarse intermittent messages, and its riot gun protectively nuzzling the backs of our necks over the edge of the rear seat—I had the sensation from time to time that this Negro, who had so long occupied my thoughts, who indeed had so obsessed my imagination that he had acquired larger spirit and flesh than most of the living people I encountered day in and day out, had been merely a crazy figment of my mind, a phantom no more real than some half-recollected image from a fairy tale. For here in the backcountry, this horizontal land of woods and meadows where he had roamed, only a few people had heard of Nat Turner, and of those who had— among the people we stopped to make inquiries of, both white and black, along dusty country roads, at farms, at filling stations, at crossroad stores— most of them confused him, I think, with something spectral, mythic, a black Paul Bunyan who had perpetrated mysterious and nameless deeds in millennia past. They were neither facetious nor evasive, simply unaware. Others confounded him with the Civil War—a Negro general. One young Negro field hand, lounging at an Esso station, figured he was a white man. A white man, heavy-lidded, and paunchy, slow-witted, an idler at a rickety store, thought him an illustrious racehorse of bygone days.

The sheriff, a smallish, soft-speaking, ruminative man, with a whisper of a smile frozen on his face as if he were perpetually enjoying a good joke, knew full well who Nat Turner was, and I could tell he relished our frustrating charade. He was a shrewd person, quick and sharp with countrified wisdom, and he soon became quite as fascinated as I with the idea of tracking down some relic of the uprising (although he said that Drewry's map was hopelessly out of date, the roads of that time now abandoned to the fields and woods, the homes burned down or gone to ruin); the country people's ignorance he found irresistible and I think it tickled him to perplex their foolish heads, white or black, with the same old leading question: "You heard about old Nat Turner, ain't you?" But few of them had heard, even though I was sure that many had plowed the same fields that Nat had crossed, lived on land that he had passed by; and as for dwellings still standing which might have been connected with the rebellion, not one of these backcountry people could offer the faintest hint or clue. As effectively as a monstrous and unbearable dream, Nat had been erased from memory.

It was late afternoon when, with a sense of deep fatigue and frustration,

I suggested to Mr. Seward and the sheriff that maybe we had better go back to Courtland and call it a day. They were agreeable—relieved, I felt, to be freed of this tedious and fruitless search—and as we headed east down a straight unpaved road, the conversation became desultory, general. We spoke of the North. The sheriff was interested to learn that I often traveled to New York. He went there occasionally himself, he said; indeed, he had been there only the month before—"to pick up a nigger," a fugitive from custody who had been awaiting trial for killing his wife. New York was a fine place to spend the night, said the sheriff, but he wouldn't want to live there.

As he spoke I had been gazing out of the window, and now suddenly something caught my eye—something familiar, a brief flickering passage of a distant outline, a silhouette against the sun-splashed woods—and I asked the sheriff to stop the car. He did, and as we backed up slowly through a cloud of dust I recognized a house standing perhaps a quarter of a mile off the road, from this distance only a lopsided oblong sheltered by an enormous oak, but the whole tableau—the house and the glorious hovering tree and the stretch of woods beyond—so familiar to me that it might have been some home I passed every day. And of course now as recognition came flooding back I knew whose house it was. For in *The Southampton Insurrection*, the indefatigable Drewry had included many photographs—amateurish, doubtless taken by himself, and suffering from the fuzzy offset reproduction of 1900. But they were clear enough to provide an unmistakable guide to the dwellings in question, and now as I again consulted the book I could see that this house—the monumental oak above it grown scant inches, it seemed, in sixty years—was the one referred to by Drewry as having belonged to Mrs. Catherine Whitehead. From this distance, in the soft clear light of a spring afternoon, it seemed most tranquil, but few houses have come to know such a multitude of violent deaths. There in the late afternoon of Monday, August 22, Nat Turner and his band had appeared, and they set upon and killed "Mrs. Catherine Whitehead, son Richard, and four daughters, and grandchild."

The approach to the house was by a rutted lane long ago abandoned and overgrown with lush weeds, which made a soft, crushed, rasping sound as we rolled over them. Dogwood, white and pink, grew on either side of the lane, quite wild and wanton in lovely pastel splashes. Not far from the house a pole fence interrupted our way; the sheriff stopped the car and we got out and stood there for a moment, looking at the place. It was quiet and still—so quiet that the sudden chant of a mockingbird in the woods was almost frightening—and we realized then that no one lived in the house. Scoured by weather, paintless, worn down to the wintry gray of bone and with all the old mortar gone from between the timbers, it stood alone and desolate above its blasted, sagging front porch, the ancient door ajar like an open wound. Although never a manor house, it had once been a spacious and comfortable country home; now in near-ruin it sagged, finished, a shell, possessing only the most fragile profile of itself. As we drew closer still, we could see that the entire house, from its upper story to the cellar, was filled with thousands of shucked ears of corn—feed for the malevolent-looking razorback pigs which suddenly appeared in a tribe at the edge of the house, eyeing us, grunting. Mr. Seward sent them scampering with a shied stick and a farmer's sharp "Whoo!" I looked up at the house, trying to recollect its particular role in Nat's destiny, and then I remembered.

There was something baffling, secret, irrational about Nat's own participation in the uprising. He was unable to kill. Time and time again in his confession one discovers him saying (in an offhand tone; one must dig for the implications): "I could not give the death blow, the hatchet glanced from his head," or, "I struck her several blows over the head, but I was unable to kill her, as the sword was dull. . . ." It is too much to believe, over and over again: the glancing hatchet, the dull sword. It smacks rather, as in *Hamlet*, of rationalization, ghastly fear, an access of guilt, a shrinking from violence, and fatal irresolution. Alone here at this house, turned now into a huge corncrib around which pigs rooted and snorted in the silence of a spring afternoon, here alone was Nat finally able—or was he forced?—to commit a murder, and this upon a girl of eighteen named Margaret Whitehead, described by Drewry in terms perhaps not so romantic or far-fetched, after all, as "the belle of the county." The scene is apocalyptic—afternoon bedlam in wild harsh sunlight and August heat.

> I returned to commence the work of death, but those whom I left had not been idle; all the family were already murdered but Mrs. Whitehead and her daughter Margaret. As I came around the door I saw Will pulling Mrs. Whitehead out of the house and at the step he nearly severed

her head from her body with his axe. Miss Margaret, when I discovered
her, had concealed herself in the corner formed by the projection of the
cellar cap from the house; on my approach she fled into the field but was
soon overtaken and after repeated blows with a sword, I killed her by a
blow on the head with a fence rail.

It is Nat's only murder. Why, from this point on, does the momentum of
the uprising diminish, the drive and tension sag? Why, from this moment in
the "Confessions," does one sense in Nat something dispirited, listless, as if
all life and juice had been drained from him, so that never again through the
course of the rebellion is he even on the scene when a murder is committed? What happened to Nat in this place? Did he discover his humanity
here, or did he lose it?

I lifted myself up into the house, clambering through a doorway without
steps, pushing myself over the crumbling sill. The house had a faint yeasty
fragrance, like flat beer. Dust from the mountains of corn lay everywhere in
the deserted rooms, years and decades of dust, dust an inch thick in some
places, lying in a fine gray powder like sooty fallen snow. Off in some room
amid the piles of corn I could hear a delicate scrabbling and a plaintive
squeaking of mice. Again it was very still, the shadow of the prodigious old
oak casting a dark pattern of leaves, checkered with bright sunlight, aslant
through the gaping door. As in those chilling lines of Emily Dickinson, even
this lustrous and golden day seemed to find its only resonance in the memory, and perhaps a premonition, of death.

> This quiet Dust was Gentlemen and Ladies,
> And Lads and Girls;
> Was laughter and ability and sighing,
> And frocks and curls.

Outside, the sheriff was calling in on his car radio, his voice blurred and
indistinct; then the return call from the county seat, loud, a dozen incomprehensible words in an uproar of static. Suddenly it was quiet again, the
only sound my father's soft voice as he chatted with Mr. Seward.

I leaned against the rotting frame of the door, gazing out past the great
tree and into that far meadow where Nat had brought down and slain Miss
Margaret Whitehead. For an instant, in the silence, I thought I could hear a

mad rustle of taffeta, and rushing feet, and a shrill girlish piping of terror; then that day and this day seemed to meet and melt together, becoming almost one, and for a long moment indistinguishable.

[*Harper's,* April 1965. Written for a special issue titled "The South Today," assembled by Willie Morris. The issue included contributions from C. Vann Woodward, Louis E. Lomax, Walker Percy, Whitney Young, LeRoi Jones, Louis Rubin, Arna Bontemps, and Robert Coles.]

A Southern Conscience

"There is a saying among the Negroes in Harlem," James Baldwin said recently, "to the effect that if you have a white Southerner for a friend, you've got a friend for life. But if you've got a white Northerner for a friend, watch out. Because he just might be the kind of friend who decides to move out when you move in." This is a sentiment which may be beguiling to a Southerner, yet the fact does remain that a Southern "liberal" and his Northern counterpart are two distinct species of cat. Certainly the Southerner of good will who lives in the North, as I do, is often confronted with some taxing circumstances. There was the phone call a number of years ago in the distant epoch before the present "Negro revolt," and the cautious interrogation from my dinner hostess of the evening: a Negro was going to be present—as a Southerner, did I mind? If I wished to stay away, she would surely understand. Or much later, when Prince Edward County in Virginia closed its schools, the deafening and indignant lady, a television luminary, who demanded that "we" drop bombs on "those crackers down there." (She got the state wrong, Virginians may be snobs but they are not crackers; nonetheless, she was proposing that "we" bomb my own kith and kin.) Or quite recently, a review in *The New Yorker* of Calder Willingham's *Eternal Fire*, a remarkably fine novel about the South which the reviewer, Whitney Balliett, praised extravagantly without knowing exactly why he was doing so, charging that the book was the definitive satire on Southern writing (though the book is funny, it is anything but satire, being too close to the bone of reality), and polishing off Faulkner, Welty, Warren, et al., with the assertion that Southern fiction in general, in which the Negroes had served so faithfully as "a resident Greek chorus," had now terminated its usefulness.[1] It is of course not important what this particular reviewer thinks, but the buried animus is characteristic and thus worth spelling out: white Southern writers, because they are white and Southern, cannot be expected to write about Negroes without condescension, or with understanding or fidelity or love. Unfortunately, this is a point of view which, by an extension of logic, tends to regard all white Southerners as bigots, and it is an attitude which one might find even more ugly than it is were it prompted by malice rather than ignorant self-righteousness, or a suffocating and provincial innocence. Nor is its corollary any less tiresome: to show that you really love Negroes, smoke pot and dig the right kind of jazz.

A tradition of liberalism has of course existed honorably in the South and is as much a part of its history as is its right-wing fanaticism and violence. The South in the nineteenth century had produced liberals of staunch fiber—the Louisiana novelist George W. Cable is a notable example—but less well known than the thread of liberalism woven into the fabric of Southern history is the fact that the South has also produced its flaming radicals. Lewis Harvie Blair was one of these. Born in Richmond in 1834, Blair came from a distinguished family which numbered among its antecedents a host of well-known theologians, college presidents, editors, generals, and even a presidential aspirant or two. After serving as a cavalry officer in the Confederate army, Blair returned to Richmond, established a fortune through the manufacture of shoes and in real estate, and then in 1889, at the contemplative age of fifty-five, and while comfortably installed in his mansion on East Grace Street, wrote a flabbergasting book called *Prosperity in the South Dependent on the Elevation of the Negro*. It received almost no attention in its time, but now, bearing the title *A Southern Prophecy*, it has been resurrected by Professor C. Vann Woodward, who has also provided an introduction that is a model of clarity and insight. Certainly, in view of the time and place it was written, *A Southern Prophecy* is one of the most amazing and powerful exhortations ever written by an American.

The original title of the book is somewhat deceptive. As Woodward points out, it was perhaps inevitable that Blair should adopt a hard-boiled tone, appealing to Southerners to regard the plight of the Negro in terms of their own economic self-interest. Nevertheless, Blair was unable really to conceal his intense humanitarian concern and moral passion; the sense of an abiding indignation over injustice is on every page and helps give the work its continuing vitality. It was the Rotarian-style boosterism of the famous editor Henry Grady of Atlanta—whose gospel of the New South included white supremacy and the permanent degradation of the Negro masses— that provided the source of Blair's initial wrath. The New South propaganda, as Blair saw it—the vision of great and glittering cities springing from the wreckage of the Civil War—was the sheerest humbug. Look rather to the "real South," he insisted: this was a land of crushing poverty for "the six million Negroes who are in the depths of indigence . . . the hundreds of miles of poor country with its unpainted and dilapidated homesteads . . ." This was the reality behind the garish fantasy, and it would remain just that—a fantasy—until the entire South attained a single goal: total equality for the Negro, economic and social. Some of Blair's chapter headings may convey a sense of the scope of the work, and also a touch of Blair's own cranky intransigence:

If Highest Caste will not Elevate, Must Crush Lowest Caste to Powder— Race Prejudice must be Mollified and Obligated—Prejudice Mark of Inferiority—Courts of Justice must be Impartial to All Colors—Why Negroes do not Enjoy Such Impartiality

Negro not a Competent Voter; neither are Millions of White Voters; but Ballot Absolutely Essential to his Freedom—Ruin of the Commonwealth that Degrades its Citizens—Tyranny Destroys the State and Demoralizes the Citizens—Southerners cannot Escape the Demoralizing Effects of Tyranny

The Abandonment of Separate Schools—The Necessity Thereof and Why—It Doubles Basis for Schools—Separate Schools a Public Proclamation of Caste

Other Things we must Do—the Negroes should be Allowed Free Admission to All Hotels, Theatres, Churches, and Official Receptions— Why Negroes should not be restricted to Places for Negroes

"Let us put ourselves in the Negro's place," wrote Blair. "Let us feel when passing good hotels there is no admission here; we dare not go in lest we be kicked out; when entering a theater to be told to go up in the top gallery; when entering an imposing church to be told rudely: no place in God's house for you . . . would not we have our pride cut to the quick? Can we expect the ignorant, degraded, poverty-ridden Negro to rise with such burdens resting upon him, and if he sees no prospect of the burden's lifting?" Although it was the South that received the full force of Blair's implacable anger, the North was not spared, and in a stern, avuncular epilogue he said:

> For the North to clear its skirts of the charge of hypocrisy, it must change its own treatment of the Negro; for until it says, Follow my example instead of doing as I exhort, the seed it sows may be good, but it will fall upon hard and stony soil. . . . Put your own Negroes in the way of supporting themselves with comfort, throw open all the avenues of life to them, encourage them to enter freely therein, relieve them of the dangers and the dread of being robbed, beaten, and imposed upon by ruthless white neighbors; in short, elevate them to the full stature of citizenship, and then you can appeal with hope of success to your white Southern brethren; but until you do these things, your purest, most unselfish efforts will be looked upon with suspicion. . . .

The year 1889 was, of course, too late for anyone—North or South—to heed Blair's prophecy. Few people cared, anyway. All the momentum of history had gathered its bleak and gigantic power, and within the decade the horrid night of Jim Crowism had settled in. There is a sad sequel to the story of Lewis Blair. Some years before his death in 1916 he suffered the occupational disease of radicals—recantation—and in his private papers disavowed almost everything he had expressed with such conviction years before. But it hardly seems to matter now, for the force and urgency still throb through these pages, reminding us that such passion is not bound by geography or time but remains, quite simply, the passion that binds us together as men. And the final words of certainty seem even more apocalyptic now than at the moment when this splendid Confederate wrote them, seventy-five years ago: "The battle will be long and obstinate, with many difficulties, delays, and dangers. . . . We older ones will not see that day, but our grandchildren will, for the light of coming day already irradiates the eastern sky."

[*New York Review of Books*, April 2, 1964.]

Slave and Citizen

I can recall with clarity from childhood my North Carolina grandmother's reminiscences of her slaves. To be sure, she was an old lady well into her eighties at the time, and had been a young girl growing up during the Civil War when she owned human property. Nonetheless, that past is linked to our present by a space of time which is startlingly brief. The violent happenings that occur in Oxford, Mississippi, do not take place in a vacuum of the moment but are attached historically to slavery itself. That in the Commonwealth of Virginia there is a county today in which no Negro child has been allowed to attend school for over four years has far less relevance to Senator Byrd than to the antebellum Black Laws of Virginia, which even now read like the code of regulations from an inconceivably vast and much longer enduring Nazi concentration camp.

As Professor Stanley Elkins has pointed out, the scholarly debate over slavery has for nearly a century seesawed with a kind of top-heavy, contentious, persistent rhythm, the rhythm of "right" and "wrong." These points of view, shifting between the Georgia-born historian Ulrich Phillips's vision of the plantation slave as an essentially cheerful, childlike, submissive creature who was also in general well treated (a viewpoint which, incidentally, dominated historical scholarship for the decades between the two world wars), and Kenneth Stampp's more recent interpretation of American slavery (*The Peculiar Institution*) as a harsh and brutal system, practically devoid of any charity at all, have each been so marred by a kind of moral aggression and self-righteousness as to resemble, in the end, a debate between William Lloyd Garrison and John C. Calhoun—and we have had enough of such debates. Granted that it seems inescapable that the plantation slave, at least, often displayed a cheerful, childlike and submissive countenance, and that plantation life had its sunny aspects; granted, too, that the system was at heart incredibly brutal and inhumane, the question remains: Why? Why was American slavery the unique institution that it was? What was the tragic essence of this system which still casts its shadow not only over our daily life but over our national destiny as well? Professor Frank Tannenbaum's brief work, *Slave and Citizen: The Negro in the Americas* (first published by Knopf in 1947 and now reprinted by Vintage), is a modest but important attempt to answer these questions.

Tannenbaum's technique is that of comparison—the comparison of slavery in the United States with that of coexisting slave systems in Latin America. Slavery was introduced by the Spanish and Portuguese into South America at the identical moment that it was brought to North America and the West Indies by the British, and its duration in time as an institution on both continents was roughly the same. But it is a striking fact that today there is no real racial "problem" in Brazil; a long history of miscegenation has blurred the color line, legal sanctions because of race do not exist, and any impediments toward social advancement for the Negro are insignificant. That this is true is due to an attitude toward slavery which had become crystallized in the Portuguese and Spanish ethic even before slaves were brought to the shores of the New World. For slavery (including the slavery of white people), as Tannenbaum points out, had existed on the Iberian peninsula throughout the fourteenth and fifteenth centuries. Oppressive an institution as it may have been, it contained large elements of humanity, even of equality, which had been the legacy of the Justinian Code. Thus Seneca: "A slave can be just, brave, magnanimous." Las Sieste Partidas, the body of law which evolved to govern all aspects of slavery, not only partook of the humanitarian traditions of the Justinian Code but was framed within that aspect of Christian doctrine which regarded the slave as the spiritual equal of his master, and perhaps his better. The law was protective of the slaves, and in conjunction with the church provided many incentives for freedom; and this attitude persisted when Negro slavery was established in South America. Despite its frequent brutality, the institution of slavery in

Brazil, with its recognition of the slave as a moral human being and its bias in favor of manumission, had become in effect, as Tannenbaum says, "a contractual arrangement between the master and his bondsman"; and in such a relatively agreeable atmosphere it is not unnatural that full liberty was attained through a slow and genial mingling of the races, and by gradual change rather than through such a cataclysm as Civil War.

We are only beginning to realize the extent to which American slavery worked its psychic and moral devastation upon an entire race. Unlike the Spanish and the Portuguese, the British and their descendants who became American slave owners had no historical experience of slavery; and neither the Protestant church nor Anglo-American law was equipped to cope with the staggering problem of the status of the Negro: forced to choose between regarding him as a moral human being and as property, they chose the definition of property. The result was the utter degradation of a people. Manumission was totally discouraged. A slave became only a negotiable article of goods, without rights to property, to the products of his own work, to marriage, without rights even to the offspring of his own despairing, unsanctioned unions—all of these were violations of the spirit so shattering as to beg the question whether the white South was populated either by tolerant, amiable Marse Bobs or by sadistic Simon Legrees. Even the accounts of brutality (and it is difficult even now, when witnessing the moral squabble between those historians who are apologists and those who are neo-abolitionists, to tell whether brutality was insignificant or rampant) fade into inconsequence against a backdrop in which the total dehumanization of a race took place, and a systematic attempt, largely successful, was made to reduce an entire people to the status of children. It was an oppression unparalleled in human history. In the end only a Civil War could try to rectify this outrage, and the war came too late.

> In Latin America the Negro achieved complete legal equality slowly through manumission, over centuries, and after he had acquired a moral personality. In the United States he was given his freedom suddenly, and before the white community credited him with moral status.

That is the problem we are faced with today: too many white Americans still deny the Negro his position as a moral human being.

Unfortunately, history does not give answers to the problems it leaves us.

Professor Tannenbaum concludes his excellent study with the reasonable implication that the attainment by the Negro of a moral status may still take a very long time. It seems apparent that a very long time might be too long for our salvation.

[*New York Review of Books,* Inaugural Issue, February 1963.]

Overcome

A mong the many humiliations of the American Negro, not the least burdensome has been the various characterizations he has had to undergo in the eyes of the white man. It is hardly an exaggeration to say that before World War II the predominant image of the Negro was that of the *New Yorker* cover of around 1935, which in a cartoon by Rea Irvin depicted a rotund and very black man in the act of chicken thievery: against a background of midnight blue the chickens are squawking their panic while the Negro, pop-eyed and comically aghast, tries vainly to shush them with a finger held against his blubbery lips.° This caricature of the Negro as a pilfering but likeable scalawag was dominant from slave days until the early 1940s, and one is bemused by the fact that it appeared on the cover of the same magazine which this year published James Baldwin's now celebrated essay.[1] Since that *New Yorker* cover, of course, reaction has set in with a vengeance. Yet though the situation has virtually reversed itself, the characterizations—the caricatures—persist. With the help of sociology and anthropology and hipster romanticism, Stepin Fetchit has been transformed into a sexual carnivore of superhuman capacities. The *New Yorker* cover was thoughtless and vapid enough—even though a fair reflection of the times—

° Rea Irvin (1881–1972), first art editor of *The New Yorker*. The cover to which Styron refers appeared on the issue for November 21, 1936.—J.W.

but the concept of "the white Negro" is equally preposterous; both arise from an imaginary notion of Negro life, both are lampoons and vulgarizations, and both are products of wish fulfillment.°

The historiography of the American Negro, especially that of Negro slavery, has likewise suffered from a career in which genteel apology has been supplanted less by perceptions than by extremist revisionism. First published in 1943 and reissued now, Herbert Aptheker's *American Negro Slave Revolts* is an attempt to repudiate such old-school apologists for the antebellum Southern plantation system as Ulrich B. Phillips, who saw in slavery a generally genial institution, the victims of which were more or less content with their lot and in any case so docile by nature as to be incapable of rebellion. Certainly it seems clear now that the Phillips viewpoint, shared by many other historians, was befogged by Southern pride and often by frank racism: and when Aptheker's book first appeared (during the same general period as Myrdal's *An American Dilemma,* a period of leftist-oriented anthropology and sociology), the reaction had begun to move into full tide. Negro slaves, according to the new canon, were not happy, servile, childlike; they were instead intractable, seething with unrest, forever chafing in the bonds of slavery. As Aptheker stated this position: "The evidence . . . points to the conclusion that discontent and rebelliousness were not only exceedingly common, but, indeed, characteristic of American Negro slaves" (p. 374).[2]

As a matter of fact, if we can accept Aptheker's evidence—and on the whole his book seems well documented—it would appear that unrest and discontent *were* considerably more widespread than earlier historians would grant, with sporadic outbreaks of violence occurring throughout the South for many years. Relying heavily on contemporary newspaper accounts and documents overlooked or ignored by other authorities, Aptheker traces the course of slave unrest from early colonial times until the Civil War, and makes a good case against the theory of universal content and docility among the slaves. A considerable number of plots and conspiracies arose among the Negroes—most of them aborted or otherwise unsuccessful—and the incidents of murderous violence which abounded from Delaware to Texas are both too numerous and too striking to be shrugged off; thus, Aptheker

° Styron is referring to Norman Mailer's essay "The White Negro," first published in the Fall 1957 issue of *Dissent.*—J.W.

offers convincing proof that some slaves, at least, were not only discontented, but through courage and out of desperation found opportunity to make their forsaken bids for freedom.

Yet the title *American Negro Slave Revolts* is badly misleading (*Signs of Slave Unrest* might have been more exact), and it is a measure of Aptheker's extremist "either-or" position that, in the preface to this new edition, he is forced to protest: "Generally speaking, this book has weathered some heavy attacks launched by individuals to whom white supremacy and the magnolia-moonlight-molasses mythology that adorns it were sacred." But one does not have to be a white supremacist to note that Aptheker fails almost completely in his attempt to prove the universality of slave rebelliousness. Save for two enthusiastic but localized conspiracies—that of Gabriel in Richmond in 1800, and that of Vesey in Charleston in 1822, both of which were nipped in the bud—there was only one sustained, effective revolt in the entire annals of slavery: the cataclysmic uprising of Nat Turner in Virginia in 1831. To say, therefore, as Aptheker does, that "discontent and rebelliousness were not only exceedingly common, but, indeed, characteristic of American Negro slaves," is not just to indulge in distortion, it is once again truly to fall into the trap of "characterization." Of unrest and disaffection there seems to have been a natural plenty; of true rebelliousness on any organized scale there was amazingly little, and in his eagerness to prove the actuality of what was practically nonexistent, Aptheker, like those latter-day zealots who demean the Negro's humanity by saddling him with mythical powers of eroticism or other attributes he neither wants nor needs, performs only a disservice to those who would understand American Negro slavery and the meaning it has for us.

It may be impossible ever to tell for certain, but it would now seem apparent that it was the monolithic structure of the institution of chattel slavery itself which generally precluded organized revolt. In his brilliant analysis *Slavery*, Stanley Elkins has demonstrated what must have been the completely traumatizing effect upon the psyche of this uniquely brutal system, which so dehumanized the slave and divested him of honor, moral responsibility, and manhood. The character (not characterization) of "Sambo," shiftless, wallowing happily in the dust, was no cruel figment of the imagination, Southern or Northern, but did in truth exist. But that the plantation slaves *were* often observably docile, *were* childish, *were* irresponsible and incapable of real resistance would seem to be no significant commentary upon the character of the Negro but tribute rather to a capitalist super-machine which swiftly managed to cow and humble an entire people with a ruthless efficiency unparalleled in history. Nat Turner, a literate preacher and a slave of the Upper South, lived outside the thralldom of organized plantation slavery; the success of his revolt was due to a combination of native genius, luck, and the relative latitude of freedom he had been granted. The many millions of other slaves, reduced to the status of children, illiterate, tranquil- lized, totally defenseless, ciphers and ants, could only accept their existence or be damned, and be damned anyway, like the victims of a concentration camp. Rebellion was not only not characteristic: to assign a spirit of rebel- liousness to human beings under such conditions is to attribute to the Negro superhuman qualities which no human being possesses. Like the comic chicken thief, like the raging hipster, the slave in revolt is a product of the white man's ever-accommodating fantasy, and only the dim suggestion of the truth. The real revolt, of course, is now, beyond the dark wood of slavery, by people reclaiming their birthright and their direct, unassailable humanity.

[*New York Review of Books,* September 26, 1963.]

Slavery's Pain, Disney's Gain

Imagineering, an adroit neologism, is the Walt Disney Company's name for the corporate unit involved in developing Disney's America, the projected mammoth theme park in northern Virginia. Not long ago, the chief imagineer, Robert Weis, described what would be in store, among other historical attractions for hordes of tourists. "We want to make you feel what it was like to be a slave, and what it was like to escape through the Underground Railroad." He added that the exhibits would "not take a Pollyanna view" but would be "painful, disturbing, and agonizing."

I was fascinated by Mr. Weis's statement because twenty-seven years ago I published a novel called *The Confessions of Nat Turner*, which was partly intended to make the reader feel what it was like to be a slave. Whether I succeeded or not was a matter of hot debate, and the book still provokes controversy. But as one who has plunged into the murky waters where the imagineers wish to venture, I have doubts whether the technical wizardry that so entrances children and grown-ups at other Disney parks can do anything but mock a theme as momentous as slavery, the great transforming circumstance of American history. If it is so difficult to render the tragic complexity of slavery in words, as I once found out, will visual effects or virtual reality make it easier to comprehend the agony?

No one knows what Disney's Department of Imagineering has up its sleeve, but whatever exhibits or displays it comes up with would have to be fraudulent, since no combination of branding irons, slave ships or slave cabins, shackles, chained black people in their wretched coffles, or treks through the Underground Railroad could begin to define such a stupendous experience. To present even the most squalid sights would be to cheaply romanticize suffering. For slavery's abyssal pain arose far less from its physical cruelty—although slave ships and the auction block were atrocities—than from the moral and legal savagery that deprived an entire people of their freedom, along with their rights to education, ownership of property, matrimony, and protection under the law.

Slavery cannot be represented by exhibits. It was not remotely like the Jewish Holocaust—of brief duration and intensely focused destruction—which has permitted an illuminating museum. In its 250-year history in America, the institution, which so intimately bound slave and master together, could not fail to produce almost unlimited permutations of human emotions and relationships. How would the Disney technicians make millions of their pilgrims feel all these things? How would they show that there were white people who suffered torment over the catastrophe? And how can they possibly render, beyond the deafening noise and the nasty gore, the infinitely subtle moral entanglements of the terrible war that brought slavery to an end?

I was born and reared in Virginia, and I am the grandson of a slave owner. I continue to be astonished that in the waning years of the twentieth century, I should possess a flesh-and-blood link with the remote past—that from boyhood I have a luminous memory of an old lady, my grandmother, who actually owned black slaves. For this very reason, she has haunted my life, become embedded in the fabric of my work as a writer, and helped make slavery an undiminishing part of my consciousness. Her story, some of which I recall being told in her own quavering and stubborn voice, would possess no appeal for those planning the wicked frisson of a Simon Legree tableau, but it has its own harrowing truth.

The drama began in 1863, the year the Emancipation Proclamation was issued, when Union troops occupied much of eastern Virginia and part of northeastern North Carolina. That spring, my grandmother, Marianna Clark, was a twelve-year-old living on a remote plantation where her father owned thirty-five slaves. Two of the slaves were girls, roughly her age, who had been given to her by deed. She had grown up with them and played with them; they had become so lovingly close that, not surprisingly, the children regarded one another as sisters. Her clearest memory was of having knitted woolen stockings for the girls during that bitter winter.

One morning, a large body of Union cavalrymen, detached from General Ambrose Burnside's forces, swept down on the plantation, stripped it bare of everything valuable and worthless, edible and movable, burned down the outbuildings, and, after a day's long plunder, disappeared. Most of the slaves departed with the troops, and the little girls also vanished. My grandmother never saw them again. She and the family verged close to starvation for several months, forced "to chew roots and eat rats." She grieved for the girls but her grief may have been absorbed into her own suffering, for she became a near skeleton, and the deprivation, I suspect, arrested her growth, making her diminutive and weak-boned (though she was amazingly resilient) to the end of her long life.

My grandmother's terror and trauma were genuine, but they have to be reckoned as no great matter in the end, for she survived the privation of Reconstruction, reared six children in reasonable comfort, and died at eighty-seven, at peace except for her feeling about Yankees, for whom she had a fund of inexhaustible rage and contempt. What has haunted me is those slave girls, her "little sisters" who vanished on that spring day and caused her to mourn whenever she spoke of them. One can be certain that they had no easy time of it. Swallowed up into the legion of disfranchised ex-slaves, they had little to look forward to in the oncoming years of poverty, the Ku Klux Klan, a storm of hatred, joblessness, illiteracy, lynchings, and the suffocating night of Jim Crow. They were truly, in the lament of the spiritual, among the "many thousand gone."

This renewed bondage is the collective anguish from which white Americans have always averted their eyes. And it underlines the falseness of any Disneyesque rendition of slavery. The falseness is in the assumption that by viewing the artifacts of cruelty and oppression, or whatever the imagineers cook up—the cabins, the chains, the auction block—one will have succumbed in a "disturbing and agonizing" manner to the catharsis of a completed tragedy. But the drama has never ended. At Disney's Virginia park, the slave experience would permit visitors a shudder of horror before they turned away, smug and self-exculpatory, from a world that may be dead but has not really been laid to rest.

[*New York Times,* op-ed, August 4, 1994.]

Our Common History

Of the many comments that *The Confessions of Nat Turner* has evoked, two have touched me with especial poignancy. One is that of James Baldwin, who is recorded as having said: "He has begun the common history—ours."[1] The other is from President Stokes, who wrote in a letter to me: "*The Confessions of Nat Turner* initiates all Negroes into our fearsome and wonderful heritage."* I would like to consider the meaning of these two statements as they merge together in my mind—the Negro's fearsome and wonderful heritage and the relevance of that heritage to the common history, *ours*—and to reflect briefly on the past that binds together all of us.

First, however, let me say that my coming to Wilberforce University represents in a curious way the fulfillment of a journey which I began years ago as a boy in Tidewater Virginia. I was born in a middle-class Southern home, of educated Southern parents who desired what are commonly known as the "best things" in learning and culture. Yet my first memories of cultural advantages are not those arising out of some white background but from the

---

* Rembert E. Stokes, president of Wilberforce University 1956–1976, who was present on the stage when Styron delivered this speech. Reverend Stokes later became Bishop of the African Methodist Episcopal Church.—J.W.

famous Negro college nearby, Hampton Institute, a campus whose trees and lovely seaside setting are more vivid in my memory than those of the segregated white Southern schools I later attended. It was there at Hampton as a boy and—surprisingly enough for the South at that time—in integrated audiences, that I first heard the Philadelphia Orchestra, the Vienna Choir Boys, the Budapest String Quartet, there that I first saw educational films which the surrounding white community had little interest in seeing. I was very young during those years and I recollect with perfect clarity how, leaving Ogden Hall after an evening concert, some concert of Mozart or Beethoven which first stirred me with a passion for music which has never left me, I would be conscious in a vague, inchoate, yet nagging way that a barrier was gradually being breached in me, that the prejudices which were a normal part of the daily life of a Southern boy were being even then eroded away. For this was a Negro college—it was under the auspices of no white school that I was being proffered such beauty—and I could not escape the dim feeling that my life would someday be bound up together with the lives of those black people who had made me this splendid gift of music and had shared it with me. And although it was a number of years before I was able completely to shake free from that racial bias which wounds nearly every person born and bred in the South, it was surely these memorable evenings at Hampton that caused me far back in childhood to begin a long process of identification with the Negro people and the Negro spirit. And, as I say, the privilege I have of speaking here at Wilberforce seems only a continuation of that privilege which was first tendered me years ago, and as a gift, at Hampton.

I no longer know when or where it was that Nat Turner entered into my consciousness. It may have been around the time when my grandmother—then an old lady almost ninety years old—first told me about the two slave girls she owned when she herself was a little girl, just before the Civil War. In any case, I do know that I was still quite young, still in high school, when something strangely brooding and troublesome stung my curiosity, when I first heard of that slave in a nearby county, Southampton, who a hundred years before had risen up and struck down his oppressors, and had been hanged and had sunk back not into history but into oblivion. I remember going to Southampton in those days; there was no trace of Nat Turner then—only a solitary highway marker—just as there is no trace today of that dim and prodigious black man, nothing, no monument, no ruin, no relic of that revolt unique in American history. Even at that time I must somehow have been aware of the startling and devastating fact: that here in a state supreme among all the American states in the obeisance it paid to history—here in the Virginia of Jamestown and Yorktown and Williamsburg, of George Washington and Patrick Henry and John Marshall, the bloody land of Chancellorsville and the Wilderness—here in this same commonwealth another man had been born and had risen up, and wreaked a cataclysm, yet unlike those illustrious others he had not been memorialized and enshrined but had had his very memory spirited away, and was now obliterated, entombed, all traces of him vanished as if he had never dwelt on earth. I could not, of course, have expressed at that early age the underlying truth of this matter; my apprehension of the tragic reality came at a later date.

What simply had happened was this: Two races of people had existed side by side on this continent, in intimacy, in the closest propinquity, for three centuries and more. One race had possessed a history, an intricate and meaningful past made up of a web of antecedents and relatives and often remembered forebears whose works and deeds were chronicled or celebrated, indexed, annotated, or otherwise imperishably recorded for a more or less grateful posterity; their names were Stuart and Calhoun and Peyton, Wyatt and Upchurch, Longstreet and Davidson and Taliaferro and Lee. Their fortunes and their failures were a matter of enduring knowledge, their romances the subject of poems and novels, the edifices they built monuments to dynasty and power. Not all were rich by any means, but even those less favored had a past and an ancestry and could claim a continuity in time which might explain and even give some meaning to their present estate.

The other race had no past at all. Generation succeeded generation without mark or record, like dead leaves, the only memorial of their existence a scrawled first name in a property ledger or a carved monosyllable on the cedar headboard in a tumbledown graveyard choked with weeds and dandelions. No tie, no link bound son to father, father to grandfather; of their earthly coming there was small celebration, of their passing scant mourning, and of the chronicling of either few words. Their names were Tom and Jim and Ella Mae, Phoebe and Lucinda, Easter and Uncle Henry and Jericho and Dred. These people were chattel, property—a terrible though inescapable truth—and even had they been able to create a meaningful history it would have been denied them, obliterated by those who held them in bondage, the worst the world has ever seen. Such common history as the two races shared—shared in passion and heartbreak and hilarity and rage and hatred and love—this common history would not be allowed even after the chains of slavery were broken and black people, at least by law, became free men. If allowed at all, this history would become partisan, factional, biased—the black slave less a subject for the intense exploration of an institution than a pawn in the battle between white men passionate to display either their past benevolence or their present self-righteousness. And no one single figure in Negro history demonstrated how effectively the white man has eradicated that very history than that messianic preacher, Nat Turner. In Southampton County, now as in my boyhood, nothing remains; all is crumbled into dust; dwellings, barns, sheds, anyplace Nat must have visited along his cataclysmic journey has vanished as if into air. Yet perhaps it was just this willful destruction of history, this very absence of anything to see or smell or touch, that for so long challenged me to discover the truth about Nat Turner, to resurrect him from a nearly nonexistent past and in that act of resurrection to try to create a paradigm not only of man in revolt but of the beautiful and tragic reality of the history that all of us, black and white, have shared for so long in common.

It is perhaps a terrible paradox that Nat Turner—certainly one of the first American Negroes to become aware of the nature of our shared history—found the very fact of his inseparable bond with white people so intolerable that he was led to the most hideous sort of slaughter and destruction. I have often been asked if there was not some moral or lesson to be drawn from the story of Nat Turner, whether out of the mythic quality of his career there was not some parallel to be drawn about the revolutionary events of our own era. I have always hesitated to answer such questions, since like most honest writers my true intent was to produce not a tract for the times but a literary work which somehow might transcend matters even of racial conflict. What a slave in his anguish produced in destruction and bloodshed a century and more ago does not necessarily find its echo in the clamor and strife of present-day events. Yet certain connections are unavoidable, and it may be well to essay one or two final reflections. Was Nat Turner mad? No, I do not think so. Obsessed, yes, fixed with a murderous, obdurate purpose but one who was not so much mad as one who, like Martin Luther, could do no other. Nat Turner was oppressed, yet like some few who are oppressed he had tasted the sweet breath of freedom. It requires only a modicum of psychological insight to reason that continued oppression in the face of the promise of freedom may result in a bloody rage on the part of the oppressed and disaster for the oppressor; that whenever oppression persists—especially when liberty and abundance in all their glory lie roundabout for others—the oppressor may expect, as surely as the dawning of the sun, the visitation upon his head of unholy wrath.

Yet still it cannot be escaped that if oppression is bound to breed hatred, rampant hatred in return can only bring on catastrophe. During Nat Turner's insurrection fifty-five white people went to their deaths, and of the slaves involved most were either transported or hanged. The scores of innocent black people slaughtered or tortured in reprisal appall the imagination. That Nat Turner's revolt prevented the state of Virginia, which had been edging toward emancipation, from freeing its slaves now seems plain, just as that same futile insurrection brought down upon the black people of the entire South cruel new repressions and burdens which lasted until the Civil War. One cannot regard the story of Nat Turner with equanimity and blandly counsel revenge. Then what is the answer? For Frantz Fanon, the distinguished Negro psychiatrist, hatred itself is a cathartic for the disinherited, the oppressed, an emotion outside of morality which, however destructive, allows men the ecstasy of a sense of worth and self-regard.° The cost in human anguish is consequently of no matter. I myself am in no position to argue against this point of view, since I cannot lay claim to a condition in life which might impel such violence. Nor can I suggest that love is the answer, for love is perhaps now both too difficult and too easy, and in any event doubtless too late. Yet it was the only answer that Margaret Whitehead had—she whom Nat Turner dearly loved and whom in despair he murdered with his sword. "Beloved, let us love one another," she said to Nat, quoting

---

° Frantz Fanon (1925–1961), a Martinique-born French psychiatrist whose best-known book is *The Wretched of the Earth*, first published in 1961, with a preface by Jean-Paul Sartre.—J.W.

John, "for love is of God; and every one that loveth is born of God, and knoweth God" (I John 4:7).

Perhaps there *is* no answer. Love was too late for Margaret Whitehead, as it was for Nat Turner, and indeed as it may be for us; but maybe when all is done it is love that remains still our last, our only hope.

[Speech at Wilberforce University, November 21, 1967. Previously unpublished.]

Acceptance

Just as I started to set down these few words my attention was caught by an advertisement for a book of essays which claimed to challenge, among other things, *The Confessions of Nat Turner* and its "condescending and degrading opinions about Negroes." It was not the modifiers—*condescending and degrading*—that bothered me so much as the key word: *opinions*. I had an old hurtful twinge of resentment, and my first impulse was to say here something mean-spirited and elaborately defensive about this familiar response to my work. I am sure there is some wisdom in my not doing so, for this award is one which by its very essence tends to make any bitterness I might still harbor quite unimportant.

It seems to me that in honoring my work this award underscores some certainties about the nature of literature. One of these is that a novel worthy of the name is not, nor ever has been, valuable because of its opinions; a novel is speculative, composed of paradoxes and riddles; at its best it is magnificently unopinionated. As Chekhov said, fiction does not provide answers but asks questions—even, I might add, as it struggles to make sense out of the fearful ambiguities of time and history. This award therefore implies an understanding that a novel can possess a significance apart from its subject matter and that the story of a nineteenth-century black slave may try to say at least as much about longing, loneliness, personal betrayal, madness, and the quest for God as it does about Negroes or the institution of slavery. It implies the understanding that fiction, which almost by definition is a kind of dream, often tells truths that are very difficult to bear, yet—again as in dreams—is able to liberate the mind through the catharsis of fantasy, enigma, and terror.

By recognizing *Nat Turner* this award really honors all of those of my contemporaries who have steadfastly refused to write propaganda or indulge in mythmaking but have been impelled to search instead for those insights which, however raggedly and imperfectly, attempt to demonstrate the variety, the quirkiness, the fragility, the courage, the good humor, desperation, corruption, and mortality of all men. And finally it ratifies my own conviction that a writer jeopardizes his very freedom by insisting that he be bound or defined by his race, or by almost anything else. For one of the enduring marvels of art is its ability to soar through any barrier, to explore any territory of experience, and I say that only by venturing from time to time into strange territory shall artists, of whatever commitment, risk discovering and illuminating the human spirit that we all share.

[Acceptance speech for the 1970 Howells Medal. Published in the *Proceedings of the American Academy of Arts and Letters and the National Institute of Arts and Letters,* 2nd series, no. 21, 1971.]

In the Southern Camp

outhern women of all classes, probably more than women anywhere
else, have for generations been valued for their physical beauty to the
exclusion of any other quality. The ethos of the plantation, with its
stress on male dominance, allowed, generally speaking, very little room for
the development of women's intellectual capacities, except in a closeted way
and then only with vast condescension on the part of the men. Generation
after generation of this form of acculturation produced droves of famously
beautiful women, but also—in combination with a diminished emphasis on
education—a kind of endemic regional dumbness too well known and too
persistently remarked upon to be dismissed.

That there are many exceptions to this state of things, especially nowadays, is another sign of the South's splendid resurgence as it joins the twentieth century; beauty and brains are not necessarily antipathetic in the same
person. But until recent years the trials of a bright but plain woman in the
South were more difficult than those of her sisters elsewhere who, though
certainly fettered in many ways too, suffered less from the stigma of possessing actual intelligence. Difficult, perhaps, but in some ways more interesting. For even as recently as the 1940s, when I was growing up in the South,
one could perceive the difference between the often stunning coed beauties
who, like their counterparts in the past, fluttered effortlessly into poses of
decorative blossoms, and those who were less favored physically but who

were far more attractive because of their wit and charm. They created their own seductiveness.

Mary Boykin Chesnut was doubtless one of these: a not really good-looking woman (self-admittedly) whose very lack of beauty helped prevent her from becoming the stereotype of a plantation mistress—frail, dependent, vacuous—and whose compensating drive toward self-expression led her to writing one of the great chronicles of the Civil War. The likeness of Mary Chesnut that regards us from the dust jacket of the new edition of her book is rather plain—the nose too long, the jaw too broad, the eyes too large and dominating—but very winning nonetheless. The picture suggests intelligence and the whisper of mischief—clearly a woman one would have liked to know. That one does get to know her is the result both of her honesty and of the meticulous way in which she records her impressions of daily life in the South between the winter of 1861 and the summer of 1865.

Yet this is not really a "personal" narrative, and despite her candor and the piercing, almost ruthless way in which she dissects her own emotions, Mary Chesnut's journal has its greatest value for the modern reader in the extraordinary panorama it presents of a culture being rent asunder. Not for its autobiography, not for its "fortuitous self-revelations," says Professor C. Vann Woodward in his introduction to *Mary Chesnut's Civil War*, will the Chesnut chronicle be remembered, but "for the vivid picture she left of a society in the throes of its life-and-death struggle, its moment of high drama in world history."

Mrs. Chesnut was blissfully fortunate in having been near the center of the political affairs of the Confederacy throughout the Civil War. Born and reared in South Carolina and married to an ardent secessionist—a onetime United States senator who, after Fort Sumter, became an aide to Jefferson Davis—Mrs. Chesnut traveled forth from her native state to the early capital in Montgomery and thence to Richmond, where she abundantly records her impressions of the great and the near-great. A well-educated woman, fluent in French and an avowed Francophile, she seems in certain rudimentary ways a Southern Madame de Staël. Although by no means a philosophical or literary innovator like de Staël, she had nonetheless the same kind of intellectual energy and, like de Staël, possessed both a ferocious interest in powerful people and the magnetism to attract such people. Thus her observations of such figures as Jefferson Davis, Robert E. Lee, Wade Hampton, and General Joseph Johnston are as fascinating in their intimacy as they are invaluable.

Here is a sketch of Jefferson Davis in June 1861:

In Mrs. Davis's drawing room last night, the president took a seat beside me on the sofa where I sat. He talked for nearly an hour. He laughed at our faith in our own powers. We are like the British. We think every Southerner equal to three Yankees at least. We will have to be equivalent to a dozen now. . . . There was a sad refrain running through it all. For one thing, either way, he thinks it will be a long war. That floored me at once. It has been too long for me already. Then said: before the end came, we would have many a bitter experience. He said only fools doubted the courage of the Yankees or their willingness to fight when they saw fit. And now we have stung their pride—we have roused them till they will fight like devils.

And an insight into the domestic life of Robert E. ("Cousin Robert") Lee:

General Lee told us what a good son Custis was. Last night their house was so crowded Custis gave up his own bed to General Lee and slept upon the floor. Otherwise General Lee would have had to sleep in Mrs. Lee's room. She is a martyr to rheumatism and rolls about in a chair. She can't walk.

Constance Cary says, if it would please God to take poor Cousin Mary Lee—she suffers so—wouldn't these Richmond women *campaign* for Cousin Robert? In the meantime Cousin Robert holds all admiring females at arm's length.

A glimpse of Lee and Davis on the same day:

Sunday Mars Kit walked to church with me. Coming out, General Lee was slowly making his way down the aisle, bowing royally right and left. I pointed this out to Christopher Hampton. When General Lee happened to look our way, he bowed low, giving me a charming smile of recognition. I was ashamed of being so pleased. I blushed like a schoolgirl.

We went to the White House. They gave us tea. The president said he had been on the way to our house, coming with all the Davis family to see me. But the children became so troublesome they turned back.

Just then little Joe rushed in and insisted on saying his prayer at his father's knee. . . . He was in his nightclothes.

But if Chesnut's journals were merely high-level gossip restricted to a circle of the celebrated men and women of the period, the book would have very limited appeal. The work is really an epic in which the accumulation of quotidian detail—the weather, parties, receptions, rumors, duels, love affairs, murders, promotions and demotions, intrigues, illnesses, celebrations— provides a sense of the rhythms of ordinary life during those chaotic four years in a way that no other book has done. We often tend to think of the Civil War in terms of its battles, all of which have been chronicled in such detail—in history and in fiction—that the savagery, say, of Chickamauga or the desperate anxiety of the ordinary soldier represented in *The Red Badge of Courage* becomes emblematic of the entire conflict. The romanticism of *Gone with the Wind* prevents that novel from furnishing us with a reliable picture of life away from the arenas of combat.

What gives Mrs. Chesnut's account such stunning verisimilitude is the way in which the war, despite its distance from the diarist and her friends in places like Richmond and Columbia, impinges on every facet of daily existence; scarcely a page of this extremely long journal does not have its allusion to the progress of the various campaigns, to the slow attrition being suffered by the Confederacy, to the hospital horrors, to privations, to lost battles and battles won, and—incessantly—to the dead, the mutilated, and men who have come home to die. Yet despite the appalling grimness of those years there is little of the morbid or despairing in Mary Chesnut's description of events. Underlying even the darkest passages is a cheerfulness of spirit, almost a buoyancy, that in effect aerates the narrative and provides much of its charm and readability.

The following passages, only a few pages apart, provide a characteristic juxtaposition of the somber and the lighthearted:

Yesterday we went to the capitol grounds to see our returned prisoners. . . . We walked slowly up and down until Jeff Davis was called upon to speak to the prisoners. Then I stood almost touching the bayonets, where he left me. Poor fellows! They cheered with all their might—and

I wept for sympathy, enthusiasm, and all that moved me deeply. Oh! these men were so forlorn, so dried up, shrunken, such a strange look in some of their eyes. Others so restless and wild looking—others again, placidly vacant, as if they had been dead to this world for years. A poor woman was too much for me. She was hunting her son. He had been expected back with this batch of prisoners. She said he was taken prisoner at Gettysburg. She kept going in and out among them, with a basket of provisions she had brought for him to eat. It was too pitiful. She was utterly unconscious of the crowd. The anxious dread—expectation—hurry and hope which led her on showed in her face . . .

✿   ✿   ✿

The church windows were closed that it might be a candlelight wedding. A woman in the gallery had a cataleptic fit, and they were forced to open a window. Mixed daylight and gas was ghastly and greatly marred the effect below. The poor woman made a bleating noise like a goat. Buckets of water were handed over the heads of the people, as if it was a fire to be put out, and they dashed water over her as fast as the buckets came in reach. We watched the poor woman from below in agony, fearing she might die before our eyes. But no—far from it. The water cure answered. She came to herself, shook her dress, straightened up her wet feathers, and put her bonnet on quite composedly. Then watched the wedding with unabashed interest—and I watched her. . . . For one thing, the poor woman could not have been gotten out of that jam, that crowd, unless, like the buckets of water, she had been handed out over the heads of the public.

Readability is perhaps an imprecise word to explain the fascination that this book exerts once one has become captured by its force and sweep, but it is there in a powerful way, and is quite simply a factor of the inherent literary nature of the work. Mrs. Chesnut clearly had the gifts of a novelist (she had written a couple of undistinguished though not unpromising works of fiction), and the novelistic talent is everywhere evident—in her dialogue, sharp observations, the felicitous use of language, the deft modulations in tone which are the novelist's stock in trade. In an essay on Mrs. Chesnut published in *Patriotic Gore* in 1962, Edmund Wilson remarked on her literary qualities: "The very rhythm of her opening pages at once puts us under the spell of a writer who is not merely jotting down her days but establishing, as a novelist does, an atmosphere, an emotional tone."

Wilson had been profoundly impressed by the journal, which he had read in an abridged form unfortunately entitled *A Diary from Dixie*. (Mrs. Chesnut herself disliked the word "Dixie," but the book was named by its editors, who brought out the work in 1905, nineteen years after her death.) He had also read and, with some reservations, admired a more recent and more extensive version of the diary put together by the novelist Ben Ames Williams. In the first version the editors had suppressed such matters as the gross injustice of slavery (thereby obscuring an extremely important aspect of Mrs. Chesnut, who was a vigorous opponent of the slave system), and Wilson's admiration for the Williams edition was due both to this enlargement of perspective and to the fact that it read like a good novel—something that appealed to the literary side of Wilson's critical sensibilities.

What Wilson could not have known was that considerably more of the novelistic imagination went into the making of Mrs. Chesnut's diary than one might think. For although she did keep an extensive journal during several of the Civil War years, it was not until 1881—sixteen years after the war ended—that she sat down and began completely to rework her chronicle, fleshing out her story through a complex series of expansions and elaborations, adding new episodes and new material, condensing here, omitting there, shifting dates, telescoping entries, until the new version was no longer the actual record of the wartime days but what might be termed a reconstruction through memory. The liberties she took in this reworking of her own material were plainly great, but the final product was not the creation of one who has distorted or falsified history but of one who, through the prism of memory and in the calm of reflection, has perhaps cast a brighter and more revealing light upon past events than might have been shed in an actual journal, with its frequent myopia.

Confessing that he began the editing of this new, complete edition with a spirit of skepticism, Professor Woodward writes that "a growing respect for the author and the integrity of her work began to replace the original misgivings. Given the kind of liberties she took . . . Mary Chesnut can be said to have shown an unusual sense of responsibility toward the history she records and a reassuring faithfulness to perceptions of her experience of the period as revealed in her original journal."

Having read with considerable admiration Capote's *In Cold Blood* and

Mailer's *The Executioner's Song*—and having been able to compare the two versions of Mrs. Chesnut's chronicle—I would say that Mrs. Chesnut played far less fast and loose with the facts and with "truth" than either of these writers, whose works we value precisely because of their fluid, interpretative nature, their refusal to be hamstrung by adhering to a mechanical account of events. (It may be that the most interesting aspect of the controversy that surrounds these books is not the blur they create between fact and fiction but the no-man's-land of terminology; as powerfully impressed as I was by *The Executioner's Song*, some stubborn intuition still tells me it is not a novel.)

In any case, we should not fault Mrs. Chesnut for her inconsistencies; she herself did not attempt to hide the fact that much of her final version was reworked and rewritten. Partly because of this, Professor Woodward has removed the word "diary" from the title, so that *Mary Chesnut's Civil War* really ends up being not a literal record but a history book *sui generis*, a new mixture of memoir and journalism to which only the most rigorously literal-minded reader could object on the grounds that it does not hew to the minutiae of chronology and fact.

If Professor Woodward had not, in the passage just quoted and elsewhere in his remarkably sensitive and careful introduction, taken such pains to explain the difference between the original diary and the later transformation, it would be somewhat easier to accept the charge made by Professor Kenneth S. Lynn, in *The New York Times Book Review*, that the Chesnut journal is a "hoax," and "one of the most audacious frauds in the history of American literature." It is offensive enough that Professor Lynn has called the book a hoax; what seems obtuse is his further insistence that Professor Woodward not only has exposed the hoax but has refused "to bestow that label upon it."[1]

But if a hoax is something that is deliberately intended to trick or dupe, which I believe to be a scrupulous definition of the word, then nothing could be more wrong. As I said before, Mrs. Chesnut did nothing to hide the reworked nature of her journals. Further, even if such charges as Professor Lynn makes were true—for instance, that she cleansed the later version of her journal of antislavery sentiments to be more in tune with the mood of the postwar years—a criticism that does not hold up—it would hardly be of great significance, when one compares the haphazard and fragmentary nature of the early diary (containing, as Professor Woodward points out, "so many indiscretions, gaps, trivialities, and incoherencies") with the reflective finished work, radiating such vitality and truth. Professor Lynn wonders whether Edmund Wilson might not have wanted to retract all his praise for Mrs. Chesnut had he known the real nature of her achievement. I doubt that he would have wanted to do any such thing, any more than he would have preferred Proust's notebooks to *Swann's Way*.

Mary Chesnut's Civil War is important because, whatever one calls it—journal, memoir, chronicle, or an amalgam of these—the book remains a great epic drama of our greatest national tragedy. Even so, when the last page is finished and the panorama begins to fade, one is still haunted by the personality of the book's extraordinary author. How thoroughly—by force of her vivacity, her compassion, and her wisdom—she helps rearrange in our consciousness certain shopworn images which might linger in regard to the emptiness of Southern women of her time is a measure of her great authority as a writer.

Doubtless there were many like her, but it was she who almost alone rose with such gallantry to the challenges of her era. For one thing, she was in certain matters decades ahead of her contemporaries of either sex. To be sure, she was not entirely alone among the women of her time and place in her detestation of slavery, but the voice she raised against the institution of slavery was among the loudest and most vehement. Reading her animadversions on the slave system, one wonders which she hated more: the plight of the slaves or that of her own female sex, doomed forever, it seemed, to the tyranny of male domination. Mary Chesnut was a passionate and outraged feminist; and one of the most fascinating aspects of her personality, and the tensions that energized her, was her constant awareness of the way in which the oppression of black slaves and the oppression of women were similar, indeed intertwined.

Have made the acquaintance of a clever woman, too—Mrs. McLean, née Sumner, daughter of the general. . . . They say *he* avoids matrimony.
"Slavery the sum of all evil," he says. So he will not reduce a woman to slavery. There is no slave, after all, like a wife.

❀   ❀   ❀

So I have seen a negro woman sold—up on the block—at auction. The woman on the block overtopped the crowd. I felt faint—seasick.

She was a bright mulatto with a pleasant face. She was magnificently gotten up in silks and satins. She seemed delighted with it all—sometimes ogling the bidders, sometimes looking quite coy and modest, but her mouth never relaxed from its expanded grin of excitement. I daresay the poor thing knew who would buy her.

I sat down on a stool in a shop. I disciplined my wild thoughts. . . .

You know how women sell themselves and are sold in marriage, from queens downward, eh?

You know what the Bible says about slavery—and marriage. Poor women. Poor slaves. . . .

Certainly one feels that she had earned the right to such awareness and to the consequent indignation; after all, these were the twin curses of the environment out of which she had sprung. Unlike Harriet Beecher Stowe—for whom she had considerable contempt—Mary Chesnut had been reared in a world where the horrors of slavery were a daily reality; just as real and just as grinding was the peculiarly Southern form of patriarchal domination— a nearly total exploitation of women by men. Her treatment of these themes, foreshadowing so much of that which has come to an upheaval in our own period, is in itself a splendid manifestation of moral courage, as well as pre-science. It is such honest turmoil within the mind and heart of this questing woman that helps to bestow upon both the work and its creator an unshakable excellence.

[*New York Review of Books*, August 13, 1981.]

A Voice from the South

I've always been surprised by my direct link to the Old South—the South of slavery and the Civil War. Many Southerners of my vintage, and even some of those who are considerably older, can claim an ancestral connection to that period only through a *great*-grandparent. "I have letters written during the war by my great-aunt," they will say, or "my great-grandfather was with Longstreet at Seven Pines." If they remember their grandparents, they usually remember elderly ladies and gentlemen whose own childhood memories are of the days of Reconstruction or afterwards. But it was from my own grandmother, who was in her late eighties when I was a boy of twelve or so, that I heard of her life as a little girl just before the war and of the sometimes remarkable events that took place in her life thereafter.

The Clark plantation, where she was born Marianna at midcentury, was a small fiefdom of several thousand acres on the lower reaches of the Pungo River in eastern North Carolina. Even now Hyde County is a remote region, low-lying, with the desolate marsh-and-pinewoods beauty of land bordering on the sea. In those days, before highways and cars, before telephones, the remoteness must have been a globe of near-perfect silence, with only the diurnal sounds of plantation business obtruding: cartwheels squeaking, a blacksmith's hammer, the fuss and grumble of livestock—at night an immense quiet. Whenever, in my fantasy of the place, I hear human voices, the voices are almost always those of black people, calling from the cabins or the fields, through an August haze. This was a mercantile enterprise after all, and the black people made up its vital force and were its essential personnel. My grandmother's father, Caleb Clark, was a major entrepreneur; he owned upwards of thirty-three slaves, a large number for the upper South. And it was they who labored to produce the plantation's crops—cotton and cotton meal, shingles and turpentine—much of which was transported by boat up through the inland waterway to Norfolk for shipment north and to Europe.

In the late nineteenth century, and well into the early decades of this century, there were many sentimental novels written by Southerners, still infatuated with life in antebellum times, in which the central figures are a child and an older person reminiscing about those bygone years; in these chronicles there was never a world so idyllic as that of the plantation, with its celebrations, its pleasant frivolities and domestic commotions, its possum hunts and horse races and sewing bees, its natural disasters that always resolved themselves benignly, the genteel collision of white people and their black servitors in encounters touching or droll but never menacing.

Curiously, I recall myself as a boy being a character in just such a novel, and the older person was none other than my grandmother, then living in the small town of Washington—popularly known as Little Washington—not many miles from that arcadian domain in Hyde County where her childhood was spent experiencing precisely those joys that the sentimental novelist described. Or at least that is the way she represented her early life to me, and of course she could be excused because of her extreme youth for having failed to be aware of the desperate and sorrowful undercurrents that lay beneath the genial surface of the Clark plantation. In the same way my own extreme youth allowed me to be beguiled by her description of the two little slave girls she owned. Approximately her own age, they had been legally deeded to her by her father, and they had the priceless names of Drusilla and Lucinda. Drusilla and Lucinda—they were names right out of one of those heartrending chronicles where the young heroine nurses her beloved charges through dire illnesses such as scarlet fever, and braids their hair, and knits woolen stockings to protect their skinny little black legs from the winter cold. But the fact is that my grandmother actually performed these good offices. They were no maudlin romantic invention. Much of what she told me had a quality of innocence, even beatitude, and she was telling the truth as she saw it, at least.

But suddenly—and why shrink from the obvious locution?—it was all gone with the wind. From the outset of the war Federal troops had occupied eastern North Carolina, and in 1862 a small force of General Burnside's men marched onto the Clark plantation and ransacked the place from end to end. They were efficient devastators and destroyed much of the property, but my grandmother recalled that the most terrible result of the Yankees' plunder was hunger. Their chief objective had been food and provisions and they stripped the premises of every edible ounce. The troops were surly, loud, and uncouth; they were from Ohio, and that state for her forever had a special stigma among the generally hated Northern states, causing her to pronounce the name with a kind of aspirated loathing, O-high-O. One particularly vivid image she left me with was the maneuver whereby the scores of smoked and cured hams and bags of meal in the cellar were removed from the house: a chain of blue-jacketed soldiers, like a bucket brigade, passing hams and bags one after another out the window and into the wagons below. The monsters waved their flags and brandished their rifles, and they used dreadful cuss words, my grandmother said, language no Southerner would use. Then they departed and the Clark family began to starve; for weeks the family—and the black people, too—subsisted on what they could scrounge from the fields and woods, until finally some meager supplies began to arrive regularly from friends in Tarboro, smuggled through the Union lines. All of us are by now acquainted with human beings who have suffered pain of nearly every description, but aside from a few of the survivors of Auschwitz, my grandmother was the only person I've ever known—certainly the only American—who could describe the harrowing pain of continual starvation.

Meanwhile, over in Little Washington, which was in the hands of the Federals, my grandmother's husband-to-be—my grandfather Alpheus Whitehurst Styron—had sneaked his way out of town to join the Confederate army. He was a rambunctious kid of fifteen with enough inbred Southern chutzpah then to lie about his age in order to sign up with one of the units of General Robert Hoke, who for many months had laid siege to the town in a campaign to drive the Yankees out. He was assigned to a job as courier, and this provided him with many scary and hairbreadth adventures as he moved in and out of the town through the cordon of Union pickets. But his splendid career as boy warrior was brief, and terminated abruptly in 1864 when the Union troops were ordered to abandon their stronghold and leave Washington. Before departing, hundreds of soldiers went on a nasty spree through the streets, pillaging stores and warehouses and private homes; then they burned down the pretty little town. One responsible historian has written that, for its size, no Southern community was so completely devastated, including those in the path of Sherman's infamous march. The wars of the twentieth century, with their hideous massacres of civilians and reprisals against the innocent, have made such episodes appear like mere gross misbehavior; a spirit of gallantry, now virtually defunct, prevailed on both sides of the Civil War, and the atrocities to which most of us have become anesthetized were in those days almost never a part of the repertory of violence. There were no Babi Yars, no Lidices, no Oradours, no My Lais. But the invaders were experts in the science of destruction, and it requires no stretch of credulity to speculate that, had the fortunes of war and geography been different, the Confederate troops would have been capable of the same evil mischief. Whatever, as Vann Woodward observed in *The Burden of Southern History,* the South in its ruination—of which the destroyed town of Washington was a symbol—became the only region in America to experience the tragic exhaustion and trauma of defeat (along with the bitterness of the vanquished) that has been the common lot of so many millions of Europeans. So it is no wonder that many years later, living serenely in a Washington now restored, my grandmother should still have been affected by the brutality and privation she had suffered as a little girl, and her gentle yet animated face turned aggrieved, pale as ice at the recollection of the barbarians who had abused and starved her. It is not difficult for me, recomposing my own memories, to see in that face the same wintry hauntedness of a Russian woman I knew whose town was overrun by the Germans. Both had psychic wounds and both were unforgiving.

When I had these memorable encounters with my grandmother I was living not far north in the Virginia Tidewater, near the small city where I was born. Newport News was indisputably a Southern community, but it lacked many of the characteristics we commonly associate with a Southern environment. It was a rootless and synthetic town, created from the ground up in the 1890s by the Northern railroad tycoon Collis P. Huntington, who perceived in the lower James River a perfect setting for his shipbuilding enterprise, while obviously being enticed by the prospect of cheap, non-union Southern labor, much of it black. My father, a graduate of North Carolina State College, was an engineer at the shipyard. Newport News also became a bustling ocean port and chief terminus for the Chesapeake and

Ohio Railroad, which was a major transporter of coal from the Appalachian mines, tobacco from the Carolinas, Virginia, and Kentucky, and grain from the Midwest. Among its lesser but continuous exports were the elderly horses saved from the Kansas City dog-food factories but headed for a more dreadful fate by being consigned to Spain, where they became the terrorized and often gored-to-death mounts of picadors in bullfights. As a boy I remember seeing hundreds of these cadaverous old nags huddled in the rain, and only learned of their purpose years later when Hemingway mentioned Newport News in *Death in the Afternoon*. I would not go so far as to say that, metaphorically, these wretched beasts represented for me the dreariness of the city, yet it was a strangely soulless community and, despite what I still reckon to have been a relatively happy childhood spent in and around the place, I never discovered its center, its identity. Certainly I could argue with myself that in writing my first novel, *Lie Down in Darkness*, I made a stab at plumbing that identity, and even perceiving glints of natural beauty, usually those of river and estuary and bay; but it was difficult to establish a spiritual connection with such a city, basically callow and without a past to supply it with those necessities of Southern life—myth and tradition.

A connoisseur of the unaesthetic, H. L. Mencken, once rated the town second in ugliness only to Altoona, Pennsylvania. It is true that those who were the most favored economically might, as is customary, build houses commanding a gorgeous view—in this case the broad James or the wide and spectacular Hampton Roads—but essentially the city was raw, clamorous, industrial, and unsightly, with a big, drab white slum and an even drabber and bigger black slum, a part of which, even in those days before cocaine or crack had been heard of, was prey to such unceasing violence that it bore the lurid name Blood Fields. Aside from all this it was hard to love a place where much of the population was transient, shifting, faceless: swarms of country boys, black and white, seeking railroad or shipyard jobs, an endless invasion of seamen from merchant ships, and a horde of soldiers and sailors from every base in the swollen military encampment which the lower Tidewater was becoming in the years before World War II. As I've implied, the city inflicted on me little actual misery. I had happy times as a kid, and I loved the great murky expanse of the James River, in which, or on which, swimming or sailing, I dwelled with such comfortable abandon that I felt it to be as fundamentally my habitat as a gull's or a shad's. But I remained an alien in my birthplace, uncharmed and unattached. Would I have so easily

fled Richmond, or Mobile, or Jackson, Tennessee, or Cheraw, South Carolina? Numberless factors shape one's needs and longings, and I may have
been forced to escape any native environment. At any rate, a line I wrote in
the diary I kept as a fourteen-year-old became a prophecy: *I've got to get the
hell away from here.*

But throughout my boyhood, whatever my dissatisfactions with the city,
I felt an acute consciousness of myself as a Southerner. I also acquired, by
that osmotic process that most Southerners experience, a hyperintense
sense of place. Despite its instability and its grimy atmosphere, Newport
News was in Dixie; you would never really confuse it with Sandusky or Du-
luth. At a time when most urban areas, both north and south, were still
predominantly white, Newport News was nearly forty percent black—or
Negro, as we were permitted to say in those days—largely owing to the vast
numbers of immigrants from the Southeastern farms who found jobs in the
shipyard. Jim Crow reigned and segregation was as omnipresent as it is
today in Johannesburg, though in those years, unlike the restive black South
Africans now, the victims of Virginia apartheid were frozen in the weird
time warp that had held them captive since the Civil War; they fitted, seemingly uncomplaining and precisely where they belonged—or where white
people wanted them to belong—within the matrix of community life, in
which the timeless status quo had smothered protest and rendered revolt
inconceivable. I didn't get the intimate connection with Negroes that I
might have had in the country or a small town. To my bemused and attentive
eye, as a boy, Negroes were participants in a bewildering magic trick, appearing and disappearing at the whim of some prestidigitator, who caused
them to throng the stage of the city by the thousands—especially at four
o'clock, the shipyard quitting time—but who then made them vanish in a
puff, so that at night the same main street would be occupied only by Cau-
casians, not a single black soul in sight; they had all been whisked away into
their baleful ghetto beyond the C&O tracks where they were occupied, according to legend, with cutting each other up in Blood Fields, and where
the only white persons present would be the merchant sailors paying visits
to the seedy whorehouses along Warwick Avenue.

This vanishing act did indeed baffle me, so much so that any awareness
of Negroes was honed to an exquisite receptivity not by their presence so
much as by their absence. I was still quite young when I began to wonder at
this absence. Why weren't they in school with me? Why didn't they belong

to the Presbyterian church, like I did? Why weren't they in the movie theaters, at the baseball games? Why were Florence, the cook, whom I was so
fond of, and old William, who mowed the lawn and told me funny stories,
finally such strangers, disappearing at night into a world of utter mystery?
Because they were absent, even though constantly visible and present, Negroes exacted a powerful and curiously exotic hold on my boyhood; their
lives, their peculiarity, their difference, their frustrating untouchability all
fascinated me, and finally comprised a kind of obsession. I wasn't dumb: I
knew that they had lives beyond the sweat of hard ill-paid labor and Saturday night mayhem and being whores, and I struggled in my way to get to
know them. For one thing, I knew they led—many of them at least—a religious life, a life of incandescent faith. The presence in the city of two messianic figures, Elder Solomon Lightfoot Michaux and his archrival Bishop
Grace—known as Daddy Grace—was testimony to that, and their competitive mass baptisms in Hampton Roads, thousands of the faithful being immersed in the briny waters while shouting songs of salvation, were spectacles
I was drawn to, agitated and wide-eyed. I had a deep hunger to divine the
nature of this spirituality, so alien to my pallid Presbyterianism, with its
numbing Sunday school sessions and querulous hymns, its purple sabbath
melancholy. There was a wild and forthright gladness in the religion of black
people. Its music—the gospel sound and those spirituals, that gave voice to
such depths of anguish and highs of almost manic ecstasy—moved me to
inexpressible feelings, feelings I'd never had before and wouldn't experience again until, on a different but equally genuine level of response, I
began to listen to Mozart and Bach.

Somehow I must have been aware that the key to my preoccupation with
Negroes and their religion was slavery. Even so, I couldn't quite shake off
the ambivalence toward them that was a product of my upbringing. Bigotry,
foolish and fangless but real nonetheless, was essentially a part of my character, as it was for nearly all my contemporaries, and what little understanding I had of Negro history must have been colored by the prevailing
platitudes. But at least I was groping for enlightenment. One of my first attempts at literary composition was a high-school theme called "Drusilla and
Lucinda, Two Little Slave Girls." I recall almost nothing about this work.
I'm sure it was as mawkish and absurd as the official state history texts which
the Commonwealth of Virginia had prepared for its youngest citizens and
whose rubrics concerning the transcendental sweetness of slave times I

innocently accepted. (Consider the historical objectivity of the set of two volumes, one of which, for freshmen, had portrayed on its cover Robert E. Lee, while the other, for sophomores, has a photograph of Lee's horse Traveller, fixed in taxidermy's timeless paralysis and on display at Washington and Lee.) I've often wondered how such prejudice and propaganda didn't desensitize me to the much closer approximations of truth I found in history books when I was later contemplating my own work on slavery.

I have not overlooked the fact that the suffering my grandmother endured as a child was the grim though perhaps not unnatural consequence of a war that was fought over the very existence of slavery. Within certain sound moral standards she may be regarded as having been the pitiable victim of a struggle in which right prevailed. This idea hadn't really penetrated my consciousness either, as a boy. I recall how in 1937, the year before she died, I looked forward to our trips down to Little Washington. She was now nearly eighty-seven years old and partially paralyzed from a stroke, but her mind was still quick; she was a tiny little lady, so frail and light that my father carried her in his arms like a child. For me the pleasure and the excitement of the trip began when our car—a 1930 Oldsmobile my father won in a raffle— left the sooty urban bloat of Newport News behind, and we passed over the James River bridge into southside Virginia. A short distance beyond the end of the bridge began the fields of peanuts and cotton; they were doubtless the northernmost cotton fields in America and were symbolic to me of the forlornly beautiful, funky rural South into which we were penetrating, the South of pine forests and unpainted farm shacks, Bull Durham signs and coffee-brown sluggish streams winding through swamps, mule teams off in the distance and shabby little Negro churches in a stand of ancient oak trees, rattletrap Fords and tumbledown graveyards and a sense of universal poorness and sadness—the eternal Southern countryside. In Washington, my grandmother, bedridden now, always greeted us with the look of startled then expanding joy of one who had waited a long and anxious time for our visit.

After the Civil War she had lived a good, satisfying, philoprogenitive (she'd had eight children) life, though one beset by many knocks and adversities. When she married my grandfather, some years after his dashing career as a boy courier, he was ambitious for good old American success and in due course built up a thriving little business manufacturing chewing tobacco and snuff. Good old American catastrophe struck one year in the

1880s, however, when those original Southern robber barons, the rapacious Dukes, *père et fils,* founders of the American Tobacco Company—my father always called them "those piratical devils" and was sorely injured when I became a student at the university bearing their name—ran my grandfather out of business through some wicked monopolistic maneuver, one which, though perfectly legal in those freebooting days, left the family nearly destitute. My grandfather somehow recovered and made a moderately decent living thereafter as the proprietor and captain of a small steamship first used for hauling farm cargo to Norfolk and later taking passenger tours through Pamlico Sound. But my grandmother had had to live a domestic life of considerable hardship and, now widowed for many years, she could not quite throw off that burden of hardship, which showed in her tired eyes and brittle-looking work-worn hands, though her spirits were unquelled and chipper.

On one of those visits my mother came along, and I recall how her presence complicated matters, for she was a Northerner, born in western Pennsylvania. It was not until that trip, perhaps because I was getting a little older and more perceptive, that I realized the strained relations that must have always existed between the two women. My grandmother was a lady of bountiful nature and kindness, and it is difficult to believe that she was intentionally rude to my mother, who herself was amiable and outgoing and possessed a desire to please and who, I'm sure, made a strenuous effort to reach out to my grandmother, as if to say, I am of a different generation. The war is long over, let us bind up the old wounds. But try as she might to avoid it, and I'm sure she had tried, the remoteness my grandmother displayed, the chilliness, the hostility she felt not toward my mother herself but toward her Northernness, had in some way made itself all too evident; on the trip back to Virginia I heard my mother say to my father in a hurt, strained voice: "She has never really liked me, has she?" And despite my father's pained explanations, his denials, I think it may have been *then* that I understood how truly lacerating to my grandmother's spirit the war had been and how unexceptional it was that she could not eradicate from memory that appalling visitation with its rampaging footfalls and deafening yells of the Ohio marauders who destroyed in a day nearly all that she knew existed. How perfectly normal and human it had been to hoard up the injustice of those weeks when her belly shriveled into a knot, and when, soon after, she saw the only community she had known burned to cinders. A few others might have had the magnanimity to forget and pardon, but my grandmother apparently did not; it was a failing I always found easy to disregard.

She once told me in those last days, squeezing my hands, "Billy, always remember you're a Southerner." She would have greatly disapproved, I fear, the choice I made to live in the North. But if I had been able, in recent years, to reach her through the void, I may have had to tell her some truths she would have found disappointing. I would have to tell her that the North is not so bad a place to make a home, certainly in the bucolic region in which I dwell, where the people are at least as good-natured and as easygoing as Southerners, just as often displaying the generosity Southerners are famous for, and where the gently rolling landscape has the harmonious contours of the uplands of north Georgia or Alabama. I would tell her that it is much too cold in the winter where I live, and that the bland native cuisine is such that I long for the sumptuous Tidewater meals I remember; but one can fly away for the winter, and as for the cuisine—you can import almost anything edible from the South now, overnight mail, and gorge on Florida oysters and Carolina quail at home. I would tell her that our back roads have noisy rednecks and the ether teems with country music.

Sometimes I miss the South, but often I don't, since, when I view the region from afar, or when I make my frequent visits, it seems to resemble the North at its most shopping mall–ridden and architecturally berserk. Walker Percy, a writer for whom my esteem is unsurpassed, once spoke in an interview of the Connecticutization of the South, or parts of it, but this seemed to me an unnecessary disparagement of my adopted state, for if anyone shrinks, as I do, from the high-tech and runaway urban glut of Georgia's capital city, the idea of the Atlantaization of the modestly proportioned cities of Connecticut creates dread. It would seem to me that the dynamism of American society in the past few decades has allowed the development of a homogeneity in which it is very hard to regard either the ills or the excellences of life as being the peculiar property of one region or another. Such are the excellences I've seen in the South recently—side by side with certain atrocities, to be sure—that I could live there with the greatest happiness, were my transplantation to the North not so long-lived and complete.

Essentially my grandmother was right, and I have heeded her counsel: I've never forgotten that I am a Southerner. A mere decade from now her descendants will celebrate her 150th anniversary—a span of time of such magnitude that I am touched with awe that I was once so intimately bound up with her being. To remember her now as she was, fading and frail, in the realization that those hands I embraced—the skin like tissue, the flesh warm with life yet invaded by a dying chill—were hands that once braided the hair of a little black girl who was her property, were hands that scratched for food in the harsh Carolina earth in a war that separated her and the little black girl forever: the remembrance of those hands is alone enough for me to forge a lasting bond with our unfathomable past, and to prevent me from being anything but a Southerner, wherever I live.

[*Sewanee Review*, Fall 1989.]

Nat Turner Revisited

Twenty-five years ago this November, I found myself in Ohio, where I was being awarded an honorary degree at Wilberforce University. The university, one of the few all-Negro institutions in the North, was named after William Wilberforce, the great British abolitionist of slavery, and so I marked the special appropriateness of this honor when I accepted the invitation a few weeks earlier. My novel *The Confessions of Nat Turner,* based on the Virginia slave revolt of 1831, had been published early in October to generally glowing reviews, had received a vast amount of publicity, and had quickly ascended to the top of the best-seller lists, where it would remain for many weeks. Only the most disingenuous of writers would, I think, fail to confess being pleased by such a reception.

I was also gratified to have the blessing of both the Book-of-the-Month Club and the *New York Review of Books*. There was a lavish movie contract from Twentieth Century–Fox and an admiring review in *The New Republic* from one of America's preeminent historians.[1] I am stressing these outward signs of success only to point up the reversal of fortune the book would soon undergo. Like any writer who is honest with himself, I knew that *Nat Turner* had defects and vulnerabilities—Faulkner remarked that we novelists will be remembered for "the splendor of our failures"—but that it was hard not to feel a certain fulfillment that fall, more than five years after having sat down at my desk on Martha's Vineyard, determined to re-create, out of an extremely sketchy and mysterious historical record, the life of a man who led the only significant slave revolt in our history, and to try to fashion in the process an imagined microcosm of the baleful institution whose legacy has persisted in this century and become the nation's central obsession. In 1962, when I began writing the book, the civil rights movement still had the quality of conciliation; Martin Luther King, Jr.'s grand and impossible dream was dreamed in a spirit of amity, concord, and the hope of a mutual understanding. The following years demonstrated the harsher truths: Birmingham, the bombings, Selma, the death of Medgar Evers, the three youthful martyrs of that Mississippi summer, churches set on fire, unbounded terror. James Baldwin, who was a friend of mine and who had made notes for his great essay *The Fire Next Time* while living in my house, had seen his prophecy come to pass in the smoke and flames of Watts and of Newark and Detroit. I've often been surprised, reflecting on this time, at the naïveté or perhaps blindness that prevented my perceiving in that tumult a suggestion of the backlash that awaited *Nat Turner*.

But on the campus of Wilberforce University there was no hint of the gathering storm. The angry word had not yet gone out. In a sea of smiling black and brown people, I was greeted with good will, thanks, praise. During lunch the university's president publicly expressed his appreciation for my story, for the way I had illuminated some of slavery's darker corners. At the convocation ceremony I made a brief talk in which I expressed the hope that an increased awareness of the history of the Negro (I used this word, which, though moribund and about to be replaced within months by black, was still acceptable), especially of Negro slavery, would allow people of both races to come to terms with the often inexplicable turmoil of the present.

There was much applause. George Shirley, a Wilberforce alumnus who was a leading tenor with the Metropolitan Opera, gave a spine-chilling rendition of "The Battle Hymn of the Republic," in which the audience joined together, singing with great emotion. Standing in that auditorium, I was moved by a feeling of oneness with these people. I felt gratitude at their acceptance of me and, somehow more important, at my acceptance of them, as if my literary labors and my plunge into history had helped dissolve many of my preconceptions about race that had been my birthright as a Southerner and allowed me to better understand the forces that had shaped our common destiny. For me it was a moment of intense warmth and brotherhood. It would have been inconceivable to me that within a short time I would experience almost total alienation from black people, be stung by their rage, and finally be cast as an archenemy of the race, having unwittingly created one of the first politically incorrect texts of our time.

The story of Nat Turner had been long gestating in my mind, ever since I was a boy, in fact, since before I actually knew I wanted to be a writer. I could scarcely remember a time when I was not haunted by the idea of slavery or was not profoundly conscious of the strange bifurcated world of whiteness and blackness in which I was born and reared. In the Virginia Tidewater region of my beginnings, heavily populated by blacks, society remained firmly in the grip of the Jim Crow laws and their ordinance of a separate and thoroughly unequal way of life. The evidence was blatant and embarrassing even to some white children, like myself, who were presumably brought up to be indifferent to such inequities as the ramshackle black school that stood on the route we traveled to our own up-to-date and well-equipped edifice, with its swank state-of-the-art public-address system, very advanced for the late 1930s. Many black schools in Virginia at that time had outside privies.

Despite our own fine local facilities, Virginia—in the era of the hidebound Harry Byrd political machine—ranked in public education among the lowest of the states, down there with Arkansas and Mississippi, and the quality of instruction in the black schools had to be even worse than what we white students were given, which (except for a few individually outstanding teachers) was desperately mediocre. I was painfully sensitive to this disparity, just as I was conscious of the utter strangeness of this whole segregated world: the water fountains and restrooms marked "White" and "Colored," the buses in which black folk were required to sit in the rear, the theaters with blacks seated in the balconies (in the larger towns there were actually separate theaters); even the ferryboats crossing the rivers and bays enforced a nautical apartheid, with whites starboard and Negroes portside. I was perpetually bemused by this division and the ensuing isolation.

It was a system both ludicrous and dreadful, and I sensed its wrongness early, probably because of my parents, who, while hardly radical, were enlightened in racial matters, but also out of some innate sense of moral indignation. Although of course I was an outsider, I fell under the spell of negritude, fascinated by black people and their folkways, their labor and religion, and especially their music, their raunchy blues and ragtime and their spirituals that reached for, and often attained, the sublime. Like some young boys who are troubled by their "unnatural" sexual longings, I felt a similar anxiety about my secret passion for blackness; in my closet I was fearful lest any of my conventionally racist young friends discover that I was an unabashed enthusiast of the despised Negro. I don't claim a special innocence. Most white people were, and are, racist to some degree, but at least my racism was not conventional; I wanted to confront and understand blackness.

Then there was the incomparable example of my grandmother. In a direct linkage I still sometimes find remarkable, I am able to say that I remain separated from slavery by only two generations and that I was related to and was familiar with and spoke to someone who owned slaves. Born in 1851 on an eastern North Carolina plantation, my father's mother was the proprietress of two slave girls who were her age, twelve or thereabouts, at the time of the Emancipation Proclamation. Many years later, when she was an old lady in her eighties and I was eleven or twelve, she told me at great length of her love for these children and of the horror and loss she felt when that same year, 1862, Union forces from an Ohio regiment under General Burnside swept down on the plantation, stripped the place bare, and left everyone to starve, including the little slave girls, who later disappeared. It was a story I heard more than once, since I avidly prompted her to repeat it and she, indulging her own fondness for its melodrama, told it again with relish, describing her hatred for the Yankees (which remained undiminished in 1937), the real pain of her starvation (she said they were reduced to eating "roots and rats"), and her anguish when she was separated forever from those little black girls, who were called, incidentally, Drusilla and Lucinda, just as in so many antebellum plantation novels. All of the deliciously described particulars of my grandmother's chronicle held me spellbound, but I think that nothing so awed me as the fact that this frail and garrulous woman whom I beheld, and who was my own flesh and blood, had been the legal owner of two other human beings. It may have determined, more than anything else, some as-yet-to-be-born resolve to write about slavery.

Nat Turner entered my consciousness through brief references to his revolt in my text on Virginia history. But most memorably he appeared in the form of a historical highway marker adjoining a peanut field in Southampton County, where I traveled with our high school football team in the fall. This was a remote, down-and-out farm region, whose population was sixty percent black. I was transfixed by the information conveyed by that marker, paraphrased thus: Nearby, in August of 1831, a fanatical slave named Nat Turner led a bloody insurrection that caused the death of fifty-five white people. Captured after two months in hiding, Nat was brought to trial in the county seat of Jerusalem (now Courtland) and he and seventeen of his followers were hanged. I recall how this sign set off in my mind extraordinary resonances, which were clearly in conflict with my grandmother's story: What was the connection, if any, between her loving memories and this cryptic notation of terror and mayhem? Perhaps more important, I remember wondering whether that bygone moment of sudden disaster didn't reflect something sinister in the divided white and black world in which I lived, so outwardly peaceable yet, except to the blind, troubled and jumpy with signs of resentment, sullenness, covert hostility, and anger. The Virginia of my boyhood, like virtually all the South, was a place where the amiable, if often edgy, relations between the races rose from an impulse that was mutually self-protective, keeping in abeyance much white fear and much black rage.

Daily life produced an unstated precariousness. There were strong, even passionate bonds of affection between individuals, black and white, but the social arrangement was a different matter; in the vast rural areas a form of pseudoslavery prevailed, and the white man's whim was law. Urban existence, not much better, gave rise to ghettos where crimes by blacks against blacks went ignored and unrecorded. At its worst, the South was filled with intimidation and brutality on a terrifying scale; in the Deep South lynchings were still more than occasional. At its best, kindheartedness and decency, along with genuine love spontaneously reciprocated, were the rule, but even so, the South suffered, in its Jim Crow shackles, from the sickness of alienation. It was a bizarre, culturally schizoid world with falsity at its core, not to speak of a glaring inhumanity. I'm sure that my early fascination with Nat Turner came from pondering the parallels between his time and my own society, whose genteel accommodations and endemic cruelties, large and small, were not really so different from the days of slavery. I think I must have wondered whether this tautly strained calmness might not someday be just as susceptible to violent retribution.

I wrote several works of fiction before I finally tackled *Nat Turner*. Then in the early 1960s I decided that the time was ripe; certainly I was never anything but intensely aware of the way in which the theme of slave rebellion was finding echoes in the gathering tensions of the civil rights movement. Although it didn't dawn on me at the time, I later realized that one of the benefits for me in Nat Turner's story was not an abundance of historical material but, if anything, a scantiness. This was a drama that took place in a faraway backwater when information gathering was primitive. While it may be satisfying and advantageous for historians to feast on rich archival material, the writer of historical fiction is better off when past events have left him with short rations. A good example might be the abolitionist John Brown, who made his prodigious mark on history only thirty years after Nat Turner but whose every word and move were recorded by enterprising journalists, producing documents enough to fill a boxcar.

The novelist attempting John Brown's story is in conflict with the myriad known details of the chronicle, and his imagination cannot simply run off in a certain direction—which is what fiction writers need their imaginations to do—because he is fettered by already established circumstances. He is in danger of being overwhelmed by an avalanche of data. That is why the writing of novels about plentifully documented figures—Lincoln, say, or John F. Kennedy—is a risky matter, constricting for the writer himself who, while quite free to take liberties with the known facts (the shopworn but sound concept of artistic license), must still take care not to violate the larger historical record. (Although even here the convention has often been broken; history has taught us, for example, that Richard III was not an unmitigated villain, nor a hunchback, but only pedants carp at Shakespeare's nasty portrayal.)

The single meaningful document having to do with the Turner revolt was a short (seven-thousand-word) transcript that gave the title to my own work. The original *Confessions of Nat Turner*, which comprised both Nat's account of his upbringing and a description of the events leading up to the revolt, as well as the details of the revolt itself, was put in writing by a court-appointed lawyer named Thomas R. Gray, who took down the words from Nat's lips as he sat chained in his jail cell during the October days before his execution. From the first word this discourse poses serious questions of veracity. At a time when justice for slaves was at best a sham, and in the aftermath of a sensational trial where the state's absolute authority must have prevailed, how reliable or authentic was anything Nat said, when filtered through the mind of this minion of the state? Still, despite this problem, the bulk of the document appeared genuine—Nat himself had nothing to lose at this point by telling the truth, and while some of Gray's interpretation is doubtless suspect, he had little to gain by substantially altering Nat's statement—and so I was generally disposed to use it as a guideline, a *loose* guideline, for my own narrative.

Aside from Nat's own *Confessions* and a number of contemporary newspaper articles, most of which added little to Gray's account (except to emphasize the immediately devastating psychological effect the event had on Southern society), there was virtually no material of that period that was useful in shedding further light on Nat Turner as a person or on the uprising. Such a near-vacuum, as I say, seemed to me to be an advantage, placing me in the ideal position of knowing neither too much nor too little. A bad historical novel often leaves the impression of a hopelessly overfurnished house, cluttered with facts the author wishes to show off as fruits of his diligent research. Georg Lukács, the Hungarian Marxist critic whose monumental *The Historical Novel* should be read by all who attempt to write in the genre, views the disregard of facts as a state of grace; the creator of historical fiction, he argues convincingly, should have a thorough—perhaps even magisterial—command of the period with which he is dealing, but he should not permit his work to be governed by particular historical facts. Rather, his concern "is to reproduce the much more complex and ramifying totality with historical faithfulness." At the time of writing *Nat Turner,* I felt that as an amateur historian I had absorbed a vast amount of reading on slavery in general, not only by way of a great number of antebellum books and essays but through much recent scholarship in the exploding field of the historiography of the slave period; thus, while my command may scarcely have been magisterial, I felt I reasonably fulfilled the first of Lukács's conditions. It was perhaps serendipitous that Lukács's other condition, regarding the relative unimportance of facts, made my task easier since I had chosen a man about whom so little was known.

Yet the facts can never be simply ignored, and the principal item I had to deal with, and freely reject, was that which involved the character of Nat Turner himself. The fact: He was a person of conspicuous ghastliness. I eventually read the original *Confessions* countless times, trying to pick up useful clues about the man and his background, but early on I was struck by the impression that our hero was a madman. A singularly gifted and intelligent madman, but mad nonetheless. No attempts on my part of sympathetic reinterpretation could alter this conclusion: his apocalyptic and deranged visions, his heavenly signs and signals, his belief in his own divinely ordained retributive mission, his obsessive fasting and prayer, his bloodthirsty megalomania and self-identification with the Deity (to a provocative question about himself by Gray, he replied, "Was not Christ crucified?")—there was no shaking the fact that on the record Nat Turner was a dangerous religious lunatic. I didn't want to write about a psychopathic monster. While the institution of slavery was so horrible that it could readily produce psychopathology, and often did, I wished to demonstrate subtler motives, springing from social and behavioral roots, that could drive a young man of thirty-one to embark on his fearsome errand of revenge. So, without sacrificing the essence of Old Testament vengeance that plainly animated Nat, I attempted to moderate this aspect of his character and in doing so give him dimensions of humanity that were almost totally absent in the documentary evidence. When stern piety replaced demonic fanaticism, the man could be better understood.

I took an enormous liberty with historical actuality when I began to deal with Nat's childhood and upbringing. I placed the boy in a milieu where he could not possibly have belonged. During the course of Nat's brief life, Southampton County, where he was born and reared, had already suffered the impoverishment that had come to Virginia long before as the result of the overcultivation of tobacco and other crops, leaving a surplus of slaves who were constantly in danger of being sold off to the thriving plantations of Alabama and Mississippi—the "Far South." Virginia's Southside, as the region below the James River is known, was in those days dotted with small farms and modest holdings, patches of cotton and corn for home use (peanuts had yet to come into their own), apples grown for cider and brandy, pigs in their wallows or rooting in the wild. This bore no resemblance to the romantic view of Old Dixie. The average farmer owned one or two deprived slaves. It was a forlorn, down-at-the-heels section of the Tidewater, where there never existed the celebrated plantations that gave the South its sheen and legendary glamour.

But I felt I had to create a plantation anyway. The plantation was an integral and characteristic part of Southern life in slave times; it was the very metaphor for the capitalist exploitation of human labor, and the plantation owners often represented the best and worst of those whom history had cast as masters in the peculiar institution, carrying within themselves all the moral frights and tensions that slavery engendered. I needed to dramatize this turmoil, and so I contrived to have Nat Turner grow up on a prosperous plantation that might have existed fifty years before far up the James River but that could not have flourished in poverty-racked Southampton. In this way I was able to expose young Nat Turner (from whose point of view the story is told) to the intellectual tug-of-war between the two Turner brothers, owners of the plantation and men diametrically opposed in their views on the morality of slavery. Such a strategy, while disdainful of the facts, enabled me to demonstrate certain critical philosophical attitudes I couldn't have done otherwise, except didactically, yet still allowed me to remain, in the larger sense, historically faithful.

Two of the most carefully pondered decisions I made regarding Nat's fictional character were ones that later provoked the greatest outrage from many of those people who became bitter enemies of the book. As is the case with disputes involving so many heroes, contemporary or departed, the bone to pick here was over the matter of sex. Why, came the bitter demand, hadn't I linked Nat with a black woman? First, in the process of using the *Confessions* as a rough guide, I was struck by the fact that Nat referred to his relationship with quite a few people—grandmother, mother, father, master, disciples—but never to a woman in a romantic or conjugal sense; apparently he had neither a female companion nor a wife. This absence was quite significant, and I had to use my intuition to guess at its meaning. A wife or companion would have had important resonance, and his mention of such a woman would have forced me to create her counterpart. But since no other reliable source ever spoke of Nat's being married (a pointless connection in the formal sense, slaves being legally forbidden to wed) or even being involved with a woman, it made it all the more plausible for me to portray a man who was a bachelor, or at least womanless, a celibate with all the frustrations that celibacy entails. Further, such a portrayal was entirely compatible with both the real Nat Turner's revolutionary passion and his religious zeal; chastity, combined with a single-minded devotion to a cause, has been the hallmark of religious rebels and reformers throughout history, and I saw a commanding reasonableness in having Nat share their condition, in which austerity clashed with feverish sexual temptation.

But by all odds my most crucial choice, as I picked my way through the facts and factoids of the original Confessions, was the one that also gave rise to the most furious misinterpretation later—and this was to invent a relationship between Nat Turner and a teenage white girl, the daughter of a small landowner. No decision I made shows so well the pitfalls waiting for the historical novelist who, however well intentioned, creates a situation or concept repugnant to ideologues; at the same time, nothing so deftly illustrates the invincible right of the novelist to manipulate historical fact and pursue his intuition concerning that fact to its artistically logical conclusion. Here are two intertwined facts, recounted by the perpetrator and recorded by Thomas Gray with the clinical dispassion of a modern-day homicide report: During most of the course of the revolt, in which fifty-five people were slaughtered, the leader of the murderers could not kill or inflict a wound on any of the victims, although he confesses that he tried more than once. This is the second fact: Toward the end of the bloody proceedings Nat is finally able to kill, and he kills—seemingly without qualm—a young woman named Margaret Whitehead, once described as "the belle of the county." It is his only murder. And after that murder his insurrection seems to quickly run out of speed. Why?

These are two of those undecipherable facts so consequential that they can't be sidestepped; indeed, for me they acquired such importance that my need to fathom their meaning became a dominant concern. And here it may be interesting to comment on the roles of the historian and the novelist, each of whom would be presented with different but overlapping opportunities to make sense of this terrible moment. Hewing more or less to the written record, both the historian and the novelist would be able to set the same scene, although the novelist would probably allow himself more descriptive breadth: the tranquillity of a hot August day in the still countryside; the band of black marauders bursting out of the pinewoods and engulfing the simple whitewashed frame house where the sunbonneted mother is swiftly decapitated by a muscular, screaming black man; the pretty young girl fleeing across the field, falteringly pursued by the Negro—irresolute at first, then determined—who, when she stumbles down in a heap, stabs her with his sword, then batters her head with a fence rail until she moves no more. Who was this Margaret Whitehead and what brought her together with Nat Turner? The facts tell us nothing else.

For this reason the historian's concern with Margaret Whitehead would most likely end here, and he would pass on to other matters. Let us pause for a moment. The killing of Margaret is near the climax of Nat Turner's chronicle, and it might be a convenient place to reflect on the immense effect the uprising had on American history and how its violence may have helped churn up a larger violence undreamed of by even the most obdurate slaveholder in 1831. Throughout that year the Virginia legislature had been engaged in a debate concerning the abolition of slavery; because of strong antislavery feeling in the Piedmont region and the western counties, where slaves were few, it appeared likely that abolition would become a reality, if not immediately, then in the near future. The Turner cataclysm caused a wave of fear to sweep through the state, as well as much of the rest of the South, and may have been the most important factor in assuring the continuation of slavery in the Old Dominion. A legislator is reported to have said in public, "We're going to lock the niggers in a cellar and throw away the key." Had Virginia, with its great prestige among the states, abolished slavery during that critical time, the impact on the future (especially in terms of the possible avoidance of events leading to the Civil War) is awesome to contemplate.

But as a novelist I couldn't abandon the relationship of Nat Turner and Margaret Whitehead to the vacuum into which it had been cast in the *Confessions*. It was nearly inconceivable that in the tiny bucolic cosmos of Southampton the two had not known each other, or had not been acquainted in some way. And if they had known each other, what was the nature of their affinity? Had she been cruel to him, slighted him, snubbed him, subjected him to some insult? Since she was his sole victim, could the entire rebellion have been conceived as his retribution against her? Far-fetched perhaps, but history is full of catastrophes in which many have been sacrificed because of one person's lethal wrath against another. Or was it something else entirely that bound them, something absurdly obvious, the very antithesis of hatred? Had they been lovers? This seemed unlikely, given one's conviction about his basic asceticism. Perhaps, however, she had tempted him sexually, goaded him in some unknown way, and out of this situation had flowed his rage.

Perhaps nothing at all had occurred between them, and her death came merely as a needful act on the part of a man who, having been unable to kill, having failed to prove his manhood in front of his followers, desperately sought to destroy the nearest living body at hand. This I very much doubted, and rejected, though no one, of course, could ever know the truth. But it was my task—and my right—to allow my imagination to range over these questions and determine the nature of the mysterious bond between the black man and the young white woman. In *The Confessions of Nat Turner* I strove to present a complex view of slavery, and Nat and Margaret's story would occupy a relatively small place in the larger scheme. But from the first page I was drawn irresistibly to that final scene of horror in the August heat, knowing that, to my own satisfaction at least, I had discovered a dramatic image for slavery's annihilating power, which crushed black and white alike, and in the end a whole society.

Several years after my novel appeared, two historians named Seymour L. Gross and Eileen Bender published a long essay entitled "History, Politics and Literature: The Myth of Nat Turner."[2] The essay was a carefully argued defense against the attacks on *The Confessions of Nat Turner,* which were chiefly embodied in a polemical book called *William Styron's Nat Turner: Ten Black Writers Respond.* Professors Gross and Bender made the interesting point that as a result of the extraordinary denunciation I had received, my book had been cast, as far as blacks were concerned, into the abyss. "Like the white schoolchildren in South Carolina at the turn of the century," they wrote, "who had to take an oath never to read *Uncle Tom's Cabin* because there was no truth in Mrs. Stowe, present-day blacks are being similarly assured that they can safely despise Mr. Styron's book without having to read it." There was a curious element of prophecy embedded in this statement, because much of the limbo status of *Nat Turner* (again insofar as black readers have been affected) has extended until the present day; as recently as the mid-1980s Paule Marshall, a fully grown black writer and a reputable one, was quoted in *The New York Times Book Review*— where she was playing a game in which writers were asked to name "Great Books We Never Finished Reading"—as saying that she never even started reading *The Confessions of Nat Turner,* since she had been assured that the work was "racist."[3]

The racist tag was affixed to the novel soon after the publication of *Ten Black Writers,* which appeared the summer after I spoke at Wilberforce. The book was published by Beacon Press, under the auspices of the Unitarian Universalist Association, a high-minded group ostensibly dedicated to preserving the truth. This collection, which contained critical pieces by largely well-known black intellectuals from various disciplines (English, sociology, psychiatry, history), along with several critics and fiction writers, was an extraordinary book by any standard; a collective *cri de coeur* of throbbing pain and rage, its overall lament was that I had written a malicious work, deliberately falsifying history, that was an affront to black people everywhere. The volume received much attention: the front page of *The New*

York Times Book Review, two consecutive reviews in the daily *Times,* and so forth.[4] There was nothing restrained about the assault; in the splenetic tone of the sixties I was labeled "psychologically sick," "morally senile," and was accused of possessing "a vile racist imagination." The major complaint was apparent from the book's first sentence: How dare a white man write so intimately of the black experience, even presuming to become Nat Turner by speaking in the first person?

Following close upon this indictment were other charges: that (aside from the outrageous business about the young white woman) I had "missed the beauty of the Afro-American idiom," that I had created an indecisive and emasculate wimp rather than the stalwart figure of history, that the text reflected an approving view of the paternalism of slavery, that my description of a fleeting homoerotic episode in adolescence meant that I regarded Nat as a "raving homosexual," that I had failed to give him a wife, that the secret agenda of the entire work was to demonstrate how the black struggle for freedom was doomed to failure—the bill of particulars was interminable. Virtually nothing in my work, according to these inquisitors, had merit; the most innocuous and tangential aspects of the novel received scathing treatment.

A couple of the essays, a bit less irate than the others, were at least well considered; they had in common the conviction that I had somehow missed the religious and emotional center of the black experience—and they may have been right. I knew from the beginning the hazards of setting foot in exotic territory and was aware that even though I was dealing with long-ago Virginia, instead of, say, Harlem or Watts (about which I would never have been able to write with authority), my stranger's perspective might not always ring true to black people. One of these more rational critics, who called *Nat Turner* a "tragedy" (in the noncomplimentary sense) and my figure of Nat "a caricature," expressed the general hurt and frustration he shared with his fellows by saying that "Styron has done nothing less . . . than create another chapter in our long and common agony. He has done it because we have allowed it, and we who are black must be men enough to admit that bitter fact. There can be no common history until we have first fleshed out the lineaments of our own, for no one else can speak out of the bittersweet bowels of our blackness." Right or wrong, this was a civilized sentiment that I could take seriously.

But the prevailing tone was strident and crude, sounding very much like the agitprop flatulence of the 1930s. Over the entire enterprise hovered the spirit of the historian Herbert Aptheker, the official United States Communist Party "theoretician," who had done pioneering work on Nat Turner and American slave revolts in the 1930s and 1940s. A militant quotation from Aptheker set the tone of the book. Aptheker's work had been groundbreaking and useful at a time when Negro history was almost totally neglected, but it was badly skewed by party dogma; his thesis that the institution of slavery was threatened by constant rebellion simply did not, and does not, hold up under scrutiny. He underestimated slavery's suffocating might. My own view, shared by many students of the history of slavery, was that the institution in the United States was almost uniquely despotic, a closed system so powerful and totalitarian that organized insurrection was almost entirely precluded, though, of course, rebelliousness on an individual level was always present.

This overview necessarily dominated my *Nat Turner.* Aptheker, upon whose preserve I had so seriously poached, was incensed by my book and for a while trudged around the university circuit preaching a gospel in which I was cast as one of the supreme liars ever to write about American history. (He never seemed to grasp the fundamental fact that I had written a novel.) It was unfortunate that in *Ten Black Writers* so many recklessly unprovable allegations were made; they were also written in shabby and slipshod rhetoric that even permeated the essays of well-thought-of black figures like the political scientist Charles V. Hamilton and the psychiatrist Alvin F. Poussaint; the impression left upon many people (including myself and those sympathetic to the black cause) was of intellectual squalor. For me the most frustrating aspect of *Ten Black Writers* was that writing filled with so much overheated absurdity should have acquired real authority in black America, causing my work to be lodged in a kind of black Index Expurgatorius from that point on, along with such overtly racist novels as *The Clansman* and *Mandingo*. Lest such a notation appear overstated, I would point out ample evidence of *Nat Turner's* being not only unread by blacks but in perpetual quarantine. This came from reports filtering back to me from black studies programs in the years up to the present. Several times I learned the dismal news that in specific courses *Ten Black Writers* would be required reading, while *The Confessions of Nat Turner* was not listed. This has echoes of Alice chatting with the March Hare. I have often felt perversely gratified that my work could inspire such fear, though scarcely such stunning mindlessness.

In my few ill-considered public appearances that year, when I was un-wise enough to accept invitations to defend my fictional choices in front of predominantly young black audiences and tried to show the inner logic that dictated my interpretation of Nat Turner and some of his relationships, the result was disastrous. Writers of novels should never defend themselves, but this was a somewhat special case. In these often raucous sessions, where the gathering was drenched with hostility, I would attempt to explain why I had made certain decisions. I observed, for example, that in the matter of one of the most inflammatory issues—that of Nat's wife—the ten black writers had simply got it wrong. There was no documentary evidence of a wife, or the equivalent, and if there had been, my conscience would have compelled me to give him one, even though as a novelist I had no such strict obligation. Likewise Margaret Whitehead. A careful reading, I insisted, would show that Nat's motivation was complex, flowing from a relationship containing hatred as well as love, but not the simple-minded lust claimed by the critics. This made little impression; the response was pitched between sneering disbelief and incomprehension, and for the first time in my life I began to share the clammy chagrin of those writers and artists who have stood before whatever intimidating tribunal, hopelessly defending their work to cold-eyed political regulators. By this time I was being stalked from Boston to New Orleans by a young dashiki-clad firebrand, who unnerved me. Some-what belatedly, I realized that *Nat Turner* was not, in this case, an aesthetic object but a political whipping boy—the most prominent one that the black activists possessed at the moment—and I quickly backed off from public view, letting others act as counsel for the defense.

I received as strong and vigorous a defense as a beleaguered writer could expect. I was especially well served by Eugene D. Genovese—who was then on his way to becoming the preeminent historian of American slavery and whose devotion to the black cause could scarcely be questioned—when he issued a massive rebuttal to the black essayists in *The New York Review of Books;* clearly as much dismayed as angered by the book's irrationality and philistinism, Genovese took up its main arguments one by one and effec-tively demolished them.[5] This inflamed the black critics and their colleagues even more, and in counter-rebuttals that filled the back pages of the *New York Review* the ugly debate raged on. Inevitably the storm died down, but the controversy has remained at a slow simmer until this day. Literally hun-dreds of articles have been written about the dispute, and at least four full-length books have appeared, including a ponderously comprehensive study of the entire affair that appeared only this year. Amid this vast scholarly debris it is possible to salvage at least a few commentaries whose insight and wisdom are worth preservation, and one of these is the Gross-Bender essay. Like Genovese, the historians deal harshly with the ten black writers and briskly dispose of their charges, but they have further illuminating things to say about the perennially enigmatic figure of Nat Turner and his place in our history.

They make the point that while Nat Turner was relatively obscure until my book appeared, he had "always belonged to those who used him—as a myth, as an imagined configuration of convictions, dreams, hopes and fears." What has helped make the man such a fascinating subject for speculation is his very inaccessibility. Neither historians nor writers of fiction have ever been able really to make much sense of the original document or to draw from it an identity with which everyone can agree by concluding: This is the historical truth. No firm truth can be established from such an incoherent text, or from the silhouette of the man, and, therefore, Nat has been the subject of wildly varying interpretation. One of the most prominent black historians of the nineteenth century, William Wells Brown, sallied forth on an ostensibly historical account but ended up drawing an elaborate imaginative portrait that resembled fiction; like me, he was repelled by Nat's religious mania, and, like me, he minimized or softened his biblical bloodthirstiness. In most other respects this chronicle by a historian plainly baffled by the obscurities and paradoxes of the record is as novelistic as mine. And Brown makes no mention of a Mrs. Nat Turner.

On the other hand, the illustrious Thomas Wentworth Higginson, ardent champion of black rights, was fascinated by Nat Turner and did supply the hero with a spouse in his account, which was quasi-historical or semifictional, depending on the reader's definition of this blurred region, but in any case almost totally fanciful. Harriet Beecher Stowe, George Washington Williams, and numerous other writers of the last century, both black and white, tried to pin Nat down, but this "black Spartacus," as he was termed by one commentator, utterly evaded a consistent portrayal; the fabled insurrectionist, mad or sane or simply beyond comprehension, was truly a chameleon. As recently as this year, in an off-Broadway play about the insurrection by a black playwright, Nat Turner's ultimate motivation for violence is the rape of his "wife" by a slaveholder—acceptable enough if one subscribes to the principle of artistic license, but a far more flagrant deviation from prima facie evidence than anything in my own work.[6] Gross and Bender conclude that my own attempt was "very much part of a tradition. Styron has 'used' Nat Turner as Gray, Higginson, Wells Brown, and, indeed, the accusing critics themselves have used him—reading into him, and out of him, those usable truths which seemed to him to coalesce about the image he was contemplating."

When I mentioned James Baldwin earlier, it was with the memory of our friendship and of the time when he was encouraging me to do what at first caused me hesitation, and that was to take on the persona of Nat Turner and write as if from within this black man's skin. Baldwin was wrestling with his novel *Another Country,* which deals intimately with white characters, and we both ultimately shared the conviction that nothing should inhibit the impulse that causes a writer to render experience that may be essentially foreign to his own world; it is a formidable challenge and among an artist's most valuable privileges. Baldwin's determination to pursue this course aroused the ire of many militant blacks, who saw such a preoccupation as frivolous and a betrayal of a commitment to the black cause. He stuck to his belief though his conscience and his persistence brought him rebuke and bitter alienation. My attempt, of course, was an even greater effrontery, and after *Nat Turner* was published, Baldwin told an interviewer most accurately, "Bill's going to catch it from black and white." Some months later, when I saw him, he offered me congratulations on the book's success and commiseration on the uproar, adding with the voracious full-throated Baldwin laughter that was one of his trademarks, "If you were just darker, it would be you, not me, who was the most famous black writer in America." It was at least partly true: my problem was less that of my work than that of my color.

Color and its tragedy, in this troubled year of 1992—which so resembles the troubled year of 1967—has made me think often of James Baldwin and the stormy career of *The Confessions of Nat Turner.* Naturally I didn't create the book with a political or social agenda in view, but as Georg Lukács points out, historical novels that have no resonance in the present are bound to prove of only "antiquarian" interest; certainly in the back of my mind I had hoped that whatever light my work might shed on the dungeon of American slavery, and its abyssal night of the body and spirit, might also cast light on our modern condition and be understood by black people, as well as white, as part of a plausible interpretation of the agony that has bound the present to the past. But while the book remains alive and well and widely read by white people, it is, as I say, largely shunned by blacks, sometimes with amazing hostility neither articulated nor explained, as if the admonitions of those ten black writers a generation ago still provided a stony taboo. I am less bothered by this boycott in itself—for despite what I've just said, I am far from believing that my book, or any novel, has any real relevance to the contemporary crisis—than the way in which it represents a continuation of that grim apartness that has defined racial relations in this country and that seems, from all signs and portents, to have worsened over the twenty-five years since *The Confessions of Nat Turner* appeared. That year much of Newark and Detroit burned down; this year the fires of Los Angeles seem anniversary fires too cruelly symbolic to accept or believe.

It was typical of Jimmy Baldwin's intransigent spirit that he never truly abandoned hope. I doubt that he would give up hope, even today. A recent essay on Baldwin quoted some brave and lovely words of Jimmy's that reminded me of the time when he and I, with our boundless and defiant ambitions, were both setting out to break through the imprisoning walls of color and into the alluring challenge of alien worlds: "Each of us, helplessly and forever, contains the other—male in female, female in male, white in black and black in white. We are a part of each other."[7]

[*American Heritage,* October 1992.]

Final Solutions

Auschwitz

Springtime at Auschwitz. The phrase itself has the echo of a bad and tasteless joke, but spring still arrives in the depths of southern Poland, even at Auschwitz. Just beyond the once-electrified fences, still standing, the forsythia puts forth its yellow buds in gently rolling pastures where sheep now graze. The early songbirds chatter even here, on the nearly unending grounds of this Godforsaken place in the remote hinterland of the country. At Birkenau, that sector of the Auschwitz complex that was the extermination camp for millions, one is staggered by the sheer vastness of the enterprise stretching out acre upon acre in all directions. The wooden barracks were long ago destroyed, but dozens of the hideous brick stablelike buildings that accommodated the numberless damned are still there, sturdily impervious, made to endure a thousand years.

Last April, as this visitor stood near Crematorium II, now flattened yet preserved in broken-backed rubble, his gaze turned and lingered upon the huge pits where the overflow of the bodies from the ovens was burned; the pits were choked with weeds but among the muck and the brambles there were wildflowers beginning to bloom. He reflected that "forsythia" was one of two loan words from Western languages that he recognized amid his meager command of Polish. The other word, from the French, was *cauchemar*—

"nightmare." At the beginning of spring, the two images mingle almost unbearably in this place.

At Auschwitz itself, in the original camp nearby, there is still the infamous slogan over the main gate—*Arbeit Macht Frei*—and only yards away, unbelievably, a small hotel. (What does the guest really order for breakfast? A room with *which* view does one request?) It is hardly a major world tourist attraction but Auschwitz is not unfrequented. Many of the visitors are Germans, festooned with Leicas and Hasselblads, whose presence does not seem inappropriate amid the *echt*-German architecture.

These grim warrens, too, were built to last the Hitler millennium. Hulking and Teutonic in their dun-colored brick, the rows of barracks where hundreds of thousands perished of disease and starvation, or were tortured and hanged or shot to death, now shelter the principal museum exhibits: the mountains of human hair, the piles of clothes, the wretched suitcases with crudely or neatly painted names like Stein and Mendelson, the braces and crutches, the heaps of toys and dolls and teddy bears—all of the heart-destroying detritus of the Holocaust from which one stumbles out into the blinding afternoon as if from the clutch of death itself. Even thus in repose—arrested in time, rendered a frozen memorial, purified of its seething mass murder—Auschwitz must remain the one place on earth most unyielding to meaning or definition.

I was unable to attend the recent symposium on Auschwitz at the Cathedral Church of St. John the Divine in New York City, but many of the aspects of the proceedings there, at least as reported, troubled and puzzled me, especially because of the overwhelming emphasis on anti-Semitism and Christian guilt.[1] My interest in the meeting was deep, since although I am nominally a Christian, my four children are half-Jewish and I claim perhaps a more personal concern with the idea of genocide than do most gentiles.

There can be no doubt that Jewish genocide became the main business of Auschwitz; the wrecked crematoria at Birkenau are graphic testimony to the horrible and efficient way in which the Nazis exterminated two and a half million Jews—mass homicide on such a stupefying scale that one understands how the event might justify speculation among theologians that it signaled the death of God.

The Holocaust is so incomprehensible and so awesomely central to our present-day consciousness—Jewish and gentile—that one almost physically shrinks with reticence from attempting to point out again what was barely touched on in certain reports on the symposium: that at Auschwitz perished not only the Jews but at least one million souls who were not Jews. Of many origins but mainly Slavs—Poles, Russians, Slovaks, other—they came from a despised people who almost certainly were fated to be butchered with the same genocidal ruthlessness as were the Jews had Hitler won the war, and they contained among them hundreds of thousands of Christians who went to their despairing deaths in the belief that *their* God, the Prince of Peace, was as dead as the God of Abraham and Moses.

Or there were the few ravaged survivors, like the once devoutly Catholic Polish girl I knew many years ago, the memory of whom impelled my visit to Auschwitz. It was she who, having lost father, husband, and two children to the gas chambers, paid no longer any attention to religion, since she was certain, she told me, that Christ had turned His face away from her, as He had from all mankind.

Because of this I cannot accept anti-Semitism as the sole touchstone by which we examine the monstrous paradigm that Auschwitz has become. Nor can I regard with anything but puzzled mistrust the chorus of *mea culpas* from the Christian theologians at the symposium, rising along with the oddly self-lacerating assertion of some of them that the Holocaust came about as the result of the anti-Semitism embedded in Christian doctrine.

I am speaking as a writer whose work has often been harshly critical of Christian pretensions, hypocrisies, and delusions. Certainly one would not quarrel with the premise that Christian thought has often contained much that was anti-Semitic, but to place all the blame on Christian theology is to ignore the complex secular roots of anti-Semitism as well. The outrages currently being perpetrated against the Jews by the secular, "enlightened," and anti-Christian Soviet Union should be evidence of the dark and mysterious discord that still hinders our full understanding of the reasons for this ancient animosity.

To take such a narrow view of the evil of Nazi totalitarianism is also to ignore the ecumenical nature of that evil. For although the unparalleled tragedy of the Jews may have been its most terrible single handiwork, its threat to humanity transcended even this. If it was anti-Semitic, it was also anti-Christian. And it attempted to be more final than that, for its ultimate depravity lay in the fact that it was anti-human. Anti-life.

This message was plainly written in the spring dusk at Auschwitz only short weeks ago for one observer, who fled before the setting of the sun. To linger in Auschwitz after nightfall would be unthinkable.

[*New York Times,* op-ed, June 25, 1974.]

Hell Reconsidered

F ew books possess the power to leave the reader with that feeling of
awareness which we call a sense of revelation. Richard L. Rubenstein's *The Cunning of History* seems to me to be one of these. It is a
very brief work—a long essay—but it is so rich in perception and it contains
so many startling—indeed, prophetic—insights that one can only remain
baffled at the almost complete absence of attention it suffered when it was
first published in 1975. When I first read Rubenstein's book about Auschwitz I felt very much the same effect of keen illumination that I did when,
in the early stages of writing *The Confessions of Nat Turner,* I happened to
read Stanley Elkins's *Slavery*—a work which shed fresh light on American
Negro slavery in such a bold and arresting way that, despite the controversy
it produced, it has become a classic study. It is perhaps a fitting coincidence
that Rubenstein discusses Elkins at some length in this book; certainly both
writers share a preoccupation with what to my mind is perhaps the most
compelling theme in history, including the history of our own time—that of
the catastrophic propensity on the part of human beings to attempt to dominate one another.

If slavery was the great historical nightmare of the eighteenth and nineteenth
centuries in the Western world, slavery's continuation in the horror we have
come to call Auschwitz is the nightmare of our own century. Auschwitz,

like the core of hell, is the symbolic center of *The Cunning of History,* and while the theological and political ramifications radiating from this center provide many of the book's most illuminating insights, it is Auschwitz—simply Auschwitz—that remains Rubenstein's primary concern. We are still very close to Auschwitz in time; its unspeakable monstrousness—one is tempted to say its unbelievability—continues to leave us weak with trauma, haunting us as with the knowledge of some lacerating bereavement. Even as it recedes slowly into the past it taxes our belief, making us wonder if it really happened. As a concept, as an image, we shrink from it as from damnation itself. "Christmas and Easter can be subjects for poetry," wrote W. H. Auden, "but Good Friday, like Auschwitz, cannot. The reality is so horrible."

To this he might have added the near-impossibility not just of poetry but of prose, even of an expository sort. That the subject is almost totally beyond the capacities of the mass media may be seen in the failure of the recent television series *Holocaust* to convey any sense of the complex nature of Auschwitz—a matter which I shall revert to later. The critic George Steiner has suggested the ultimate response: silence. But of course writers cannot be silent, least of all a searching writer like Rubenstein, who has set himself the admirable but painful task of anatomizing the reality within the nightmare while the dream is still fresh.

As near in time as Auschwitz is to us, it is nonetheless a historical event, and one of the excellences of Rubenstein's book is the audacious and original way in which the author has confronted the event, wringing from its seeming incomprehensibility the most subtle and resonant meanings. This is an unusual achievement when one considers how frequently analyses of the historical process become little more than tendentious exercises reflecting the writer's bias, which in turn corresponds to the pieties of the era in which he writes. So often the product is less history than wish-fulfillment, reinforcing the prejudices of his contemporaries and their hearts' desire.

A brief word about the dramatic shift in attitudes in the writing of the history of American Negro slavery may serve to illustrate this. During the roughly three-quarters of a century between the Emancipation Proclamation and World War II, the historiography of slavery generally reflected the mood of a society which remained profoundly racist, committed to the notion of racial inferiority and to the unshakable virtues of segregation. Towering above all other historians of slavery in the decades before the war was the Georgia-born scholar Ulrich B. Phillips, whose work, despite certain undoubted merits of scholarship, was heavily weighted in favor of the portrayal of slave times as an almost Elysian period, in which contented slave and indulgent master were united in an atmosphere of unexacting, productive labor and domestic tranquillity.

By the 1940s, however, the social upheavals of the preceding decade had drastically affected the national consciousness, bringing with them a perception of the outrages and injustices still being perpetrated on the Negro. Also, a certain sophistication had evolved regarding the psychology of suffering. It would thus seem inevitable, in this new atmosphere of nagging guilt and self-searching, that the writing of the history of slavery would undergo drastic revisionism, and it was just as likely that the new portrait of antebellum times would be the very antithesis of Ulrich B. Phillips's softly tinted idyll; most of the new scholarship (epitomized by Kenneth M. Stampp's *The Peculiar Institution*) represented slavery as unremittingly harsh, cruel, and degrading, with few if any redeeming aspects. It was one of the great virtues of Elkins's *Slavery,* coming a few years later, that it struck violently through the obfuscations and preconceptions that had dictated, often self-righteously, the views of the apologists for slavery on the one hand and its adversaries on the other, and, in effect, demanded that the institution be examined from any number of new and different angles objectively, in all of its difficult complexity.

Unlike slavery—which, after all, has had its quixotic defenders—Auschwitz can have no proponents whatever. Therefore I am not suggesting that in *The Cunning of History* Rubenstein is acting as an intermediary in a debate or is synthesizing opposing points of view. I am saying that, like Elkins, Rubenstein is forcing us to reinterpret Auschwitz—especially, although not exclusively, from the standpoint of its existence as part of a continuum of slavery which has been engrafted for centuries onto the very body of Western civilization. Therefore, in the process of destroying the myth and the preconception, he is making us see that that encampment of death and suffering may have been more horrible than we had ever imagined. It was slavery in its ultimate embodiment. He is making us understand that the etiology of Auschwitz—to some, a diabolical, perhaps freakish excrescence which vanished from the face of the earth with the destruction of the crematoriums in 1945—is actually embedded deeply in a cultural tradition which stretches back to the Middle Passage from the coast of Africa, and beyond, to the enforced servitude in ancient Greece and Rome. Rubenstein is saying that we ignore this linkage, and the existence of the sleeping virus in the blood-stream of civilization, at risk of our future.

If it took a hundred years for American slavery to become demythified, we can only wonder when we can create a clear understanding of Auschwitz, despite its proximity to us in time. For several years now I have been writing a work—part fiction, part factual—which deals to a great extent with Ausch-witz, and I have been constantly surprised at the misconceptions I have encountered with enlightened people whenever the subject has come up in conversation. The most common view is that the camp was a place where Jews were exterminated by the millions in gas chambers—simply this and nothing more. Now, it is true that in their genocidal fury the Nazis had con-secrated their energies to the slaughter of Jews en masse, not only at Ausch-witz, where two and a half million Jews died in the gas chambers, but at such other Polish extermination centers as Belzec, Treblinka, Majdanek, and Chelmno. And, of course, countless victims died at camps in Germany. A directive from the Reichsführer SS, Heinrich Himmler, in 1943 plainly stated that all European Jews would be murdered without exception, and we know how close to success the carrying out of that order came.

But at Auschwitz—the supreme example of that world of "total domina-tion" which Rubenstein sees as the arch-creation of the Nazi genius—there was ultimately systematized not only mass murder on a scale never known before but mass slavery on a level of bestial cruelty. This was a form of bond-age in which the victim was forced to work for a carefully calculated period (usually no more than three months) and then, through methods of depriva-tion calculated with equal care, allowed to die. Slaving at the nearby factory of I. G. Farben or at the Farben coal mines (or at whatever camp mainte-nance work the SS were able to contrive), the thousands of inmates initially spared the gas chambers were doomed to a sick and starving death-in-life perhaps more terrible than quick extinction, and luck was more often than not the chief factor involved in their survival.

As Rubenstein points out, only in a situation where human bodies were end-lessly replaceable could such a form of slavery attempt to be efficient—but the Nazis, who aspired to be among this century's leading efficiency experts, had no cause for concern on this count, supplied as they were with all the

Jews of Europe, besides thousands of Poles, Russian prisoners of war, and others. And although the concept was not entirely unique in the long chronicle of bondage (for a period in the West Indies the British, with a glut of manpower, had no qualms about working slaves to death), certainly no slaveholders had on such a scale and with such absolute ruthlessness made use of human life according to its simple *expendability*. It is this factor of expendability, Rubenstein explains in his persuasive first chapter—an expendability which in turn derives from modern attitudes toward the stateless, the uprooted and rootless, the disadvantaged and dispossessed—which provides still another essential key to unlocking the incomprehensible dungeon of Auschwitz. The matter of populations declared to be surplus (whether by Nazi Germany or other superstates, past and future), which Rubenstein touches upon again and again, haunts this book like the shadow of a thundercloud.

But slave labor is pointless without an end product, and what did slave labor produce at Auschwitz? Of course, on one level, slaves—Jews and non-Jews—slaved to kill Jews. On April 4, 1943, it was decreed that the Auschwitz gas chambers—previously employed to exterminate Jews and gentiles without differentiation—would be used to kill only Jews. Therefore much of the energies of those able-bodied prisoners selected to live for a while was either directly or peripherally expended in the business of getting on with the Nazis' main obsession: the murder of all the Jews in Europe.

But this was not all. One of the gaps in the knowledge of many people I have talked to is their ignorance of the fact that one of the chief functions of Auschwitz was to support a vast corporate enterprise involved in the manufacture of synthetic rubber. Anyone who has studied the Nazi period, especially that aspect of it having to do with the concentration camps, is usually both impressed and baffled by seemingly unresolvable contradictions, by the sheer caprice and irrationality of certain mandates and commands, by unexplainable cancellations of directives, by *Ordnung* in one area of operation and wild disorder in another. The SS, so celebrated for their discipline and methodicalness, seemed more often than not to have their collective heads in total disarray. Witness Himmler's order early in 1943 concerning the annihilation of the Jews; nothing would seem more unequivocal or more final. Yet this imperious command—surely one of the most awesome and terrible in history—was completely countermanded soon after it was conceived and handed down, replaced by a directive which ordered all able-bodied Jewish adult arrivals at Auschwitz not to the crematoriums but to work.

We can only surmise the reason for this quick reversal, but it should not take too long to conclude that pressures from I. G. Farben–Auschwitz, operators of the rubber factory, were among the decisive factors in Himmler's decision, and that at the behest of the directors of the company (which only a few years before had been helping to supply peaceful European households with tires and doormats and cushions and ashtrays), thousands of Jews each day would rejoice in their "reprieve" from the ovens at Birkenau, only to realize that they had joined the legions of the walking dead.

It is ironic that the immolation of these doomed souls (and there were among them, I think it necessary to emphasize, hundreds of thousands of non-Jews) came to naught; we know now that for various reasons the nearby factories produced very little synthetic rubber to aid the struggles of the Wehrmacht, yet it was through no lack of effort on the part of either I. G. Farben or the SS that the enterprise was fruitless. There was a constant conflict, within the SS, between the lust for murder and the need for labor, and thus the Farben works were often supplied with sick or incapacitated prisoners temporarily saved from the crematoriums. But chiefly the failure to produce matériel was less the result of insufficient or inadequate manpower than of a technological mismanagement which, as it so often did, belied the Nazis' claims to being paragons of efficiency. What had really been demonstrated was the way in which the bureaucratization of power in the service of a new kind of soulless bondage could cause total domination of human beings that makes the oppression of traditional, old-fashioned Western slavery—with its residue of Christian decency and compassion— seem benevolent by comparison.

As Rubenstein says in an important passage:

> The death-camp system became a society of total domination only when healthy inmates were kept alive and forced to become slaves rather than killed outright. . . . As long as the camps served the single function of killing prisoners, one can speak of the camps as places of mass execution but not as a new type of human society. Most of the literature on the camps has tended to stress the role of the camps as places of execution. Regrettably, few ethical theorists or religious thinkers have paid atten-

tion to the highly significant political fact that the camps were in reality a new form of human society.

And in another passage Rubenstein concludes with stunning, if grim, perception: "The camps were thus far more of a permanent threat to the human future than they would have been had they functioned solely as an exercise in mass killing. An extermination center can only manufacture corpses; a society of total domination creates a world of the living dead."

Sometime ago I watched a late-night discussion program on television, the moderator of which was the entertainer David Susskind. Assembled for the event that evening were perhaps half a dozen writers whose expertise was in the subject of the Nazis and their period, and also in the continued presence of a kind of *Lumpen* underground Nazism in America. I believe most of these men were not Jewish. I remember little about the program save for the remarkably foolish question posed by Susskind near the end. He asked in effect: "Why should you gentiles be interested in the Nazis? Why, not being Jewish, are you concerned about the Holocaust?"

There was a weak reply, sotto voce, from one of the participants to the effect that, well, there were others who suffered and died too, such as numerous Slavs; but the remark seemed to be ignored and I bit my tongue in embarrassment for all concerned, of course unable to utter what I was longing to say, namely, that if the question was unbelievably fatuous, the reply was shamefully feeble and off the mark. Most emphatically (I wished to say) Mr. Susskind *should* be enlightened about the vast numbers of gentiles who partook in the same perdition visited upon the Jews, those who were starved and tortured to death at Ravensbrück and Dachau, and the droves who perished as slaves at Auschwitz. Such ignorance seemed to me by now impermissible.

In this respect the fatal date April 4, 1943, which I referred to before, is instructive. For if that day demonstrates the way in which the dynamo of death was cranked up to ensure the Final Solution, it also plainly shows how the policy of extermination had never been limited to the Jews. Nor did the new policy indicate any preservative concern on the part of the Nazis for the Poles and other undesirables—only that their deaths as slaves would come about less methodically than the deaths of the Jews, who had been suddenly tendered unquestioned priority in the process of annihilation by gas.

The statistics are meager, and so we have no way of knowing the number of non-Jews who were murdered in the gas chambers prior to this cutoff date; not many, compared to the Jews, but certainly they numbered in the tens of thousands. Yet to escape the crematoriums was, of course, to gain only the most feeble hold on the possibility of survival. Statistics regarding the non-Jews who perished during the four years of the existence of Auschwitz as a result of starvation and disease are likewise inexact but somewhat more reliable. It would appear that out of the four million who died, perhaps three-quarters of a million—or approximately a fifth of the total—fell into the category which the Nazis termed Aryan. This was at Auschwitz alone. Multitudes of innocent civilians were murdered elsewhere.

These vast numbers would possibly seem less meaningful if the victims had been part of the mere detritus of war, accidental casualties, helpless by-products of the Holocaust; but such was not the case, and there can no longer be any doubt about which other people were to fall within the scope of the Nazis' master scheme for genocide. Rubenstein quotes from a letter written in the fall of 1942 by Otto Thierack, the German minister of justice, who stated his intention of granting to Himmler "criminal jurisdiction" over Poles, Russians, and Gypsies, as well as Jews, and whose use of the word "extermination" is blunt and unequivocal. There is, I think, something profoundly minatory and significant—telling much about the Nazis' eventual plan for these "subhuman" peoples of the East—in the little-known fact that the first victims of Zyklon B gas at Auschwitz were not Jews but nearly one thousand Russian prisoners of war.

In the face of the destruction of the European Jews, so nearly completely successful and so awesomely the product of a single-minded evil beyond comprehension, one hesitates before bringing up the suffering of these other people. Nonetheless, the unutterable degradation, horror, and vile deaths which they so often shared with the Jews remain to trouble the mind—all the more so because of the continuing ignorance regarding their fate. Theirs is a history of anguish which still seems to dwell dimly if at all in the public consciousness. It also must be remembered that these human beings perished not randomly but often by systematic means and in prodigious numbers. A man who is possibly our most unimpeachable witness, Simon Wiesenthal, the head of the Jewish Center of Documentation in Vienna, expressed his feelings on the matter in a recent interview:

I always insist that the victims must not be divided into Jews and non-Jews. I brought over eleven hundred Nazis before courts in different countries, Nazis who killed Jews and gentiles and Gypsies and Serbs and so on, and I've never thought about the religion of the victims. I've battled for years with Jewish organizations, warning them that we shouldn't always talk about the six million Jews who died in the Holocaust. I say let's talk about *eleven million* civilians, among them six million Jews, who were killed. It's our Jewish fault that in the eyes of the world this whole problem became reduced to the problem between the Nazis and the Jews; the problem obviously was much broader. The Jews need the help of others to prevent new holocausts.

But the point I struggled vainly to make, looking at David Susskind and murmuring to myself in the dark, was that even if all this were not true—even if the Jews had been without any exception the inheritors of Hitler's hatred and destruction—his question would have been very close to indecent. I could not help thinking whether there was something paradigmatically American (or certainly non-European) in that question, with its absence of any sense of history and its vacuous unawareness of evil.

By contrast, how pervasive is the sense of evil in Rubenstein's essay, how urgent is the feeling that an apprehension of the devil's handiwork and an understanding of the Holocaust are the concern of Jew and non-Jew alike. We are all still immersed in this deepest pit. In *The Cunning of History,* written by a Jewish theologian, the fact of the Holocaust as *the* cataclysmic tragedy of the Jewish people is assumed, *a priori* as it should be, just as it is assumed that the annihilation of the Jews acquired a centrality in the Nazis' monstrous order of things. Rubenstein's analysis of the historical sources of anti-Semitism provides some of his most illuminating passages.

But among the qualities which I find so powerful about Rubenstein's book, as opposed to a great deal which has been written about Auschwitz, is how, despite the foregoing, he has acquired a perspective—a philosophical and historical spaciousness—that has allowed him to anatomize Auschwitz with a knowledge of the titanic and sinister forces at work in history and in modern life which threaten *all* men, not only Jews. I intend no disrespect to Jewish sensibility, and at the same time am perhaps only at last replying to Mr. Susskind, when I say how bracing it is to greet a writer who views totalitarianism as a menace to the entire human family. As an analyst of evil,

Rubenstein, like Hannah Arendt, is serene and Olympian, which probably accounts for the unacceptability I have been told he has met with in some quarters.

Rubenstein's apprehension of the larger menace of Nazism, and Simon Wiesenthal's insistence that we must recognize the ecumenical nature of its evil—the "broader problem"—found little echo or corroboration in last April's television series *Holocaust*. It must be clear by now that even with good intentions the rendering of major historical events in their subtlety and complexity is quite beyond the power of American television. And *Holocaust* may have been, in its soft-headed vulgarity, one of television's more creditable dramatic efforts. Like *Roots*, the earlier TV extravaganza about American Negro slavery, the program was obviously "carefully researched," and its nine and a half hours of slick footage possessed, one felt, an underpinning of authenticity that seemed to permit little major violation of the basic historical record. In fact, as in the earlier sequences of *Roots*, which captured some of the aspects of the African slave trade with surprising verisimilitude, the initial parts of *Holocaust*, in episodes depicting the effects of the Nazi poison as it invaded the lives of Jews and incipient fascists alike, had moments of striking and cautionary power. It became all the more oppressive, then, that aside from its totally objectionable features in matters of taste—mainly the strident commercials which intruded at intervals like chanted obscenities—the series slid into rhythmically spaced troughs of sentimentality and melodrama.

When drama erodes into melodrama one of the warning signals is the appearance of token figures. In *Roots*, which soon vitiated its early promise by turning the history of slavery into an equation in which all black was good and all white was evil, tokenism came in the form of a single decent white man; in *Holocaust*, the brief glimpses of an anti-Nazi Christian prelate and a "good" Nazi official (and also one or two Jewish Kapos and finks) served as a kind of bogus leavening to what had degenerated into skillfully rigged but hollow theatrics. Least of all did the program deal satisfactorily with that appalling edifice which provided the culminating scenes and, presumably, lent to the series its metaphorical meaning—Auschwitz.

The scenes of naked Jews being consigned to the gas chambers, though embarrassingly staged, were presented with graphic emphasis. But despite an offhand allusion to I. G. Farben, which seemed both strained and obvious, and a brief reference to the Poles, which, in the context in which it was made, gave the mistaken impression that theirs was an infinitely more pleasant lot than that of the Jews, there was conveyed no sense whatever of the magnitude and deadliness of the slave enterprise. There was no suggestion that in this inconceivably vast encampment of total domination (predominantly gentile at any given time) there were thousands of Poles and Russians and Czechs and Slovenes dying their predetermined and wretched deaths, that in droves Catholic priests and nuns were being subjected to excruciating and fatal medical experiments, that members of Polish and other European resistance groups (whose struggle and great courage were never once hinted at in the program) were being tortured and, in some cases, gassed like the Jews. In short, the suffering and martyrdom of these others were ignored, to the great loss of historical accuracy and, I am afraid, of moral responsibility. We shall perhaps never even begin to understand the Holocaust until we are able to discern the shadows of the enormity looming beyond the enormity we already know.

[*New York Review of Books,* June 29, 1978.]

In his 1980 Nobel Prize acceptance speech, Czeslaw Milosz expressed alarm over the fact that the actual existence of the Holocaust was being questioned in books and pamphlets published throughout Europe and America. He then went on to say: "[The poet] feels anxiety, though, when the meaning of the word Holocaust undergoes gradual modification, so that the word begins to belong to the history of the Jews exclusively, as if among the victims there were not also millions of Poles, Russians, Ukrainians, and prisoners of other nationalities. He feels anxiety, for he senses in this foreboding of a not distant future when history will be reduced to what appears on television, while the truth, because it is too complicated, will be buried in the archives, if not totally annihilated."—W.S. (1982)

Auschwitz and Hiroshima

Toward the end of World War II, in the winter of 1945, two momentous events took place simultaneously at distant parts of the earth. It can be safely assumed that none of the participants in either of these grim dramas had the remotest knowledge of the others' existence. In southern Poland, the army of the Soviet Union had finished evacuating the German concentration camp of Auschwitz. In the Pacific Ocean, eight hundred miles south of Japan, three United States Marine divisions were commencing the invasion stage of one of the bloodiest campaigns ever fought, the battle for the island of Iwo Jima, which would be of critical importance as a way station for the flight carrying the first atomic bomb.

It might be said that the war in Europe and the Pacific conflict took place on different planets. Most servicemen engaged in war against the Japanese gave little thought to remote campaigns like the ones in Italy and France. It was a global struggle too vast to comprehend while it was happening. But when it was over and somewhat more comprehensible, we could see that the war left us with, if nothing else, two prodigious and enduring metaphors for human suffering: Auschwitz and Hiroshima. History has carved no sterner monuments to its own propensity for unfathomable evil.

After VJ Day, there was a space of a year or so when it was truly possible to conceive of a world without war. Progenitors of the baby boom, most veterans were diligently amorous. It may be that the gloom descended soon after Winston Churchill's Iron Curtain speech. For me the sense of the future closing down permanently came only six years later, when as a Marine reserve I was called up for duty in the Korean War. Back in infantry training again, I had the nightmarish perception of war as a savage continuum, not a wholesale if often lethal adventure men embarked upon, as in World War II, to strike down forces of evil, but a perpetual way of life in which small oases of peacetime provided intermittent relief. In Asia there was an explosion waiting to happen; America stood ready to light the fuse the French had laid down, and in the next decade the sequel of Vietnam came as no surprise.

In that same decade of the 1960s I became engrossed in the issue of racial conflict in America—especially as it was reflected in the history of slavery—and found myself pondering the extent to which race and racial domination played a part in the recent wars. The stunning late-nineteenth-century insight of W. E. B. Du Bois—that the chief problem of the coming century would be that of color—had swiftly become a self-fulfilling prophecy. Du Bois was speaking of his own African-American people but his prophecy would embrace the globe. If in the First World War nationalistic ambitions largely fueled the conflict, World War II was the incubator of a poisonous worldwide racism. A poster I recall from the Pacific war was of a bucktoothed and bespectacled rat, with repulsively coiled tail and Japanese army cap; the caption read KNOW YOUR ENEMY.

All Americans fighting in the Pacific were racists. Marines were indoctrinated to regard Japanese soldiers as dangerously rabid animals. The paucity of enemy prisoners taken by our troops was due in part to the Japanese creed of fighting to the last breath, but it was also because of our own policy of extermination, often with an intriguing new weapon, the flamethrower, which roasted our adversaries in their bunkers and burrows. The enemy repaid our racism in kind and generally surpassed us; few people were treated more barbarically than those starving prisoners, many of them European and American but also Asian, who existed amid squalor and privation in the Japanese camps.

Hiroshima had a profound direct effect on my life; Auschwitz would come much later. In the summer of 1945 I was a young Marine officer slated to lead my rifle platoon in the invasion of Japan. Most of us were spunky but scared, and we had much to be scared about. The carnage had reached a surreal intensity. Already on Iwo Jima and Okinawa, 17,000 Americans had lost their lives, including many of our friends. It had been predicted that the invasion would produce over half a million American casualties, while perhaps as many as three times that number of Japanese would be killed or wounded, including countless civilians.

Herman Melville wrote, "All wars are boyish, and are fought by boys." I cannot say, from this distance in time, what is more firmly lodged in my memory—the desperate fatalism and sadness that pervaded, beneath our nervous bravado, the days and nights of us young boys, or the joy we felt when we heard of the bomb, of Hiroshima and Nagasaki, and of the thrilling turnaround of our destiny. It was a war we all believed in and I'd wanted to test my manhood; part of me mourned that I never got near the combat zone. But Hiroshima removed from my shoulders an almost tactile burden of insecurity and dread. Later I often used the word "ecstasy" to describe my reaction. I used it again only a few years ago in, of all places, Tokyo, when a TV interviewer asked me to express my views about Hiroshima and related matters.

Afterward I had the feeling I'd misspoken badly. But later, at a party, a Japanese man of my vintage approached me, murmuring a little surreptitiously that he'd seen me on television and wanted to tell me something he'd never told anyone before. He said he'd also been a young infantry officer, the leader of a heavy mortar unit training on Kyushu to repel our invasion, when word came of the bomb and the end of the war. We might have blown each other up, he added, and when I asked him how he'd taken the news he said, "I felt ecstasy, like you."

This brings me to an issue which has incited more controversy than perhaps any other in the writing of the history of World War II; and that is the justification for the dropping of the atomic bomb.

As I've said, I belong to that small body of veterans who were headed for the invasion; we're getting smaller each year through obvious reasons of attrition, and many of us remain extremely sensitive to the moral implications of the bomb. We were never a large group, in terms of the general population; there were originally a quarter of a million of us. Perhaps less than 100,000 are left. Despite what I've just said about the lifelong gratitude most of us felt for the bomb and its makers, there are a few of us, I suspect, who wouldn't be troubled if it were never shown conclusively that Hiroshima and Nagasaki could have been avoided. Even the most callous ex-serviceman might be shaken by proof that his own salvation was bought by the needless sacrifice of 200,000 innocent human beings. Therefore, there were more than a few of us who were disturbed by the revisionist view espoused by numerous historians who, on the fiftieth anniversary of the bomb, two years ago, took the occasion of the *Enola Gay* exhibit at the Smithsonian Institution to make what was tantamount to a dreadful accusation: namely, that President Harry Truman behaved in an irresponsible, even criminal, fashion in ordering the bomb dropped when he was aware that the weapon was really not necessary for ending the war. The *Enola Gay*, of course, was the B-29 aircraft that dropped the bomb on Hiroshima. The *Enola Gay* exhibit, many of you will recall, became the focal point of the controversy, and the dispute became nasty when such groups as the American Legion and the Air Force Association protested the underlying assumptions of the display, claiming that it was anti-American, that it muddied the patriotic waters with ambiguities and bothersome questions about the bomb's ultimate worth, as if its use were not absolutely just. Quite simply, the critics of the exhibit wanted a celebration. The Smithsonian backed down, and the exhibit became a tame and harmless sideshow. This was unfortunate since the original text reveals that the questions raised were legitimate. It is still worth pondering, as the Dutch-born historian Ian Buruma has pointed out, "whether [dropping atomic bombs] was an act of racism; whether the bombs were dropped to warn the Soviets, and keep them from invading Japan; whether Truman should have paid more attention to Japanese peace initiatives; and whether there were better ways than nuclear bombing of ending the war swiftly." But perhaps most importantly the Smithsonian's capitulation to the American Legion sent the wrong message to the Japanese, who have been scandalously negligent in facing up to many of the enormities of their own past. If the Americans can continue to insist on their own righteousness, the Japanese are now able to say: why can't we do the same? I will return to this Japanese historical amnesia in a moment.

One does not wish to regard these revisionist historians with impatience or contempt. They are, by and large, serious and dedicated scholars who have invested much intellectual capital in presenting their theses. One of the best known, Gar Alperovitz, has written hundreds of pages in several books attempting to prove that Truman dropped the bomb to show our supremacy to the Soviet Union. Other critics, notably the psychiatrist Robert Jay Lifton, are convinced that the Japanese would have surrendered anyway, and that therefore Truman, knowing of this, must have possessed the capacity for irrational behavior bordering on madness; in other words, Truman's decision was an act of megalomania. One of the revisionist scholars, Philip Nobile, went so far as to canvass various writers, especially writers who were also veterans of World War II like myself, asking if they would sign a petition to President Clinton, the purpose of which would be that he apologize to the Japanese people. Needless to say, I declined, but in a book he edited, *Judgment at the Smithsonian,* to which I contributed my dissent,[1] he made clear that his own anti-bomb, anti-Truman viewpoint was based largely on moral outrage, on outrage which in turn derived from some religious wellspring: Nobile is an active Catholic layman and often uses words like "atonement," "repentance," and "original sin." As if all this were not enough, an ABC television news special, led by Peter Jennings, a Canadian, was unequivocally slanted against the bomb and Harry Truman.[2]

Of course, it is entirely understandable that a phenomenon as unique and monstrous as the atomic bomb, and the indescribable suffering it caused, should arouse much soul-searching. And it is doubtless healthy, too. The use of any weapon so terrible, and the political power that puts that use into play, needs vigilant scrutiny not merely now but for generations. Therefore revisionism, puzzling and exasperating as it often has been, is a welcome activity, especially in an America too often blind to its own global propensity for *force majeure*. One must honor doubts, whether their roots are psychological, political, or religious. Never let it be forgotten that, even as I speak, there are innumerable atomic weapons stashed away all around the world, and that the end of the Cold War did not relieve us from the necessity of constantly pondering their existence. Yet as I reflect on that event of 1945 I can't help being convinced that Truman had no alternative to his decision, and that his choice was the right one, even though its absolute rightness can never really be proved. Its rightness can never be proved, at least to universal satisfaction, because so much of the decision was bound up in the understandably bellicose psychology of the moment. Might not Truman have behaved differently if he, like most of his fellow Americans— especially young marines such as Lieutenant William C. Styron—were not consumed with a need for retaliation and with the savage rage against the enemy that three and a half years of brutal fighting had engendered? It is easy, from the comfortable perspective of hindsight, for a psychiatrist like Robert Jay Lifton, who through no fault of his own did not serve in the war, to confuse such rage with megalomania and to regard the decision to use the bomb as a form of madness. Perhaps only those who literally and truly re-member Pearl Harbor can comprehend the national fury.

Yet it is hard to see how even a Harry Truman totally dispassionate and unaffected by rage could have acted in any other way. And this opinion de-rives from two hard facts embedded in the conduct of the war itself. First, it must be remembered that by the time the first atomic weapon was dropped, in August 1945, the mainland of Japan had been subjected to the most ruth-less destruction visited upon a nation in the history of warfare. On a single night in March over 100,000 civilians died when General LeMay's B-29s firebombed Tokyo. The bombs had produced an incendiary storm destroy-ing helpless hordes in heat so violent that those who had sought shelter in underground tunnels suffered an actual liquefaction—not lucky enough to be swiftly incinerated but broiled alive—while people who had tried to find safety in the river shallows were burnt to ashes. I still have a letter from a marine friend of mine who was on the island of Saipan when those B-29s took off, and he watched them in their flight toward Tokyo. "Why I was un-able to feel repelled or to be touched by a tremor of pity, I could not say," he wrote, "even as I gazed through the twilight at the howling monsters speed-ing northward to drop their cargoes on numberless cowering Yokohama mamas and the toothless slant-eyed old farts in baggy drawers and school-girls and roly-poly wee baby-sans. My Presbyterian conscience bade me weep but I was dry-eyed. Which is what war does to you," he concluded, "it fucks up your heart."

What my friend was witnessing happened to be a routine example of strategy that began in the 1930s with Japanese bombing of civilians in China, resumed in the Nazi destruction of Guernica in Spain, and continued with the firebombing by the Germans of London and Coventry and Manchester and other urban centers in Britain. Let us not minimize the primitive moral appeal of the question: "Who started it, after all?" Our own evil was bound to follow. The British and Americans' senseless air attack on Dresden, in which multitudes were cremated, was a horrible amplification of this bar-baric custom. Now, there is no moral justification for the destruction of civil-ians under any circumstance. But it has to be understood that by August, Harry Truman and his advisors saw the dropping of the atomic device as a logical extension of strategic bombing. As the late McGeorge Bundy wrote: "[By the summer of 1945] both military and political leaders gradually came to think of urban destruction not as wicked, not even as a necessary evil, but as a result with its own military value."[3] One need not justify the morality of his decision to understand that Truman regarded the atom bomb as just another, only more effective, weapon in the arsenal of total destruction. In their different ways, Hitler, Stalin, and Churchill would have all approved.

But ultimately the rightfulness of Truman's judgment rests on one crucial question. And that is whether or not the Japanese were ready to surrender. If, as virtually all of the revisionists seem to assume, the enemy was prepared to accept Allied peace terms then indeed the dropping of the bomb was not only unnecessary but morally indefensible. But there is no indication that the Japanese were going to throw in the towel, and this is a matter that the critics refuse to confront, either pussyfooting around such a critical issue or pretending that surrender was imminent, while offering no evidence to support the fact. Ian Buruma, whose analysis of the atom bomb controversy is a model of objectivity, has written: "Closer examination of what went on in Tokyo shows that the Japanese were not on the verge of capitulation before the destruction of Hiroshima. So long as there was no unanimity in the war cabinet and the Emperor remained silent, the war would go on."[4] On a purely military level, too, all indications were that Japan was prepared to fight to the last man and, indeed, the last woman and child; proclamations had gone out to this effect, and if this were not enough there were the recent examples of Iwo Jima and Okinawa, where the ferocious resistance of the enemy provided a foretaste of the butchery awaiting both sides when the Americans embarked on their mainland invasion. Suppose, it has been asked, that Harry Truman—for whatever reason behind his caution—had not dropped the bomb, and suppose then that Americans and Japanese had engaged in the predicted battle, a savage struggle which, following the pattern of the bloody stalemate on Okinawa, would have taken months and consumed tens of thousands of lives. Suppose after the inevitable American victory it had been revealed that the President of the United States had possessed all along a weapon that most likely would have ended the war, but had not used it. What would countless bereaved parents have thought about that? What would have been the reaction in America and throughout the world? The question gives rise to such an awesome moment of hushed speculation that one must necessarily end the matter by affirming the truth that for Truman there was no other choice.

A journalist friend of mine who lives in Honolulu has several times interviewed Japanese tourists who visit the memorial site at Pearl Harbor. Japanese tourists are, to say the least, numerous in Hawaii (Japan Air Lines flies an unbelievable seventy-two flights a day from Tokyo) and my friend has buttonholed quite a few of them. Some of the visitors are fairly sophisticated about modern history but most are not; the great majority tell the journalist that America started the war and the Japanese attack on Pearl Harbor was in retaliation for our aggression. This is an example of the historical amnesia afflicting the Japanese people which I mentioned earlier. Except among a relatively small group of the intelligentsia it is a national article of faith that the devastation and death wrought in Hiroshima and Nagasaki was an evil phenomenon, the result of American inhumanity, with no causation rooted in the Japanese militarism of the 1920s and '30s. History books at the elementary and high school level avoid mention of the Rape of Nanking or the barbaric plunder of Manchuria. I alluded earlier to the Japanese oppression of prisoners. Nowhere is there reference to the enslavement, during World War II, of hundreds of thousands of Koreans, many of them women forced to serve in Japanese army brothels. The atrocities committed by Imperial troops during the course of the war, from Bataan in the Philippines to the farthest reaches of Southeast Asia, exist in a vacuum, unrecorded. A recent work by an Australian-born scholar, Gavan Daws, called *Prisoners of the Japanese*,[5] has meticulously documented the depredations of the Japanese army in Indonesia and Malaysia; employing new and original research, and interviewing dozens of Australian, Dutch, British, American, and Asian survivors, Daws provides a panorama of butchery and torture far scarier than could have been previously imagined. It shows a deliberate, carefully executed program of slave labor designed to work captives until they died of starvation and exhaustion; it was a technique of total domination every bit as ruthless as that of the Nazis at Auschwitz, and might have been considered genocidal except for the fact that it was even worse; it was panracial, condemning everyone to death without ethnic partiality. The Japanese people today, of course, refuse themselves access to such terrible knowledge, preferring the cultural comfort of timeless victimhood.

Having said this about postwar Japan, I must stress an obvious truth: no nation is without shame, or the stain of past dishonor. To the everlasting credit of the Germans, the horrors of Nazi despotism have been anatomized and dissected until scarcely a personality or event of that era remains unexamined. We Americans have pored over the disgraceful episodes of our past with nearly morbid zeal; slavery, the decimation of our Native Americans, our unconscionable racism, the nightmare of Vietnam—all of these have received our impassioned, sometimes even masochistic scrutiny. But the Japanese have averted their eyes from history, and in so doing have jeopardized their future and perhaps our future, too. People who have no lessons to learn from their past are likely to be extremely dangerous.

I want to close with a few final reflections on racism, and on Auschwitz. When in the mid-1970s I decided to write about another racism—the Nazi racism of total domination—I realized that in dealing with the German mind of that period I had to confront certain exquisite paradoxes. Anglo-Saxons, for example, however bitterly abhorred, did not belong among the despised *Untermenschen* and were granted a certain provisional respect. A loony relativism at the heart of Hitler's racial policy is demonstrated by the treatment of various POWs. The captured British and American soldiers and airmen were usually confined in a prison where conditions were basically civilized and in fact so comparatively congenial that the farcical image conveyed in *Hogan's Heroes* or *Stalag 17* is not too far off the mark. It was reputed Nordic identification that prevented all but a small percentage of these prisoners from dying.

In contrast there is the appalling saga of the Soviet prisoners of war, who were, after the Jews, the numerically largest group of victims and whose partial annihilation—over three million, or nearly sixty percent of all Soviet POWs—is commentary enough on the Nazis' view of the humanity of the Russians and other Slavs. Which brings me to Auschwitz. I was always struck by the fact that the first executed victims of Auschwitz were not Jews but six hundred Soviet POWs. Although the Holocaust was uniquely Jewish, its uniqueness becomes more striking when we can see that it was also ecumenical, but in ways that can only emphasize the peculiar nature of Jewish suffering.

I have been criticized in some quarters for "de-Judaizing" and "universalizing" the Holocaust by creating, in my novel *Sophie's Choice,* a heroine who was a gentile victim of Auschwitz. Such was not my intention; it was rather to show the malign effect of anti-Semitism and its relentless power—power of such breadth, at least in the Nazis' hands, as to be capable of destroying people beyond the focus of its immediate oppression. At Auschwitz, as in the Inferno, Jews occupied the center of hell, but the surrounding concentric rings embraced a multitude of other victims. It would be wrong for them to be forgotten. For years, all of them were largely forgotten, beyond the borders of Jewish remembrance. It wasn't until the late 1970s that the word "Holocaust" fully entered the language; before then, the horror of the camps had a less discernible shape.

As for that other dreadful monolith, Hiroshima, it might be said that the sacrifice of its victims presented an object lesson and perhaps a priceless warning, preventing the future use of the weapon that achieved such destruction. If so, the many deaths and the suffering—the same that assured my probable survival and that of my Tokyo comrade in arms along with legions of others—may be justified, if we who have lived so long afterward are fit to justify such a fathomless event. Certainly the bomb did nothing to eliminate war and aggression, and I am still amazed at the memory of myself, a boy optimist returned home after Hiroshima, firmly convinced—for one brief and intoxicating moment—that the future held out the hope of illimitable peace. Over fifty years after that moment the fratricidal horrors and ethnic atrocities that the world has endured, and still endures, remain at the quivering edge of tolerance and are past comprehension. Yet we go on, the earth turns. If you do what I do, you write—as the canny Isak Dinesen said you must do—you write without hope and without despair.

[*Newsweek*, January 11, 1993. The magazine text was abbreviated; the full text published here is from Styron's surviving manuscript, among his papers at Duke University.]

A Wheel of Evil Come Full Circle

Edmund: The wheel is come full circle. I am here.
— *King Lear* V.III.185

During the late 1960s I developed a brief but warm relationship with Hannah Arendt. We were both members of the editorial board of *The American Scholar,* which met twice a year alternately in New York and Washington. After these long and rather soporific meetings, Hannah and I would retire to a bar and drink scotch, for which we both had a fairly enthusiastic taste. I was an ardent admirer of her work, though as one untrained in philosophy I found much of it rough going, and the thickets of her English sometimes verging on the impassable; still I regarded *The Origins of Totalitarianism* as a great illumination, and had made *Eichmann in Jerusalem* a kind of handbook. My novel *The Confessions of Nat Turner* had recently appeared, and had been furiously attacked by members of the black intelligentsia. A book of essays had been published—*William Styron's Nat Turner: Ten Black Writers Respond*—in which I'd been accused of racism and of falsifying and distorting the story of the rebel slave leader. This assault had left me with a residue of indignation, although I was cooling off.

Hannah had read my book, and I'm sure that some small part of the affinity we felt for each other came from a shared sense of aggravation: she was still vexed over the rancorous criticism of *Eichmann in Jerusalem,* and while she had cooled off, too, I sensed a touch of bitterness about what she continued to view as an absurd misreading of her work. She insisted that those who had accused her of asserting that the European Jews had capitulated, in a form of self-murder, before the Nazi onslaught were guilty of gross misinterpretation. I felt she was still resentful, as I was, over being hounded by special-interest groups. And so she chain-smoked, which I mildly chided her for; and we drank our scotch in a glow of rueful sympathy and mutual martyrdom.

I recall her asking me how it was that a Southern-born writer, connected tenuously to the modern European experience, could reveal a compulsive interest in anything so essentially European as the Nazi camps. Hannah always used the word "camps," or, occasionally, "Auschwitz," as a generic term for the Nazi terror—never "Holocaust," which doesn't appear in *Eichmann in Jerusalem,* and which, in the late sixties, was largely a scholarly characterization, one that would begin to enter the common speech only a decade or so later. I reminded her that totalitarianism, on which she was perhaps the leading authority, had found its expression in America in the form of chattel slavery; she agreed that, in a broad and abstract way, at least, the leap from the slave South to Auschwitz formed a logical transition. It was plain that both of us were fascinated by those wellsprings of human nature out of which there boils over the need for subjugation and oppression.

I remember our discussing a book which we'd both read, a work I had encountered just after the war, when, following service in the Marines, I had returned to college. This account of Auschwitz, *Five Chimneys,* was written by Olga Lengyel, a doctor's wife who with her family had been transported to the camp from Transylvanian Hungary in 1944. Curiously enough, she does not identify herself as Jewish, although this would appear almost certain, given the chronology of the transports from Hungary. The book was one of the first narratives of its kind published in postwar America; it had affected me in powerful, unsettling ways that had lingered over the years.

Five Chimneys deals graphically with the barbarities and deprivations of life at Auschwitz, and contains stark images of the extermination process, seen close-up. It also then provided the world with some of the earliest portraits of Dr. Josef Mengele and the awesomely depraved ogress Irma Grese. The work is still capable of evoking near-incredulity and a sense of horror beyond horror. But most chilling of all, somehow, surpassing the butcheries and beatings, was the description of the author's arrival at the camp in a boxcar, and the decision she was forced to make about her mother and one of her children. Confused, and unaware of the lethal workings of the selection process, Lengyel lies about her twelve-year-old son's age, telling the SS doctor that the boy is younger than he is, in the mistaken belief that this will save him from arduous labor. Instead of being spared, the boy is sent to the gas chambers, along with his grandmother, whom Lengyel, again in ghastly error, helps kill. She asks the doctor that her mother be allowed to accompany the child in order to take care of him. For me, this transaction, with its imposition of guilt past bearing, told more about the essential evil of Auschwitz than any of its most soulless physical cruelties.

On another evening with Hannah Arendt, I recall that the matter of "authenticity" came up. I told her that someday I hoped to write about Auschwitz—I had in mind, specifically, a Polish Catholic survivor of that camp, a young woman named Sophie, whom I had known in Brooklyn after the war—but I was troubled by how authentic my rendition might be. What did I know about midcentury Europe in its torment and self-immolation? She scoffed lightly at this, countering with this question: What, before writing *Nat Turner*, had I known about slavery? An artist creates his own authenticity; what matters is imaginative conviction and boldness, a passion to invade alien territory and render an account of one's discoveries. That was the task of a writer, she said, and I was heartened, though still doubtful. When I demurred a little—I remember saying that I could foresee dodging an assault entitled *Ten Rabbis Respond*—she kept up her encouragement, though not without conceding that I'd probably receive flak from those who might feel, as certain blacks had, that I was, as she put it, poaching on their turf.

One matter that never came up in our talks was the idea that I shouldn't write about the subject at all—that after Auschwitz the only appropriate response was silence. I think Hannah would have been puzzled and skeptical about any such notion, if not downright offended. I became aware of this thesis much later, when I was well along in the writing of *Sophie's Choice*; and though the view was advocated by writers whom I admired, like George Steiner, it was an exhortation I refused to accept, especially when I noted that the demand for silence was often coming the loudest from those who were busy scribbling books about Auschwitz. Certainly the subject required almost unprecedented caution and sensitivity, and respect verging on reverence; but to make Auschwitz, in the literary sense, sacrosanct and beyond reach of words was a pietism I had to reject, if only because it made no sense to me that this monumental human cataclysm should remain buried and lost to memory. Why should writers be denied the chance to illuminate these horrors for future generations?

In my own case, I began to realize, it came down chiefly to the problem of distance. I knew it would be presumptuous of me to try to duplicate the brutal atmosphere of the camps already described in the narratives of Bruno Bettelheim and Eugen Kogon and Raul Hilberg and Primo Levi—or to amplify upon such searing fictional works as André Schwarz-Bart's *The Last of the Just* or Jean-François Steiner's *Treblinka*. These books had exposed the camps' pathological anatomy, the seething cauldron of the interior of places like Buchenwald and Belsen, in sometimes microscopic close-up. What I needed was a new strategy and a dominant metaphor, and both of these came to me with flashing suddenness one morning in 1974. I had been stymied for a long time with a work in progress, and was open to new inspiration. Awaking on that spring day from a confused dream of the Sophie I had known in Brooklyn so many years before, and being swept at almost the same instant by the memory of Olga Lengyel's ordeal in *Five Chimneys,* I sensed dream and memory merging into a dramatic concept of stunning inevitability. What if I were to convert my brief encounter with Sophie in Brooklyn—she whose past had been a mystery to me, save for one or two tantalizing tales of wartime Poland she had told me, and whose tattooed arm had evoked questions I dared not ask—into a fictional narrative in which I actually got to know this young woman over a long and turbulent summer?

During that summer she would reveal to me—the callow and credulous, but not entirely unsophisticated, narrator—the secrets of her past, which would include her Polish upbringing, and the arrival of the war, and of her imprisonment in Auschwitz, and a host of other matters bearing on the Nazi terror. All of these details would be unpeeled, layer after layer like an onion, until at last there would be uncovered the most terrible secret of all: the day of her arrival at Auschwitz, and a fatal decision she would be forced to make, one that involved the lives of her children. Here, it seemed to me, was the ultimate expression of totalitarian evil: a system that could force a mother to become her child's murderer was one that had refined the infliction of human suffering to a point at which all other cruelties—the beatings, the tortures, the medical experiments—were an infernal background. And that morning, even as I realized the metaphorical authority of Sophie's dreadful choice, I realized too that I had solved the problem of distance. I would never place Sophie inside the confines of Auschwitz, where as narrator I dared not tread. Sophie would instead, in her memory, always be located in the house of the camp's commandant, outside Auschwitz yet near enough that its vile stench and daily pandemonium would compose that infernal background.

From the beginning it never occurred to me that the Jewish experience under the Nazis was not unique, or that the victimization of the Jews was not of a far greater magnitude than the oppression of others. That others were oppressed, however, and agonizingly so, remained a fact; and among these victims was the Sophie I had known, who remained to me the embodiment of the hundreds of thousands of Polish Catholics whom the Nazis enslaved and, in numerous cases, tortured and killed. As I set out to write the novel, I had no idea how to reconcile these matters within the framework of the narrative, only trusting that my instinct, along with a regard for the historical necessities, would permit me to portray Sophie's tragedy within the more spacious context of the Jewish catastrophe. About a hundred pages into the story of Sophie, I interrupted my work in order to make a trip to Poland and visit Auschwitz. It was an essential trip—among other needs, I had to absorb some of the atmosphere of Cracow, where the real Sophie had spent her childhood—and when I returned home, picking up the narrative where I had left off, I had an amazing revelation: it was a moment that showed, to an extraordinary degree, the autonomy of the subconscious in the process of literary creation.

At this point in the novel, Sophie is describing to Stingo, the narrator and my alter ego, the nature of her relationship to her dead father, a professor of law at the Jagiellonian University of Cracow. She begins to tell Stingo of her love for her father, and of her admiration for his character and his works; among the noble deeds he performed, she says, was that of protecting and hiding Jews during the war, risking his own arrest and execution. I recall halting in midpassage as I wrote this part, saying to myself: *The girl's a liar.* I suddenly understood, of course, that Sophie, lying to Stingo as well as to me—the hapless, gullible author—was really trying to conceal from us both one of her most dire and sinister secrets. Her father, the distinguished professor, far from being the gentle humanist Sophie claimed him to be, was in truth a poisonous anti-Semite of frightening dimensions, a man she loathed. And this secret, gradually revealed as the story went forward, became a key to the entire novel, for the book in large part has to be read as a parable of the devastation of anti-Semitism, not only of the Nazi brand run amok, but of the genteel, intellectual variety that had transformed Poland from a nation hospitable to Jews into one seething with anti-Jewish menace.

Hannah Arendt died before my novel was finished, and I often have regretted that she never read it and was unable to observe its reception. Unlike *Nat Turner, Sophie's Choice* was spared a bitter onslaught of criticism, though it had its detractors. In certain quarters I was accused of "universalizing" or "eroticizing" the Holocaust, whatever these strange terms may really mean, while Elie Wiesel, a writer I respect, took me to task for what Hannah would have regarded as poaching on his turf; Wiesel wrote that, in regard to Auschwitz: "Only those who lived it in their flesh and in their minds can possibly transform their experience into knowledge. Others, despite their best intentions, can never do so."[1] One other response stands out particularly, and if its fear and inflexible rage were any gauge of the effectiveness of my work, they caused me a certain satisfaction. For, although *Sophie's Choice* was translated into more than two dozen languages, including Hebrew, it was denied translation for over a decade into Sophie's native tongue. The Polish government forbade its publication on the grounds that the book's depictions of anti-Semitism were a slander against the Polish people; indeed official anger was so great that in 1982, when calls went out for Polish actors to appear in the film version, then being made in Zagreb, the authorities warned that anyone responding to the offers would be severely punished.

After the Communist downfall, the book was published in large printings and was received generally with enthusiasm. Even so there were fierce holdouts among those Poles who refused to accept the fact that Sophie and her children, while surely victims of the Nazis, were also sacrificed to a native-born enmity. They would not allow themselves to see that Sophie, through her father and his Jew-hatred, is lost beneath a wheel of evil come full circle. It is his doctrine, after all, that crushes his innocent daughter and his even more innocent grandchildren with lethal finality. Such hatred, knowing no boundary, eventually will achieve absolute destruction, consuming everyone, Jews and Christians, even one's own flesh. The annihilation that came from this vicious advocacy, Hannah Arendt perceived, was more than a crime against the Jewish people: "Mankind in its entirety was grievously hurt and endangered."

[*Sewanee Review*, Summer 1997.]

Disorders of the Mind

Why Primo Levi Need Not Have Died

Why did the eminent Italian writer Primo Levi die in the shocking way he did?

In the depths of a clinical depression, Mr. Levi, an Auschwitz survivor who had written eloquently of his ordeal under the Nazis, jumped down a stairwell in Turin in 1987.

The question appeared to haunt—indeed, nearly dominate—a recent symposium held at New York University and dedicated to Mr. Levi and his work, according to an article in *The New York Times*.[1] Some participants reacted with simple incredulity.

Alfred Kazin, a distinguished literary critic, was quoted as saying: "It is difficult for me to credit a will to blackness and self-destruction in a writer so happy and full of new projects."

A friend, rejecting the idea that the writer had planned to kill himself, saw the death as the result of a "sudden uncontrollable impulse"—as if rational deliberation might have somehow colored the act with wrongdoing. In this and other statements, there was at least a tinge of disapproval, an unspoken feeling that through some puzzling failure of moral strength Mr. Levi had failed his staunchest admirers.

Apparently not expressed at the symposium, though quoted in the article, was the harshest example of such a viewpoint: a suggestion in *The New*

Yorker that "the efficacy of all his words had somehow been cancelled by his death."[2] This idea leaves the implication that the force and fervor of a writer's work is rendered invalid if, instead of expiring of natural causes, he takes his life.

What remains most deeply troubling about the account is the apparent inability of the symposium participants to come to terms with a reality that seems glaringly obvious. It is that Mr. Levi's death could not be dissociated from the major depression with which he was afflicted, and that indeed his suicide proceeded directly from that illness.

To those of us who have suffered severe depression—myself included— this general unawareness of how relentlessly the disease can generate an urge to self-destruction seems widespread; the problem badly needs illumination.

Suicide remains a tragic and dreadful act, but its prevention will continue to be hindered, and the age-old stigma against it will remain, unless we can begin to understand that the vast majority of those who do away with themselves—and of those who attempt to do so—do not do it because of any frailty, and rarely out of impulse, but because they are in the grip of an illness that causes almost unimaginable pain. It is important to try to grasp the nature of this pain.

In the winter of 1985–86, I committed myself to a mental hospital because the pain of the depression from which I had suffered for more than five months had become intolerable. I never attempted suicide, but the possibility had become more real and the desire more greedy as each wintry day passed and the illness became more smotheringly intense.

What had begun that summer as an off-and-on malaise and a vague, spooky restlessness had gained gradual momentum until my nights were without sleep and my days were pervaded by a gray drizzle of unrelenting horror. This horror is virtually indescribable, since it bears no relation to normal experience.

In depression, a kind of biochemical meltdown, it is the brain as well as the mind that becomes ill—as ill as any other besieged organ. The sick brain plays evil tricks on its inhabiting spirit. Slowly overwhelmed by the struggle, the intellect blurs into stupidity. All capacity for pleasure disappears, and despair maintains a merciless daily drumming. The smallest commonplace of domestic life, so amiable to the healthy mind, lacerates like a blade.

Thus, mysteriously, in ways difficult to accept by those who have never suffered it, depression comes to resemble physical anguish. Such anguish can become every bit as excruciating as the pain of a fractured limb, migraine, or heart attack.

Most physical distress yields to some analgesia—not so depression. Psychotherapy is of little use to the profoundly depressed, and antidepressants are, to put it generously, unreliable. Even the soothing balm of sleep usually disappears. And so, because there is no respite at all, it is entirely natural that the victim begins to think ceaselessly of oblivion.

In the popular mind, suicide is usually the work of a coward or sometimes, paradoxically, a deed of great courage, but it is neither; the torment that precipitates the act makes it often one of blind necessity.

The origins of depression remain a puzzle, despite significant advances in research. Many factors seem to be involved. Aside from the basic chemical disturbance in the brain and behavioral and genetic influences, psychological reasons must be added to the equation. Mr. Levi may have been bedeviled by buried conflicts unrelated to Auschwitz.

Or, indeed, his ordeal at Auschwitz may have imposed on his soul an insupportable burden; other writers wounded by the Holocaust (Paul Celan and Tadeusz Borowski come to mind) decided upon suicide as a way out of the blackness of memory. But the overwhelming majority of camp survivors have chosen to live, and what is of ultimate importance to the victim of depression is not the cause but the treatment and the cure.

What is saddening about Primo Levi's death is the suspicion that his way of dying was not inevitable and that with proper care he might have been rescued from the abyss.

Depression's saving grace (perhaps its only one) is that the illness seems to be self-limiting: Time is the real healer and with or without treatment the sufferer usually gets well.

Even so, presumptuous as it may be to speculate from such a distance, I find it difficult not to believe that if Mr. Levi had been under capable hospital attention, sequestered from the unbearable daily world in a setting where he would have been safe from his self-destructive urge, and where time would have permitted the storm raging in his brain to calm itself and die away, he would be among us now.

But, in any event, one thing appears certain: He succumbed to a disease that proved to be malignant, and not a shred of moral blame should be attached to the manner of his passing.

[*New York Times,* op-ed, December 19, 1988.]

After the essay on Primo Levi was published in *The New York Times* I received an enormous number of letters, almost all of them from people who had experienced depression, directly or as a result of being associated with victims of depression, and who felt I had given voice to a subject too-long buried. The essay prompted an invitation from the department of psychiatry of the Johns Hopkins School of Medicine for me to speak at a symposium on mood disorders; this speech was eventually expanded into a long article in *Vanity Fair,* and eventually into a book, *Darkness Visible.*—W.S. (1993)

Prozac Days, Halcion Nights

In the spring of 1991 I was invited to give the keynote address at a symposium to be held in Washington, D.C., for the purpose of discussing depression and the ways to cope with the disease. The gathering, I was told, was to be made up of what might loosely be called semiprofessionals, that is, people who, though not psychiatrists or therapists, had an interest in knowing more about depressive illnesses; they would include social and welfare workers, hospital administrators, public health and police officials, paramedics, and the like. As a result of my book *Darkness Visible*, in which I describe my successful struggle with severe clinical depression, I have received a lot of such invitations, and accepted a few (perhaps more than I should have) out of some missionary urge; many people who finally vanquish melancholia's unspeakable demons have the charitable impulse to tell others similarly afflicted not to give up hope, that they can get well. Such support is of critical importance to someone felled by depression. Since countless people *don't* think they can make it, and play seriously with the idea of suicide, the recovered victim is walking testimony to the radiant fact that most sufferers, despite their nearly unbearable ordeal, do indeed get well; the very presence of the survivor and his words of encouragement can be lifesaving.

This message of hope was central to my little book; its upbeat nature, not falsely optimistic but rooted in the simple reality that treatment is available and usually effective, would make the foundation for the opening speech I had been asked to give. But I began to have second thoughts. While I still felt the note of cheer was important, and resolved to begin in that spirit, it seemed to me that this might be an opportune moment to sound a warning. And the warning should be one especially meaningful to the participants in the symposium, who I felt had to be put on their guard about a matter that I continue to feel is neglected or consciously shunted aside in most forums on the treatment of depression, and that is the misuse of medications, primarily tranquilizers. Tranquilizers should not be confused with antidepressants, although they are often prescribed to sedate people with depression. I wanted to point out that my own bleak experience had convinced me that virtually all the commonly prescribed minor tranquilizers (also known as benzodiazepines) are of questionable value even for healthy people; for those suffering from depression they should be shunned like cyanide, and of them all the most indisputably monstrous is a tiny gray-green oval called triazolam, better known by the brand name Halcion.

Halcion has become a kind of famous national gargoyle, part nightmare, part joke. People who haven't heard of Listerine know the name Halcion. Wasn't Halcion the sleeping medicine George Bush was on when he barfed in the lap of the prime minister of Japan? TV comics have made sport of it. But Halcion is not a very funny pill, as I discovered through personal experience. I took this tranquilizer as a remedy for the insomnia that so often accompanies depression. Although the depression I describe in my book was not directly caused by Halcion, and I said as much, I've become convinced that the pill greatly exaggerated my disorder, intensified my suicidal feelings, and finally forced me to be hospitalized. I was not aware of this cause-and-effect relationship at the time, for when my illness occurred, in 1985, Halcion had yet to be implicated as the origin of such dire mischief, and I made no connection myself.

Five years later, however, when I was writing *Darkness Visible*, I was able retrospectively to perceive the connection, greatly helped by the amount of information that was suddenly being made public concerning Halcion's malign effects. When the book was published I was stunned by the volume of mail I received, but nothing impressed me more than the large number of correspondents—I would estimate perhaps as many as fifteen or twenty percent—who spoke of their own Halcion-induced horrors, homicidal fantasies, near-suicides, and other psychic convulsions. This outpouring has given me a rare perspective on all aspects of depression, including the effect (or non-effect) of medications. Other pills were mentioned, notably Prozac, the antidepressant, which appears to be beneficial for many people; the spontaneous testimonials in favor of that medication convince me that, if my thick archive of correspondence is a revealing cross section, Eli Lilly's bonanza drug cannot be lightly dismissed. But Prozac, scarcely an all-purpose miracle medicine, is merely an improvement on an old formula. What is distressing is the fact that a significant number of people do have very bad reactions to Prozac, chiefly suicidal impulses (the letters to me reflect this), and it is Lilly's concerted efforts to minimize such sinister side effects that remain even now indefensible.

In a recent *Nation* column ("Beat the Devil," December 7, 1992), Alexander Cockburn describes how Lilly, annoyed by evidence that its remedy might cause such harmful reactions (while already suffering a $150 million lawsuit based on this proposition), and further distressed by attacks on their product by the Church of Scientology, turned matters around by enlisting the press in a campaign that resulted in lurid onslaughts against the church in *The Wall Street Journal* and in *Time*, where the church was the subject of a cover story. There were other craftily orchestrated PR tie-ins, but this was basically the old chronicle of overpowering corporate muscle and deafening propaganda, successfully applied. Meanwhile, the advisory committee of the Food and Drug Administration that was organized to study Prozac—five of whose eight members, according to Cockburn, had "serious conflicts of interest, including substantial financial backing from Lilly"—gave the medication its OK.

I'm afraid my esteem for the Church of Scientology, unlike that of Cockburn, is lower even than my esteem for *Time*. The church's indiscriminate attacks on virtually all psychiatric medicines is nothing but medieval zealotry, and one would wish that the adversarial voice raised against Lilly were backed by credentials sounder than those deriving from L. Ron Hubbard's loony theology. While Cockburn's attempt to incriminate Lilly for its sorry excesses is a worthy one, he never addresses the nature of Prozac, which for many people is a very effective antidepressant. It is not a wonder drug, but it is by no means without value, and, as I say, my correspondence has reflected this fact. Lilly's wrong springs not so much from its product as from a hucksterism that admits to no deficiencies.

But no one who wrote to me had anything but ghastly tales to tell about

Halcion, and in my Washington talk it seemed necessary to focus on my own devastating experiences with this pill, made by the Upjohn Company. Many years ago the phrase "ethical drug manufacturers" came into being as a result of the industry's justifiable desire to differentiate its members from the patent-medicine makers, ostensibly ethical cretins, who peddled Lydia E. Pinkham's Vegetable Compound, snake oil, Dr. Moog's Love Balm, magic crystal beads, Spanish fly, Peruna, and other shady nostrums. But even the noblest ethics suffer attrition, and it is plain that various corporations have become less ethical than others, some to the point of knavery. If there are the Tiffanys of the trade—I've heard people in the know about such topics murmur Merck with reverence—there are also those at the bottom end, and there Upjohn is clearly the Crazy Eddie of the industry. Not long ago *The Nation* ran a piece describing the disgraceful hype Upjohn brought to bear in advertising its potent and (like all benzodiazepines) potentially hazardous anti-anxiety drug Xanax, another multimillion-dollar winner, attempting to make it appear as free of the need for precaution as Gatorade. (See Cynthia Cotts, "The Pushers in the Suites," *Nation*, August 31/September 7, 1992.) Even closer to its snake-oil origins is Upjohn's recent campaign for liquid Rogaine, an only marginally effective treatment for baldness whose capacities, according to *Consumer Reports,* the company has attempted to inflate by putting it into a totally ineffective shampoo called Progaine.

But beyond this relatively commonplace sleaze lies Upjohn's refusal to face up to the Frankenstein's monster its Kalamazoo laboratories let loose in the shape of Halcion. Public awareness of the dangers of the pill dates back to 1979, when a Dutch psychiatrist, Dr. C. van der Kroef, disquieted by the psychotic symptoms reported by many patients taking Halcion, carried out an in-depth investigation and sounded the alarm; the pill was soon categorically banned in the Netherlands. Shamefully, Upjohn's own awareness of the serious risk inherent in its medication goes back to the early 1970s, when the company's experiments with a volunteer group of inmates at the Jackson State Prison in Michigan came up with disturbing—or what should have been disturbing—results. The human guinea pigs developed all sorts of aberrant reactions—memory loss, paranoid feelings—that were not consonant with the safe, readily tolerated hypnotic that Halcion was intended by its makers to be.

About a year ago, both in a *60 Minutes* program and a BBC documentary (in which I had a cameo role as a damaged but recovered victim), evidence that can only be described as revolting revealed that Upjohn had had full knowledge of the injurious nature of its product but put it on the market anyway. After that, sales of Halcion, which had been a top earner for years, were mercifully slowed by the adverse publicity it received; the pill has been implicated in numerous suicides and acts of violence, including several murders, the most recent of which, in Dallas County, Texas, resulted in a jury deciding that the drug was partly responsible for the killing.[1]

Halcion has now been banned in Britain and four other countries. Despite this and its appalling record, and the obvious fact that other readily available tranquilizers don't produce such calamitous side effects, Halcion last spring was once more approved by the ever-supine Food and Drug Administration, which insisted only that Upjohn strengthen its warning about dosage. In fairness, it should be pointed out that it is frequently an inadvertent overdose—though more often than not an extremely small one, amounting to a fraction of a milligram—that produces these evil reactions. Even so, the normally prescribed dosage has many times precipitated disastrous behavior. In any case, viewing the FDA's cavalier decision, one wonders how long aspirin would remain on the market if a small overdose of one more than the commonly recommended two tablets caused some people to lapse into paranoia and violence.

At the beginning of his new novel, *Operation Shylock,* which I've read in manuscript and which will be published this year, Philip Roth has a brilliant and harrowing description of Halcion-induced madness, based on his own experience in 1988, when he had been innocently taking the pill for sleep after minor knee surgery. "I thought about killing myself all the time. Usually I thought of drowning: in the little pond across the road from the house . . . if I weren't so horrified of the water snakes there nibbling at my corpse; in the picturesque big lake only a few miles away . . . if I weren't so frightened of driving out there alone. When we came to New York that May . . . I opened the window of our fourteenth-floor hotel room . . . and, leaning as far out over the interior courtyard as I could while still holding tight to the sill, I told myself, 'Do it. No snakes to stop you now.' "[2]

Withdrawal from Halcion invariably results in a disappearance of the symptoms, and Roth of course survived, as did I. But the ordeal verges on being beyond description in its nearly unalleviated anguish. Like Roth, I thought about drowning. And like Roth's, my own trial began with a surgical problem: A long-ago injury to my neck, received when I was a marine in the Korean War, had caused a nerve compression that resulted in my losing much strength in my right arm. An operation in Boston was imperative but was delayed, and during the two-week wait I had time to brood and was ravaged by anxiety. The anxiety began to hinder sleep, and to conquer the sleeplessness I commenced taking Halcion, still serenely unaware of the pill's involvement in my breakdown four years before, which was described in *Darkness Visible*. I had gone to California, fulfilling an obligation to teach at Claremont College. There, in that sunny landscape, I was all but totally consumed by thoughts of suicide that were like a form of lust. Somehow I managed to get through my classroom duties, but my mind was never free of exquisite pain, a pain that had but one solution—self-extinction. One night, visiting at my daughter's house in Santa Monica, I stayed awake for hours thinking only of walking out into the ocean and being engulfed by the waves. At Claremont, I kept constant schemes in mind to have my wife lured away so I could secrete myself in a closet and end it all with a plastic bag.

I held on to my sanity long enough to fly back to Boston for the operation. Although the procedure was a complete success, the raging depression hung on during the postoperative convalescence. Many times I contemplated sneaking out of the hospital and leaping into the Charles River from the bridge I could see from my window. Then suddenly a curious intervention occurred. I was consulting with a staff psychiatrist, and he asked about my sleeping habits. I told him that I was sleeping poorly but that what sleep I did get was courtesy of Halcion. The eyes of the doctor, a man plainly privy to the latest pharmaceutical alarms, sharpened interestingly, and it required no more than a few seconds for him to tell me that he was switching me immediately to a new drug. A day or two later, peering into my shaving mirror, I realized the bizarre configuration around my lips was a smile. Thus began my education about Upjohn's baneful remedy, and my shaky and haunted but eventually full recovery. . . .

This was the chronicle I related to the audience in Washington, not the gladdening sermon that had been expected of me, perhaps, but a cautionary tale that I felt very much needed telling. But I must back up for a moment. Just a few days before my appearance, the lecture agent who had arranged my visit called me with some stimulating but hardly surprising news. The fee I was receiving for my lecture, he said, would be paid by Eli Lilly and

Company, makers of Prozac, which was underwriting the symposium. Did I have any qualms about the pharmaceutical tie-in? Not really, I said, though it might depend on the company; I'd never take a penny from Upjohn. Drug companies often finance psychiatric conferences. It was not a practice I was enthusiastic about, and if I were in the profession I might feel embarrassed; as a layperson, however, I would feel compromised only if an attempt was made to censor or fiddle around with what I had to say. I told the lecture agent that I planned to make a vigorous attack on Halcion. I heard the agent catch his breath, saying he was happy the pill wasn't made by Lilly.

The word of my coming animadversions must have been leaked in advance. Minutes before the lecture I was confronted by a gentleman who identified himself as the acting director of the National Institute of Mental Health. Although friendly enough, he appeared a little distracted and nervous. After my talk, which was in a hotel ballroom, there was a press meeting billed as "A Conference with William Styron." At the conference, where there was a microphone and podium, I faced twenty-five or thirty journalists, most of them reporters from medical and other scientific publications. They seemed generous in spirit and attentive as I approached the podium, and I felt they had reacted with considerable interest to my talk. I sensed the acting director hovering near. The first question was, "Mr. Styron, that was quite a story about Halcion. Now, what is your opinion concerning Prozac?" I replied that I had very mixed feelings about Prozac. Although I had never used it myself, I had gained contradictory evidence that it was quite beneficial for many people, while for some others it had no effect at all; for a significant few it produced sinister reactions, primarily suicidal fantasies. The many letters I had received, I continued—

But I got no further. Courteously, the acting director of the National Institute of Mental Health edged me away from the microphone. Every medication has unpredictable side effects, he said, in an I'm-taking-charge voice, but it has been clearly determined that Prozac is virtually free of the serious reactions that have plagued antidepressants in the past. No safer and more reliable treatment for depression has ever been available to therapists and physicians—a truly remarkable development in psychopharmacology. Any more questions?

There were, indeed, quite a few more questions, but none were—or could be—addressed to me, since the microphone had been, as far as I could tell, unbudgeably preempted. As the minutes ticked past I found myself sidling ever more lonesomely off to the side of the podium. The gathering had become a conference with the acting director of the National Institute of Mental Health. There was no more talk of Halcion but a great deal of talk about Prozac, most of it from the acting director, all of it fulsome and rich with commendation. After fifteen minutes the acting director briskly declared the meeting closed. As I wandered out I felt so ludicrously discomfited that I barely heard the canny, sympathetic Deep South voice of one of the journalists: "Boy, the guv'ment sure did shut you up, didn't they?"

[*Nation*, January 4/11, 1993.]

"Interior Pain"

The harrowing episodes I experienced during my period of grave depression eight years ago were so numerous that I could not possibly have recorded them all in *Darkness Visible*. But if I were revising the book, I would include my memory of an excruciating evening a week or so before my suicidal impulses overwhelmed me and I committed myself to a hospital. My wife and I had been invited to dinner with half a dozen friends at a fine Italian restaurant in New York. I very much feared the hour. The majority of people suffering from depression go through their worst pain in the morning. As the hours wear on there is some alleviation, and, with effort, they are often able to cope. With me this situation was reversed. Beginning in midafternoon the anxiety and gloom would slowly accelerate, until by dinnertime I felt virtually suffocated by psychic discomfort. Of course, that evening I could have stayed at home. Anyone suffering the equivalent pain of almost any other disease would surely remain in bed, or at least sequestered from social life. But in depression the anguish is lodged in the mind, so it matters little where the corporeal self is located; one will feel equal desolation at home in one's armchair or trying to eat dinner at La Primavera.

I say "trying" to eat dinner because my appetite had decreased over the previous week to a point where I was eating purely for sustenance. Two of my table companions were charming friends I had known for years. I picked at what must have been excellent pasta without tasting it. For no particular reason, the sense of encroaching doom was especially powerful that night. But the demented stoicism that depression imposes on behavior caused me to register scarcely a flicker of this inner devastation. I chatted with my companions, nodded amiably, made the appropriate frowns and smiles.

The restroom was nearby, down a flight of carpeted stairs. On my way there the fantasies of suicide, which had been embedded in my thoughts daily for several weeks, and which I had kept at bay during the dinner conversation, returned in a flood. To rid one's self of this torment (but how? and when?) becomes the paramount need of all people suffering depression. I wondered desperately whether I would make it through the rest of the evening without betraying my condition. On my return to the floor above I astonished myself by expressing my misery aloud in a spontaneous utterance which my normal self would have rejected in shame. "I'm dying," I groaned, to the obvious dismay of a man passing down the stairway. The blurted words were one of the most fearsome auguries of my will to self-destruction: within a week I would be writing, in a stupor of disbelief, suicide notes.

Some months later, after I had been hospitalized and recovered from the illness, my two table companions recollected that I had appeared to be behaving quite normally. The monumental aplomb I exhibited is testimony to the almost uniquely interior nature of the pain of depression, a pain that is all but indescribable, and therefore to everyone but the sufferer almost meaningless. Thus the person who is ill begins to regard all others, the healthy and the normal, as living in parallel but separate worlds. The inability to communicate one's sense of the mortal havoc in one's brain is a cruel frustration. Sylvia Plath's bell jar is an apt metaphor for the isolation one feels, walled off from people who, though visible and audible, are essentially disconnected from one's own hermetically sealed self.

In recent months the press has engaged in an orgy of speculative stories about the circumstances surrounding the death of Vincent Foster.* What has been largely forgotten is that there were clear signs in the months leading up to his suicide that he was suffering from a major depression. He had reportedly lost his appetite and his weight had dropped by fifteen pounds,

---

* Foster, a deputy counsel at the White House early in the first Clinton administration, committed suicide on July 20, 1993.—J.W.

he had developed insomnia, he had spoken of feeling worthless, he had felt his concentration diminish—all signs of a serious affective illness. His closest friends seem to have been aware of his despondency and mystified by it.

The pattern of each person's depression is different, but there are also marked similarities. The psychic torment of depression is, quite simply (albeit mysteriously, defying analysis or explanation), as exquisite as any imaginable physical pain. I recall telling my daughter with desperate seriousness, while in the depths of my own illness, that I would greatly prefer to undergo amputation. It was reported that Foster, during the weekend before the Tuesday that he killed himself, visited friends in Maryland, where he jogged, learned to crack crabs, and talked sports. To nearly everyone this conjures up a congenial image of summertime pleasure, but to those who themselves have confronted the horror, there is the almost certain knowledge that the jogging session was beset by demonic imaginings, the cracking of crabs was accompanied by thoughts of doom, and the sports talk became a conversational mask hiding a frantic inner quest for oblivion. A close friend of Foster's has confided that, though he was clearly depressed, he never mentioned suicide, but this tells us little. Many people who kill themselves fail to give a hint of their intentions.

If Foster had suggested aloud that he was thinking of doing away with himself, would it have made any difference? Psychiatry cannot assure victory over depression, especially in its severest form, but its strategies, both pharmacological and psychological, have shown considerable success in recent years. A person suffering from depression who consults a psychiatrist has commenced a process that, however faltering, can be one of catharsis and psychic ventilation.

Like many men, in particular certain highly successful and proudly independent men, Vincent Foster may have shunned psychiatry because, already demoralized, he felt it would be a final capitulation of his selfhood to lay bare his existential wounding in front of another fallible human being. When my own depression engulfed me, I had to overcome a lifelong skepticism and mistrust of the psychiatric profession in order to seek help. A Southerner like Foster, I attended the same college he graduated from— Davidson, in North Carolina, a small Presbyterian institution of outstanding academic quality. The college's venerable Calvinism, although liberalized in recent decades, has inculcated in its students a belief that hard work, material success, civic virtue, and creative achievement are the real guarantors of mental health. Although Foster himself was Roman Catholic, there is little doubt that Davidson's values left their mark.

The South, including Arkansas, is not fertile ground for psychiatry, and lawyers and writers who have been brought up in the tradition of Southern Presbyterianism are reluctant candidates for therapy. It has been said that Foster had been given the names of two psychiatrists whom he never contacted. Among the most troubling details in his sad chronicle is the one concerning his consultation by telephone, only the day before his death, with his family physician back in Little Rock, who prescribed an antidepressant. This long-distance procedure would seem to be appallingly insufficient, and not only because of the absurd insufficiency of antidepressant medication at that critical moment. Foster was near the brink. He needed to see a skilled practitioner who most likely would have insisted that he go to a hospital, where he would be safe from himself. There, after treatment but, as importantly, after relief from the fierce pounding of the partly real but mostly imagined afflictions he had endured, he would have eventually recovered, as the vast majority of people do. Far from destroying him, his breakdown would have been a deliverance. In a Washington he had learned to hate, the failure to survive his career in government would have been seen, after time, as of no consequence.

There remains only the need to ask why Vincent Foster became one among the legions of men and women who have suffered this shipwreck of the soul. One of the hallmarks of depression is the way it causes its victims to magnify troubles out of all proportion to their true measure. Paranoia reigns, harmless murmurs are freighted with menace, shadows become monsters. Such harassments as Foster endured in Washington could not have been entirely negligible, and they plainly triggered his collapse. One can understand why he felt betrayed and maligned, why his sense of self-worth may have been compromised. Countless stories have been written since the insinuating *Wall Street Journal* editorials about Foster. The articles claim that he must have feared exposure for some misconduct, probably connected to the Whitewater affair. But even an anxiety like this rarely leads to thoughts of drastic solutions in a normal mind. Only in someone vulnerable to depression would such worries give rise to the dementia that leads to self-murder. Foster may well have been at risk since infancy. If—as in many such cases—he had a genetic predisposition toward depression, he would always harbor the potential for chaotic behavior in the face of crisis. This was no defect of character but one symptom of a complex and mysterious illness that afflicts millions.

The fact that Foster's destruction took place in Washington rather than Little Rock could have also been, in the end, a mere quirk of geography, for though it is unlikely that in the placid landscape of Arkansas, had he stayed there, he would have met the pressures and anxieties that so bedeviled him, it is not inconceivable. A hometown scandal, some sudden fiasco, an unforeseen grief or loss (such as his father's recent death)—any of these might have caused in Foster the same devastation. One thing, in any event, is certain: it was not Washington that became the real proscenium for Vincent Foster's tragedy. It was the stage inside the mind upon which men and women enact life's loneliest agony.

[*Newsweek*, April 18, 1994.]

Warfare and Military Life

MacArthur

The *Reminiscences* by General of the Army Douglas MacArthur would be remarkable if for no other reason than that they may very well comprise the only autobiography by a great man which is almost totally free of self-doubt. There is no soul-searching here, none of the moments of despair, inquietude, fits of gloom that are recorded in the lives of even the most self-possessed of heroic men. MacArthur's solitary attack of desperation—so far as one can tell—occurred when he was nineteen, while still a plebe at West Point. The occasion was the investigation of a hazing incident in which young Douglas had been one of the victims. Called upon to divulge the names of the upperclassmen involved, he was naturally thrown into a state of anguish—all the more wrenching because of the presence at the Point of his mother, who had taught him stern rules about lying and tattling. This same lady (she was of an old Virginia family, and made her home for long periods with the General until he was past fifty) sent him the following poem during a recess of the court:

> Do you know that your soul is of my soul such a part
> That you seem to be fiber and core of my heart?
> None other can pain me as you, son, can do;
> None other can please me or praise me as you.
> Remember the world will be quick with its blame

If shadow or shame ever darken your name.
Like mother, like son, is saying so true
The world will judge largely of mother by you.
Be this then your task, if task it shall be,
To force this proud world to do homage to me.
Be sure it will say, when its verdict you've won,
She reaps as she sowed: "This man is her son!"

"I knew then what to do," MacArthur adds. "Come what may, I would be no tattletale."

The last remark is characteristic. For if a serene confidence untouched by that daily incertitude which afflicts most humans is one of the most immediate and striking features of this book, so too is the style, which, it should be said at the outset, is disappointingly juvenile. When one recalls those august periods which had rallied so many Americans during World War II, it comes as a surprise that here the tone is distinctly flat and insipid, the laborious prose having been set down with that gauche, manly earnestness that one recollects as a prominent characteristic of the adventures of Tom Swift. One wonders whatever happened to the grandiloquent MacArthur, the MacArthur who endeavored through rhetoric to transform the drab reality of American military life into something as rich and as mythic as medieval knighthood—an ideal typified in the address in 1935 to the veterans of his own World War I Rainbow Division:

> Those days of old have vanished tone and tint: they have gone glimmering through the dreams of things that were. Their memory is a land where flowers of wondrous beauty and varied colors spring, watered by tears and coaxed and caressed into fuller bloom by the smiles of yesterday. . . . We listen vainly but with thirsty ear for the witching melodies of days that are gone. . . . Youth . . . strength . . . aspirations . . . wide winds sweeping . . . beacons flashing across uncharted depths . . . movements . . . vividness . . . faint bugles sounding reveille . . . far drums beating the long roll call . . . the rattle of musketry . . . the still white crosses.

This is terrible junk, but it has at least a certain impassioned rhythm, while the greater part of the autobiography, when it is not simply boyish in tone, is set down in that lusterless Eisenhowerese which is so favored by corporation executives and which may be the result of MacArthur's later years at Remington Rand.° At any rate, the book is often something of a struggle to get through.

The quotation above, incidentally, is taken from Richard H. Rovere and Arthur M. Schlesinger, Jr.'s less than admiring but very fair *The General and the President*, published in 1951. A course of supplementary reading is as essential to the *Reminiscences* as it is to Parson Weems's life of Washington; and the Rovere-Schlesinger work, although it is primarily concerned with the last, or Korean, phase of MacArthur's career, is the most informative of an abundant selection. Noting the seventeen years MacArthur spent out of the United States before his recall from Korea in 1951, Rovere and Schlesinger make the observation that "MacArthur is our greatest military expatriate; he was as much in rebellion against our civilization as ever Henry James or Henry Miller was, and he probably symbolized the non-homesick American better than they ever did." The key phrase here is "non-homesick," and certainly Rovere and Schlesinger's contention is more than supported by MacArthur's autobiography. For in trying to understand MacArthur it is important to remember how completely his life was dominated by the Army, by the concept of the professional soldier, and how from the moment of his birth the Army became his home and his only home.

Born in 1880, MacArthur was the son of an ambitious and extremely gifted young officer from Wisconsin, a Union veteran who married a Southern woman whose brothers had fought under Robert E. Lee; the family atmosphere seems to have been one of an exhilarating preoccupation with the military tradition and its achievements, past and present. MacArthur's father, Arthur MacArthur, eventually became the highest ranking officer in the Army. Douglas MacArthur's boyhood was spent almost entirely on Army posts, mainly in the Southwest, and after an Army education at West Point (his career there was illustrious; MacArthur does not dwell upon the exact nature of his education, but it must have been, at that time, parochial in the extreme), he rose with amazing speed to become, at thirty-eight, a brigadier general and the youngest divisional commander in the American Expeditionary Force. His military record in France was truly spectacular, and his

° Or perhaps it is the influence of MacArthur's biographer, Major General Courtney Whitney. Although MacArthur claims to have "penned this book by my own hand," lines have been blandly plagiarized from Whitney's sycophantic *MacArthur: His Rendezvous with History* (1956).—W.S. (1982)

personal courage has never been in doubt; he returned from World War I loaded down with decorations and glory.

For a man of such—let it be cautiously called—egocentricity, there is little wonder that the following fifteen years and more, dutiful and dedicated as they were, lacked savor, and therefore make dull reading in the *Reminiscences:* a colorless tour of duty as Superintendent at West Point, a brigade command in the peaceful Philippines, a corps command in Baltimore, directorship of the Olympic Games committee. Even his five years as Army Chief of Staff (MacArthur writes with perfect aplomb that he accepted this high post solely at the demand of his mother, which must be the most awesome example we have of the influence of motherhood upon the national destiny) were singularly devoid of glamour, their only bright moment being his celebrated skirmish with the bedraggled Bonus Army on Anacostia Flats. This wasn't much of a war. It is understandable that at the age of fifty-five, having risen as high as one can rise in the Army, burdened with too much rank and heading for premature retirement, MacArthur was rent by such a keen nostalgia for the wartime days that it was like a gaping wound, and that in the midst of the early Roosevelt era—when military men were *déclassé,* anyway—he felt the need to give his Rainbow Division speech with its desperate and frustrated longing, its "thirsty ear" for "far drums beating the long roll call, the rattle of musketry, the still white crosses." He resigned to become chief military adviser to the Philippines, six years before the cataclysm at Pearl Harbor.

If it is impossible to share MacArthur's nostalgia for war, to share his passionate identity with the world of soldiering, it is at the same time easy to understand that nostalgia in the light of these fifty-five years. Anyone who has lived as a stranger for any length of time among professional military men, especially officers, is made gradually aware of something that runs counter to everything one has been taught to believe—and that is that most of these men, far from corresponding to the liberal cliché of the superpatriot, are in fact totally lacking in patriotism. They are not unpatriotic; they simply do not understand or care what patriotism is. Most of them, having been molded within the microcosm of service—Army, Marine Corps, Navy, whatever—are spiritually bound to a service, not a country, and the homage they pay to Old Glory they could pay to anyone's flag. A true military man is a mercenary (the calling is not necessarily ignoble, but certainly

MacArthur's role in the Philippines was for all intents and purposes that of a mercenary soldier), and it is within the world of soldiering that he finds his only home. This is why MacArthur, owing no spiritual allegiance to his native land, was able to become the very archetype of an expatriate, hostile to America and understanding almost nothing of it. This is also one of the reasons why, during World War II and to a nearly disastrous degree in Korea, he found it so easy to defy civilian authority: what did these secretaries of the Army and fussy presidents—who, after all, were only Americans—know about the service, which transcends all?

Nevertheless, if one understands the nostalgia for war which marked these years of his break with America, it still remains a nostalgia that is empyreal and histrionic. Only once in his career did MacArthur lead as small a body of men as a company—one somehow feels that the idea of MacArthur, even as a boy, in command of anything less than a division verges on the ludicrous—and this helps explain why his attitude toward the drab brown, smeary side of military life seems so rosy, and why the rare notice he pays to enlisted troops, whether singly or as a lacerated frontline unit, is always so condescending. MacArthur was a genuine militarist, but like all of this breed he was a hopeless romantic and almost totally without humor; it was his misfortune to collide head-on many times with that strain in the American character which is obdurate, wry, realistic, and comical. Americans have in many ways been a bloodthirsty people, but except in odd spasms they have never been militaristic, and it is this important distinction that one must take into account when one contemplates MacArthur's amazing career. For MacArthur, military life may be symbolized by "beacons flashing across uncharted depths . . . faint bugles sounding reveille," but for many if not most of his countrymen it is something else: It *is* reveille. It is training manuals and twenty-mile hikes, stupefying lectures on platoon tactics and terrain and the use of the Lister bag, mountains of administrative paperwork, compulsive neatness and hideous barracks in Missouri and Texas, sexual deprivation, hot asphalt drill fields and deafening rifle ranges, daily tedium unparalleled in its ferocity, awful food, bad pay, ignorant people, and a ritualistic demand for ass-kissing almost unique in the quality of its humiliation. The world that MacArthur thrills to makes most of his fellow Americans choke with horror.

Early in his narrative, describing how careful preparation allowed him to win the highest marks in high school, MacArthur says: "It was a lesson I never forgot. Preparedness is the key to success and victory." In 1939, in a statement not quoted in this book, he was saying complacently of the Philippines: "It has been assumed, in my opinion erroneously, that Japan covets these Islands. Proponents of such a theory fail fully to credit the logic of the Japanese mind." But the evidence is now that inadequate preparedness on MacArthur's part was a central factor in the catastrophe that engulfed the Philippines immediately after Pearl Harbor, and that the General's failure to implement properly certain crucial plans involving supply led directly to the eventual defeat on Bataan. MacArthur naturally does not linger on these matters, querulously placing the blame on the Navy, on something he calls "Washington," or an even more nebulous something called "my detractors"—a group that crops up with increasing frequency as the book drags on. There is one bracing passage from the Bataan-Corregidor section of the book, however: it is MacArthur's description of his departure by PT boat from the dock of the island, in the midst of incredible devastation:

> The desperate scene showed only a black mass of destruction. Through the shattered ruins, my eyes sought "Topside," where the deep roar of the heavy guns still growled defiance. Up there, in command, was my classmate, Paul Bunker. Forty years had passed since Bunker had been twice selected by Walter Camp for the All-American team. I could shut my eyes and see again that blond head racing, tearing, plunging—210 pounds of irresistible power. I could almost hear Quarterback Charley Daly's shrill voice barking, "Bunker back." . . .

It is at this point that MacArthur begins increasingly to yammer against censorship. He had been incensed when "Washington" forbade the release of information about the Death March on Bataan, and he writes of this incident: "Here was the sinister beginning of the 'managed news' concept by those in power." This statement was made by a man who could not have been unaware that it was public knowledge that he himself ran the most tightly controlled news agency of the war—an organization dedicated to glorifying MacArthur and so firmly under the General's thumb that one correspondent who was there called it "the most rigid and dangerous censorship in American history." ("If you capture Buna," MacArthur once said to General Eichelberger during the New Guinea campaign, "I'll give you a

Distinguished Service Cross and recommend you for a high British decoration." Then he added: "Also, I'll release your name for newspaper publication.") Nevertheless, most of the field generals and even some of the admirals had enormous respect for MacArthur's strategical sense, and his fight back to the Philippines from Australia by way of New Guinea remains a brilliant achievement. Maybe it is unfair to complain that the General's account of these operations—which rank high among his genuine triumphs—seems to be abstract, distant, skimpy in its total effect. While it would be wrong to expect a commander of MacArthur's position to have spent much time on the front lines (although often during the war, communiqués from "MacArthur's Headquarters" misled many newspaper readers into believing that he had done just that), and therefore his account cannot be filled with the smoke of battle and the feel of troops and movement, it is precisely this lack that makes for dull reading when a general has reached that stage of command which is both Olympian and "global." Thus MacArthur writes: "On January 2, 1943, Buna Mission fell; Sanananda followed, and the Papua campaign . . . ended." This is the General's single allusion to Sanananda, a bitter and horrible struggle—unknown by name to most Americans—which resulted in as many deaths as the bloody and far more famous battle by the Marines for Tarawa. Another reason comes to mind for such a cavalier reference, and it is less pleasant. It is that in this book no less than in his wartime dispatches, MacArthur is concerned with minimizing his own loss of men.

MacArthur's habit of self-congratulation, beating its rhythmic way through these pages in a rattle of medals, decorations, flattery from underlings, and adulatory messages from chiefs of state, reaches a crescendo as the Philippines are retaken and it becomes clear that the war is going to be won. Certainly the work of no modern military leader is filled with so many utterances of admiration, love received and bestowed, and pure vanity; by comparison, the autobiography of Fleet Admiral Halsey, no mean hand himself at the immodest appraisal, seems a work of anemic self-abasement. Indeed, by the time MacArthur has reached Manila, the need to describe the charisma of his own physical presence has become so obsessive, and the narcissism is so unremitting, that the effect is somehow vaguely sexual, as if the General had begun to lure the unwilling reader into some act of collaborative onanism. He describes, for example, his first visit to the infamous Santo Tomás prison camp.

When I arrived, the pitiful, half-starved inmates broke out in excited yells. I entered the building and was immediately pressed back against the wall by thousands of emotionally charged people. In their ragged, filthy clothes, with tears streaming down their faces, they seemed to be using their last strength to fight their way close enough to grasp my hand. One man threw his arms around me, and put his head on my chest, and cried unashamedly. A once-beautiful woman in tatters laboriously lifted her son over the heads of the crowd and asked me to touch him. . . . I was kissed. I was hugged. . . .

It is callous and offensive enough—even more so since it was written from the vantage point of mellow reflection—that this passage has for its dominant image not that wretched suffering itself but a man confusing himself with Christ. It becomes unspeakable when it seems very likely that MacArthur was employing characteristic fantasy in order to obscure the pathetic truth. Protesting MacArthur's similar description of the "liberation" of another Manila prison camp, Bilibid, a survivor recently wrote a letter to *Life* magazine—where part of this book was first published—and claimed bluntly that the General's account was a lie. The prisoners were freed and taken elsewhere, he said, then "unaccountably" brought back to the prison, where MacArthur shortly joined them with his entourage of newspapermen. There was no grateful outburst of welcome, only "wobbly ranks of thin, terribly tired men standing in stony silence."

MacArthur's Southwest Pacific command was one prong of a two-pronged assault on Japan, the other being Admiral Nimitz's Central Pacific force composed primarily of the Navy and Marine Corps. At the beginning of the war MacArthur bitterly opposed this division of the power, and he hated the Navy with a passion; it comes as a pleasant surprise, therefore, that he nowhere makes the claim of having won the war in the Pacific single-handedly; and the General earns points by offering praise where praise is due, paying tribute to Halsey and Kinkaid and such Air Force men as Kennedy and even Major Bong, who contributed so much to the success of his own operations. MacArthur's unselfish respect for the achievements of other military men is very Prussian. Also it cannot be denied that his own great sweep up through New Guinea and its island outriders to the Philippines was a brilliant feat of aggressive warfare.

A kind of exultant momentum seems to take hold of MacArthur as the war concludes, and it carries him through to his undoubtedly fine achievements as the absolute dictator of a conquered Japan. Free of "Washington" at last, MacArthur seems to have undergone in Tokyo a kind of benign metamorphosis. Sternly aloof, authoritarian, he was able nonetheless to display enormous understanding, tact, and even a heretofore concealed strain of magnanimity—as when he firmly resisted the yowls from America and its allies that Emperor Hirohito be tried as a war criminal. No less able a witness than Ambassador Edwin O. Reischauer has paid his earnest compliments to MacArthur's job of democratization, and similarly Roger Baldwin of the American Civil Liberties Union returned from Japan impressed by his reforms in such areas as constitutional rights, labor, and the enfranchisement of women. Yet both Reischauer and Baldwin think that he outwore his stay, and Baldwin has felt that with such central issues as the unionization of government workers the General sided with reaction.

Typically, MacArthur's long account of his visitation to Japan is Promethean and lacking in any flaw; it is one of the General's failings that often as soon as he has begun to win the reader over with a sort of hulking charm, he doses him by a sudden convulsion of self-righteousness. Thus, despite his magnanimous treatment of the emperor, he was ruthless in his disposal of the case of General Homma, "the Beast of Bataan," who had reputedly engineered the Death March. In his excellent book *But Not in Shame,* John Toland has offered convincing evidence that MacArthur was simply out to get his old enemy of the Philippines and that he rigged a trial that did not faintly resemble a display of justice. Homma, aside from being a man of great personal dignity and humanity, had no inkling of the atrocities taking place at that distant edge of his command. Our hero must have known this, yet in reviewing the trial he ordered Homma peremptorily executed with a statement priggish and insufferable even for MacArthur:

> The proceedings show the defendant lacked the basic firmness of character and moral fortitude essential to officers charged with the high command of military forces in the field. No nation can safely trust its martial honor to leaders who do not maintain the universal code which distinguishes between those things that are right and those things that are wrong. . . .

In 1951, recalled from his command in Korea by President Truman, MacArthur received the grandest welcome ever accorded by the American people. The General notes this fact with pride in his *Reminiscences,* though perhaps at last it is some aberrant modesty that prevents him from recording what had already been spoken and written of him: "the greatest living master of English" (this from Dr. Norman Vincent Peale), "the greatest man alive," "the greatest man since Christ," "the greatest man who ever lived." To these must be added the highest encomium ever received by an American—certainly in the halls of Congress—when after MacArthur's famous speech to that body, Representative Dewey Short of Missouri, a man educated at Harvard and Oxford, said, "We heard God speak here today, God in the flesh." (In the *Congressional Record* he later revised this statement to read: "A great hunk of God in the flesh.") MacArthur had made a tragic blunder in Korea—failing, as he had with the Japanese in the Philippines, to prepare adequately for Chinese aggression—yet his terrifying plan to extend the war onto the Chinese mainland had been cheered on, in one of those rare militaristic spasms, by vast numbers of Americans. Why they had done so may have best been explained by the British scholar Geoffrey Barraclough:

> Whatever view one may otherwise take of his actions, he took his stand on American interests. It is perhaps understandable, in the tense international situation of 1950, that Truman and his advisers found it difficult to acknowledge in the face of the world that the United States had an imperial role in Asia, shaped by long history, which it was going to defend. MacArthur made no bones about it. He cleared the air of cant.

That "Washington," this time in the form of Harry Truman and the Joint Chiefs of Staff, foresaw that he would "involve us in the wrong war, at the wrong place, with the wrong enemy, at the wrong time," provided the margin of our salvation.

In spite of his noble protestations, MacArthur had a simple lust for war. Though he was an alien to our civilization, perhaps in the end he was really not so remote from it that it is possible for us to rest easy with his sentiments, his yearning, and with those men who share his yearning. Toward the last days of his career he claimed over and over to be a lover of peace, a man who hated more than anything the idea of war. Yet he gave a final, suppos-

edly extemporaneous speech at West Point. And the lines of farewell from
that speech recorded on the last page of the book—for a peace-lover they
seem inappropriate but they do not surprise us; we have seen those very
words before—are filled with the same old nostalgia:

> The shadows are lengthening for me. The twilight is here. My days of
> old have vanished tone and tint; they have gone glimmering through the
> dreams of things that were. Their memory is one of wondrous beauty,
> watered by tears, and coaxed and caressed by the smiles of yesterday. I
> listen vainly, but with thirsty ear, for the witching melody of faint bugles
> blowing reveille, of far drums beating the long roll . . . the crash of
> guns . . .

[*New York Review of Books,* October 8, 1964.]

The Red Badge of Literature

Why is it that the war in Vietnam has inspired tons of journalism, most of it ordinary, yet such a small amount of imaginative literature? Could this be merely the continuation of a negative trend which began during the Korean War—a conflict which also produced little that was notable in the way of fiction, drama, or poetry? For up until the past two decades the wars America engaged in proved to be the catalyst for memorable work from some of our finest writers. In the best of these works—those of Whitman and Melville, Hemingway, Dos Passos, E. E. Cummings, Mailer, James Jones—the writers seemed possessed by an almost Euripidean need to demonstrate the eternal tragedy and folly of warfare, its persistence as a mysterious and destructive force dwelling in the very matrix of our nature, its stupidity, its boredom and anguish, and the glorious heroism it sometimes calls forth in spite of itself. In retrospect, it may be that both the appeal and the vitality of these novels and poems—and of lesser yet beautifully crafted works like John Horne Burns's novel of World War II, *The Gallery*—had to do with a kind of residual unconscious romanticism. After all, the Civil War and the two world wars of this century, whatever their horrors and whatever the historical blunders and idiocies that propelled them into being, possessed moral aspects which could make an individual's participation in the conflict not entirely ignoble. Both Stephen Crane and Hemingway were conscious of the insanity, the brutalization of war, but there were still a few idealistic principles embedded in the Civil War and World War I, thus lending to *The Red Badge of Courage* and *A Farewell to Arms* certain ironies and contradictions which helped give to each, finally, a romantic and tragic resonance.

It is possible, then, that the further we remove ourselves from wars in which a vestige of idealism exists or—to put it the other way around—the more we engage in waging wars that approach being totally depraved, the less likely we are to produce imaginative writing that contains many plausible outlines of humanity. It is a long leap, both historically and aesthetically, from the clear, frightened, distinctive identity of the hero of Stephen Crane to the blurred, undifferentiated, curiously one-dimensional twentieth-century victims wandering or staggering through the Vietnamese landscape of Ronald J. Glasser's *365 Days;* yet it is a tribute to Glasser's great skill as a writer that from this most morally loathsome of wars, which has in some way degraded each person who has been touched by it, he has fashioned a moving account about tremendous courage and often immeasurable suffering. It is therefore a valuable and redemptive work, providing as it does a view of the war from the vantage point of a man who has not only been there but has himself, obviously, seen and suffered much.

Glasser is a physician, a former Army major who found himself assigned in 1968 to the U.S. Army hospital at Zama, in Japan. It was here that he first encountered the evacuated wounded from Vietnam, "the blind 17-year-olds stumbling down the hallway, the shattered high-school football player being wheeled to physical therapy." Trained as a pediatrician, Glasser relates how he began to feel a special empathy for these blown-apart, uncomplaining, sometimes hideously mangled casualties of war. "I soon realized," he writes, "that the troopers they were pulling off those med evac choppers were only children themselves. . . . At first, when it was all new, I was glad I didn't know them; I was relieved they were your children, not mine. After a while, I changed." In the act of changing, in the process of becoming involved with these boys, Glasser listened to many stories about the horrors of combat in Vietnam. They were grim stories mostly, touched with the cold hand of mortality and having to do with slow or sudden death and unspeakable wounds, yet some of the tales were wildly improbable and overlaid by the graveyard hilarity that inevitably accompanies any chronicle of warfare.

Recounted in a dry, dispassionate, superbly controlled, and ironic voice, these anecdotes mingle at random with Glasser's own vividly observed, firsthand sketches of hospital life in Japan. The effect is disorganized, laconic, rather unsettlingly fragmentary, until one realizes that such a disjointed technique is perfectly suited to the outlines of the lunatic war itself: its greedy purposelessness, its manic and self-devouring intensity, its unending tableaux of helicopters crashing on missions to nowhere, futile patrols ending in bloody slaughter, instantaneous death in some remote mess area miles behind the action. Glasser's yeoman soldiers, aided by modern technology, are as miserably up to their necks in war as were those of Shakespeare. They trip over mines and are reduced to vegetables; after a night of grisly hand-to-hand murder they are enraged when the cook runs out of cornflakes; they nervously conspire to kill their swinish senior officers, and then chicken out. These awful vignettes are rendered with splendid understatement. It is a banal and senseless war, lacking either heroes or a chorus. Perhaps only an ear exquisitely attuned to the banal and senseless, like Glasser's, could do justice to such a nightmare: certainly many of these pages of callow, dyspeptic dialogue—uttered out of young souls quite trampled down with despair and fatigue—are as authentic and as moving a transcription of the soldier's true voice as any written in recent memory.

But if the war has been a war made up of victims and has been denied its true heroes, it has nonetheless had its moments of great sacrifice and courage in the face of incredible suffering. It is through Glasser's calm, unsentimental revelation of such moments that we are able to shake off some of the horror with which these pages are so often steeped and to see *365 Days* as the cleansing and redemptive document it is. Nearly all of Glasser's stories of combat, although admittedly secondhand (as was *The Red Badge of Courage*), are remarkable miniature portraits of men at war. It is in the hospital episodes, however, where the force of Glasser's professional concern melts with the compassion and sensibility of a gifted storyteller, that we are given scenes of wrenching power. In the last story in the book, Major Edwards, a doctor in the hospital burn unit, is faced with the hopeless task of saving a young soldier cruelly burned across 80 percent of his body. The tale is simple, the situation uncomplicated: a dedicated physician, through no other motive than that resulting from the mighty urge to hold back death, trying against all odds to salvage someone who himself is suffering, without complaint, ecstasies of pain. Two human beings, then, locked in the immemorial struggle against inexplicable fate. This is a familiar story and one that could have been both clinical and cloying, but Glasser's hand is so sure, his eye so clear, that the moment of the boy's imminent death and his last cry to the doctor—"I don't want to go home alone"—seem to rise to form a kind of unbearable epiphany to the inhuman waste and folly of war.

It is this quality, reverent at its best, enormously touching in its concern for the simple worth and decency of life, that gives *365 Days* its great distinction and may cause it—one hopes—to become one of those rare chronicles we can use to help alleviate the killing pain of this war, and its festering disgrace. For it shows that in the midst of their most brutish activity there is a nobility in men that war itself cannot extinguish. As Glasser says, in one of the most poignant of his passages, about the "medics":

> In a world of suffering and death, Vietnam is like a Walt Disney True-Life Adventure, where the young are suddenly left alone to take care of the young. . . . A tour of Nam is 12 months; it is like a law of nature. The medics, though, stay on line only seven months. It is not due to the good will of the Army, but to their discovery that seven months is about all these kids can take. After that, they start getting freaky, cutting down on their own water and food so they can carry more medical supplies; stealing plasma bottles and walking around on patrol with five or six pounds of glass in their rucksacks; writing parents and friends so they can buy their own endotracheal tubes; or quite simply refusing to leave their units when their time in Nam is over.
>
> And so it goes, and the gooks know it. They will drop the point, trying not to kill him but to wound him, to get him screaming so they can get the medic too. He'll come. They know he will.

[*Washington Monthly*, March 1972.]

There was a rather grotesque aftermath to *365 Days*. In 1981, long after its publication, the book became a *cause célèbre* in the state of Maine, where it went on trial for the obscenity of its language. Glasser and his book were acquitted, but the case remains a remarkable example of the perennial confusion in the United States over the difference between the relatively benign obscenity of certain words and the total obscenity of war.—W.S. (1982)

A Farewell to Arms

A short time ago, while talking to a group of students at a college in Virginia, I was seized by a dismal insight. The subject of war literature had come up and I said that it occurred to me suddenly that at the age of fifty-one—perhaps a mellow age but one I refused to regard as being advanced or venerable—I had lived through three wars, in two of which, both as an officer and as an enlisted man in the Marine Corps, I had been an active participant. I reviewed the wars in reverse order. Although I had been spared the war in Vietnam, except as an outraged and frustrated onlooker, I had been involved in the war against the Chinese and the North Koreans as well as the Japanese in World War II (the Marines have in recent years specialized in Oriental foes); as a matter of curiosity I threw in the fact that World War I—that pointless and heartrending conflict—ended only seven years before my birth.

The Virginia springtime was peaceful and bright as I brooded in this fashion, but I wondered aloud on the illusory nature of this peace. Was it going to last? Was it really peace? The students appeared to be perplexed, maybe a little bored. I reflected that given the almost cyclical nature of these terrible conflicts in our century—the seemingly inexorable pattern of their recurrence—no one could imagine an experienced oddsmaker like Jimmy the Greek or, let us say, a sound actuarial mind regarding as anything but an outside chance the notion that war of serious magnitude involving

American forces would not happen again. Perhaps soon, certainly within your own lifetime, I concluded somberly to the students—but since on those fresh young faces I saw nothing but incomprehension, we talked of other matters. I had the feeling that the battles of Vietnam for them were as remote as Shiloh or Belleau Wood.

It was with the memory of this episode that I turned to Philip Caputo's remarkable personal account of the war in Vietnam, *A Rumor of War,* and experienced from the very first page a chilling sense of déjà vu. Caputo and I are separated in age by approximately twenty years, and although there were significant differences in his Marine Corps experience and mine, I was struck immediately by the similarities. Born like me into a middle-class family, Caputo joined the Marines in 1960 (as I did during World War II) for the glory and the adventure, for the need to "prove something—my courage, my toughness, my manhood." In my own case, the Japanese were already our sworn enemy and it may be that patriotism inspired by war against a proven aggressor helped to motivate my choice; to wait and be drafted into the *Army* was unthinkable.

Caputo, enlisting in a time of nominal peace, concedes that "the patriotic tide of the Kennedy years" was an element for him in choosing the Marines (early in the book he bitterly, and correctly, speaks of John Kennedy as being "that most articulate and elegant mythmaker," who was as responsible as anyone for the Vietnam enterprise and for his own final disillusionment), but Caputo and I shared, quite unequivocally, I think, the quest for war's heroic experience: "war, the ultimate adventure, the ordinary man's most convenient means of escaping from the ordinary."

In the opening passages of his book, Caputo describes how directly from his classes in English literature he entered Marine Corps training at Quantico, where as an officer candidate he learned to slaughter people with rifles and knives and explosives or to blast them to pieces with rocket launchers. These passages could serve almost perfectly (excepting one or two trivial technological details) as the introduction to my own youthful military reminiscences. We went through virtually the same training ordeal, which in the Marine Corps remains unchanged to the present moment: the remorseless close-order drill hour after hour in the burning sun, the mental and physical abuse, the humiliations, the frequent sadism at the hands of drill sergeants, all the claustrophobic and terrifying insults to the spirit that can make an outpost like Quantico or Parris Island one of the closest things in the free world to a concentration camp. (I have learned that revolutionary changes have taken place, but only in recent months.) Yet this preparation, a form of meat processing which I do not think it hyperbolic to call infernal (it has on too many occasions actually maimed or killed), is intended to create an esprit de corps, a sense of discipline and teamwork, above all a feeling of group invincibility which sets the Marine Corps apart from the other branches of the service. And that the training has been generally successful can be demonstrated by the fierce pride with which it stamps its survivors.

It is for me a touchstone of the Marine Corps' fatal glamour—that training nightmare—that there is no ex-Marine of my acquaintance, regardless of what direction he may have taken spiritually or politically after those callow gung-ho days, who does not view the training as a crucible out of which he emerged in some way more resilient, simply *braver* and better for the wear. Another measure of the success of that training is that it could transform Philip Caputo of Westchester, Illinois, from an ordinary, bright suburban lad with amorphous ambitions into a highly trained technician in the science of killing, who in March of 1965, during those palmy "defensive" or "expeditionary" days of the war, landed at Danang eager for the fight, for the excitement, for medals, anxious to prove himself as a Marine officer, above all drawn to war with "an unholy attraction" he could not repress. One of the indispensable features of Caputo's narrative is that he is never less than honest, sometimes relentlessly so, about his feelings concerning the thrill of warfare and the intoxication of combat. At least in the beginning, before the madness. After sixteen months of bloody skirmishes and the ravages of disease and a hostile environment, after the psychological and emotional attrition, Caputo—who had begun "this splendid little war" in the jaunty high spirits of Prince Hal—was very close to emotional and physical collapse, a "moral casualty," convinced—and in 1966!—that the war was unwinnable and a disgrace to the flag under which he had fought to such a pitch of exhaustion.

There is a persuasive legitimacy in this hatred of a war when it is evoked by a man who has suffered its most horrible debauchments. But perhaps that is why we are equally persuaded by Caputo's insistence on a recognition that for many men, himself included, war and the confrontation with death can produce an emotion—a commingled exultation and anguish—that verges on rapture. It is like a mighty drug; certainly it approaches the transcendental. After becoming a civilian, Caputo was engaged for a long time in the antiwar movement. But, he says, "I would never be able to hate the war with anything like the undiluted passion of my friends in the movement." These friends, he implies, could never understand how for him the war "had been an experience as fascinating as it was repulsive, as exhilarating as it was sad, as tender as it was cruel." Some of Caputo's troubled, searching meditations on the love and hate of war, on fear, and the ambivalent discord that warfare can create in the hearts of decent men, are among the most eloquent I have read in modern literature. And when in a blunter spirit he states, "Anyone who fought in Vietnam, if he is honest about himself, will have to admit he enjoyed the compelling attractiveness of combat," he is saying something worthy of our concern, explaining as it does—at least in part—the existence of preparatory hellholes like Quantico and Parris Island, and perhaps of war itself.

Of course no war can be reckoned as good. Yet aside from the fact that for the Marines in the Pacific, World War II was at least a struggle against aggression, while the war in Vietnam was a vicious and self-serving intrusion, what finally differentiated the two conflicts from the point of view of the dirty foot soldier? Caputo's war and mine? As the earlier war recedes, and the Pacific battlefields become merely palm-shaded monuments in the remote ocean, there is a tendency to romanticize or to distort and forget. Bloody as we all know that conflict was, it becomes in memory cleaner and tidier—a John Wayne movie with most of the gore hosed away for the benefit of a PG-rated audience. The Marines in that war seem a little like Boy Scouts, impossibly decent. Could it be that the propinquity of the unspeakable horrors of Vietnam forces us to this more tasteful view? Yet it should be noted that World War II produced its own barbarities. As a young Marine lieutenant I knew a regular gunnery sergeant, a mortar specialist, who carried in his dungaree pocket two small shriveled dark objects about the size of peach pits. When I asked him what they were he told me they were "Jap's nuts." I was struck nearly dumb with a queasy horror, but managed to ask him how he had obtained such a pair of souvenirs. Simple, he explained; he had removed them with a bayonet from an enemy corpse on Tarawa—that most hellish of battles—and had set them out at the end of a dock under the blazing sun, where they quickly became dried like prunes. The sergeant was highly regarded in the company and I soon got used to seeing him fondle his keepsakes whenever he got nervous or pissed off, stroking them like worry beads.

I have been prompted to set down this vignette because of its resemblance to Caputo's Vietnam, where in a trance of comparable horror the young officer, still innocent and untried in battle, watches one of his Australian allies display a couple of mementos taken from the Vietcong—"two dried and bloodstained human ears." With his tough fair-mindedness Caputo is quick to point out in a somewhat different context how ready the Vietcong and ARVN were to commit similar desecrations; and the cruelty of the French in the earlier Indochinese war is too well documented to dispute. Nonetheless, there is a continuity of events, a linkage of atrocity from war to war, that forces the conclusion that we are capable of demonstrating toward our Asian adversaries a ruthless inhumanity we would doubtless withhold from those less incomprehensibly different from us, less likened to animals, or simply less brown or yellow.

Racism was as important, ideologically, to the conduct of the Pacific war as racism was to the war in Vietnam. As a matter of fact, racism may have been more important to the Marines in the Pacific, since there was no such propagandistic cause as anti-Communism to impel those peach-cheeked youngsters to wage a war against an enemy caught up in the thrall of a fanatical, even suicidal nationalism. Pearl Harbor was a powerful incentive—as were the Japanese cruelties on Bataan—but still, these were not enough. Racism in warfare had already been initiated by the Germans, who, imputing to them a subhuman status, had begun to exterminate hundreds of thousands of Russian prisoners of war (many gassed at Auschwitz) while in general treating their Anglo-Saxon foes with acceptable decency. As for the Japanese, it was enough for us to establish an anthropoid identity and thus, having classified them as apes, we found it easy to employ the flamethrower—that ghastly portable precursor of the napalm bomb used in Vietnam—and fry them in their bunkers and blockhouses. ("They sizzle like a bunch of roaches," I remember being told by a flamethrowing corporal, who was delighted with the weapon.) There was also a normal amount of casual murder, torture of prisoners, and other crimes. (A friend of mine admitted to having slit the throats of two prisoners while he was a sergeant leading a patrol on

Guam, though he later expressed honest remorse for the deed. A retired colonel now, he lives in La Jolla, where he grows prize dahlias.)

Psychologically, however, the Pacific war differed from Vietnam in that the Marines had not only a clearly defined commitment, a sense of purpose, but a decisive, freewheeling (albeit at times badly flawed) strategy which almost never allowed them to feel that they had settled into a pointless morass. The Marines were too busily on the go, too happy at their lethal task, to dabble in atrocity. After Guadalcanal the Marine Corps was constantly on the offensive (a state most conducive, for the infantryman, to that sense of qualified bliss Caputo dwells on), in battle not against a guerrilla enemy maddeningly lurking in the jungles of a huge landmass but against soldiers immured for the most part within plainly visible fortifications on plainly visible islands where there were few or no civilians.

Behind the fighting men, too, was a perpetual surge of national pride. It was a madly popular war. It was a war which accomplished successfully what history demanded of the Marine Corps: the almost total annihilation of the enemy—more bliss. That is what fighting men are for, to kill, but to kill purposefully and with a reasonably precise goal in view—not as in Vietnam to produce mere bodies for General Westmoreland's computer. And certainly not to get fouled up with civilians.

Thus the Pacific war may be viewed in retrospect as a discussible moral enterprise. It was an awful war, one of the worst: in it one could experience battle fatigue, unconscionable misery and pain, insane fear, deprivation, loathsome disease, stupefying boredom, death, and mutilation in places with names like Tarawa, Peleliu, Iwo Jima—arguably the most satanic engagements in which men have been pitted against one another since the birth of warfare. But those who fought in the Pacific war, whatever the nature of their wounds or their diminishment, could emerge undefiled. What Philip Caputo demonstrates by contrast in his ruthless testament is how the war in Vietnam defiled even its most harmless and well-meaning participants. His is the chronicle of men fighting with great bravery but forever losing ground in a kind of perplexed, insidious lassitude—learning too late that they were suffocating in a moral swamp.

I have said that one of the most remarkable features of *A Rumor of War* is the fact that Caputo's bitter disaffection with the Vietnamese war and all it represented came when the war was in its infancy, 1966. Not that the war

was anything but corrupt to begin with; still, there is something almost phenomenal in Caputo's microcosmic sixteen-month odyssey, as if compressed
within its brief framework was the whole foul and shameful drama of the
conflict which was to drag on for many more years.

Of course, as I have also said, the war began for Caputo in a spirit that
was anything but shameful. Gung ho, a knife in his teeth, he was pining for
the glamour, the action, and he got it. After a stagnant period of waiting and
chafing at the bit on the perimeter around Danang, Caputo and his men
went on the offensive in perhaps the very first engagement by American
forces in Vietnam. It was not a big engagement, only a skirmish with the
Vietcong, but it was filled with noise and excitement and a certain amount
of danger, and this baptism under fire made Caputo "happy . . . happier than
I have ever been." Reading this early episode from the vantage point of
hindsight, knowing what the outcome had to be in the ensuing dreadful
years, one feels a chill at all that youthful machismo and reckless bloodlust:
it evokes all that is unripe and heedless and egregiously romantic in the
American spirit.

Already the United States—bursting with unspent power and unused
armaments, slowly and inexorably being maneuvered from "defense" into
aggression by the generals and the politicians—was beginning to move from
its phase of "expedition" into the colossal entanglements of a full-scale war.
How easy it would have been at that point, one thinks, for the Marine Corps
to have packed up its seabags and departed, leaving our Asian brothers to
resolve their strife in whatever way destiny willed. But we had fatally intervened, and one of the critical instruments of our intervention was dauntless,
hot-blooded Lieutenant Philip Caputo, who, it must be remembered, was
hardly dragooned into the fray. He was also a man without whom (together
with his tough, resolute brothers in arms) the war could not have proceeded
a single inch into those treacherous and finally engulfing jungles.

Caputo writes brilliantly about these early days around Danang, that period
of eager expectation before the horrors descended and the war began to
taste like something incessantly loathsome on his tongue. Even then, in that
time of cautious waiting—a stationary war of skirmishes and patrols and
skittish engagements with the Vietcong—it was not pleasant duty, but after
all, this is what Caputo had bought and bargained for: the unspeakable heat

and the mosquitoes, the incessant clouds of dust, the boredom, the chicken-shit from upper echelons (often described with ferocious humor, in the spirit of *Catch-22*), the dreary nights on liberty in the ramshackle town, the impenetrably lush and sinister mountain range hovering over the flyblown domestic landscape, already smeared with American junk.

> The convoy slows to a crawl as it passes through Dogpatch. The filth and poverty of this village are medieval. Green pools of sewage lie in the culverts, the smell mingling with the stench of animal dung and nuoc-maum, a sauce made from rotten fish. . . . Water buffalo bellow from muddy pens shaded by banana trees whose leaves are white with dust. Most of the huts are made of thatch, but the American presence has added a new construction material: several houses are built entirely of flattened beer cans; red and white Budweiser, gold Miller, cream and brown Schlitz, blue and gold Hamm's from the land of sky-blue waters.

Boredom, inanition, a sitting war; drunken brawls in Danang, whores, more chickenshit, the seething lust for action. All this Caputo embroiders in fine detail—and then the action came in a powerful burst for Caputo and his comrades. Suddenly there were pitched engagements with the enemy. There were the first extended movements into enemy territory, the first helicopter assaults, the first real engagements under heavy fire, and, inevitably, the first shocking deaths. War became a reality for Caputo; it was no longer a film fantasy called *The Halls of Montezuma,* and there is great yet subtle power in Caputo's description of how—in this new kind of conflict, against a spectral enemy on a bizarre and jumbled terrain (so different from such textbook campaigns as Saipan or even Korea)—the underpinnings of his morale began to crumble, doubt bloomed, and the first cynical mistrust was implanted in his brain. These misgivings—which later became revulsion and disillusionment—arrived not as the result of a single event but as an amalgam of various happenings, each one repellent, which Caputo (as well as the reader) begins to perceive as being embedded in the matrix of the war and its specifically evil nature.

It is an evil more often than not underscored by a certain loathsome pointlessness. A nineteen-year-old marine is discovered cutting the ears off a dead VC. After a huge engagement in which the battalion expends thousands of rounds of ammunition there are only four Vietcong dead. (Later three thousand troops supported by naval gunfire kill twenty-four VC in three days.) In pursuit of the enemy and fearing an ambush, one of the platoons goes berserk and burns down a hamlet, devastating the place entirely. In this instance none of the villagers is seriously hurt, yet there is a peculiar primitive horror about the scene, and Caputo does not even bother to make the point all too ominously adumbrated by his powerful description: hovering in that smoke and the sound of wailing women is our common knowledge that My Lai is only a few years away.

There were many brave men who fought in Vietnam, and many performed brave deeds, but the war itself disgraced the name of bravery. That "uncommon valor" of which the Marines are so justifiably proud—which still stirs men when they hear names like Belleau Wood and Guadalcanal and Peleliu—was as much in evidence on the banks of the Mekong and on the green walls of the Annamese Cordillera, about which Caputo writes with such strength and grace, as in those early struggles. But what names blaze forth from Vietnam? Men's courage passes from generation to generation and is never really extinguished; but it is a terrible loss that, try as we might, we cannot truly honor courage employed in an ignoble cause.

In this book Philip Caputo writes so beautifully and honestly about both fear and courage, writes with such knowing certitude about death and men's confrontation with the abyss, that we cannot doubt for an instant that he is a brave man who fought well long after that "splendid little war" became an obscene nightmare in which he nearly drowned. But he was dragged downward, and indeed the most agonizing part of his chronicle is found not in the descriptions of carnage and battle—as harrowingly re-created as they are—but in his own savage denouement when, driven into a raging madness by the senseless devastation he has witnessed and participated in, he turns into a monster and commits that mythic Vietnam-stained crime: he allows the murder of civilians. Although he was ultimately exonerated, his deed became plainly a wound forever engrafted on his soul. It seems the inevitable climax to this powerful story of a decent man sunk into a dirty time, in a far place where he was never intended to be, in an evil war.

In a passage near the beginning of A Rumor of War, Caputo—happy, optimistic, thirsting for battle—sits in an observation post overlooking the sun-dappled rice paddies, the green hills, the majestic ageless mountains of the Annamese range. He cannot even dream of the horrors yet to come. He is reading Kipling and his eyes fall upon some lines which may be among the most lucid ever written about the mad, seemingly unceasing adventures which bring young boys from Illinois to such serene, improbable vistas:

> The end of the fight is a tombstone white with the name of the late
> deceased,
> And the epitaph drear: "A Fool lies here who tried to hustle the East."

[*New York Review of Books,* June 23, 1977.]

Calley

Whole seas, one feels, could not contain the tears that humanity must shed at the knowledge of the horror at My Lai. As one goes over the event yet another time—as one rereads Seymour M. Hersh's brilliant, pitiless account *My Lai 4,* published last year—one has to try to insulate one's self from the details of the massacre, protectively conjuring up visions of other atrocities, saying to oneself: "Keep thinking of Bengal, of the murder of the Huguenots, the sack of Magdeburg, of Lidice, Malmédy. Isn't this only what men have always done to other men?"

> Near them [writes Hersh] was a young Vietnamese boy, crying, with a bullet wound in his stomach. . . . The radio operator then stepped within two feet of the boy and shot him in the neck with a pistol. Blood gushed from the child's neck. He then tried to walk off, but he could only take two or three steps. Then he fell onto the ground. He lay there and took four or five deep breaths and then he stopped breathing. The radio operator turned to Stanley and said, "Did you see how I shot that son of a bitch?"

❖ ❖ ❖

Nineteen-year-old Nguyen Thi Ngoc Tuyet watched a baby trying to open his slain mother's blouse to nurse. A soldier shot the infant while it was struggling with the blouse, and then slashed at it with his bayonet.

* * *

Nguyen Khoa, a thirty-seven-year-old peasant, told of a thirteen-year-old girl who was raped before being killed. G.I.'s then attacked Khoa's wife, tearing off her clothes. Before they could rape her, however, Khoa said, their six-year-old son, riddled with bullets, fell and saturated her with blood.

Until recently America had by luck or through divine providence been saved from being a truly militaristic nation, but it has in the past been a bloodthirsty one. Such passages as those just quoted therefore do not so intolerably rend the heart merely because they describe atrocities at the hands of wholesome American boys—these clean-cut American boys, after all, butchered the Indians and inflicted tortures on the Filipinos—but because just as we grieve for its victims we grieve for an America which, twenty-six years after the end of a war to save the world for democracy, finds itself close to moral bankruptcy—the criminal nature of its war in Southeast Asia symbolized by the My Lai carnage and by its flyblown principal executor, First Lieutenant William Laws Calley.

For this reason Calley commands our most intense interest. Banal, stunted in mind and body, colorless, lacking even a native acumen, with an airless, dreary brain devoid of wit—he is not the first nobody whose brush with a large moment in history has personified that moment and helped define it. One thinks of Eichmann. Almost all comparisons between America and Hitler's Germany are strident and inept, but here the analogy seems appropriate. Both of them, the Nazi functionary and the loutish American officer, attempted exculpation of their enormous crimes through insistence that they were merely cogs in a great machine, that they were only carrying out orders, that the true guilt lay with others. Both of them finally, in their rancid ordinariness, symbolized the historic moment more dramatically than the flamboyant leaders they served.

Thus, as the Nazi concentration camps recede into the past, Eichmann seems to embody their memory, and even that of the entire Nazi regime, more significantly than does a Goebbels or a Himmler. It would slander the young men who have been forced to fight and die in Vietnam to say that Calley is an archetype of the soldier in this war. He may in the perspective of time, however, become more archetypal of the war's total moral degeneracy than its actual perpetrators—miscreants of the White House and the

Pentagon too well known, too numerous, and enjoying at the moment too much exposure to need naming here.

This is not to assume that on lower levels of authority there are not those who share in Calley's guilt. It is spelled out in Hersh's book, and one's conviction that other officers were criminally involved is reinforced by Richard Hammer's *The Court-Martial of Lt. Calley,* an excellent, straightforward piece of reporting which pursues the theme of Calley's individual guilt with almost puritanical zeal but which cannot help leaving the impression of the culpability of others. It is difficult to believe, for instance, that Lieutenant Colonel Barker, the task force commander who was whirling over the area in his helicopter as Charlie Company went about its bloody work, was not aware of the true nature of what was happening and should not have stopped it; but this can probably never be proved, for Barker was killed in another action.

But to focus upon the guilt of others is largely begging the question when it comes to judging Calley, for, as Hammer points out, we do not exonerate a criminal merely because his accomplices in the crime had the good luck to escape justice. Military life may be a repugnant notion to most of us; but the idea commonly nurtured by those civilians who most detest, or misunderstand, or indeed admire the military as an institution—that because it is engaged in killing it is an amoral place, or a place in which ordinary considerations of morality are irrelevant—is tempting and romantic but false. Despite the paradoxes involved, the military may remain our most intransigently "moral" institution;* and it was an unawareness of this fact on the part of those millions of Americans who thought Calley was persecuted, or considered him a sacrificial lamb, that led to their confusion.

Much, for instance, has been made of Calley's "orders." Is it not the first duty of a military man to obey orders from a superior? The answer is yes, but a strictly qualified yes. Calley and other witnesses contended that at Captain Ernest Medina's briefing the night before the assault, the captain ordered the company to "kill everything." Medina and still other witnesses have disclaimed such an order, maintaining that by "kill" or "waste" or "de-

---

* The reduction of Calley's sentence from life to twenty years, probably influenced by President Nixon's sympathy for the lieutenant, and which occurred after this review was written, tends to undercut any such venerable premise about the military service, and may simply be an indication of how corruptible it has really become.—W.S. (1982)

stroy" he did not mean unarmed men, women, and children. This issue, in detail, remains obscure.

Yet the point is that if Medina did indeed give an order specifying the wholesale murder of helpless civilians, it was an illegal order, which Calley—especially as a commissioned officer, whose very commission implies that he is supposed to know better—was obliged to refuse to execute. His own orders to his troops to kill and the alacrity with which he himself sprang to the slaughter, on the other hand, in contrast to those of the men who declined to join the bloodletting, illustrate dramatically how there existed that morning at My Lai the element of choice; and this is another dimension by which Calley must be judged and condemned.

It is a lamentable fact—though one perhaps not too surprising—that some of the GIs under Calley's orders embarked on private orgies of murder that defy words. But others of those "grunts" so ably depicted in Hammer's book drew back in shock and shame. Those white and black dogfaces from places like Holyoke, Massachusetts, and Providence and New Orleans, the deprived or the semideprived with their comic books and their bubble gum and their grass, these melting-pot types bearing names out of a patriotic World War II movie, Dursi and Maples and Grzesik—they were benumbed by the horror and they refused to kill; and their presence at Fort Benning as they bore witness against Calley brought out perhaps more than anything else the lieutenant's fathomless dereliction.

If this were not sufficient, there was the testimony of a fellow officer, Lieutenant Jeffrey LaCross, the leader of the third platoon, who said that he neither heard Medina give the command to kill everyone in the hamlet nor did he himself assume that anything should be done to the civilians other than to employ the usual practice of gathering them together and submitting them to interrogation. Having done just this on that day, he too demonstrated by contrast the measure of his fellow platoon leader's irresponsibility; and his testimony was badly damaging to an already brutally damaged Calley, who, it seemed plain as the trial drew to an end, had got his name entered on the rolls of history's illustrious mass murderers.

But what of Calley himself? Hammer's book is an honest, penetrating account of a crucially significant military trial; but his loathing for Calley is manifest on every page. Surely, one thinks, there must be some extenuation, some key to this man's character which will allow us a measure of compassion or at least of understanding so that despite his crimes some beam of warmth or attractiveness will flow out—some tragic or, God knows, even comic dimension that could permit us to mourn a little over this good ole boy from Florida gone wrong. Hammer stalks Calley so relentlessly that, despite resistance, one begins to feel the sweat of Christian charity being coaxed from one's pores. We therefore turn with eagerness to *Lieutenant Calley: His Own Story*, as told to John Sack, hoping for that ameliorative detail or insight that might help cast a gentler light on the transgressor.

Alas, it is a vain hope, for Calley's whole identity—as recorded, according to his Boswell, "on five hundred thousand inches of magnetic tapes and a fiftieth ton of transcripts"—impresses the reader as being one of such stupefying vacuity, of such dwarfishness of spirit that one is relieved that his account does not yield us the luxury of even a fleeting affection. Furthermore, the book is an underhanded, self-serving document, one of those soulless apologias that have emanated many times before from base men. Simulating honesty, it attempts a cheap vindication, and in so doing, more firmly ratifies the guilt.

In his preface, after anesthetizing us with more statistics ("I talked to Calley for a hundred days. I asked him somewhere near ten thousand questions, or one question for each three-fourths of a sentence here"), Sack tells us how impressed he became with Calley's sincerity and appeals to the reader not to lose sight of it. One reader lost sight of it after about the tenth and a half page, although in fairness to Calley this may in part be the fault of the style, or technique rather: those five hundred thousand inches of magnetic tape ending up on the page as indigestible splinters and strips—one feels choked on acetate.

That a tape recorder, in proper hands, can be an effective amanuensis and collector of thoughts and voices was proved by the late Oscar Lewis, whose guiding intelligence brought an almost Balzacian sweep to his works of social anthropology. But Sack's intelligence does not guide. This lapse, in conjunction with the boyish squalor of Calley's mind, gives the book a fragmented, groping, almost hysterical quality, as if spoken by a depraved Holden Caulfield. There is an irresistible temptation to believe, in fact, that Sack, perhaps without knowing it, is bent upon hanging Calley on the gallows of his own "sincerity." Otherwise, it is hard to make sense of such a remarkable passage as that which comes near the beginning of the book, in which Calley describes his reaction to the news that he is likely to be prosecuted for the murders:

I thought, *Could it be I did something wrong?* I knew that war's wrong. Killing's wrong: I realized that. I had gone to a war, though. I had killed, but I knew. *So did a million others.* I sat there, and I couldn't find the key. I pictured the people of Mylai: the bodies, and they didn't bother me. I had found, I had closed with, I had destroyed the VC: the mission that day. I thought, *It couldn't be wrong or I'd have remorse about it* [italics Sack's].

Here in these few lines, which are fairly typical of the book in both style and substance, Calley manages to reveal at least three appalling facts about himself: that he is still unaware, or pretends to be unaware, of the difference between a massacre and lawful killing in combat; that he is still unmoved by the effects of his butchery at My Lai, when others who were there had been gruesomely haunted by the sight for months, at least one of them driven to the brink of mental breakdown; and that he is a liar. He is a liar, we see, because it is impossible that so many months after the event he still thinks that the victims of his slaughter—old men, women, and children—had been really his enemies, the Vietcong.

Or what is one to say about a truly flabbergasting passage in which, at the very height of the carnage at My Lai, Calley describes how he rushes to prevent a GI from forcing a girl to perform a sexual act, and then asks himself rhetorically why he had been so "saintly"?

Because—if a GI is getting sex, "he isn't doing his job. He isn't destroying communism." Calley's puzzlement over moral priorities and options seems typically in the American grain, for he then goes on to brood:

Of course, if I had been ordered to Mylai to rape it, pillage, and plunder—well, I still don't know. I may be old-fashioned, but I can't really see it. Our mission in Mylai wasn't perverted though. It was simply "Go and destroy it."

Or this episode, a few pages later, describing his encounter at My Lai with a defenseless civilian (apparently a Buddhist priest), whom he was convicted of murdering:

You sonofabitch. And bam: I butted him in his mouth with my M-16. Straight on: sideways could break the M-16. He had frustrated me!

Sack should have been advised that sometimes sincerity does not appear to be a winning virtue. Yet, if indeed sincerity were a truly consistent component of this book, we might be able to accept at least part of it. The story is, however, implausible when it is not being greasily devious, and it is dominated by two tendentious themes. One of these themes—Calley's fear that civilians, whether they be old men or women or children, are really the enemy in disguise—pervades, indeed saturates, the narrative. It is allied with another theme—his hatred of Communism, which he cheerfully admits as a "run-of-the-mill average guy" that he doesn't understand—and together they form a linked motivation which even a very unperceptive reader would begin to perceive he is going to use to rationalize his crimes at My Lai.

Page after page is filled with his animadversions, if such they may be called, on the Communist menace. These passages alternate with those which express his terror of the civilian populace, his frantic suspicion that each innocent-appearing Vietnamese may in truth be a Vietcong concealing a weapon or ready to throw a bomb.

Curiously, when describing his fear, Calley is sometimes rather effective. His fear is certainly real enough, and understandable; and in his reflections on this fear and on the omnipresence of death amid the Vietnamese landscape he achieves on one or two pages, almost as if by accident, a kind of slovenly eloquence. Surely no one acquainted with the demoralizing character of the war in Vietnam would deny the legitimacy of such a fear.

Yet long before the book's halfway point—where Calley in his inimitably charmless way has even begun to invoke General Sherman's tactics in Georgia to justify atrocities against civilians—his tone has become so hectoring, so shrill, that we simply know he is out to hoodwink us into believing that he honestly thought the Vietcong were his victims that day at My Lai. It is an ineffably shabby performance; and by the time we arrive at the end, cringing as we observe Calley try to discredit the witnesses who had appeared against him at Benning, we are able to see why he inspired in Richard Hammer such healthy revulsion.

Certainly the loathsome and festering nature of the war in Vietnam provided fertile ground for such a catastrophe as My Lai. It is a particularly iniquitous war, this criminal venture which has implanted in the hearts of our apple-cheeked young warriors such a detestation of "slopes" and "slants" and "gooks." That there have been other atrocities and other My Lais may be painful to accept but not difficult to believe. To those numerous letters he received from other servicemen confessing to their own atrocities, Calley points with distorted pride, failing to realize—just as millions of people have failed to realize—that one outrage does not expunge another. Neither does the obvious culpability of others in this horror absolve Calley, whose trial and conviction may be one of the most critically significant events of recent times, in that it has been able to show in vivid outline the extent of the degeneracy to which this war and its leaders have brought us.

Mankind is sick nearly unto death of warfare, but until that remote day when its abolition is achieved, the wars our folly leads us to will have to be fought within the framework of those sometimes inadequate but necessary laws we have shaped to govern their course. In abstract, at least, it is obedience to this principle which has so far prevented our reaping the whirlwind of nuclear destruction. It is the depth of moral stupor to assume that in the pursuit of war, barbarous as it may seem to be, we must not be bound by rigorous codes.

Few of us may be enamored of the military, but the military is both a fact of life and an institution; and like any institution—like law or business or government itself—it must stand guard against the venal, the felonious, and the corrupt. Thus to ignore the lesson of Lieutenant Calley is to ignore a crucial reality: that war is still steadfastly a part of the human condition, and that our very survival as human beings continues to depend on accommodating ourselves to ancient rules of conduct.

[*New York Times Book Review,* September 12, 1971.]

Arnheiter

Neil Sheehan's *The Arnheiter Affair* is a lively and thoroughly fascinating account of one of the most important controversies in modern American military history. The central figure of this true story, Lieutenant Commander Marcus Aurelius Arnheiter, was a naval officer of questionable ability in all departments when he was somehow given command of the destroyer escort *Vance* in the latter part of 1965. An Annapolis graduate, a fatuous worshiper of Lord Nelson, an ambitious, overbearing, thick-skinned man, he appeared to have almost none of the lambent human qualities that even the most zealous military officer must possess if he is effectively to command men, and his behavior from the outset was something less than auspicious. He made it plain that he knew little and cared less about the mechanics of running a ship, and soon established aboard a regime that Sheehan aptly describes as one of "whimsical tyranny." This extended from his insistence on saluting and upon immaculately clean daily dress—items of routine usually dispensed with on a small ship at sea—to the humiliating impromptu lectures he required of his officers after dinner, on such recherché subjects as how to use a finger bowl. A Protestant himself, he enforced (against regulations) strict attendance at his Protestant-oriented religious lectures, to the chagrin and outrage of the many Catholics among the crew. Sedulous in regard to his own creature comforts, he smoked cigars bought with money paid to a "Boner Box" by officers guilty of small infractions of the rules, and enjoyed twenty-minute showers with preciously hoarded water while the rest of the crew, bathless, sweated in the dreadful heat of the Gulf of Siam.

Arnheiter's lack of sensitivity about the nuances, the proprieties inherent in rank and privilege was almost boundless, but his official behavior as commanding officer of the *Vance* while patrolling the Vietnamese coast was even more bizarre. In a zone of the sea relatively far removed from any important enemy activity, Arnheiter was forced to resort to ever more quixotic maneuvers in order to satisfy his bellicose fantasies. He once nearly ran his ship aground as he invented targets and emplacements onshore which he claimed were "demolished" by his three-inch guns. He "annihilated" detachments of Vietcong guerrillas (they turned out to be a flock of chickens), and dangerously set out to stalk a Red Chinese submarine. Also, in a desperate spasm of *machismo,* he radioed a series of false position reports in order to give the impression of intrepid seamanship. Finally, to cap it all, the relentless skipper fabricated an engagement with the enemy in which he claimed to have performed personally with conspicuous gallantry, and dictated a totally spurious commendation, the intent of which was to award himself the Silver Star. At this point, mercifully, the *Vance* and its by now despairing and morally bedraggled crew were spared further misery. The cumulative effect of Arnheiter's conduct could not go disregarded for long even in a navy that tends to insist that its officers can do little wrong. Arnheiter was relieved of his command at Manila Bay, some four months after the excruciating, hair-raising, sometimes wrenchingly comic odyssey began.

On the level of a nautical adventure alone, Sheehan's book makes an engrossing tale. The parallels with Captain Queeg in *The Caine Mutiny* are, of course, obvious. Like Queeg—indeed, like all fanatics—Arnheiter seemed cursed with a fatal humorlessness. Whimsy, yes, but no humor. One feels that even a vestige of a real sense of humor might have allowed the bedeviled captain some insight into the more ludicrous consequences of his own monomania; and his dire self-obsession and its tragicomic effects are unfolded by Sheehan with the skill and subtlety of a first-rate novelist. But examined on another level, *The Arnheiter Affair* tells us some important and disturbing things about the American people and their relationship to the military establishment. The Arnheiter affair did not end with the captain's relief from his command in the Philippines: it only began there. For with the single-minded self-righteousness of his breed, Arnheiter disclaimed the accusations against him and mounted a vociferous campaign to exonerate himself, protesting that he had been victimized by his subordinate officers, who had slandered him with trumped-up charges. For a brief but agreeable period it must have seemed to Arnheiter that his efforts in his own behalf would bear fruit. Valiant support chugged up to his side from the left and right, from the middle, from every hand. Americans have never fully understood the role of the military in their own society, and perhaps it is their native egalitarianism that has caused the citizenry to harbor an inane and nearly indefatigable passion for whoever appears to be the underdog— witness the example of Lieutenant William Laws Calley.

Initially, Arnheiter was made to look like a martyr by the press and the other media. (Sheehan covered the story for *The New York Times,* and one of his winning points is a gentlemanly admission of his own knee-jerk liberal reaction to what then seemed Arnheiter's beleaguered plight.) Yet the captain also found some of his most ardent defenders among the high Navy brass, including an illustriously placed officer who risked and ultimately ruined his career by campaigning in Arnheiter's defense. As usual it was a case of feverish wish-fulfillment—the captain as symbol satisfying every immediate and shoddy fantasy while failing to instill in anyone the desire to inspect the hard moral and legal aspects of the issue at hand. "To the liberals," Sheehan writes, "he was a little man who was victimized by an impersonal military institution. To the conservatives, the mutinous behavior of Arnheiter's subordinates was a manifestation of the general disorder and mockery of authority that was polluting the qualities of national life." But an official review of Arnheiter's case and Sheehan's own careful investigation amply demonstrated that neither of these situations was the case. To put it in the simplest terms, the captain was exposed as a fraud and a menace.

Unlike the actions of Lieutenant Calley, Arnheiter's conduct did not result in injury or the loss of any human lives (although it clearly contributed to the mental breakdown of a crewman and helped wreck the career of at least one of the ship's officers), and consequently the case lacked some of the sensational aspects of the more recent scandal. Yet just as one of the revelations of Calley's court-martial lay in the shocking fact that a man of the lieutenant's wretched caliber and qualifications should never have been made an officer in the first place, so the Arnheiter affair demonstrated that the Navy likewise had much to answer for in justifying the promotion of an Arnheiter to such a delicate position of command. Arnheiter often appeared to be a simple clown, and the story as Sheehan has put it down does contain much comic flavor of the *Mister Roberts* variety—this is what helps make the book so consistently entertaining—but the narrative is also filled with somber and sobering overtones. The author is not being at all facetious when he speculates upon how Arnheiter's imbecilic game of hide-and-seek with the Chinese submarine might easily have helped precipitate another world war. On this plane, the Arnheiter affair no less than that of Calley demonstrates the potential for disaster that exists for us when at any level of authority there is a crucial abdication of personal responsibility, and shows the danger that is always present when even one small device in the grotesque, precariously balanced supermechanism of war we have fashioned for ourselves is handed over to cranks and fanatics.

[*American Scholar,* Summer 1972.]

The Wreckage of an American War

T he marines who fought in the Pacific during World War II had much to fear, for the fighting was often lethal and barbaric. Yet because they were marines, with an intense feeling of identity, and were caught up in that mysterious group trance known as esprit de corps, they really did assume that they were invincible. Some of this hubris came from their brutal and very efficient training, but a great deal of their deepest confidence flowed from their leaders. Their officers, both commissioned and noncommissioned, were arguably the best in the world, and of these leaders no marine commanded more admiration than a colonel with a beguilingly menacing countenance and a pouter-pigeon strut named Lewis Burwell Puller.

Puller—the father of the author of *Fortunate Son,* a dark and corrosive autobiography—was nicknamed Chesty for the aggressive thrust of his carriage; he was and still is a legend, an embodiment of the Marines in the same way that Babe Ruth embodies baseball or that Yeats stands for Irish poetry.

A native of the Virginia Tidewater, Puller was born at the end of the last century, close enough to the Civil War to be haunted by it and to be mesmerized by its Confederate heroes and victims. Like many of the high-level marine officers, disproportionately Southern by origin, who helped defeat the Japanese, Puller learned his infantry tactics while chasing and being chased by the guerrilla forces of Augusto Sandino in the Nicaraguan jungles; his spectacular exploits there won him two Navy Crosses.

During World War II, the last truly just war fought by Americans, Puller was awarded the Navy Cross two more times for gallantry under fire, at Guadalcanal and at Cape Gloucester, and his legend blossomed. Stories about him abounded. Respected extravagantly, he was also greatly feared, especially by very junior officers. It was rumored that he literally devoured second lieutenants; after all, at the gruesome battle of Peleliu, a derelict shavetail was summoned into Chesty Puller's tent and never a shred of him was seen again—he plainly had been eaten.

Puller exhibited little tact, especially with the press. In the aftermath of the deadly Guadalcanal campaign, an asinine journalist inquired, "Colonel, could you tell the American people what it is you're fighting for?" Puller replied, "Six hundred and forty-nine dollars a month." His fairness and concern for his troops were celebrated and were never so evident as during the retreat from Chosin Reservoir, during the Korean War, when as a regimental commander he led a rearguard action of such tactical mastery that it manifestly saved countless American lives; this feat won him a fifth Navy Cross and promotion to brigadier general.

As Burke Davis portrays him in his fine 1982 biography, *Marine!*, Chesty Puller, despite the glory he gained in the mechanized setting of modern warfare, was a God-fearing fighting man of the old school, cast in the mold of Lee and Jackson, both of whom he idolized. Amid the most foulmouthed body of men in Christendom he was, if not prudish, restrained in speech. Some of the letters he wrote to his wife from various exotic hellholes are poignant, old-fashioned utterances that touch on the horrors of war but speak of a longing for repose in tones of spiritual anguish reminiscent of Stonewall Jackson. After he retired to his Tidewater village, nearly two decades before his death in 1971, he was proud when his only son, born when he was nearing fifty, went off as a second lieutenant to combat duty in Vietnam. That twenty-year-old man, his namesake—the "fortunate son" of this bitter though redemptive narrative—became one of the most grievously mutilated combatants to survive the ordeal of Vietnam.

The catastrophe happened on a blazing October day in 1968, when Lewis Puller, Jr., was leading his platoon on a routine patrol through an especially sinister area of the countryside nicknamed the Riviera, a strip of rice paddies and wooded hills bordering the South China Sea. Mr. Puller had served in the combat zone for less than three months, but his activity had been intensely concentrated and appallingly violent. He had seen marines wounded and killed, had engaged in fierce firefights, had been exposed to booby traps; during an attack on a local village one of his men had inadvertently blown off the arm of an eight-year-old girl.

Mr. Puller is a gripping writer when he describes the heat and exhaustion, the physical brutalization, the incessant anxiety and danger suffered by young men engaged in that demented strife nearly a quarter of a century ago. Not without good reason he may be at his most vivid when he tells what happened to him.

That October day he stepped on a booby-trapped howitzer round and was rocketed sky-high. He "had no idea that the pink mist that engulfed me had been caused by the vaporization of most of my right and left legs. As shock began to numb my body I could see through a haze of pain that my right thumb and little finger were missing, as was most of my left hand." In addition, the explosion destroyed massive parts of both buttocks, ruptured an eardrum, split his scrotum, and sent slivers of shrapnel through most of the rest of his body.

Hovering near death for many days, Mr. Puller developed a stress ulcer that required the removal of two-thirds of his stomach, augmenting the already intolerable pain. Transported stateside, he remained for nearly two years at the Philadelphia Naval Hospital, where, through the early phases of his stay, he was utterly helpless and so dependent on morphine that when he was briefly taken off it he was, as he says, "quickly reduced to the level of a snarling animal." When his weight dropped to less than sixty pounds and his stomach resisted food, he was given nourishment through a nasal tube.

These pages exude the whiff of authentic hell and are, accordingly, sometimes difficult to read. But because Mr. Puller writes with simplicity and candor, with touches of spontaneous humor, his outcry of agony and isolation, while harrowing, leaves one primarily overwhelmed with wonder at the torture a human being can absorb this side of madness.

Slowly the worst of the torment receded and slowly the recuperative process began: skin grafts, reconstructive surgery, endless hours on the operating table, all enacted in a continuum of diabolical pain. He regained some extremely limited use of his mangled hands, but the efforts to restore mobility to his legs through prosthesis, while tireless, were in vain; he would have to spend the rest of his life in a wheelchair. There were compensations, however, for his sacrifice: his face was unscathed and his basic senses, including his eyesight, remained intact. So did his sexual functioning. His young wife, who was pregnant when he went off to Vietnam, presented him with a son. Escaped like Ishmael from the vortex of oblivion, he had a future and also, clearly, a tale to tell.

Fortunate Son is an amazing tale, but in many ways an artless one, with great cumulative power yet more compelling as a raw chronicle than a work offering literary surprises. If its prose does not resonate as does Philip Caputo's eloquent *Rumor of War,* if the book lacks the surreal wackiness and scathing insights that made Michael Herr's *Dispatches* such an original tour de force, its act of bearing such passionate witness to a desecrated moment in history has its own importance and gives it a place among the meaningful works on the Vietnam nightmare.

As for Mr. Puller's future, it seemed in certain respects almost as calamitous as the experience of war. He acquired a law degree and an ambition to run (as a Democrat) for a congressional seat in Virginia. By this time he had undergone the same traumatic insult as numberless veterans whose brother and sister Americans detested them for an event they conceived to be the handiwork of the warriors themselves. Smarting at this mad response but in a rage at the war and its real instigators in Washington, he made his feelings public, proclaiming that if he were called up again he would refuse to go.

Such statements, coming especially from the son of Chesty Puller, did not go down well in a state as profoundly hidebound as Virginia, where Mr. Puller also was rash enough to choose to run in a district bordering Hampton Roads—the very marrow of the military-industrial complex and a busy hive of patriots ill-disposed to contemplate any such paradigm of the monstrousness of war.

His image as a horribly maimed veteran, rather than inspiring compassion and patriotic rapport, aroused resentment and guilt among the voters and plainly contributed heavily to his defeat. Then he slid into perhaps his deepest peril yet. He had always been an enthusiastic drinker, but shortly after his political loss his dependency became overpowering; he subsided into the near-madness of alcoholism, becoming so deranged and incapacitated that he came close to killing himself. With the help of Alcoholics

Anonymous he recovered, and his wretchedly difficult but successful climb out of still another abyss makes up the rest of *Fortunate Son,* the coda of which culminates in a revealing irony: apparently at peace with himself and the world, Mr. Puller is currently a senior attorney in the office of the general counsel of the Department of Defense.

Or the irony may not be so striking after all. Throughout the book one senses in Mr. Puller a hesitation, an ambivalence about the Marines that he seems unable to resolve. About the Marine Corps, he wonders at one point how "I could love and despise it with such equal ardor." This tells much about the powerful hold that military life, at its most idealistic, can have upon thoroughly decent men, quite a few of whom are capable of complex quandaries and apprehensions about what they are called upon to do.

What Mr. Puller was called upon to do was to fight in a war that never should have begun, but once begun tainted the souls of all those connected with it. Yet the quality of devotion sometimes inexplicably and maddeningly remains. Just before the famous gathering of 1971, when protesting Vietnam veterans planned to discard their medals on the steps of the Capitol, the author debated agonizingly with himself before putting his medals back in the closet.

"They had cost me too dearly," he writes, "and though I now saw clearly that the war in which they had been earned was a wasted cause, the medals still represented the dignity and the caliber of my service and of those with whom I had served."

It would be wrong for flag-wavers to misinterpret these words and cheer Mr. Puller's nobility, and just as wrong for those who reflexively condemn all wars to read them as the sentiments of the enslaved military mind. Like his father, who served heroically in several just wars—or at least understandable ones—Mr. Puller was a professional engaged in what many men of good will still regard as an honorable calling, and one likely to remain so until wars are made extinct; yet he was too young and too unaware, at least at the beginning, to realize the nature of his involvement in a national dishonor.

His father, Mr. Puller notes, came home twice from the Far East in triumph, while his own reception was one of scorn and jeers. The old man, he writes, almost never gave vent to his deepest emotions. But no wonder Chesty Puller finally wept, looking down at his legless and handless son, wreckage of an American war in which random atrocities would serve as the compelling historical memory, instead of the suffering and sacrifice, and for which there would be no Guadalcanal or Iwo Jima, no Belleau Wood, no Shiloh or Chickamauga.

[*New York Times Book Review,* July 16, 1991.]

A Father's Prophecy

In July 1943, I had just turned eighteen and had been a private in the Marine Corps for about five months. The American war against the Japanese and Germans had not yet reached the halfway point. The look of innocence and optimism on my face, in a photograph I have preserved from that time, reminds me of the similar expressions I've seen on the faces of some of the young marines preparing for combat in Saudi Arabia. I recall having little real fear of being wounded or killed—that fear came later on. The conflict in the Pacific was still far off, and while there had been some terrible battles, with many Army, Navy, and Marine casualties in the Solomon Islands (and large Army losses in New Guinea and the Aleutians), the carnage was a remote abstraction to me; besides, I was eager to test my manhood. I couldn't know that the worst was yet to come.

For most Americans World War II was suffused by an authentic love of country, reflecting matters of necessity and idealism that were far more scrupulously defined than those of the war in the Persian Gulf. There have been grievous moral deficiencies on both sides in the war with Iraq. This was not the case in that other war, a Manichaean collision of good and evil which probably allowed America its last moment of true decency. In those years we felt almost physically defiled: our security had been menaced, our survival was at risk, our national soil had been violated by the Japanese atrocity at Pearl Harbor, which had left nearly 2,500 Americans dead. (There was Hitler, too, but we marines gave little thought to the European war, which was an Army and Navy operation.) Beautiful ideas like courage and sacrifice and pride had thrilling resonance for American kids, especially one like me who had pined to become a marine long before Hirohito became a household name. Culture and tradition merged in me to generate a surging passion for military honor. But to this day I don't find such passion freakish or even unusual. Despite the niceties concerning peace and peacemaking, our society has always possessed a bloodthirsty streak, encouraging most boys to cherish the arts of war and to relish becoming legal killers.

More than once I heard my father, who sheltered the spirit of a poet-philosopher within the person of a naval engineer, say with acid distaste that America's natural destiny was war. He should have known because war roosted like a bad memory in our family's past—my grandfather had been a fifteen-year-old Confederate soldier, two great-uncles were killed in that conflict—and the steely hand of the military touched every corner of our environment. This was in Virginia, the most bellicose of American states (not excepting Texas) and in a part of the commonwealth so thoroughly militarized that by the mid-1930s it resembled an armed encampment. Within twenty miles from home were the Norfolk naval base and air station, Langley Field (now Langley Air Force Base), the Army Transportation Corps facility at Fort Eustis, the coast artillery base at Fortress Monroe, the naval mine depot at Yorktown, the naval shipyard at Portsmouth. These places, in the midst of the Depression, brought a measure of local prosperity. My father was both dependent on the military and bruised by it—he was basically a peace-lover—and it made him a prophet.

I'll never forget his high moment of prophecy. He was employed by Newport News Shipbuilding, then as now the largest private yard in the nation, where as a middle-level engineer he helped create such behemoths as the aircraft carriers *Ranger, Yorktown, Enterprise, Essex,* and *Hornet.* One of my luscious childhood memories is of being taken to the launching of *Ranger,* the first American carrier built from the keel up, and of watching the wife of the president, Mrs. Herbert Hoover (whose slip was showing), make three attempts at bashing a champagne bottle over the ship's prow before she succeeded, drenching herself in a sacrament of foam. The shipyard adjoined an apartment building where we lived and where the bedlam from riveting hammers and pile drivers and other machinery caused my mother hectic distress. As if this noise weren't enough, there was often the roar of the new B-17s—the Flying Fortresses—as they climbed out of Langley Field, sometimes joined by the racket of naval fighter planes, and on one such hot summer day my mother had been driven frantic. Ordinarily a patient and reasonable woman, she began to complain bitterly of the ghastly noise, its effect on human beings, the waste of money, the chaos, the futility—all, she said, to maintain a bloated military establishment in peacetime. My father, usually so gentle with my mother, erupted, calling her an ostrich, blind to reality. "We are preparing for *war!*" he exclaimed with a gesture toward me. "For a war which I pray our son will survive and—if we're lucky—wars our grandchildren will survive, too. War, my dear, is the destiny of this nation—was, is now, and ever shall be. We will be fighting wars *forever*—as long as we have the money and the guns!"

Those prescient words still give me a chill. At the time they scared me. Still, my father's rage and apprehension didn't prevent me from signing up as a marine not many years later, making me an eager apprentice in one of the wars he had so accurately predicted. I was an officer candidate. To become a second lieutenant in the Marine Corps seemed to be the most elegant destiny in the world. Much of the giddy crush I had on the Marine Corps derived, of course, from the sheer glamour of the outfit. I longed to be among the toughest and the best, these hellraising leathernecks with their grand history of machismo and martyrdom—and there was also the uniform. Countless young men have been lured to their deaths by the promise of a sexy uniform. The gold bars, the smart blouse of forest green, the mirror-bright cordovan shoes, the trim barracks cap with the braided quatrefoil—such dash would cause a splendid flutter among the bevy of girls one hoped to conquer while home on leave. But that brief lull would be a pathetic trade-off for the reality of Pacific combat, with its dirty dungarees and horror, which loomed more threatfully close when I did finally receive my commission in the summer of 1945. The war against Japan had produced murderous pandemonium, and there were few of us second lieutenants who were not conscious, sick to our souls, of the fate of our fellow fighting men at two recently concluded slaughters: Iwo Jima (Dead: Americans, 6,800; Japanese, 20,000) and Okinawa (Dead: Americans, 12,500; Japanese, 135,000). I became a connoisseur of such appalling statistics.

My comrades and I were spared the fate of so many others by an incandescent event of history: the atom bomb. It was while I was in training to lead a platoon of riflemen in the invasion of the Japanese mainland that the cataclysm occurred. Had the war not terminated with such a prodigious bang, my platoon would almost certainly have been participants in that final bloodbath (Predicted dead: Americans, 100,000; Japanese, upward of 1,000,000). During the quiescent time that immediately followed my return to civilian life the idea of war seemed so inconsequential that my father's augury faded from my mind. Peace seemed to stretch out into the limitless future. The hiatus, however, was but an historical split second; the conflict in Korea commenced in 1950 and I, who had been reckless enough to remain in the reserves, was called back to active duty. Softened and sweetened by peacetime pleasures, I was no longer the gung-ho marine and in near-disbelief I struggled for long nightmare months in the swamps of North Carolina, relearning infantry tactics I would use in the killing of—or in being killed by—a new and ferocious Asian enemy.

My luck held out. I was released from duty because of an eye defect, and as the upheaval on the Korean peninsula receded in time it seemed significantly less a just war than World War II, and one I felt no guilt in having been excluded from, though good friends died at places like the Chosin Reservoir and though I experienced anguish over the eventual carnage (Dead: American, 33,000; South Korean and U.N., 75,000; all Communist forces, in excess of 2,000,000).

I was too old for the war in Vietnam, but it aged me nonetheless. My father's bleak pronouncement on that summer day returned over and over again as the war in Southeast Asia unfolded throughout a decade. The sons of friends were killed; my soul felt snapped during those ugly years. It was an unutterably sordid catastrophe (Dead: Americans, 58,000; South Vietnamese, 99,000; North Vietnamese, at least 1,000,000) and it so undermined the American Dream that it did seem scarcely possible that we could allow in our lifetime another such death-happening.

But now as I set down these reflections I see the grave faces of the boys in the Arabian desert—faces luminous and attentive like mine was over four decades ago—and I realize with a shock that these kids are the age, not of my father's grandchildren, but of his great-grandchildren, and that if he were alive today he would have lived to see his harsh vision not merely made true but realized in ways beyond his darkest imagining. He would have been verified in his belief that war was the destiny of America and he would have wondered, as I do now, how many young human beings of whatever nation would ultimately be fitted into those bleak parentheses historians use to list the warrior dead. Perhaps few, perhaps many, but in any case it will be a prophecy fulfilled.

[Previously unpublished. Styron wrote this essay in February 1991 at the invitation of *Life* magazine. It was to be part of a special issue on the upcoming full ground invasion of Iraq during the Persian Gulf War. The issue was canceled when a cease-fire was negotiated in March 1991. The text here is taken from the surviving typescript, preserved among Styron's papers at Duke University.]

Prisoners

The Death-in-Life of Benjamin Reid

T he Connecticut State Prison at Wethersfield is a huge, gloomy Victorian structure whose very appearance seems calculated to implant in the mind of the onlooker the idea of justice in its most retributive sense. It is one of the oldest prisons in America. Uncompromisingly somber, the penitentiary suggests not only that crime does not pay but that whosoever is a wrongdoer is quite conceivably beyond redemption. On death row, the condemned cells were built for an epoch when, after a man was told he must die, the supreme penalty was administered far more swiftly than in these present days of interminable legal postponements. Each cell still measures only seven by seven feet, implying momentary residence. A strong electric light shines in the face of the condemned all night and all day. The condemned are not allowed to communicate with one another, and until very recently, were denied even the solace of an earphone radio. To live on death row at Wethersfield is in effect to dwell in solitary confinement until the day of one's execution. As I write these words (mid-October 1961) the state of Connecticut is preparing to kill a twenty-four-year-old felon named Benjamin Reid. Reid is no Caryl Chessman.[1] As a matter of fact, he is subliterate and possesses an intelligence which, if not so low as to be called defective, can only be described as marginal. The condemned at Wethersfield are allowed to read and to write letters, but it is doubtful that Ben Reid has availed himself much of these privileges; and this is a circumstance which must have made his confinement all the more forsaken, because Reid has lived in the presence of the electric chair for four years and three months.

On a bitterly cold night in Hartford in January of 1957, Ben Reid, who was nineteen at the time, waylaid a middle-aged woman in a parking lot and beat her to death with a hammer. His avowed and premeditated motive was profit (the woman was a friend of his mother's and had been known to carry large sums of money with her), but this aspect of his crime he so ruinously botched that he got nothing. Over $2,000 was discovered on the woman's frozen body, which Reid in his final panic had jammed into a car. It would appear that Reid scarcely bothered to conceal his tracks, fleeing to the home of a relative in New Haven, where he was found in short order by the police. He seemed rather relieved to be caught. He made several confessions, and in the summer of that same year, was brought to trial by jury in the Superior Court at Hartford. The trial was a fairly brief one, as murder trials go. On June 27, 1957, Reid was sentenced to die by electrocution. He was taken to Wethersfield (a suburb of Hartford, and except for the eyesore of its prison and several small factories, a lovely elm-lined New England town) and there in his tiny cell, brightly illuminated night and day, he has been for more than four years, awaiting what must be, for him, the ever present but always undiscoverable moment of his death.

There is, of course, no such thing as absolute justice, but even advocates of capital punishment will grant that when a human's life is at stake, there should be the closest approximation of absolute justice the law can attain. In terms of absolute justice, to make evident the reasonableness of Ben Reid's execution for murder it would have to be proved that his crime was morally more reprehensible than a similar crime for which some other murderer received a lesser sentence. There have been, and still are, murderers whose crimes repel us by their violence and brutality quite as strongly as does Ben Reid's. Some of these criminals have been put to death as creatures past salvation; more frequently sparing their lives, the state has sentenced them to serve a life term, with the possibility of parole, or a number of years, and by this relative leniency has granted, at least theoretically, the rather more lucid assumption that some men's crimes are not so depraved as to place them forever beyond redemption. But the logic of this random choice is as fearful as it is mysterious. The wickedness, the inherent immorality, of any crime is a quality which it is beyond the power of any of us to weigh or measure. Ben Reid's crime, however, has been weighed, and Reid himself has been found completely and irrevocably wanting. Neither absolute justice nor any kind of justice, so far as the eye can see, has been served. It might be interesting to learn something about this young man, and perhaps discover why the state has judged him irredeemable, past hope of recovery.

Warden Lewis E. Lawes of Sing Sing, an expert foe of the death penalty, once said that in order to be executed in America a person had to be three things: poor, a man, and black. He was speaking of the North as well as the South. He was also admittedly generalizing, if not being somewhat facetious, for a great many white men and a few women of both races have, of course, been executed, and on exquisitely rare occasions the state has taken the life of a criminal of wealth. But the implication of his remark, it is safe to say, is borne out by the statistics—North and South—and Ben Reid fills the bill: he is a poor black man. To read of his background and career is to read not only of poverty and neglect and a mire of futile, petty crime and despair, but, in the end, of a kind of wretched archetype: the Totally Damned American. If one wished to make a composite portrait of the representative criminal upon whom the state enacts its legal vengeance, one's result would be a man who looked very much like Ben Reid. Like his victim, who was also a Negro, he was born in a dilapidated slum area on the north side of Hartford. When he was two his father died, leaving his mother virtually destitute and with several children to support besides Ben. These years toward the end of the Depression were bleak enough for a large number of Americans; for people in the situation of Ben Reid and his family the times were catastrophic and left ineradicable scars. When Reid was almost eight his mother got into a shooting scrape and was grievously wounded; she was left crippled for life and partially paralyzed. At this point Reid was forced to enter the Hartford County Home, and there he remained for eight years. He was not alone among his family to become a ward of the People; during the time he was at the county home his twin brother was committed to the state hospital for the insane at Norwich, while an older sister, adjudged to be mentally deficient, was sent to the Mansfield State Training School. Most children are released from the county home at the age of fifteen, but since no one wanted Reid, he received the dispensation granted, in special cases, to the totally unwanted and was privileged to stay an extra year. One pauses to speculate, hesitates, goes on, feeling presumptuous (there is no other word) as one tries to imagine Ben Reid's thoughts during this weary, bedraggled era. He was never too bright, so probably—unlike other adolescents somewhat more richly endowed in mind as well as circumstance—he entertained no Deep Thoughts about life at all. To Reid, coming out of oblivion into this existence which, so far as one can tell, had seemed to guarantee the unfulfillment and frustration of every ordinary childish yearning, life must have begun to appear simply and demonstrably lacking in significance. Lacking in significance, it must necessarily have lacked any values whatever, and it is not at all surprising that Reid, soon after he was sent away from the county home, began feloniously and empty-headedly to trifle with those values in life which society so highly regards.

When the county home finally discharged him, the nation was experiencing a time of prosperity such as no country has ever seen, but very little of this abundance rubbed off on Ben Reid. For a year or so he was shunted from one foster home to another; he went hungry again from time to time, and there were occasions when he was reduced to foraging from garbage cans on the backstreets of Hartford. It was during this period that Reid had his first brush with the law, in an involvement which has come to seem numbingly typical of his age and background: he was caught acting as a runner for a narcotics peddler, and for his offense was placed on probation. A few months later he tried to rob a store, hopelessly bungled the endeavor, and was sentenced to serve a term in the state reformatory at Cheshire. It is apparent that he was in no way reformed. However, it may be said that after his release from the reformatory, an episode occurred in Reid's life which tends in some small way to alleviate the harshness and ugliness of his career until then. He met a girl. She was a few years older than he, but they began seeing each other and presumably fell in love, and they were married in 1956. It might have been an answer to Reid's trouble, but it wasn't. He was unable to get a job. Not long after their marriage Ben began to brood about money and commenced hitting the wine bottle. His wife apparently did her best to straighten him out, but these efforts led to nothing. She was pregnant and had just left him when Reid, thinking about money, went out into the snow that night and committed the crime for which he is now scheduled to die.

Often, it seems, what appears to be justice is merely a shadow image of justice, determined by queer circumstances which can only be discerned in retrospect. This sinister element in the law might alone be enough to cast final doubts upon the infliction of the death penalty; for only under conditions of absolute justice—a kind of aseptic legal vacuum completely invulnerable to fleeting social panic, hysteria, shifts in public temper—could we presume to condemn a man utterly, and absolute justice nowhere exists. It of course cannot strictly be proven, but it seems at least probable that had Ben Reid not come to trial at the particular time he did, he would not have been condemned to die. The reason for this conjecture is the existence in Hartford at that same time of two particularly vicious criminals: a huge, lantern-jawed ex-con and ex-resident of death row named Joseph ("The Chin") Taborsky and his moronic accomplice, Arthur Culombe. Taborsky, who was a psychopath of fearfully sadistic dimensions, and Culombe, a kind of torpid, blinky-eyed caricature of the dim-witted henchman, had finally been apprehended after a series of holdup-murders which had terrorized central Connecticut and, quite literally, sent many of the people of Hartford in off the streets. A notable feature of their *modus operandi* was to make their victims kneel down at their feet before shooting them. Taborsky and Culombe had been dubbed by the newspapers, with scant originality though in luminous headlines, "The Mad Dog Killers," and when they came to be tried there can be no doubt that the public, which attended the trial in droves, was in something less than a mood of composure. Ben Reid was tried at the same time and in the same building. His mother, crippled and woefully concerned, was the only spectator on the first day of the trial, when the jurors were sworn in, and except for Reid's wife and one or two interested onlookers, remained the only spectator until the trial's end. The People's interest was in the Mad Dogs, not in Ben Reid. There seems little doubt that the Taborsky-Culombe affair next door, with its public hubbub and its reverberant atmosphere of mass outrage, did nothing to help Ben Reid's case, and in fact subtly contaminated his own courtroom with the odor of vengeance.

The trial, as I have said, lasted only a few days. Reid's defense was almost nonexistent; he had, after all, killed someone with what in the legal sense is surely malice and premeditation. His defense counsel (since Reid had no money, this job fell to the public defender) made strenuous efforts in his client's behalf, outlining his squalid background and the nature of his upbringing. But the jury (Respectability in its pure, concentrated essence, disarmingly mild-eyed and benign, like a Norman Rockwell tableau: five Christian housewives and among the rest, as might be anticipated in Hartford, a clutch of insurance adjusters) was not terribly moved. Testifying in his own behalf, Reid seemed confused. Once when asked why, after his first blow, he continued to strike the woman, he replied that she had seemed to be suffering so that he wanted to put her out of her pain. Now, asked the same question by the prosecutor, he could only mumble hopelessly, "I don't know. I started to shake. I lost control of myself. I didn't want her to die." In his final summation, the prosecuting attorney expressed a few personal regrets but went on to add that we must not be swayed by the fact of a person's sordid environment; after all, some of our most valued citizens have struggled up to eminence from the lower depths, fighting their way to fame and fortune, ladies and gentlemen, while people like this criminal sitting here, etc. It had the echo of a thousand courtrooms: Look at Al Jolson and Eddie Cantor. Look at Joe Louis! It was the old American death-cry, and there is no reply to it, save the negative one, to be spoken in a whisper, that when life is an issue we have no God-given right to measure the gallant strength of a few men against the imponderable weakness of a foundling like Ben Reid. The jury was asked if it would like to retire and deliberate right away, or if it would like to have lunch first. It replied that it would like to have lunch. After it fed itself it retired and came back with the verdict in a little over an hour. As happens with rather enigmatic frequency in capital trials, the judge flubbed the reading of the death sentence. In setting the date of execution, he said, "the year 1958," instead of "the year 1957," and the entire pronouncement, for the record, had to be read over again. Up until this time Reid had showed very little emotion during the trial, except for the moment when the prosecutor began to describe his crime in its bloody detail, at which point, in a gesture which can only be described as childlike, he furiously clapped his hands over his ears. Now perhaps he felt that the judge was damning him twice. At any rate, he broke down and wept.

One curious fact which tends to underline the basic senselessness of capital punishment is the way in which we are regularly brought into touch with an evil apart from the nagging, chronic, yet somehow endurable distress which the death penalty itself causes us: this is the almost unendurable incongruity it manifests in its choice of victims. If in Caryl Chessman, for instance, we were confronted with a plucky, dogged, intelligent man (so intelligent, in fact, as to have blurred in the minds of many people the nature of his morality, which was that of a cynical, self-justifying hoodlum; he verged as close to an embodiment of the perfect son of a bitch as the mind can conceive) who possessed the right at least to the possibility of redemption, in Ben Reid we are faced with a man so egregiously lacking in gifts, so totally desolate in circumstance, in quality of mind and spirit, that though he bears an almost antipodean relationship to Chessman as a man, we find ourselves questioning by this very contradistinction his implacable abandonment by society. Of course, the facts of heredity and environment cannot be allowed completely to eliminate responsibility and guilt. Reid's crime was an appalling one—one of such blind ruthlessness that it should have been apparent at the outset that he must be removed from the community until that time when it might reasonably be made certain that he could take his place again among his fellow men. Failing this approximate certainty, it would have to be made sure that he was incarcerated for good. But here we are not speaking of correction. We are not even speaking of that reasonable punishment which might carry with it vitalizing connotations of remorse and contrition. We are speaking of total abandonment. Perhaps not so wise but no less unfortunate than Chessman, Reid too had been judged beyond salvation. It is this abrupt, irrevocable banishment, this preemption by the state of the single final judgment which is in the providence of God alone— and the subtle but disastrous effect this act has upon the whole philosophy of crime and punishment—that wrecks the possibility of any lasting, noble concept of justice and causes the issue of the death penalty to become not peripheral, but central to an understanding of a moral direction in our time.

Against an awesome contemporary backdrop of domestic trouble and crisis, and the lingering image of concentration camps, and the threat of mass annihilation, the case of Ben Reid might seem an event of such small moment that there is hardly any wonder that it has commanded no one's attention. It is a case little enough known in Hartford, much less in the state of Connecticut or the broad, busy world. If it is true that crime in general, save in its most garish, tabloid aspects, fails to gain our serious regard, it may also be said that the question of capital punishment commands even less interest on the part of thinking people, especially in America. It becomes one of those lofty moral issues relegated to high school debates. To most thinking people, crime is something we read about at breakfast. The infliction of the death penalty, even further removed from our purview, is a ceremony which takes place in the dead of night, enacted, like some unnamable perversion, in shame and secrecy, and reported the next morning, on a back page, with self-conscious and embarrassed brevity. Our feelings are usually mixed; conditioned by two decades of James Cagney movies, and the memory of the jaunty wisecrack when the warden comes and the last mile commences, few of us can escape a shiver of horrid fascination which the account of a man's judicial execution affords us. But the truth is that few of us, at the same time, are left without a sense of queasiness and discomfiture, and indeed there are some—not simply the quixotic or the "bleeding hearts," as Mr. J. Edgar Hoover describes those who abhor the death penalty—who are rendered quite inescapably bereft. "For certain men, more numerous than is supposed," wrote Albert Camus, "knowing what the death penalty really is and being unable to prevent its application is physically insupportable. In their own way, they suffer this penalty, too, and without any justification. If at least we lighten the weight of the hideous images that burden these men, society will lose nothing by our actions." This is not alone an interior, personal viewpoint which would subvert a general evil in the name of delicate feelings; Camus's other arguments against capital punishment are too fierce and telling for that. The fact remains that all of us, to some degree, are spiritually and physically diminished by the doctrine of legal vengeance, even though it manifests itself as nothing more than a chronic, insidious infection beneath the public skin. We need only the occurrence of a sudden Chessman, flaunting his anguish like a maddened carbuncle, to make evident the ultimate concern we have with our own debilitating and corrupting sickness. That we do not discuss this problem until a Chessman appears is only an indication of one of our most ruinous human feelings—our inability to think about any great issue except in the light of the unique, the glamorous, the celebrity. Chessman was indisputably unique as a criminal and as one condemned; it is not to demean that uniqueness to declare that we shall never resolve the issue of capital punishment until we ponder it in terms not alone of Chessman, but of Ben Reid.

It is more than likely that apathy about the question is generated by the knowledge that capital punishment is on the decrease. With great pride the commonwealth acknowledges that, on the average, it now exterminates only about fifty people a year—like stars on a flag, one for each sovereign state. A common attitude might be articulated in the words of *Time* magazine, which said during the Chessman affair: "If opponents of capital punishment were patient enough, they could just sit back and wait for it to fade away—in practice, if not on the statute books. But abolitionists try to hasten that fade-away by argument." Aside from the fact that very few evils have been hastened into extinction without the benefit of incessant argument, such a statement represents a blindness to the profounder truths which seems to seize *Time* at intervals. There is very little patience among men who are waiting to die. "To sit back and wait for it to fade away" is of small consolation to the "160 or so" people (including Ben Reid) who *Time* in the same article stated were awaiting execution on death rows all over America at the time of the Chessman affair. I do not know how *Time's* writer visualized the number 160—if indeed he tried to visualize it at all: larger than fifty maybe? less than a thousand? As for myself, the more I ponder 160 condemned faces, the more the number acquires a queerly disproportionate hugeness, and to use any phrase which implies such a gradual, far-off diminution seems to me, quite simply, a triumph of indifference.° Moreover, I am not at all sure that capital punishment will in fact fade away, as long as Mr. J. Edgar Hoover, the guardian of our public morals, has any say in the matter.

Mr. Hoover, according to a news item last June in the *New York Herald Tribune,* for the first time in his long career as our premier law-enforcement officer, has allowed himself, in what I suppose must be called a policeman's trade journal, to proclaim his belief in the efficacy of the death penalty. The article went on to describe the particular malfeasance which had impelled Mr. Hoover to take this position. It was a singularly hideous crime. A California woman, who happened, incidentally, to be pregnant, enticed a little girl of six into a car. There in the woman's presence her thirty-year-old husband raped the "screaming" child, who thereupon was bludgeoned to death by the wife with a tire jack. Apprehended and tried swiftly, the man was sentenced to die in the gas chamber, while his wife received life imprisonment. Past any doubt this was a deed so horrible as to tempt one to view it almost metaphysically, as if it were enacted in a realm beyond even abnormal behavior. All of our emotions are unhinged, displaced, at the contemplation of such a monstrous crime. As Anthony Storr, writing in a recent issue of the *New Statesman,* remarks: "To rape and murder a little girl is the most revolting of crimes. It is easy to sympathize with those who feel that a man who could do such a thing should be flogged or executed. . . . We think of our own young daughters and we shudder. The child rapist has alienated himself from our society, and we want to eliminate him, to suppress him, to forget that he ever existed."

° In 1982, there were nearly 1,000 American prisoners on death row. Although actual executions have decreased, the number of condemned has vastly increased, and the United States remains the single major Western nation in which the death penalty not only exists but is on the march.—W.S. (1982)

Yet as one thinks about the *Herald Tribune* article and the crime and, more particularly, Mr. Hoover's attitude toward it, it seems evident that in lending his great prestige to the furtherance of capital punishment and, moreover, in using this particular case as an example of its presumed "efficacy," Mr. Hoover (who, after all, is not a law-giver, but a law-enforcement officer) is committing a two-fold error. Because where one might say, *purely for the sake of argument,* that the death penalty was effective in preventing such crafty and meticulously deliberate crimes as kidnapping for ransom, or treason, or even the hijacking of airplanes, one would be almost obliged to admit, if he had any understanding of criminal behavior, that its value in a crime of this type was nil. For the two wretched people who perpetrated this outrage were not, in any sense of the word, rational, and clearly not susceptible to rational controls. To believe that by taking away the life of even one of these sickening perverts we shall deter others from similarly mad acts is demonstrably a false belief: only one conceivable end is served, and that is vengeance, an emotion which—instinctive as it may be—society can no longer afford. As Anthony Storr goes on to say: "It is also important that we should not simply recoil in horror, but that when we catch the child rapist we should study him and the conditions which produced him. In that way only may we be able to . . . offer help to those who are driven by similar desires. . . . You and I may imagine that we could never rape a child and then murder it: but, if we are honest with ourselves, we have to admit that even this potentiality exists within us. We do not know what internal pressures drive the rapist, nor what conditions determine his dreadful acts. But he cannot be regarded as a different kind of animal with different instincts; for he is also human, and subject to the same laws and the same forces which determine the desires of every one of us. It is tempting to treat him as something utterly foreign from ourselves and so avoid looking into our own depths. . . . To condemn him as inhuman is to fall into the trap of treating him as he treated his victims: as a thing, not a person, a thing on whom we can let loose our own sadistic impulses, not a fellow creature who might, even yet, be redeemed."

At this juncture, whether we are viewing a child rapist or Ben Reid, we are admittedly faced with problems that do not lend themselves to ready solutions. For one thing, there is the familiar question: "Wouldn't Ben Reid, when all is said and done, be better off dead if he had to serve a life sentence in prison?" This, or something like it, is a commonly heard sentiment, often uttered by people who are compassionate and well-meaning. But in the end it only emphasizes a corollary evil of capital punishment—the equally vengeful notion that there is no alternative to the death penalty save a sentence of perpetual incarceration. Significantly, if it is true that a life term with no hope of parole is worse than death (and one cannot help but agree that it may be worse), it becomes necessary to ask why we do not sentence our most villainous offenders to life, reserving the death penalty for lesser criminals. But more importantly, to assume that short of killing a man, we must doom him to a lifetime behind prison walls is to succumb to the doctrine of retaliation in its most hateful sense; and it is the practice of capital punishment more than any other single factor that tends to blight our administration of justice and to cast over our prisons the shadow of interminable revenge and retribution. Now, it would appear that some criminals are hopelessly incorrigible. Taborsky would seem to be mad or half mad, or, though sane within the legal sense of the word, seemingly devoid of any kind of understanding of right or wrong; from these people it would certainly be clear that we must protect ourselves by keeping them behind high walls forever. At the very least, as Anthony Storr points out, we can study them and learn why they and their kind behave as they do. A majority of criminals, however—including those whose deeds have been quite as ugly as Ben Reid's—are amenable to correction, and many of them can be, and have been, returned to society. As for Ben Reid, in arbitrarily inflicting upon him the sentence of death, in denying him even the chance of rehabilitation that we have just as arbitrarily granted others, we have committed a manifest injustice; and the death penalty, once again, reveals its ignoble logic.

It has been argued that opponents of capital punishment are swayed by emotion, that they are sentimental. To the degree that sentimentality may be considered a state of mind relying more upon emotion than reason, it would seem plain that it is the defenders of the death penalty who are the sentimentalists. If, for example, it could be proved that capital punishment was an effective deterrent to crime, even the most emotionally vulnerable, die-hard humanitarian would be forced to capitulate in favor of it. But, unable to fend off the statistical proof that it is no deterrent at all, proponents of capital punishment find themselves backed into a corner, espousing emotional, last-ditch arguments. In the present instance, its lack of deterrent effect may be shown in the fact that it did not deter Ben Reid. Even more strikingly it is true in the case of the terrible Taborsky, finally executed, who had barely escaped electrocution for murder once (he was released from death row on a judicial error and freed from prison), whereupon he committed the series of brutal slayings I have mentioned. If it is evident that Taborsky should never have been released into society, it seems almost as clear that he is a case in point of that theory, proposed by a number of serious observers, that the death penalty in significant and not too rare instances actually exerts a fatal lure, impelling certain unbalanced people to crimes which ordinarily they would not commit. (In a recent English case one Frederick Cross of Stockport, near Manchester, said in testimony: "When I saw the man in his car I got the idea that if I was to kill him I would be hanged. . . . I don't wish to be defended at all. I killed him so that I would be hanged." The victim was a complete stranger. Cross achieved his desire: he was hanged.) Finally, in order to make reasonable the argument that capital punishment is a deterrent, why is it that the public is not incessantly exposed to its horrible finality, forced to witness the barbarous rite itself, and thereby made to reflect on the gruesome fate awaiting malefactors? But it remains a secret, shameful ceremony and except for the most celebrated cases, it is even indifferently reported in the press. Until by legislative mandate all executions are carried on the television networks of the states involved (they could be sponsored by the gas and electric companies), in a dramatic fashion which will enable the entire population—men, women, and all children over the age of five—to watch the final agonies of those condemned, even the suggestion that we inflict the death penalty to deter people from crime is a farcical one.

Shorn of all rational, practical arguments, those who favor the death penalty must confront those who would eliminate it upon the solitary grounds of vengeance, and it is here, upon these grounds and these grounds alone, that the issue will have to be resolved. There is no doubt that the urge for revenge is a strong human emotion. But whether this is an emotion to be encouraged by the state is a different matter. As for Ben Reid, how much actual vengeance society still harbors toward him can only be a matter of conjecture. It would be a disgrace to all of us to say that it could be much. Having dwelt in his seven-by-seven cell on death row, as I have said, for over four years, he would seem to have endured such a torture of bewilderment, anxiety, and terror as to make the question of vengeance academic. Since that day in June 1957 when he entered his cell on death row, there have been numberless writs, reprieves, reversals, stays of execution, all carried out in that admirable spirit of Fair Play which marks American justice but which, like a pseudosmile masking implacable fury, must seem to a condemned man pitiless and sadistic beyond any death sentence. A year and a half ago, indeed, it appeared that Ben Reid would have his opportunity for redemption; the judge of the U.S. District Court vacated his conviction on the grounds that his trial had been "fundamentally unfair" because the police had exacted his confessions without informing him of his rights to counsel or, for that matter, of any of his rights. At this point Reid's attorney told him the good news: it looked as if he was going to live. This past September, however, the U.S. Circuit Court of Appeals in New York took a different view: since counsel had not brought up the point of illegal confessions at the trial, Ben had in effect "waived his rights." Thus the lower court was overruled—not without, however, a vigorous dissenting opinion by one of the justices, Judge Charles E. Clark, onetime dean of the Yale Law School, who said that the view that Reid waived his rights "borders on the fantastic in any human or practical or, indeed, legal sense." Reid has just recently been granted a reprieve, until April 30, 1962, in order that his case may be argued before the U.S. Supreme Court. Especially in the light of Judge Clark's angry dissent, it seems likely that Reid's case will at least be accepted for review. Whether by these nine old metaphysicians, as Mencken called them, the legal point will be resolved in Reid's favor remains, as usual, a mystery. In any event, for Reid it has been a splendid ordeal. His present lawyer (who, incidentally, is also a Negro) has protested to the state, asking his removal from the tiny cell. After four years there, he contends, Ben's mind has badly deteriorated. Nowhere else on earth is a man dragged by such demoralizing extremes to the very edge of the abyss.

"The little man, despite the pratings of Democracy," Judge Curtis Bok has written of the death penalty, "is still the scapegoat." And he added this observation: "Someday we will look back upon our criminal and penal processes with the same horrified wonder as we now look back upon the Spanish Inquisition." Should the U.S. Supreme Court turn down his appeal, I am told that there is an outside chance at least that Ben Reid—due to those considerations of environment and mentality which his lawyer initially argued for in vain—may have his sentence commuted by the State Board of Pardons. This is highly unlikely: the Board of Pardons has never yet commuted a death sentence of a man convicted under the same Connecticut law. But there is a chance. If this comes to pass and Reid is allowed to live, he will gain, aside from the fragments of his life, an ironic kind of victory: nothing could demonstrate more cruelly the travesty of justice which is capital punishment than this shabby and belated mercy, predicated upon the identical arguments which were advanced in his favor in a court of law nearly five years before. On the other hand, should the fact if not the spirit of justice be served, and Ben Reid goes to the electric chair one night this spring, it may be said that the soul which is taken will already have been so diminished by our own inhumanity that what shall be lost is hardly a soul at all, and that the death penalty—having divested a man not alone of his life but of that dignity with which even the humblest of men must be allowed to face death itself—has achieved its ultimate corruption. *Or when saw we thee sick, or in prison, and came unto thee!* It is perhaps a late date in history to summon up the Gospel in behalf of a derelict Negro boy; having abandoned him, it does not become a Christian society to waste a shred of its jealously guarded piety upon him whom it has cast out into darkness. Only the condemned can truly know the heaviness of guilt, it settles upon their spirits like the weight of all the universe, and the quality of their bereavement is solitary and unique among humankind. To attempt to soothe this bereavement through Christian homilies would seem to be, like that final promenade with the chaplain whispering from Holy Writ, an act of outrageous hypocrisy. Yet somehow, try as we might to evade the verdict, we find ourselves being measured: *Inasmuch as ye have done it unto one of the least of these my brethren, ye have done it unto me.* Until, searching our hearts, we can reconcile these words with the murder we inflict, in the name of justice, upon Ben Reid, and his fellows likewise outcast and condemned, we stand ourselves utterly condemned.

[*Esquire*, February 1962.]

Benjamin Reid: Aftermath

The administration of criminal justice in Connecticut is unique in really spectacular ways. Although in many practical respects, of course, the state is among the most advanced in the union, there are aspects of its criminal code which echo that of Sicily in the fifteenth century. Connecticut is one of the few states in the United States which vest pardoning power in a board. Its Board of Pardons, established in 1883, consists of five responsible citizens appointed by the governor with the advice and consent of the state Senate. Fundamentally, the concept of a separate board was well-intentioned, in that it removed the awful responsibility of the pardoning power from a single man (and also from the political arena), while at the same time it placed that power in the hands of a body of people better equipped in terms of both time and experience to judge each individual plea. Yet insofar as a condemned man is concerned, the existence of a board of pardons constitutes an unprecedented and, it might be said, almost intolerably cruel paradox. For where in other states the governor could be expected to exercise his power of commutation by granting clemency without ceremony on any day far in advance of the date of execution, the Connecticut Board of Pardons sits as a sort of second, final tribunal, and it convenes on the morning of the day that the condemned man is scheduled to die. Thus, as the minutes tick away toward the fatal evening the condemned man, who is likely to be present at the proceedings, is forced to endure what amounts to the simulacrum of another trial, sweating out this ultimate, ghastly ritual whose climax is the proclamation, quite irreversible, either of mercy totally belated (else why not mercy in the beginning?) or of immediate death. Society has perhaps conceived of nothing quite so subtly undermining to the soul since the Inquisition.

But this is not all Ben Reid would have to endure at the hearing. He would have to endure the knowledge that in over ten years the Board of Pardons had not once commuted the sentence of a man convicted under the 1951 law. This was not due necessarily to a failure of mercy; it was due rather, once again, to failure of the Connecticut law, which in criminal matters is so freakish and capricious as to stun the reason, and at best is permeated by the kind of stubborn, ominous reverse logic that haunts *Alice in Wonderland*. It doubtless begins with the fact that Connecticut, unique in so many ways, is the only state in the United States (and indeed probably the only jurisdiction in the civilized world) that does not consider its first-degree life prisoners to be eligible for parole. This in turn results from a state of mind which assumes all murderers (who are in reality overwhelmingly better parole risks than forgers and thieves) to be a species of uncontrollable brute likely to run amok in the streets. (Even second-degree murderers get a tougher break in Connecticut than anywhere else in the United States. The average time served for second-degree murderers before parole in Connecticut over a recent eleven-year period was the highest in the nation: eighteen years, vs. ten years in California and eight years in New Jersey.) Further, in 1951, in a well-meaning effort to rid the state of an archaic law calling for mandatory execution in all convictions for first-degree murder, the legislature passed an act (mentioned above), now in effect, which states: "Any person who commits murder in the first degree . . . *shall* suffer death *unless the jury* . . . recommends imprisonment in the State Prison for life, in which case the sentence of the court *shall* be imprisonment for life without benefit of release. . . ." (Italics mine.) In actuality, this statute was an enormous step backward, and its consequences need to be explained. One of the results of the act—without precedent in any state in the union—is loony and nightmarish in the extreme: what it means is that a first-degree murderer *must* be sentenced to a sort of living death without any possibility whatever of release, or that he *must* be sentenced to actual death, like Reid, whereby he stands at least a chance to live through intercession of the Board of Pardons, and in such a case is likely to be eventually paroled. Here the dilemma and anguish of our contemporary attitudes toward punishment reach their mad climax. Under such circumstances, what convicted felon would not opt for the sentence of death? Even so, his chances to live are only theoretical, since the Board of Pardons—which under the mandatory-death-penalty statute felt free to commute death sentences to life imprisonment when they thought that the nature of the case demanded it—has been understandably reluctant to overrule a jury which, representing the will of the people, had had two sentences from which to choose. Therefore, no person condemned after the 1951 act in Connecticut has ever had his sentence commuted by the board. It was mainly because of this complex and wholly irrational situation that thoughtful observers were not giving Ben Reid much of a chance.

The hearing took place last June 25. It was public, and it began promptly at ten o'clock in an airy, spacious, newly painted conference room on the second floor of the administration building of the state prison at Wethersfield. It was a beautiful, sunny day, hot but tolerably so because of a pleasant breeze, and through the windows one could see the great elms and neat lawns of the town of Wethersfield, and watch children bicycling along the streets, so that the effect—save for the presence of two or three guards— was hardly that of a prison at all, but of a meeting room in some New England school or college. The irony was almost too explicit: it did not seem either the day or the place to ponder death. At the far end of the room, at a table perhaps twenty feet long, sat the five members of the board—two lawyers, a judge of the state Supreme Court, a professor emeritus of political science at Wesleyan University, and a physician. All men in their fifties and sixties, they were gray-haired, solemn, and distinguished-looking; indeed, several of them so combined steely-gray handsomeness and juridical gravity that they seemed ready to be cast as judges in a movie. They were also, as I say, extremely solemn, almost forbidding in manner, Connecticut Yankees to a man, and I had the distinct feeling that mercy might be wrung from their hearts, but only under mighty compulsion. The spectators—sixty or so in all—sat on hard chairs at the other end of the room. Between spectators and the board there was another table, and on opposite sides of this table sat members of Reid's counsel, who would argue for clemency, and the state's attorney and his aides, who, presumably, would present reasons why Reid should be executed.

Shortly after ten, Reid was brought in by a guard. Dressed in freshly pressed prison khaki, shirt open at the throat, he was a tall muscular young Negro, and his face seemed to me curiously impassive and expressionless as he slumped down into a wooden armchair. I realized with a start that he was the first person I had ever seen whose death seemed almost inevitable and only twelve hours away.

Now, it should be said here that no longer was Reid completely friendless and alone, as he had been during the five years he had spent in his condemned cell. Since the previous winter, after a young Trinity College student named George Will had learned of Reid's predicament and imminent execution, an extraordinary amount of activity had been organized in his behalf. Will had written an impassioned letter which was published in the college newspaper. This had resulted in a committee, composed of three Trinity faculty members, three members of the Trinity administration, and six students, which had set about energetically during the ensuing months to try to save Reid's life. The committee was headed by George Will and Albert E. Holland, the latter the vice president of Trinity College and a man who might be expected to have rather severe strictures about capital punishment. Holland had spent several years in a Japanese prison camp during World War II and had endured more than one bad moment when his custodians began promiscuously lopping off heads. Like such vocal opponents of capital punishment as Arthur Koestler and Jean-Paul Sartre—who suffered similar experiences in Spain during the Civil War and for whom the issue of the death penalty has grim personal relevance—Holland was no quixotic adventurer, and his efforts to save Reid had consumed a large part of his time for over four months. With other members of the committee, Holland had dug deep into Reid's past. It had been a past of nearly monumental poverty and neglect, and much information about his squalid upbringing, it is important to note, had not been admissible as evidence at Reid's trial. The committee had pored over dozens of the melancholy records and documents scattered back through almost all the years of his wretched career— welfare records of the Reid family; juvenile-court reports; records of the Hartford County Temporary Home, where Reid had spent eight of his youthful years, and those of the state reformatory where he had also been lodged for a time; psychiatric reports and trial transcripts and records of Reid's unsuccessful appeals to higher courts. They had also interviewed a score of people who had been associated with Reid at one time or another—

parole officers, social workers, officials of various welfare and correctional institutions where he had spent the greater part of his life. In addition, the committee had engaged itself in a great deal of legal research: even on the surface of Reid's case it had been shockingly apparent that, in terms of equality of justice, his death sentence had caused him to be a singular victim in more than one respect, and the exhaustive, meticulous investigation which the Trinity group made of capital cases in the state over a period of forty years brought forth some remarkable conclusions, best expressed in a single statement made in the bulky mimeographed dossier which the committee presented to the board that morning: "Our study shows that prior to 1957 [the year of Reid's conviction] the State of Connecticut had not even tried on a first-degree murder charge, let alone sentenced to death, a person like Benjamin Reid who at the time of his crime was an adolescent, with a mental capacity of an eleven-year-old child, with a most unfortunate family heritage and background, and with no previous record of violence."

Now as we sat in the hot, still meeting room, it was Holland's task to present these facts to the board. One of the first persons he called to testify also made one of the most dramatic pleas of the day. This was Robert Satter, a prominent Hartford lawyer who had followed Reid's post-trial career with an abiding interest. It had for a long time been Satter's belief—shared by others—that of the multitude of injustices surrounding Reid's conviction one of the worst was that involving the sinister connection between Reid and the notorious mass-murderer Joseph Taborsky. It was Satter's contention that it had been the public furor and vengeful outcry attending Taborsky's trial that had infected Reid's own nearby courtroom and similarly sealed Reid's fate. A mild, scholarly-looking, sandy-haired man, Satter asked the board to consider a literary allusion. "You may recall the conclusion of *Moby-Dick*," he said, "how, as the ship *Pequod* sinks beneath the waves, the arm of a sailor appears from the depths to hammer a pennant against the mast. Just as the nail is being driven home, a gull flies by, and its wing, interposing itself between hammer and mast, is nailed fast to the spar, so that the final glimpse of the doomed ship is this bit of fluttering life being dragged with it into the deep." There was nothing histrionic about Satter and his manner; his words were splendidly afire. Pausing, he gestured toward Reid. If Benjamin Reid should die this night, he continued, his life, like that of Melville's gull, would have been sacrificed just as surely as if the arm of Joseph Taborsky had reached from the grave to drag him down into oblivion. It was a marvelously delivered speech, all in very low key, and when Satter had finished there was a long, rather uneasy silence in the room.

The first hour or so of the general plea, including Satter's statement, was based on the question of equality of justice, and Holland had plenty of statistics at hand to show that the state of Connecticut had granted clemency or given lesser sentences to many criminals whose background and mental capacity were infinitely superior to Reid's, and whose crimes had often been far more cold-blooded and ruthless. But this was only the first part of the plea. Now, as the morning lengthened, Holland began to call witnesses to testify to Reid's fearful and blighted upbringing. There were a dozen or so in all, and they included a Negro policewoman who had been assigned to the slum area where Reid had been reared (she described the section as a "jungle"), various welfare workers and parole officers who had known and worked with Reid, and finally, a gentle-spoken middle-aged white woman named Mrs. Neva Jones, who had been the nurse at the Hartford County Home during the eight years Reid was there, and who had flown up from North Carolina to be present at the hearing. Partly due to the fact that he was at first barely literate, Reid had corresponded with no one during his long and lonely stay on death row, but late in 1961, as his execution approached, he and Mrs. Jones began to exchange letters. Excerpts from his letters were read at the hearing. They were remarkable, in style often resembling nothing so much as that of a man who in a general sense was quite lost but on the verge of a miraculous verbal discovery (actually, as he told Mrs. Jones, his main reading matter had been the Bible and a dictionary): "In your most recent letter you made mention of my vocabulary as being increase, well the reason is due to the fact that I do read quite a bit, and by doing this, I feel that I can express myself more clearly logically speaking, by studying neologistical expressions excerpted from the different literature I study." But there was no doubt, as Holland pointed out to the board, that the letters were those of a man profoundly conscious of his wrongdoing ("I do not want sympathy, I just merely want a chance to show everyone that I have reformed and repented of my wrong that was done thoughtlessly senselessly") and, even more important, were the expression of one struggling toward some kind of enlightenment. There was an unconscious irony in one questioning statement, which might sum up the thoughts of condemned, miserable, desolate, guilty men everywhere: "I know that I have done wrong but have I done worse than the worse or am I the worse period."

As the hearing began to draw to a close between noon and one o'clock, and with Reid's moment of execution only hours away, I became uneasily aware that all through the proceedings one member of the board had been in the habit of gazing abstractedly for long periods out the window. But there was no diminution of attention among the audience when the final witness appeared: Reid's mother, badly crippled with an arm adrift from her side like a helpless wing, who said, almost inaudibly, "I ask you, would you grant him life, please"; and Reid himself, who stood stiffly in his khaki uniform in a strained, awkward half-bow and, his voice almost a whisper, made a brief plea for mercy.

The next-to-the-last presentation was made by Louis Pollak, professor of law at Yale, who capped even this morning's mountainous evidence of injustice with a brilliant analysis of the possibility of constitutional infirmities in Reid's case. He pointed out that although it was true that the United States Supreme Court had declined to hear Reid's appeal, there had been, in the long history of the case as it proceeded from court to higher court, enough dissent and doubt (as to whether Reid's rights had been violated) on the part of a few distinguished jurists to make it incumbent upon the board to consider this grave aspect of the case before consigning Reid to oblivion. It was a masterly plea, and it seemed difficult to surmount in terms of force and effect, but it was at least equaled by the presence of the final person to speak. This was a tall, athletically built, trimly tailored man, very grim, who approached the board and formally identified himself as Judge Douglass Wright. He had been the prosecutor in the original Reid trial and has since become a judge. The hearing room was utterly still, for this was a spectacle almost unique in American jurisprudence: a prosecutor interceding in behalf of the prisoner only hours before his doom. Wright was brief and to the point: there was no doubt of Reid's guilt; the trial had been conducted with strict fairness. But such factors as Reid's youth at the time of his crime, his slum background, his marginal mentality, had caused Wright, in the years since the sentence of death, to feel that execution would be an injustice. He joined therefore with the others in making a plea for clemency.

After this, the case for the state seemed almost anticlimactic. The state's attorney, John D. LaBelle, an owlish, methodical man who kept shuffling through his notes, was quick to indicate in the strongest terms that Reid had been guilty, that in this "classic case of first-degree murder," justice, insofar as the state was concerned, had been done. But, like Judge Wright, he conceded that the board, constituted to dispense mercy, might grant such mercy in this case, and he added, "Whatever you do, it isn't going to upset our office one bit." The proceedings were ended. The board would announce its decision at three o'clock that afternoon.

Downstairs in the prison reception lobby a large group of God's underground, the Quakers, had assembled. They numbered a score or so. Some of them had attended the hearing, and all of them were now prepared to participate that night in a vigil at the prison should the appeal for clemency fail. I spoke to one Quaker, a Hartford businessman. "We will pray for Reid," he said, "which is all we can do." He began to speak with a kind of fury for a Quaker. "It is a fearful thing, isn't it? What right has the state to coop up a man—a boy—in a tiny cell for five years, and then exterminate him like a dog?"

Outside, the day was still blooming with summer and sunlight, and along the streets of Wethersfield, one of the supremely lovely New England towns, the children were still pedaling their bicycles. I met Louis Pollak; he was chatting with the Reverend William Coffin, Jr., the chaplain of Yale University, who had taken a personal interest in the Reid case. We were joined by Mrs. Jones, and the four of us decided to have lunch in a coffee shop on one of Wethersfield's elm-lined streets.

At lunch, Mrs. Jones, seeming only a little nervous about the outcome of the appeal, said, "Oh, I knew Ben real well. He was a sort of lonely little boy. And a bit lazy, I guess. But there was nothing mean about him. He was really so proud of himself whenever he accomplished anything good. You know, he was a trombone player and assistant leader of the band. He was a good trombone player, too. I'll never forget how proud he was, dressed up in that band uniform."

"How long did you know him, Mrs. Jones?" Coffin inquired.

"Oh, the whole time he was there. It must have been eight years. Imagine, eight years in the County Home! I guess he was sixteen when they let him go. But, you know, he wasn't *ready* to go back—back to that terrible slum. It's society's fault, really. I mean, all of us. People should know more about this situation, where these poor abandoned children are taken in for a while, and then sent back just at the wrong age to that awful environment. It's just a shame, really, and people should know about it."

At around two o'clock, as Coffin and I drove back to the prison, we saw Reid's mother. Quite alone, she was hobbling laboriously down the deserted, elm-shaded sidewalk in front of the prison toward a small sheltered enclosure that serves as a bus stop. There she sat down and began to fan herself. Coffin went up and greeted her. It was rather difficult to make conversation but I couldn't help asking where she was going.

"Well, I expect I'll just go on home," she said. "The Lord done answered my prayers, so I expect I'll just go right on home."

"Then you think the hearing went well?" I said.

"Well, I figures if they was going to do anything they would say so at the end of it. But they ain't said nothing, so I figures they going let Benjamin off, praise God. I knew Ben has repented, so the mercy's coming to him. The Lord sure done answered my prayers."

Of course, she hadn't gotten this quite straight, and no one seemed to have advised her of the board's operations, but neither Coffin nor I, exchanging glances, could figure out a way to correct her. In the end it didn't seem to matter, for as she left us with these words and the bus came lumbering up, I had the feeling for the first time that day that all was going to be well.

The decision, which came to the gathering in the reception room of the prison at 4:05, was that Reid's sentence had been commuted to life imprisonment, with the possibility of parole. There would be no necessity for the Quakers to keep their vigil. And a rent had appeared in the veil of immutable law.

It is of course important that Reid's life was saved. It is more important that he will not be left to rot. Whether the five years spent in the shadow of the electric chair have worked irreparable damage upon his spirit is something no one can say for sure, but judging from his letters alone, there is a sense of something struggling and questing, and therefore salvageable. At some time in the future he will be eligible for parole, and in the meantime the Trinity group has pledged itself to help him in his search for an identity. It may be said perhaps that in prison a man's identity cannot be much, but we who are on the outside looking in—we who are so prone to forget that all men must be given at least the possibility of redemption—are in no position to judge. Not only capital punishment, but all punishment in general, is one of our most crucial dilemmas; the death penalty is the wretched symbol of our inability to grapple with that dark part of our humanity which is crime. Equally as important as Reid's own salvation is the fact that his case and the struggle to save his life, which attracted so much attention, will have caused people to rearrange entirely their ideas about some of our penal and criminal processes. Certainly the law in Connecticut in regard to capital offenders is archaic and monstrous; and already, largely as a result of the Reid case, there is talk in some circles about pressing in the legislature for a "triple verdict" law, now in effect in California and Pennsylvania (1, to determine guilt; 2, to determine sanity; 3, to determine sentence), which will permit evidence to be introduced at trial that was generally denied to Reid, this denial contributing greatly to the fact that he was initially sentenced to death. If just this act is accomplished, Reid's anguish will not have been in vain, and the simple victory won that afternoon in Wethersfield—the victory of life over death—will have been transformed into something even larger in our unending search for justice.

[*Esquire*, November 1962.]

Aftermath of "Aftermath"

This may be a good place to examine briefly certain aspects of the power of the written word. I have never wanted to claim credit for having saved a man's life, but as I was reminded years later by George F. Will (the "young Trinity College student," mentioned in "Aftermath," who has become a celebrated national columnist), the original essay did have the effect of causing the Trinity people and others to spring into action. So I suppose it may be inferred that had I not written the original essay, Ben Reid would most likely have gone to his doom. On a somewhat less dramatic note, I was pleased to learn that the second piece I wrote on Reid had the effect of changing the Connecticut law regarding capital punishment along the lines I detailed in the concluding passage. Robert Satter, now a judge, whose wonderful speech about *Moby-Dick* still lingers in my memory among the bright moments of that day, later became a state legislator. It was he who, taking a cue from my article, introduced legislation that eventually brought about a more equitable procedure regarding capital offenders. So I felt that my initial ventures into journalism had hardly been wasted time.

But what about Benjamin Reid? Rereading the two pieces I wrote on his case, I became aware of how important to my argument against the death penalty was the Christian doctrine of redemption. This interests me now, because I thought that by the time I was past thirty-five—at the very least agnostic and surely swept by the bleak winds of existentialism—I had abandoned the Presbyterian precepts of my childhood. But I can see that the Gospels were as much a mediating force in my attempt to save Reid's life as were Camus and Heidegger. And how sweet it was to see this candidate for redemption come alive from his benighted dungeon in a way that would quicken the heart of any Christian salvationist. How beautiful it was to witness this outcast victim flower and grow, once rescued and given that chance for which those honest Quakers had prayed on their knees. For the simple fact is that Ben Reid—now that he was snatched from the electric chair and released into the general prison population—demonstrated qualities of character, of will, and above all, of intelligence that defied everyone's imagination. All of the people connected with Reid's case had been deluded about his mental capacity, which was as much a victim of having been underestimated as Reid himself was a victim of foster homes and deprivation. Far from being the borderline defective he had been described as by many observers (including myself), Reid, it turned out, was quite bright, in certain ways even brilliant, and the metamorphosis he underwent in prison was something to marvel at. He became a star baseball player, a leader among the inmates; he secured his high school equivalency diploma, began to take college work. A model prisoner he was—in every sense of that worn and risky description. A triumph of faith over adversity. Maybe someday a winner.

Reid spent eight more years in prison before his time came up for parole. In the middle of March 1970 I received a telephone call from some of the people at Trinity College who had taken an interest in Reid and had followed his career through prison. It was highly probable that Reid would be paroled in April, they said. What they proposed to do was enroll Reid as a special student at Trinity, where he would begin courses at summer school. Would I be willing, they wondered, to let Reid stay in my house in Roxbury for a few weeks while they put things in order at Trinity and began to ready a permanent place for him there? My willingness would be a not inconsiderable factor in obtaining the parole. I immediately replied that I would indeed take Ben in. Although I had never visited Reid in prison, we had corresponded quite a few times over the years since his commutation. His letters were well-reasoned, grammatically correct, persuasive—so impressive, really, and showing such signs of growth and blossoming that I could not stop reproaching myself for having helped cast him as mentally deficient. A week or so before he was to be released into my custody, I visited him in the new state prison at Somers, near the Massachusetts border. I was impressed by his poise, his verbal agility, his warmth, his intelligence. The idea of my studio in Roxbury becoming Ben Reid's halfway house filled me with pleasure, and I understood the blessings of redemption.

Early in April, only a few days before the magical date, Reid walked off into the woods from a work detail just outside the gates of the prison. An alarm was sounded, and Reid was pursued by state police with dogs, but his trail was lost. After a night in the woods, during which time Reid had strayed into Massachusetts, he lingered through the early daylight hours outside a house in Longmeadow, a well-to-do, semirural suburb of Springfield. Reid found an automobile antenna and sharpened it into a weapon. He then entered the house where a thirty-seven-year-old woman was preparing breakfast for her two young children and the child of a friend. Forcing the woman and the children into her car, he made her cruise up and down the Connecticut River Valley for a large part of the day. At one point during the abduction, Reid told the woman to drive into the parking area of a deserted state park. There, he raped her. (In subsequent testimony some conflict developed as to whether there was an element of consent on the part of the woman, but this would seem to be an almost frivolous point.) Later on in the day, after the woman had driven him to Holyoke, he boarded a bus for New York but was spotted by a prison official and was quickly arrested. Tried that summer in Springfield for an assortment of crimes—including rape, kidnapping, forcible entry, and assault with a deadly weapon—Reid was sentenced to ten to fifteen years in state prison. These horrible, bizarre, and seemingly improbable events took place twelve years ago. At this writing—in the spring of 1982—Reid is approaching the end of his sentence at the Bridgewater facility in southeastern Massachusetts. This is a medium-security prison where, as before, he has been a model inmate. At the age of forty-four, he has spent all the years since the age of nineteen behind bars. Could it be—as I suspect—that Reid's frantic flight from freedom was a way to ensure staying incarcerated?

In the summer of 1981, when Jack Henry Abbott—Norman Mailer's protégé—knifed to death a young aspiring playwright on a Lower Manhattan sidewalk, a tempest of public rage roared around Mailer's head. Had it not been for Mailer's misguided zeal—it was said—had it not been for the

sentimental ardor which impelled him to espouse the freedom of a murderous convict simply because he displayed a literary gift, this terrible
crime would not have taken place. Well, yes and no. There was no doubt
that the tragedy happened, that it would not have happened had Abbott
remained in prison, and that Mailer was a critical factor in Abbott's release.
But as I replayed over and over again those ugly events, I could find no
possible way—with the memory of Ben Reid's own near-release into my
custody so immovably fixed in my mind—to condemn Mailer for his role in
the awful story. There were significant differences, of course. For one
thing, Reid had escaped before his parole took effect, although this is an
academic point. Unlike Abbott, Reid had displayed no artistic talent worth
nurturing; he had seemed to be merely an attractive and salvageable
human being who had behaved well in prison (unlike Abbott, who, whatever the motivation, had killed a fellow inmate). Then, too, their last
crimes on the outside had been of different magnitudes—manslaughter
even in this day being an atrocity greater than rape.

Nonetheless, the similarities of background were wickedly familiar:
broken homes, poverty, neglect, abuse, foster parents, and the loathsome
taste of incarceration at an early age. And years and years of the inhumanity of prison life. It is hardly possible to feel anything but revulsion for both
Reid's and Abbott's ultimate crimes, but it is plain that each crime in its
way was the result of perceptions wrenched and warped by the monstrous
abnormality of long imprisonment. An almost unbearable fact here signals
for attention: both Reid and Abbott were in prison as *children*. Much was
made during the Abbott case about the alleged romanticism of writers in
their conjunction with prisoners; some of us have been called, with a certain appropriateness, "jail groupies," and certainly there are writers who
have had to answer for their silly love affairs with criminals. But I am quite
sure that romance alone does not explain the fascination or the constant
devotion that many writers pay to those that live half-lives behind bars. Remembering one's own Elysian childhood in juxtaposition with that of Reid
and of Abbott, I think it is fair to say that a concern for either of those
wretched felons has to do less with romanticism than with a sense of justice, and the need for seeking restitution for other men's lost childhoods.

It could be argued that the power of the written word, effective in
helping to save Ben Reid from death, had the unanticipated and certainly
pernicious result of causing a suburban housewife terror and suffering. So

there we are. Do we abandon our efforts to salvage prisoners because of the savage acts of Reid and Abbott? Almost as important is the question: Do we indeed now abandon Reid and Abbott themselves? As for the first question, neither Mailer nor I would have acted as big brothers—or as surrogate fathers, or role models, or simple sponsors—to these men had we known what they might perpetrate on two innocent people. But daily throughout this country prisoners whose records are every bit as flawed with violence as Abbott's and Reid's are released into freedom, and maintain clean records thereafter. Such a statistical consideration was not in my mind when I vouched for Reid (nor do I imagine it was in Mailer's), but our mistakes were committed within limits already well established by precedent. Therefore—speaking for myself alone—I can feel (and at times have felt) aching regret, but no guilt. We are neither the first nor the last to be shattered by this dilemma. And others will make fearful errors in helping their disadvantaged brothers seek redemption.

But, finally, do we abandon Jack Abbott and Ben Reid? Since Abbott was sentenced to fifteen years to life for his New York crime, he would now seem to be placed beyond any such consideration, at least for the time being. Reid's case is considerably more simple, since in only a few more years he will have paid his debt and will go free. When I asked Robert Satter—who had invested almost as much time as anyone in working selflessly in Reid's behalf—what he felt when he first heard of the escape and the rape, he replied that he experienced a sense of utter betrayal. So, I must confess, did I, and I have often wondered what might have been the consequences for me and my family had Reid—suffering the emotional upheaval that caused him to erupt so violently—actually taken up residence with me as planned. In my grimmest imaginings I could not help thinking that he might have raped my daughter instead of the Longmeadow housewife. Yet—and I can only try to dream of the stoicism it required—Satter immediately went to Reid's aid again during the Springfield trial, offering legal and moral support to a man whom most people might have written off for good.

My own sense of betrayal has been strong, but not so complete that I have been able to turn my back on Reid's destiny. His conduct in the Massachusetts prison system has been once more, as I say, exemplary, and even if he has to serve a year or two more in Connecticut for his escape (he is hoping to be pardoned from this), it will not be long before he is free, after more than twenty-five years. It will doubtless become a difficult matter for Reid to adjust to freedom, and his return to society will have to be monitored with delicacy and care. But hope persists. I have talked to Ben Reid several times; he speaks of his remorse and his repentance, and of his conviction that he will make good on the outside, and I cannot explain why I believe him.

[Written by Styron for *This Quiet Dust* and published first in the 1982 edition of that collection.]

The Joint

Twenty years ago, when he was thirty, a talented white college-educated jazz pianist named James Blake found himself serving a two-year sentence in the Duval County jail in Jacksonville, Florida, charged with petit larceny and breaking and entering. It was his first experience at doing time, and although Blake was absurdly out of character as a criminal type and, by his own admission, the world's most inept burglar, he discovered that confinement offered such sovereign satisfactions and fulfillments that he caused himself to be incarcerated at the Jacksonville jail or, even more happily, at "The Joint," the Florida State Penitentiary at Raiford, for thirteen of the next twenty years.

Blake's work—a collection of letters written to various friends, including two writers he had come to know and who had befriended him, Nelson Algren and James Purdy—comprises a vivid and illuminating chronicle. It is one of the most wickedly entertaining of its kind, a thief's journal that reflects the mordant, droll, nervously sensitive consciousness of a man for whom prison was far less a purgatory than a retreat, a kind of timeless, walled Yaddo for the gifted misfit.

Since the Marquis de Sade there has been a paucity of significant prison literature and there have been too few articulate recorders of prison life. In our own time, save for the work of Jean Genet, writings by and about prisoners have not often surpassed in quality the level of the Sunday supplements.

Our legacy of inside accounts has tended to be characterized by garishly colored tall tales about escapes from Devil's Island, pedestrian reminiscences by celebrity cons, death-row sensationalism on the order of *The Last Mile,* and characteristically American examples of uplift and redemption, such as *The Birdman of Alcatraz.*

Many of these are well-meaning and even informative but often grossly lurid and, in any case, lacking the perceptions and insights necessary to render the prison environment and the lives of its victims with the complexity they deserve. There has been much earnest sociology, some of it readable, useful polemics by knowledgeable observers like John Bartlow Martin, and sympathetic accounts by such humane officials as Warden Lewis E. Lawes and Warden Clinton T. Duffy, who despite their sincerity and compassion retain the point of view of the overlord, the Establishment.

To some extent, this situation resembles that of the historiography of American Negro slavery. Of those "many thousand gone," only a few such eloquent witnesses as Frederick Douglass, William Wells Brown, and Josiah Henson (all ex-slaves) survived to tell us what it was truly like to live under that unspeakable oppression. In particular Douglass, a superb psychologist who would be horrified to observe the foolishness being purveyed about Negro history by many present-day black militant intellectuals, knew that slavery (which to an important degree resembles prison in that both are closed, totalitarian systems) could foster rebelliousness and the wildest desire for freedom in the breasts of many men while at the same time the very ruthless and monolithic nature of its despotism might, in certain circumstances, wreck the personalities of other men, making them supinely content with bondage, eager and happy to genuflect before authority.

Like slavery, prison life is an abominable but nonetheless human situation in which men will respond to their predicament in diverse ways that still reflect their individuality and humanity. It is a measure of the excellence of James Blake's work and the grace of his survival that he has given us a record that is both an enormously revealing chronicle of life behind walls and a fascinating self-portrait by a man who continues to be steadfastly an individualist, telling his own truths.

Like Genet, Blake is both a prose stylist of distinction and a homosexual; the incandescent homosexual activity of prison life is of course the preoccupying concern—the obsession—of Genet and the entire jailhouse mystique of carnal love is a large element in Genet's recidivism, as, at least implicitly, it is for Blake. But here the resemblance ends. Genet is a visionary and a mystical genius, and Blake's gift, however beguiling, is a minor one. Then, too, his voice, unlike that of the Frenchman whose tone is passionately embroiled, remains detached, ironic, witty, lyrical.

If Genet is the rhapsodist of criminals and their greatest metaphysician, Blake is an artificer in light verse, the criminal's best satirist, a sardonic voice that is often surprisingly poignant—one is somehow reminded of Chaplin. An epistolary collection runs the risk of monotony, however; the reader begins to detect that solitary, self-concerned, droning sound. One of the strengths of Blake's letters is their consistent readability, the secret of which is a lilting, rueful, bittersweet awareness of the sheer monstrousness of things, and a gift for hilarity in the midst of a depiction of grim events that blows like a fresh wind through the pages and keeps them mercifully cleansed of self-pity.

Blake is especially brilliant in his descriptions of his fellow convicts— both the "straight" ones and those with whom he is having homosexual relationships—and often writes with a fine novelist's canny eye for detail, incorporating so much in a brief passage that its resonance, physical and moral, haunts one bleakly long afterwards:

> So now I am back on the J-Range where I feel more comfortable, and my cell partner is a check artist from Maryland who has been ostensibly rehabilitated to the extent that he is leaving on parole next week. Glib, devious, sadly shallow and incredibly beautiful, the Narcissine mirror that goes everywhere with him has prevented him from absorbing anything. (He was locked up with David Siqueiros in Mexico City and could only shrug when I asked him about it.) He claims he is the way he is because his mother held his hand in the fire when she caught him stealing. She should have put his head in the fire. No no no, that is quite wrong. He has been amiable, pleasant and almost completely absent, it has been like coming together with a Popsicle. Put the blame on the cosmos, put the blame on Mame. His prognosis, murky, and what is not?

Or, describing another relationship, Blake indulges his flair for extravaganza:

> I'm sharing a cell now with a young cat sentenced to the chair for gangbang. He's a beautiful child, a little solemn sometimes, which I guess is

allowable under the circumstances. He asked me what I thought Eternity was like, and all I could offer was a guess—an Olivia de Havilland movie on television. . . . In a laudable attempt to dodge the thunderbolt (his case is on appeal) he has been improving each shining hour by hitting the Glory Road with the travelling bands of flagellants that haunt the jail—Holy Rollers, Mormons, Baptists, Anabaptists—and he has become an Eleventh Hour postulant in the Seventh Day Opportunists. These pious acts swing a lot of weight, such is the Kingdom of Heaven. Bless the boy, he's far too beautiful to go down for such a flimsy transgression, and I hope he makes it. The Holy Ones have a lobby in Tallahassee that don't quit.

Yet I should not want to give the impression that the tone of these letters is one of unalloyed facetiousness in the face of adversity, for Blake is a profoundly serious writer, and the jocular tone often is merely a decorative gloss upon insights that are original and startling: "I remember a black lover I had. . . . Our arrangement was an eminently workable one. We were aware that the powerful attraction we felt was because we were bizarre to one another, and we were also aware that hate was just as much present as love in our relationship. That was a really swinging affair, no nonsense at all. Not a hell of a lot of conversation, but then there wasn't much time for it, either."

But why is it that so many felons return to The Joint, abandon freedom in favor of prison's seductive lure? We know through their own confessions that many men—more than is comfortable to think about—have murdered for the very reason that they were aware that the consequence of their act would be the noose or the electric chair. If this alone is almost sufficient justification for the abolition of the death penalty, it would likewise seem that the hunger, the visceral longing, the truly quivering nostalgia that Blake, representing so many other men, felt for The Joint when away from it would be sound enough reason to abolish the institution of the prison itself. More than once Blake committed crimes—chiefly burglary as a result of the need for drugs—through a barely subliminal impulse to achieve his reincarceration; it is this mighty urge to return to the smooth, amniotic surroundings of The Joint—where all things are provided and the tensions of a too-often-terrifying and monstrous outer world are erased—that Blake anatomizes better than any convict before him and, together with the theme of homo-sexuality with which that urge is so closely connected, helps give the book the quality of revelation.

If some of the true horrors of prison life are absent from *The Joint* and if one does not obtain a sense of the dark midnight of the soul that one gets from such prison sojourners as Wilde and Dostoevsky, it is simply that for a man for whom prison is a shelter and a haven—a spiritual home—the hor-rors cannot seem so oppressive after all. Also, Blake is a self-confessed mas-ochist; such a predilection for suffering, needless to say, takes care of a lot of things when one's associates, as Blake describes them once with a kind of half-hearted antipathy, are "dull and brutal and often more square than the squares outside."

In a remarkable passage written from freedom, Blake describes what it is about prison that he finds so irresistibly appealing; how many legions of men have felt the same way can only be a matter of conjecture, though it must assuredly be vast.

You know what's in my mind? The Joint. I thought I was getting off free from that experience. I thought they hadn't managed to touch me, but it colors every moment and every action of my life. I think always of the peace that I had there—this working to survive and surviving to work seems increasingly like an arrangement I would not have chosen were it up to me. Those gates, man, they're inviting. So much lovely time stretches out before you, time to read, to write, to play, to practice, to speculate, contemplate—and without the idiot necessity to Hold Up Your End. It is so well understood, the lines are so definitely drawn: I am Society and you are Not, and there is such a weary patience with non-conforming, it is infinitely restful.

Elsewhere:

[I feel] the inexplicable pull of The Joint, trying to fathom the Why of this incredible homesickness, trying to name for myself the kinship of the doomed I felt for the other cons when I was in.

Nearing the time of one of his paroles, Blake wrote to a friend:

There's a steady and joyful surge of anticipation when I think about the Outside. I think of the freedom to walk in the night under the stars in the blessed dark, after these endless months of living my life in the shrillness of daylight—savoring again the poignancy of twilight. When I think of how shining new things will seem to me, I am filled with excitement.

This of course is fustian (though truly meant at the time) and, significantly, the tribute it pays to liberty strikes perhaps the only false note in a unique, honest, moving book which, telling us much about the paradoxes of one man's mind, enhancing our knowledge about the nature of freedom (if only because it demonstrates that we are still unable to define it), also tells us much about ourselves and our most fallible institution, The Joint.

[*New York Times Book Review,* April 25, 1971.]

A Death in Canaan

Toward the end of Joan Barthel's excellent book about Peter Reilly, Judge John Speziale—the jurist who presided over the trial and who later granted Peter a new trial—is quoted as saying: "The law is imperfect." As portrayed in this book, Judge Speziale appears an exemplary man of the law, as fair and compassionate a mediator as we have any right to expect in a system where all too many of his colleagues are mediocre or self-serving or simply crooked. Certainly his decision in favor of a retrial—an action in itself so extraordinary as to be nearly historic—was the product of a humane and civilized intellect. Judge Speziale is one of the truly attractive figures in this book, which, although it has many winning people among its dramatis personae, contains more than one deplorable actor. And the judge is of course right: the law *is* imperfect. His apprehension of this fact is a triumph over the ordinary and the expected (in how many prisons now languish other Peter Reillys, victims of the law's "imperfections" but lacking Peter's many salvaging angels?), and is woven into his most honorable decision to grant Peter a new trial. But though he doubtless spoke from the heart as well as the mind and with the best intentions, the judge has to be found guilty of an enormous understatement.

The law (and one must assume that a definition of the law includes the totality of its many arms, including the one known as law enforcement) is not merely imperfect, it is all too often a catastrophe. To the weak and the underprivileged the law in all of its manifestations is usually a punitive nightmare. Even in the abstract the law is an institution of chaotic inequity, administered so many times with such arrogant disdain for the most basic principles of justice and human decency as to make mild admissions of "imperfection" sound presumptuous. If it is true that the law is the best institution human beings have devised to mediate their own eternal discord, this must not obscure the fact that the law's power is too often invested in the hands of mortal men who are corrupt, or if not corrupt, stupid, or if not stupid, then devious or lazy, and all of them capable of the most grievous mischief. The case of Peter Reilly, and Joan Barthel's book, powerfully demonstrate this ever-present danger and the sleepless vigilance ordinary citizens must steadfastly keep if the mechanism we have devised for our own protection does not from time to time try to destroy even the least of our children.

Naturally the foregoing implies, accurately, that I am convinced of Peter Reilly's innocence. I had begun to be convinced of at least the very strong possibility of his innocence when I first read Mrs. Barthel's article in the magazine *New Times* early in 1974.[1] I happened on the article by sheerest chance, perhaps lured into reading it with more interest than I otherwise might have by the fact that the murder it described took place in Canaan, hardly an hour's drive away from my home in west-central Connecticut. (Is there not something reverberantly sinister about it, and indicative of the commonplaceness of atrocity in our time, that I should not until then have known about this vicious crime so close at hand and taking place only a few months before?) The Barthel article was a stark, forceful, searing piece, which in essence demonstrated how an eighteen-year-old boy, suspected by the police of murdering his mother, could be crudely yet subtly (and there is no contradiction in those terms) manipulated by law-enforcement officers so as to cause him to make an incriminating, albeit fuzzy and ambiguous, statement of responsibility for the crime. What I read was shocking, although I did not find it a novel experience. I am not by nature a taker-up of causes but in the preceding twelve years I had enlisted myself in aiding two people whom I felt to be victims of the law. Unlike Peter, both of these persons were young black men.

In the earlier of these cases the issue was not guilt but rather the punishment. Ben Reid, convicted of murdering a woman in the black ghetto of Hartford, had been sentenced to die in Connecticut's electric chair. His was the classic case of the woebegone survivor of poverty and abandonment who, largely because of his disadvantaged or minority status, was the recipient of the state's most terrible revenge. I wrote an article about Ben Reid in a national magazine and was enormously gratified when I saw that the piece helped significantly in the successful movement by a lot of other indignant people to have Ben's life spared. The other case involved Tony Maynard, whom I had known through James Baldwin and who had been convicted and sentenced to a long term for allegedly killing a marine in Greenwich Village. I worked to help extricate Tony, believing that he was innocent, which he was—as indeed the law finally admitted by freeing him, but after seven years of Tony's incarceration (among other unspeakable adversities he was badly injured as an innocent bystander in the cataclysm at Attica) and a series of retrials in which his devoted lawyers finally demonstrated the wretched police collusion, false and perjured evidence, shady deals on the part of the district attorney's office, and other maggoty odds and ends of the law's "imperfection," which had caused his unjust imprisonment in the first place.

These experiments, then, led me to absorb the Barthel article in *New Times* with something akin to a shock of recognition; horrifying in what it revealed, the piece recapitulated much of the essence of the law's malfeasance that had created Tony Maynard's seven-year martyrdom. It should be noted at this moment, incidentally, that Mrs. Barthel's article was of absolutely crucial significance in the Reilly case, not only because it was the catalytic agent whereby the bulk of Peter's bail was raised, but because it so masterfully crystallized and made clear the sinister issues of the use of the lie detector and the extraction of a confession by the police, thereby making Peter's guilt at least problematical to all but the most obtuse reader. Precise and objective yet governed throughout, one felt, by a rigorous moral conscience, the article was a superb example of journalism at its most effective and powerful. (It was nearly inexcusable that this piece and its author received no mention in the otherwise praiseworthy report on the Reilly case published by *The New York Times* in 1975.) [2] Given the power of the essay, then, I have wondered later why I so readily let Peter Reilly and his plight pass from my mind and my concern. I think it may have been because of the fact that since Peter was not black or even of any shade of tan he would somehow be exempt from that ultimate dungeon-bound ordeal that is overwhelmingly the lot of those who spring from minorities in America. But one need not even be a good Marxist to flinch at this misapprehension. The truth is simpler. Bad enough that Peter lived in a shacklike house with his "disreputable" mother; the critical part is this: *he was poor.* Fancy Peter, if you will, as an affluent day-student at Hotchkiss School only a few miles away, the mother murdered but in an ambience of coffee tables and wall-to-wall carpeting. It takes small imagination to envision the phalanx of horn-rimmed and button-down lawyers interposed immediately between Peter and Sergeant Kelly with his insufferable lie detector.

This detestable machine, the polygraph (the etymology of which shows that the word means "to write much," which is about all that can be said for it), is to my mind this book's chief villain, and the one from which Peter Reilly's most miserable griefs subsequently flowed. It is such an American device, such a perfect example of our blind belief in "scientism" and the efficacy of gadgets; and its performance in the hands of its operator—friendly, fatherly Sergeant Timothy Kelly, the mild collector of seashells—is also so American in the way it produces its benign but ruthless coercion. Like nearly all the law-enforcement officers in this drama, Sergeant Kelly is "nice"; it is as hard to conceive of him with a truncheon or a blackjack as with a volume of Proust. Plainly, neither Kelly nor his colleague Lieutenant Shay, who was actively responsible for Peter's confession, are vicious men; they are merely undiscerningly obedient, totally devoid of that flexibility of mind we call imagination, and they both have a passionate faith in the machine. Kelly especially is an unquestioning votary. "We go strictly by the charts," he tells an exhausted boy. "And the charts say you hurt your mother last night."

In a society where everything sooner or later breaks down or goes haywire, where cars fall apart and ovens explode and vacuum cleaners expire through planned obsolescence (surely Kelly must have been victim, like us all, of the Toastmaster), there is something manic, even awesome, about the sergeant's pious belief in the infallibility of his polygraph. And so at a point in his ordeal Peter, tired, confused, only hours removed from the trauma of witnessing his mother's mutilated body, asks, "Have you ever been proven totally wrong? A person, just from nervousness, responds that way?" Kelly replies, "No, the polygraph can never be wrong, because it's only a recording instrument, reacting to you. It's the person interpreting it who could be wrong. But I haven't made that many mistakes in twelve years, in the thousands of people who sat here, Pete." Such mighty faith and assurances would have alone been enough to decisively wipe out a young man at the end of his tether. Add to this faith the presumed assumption of Peter's guilt on the part of the sergeant, and to this the outrageously tendentious nature of his questioning, and it is no wonder that a numb and bedraggled Peter was a setup for Lieutenant Shay, whose manner of extracting a confession from this troubled boy must be deemed a triumph of benevolent intimidation. Together the transcripts of the polygraph testimony and Peter's confession—much of which is recorded in this book—have to comprise another one of those depressing but instructive scandals that litter the annals of American justice.

Yet there is much more in the case of Peter Reilly, set down on these pages in rich detail, which makes it such a memorable and unique affair. What could be more harmoniously "American," in the best sense of that mangled word, than the spectacle of a New England village rising practically en masse to come to the support of one of their own young whom they felt to be betrayed and abandoned? Mrs. Barthel, who lived with this case month in and month out during the past few years, and who got to know well so many of Peter's friends and his surrogate "family," tells this part of the story with color, humor, and affection; and her feeling for the community life of a small town like Canaan—with its family ties and hostilities, its warmth and crankiness and crooked edges—gives both a depth and vivacity to her narrative; never is she lured into the purely sensational. As in every story of crime and justice, the major thrust of the drama derives from its central figures, and they are all here: not only the law's automata—the two "nice" cops whose dismal stratagems thrust Peter into his nightmare at the outset—but the judge, prosecutor, and counsel for the defense. Regarding these personages, Mrs. Barthel's art most often and tellingly lies in her subtle selectivity—and her onlooker's silence. What she allows the State's Attorney, Mr. Bianchi, simply to utter with his own lips, for instance, says more about Mr. Bianchi and the savagery of a certain genus of prosecutorial mind than any amount of editorializing or speculative gloss. As for the fascinating aftermath of the trial—Arthur Miller's stubborn and deservedly celebrated detective work in company with the redoubtable Mr. Conway, the brilliantly executed labors of the new defense counsel, the discovery of fresh evidence that led to the order of another trial, and other matters—all of these bring to a climax an eccentric, tangled, significant, and cautionary chronicle of the wrongdoing of the law and its belated redemption.

Joan Barthel's book would deserve our attention if for no other reason than that it focuses a bright light on the unconscionable methods which the law, acting through its enforcement agencies and because of its lust for punishment, uses to victimize the most helpless members of our society. And thus it once again shows the law's tragic and perdurable imperfection. It also reminds us that while judicial oppression undoubtedly falls the heaviest on those from minority groups, it will almost as surely hasten to afflict the poor and the "unrespectable," no matter what their color. But rather triumphantly, and perhaps most importantly, *A Death in Canaan* demonstrates the will of ordinary people, in their ever astonishing energy and determination, to see true justice prevail over the law's dereliction.

[Introduction to *A Death in Canaan,* by Joan Barthel; Dutton, 1976.]

Death Row

In October 1983, four days before he was scheduled to be executed in the electric chair at the Florida state prison at Starke, something took place that enraged Shabaka Sundiata Waglini more than any single event during his nearly ten years on death row. They came into his cell and measured him for his burial suit. The bloodlessly finicky, mechanical tailoring procedure upset him violently.

I recently met him, and he said, call me Shabaka. Shabaka—thirty-four years old when he faced death, born Joseph Green Brown in Charleston, South Carolina—had been convicted for the 1973 murder, along with the robbery and rape, of a Tampa white woman. "Shabaka," a name he took before going to prison, means "uncompromising" in Swahili.

Shortly after the suit was measured, Shabaka was asked to order his last meal—he could have virtually anything he wanted—but he rejected the offer as gratuitously insulting.

One shrinks from thinking how a man prepares himself to face this form of extinction. While little can be said in favor of any type of execution, death by electric current is truly primitive, a method that has not really been improved—if improvements are imaginable—since a convicted murderer received the inaugural 2,000 volts at New York's Auburn prison in 1890. It is a broiling process at intensely high temperature. The doctors who ascertain death must wait six or seven minutes for the body to cool down so they can touch it. Pigs and cattle go more expeditiously into that good night. Shabaka thought about the manner of his dying more than once.

He had good reason to believe that because he was black he had been dealt cards from a stacked deck.

As it happened, a juror at his trial had sent an affidavit to Shabaka's minister, the Rev. Joe Ingle of the Nashville-based Southern Coalition of Jails and Prisons, asserting that a jury member had advocated the chair for Shabaka, a former Black Panther, because "that nigger's been nothing but trouble since he came down here, and he'll be trouble until we get him off the streets."

One's mouth goes dry at such an utterance, especially in light of the recent United States Supreme Court decision that racial prejudice, as a decisive factor in the administration of the death penalty, is theoretical and therefore of no importance.

In truth, racial discrimination, far from being of no importance, has an omnipresence that the remarks of that Florida juror utterly confirm. After trials like Shabaka's, how can the Court's ruling appear anything but a cruel and monumental deceit?

In the United States, blacks and Hispanics suffer the death penalty in grave disproportion. They also tend, like Shabaka, to be poor, and therefore they receive legal counsel that more often than not is slipshod and deficient. Shabaka possessed a couple of sorry impediments when he went into his trial: He was black and penniless. These conditions represent one of several arguments amid a constellation of many arguments against the death penalty.

But what would be the case in favor of killing Shabaka? (A previous armed robbery hardly gained him sympathy.) There is no doubt that the crime of which he had been convicted was terrible. Those who felt no qualms about placing him in the electric chair, including many of clear and subtle intelligence, might have wished to justify his execution on one or the other, or both, of two grounds. There really aren't any more. The most obvious of these is deterrence: By putting Shabaka and all other brutal killers to death, we think we dissuade the like-minded from committing similar crimes.

But it never has been proved that the death penalty prevents murder.

Indeed, there is convincing evidence—displayed among other damning exhibits in Amnesty International's recent report on the death penalty in America—that executions frequently cause an increase in violent crimes.

In some countries—Canada, for example—the murder rate has fallen after abolition of the death penalty. Sincere foes of that penalty rarely are sentimentalists. There are those who would have opposed Shabaka's execution for any reason—feeling it was cruel and barbaric, or merely because it violated the sanctity of life. The resolve of many pragmatic opponents would be undermined were there hard proof that the death penalty prevents murders—but proof does not exist.

The crime that sealed Shabaka's fate was one that would bring out retributive fury in most people. Simple vengeance would have been the other rationale for seeking his death. The impulse toward vengeance is understandably relentless; many people, not necessarily bloodthirsty, would without shame declare a wish to have Shabaka killed just as a way to get even. And why shouldn't we acknowledge this? For, paradoxically, it is in the realm of vengeance that the feelings of many death penalty supporters and some opponents converge, though they do not coincide.

Any harsh sentence imposed for a particularly brutal crime contains an element of retaliation, satisfying a need on the part of the victim's ghost, the close survivors, and perhaps even society.

At the time of Shabaka's trial, there were quite a few onlookers who, though they rejected the death penalty, admitted they wanted to see Shabaka suffer a very hard time. But they also rejected a vengeance that extended to the electric chair, with its irremediable finality.

By the time Shabaka's date with the executioner neared in 1983, he had made as good use of his time as a man can under the circumstances. He worked on his case, wrote letters, and, like many inmates, became a devoted reader. He greatly fancied modern American novels and developed a love for classical music. As he sweated it out, there were scores of convicts throughout America's prison system who were doing time for crimes that were almost identical to the one for which Shabaka had been condemned.

Those who were truly dangerous among these criminals would, or should, never be released. Others, after serving long terms—an average of twenty years or more—would be released on parole, and scarcely a soul among them would be returned to prison for a subsequent crime.

Why hadn't Shabaka been permitted to join this favored majority? Why had he and a small fraction of other felons been singled out to die while vastly larger numbers of criminals paying penance for misdeeds virtually the same as his were allowed to work out their destinies?

The absence of answers—which emphasizes the blind inequity of the death penalty—is another major reason why its use is immoral and unacceptable. But in Shabaka's case, the questions were really academic—because he was innocent.

The legalized killing of innocent people is the final indictment of capital punishment. For years, Shabaka had insisted on his innocence of the rape, robbery, and murder. All along, he had admitted to a robbery—but this at a time and place different from those of the murder.

Only fifteen hours before Shabaka's appointment with death, a three-judge panel of the federal circuit court of appeals in Atlanta stayed the execution on grounds that the case merited further examination. Shabaka returned to his cell and began to petition for a new trial.

In the years that followed, ugly details came to light: During the first trial, the prosecutor had concealed Federal Bureau of Investigation evidence showing that the fatal bullet could not have been fired from Shabaka's gun. Shabaka based his new claim on this fact and on his assertion that the prosecutor had allowed a crucial witness to lie, while also misleading the jury in his closing argument.

Last year, the circuit court ordered a new trial. Before it could begin, the original witness admitted he had lied. Florida, sensing it had no case, abandoned its prosecution, and early last March Shabaka left jail a free man, his only possessions being the clothes on his back and his legal papers. Between the ages of twenty-three and twenty-seven, he had spent the rich marrow of his youth on death row.

The Shabaka story illuminates the most sordid defects of capital punishment. His blackness and poverty helped doom him. He was ruthlessly cheated; it was never his privilege to be granted—even for a phantom crime—the incarceration that it meted out to others and that carries the possibility of redemption.

He would have died not a criminal but a victim whose innocence would have been as surely entombed as his body in its burial suit.

Today, Shabaka makes his home in Florida. There "decompressing," as he puts it, from his years in a cell, he reads and listens to tapes of classical symphonies. May he live in peace.

[*New York Times,* op-ed, May 10, 1987.]

Presidential

Havanas in Camelot

L ike millions of others, I watched transfixed in late April 1996 as the acquisitive delirium that swept through Sotheby's turned the humblest knickknack of Camelot into a fetish for which people would pony up a fortune. A bundle of old magazines, including *Modern Screen* and *Ladies' Home Journal*, went for $12,650. A photograph of an Aaron Shikler portrait of Jackie—not the portrait itself, mind you, a photo—was sold for $41,400. (Sotheby's had valued the picture at $50 to $75.) A Swiss "Golf-Sport" stroke counter, worth $50 to $100 by Sotheby's estimate, fetched an insane $28,750. But surely among the most grandiose trophies, in terms of its bloated price, was John Kennedy's walnut cigar humidor, which Milton Berle had given the president in 1961 after having attached a plaque reading "To J.F.K. Good Health—Good Smoking, Milton Berle 1/20/61." The comedian had paid $600 to $800 for it in that year. Thirty-five years later, poor Berle tried to buy the humidor back at Sotheby's but dropped out of the bidding at $185,000.

The winner was Marvin Shanken, publisher of the magazine *Cigar Aficionado,* who spent $574,500 on an object the auctioneers had appraised at $2,000 to $2,500. Even at such a flabbergasting price the humidor should prove to play an important mascot role in the fortunes of Shanken's magazine, which is already wildly successful, featuring (aside from cigars and cigar-puffing celebrities) articles on polo and golf, swank hotels, antique cars, and many other requirements for a truly tony lifestyle in the 1990s. After all, John F. Kennedy was no stranger to the nobby life, and what could be more appropriate as a relic for a cigar magazine than the vault in which reposed the Havanas of our last genuine cigar-smoking president?

I never laid eyes on the fabled humidor, but on the occasions I encountered Kennedy I sensed he must have owned one, protecting his precious supply, for he approached cigars with the relish and delight of—well, an aficionado. Indeed, if I allow my memory to be given a Proustian prod, and recollect Kennedy at the loose and relaxed moments when our lives briefly intersected, I can almost smell the smoke of the Havanas for which he'd developed such an impetuous, Kennedyesque weakness.

After the clunky Eisenhower years it was wonderful to have this dashing young guy in the spotlight, and soon there was nothing unusual in seeing the president posed, without apology or self-consciousness, holding a cigar. I had become friendly with two members of the Kennedy staff, Arthur Schlesinger, Jr., and Richard Goodwin, both of whom were so passionate about cigars that smoking appeared to me to be almost a White House sub-culture. They would lecture me about cigars whenever I saw them in Washington. Havanas were, of course, the sine qua non, and, as an ignorant cigarette smoker still clinging miserably to an unwanted addiction, I found myself fascinated but a little puzzled by all the cigar talk, by the effusive praise for a Montecristo of a certain length and vintage, by the descriptions of wrappers and their shades, by the subtle distinctions made between the flavors of a Ramon Allones and a Punch. Stubbornly, I kept up my odious allegiance to cigarettes, but in my secret heart I envied these men for their devotion to another incarnation of tobacco, one that had been transubstantiated from mere weed into an object plainly capable of evoking rapture.

In late April of 1962 I was one of a small group of writers invited to what turned out to be possibly the most memorable social event of the Kennedy presidency. This was a state dinner in honor of Nobel Prize winners. Schlesinger and Goodwin were responsible for my being included—at the time, Kennedy didn't know me, as they say, from Adam—and it was a giddy pleasure for my wife, Rose, and me to head off to the White House on a balmy spring evening in the company of my friend James Baldwin, who was on the verge of becoming the most celebrated black writer in America. I recall that it was the only time I ever shaved twice on the same day.

Before dinner the booze flowed abundantly and the atmosphere crackled with excitement as J.F.K. and his beautiful lady joined the assembly and presided over the receiving line. Jack and Jackie actually shimmered. You would have had to be abnormal, perhaps psychotic, to be immune to their dumbfounding appeal. Even Republicans were gaga. They were truly the golden couple, and I am not trying to play down my own sense of wonder when I note that a number of the guests, male and female, appeared so affected by the glamour that their eyes took on a goofy, catatonic glaze.

Although I remained in control of myself, I got prematurely plastered; this did not damage my critical faculties when it came to judging the dinner. I'd spent a considerable amount of time in Paris and had become something of a food and wine snob. Later, in my notebook, I ungratefully recorded that while the Puligny-Montrachet 1959, served with the first course, was "more than adequate," I found the Mouton-Rothschild 1955, accompanying the filet de boeuf Wellington, "lacking in maturity." The dessert, something called a bombe Caribienne, I deemed "much too sweet, a real bomb."

Reviewing these notes so many years later, I cringe at my churlishness (including the condescending remark that the meal was "doubtless better than anything Ike and Mamie served up"), especially in view of the thrilling verve and happy spirits of the entire evening. Because of the placement of the tables I was seated at right angles to the president, and I was only several feet away when he rose from his own table and uttered his famous bon mot about the occasion representing the greatest gathering of minds at the White House since "Thomas Jefferson dined here alone." The Nobelists roared their appreciation at this elegant bouquet, and I sensed the words passing into immortality.

The White House was anything but smoke-free, and the scullions among us lit up our cigarettes. I noticed with my usual sulkiness and envy that many gentlemen at the tables around the room had begun to smoke cigars; among them was Kennedy, who was engaged in conversation with a stunning golden-haired young woman and plainly relishing her at least as much as his Churchill. Following coffee, we moved into the East Room for a concert of chamber music. After this, just as the party was breaking up and we were about to be converted into pumpkins, I was astonished to learn from an army captain in full dress that Rose and I were invited upstairs for something "more intimate" with President and Mrs. Kennedy. Although I had an instant's impish fantasy about what "more intimate" implied—this was, after all, the dawn of the Swinging Sixties—I was in fact rather relieved to discover that the small room into which we were ushered was filled with cigar smokers and their lady companions.

The president hadn't arrived yet, but Jackie was there, as were Goodwin and Schlesinger and Bobby Kennedy and Pierre Salinger, together with their wives, and all the men were focusing on their Havanas with such obvious pleasure that one might have thought the entire Nobel dinner had been arranged to produce this fragrant climax. Only in fine Paris restaurants, where—unlike in America—cigar smoking was encouraged, had I inhaled such a delicious aroma. I had by this time taken aboard too many of the various beverages the White House had provided, including the dessert champagne (Piper-Heidsieck 1955), and sank down unwittingly into the president's famous rocking chair.

Rocking away, I talked with Lionel Trilling, the renowned critic; he and his wife, Diana, were the only other literary people invited upstairs. He was also the only other cigarette smoker, as far as I could tell—indeed, a real chain-smoker, with a haggard, oxygen-deprived look—and we made book chat and indulged in our forlorn habit while the others convivially enjoyed their great cigars. It was not until Schlesinger discreetly asked me to let the president sit down in the rocker, for the sake of his dysfunctional back, that I realized that J.F.K. had been standing in the room for some time, too polite to shoo me out of his chair. When I leapt up, mortified, and Kennedy apologetically took my place, I noticed that he was still fondling his Churchill. The leader of the Free World wreathed in smoke, gently rocking: this was the relaxed and contented image I took away with me when, well after midnight, we wobbled our way homeward from one hell of a party.

In the months that intervened before I saw Kennedy again, I waged a demonic struggle with my cigarette habit. Thanks to my two White House gurus, I was also gingerly experimenting with cigars. The embargo against Cuba, instituted officially by Kennedy himself, was now in force; Havanas had become nearly unavailable overnight, and so I found myself buying the next-best cigars, which were then being made in the Canary Islands. These cigars were actually very good, and many of them were outstanding.

But I was still hesitant to commit myself. Although I was fully aware that I was undermining my health with an addiction that had held me captive since the age of fifteen, I was unable to make the transition to cigars without going through convulsions of moral doubt. Actually, I was a victim of the conventional wisdom. This was because in America, an essentially puritanical society that is as absolutist in its views about health as it is about many other issues, there was little distinction to be made between cigarettes and cigars.

After all, in a country which some years later, in its panic over the cholesterol in eggs, would virtually banish this agelessly invaluable food from the national diet rather than merely caution moderation, it was entirely natural that the relatively harmless pleasure of moderate cigar smoking should suffer the same opprobrium as the lethal addiction to cigarettes. If I stopped cigarettes, there were a lot of old nannies of both sexes eager to tell me: cigars are just as bad!

Well, they plainly are not, and indeed, unlike cigarettes, they possess an intrinsic good. At that time, in notes I made for a 1963 review (in *The New York Review of Books*) of *The Consumers Union Report on Smoking and the Public Interest,* which was a precursor to the original surgeon general's report on the hazards of tobacco, I wrote:

> It is a grim irony that in our health-obsessed society an addiction as plainly ruinous as cigarette smoking should be condoned and promoted while the comparatively benign use of cigars should be condemned as if it were a plague. Cigars are a genuine pleasure; cigarettes are a pseudo-pleasure, of the same kind experienced by laboratory rats. The stigma against cigars has as much to do with economics and social class as it has with misplaced moralizing. The nearly universal habit of cigarette smoking is the property of the vast middle class, while cigar smokers are confined to the upper and lower ends of the economic scale. (There are overlappings and intersections, of course, but this is the basic contour.)
>
> Among middle-class cigarette smokers, cigars are regarded either as the overpriced indulgence of bankers, rich corporate board members, and movie moguls like Darryl Zanuck or, at the lower end, the cheap habit of White Owl chompers who inhabit low-class saloons and sleazy gyms. The comic-strip figure of the 1930s "Pete the Tramp" best illustrates this dichotomy: the little drifter always on the lookout for plutocrats' quality cigar butts, which he'd pluck from the gutter and impale on a toothpick.
>
> Cigars have never found a comfortable middle ground of accep-

tance. What compounds the irony is that White Owls and Dutch Masters do in fact offend the nostrils—certainly mine—and women, especially, with their canary-like sensitivity, are often justifiably upset by such effluvia. Women disturbed by cheap mass-produced cigars have innocently helped give all cigars a bum rap. What is so fascinating is that the same women, when exposed to the smoke of a prime Montecristo, will often emit genuine swooning sounds, thus demonstrating that cigars of high quality need not endure prejudice forever. Women someday will be smoking cigars. I predict, too, that at some point in the future, after society has become aware of the awful hazards of cigarettes, many of the middle class will begin gradually to embrace cigars—cigars of excellence which, coming from countries other than Cuba, will also become more and more affordable.

I'm pleased to find that my crystal ball, so often dismally clouded, was quite clear when I set down those last lines.

The following summer I quit smoking cigarettes for good, cold turkey. It was just a few weeks before Jack Kennedy invited Rose and me out for a ride on his cabin cruiser, the good ship *Patrick J.* He and Jackie crossed over from the Cape to Martha's Vineyard, where I had rented a house, and took us out on an overcast August day for a wallowing luncheon afloat. Aside from my friends John and Sue Marquand, who accompanied us, the only other passenger aboard was the late Stephen Smith, J.F.K.'s brother-in-law. A Coast Guard cutter hung around not far away for security reasons, but otherwise the seven of us had the rolling waves to ourselves. The sea was moderately rough, though alcohol soothed the mal de mer. The Bloody Marys, poured out by a rather jittery Filipino mess steward, overflowed their glasses; there was a lot of chitchat between the Marquands and Jack and Jackie, who had known each other for years, about mutual friends; variations on the twist, and other hip music of that year, blared from a record player; and the general pre-luncheon mood was frisky despite the gray weather.

The talk became a little bit more serious when we sat down to eat. At the table of the *Patrick J*'s open cockpit, no one paid much attention to the disastrous lunch. It was a mad joke of cold hot dogs in soggy buns, gooey *oeufs en gelée,* spoons dropped by the nervous Filipino into everyone's laps, glasses of beer not merely iced but frozen solid. We got involved instead in the conversation, which ranged from Massachusetts politics and the racial situation heating up in the Deep South—the previous fall's violent events in Oxford, Mississippi, had plainly shaken J.F.K.—to the old chestnut about whether Alger Hiss was guilty (Kennedy thought he was) and the president's obvious pique over an article in *The American Scholar* by the critic Alfred Kazin questioning his intellectual credentials.[1] I was both amused and impressed that Kazin should bug him so.

A lot of the time Jackie kept her shapely but rather large bare feet in the presidential lap. At one point J.F.K., in a personal aside to me, asked what I was writing, and when I told him it was a novel about Nat Turner, who had led a nineteenth-century slave insurrection in Virginia, he became immediately alert and probed me brightly and persistently for information, which I was happy to provide. He seemed fascinated by my story of the revolt. The issue of race was plainly beginning to bedevil Kennedy, as it was nearly everyone else. At that time few Americans had heard of Nat Turner. I told Kennedy things about slavery he had obviously never known before.

Then, after the ice cream and coffee, the president passed out to the men Partagas cigars, made in Havana and encased in silver tubes. I rolled mine around between my fingers delightedly, trying not to crack too obvious a smile. I was aware that this was a contraband item under the embargo against Cuban goods and that the embargo had been promulgated by the very man who had just pressed the cigar into my hand. Therefore the Partagas was all the more worth preserving, at least for a while, in its protective tube, as a naughty memento, a conversation piece with a touch of scandal. I watched as the president began to smoke with pleasure, displaying no sense of the clandestine. I palmed the Partagas into my pocket while Kennedy wasn't looking, resolved to smoke it on some special occasion, and lit up one of my Canary Island coronas. Soon afterward, however, I began feeling a certain odd, fugitive sadness at this little gift from Kennedy, a sadness I couldn't quite fathom, though it may have been only the same poignant regret that prompted me to write, later on, when I remembered the boat trip, "of the irreconcilable differences, the ferocious animosity that separated Castro and Kennedy. Of all the world's leaders the Harvard man and the Marxist from Havana were temperamentally and intellectually most alike;

they probably would have taken warmly to each other had not the storm of twentieth-century history and its bizarre determinism made them into unshakable enemies."

I saw Kennedy again the following November at a crowded, elegant party one Friday night in New York. I'd thought, before going, that we might get a brief glimpse of him and nothing more. But Rose and I, entering the dinner, discovered him at the bottom of a flight of stairs looking momentarily lost and abandoned. As if arrested in an instant's solitude, he was talking to no one and pondering his cigar. He had a splendid Palm Beach tan. He threw his arms around us and uttered a line so cornily ingratiating that it gave blarney new meaning: "How did they get you to come here? They had a hard enough time getting me!" He asked me how the novel was coming, and once again he began to talk about race. Did I know any Negro writers? Could I suggest some Negro names for a meeting at the White House? And so on. Finally someone distracted him and he disappeared into the crowd. Sometime later, on his way out, he caught my eye and, smiling, said, "Take care."

They were words I should have spoken to him, for exactly two weeks later, on another Friday, he was dead in Dallas.

I smoked the Partagas in his memory.

[*Vanity Fair,* July 1996.]

Les Amis du Président

In 1948, when I had just become old enough to participate in an election, I cast my first vote for that durable old socialist presidential candidate Norman Thomas. This, of course, was a protest against both Harry Truman and Thomas E. Dewey—a throwaway vote—and I have always cast a Democratic ballot since then, although many times despairingly. And so, this past May, when I received a personal invitation to attend the inaugural of François Mitterrand as the president of France, my great surprise was accompanied by a fleeting wonder whether the honor was not perhaps acknowledgment of that lonely vote cast thirty-three years ago. But of course not: François Mitterrand, perhaps alone among chiefs of state of our time, cares for writers more than the members of any other profession—more than lawyers, more than scientists, more even than politicians—and his invitation to me and to six other writers was a simple confirmation of that concern. This nonpolemical account is that of a partisan.

It is interesting, I think, that among *les amis du président*—the small group of 125 or so of us who gathered at the Arc de Triomphe for the inaugural ceremony—there were no representatives whatever of the diplomatic corps, no members of international officialdom, and a very minimum of pomp and circumstance. Interesting, too, that there were no French writers—obviously to avoid factionalism and jealousy. Two American writers stood with me, all of us dressed informally in ties and jackets: the playwright

Arthur Miller and Elie Wiesel, novelist and essayist, chronicler of the Holo-caust. The others, dressed similarly, were the Colombian novelist Gabriel García Márquez, the Mexican writer Carlos Fuentes, Julio Cortázar from Argentina, and Yachar Kemal of Turkey. Having gathered early, a little after noon under a gray sky threatening rain, we were able to observe the other guests as they arrived beneath the great arch with its engraved roll call of battles.

What these personages represented was unequivocal: the heart and marrow of world socialism. They came almost at random, without ceremony. Willy Brandt arrived, followed by Felipe González, head of Spain's Socialist Workers' Party. There was Olof Palme of Sweden. After him came socialist leaders Mário Soares of Portugal and Bettino Craxi of Italy. Léopold Sen-ghor, the president of Senegal and also a poet and writer, arrived, and shortly after came Andreas Papandreou, leader of the Socialist Party of Greece. But this was not an all-male gathering. Papandreou walked side by side with a radiant Melina Mercouri, whose post as member of the Greek Parliament now competes with her career as actress. Finally, in rather somber reminder of the tragic events of Chile and the eclipse of democracy there, Hortensia Allende appeared. The widow of the slain president was accompanied by another widow, the wife of Pablo Neruda, Chile's great poet. All in all, it was an extraordinary sight, this gathering of illuminaries and votaries of a cause which had been lost so often throughout European history that its unex-pected triumph here had left everyone looking a little bit stunned and sol-emn. Plainly the mood was celebratory, but the shock of the win was too great and the people seemed to move unsteadily, a little as if at a funeral.

The arrival of Mitterrand was rather anticlimactic. The new president is the quintessential Frenchman: in his plain dark business suit he would merge into a Parisian crowd as indistinguishably as yet another rather well-fleshed lycée professor or lawyer or even the patron of a good restaurant. Thus he looked undeniably the common citizen when he bent down and placed flowers in front of the Eternal Flame, but the sound of "La Marseil-laise" played by the army band raised in all of us, I could tell, the same old familiar chill.

At the luncheon at the Élysée Palace I found myself seated next to Claude Cheysson, who had not yet been named foreign minister but who, in an unpretentious way, gave the impression that he knew he was about to be tapped. He is an engaging and articulate man, and he asked me what I thought of the occasion, especially what my feelings were in regard to having been invited, along with the other writers. I said I was certain that all of the writers felt they were paying their respects to a man who, more than any other leader of a major Western nation, seemed prepared to insist on fuller measures on behalf of human rights, and that his presence on the world stage would be a significant corrective to the general rightward drift of power. In a lighter context, I added, writers were very rarely accorded this kind of recognition, especially in the United States—where, since John F. Kennedy at least, such honor was usually heaped upon rock stars, stand-up comedians, and golf champions—and that it was simply fun to help celebrate this day with a president who was so obviously and passionately in love with the written word. (Richard Eder, Paris correspondent of *The New York Times,* later alluded to our literary presence as part of the "froth" of nouveau radical chic surrounding Mitterrand, but he is wrong. A concern for culture and the intellect is not mere style with Mitterrand but central to his being.) As for Reagan, I told Cheysson, who seemed puzzled by our leader, it was not at all surprising that Americans would finally elect a movie actor as president. To the contrary, it was inevitable, since the American people have glorified movie stars to the point of lunacy and ever since the dawn of the cinema have yearned for a matinee idol to run the ship of state. Cheysson looked depressed but seemed to understand.

The socialist leveling process did not, at this luncheon, extend to the food, which began with *pâté de foie gras truffé des Landes* (a delectable dish originating in Mitterrand's native region), accompanied by a Château d'Yquem 1966, and ended, after an incredible raspberry dessert, with Dom Pérignon champagne 1971. *Time* magazine had reported that Mitterrand is indifferent to food, but here again the reporting was wrong. I was sitting only a few seats away from the president, and one could tell from the gusto with which he put away the elegant white spears of asparagus that he cares at least as much about eating as he does about attractive young women—all of these admirable tastes transcending party politics.

Afterward we stood in the garden of the palace and chatted with Mitterrand. For better or for ill, I was aware of no cordon of security guards, only Mitterrand himself looking a little withdrawn and ill at ease, but enjoying himself nonetheless as he talked with the well-wishers. There was a remarkable atmosphere of casualness. It might have been a garden party almost anywhere in France. The conversation, while not exactly momentous, sticks in the mind. When we spoke of America, Mitterrand seemed as mystified about the country as Cheysson had been about Reagan. "A vast, strange continent," he said, "so enormous and mysterious, so difficult to understand. But the people are wonderful. I wish I could say the same for your foreign policy."

When Elie Wiesel asked what it felt like to be president, Mitterrand paused, and a look of honest surprise came to his face. "I still can't believe it," he murmured. Such fine candor required from me—the old Norman Thomas rooter—a compliment, and I told him that I had voted for him in my heart. He spoke in English for the first time. "I appreciate that," he said.

Toward the end of the afternoon we were scheduled to join with the other *amis du président* for a triumphal walk up the short street that leads at a right angle from the boulevard Saint-Michel to the Pantheon. Miller, Wiesel, Fuentes, and myself set off in our car, but the driver became confused and let us off not at a point where we could gain admission to the intersection but at a corner in the midst of the crowd. The throng in the streets was enthusiastic, noisy, wildly cheerful, and unbelievably huge. Both Fuentes, who had been Mexican ambassador to France in the mid-1970s, and Wiesel, who had lived for a long time in Paris after World War II, said they had never seen such droves of people in the streets. Only the very cheerfulness of the mob prevented it from seeming menacing. People were everywhere—along the curbs, in the alleys, and on the sidewalks, waiting for the presidential motorcade to cruise up the boulevard to the intersection.

Meanwhile, the four North American writers were unable to penetrate the crowd or to get past the barricades that firmly lined the boulevard. Over and over again we tried to push through, waving our cards of admittance, but there was simply no way to penetrate the throng. In despair, we were about to give up and go to a bar and look at the proceedings on television when we spied Melina Mercouri in her car, accompanied by Andreas Papandreou, also hopelessly blocked. It was she who saved the entire situation. After a hurried conference with the four of us, she debarked from the car and pushed her way to the barricade. There, with pleading, with Greek gesticulations, and with overwhelming charm, she persuaded a very senior police official to let us through the barricade.

And now ensued the most remarkable procession any of us could remember. The broad boulevard Saint-Michel, utterly deserted but lined on either side by tens of thousands of people. Starting up its center four writers, the president of the Socialist Party of Greece, and Melina Mercouri, whose presence brought forth a vast roar from the crowd as she grinned gloriously and brandished a socialist rose. A heady and thrilling moment indeed, even when—as Fuentes pointed out—the crowd surely thought that the five gentlemen in their raincoats were Mercouri's bodyguards.

This is not the place to reflect on the future of socialism in France. That night at dinner some very rich Parisians I know dined on lobster as if at a wake, casting bleak auguries for the future, their voices heavy with bereavement. The history of the Socialist Party in Europe is hardly one of unalloyed success, and who knows what vicissitudes of the future might mock François Mitterrand's day of glory, as they might mock Ronald Reagan's or, for that matter, that of any man bold and brave enough to seek power. But as a fellow writer I found it very difficult—as we all stood in drizzling rain on the ancient gray steps of the Pantheon, listening to Beethoven's "Ode to Joy" while Mitterrand basked serenely in his hard-earned triumph—not to reciprocate the feeling of the inscription to me he wrote that day in one of his own books: "In gratitude and in hope."

[*Boston Globe,* July 26, 1981.]

François Mitterrand

A truth worth repeating is that the quality of being intellectual does not guarantee excellence, or even competence, in a political leader. Nonetheless, it would be hypocrisy to say that, in their secret hearts, intellectuals do not wish to see authentic members of their kind ascend to seats of power. With what passion the souls of thinking men and women were stirred when John F. Kennedy became president. Kennedy, of course, was no intellectual; but he was the first American president in many years to give the impression that a book was not an alien object. Also, in fairness to the Kennedy image, which has become much tarnished in recent years, it has to be said that at least he had a touching and—for a president—perhaps unique concern for what intellectuals thought of him. During one of the two conversations I had with Kennedy he was gloomily preoccupied, and clearly much hurt, because Alfred Kazin, in an *American Scholar* article, had belittled his pretensions to a place among the intelligentsia. With real pain, like a jilted lover, he spoke of Kazin and while his somewhat callow discomfiture if anything helped validate Kazin's conclusions, it also revealed to the writer in his presence something quite appealing about the Kennedy sensibility. A president fussing about the animadversions of a literary critic: after the Eisenhower doldrums, it was fresh and a little amazing.

It was not publicized that, on the day after his inaugural, one of François Mitterrand's first official acts was to grant citizenship to Julio Cortázar of

Argentina and Milan Kundera of Czechoslovakia, two exiled writers who had long and vainly petitioned the preceding administration for the right to become Frenchmen. Mitterrand's act was both symbolic and fraternal—the gesture of a politician who is also both an intellectual and a literary man. Mitterrand would doubtless object to the latter designation for, as he tells us in his remarkable book *The Wheat and the Chaff,* he always insists upon being called a politician, preferring action to words.

Yet, one feels a certain lack of commitment in this—at the very least an ambivalence—for although he says, "I could never have been an imaginative writer," he immediately adds: "I observe—and I write. I like the written word. Language, philology, grammar. I believe that real literature is born from the exact correspondence of word and thing. I was brought up in that classical school where essays in French and recitations in Latin taught me the proper order and cadence of words and phrases." This concern with literary style is very much in evidence in *The Wheat and the Chaff,* which is a free-flowing account of Mitterrand's life and thought during most of the years of the 1970s. Mitterrand calls the book a hybrid, neither diary nor chronicle; but if so it is a hybrid in other interesting ways.

Written in the days when the idea of a Socialist victory in France was a daydream, the book is in part an underdog's view of contemporary events and at the same time a blueprint for Socialist action. These passages are deft, abrasive, resolute, and (one realizes with something akin to shock) prophetic. An uncanny feeling comes over one with reflection that such matters as the nationalization of commerce—an ideal which, when Mitterrand was brooding on it, must have seemed millennial in its improbability—have begun quietly to be realized. But if the book were a mere political document it would, I suspect, despite the admirable contours of the writing, appear dated already, and could not possibly seize our attention.

What distinguishes the work, and makes it the exciting "hybrid" it is, is precisely that multifaceted literary gift that Mitterrand deprecates in himself, but which makes page after page spring into vivid life. Mitterrand may not be an "imaginative writer," but among the attractions of his book—removing it light-years from the lackluster volumes of most of the world's politicians—is the way in which so much that is observed seems filtered through the sensibility of a first-rate novelist. Whether it is nature that he is writing about, or his basset hound Titus, or encounters with such figures as Mao Tse-tung or Golda Meir or Pablo Neruda, Mitterrand has the good novelist's knack of looking past the obvious for the immanent, the particular, the revealing detail. It is relatively rare, in the writing of politicians, to experience colors and smells and the actual presence of human flesh; thus how refreshing it is to come upon this description of Mao in 1961: ". . . of medium height, wearing a gray Sun Yat-sen uniform, with one shoulder lower than the other, slow of step, his face round and seemingly quite at peace, short of breath and soft of voice . . . his small, well-manicured hands, his laugh . . . the serenity that pervaded the room. By comparison what a bunch of marionettes our Western dictators are, with their flashy uniforms, their strident voices, their theatricality."

As one who aspired to the presidency, Mitterrand has been perhaps more than normally fascinated by power and those who wield it. His longtime position as First Secretary of the French Socialist Party allowed him propinquity to the movers and shakers of his time—both at home and abroad—and some of the most engaging passages of the book are those having to do with these figures. It must be painfully difficult for any political leader to write without rancor about his rivals, past or present, especially after years of defeat, near-misses, and repeated disappointments. It is all the more impressive, therefore, to view the large-hearted fairness with which Mitterrand treats the character and career of two whose ideals he has the most strenuously opposed: de Gaulle and Malraux. To feel a certain irony in Mitterrand's retrospective treatment of his predecessor is nonetheless to admire the civilized restraint he employed in his analysis of Gaullism, as well as the sympathy he displays for the General's faults, even extending to his chauvinism and megalomania. These Mitterrand can understand even when he cannot condone. Hating de Gaulle's ideas or, as he implies, lack of them, he can still respect the man for some ineluctable historical presence.

His experience in the Resistance during the war was plainly a pivotal perception in Mitterrand's life—just as the war, in a different way, was crucial to de Gaulle's. Mitterrand is able to vibrate sympathetically to certain aspects of de Gaulle's personality because of this shared experience; one feels that Mitterrand's love of France is as passionate as that of the General, though mercifully shorn of its mysticism. "I live France," Mitterrand writes. "I have a deep instinctive awareness of France, of physical France, and a passion for her geography, her living body. There is no need for me to seek the soul of France—it lives in me." One feels no chauvinistic fever in these honest lines.

Again, Mitterrand's treatment of Malraux is a measure of his magnanimity and amplitude of vision. (Even as I write these words I am brought up
short by the improbable idea of presidential concern with a novelist: imagine Ronald Reagan in serious meditation about the career of even so public
a writer as Hemingway!) However, lest it be construed that Mitterrand is
possessed of angelic forbearance, it must be said that his intellectual judgments can be as tough as rawhide. For Malraux's poorer work he has nothing
but distaste, just as he loathes the grandiose posturing of his "official" life.
But—having uttered his scathing observations—how warm-hearted he is
when, shortly after Malraux's death, he finds himself assessing that long,
contradictory, and complex career. His final tribute to this man is a fine
example of the generosity that seems to animate Mitterrand's private and
political life. Even his detailed response to the character and vocation
of Georges Pompidou, for whom he has almost unbounded contempt, is
shot through with a rueful compassion. One keeps marveling at the sheer
patience Mitterrand exhibits during these years of disappointment and
waiting.

I was among several writers invited to Mitterrand's inaugural in May of
1981. After lunch on that day, as we stood in a small informal group in the
bright springtime garden of the Élysée Palace, Mitterrand spoke of America. He spoke of it, I felt, with something of a feeling of mystery, alluding to
it as that "vast continent, quite incomprehensible." Mitterrand has been an
indefatigable traveler; America has become a frequent way station on his
itinerary during recent years. Some of that same incomprehensibility and
mystery which he mentioned to us will be found in this book, along with his
sense of ever-renewed wonder. He has an undisguised fondness for the
United States, and even in 1972—haunted by the awareness of our bombers
then devastating Vietnam—he could meditate with eloquence on the land
and its destiny. Like all sensible Europeans, he seems to temper his fondness with profound unease over our perpetually alarming foreign policy; but
even here there is a certain philosophical patience in his point of view—his
description of a long conversation with Henry Kissinger in 1975 is fascinating, both in its scope of exchanged ideas and in the sympathy (or at least lack
of acrimoniousness) brought to bear on his portrayal of a statesman opposed
to nearly everything socialism stands for. (In an earlier passage Mitterrand
notes the appalling irony inherent in the award to Kissinger of the Nobel
Peace Prize; even then, however, one feels Mitterrand's justified animus is

directed more against official idiocy on the part of the bestowers than against Kissinger.)

Mostly, one cannot help being beguiled by Mitterrand's reflections on the United States: perplexed and troubled, one feels, by America's collective mind, wryly aware of the mediocrity of its political leaders (Ronald Reagan, not yet elected president, has received his reputation "thanks to the qualities he revealed in the exercise of his profession as television master of ceremonies, and has seduced the old machine that produced Lincoln"), Mitterrand still regards us with affection and hope. From near the top of Rockefeller Center he notes a flight of mallard ducks ascend from the East River; in the midst of this "poetic geometry" of the city which so moves him, the wild birds are a reaffirmation of the natural order of things, even here.

There are certain passages in *The Wheat and the Chaff* that will perhaps appear less compelling to the American reader than those that I have just described. Those having to do with the aspirations and programs of the Socialist Party during the 1970s, and Mitterrand's own musings upon certain current events, may now lack the urgency they once had. But the same could be declared, let us say, for some of the meditations of George McGovern or Adlai Stevenson on the policies in their times of the Democratic Party. What finally gives this book its extraordinary savor is the range of curiosity of its author, its mirror-bright reflections on people and places, its often intense feeling for nature, and its ubiquitous and passionate concern for the destiny of human beings in a calamitous century.

In saying this I do not want to minimize Mitterrand's justifiable preoccupation with Socialist principles, which everywhere energizes the book and is, after all, the prime reason for its being. About socialism, Mitterrand is passionate, but at the same time unpretentious. He is wary of Socialist dogma, which he sees as being as potentially dangerous as any other dogma.

"Socialism does not represent values that are superior to the humble truth of facts," he writes. "Nor yet does it constitute truth in itself. It argues, seeks, approximates. It knocks down idols and taboos." Which is as modest, eloquent, and appealing a description of a political ideal as one could imagine. But as I say, *The Wheat and the Chaff* is anything but a tract. In it the play of intellect and the range of curiosity and interest constantly fascinate. Is it an ingenuous reaction on my part—the reflex of an American anaesthetized by contemplation of one chief magistrate after another who more or less thinks and looks like Gerald Ford—that I have to pinch myself from time to time to realize that the president of a great nation has written this book? Perhaps so; perhaps such a connection is in the end of little importance. Nevertheless, it is a happy surprise to come across Mitterrand's sardonic reflections on certain bizarre funeral rites beginning to be practiced in France (and imported from the USA), and his gleeful scorn modulating beautifully into this final conclusion: "A society which hides death from the eyes of the living . . . is not magnifying life but corrupting it. Birth and death are the two wings of time. How can man's spiritual search come to fulfillment if he ignores these dimensions?"

The sensibility that produced such lines is rare not alone in a politician but in anyone, and this is what helps give *The Wheat and the Chaff* its commanding vigor. It is to be expected that a man whom nature touches so poignantly, and who writes about natural things with such sensitivity and affection, should express a constant concern with the environment and the proliferation of ecological blights and horrors. But even so delicately attuned a person as Mitterrand can hardly claim to be alone in these perennial anxieties. The superb moments in the book come when the thoughts of the political creature and those of the artist (I do not think that too extravagant a word) merge together, creating insights which it may be of critical importance for the present-day reader to attend to. I am thinking not only of Mitterrand's loving appreciations of two poets who were also his friends— Theodorakis and St. John Perse—but in particular of his description of Pablo Neruda, old and dying, his own agony refracted in the murder of Salvador Allende and the terrible betrayal of Chile. It was none other than Neruda, Mitterrand tells us, who urged him to read for the first time Gabriel García Marquez's *One Hundred Years of Solitude*, that dark yet dazzling masterpiece whose pages open up so many doors of perception about Latin America and its prodigious destiny. Mitterrand remains haunted by the book, and throughout his own work there is a concern with Latin America— especially the outrages perpetrated there—that amounts almost to an obsession. But what a splendid obsession! As much an outsider to that world as, say, Alexander Haig, Mitterrand has acquired touchstones to the secrets of our southern hemisphere that may transcend the brute demands of *Realpolitik*. Neruda. Gabriel García Márquez and the tragic village of Macondo. How exhilarating it is to discover a man of politics gleaning new insights from these poetic visions. It may be naive, as I implied at the outset, to think that the world can be saved by men who respond with passion to these visions. But I for one feel cleansed, at least briefly, by the notion of such grace and tenderness dwelling together with the exigencies of power.

[Introduction to *The Wheat and the Chaff*, Seaver, 1982.]

Family Values

None of the members of my family is a cheerleader for the values so stridently celebrated at this past summer's convention in Houston. But I want to describe how the rescue team they organized on Christmas Day of 1985 helped ensure my survival and, perhaps paradoxically, confirmed a lovely statement by Barbara Bush at the same event.*

For weeks I had been confined to a room in a mental hospital, suffering from one of the darkest pains known to humankind—clinical depression. They burst into that grim green cell at noon, all twelve of them, my wife and son, three daughters and their extended families. They had brought with them an enormous turkey dinner complete with napkins and silver which they laid out on my bed. Cajolery or bribery had created this miracle, along with the very presence of such a mob—regulations stipulated no visitors in excess of two.

Even more impressive was their feat of muscling past the custodians a television set and VCR. My oldest daughter, a movie director, had pieced together—out of 8 mm film I had shot—a ribbon of scenes from the distant past, much childish mugging and antic tomfoolery set to Mozart. How deli-

---

* Styron refers to Barbara Bush's speech on "family values," delivered on August 19, 1992, at the Republican National Convention, held in the Astrodome in Houston, Texas.—J.W.

cious it was, in that chill and laughterless place, to hear the sound of pure hilarity and feel appetite stir again, and perceive the first glimmer of light in the dungeon of madness. I had a long way to go, yet months afterwards it was possible for me to situate recollections of this noisy explosion of love at the very start of my recovery.

That Christmas Day my family presented, by most common American standards, an unorthodox profile. One of my daughters was living in sin with her lover, who was present. Another daughter's stepson—he was also on hand—was born out of wedlock and had been reared with great proficiency and tenderness by a single mother who happens to be a lesbian. A favorite godson was likewise illegitimate. Had I been able to take a poll among them I would have found that then, as now, none of the members of my family believed in the power of prayer, or the need for it in or out of school (or hospital). All of them at one time or another have smoked pot, and inhaled it. None considers homosexuality to be either wrong or unnatural, and they all support a woman's right to abortion. They can take pornography or leave it but in any case do not judge it to be evil. Family values? The phrase would make them hoot. Family, as Barbara Bush said, "means putting your arms around each other, and being there." This was the only consideration which had value on that day of the beginning of my own rebirth.

[Previously unpublished. Styron wrote this reminiscence in 1992 at the invitation of *Time* magazine for a projected series on "The Family." The series was canceled; Styron's statement is preserved among his papers at Duke University.]

Clinton and the Puritans

I n France the Clinton Tragedy—no longer too strong a word, in English or French—has prompted commentators to try out every possible variation on the theme of American puritanism. For years I've been attempting to convince my friends in France that Americans are collectively quite as broadminded as the French. In fact, the tenor of public opinion in respect to our president's sex life has proved the point that Americans are generally as tolerant as the French in matters like lust and its capacity to unhinge otherwise reasonable human beings. What the French don't possess is the equivalent of the American South, where a strain of Protestant fundamentalism is so maniacal that one of its archetypal zealots, Kenneth Starr, has been able to really dismantle the presidency because of a gawky and fumbling sexual dalliance. No wonder that the French, along with much of the rest of the world, view Clinton's Tormentor as the embodiment of America's terrifying puritanical spirit.

Absent too from the French scene is a media with fangs bared to go to work on the presidential throat. *Newsweek*'s early rooting about for dirt in the Lewinsky affair would not have found a French equivalent. Nor would a French paper have printed a preposterous headline about Clinton's wretched little liaison such as that which ran above Peggy Noonan's column in *The Wall Street Journal:* "American Caligula."[1] While the French press is as celebrity-sodden and, in certain ways, as prone to sensation-mongering as our own, and while its members can behave like attack dogs in political affairs, almost all journals have continually honored the privacy of those in high office; their restraint has helped them avoid the sins of their American counterparts, some of whose indecent prying helped lay the groundwork for Clinton's ghastly public denuding at the hands of Kenneth Starr.

In May of 1981, on the day of François Mitterrand's inaugural, I stood amid a small circle of people gathered near the new president in the bush garden of the Élysée Palace. Mitterrand had a fondness for writers, and I, along with Arthur Miller and Carlos Fuentes, had been invited to the occasion. The sunny weather was almost perfect, the historic nature of the moment caused people to speak in excited, mildly alcoholic murmurs, and Mitterrand himself rocked back and forth on his heels, wearing his new grandeur with a look of numb surprise. But mainly I recall a subtle and hovering eroticism. Sex drenched the air like perfume. Seven of the admirers surrounding Mitterrand were lovely young women in their spring dresses; as time wore on and they left his side, one by one, each twittered, *"A bientot, François!"* A French journalist whom I knew, standing next to me, whispered amiably, "And you can bet they *will* be back soon."

Mitterrand had a wife and he had a mistress, who bore him a daughter—this is old news by now—and he also had a slew of girlfriends. Everybody knew about it and nobody gave a damn, least of all the members of the press, who had been aware for years of Mitterrand's robust appetites. They never mentioned his diligent womanizing. In a touching memoir about Mitterrand's last months of life—published this past spring in English under the title "Dying without God"—the journalist Franz-Olivier Giesbert spoke with the ex-president about numerous matters—politics, literature, history—but the subject of women came often to the fore. Giesbert knew Mitterrand in the days before his presidency and he recalls mornings when he would run into this avid lover, resembling "not so much a night owl as a wolf that had been out on the prowl until dawn." Giesbert adds that women "were not merely his passion but the only beings on the face of the earth capable of making him abandon his cynicism."

Mitterrand liked and admired Bill Clinton (as opposed to Reagan, whom he called a "dullard" and a "complete nonentity") and was especially fascinated by what he described as his "animality," which doubtless meant something steamier. It's easy to perceive a kinship between the two chiefs of state. Clinton's own tumultuous sexual past—the Arkansas bimbo eruption, "the hundreds of women" he spoke about to Monica Lewinsky—might find a correspondence in the wonderfully candid remark uttered by the dying Mitterrand: "To be able to yield to carnal temptation is in itself reason enough to govern."

Mitterrand was a deeply flawed character—many Frenchmen still hate him—but his presidency was creative and illustrious. Clinton's self-admitted wrongdoing, his lies and his nearly incomprehensible recklessness, helped produce Starr's inquisition—an ordeal that has left his career and his ambitions in wreckage. But if Clinton is the victim of a sexual "addiction," whatever that means, so clearly was Mitterrand; the difference is that in France a compact between the press and the public allowed the president to deal with his obsession, and even perhaps to revel in it, so long as he governed well.

In America a complicity between the public and the media has generated an ignoble voyeurism so pervasive that we have never permitted a man like Bill Clinton to proclaim with fury that his sex life, past and present, is nobody's business but his own. Long before Kenneth Starr set up his cruel and indefinable pillory there had begun to evolve a climate where privacy—*la vie privée*—to be cherished above all rights—was all but gone, leaving the way clear for the Starr Report itself, and its invincible repulsiveness.

[*New Yorker,* October 12, 1998. The text published here is the full version, preserved in a handwritten draft in the Styron collection at the Hollings Special Collections Library, University of South Carolina.]

Reports

Chicago: 1968

I t was perhaps unfortunate that Richard J. Daley, the hoodlum suzerain of the city, became emblematic of all that the young people in their anguish cried out against, even though he plainly deserved it. No one should ever have been surprised that he set loose his battalions against the kids; it was the triumphant end product of his style, and what else might one expect from this squalid person, whose spirit suffused the great city as oppressively as that of some Central American field marshal? And it was no doubt inevitable, moreover, a component of the North American oligarchic manner—one could not imagine a Trujillo so mismanaging his public relations—that after the catastrophe had taken place he should remain so obscenely lodged in the public eye, howling "Kike!" at Abe Ribicoff, packing the galleries with his rabble, and muttering hoarse irrelevancies about conspiracy and assassination, about the *Republican* convention ("They had a fence in Miami, too, Walter, nobody ever talks about *that!*") to a discomfited Cronkite, who wobbled in that Oriental presence between deference and faint-hearted suggestions that Miami and Chicago just might not be the same sort of thing.

That is what many of us did along about Thursday night in Chicago—retreat to the center, the blissful black interior of some hotel room, and turn on the television set. For after four days and nights in the storm outside, after the sleepless, eventually hallucinated connection with so many of the appalling and implausible events of that week, it was a relief to get off the streets and away from the parks and the Amphitheater and the boorish, stinking hotel lobbies and to see it as most Americans had seen it—even if one's last sight was that of the unspeakable Daley, attempting to explain away a shame that most people who witnessed it will feel to their bones for a very long time.

Yet, again, maybe in the immediate aftermath of the convention it was too bad that Daley should have hogged a disproportionate share of the infamy that has fallen upon the Democratic Party; for if it is getting him off the hook too easily to call him a scapegoat, nonetheless the execration he has received (even the New York *Daily News,* though partly, of course, out of civic rivalry, carried jeering stories about him) may obscure the fact that Daley is only the nastiest symbol of stupidity and desuetude in a political party that may die, or perhaps is already dead, because it harbors too many of his breed and mentality. Hubert Humphrey, the departed John Bailey, John Connally, Richard Hughes, Ed Muskie—all are merely eminent examples of a rigidity and blindness, a feebleness of thought, that have possessed the party at every level, reaching down to those Grant Wood delegates from North Dakota who spilled out from the elevators into my hotel lobby every morning, looking bright-eyed and war-hungry, or like Republicans, whom they emulated through becoming one of the few delegations that voted against the pacific minority Vietnam plank *en bloc.* It has been said that if various burdensome and antiquated procedural matters—the unit rule, for instance—had been eliminated prior to this convention, the McCarthy forces might have gained a much larger and more significant strength, and this is at least an arguable point of view; for a long while I myself believed it and worked rather hard to see such changes come about (some did), but now in retrospect it seems that the disaster was meant to be.

Recalling those young citizens for Humphrey who camped out downstairs in my hotel, that multitude of square, seersuckered fraternity boys and country-club jocks with butch haircuts, from the suburbs of Columbus and Atlanta, who passed out "Hubert" buttons and "Humphrey" mints, recalling them and their elders, mothers and fathers, some of them delegates and not all of them creeps or fanatics by any means, but an amalgam of everything— the simply well-heeled, most of them, entrenched, party hacks tied to the mob or with a pipeline to some state boss, a substantial number hating the war but hating it not enough to risk dumping Hubert in favor of a vague professorial freak who couldn't feel concern over Prague and hung out with Robert Lowell—I think now that the petrification of a party that allowed such apathy and lack of adventurousness and moral inanition to set in had long ago shaped its frozen logic, determined its fatal choice months before Eugene McCarthy or, for that matter, Bobby Kennedy had come along to rock, ever so slightly, the colossal dreamboat. And this can only reinforce what appears to me utterly plausible: that whatever the vigor and force of the dissent, whatever one might say about the surprising strength of support that the minority report received on the floor, a bare but crucial majority of Americans still is unwilling to repudiate the filthy war. This is really the worst thought of all.

Right now, only a day or so after the event, it is hard to be sure of anything. A residue of anguish mingles with an impulse toward cynicism, and it all seems more than ever a happening. One usually sympathetic journalist of my acquaintance has argued with some logic but a little too much levity that the violent confrontations, like the show of muscle among the black militants, were at least only a psychological necessity: after all, there were no killings, few serious injuries; had there been no violence the whole affair would have been tumescent, impossibly strained, like *coitus interruptus,* and who would have had a bruise or a laceration to wear home as a hero's badge? As for myself, the image of one young girl no older than sixteen, sobbing bitterly as she was being led away down Balbo Avenue after being brutally cracked by a policeman's club, is not so much a memory as a scene imprinted on the retina—a metaphor of the garish and incomprehensible week—and it cannot be turned off like the Mr. Clean commercial that kept popping up between the scenes of carnage. I prefer to think that the events in Chicago were as momentous and as fateful as they seemed at the time, even amid the phantasmagorical play of smoke and floodlights where they were enacted.

One factor has been generally overlooked: the weather. Chicago was at its bluest and balmiest, and that gorgeous sunshine—almost springlike—could not help but subtly buoy the nastiest spirit and moderate a few tempers. Had the heat been as intense and as suffocating as it was when I first arrived in the city the Tuesday before the convention began, I feel certain that the subsequent mayhem would have become slaughter. I came at that time to the Credentials Committee meeting in the Conrad Hilton as one of four "delegate challengers" from Connecticut, presenting the claim that the popular vote in the state primaries had indicated that 13 delegates out of 44 should be seated for Eugene McCarthy, rather than the 9 allowed the McCarthy forces by John Bailey. Although logic and an eloquent legal brief by Dean Louis Pollak of the Yale Law School were on our side, the megalithic party structure could not be budged, and it was on that stifling day—when I scrutinized from the floor the faces of the hundred-odd cozy fat cats of the committee, two from each state plus places like Guam, nearly all of whom were committed to the Politics of Joy and who indeed had so embraced the establishment mythopoeia that each countenance, male or female and including a Negro or two, seemed a burnished replica of Hubert Humphrey— that I became fully aware that McCarthy's cause was irrevocably lost. Nor was I encouraged to hedge on this conviction when, sweating like a pig, I made a brief *ad hominem* plea in summation of our case, finished, and sat down to the voice of the committee chairman, Governor Richard Hughes of New Jersey, who said, "Thank you, Mr. Michener." Later, the governor's young aide came up to apologize, saying that the governor knew full well who I was, that in the heat and his fatigue he must have been woolgathering and thinking of James Michener, who was a good friend of Mr. Hughes— a baffling explanation, which left me with ominous feelings about life in general.

When I returned as an observer to Chicago the following Sunday, the lobby of the Conrad Hilton resembled a fantasy sequence in some Fellini movie, people in vertical ascent and horizontal drift, unimaginable shoals of walleyed human beings packed elbow to elbow, groin to rump, moving sluggishly as if in some paradigmatic tableau of the utter senselessness of existence. It took me fifteen minutes to cross from one side of the hotel to the other, and although I endured many low moments during the convention, I think it was at this early point, amid that indecent crush of ambitious flesh, that my detestation of politics attained an almost religious passion.

The Conrad Hilton is the archetypal convention hotel of the universe, crimson and gold, vast, nearly pure in its efficient service of the demands of power and pelf, hence somehow beyond vulgarity, certainly sexless, as if dollar hustling and politicking were the sole source of its dynamism; even the pseudo-Bunny waitresses in the Haymarket bar, dungeon-dark like most

Chicago pubs, only peripherally distract from the atmosphere of computers and credit cards. Into the Hilton lobby later that week—as into the lobbies of several other hotels—the young insurgents threw stink bombs, which the management misguidedly attempted to neutralize with aerosol deodorants; the effect was calamitous—the fetor of methane mingled with hair spray, like a beauty parlor over an open sewer—and several of the adjoining restaurants seemed notably lacking in customers. Not that one needed any incentive to abandon the scene, one fled instinctively from such a maggot heap; besides, there was much to study, especially in downtown Chicago on the streets and in the park, where the real action was, not at the convention itself (I only went to the Amphitheater once, for the vote on the minority report), whose incredible atmosphere of chicanery and disdain for justice could best be observed through television's ceaselessly attentive eye.

Since I somehow felt that sooner or later the cops would make their presence felt upon me more directly (a hunch that turned out to be correct), it appeared to me that they deserved closer scrutiny. They were of course everywhere, not only in the streets but in the hotel lobbies and in the dark bars and restaurants, in their baby-blue shirts, so ubiquitous that one would really not be surprised to find one in one's bed; yet it was not their sheer numbers that truly startled, as impressive as this was, but their peculiar personae, characterized by a beery obesity that made them look half again as big as New York policemen (I never thought I might feel what amounted to nostalgia for New York cops, who by comparison suddenly seemed as civilized as London constables) and by a slovenly, brutish, intimidating manner I had never seen outside the guard room of a Marine Corps brig. They obviously had ample reason for this uptight façade, yet it was instantly apparent that in their sight not only the yippies but all civilians were potential miscreants, and as they eyed passersby narrowly I noticed that Daley, or someone, had allowed them to smoke on duty. Constantly stamping out butts, their great beer guts drooping as they gunned their motorcycles, swatting their swollen thighs with their sticks, they gave me a chill, vulnerable feeling, and I winced at the way their necks went scarlet when the hippies yelled "Pigs!"

On Tuesday night I left a party on the Near North Side with a friend, whom I shall call Jason Epstein, in order to see what was going on in nearby Lincoln Park. There had been rumors of some sort of demonstration and when we arrived, a little before midnight, we saw that in fact a group of young people had gathered there—I estimated a thousand or so—most of them sitting peacefully on the grass in the dark, illuminated dimly by the light of a single portable floodlamp, and fanning out in a semicircle beneath a ten-foot-high wooden cross. The previous night, testing the 11 P.M. curfew, several thousands had assembled in the park and had been brutally routed by the police, who bloodied dozens of demonstrators. Tonight the gathering was a sort of coalition between the yippies and the followers of a group of Near North Side clergymen who had organized the sit-in in order to claim the right of the people of the neighborhood to use the park without police harassment. "This is our park!" one minister proclaimed over the loud-speaker. "We will not be moved!"

Someone was playing a guitar, and folk songs were sung; there was considerable restlessness and tension in the air, even though it was hard to believe that the police would actually attack this tranquil assembly, which so resembled a Presbyterian prayer meeting rather than any group threatening public decorum and order. Yet in the black sky a helicopter wheeled over us in a watchful ellipse, and word got back to us that the police had indeed formed ranks several hundred yards down the slope to the east, beyond our sight. A few people began to leave and the chant went up: "Sit down! Sit down!" Most of us remained seated and part of the crowd began singing "The Battle Hymn of the Republic." Meanwhile, instructions were being given out by the old campaigners: Don't panic; if forced to the street, stay away from the walls and blind alleys; if knocked to the ground, use your jacket as a cushion against clubs; above all—walk, don't run.

The time was now about twelve-thirty. Vaseline was offered as a protection against Mace, wet strips of cloth were handed out to muffle the tear gas. The tension was not very pleasant; while it is easy to overdramatize such a moment, it does contain its element of raw threat, a queasy, visceral suspense that can only be compared to certain remembered episodes during combat training. "They'll be here in two minutes!" the minister announced.

And suddenly they were here, coming over the brow of the slope fifty yards away, a truly stupefying sight—one hundred or more of the police in a phalanx abreast, clubs at the ready, in helmets and gas masks, just behind them a huge perambulating machine with nozzles, like the type used for spraying insecticide, disgorging clouds of yellowish gas, the whole advancing panoply illuminated by batteries of mobile floodlights. Because of the smoke, and the great cross outlined against it, yet also because of the helmeted and masked figures—resembling nothing so much as those rubberized wind-up automata from a child's playbox of horrors—I had a quick sense of the medieval in juxtaposition with the twenty-first century or, more exactly, a kind of science fiction fantasy, as if a band of primitive Christians on another planet had suddenly found themselves set upon by mechanized legions from Jupiter.

Certainly, whatever the exact metaphor it summoned up, the sight seemed to presage the shape of the world to come, but by now we were up, all of us, off and away—not running, *walking*, fast—toward Clark Street, bleeding tears from the gas. The streets next to the park became a madhouse. The police had not been content to run us out of the park, but charging from the opposite direction, had flanked us, and were harrying people down the streets and up alleys. On a traffic island in the middle of Clark Street a young man was knocked to his knees and beaten senseless. Unsuspecting motorists, caught up in the pandemonium, began to collide with one another up and down the street. The crowd wailed with alarm and split into fragments. I heard the sound of splintering glass as a stone went through the windshield of a police car. Then somehow we disengaged ourselves from the center of the crowd and made our way down Wells Street, relatively deserted where in the dingy nightclubs go-go girls oblivious to the rout outside calmly wiggled their asses in silhouette against crimson windows.

It hardly needs mention that Daley might have dealt with these demonstrators without having to resort to such praetorian measures, but violence was the gut and sinew of Chicago during the week, and it was this sort of scene—not the antiseptic convention itself, with its tedium and tawdriness and its bought and paid-for delegates—that makes its claim on my memory. Amid the confusion, I recall certain serene little vignettes: in the lobby of the Pick-Congress Hotel, Senator Tom Dodd flushing beet-red, smiling a frozen smile while being pounded on the back by a burly delegate, steelworker type, with fists the size of cabbages, the man roaring, "I'm a Polack! We know how to ride that greased pig, too!" Or the visit I made—purportedly to win over delegates to McCarthy—to the Virginia delegation, where I was told by at least three members of the group that, while nominally for

Humphrey, they would bolt for Teddy Kennedy in a shot (this helped to convince me that he could have won the nomination hands down had he come to Chicago).

But it is mainly that night scene out of Armageddon that I recollect or, the next day, the tremendous confrontation in front of the Hilton, at the intersection of Michigan and Balbo (named for Italo Balbo, the Italian aviator who first dumped bombs on the Ethiopians) where, half blinded from the gas I had just caught on the street, I watched the unbelievable melee not from the outside this time, but in the surreal shelter of the Haymarket bar, a hermetically sealed igloo whose sound-resistant plate-glass windows offered me the dumbshow of cops clubbing people to the concrete, swirling squadrons of people in Panavision blue and polystyrene visors hurling back the crowds, chopping skulls and noses while above me on the invincible TV screen a girl with a fantastic body enacted a comic commercial for Bic ballpoint pens, and the bartender impassively mooned over his daiquiris (once pausing to inquire of a girl whether she was over twenty-one), and the Muzak in the background whispered "Mood Indigo." Even the denouement seemed unreal—played out not in the flesh but as part of some animated cartoon where one watches all hell break loose in tolerant boredom—when an explosion of glass at the rear of the bar announced the arrival of half a dozen bystanders who, hurled inward by the crush outside, had shattered the huge window and now sprawled cut and bleeding all over the floor of the place while others, chased by a wedge of cops, fled screaming into the adjacent lobby.

I left Chicago in a hurry—like many others—pursued by an unshakable gloom and by an even profounder sense of irrelevance. If all this anguish, all this naked protest, had yielded nothing but such a primitive impasse— perhaps in the end best symbolized not even by the strife itself but by a "victorious" Hubert Humphrey promising us still another commission to investigate the violence he might have helped circumvent—then the country truly seemed locked, crystallized in its own politics of immobility. There were, to be sure, some significant changes—removal of the unit rule, for one—at least partially brought about by those who worked outside the establishment, including many amateurs in politics; had they been effected in less hysterical circumstances, they might have been considered in themselves prodigious achievements.

And there were some bearable moments amid all the dreck: the going to bed unblanketed on the cold ground by the fires in Grant Park when I came back just before dawn after our encounter with the police in Lincoln Park, the crowds by the hundreds hemmed in by National Guard troops (themselves Illinois plowboys or young miners from places like Carbondale, most of them abashed and ill at ease—quite a contrast to the brutal belly-swagger of the cops—but all of them just as ignorant about the clash of ideologies that brought them up here from the prairies); or the next night when again there was a vigil in the park and over a thousand people, including protesting delegates from the convention, came bearing candles and sat until dawn beneath the stirring leaves singing "Where Have All the Flowers Gone?" as they waved their candles, a forest of arms; or the moment in the daylight, totally unexpected, when a busload of children, no more than six or seven years old, rode up from somewhere on the South Side with a gift of sandwiches for the demonstrators and slowly passed by in front of the park, chanting from the windows in voices almost hurtfully young and sweet: "We want peace! We want peace!" But these moments were rare and intermittent and the emotional gloss they provided was unable to alleviate not just the sense of betrayal (which at least carries the idea of promise victimized) but the sorrow of a promise that never really existed.

[*New York Review of Books*, September 26, 1968.]

Down the Nile

In the autumn of 1849, Gustave Flaubert and a friend, Maxime Du Camp, made a wonderful trip to Egypt. At twenty-eight, Flaubert was a handsome, tall, high-spirited, neurotic young man with an ardent yearning for the exotic enchantments of the Orient. It may have been flight from his adored but incredibly dominating mother that in part impelled this journey, or perhaps it was disappointment over his first serious literary effort, *The Temptation of Saint Anthony*. More understandably, he had a serious and informed taste for antiquity and an irrepressible love of prostitutes, and in Egypt he knew he would find both in abundance. In any case, Flaubert, who was unknown as a writer (*Madame Bovary* would not appear until seven years later and bring him instantaneous fame), was even then indefatigably recording his impressions of the world, and his travel notes and letters from that nine-month odyssey along the Nile remarkably foreshadow the powers of observation and the acute sensibility that brought his masterpiece into being. By turns beautiful, rapturous, bawdy, hideous, and brutal, his record is also from time to time quite funny. Not only because of the contrasts it presents between the Egypt of now and then but because of the similarities, it comprises a fascinating and instructive document, delicious reading in itself but required reading—let me assign it as a text: *Flaubert in Egypt,* translated and edited by Francis Steegmuller, Academy Chicago Limited Edition, 1979—for all present-day voyagers along the Nile.

It can accurately be said that there is almost no place on earth that any longer is safe from tourism. When cruises to the Galápagos Islands are within reach of middle-class vacationers, and jumbo jets from New Zealand fly past the ice mountains of Antarctica for panoramic sightseeing trips (and tragically crash, as one plane did not long ago), we have truly begun to inhabit the "global village." Not only is the Nile no exception, it was beginning to be overrun by tourists even in Flaubert's time, when the exigencies of transportation were complicated to a degree that people accustomed to modern luxury travel can only reflect upon with discomfort. In the Egypt of the mid-nineteenth century, the invaders were already on the scene, inflicting their characteristic wounds. Their ubiquitous spoor—the inescapable graffiti—caused Flaubert some of his deepest moments of depression. "In the temples we read travelers' names; they strike us as petty and futile. We never write ours; there are some that must have taken three days to carve, so deeply are they cut in the stone. There are some that you keep meeting everywhere—sublime persistence of stupidity." At the Pyramid of Khepren his despair deepens. Under the name of Belzoni, the great archaeologist, he discovers "no less large, that of M. Just de Chasseloup-Laubat. One is irritated by the number of imbeciles' names written everywhere: on the top of the Great Pyramid there is a certain Buffard, 79 rue Saint-Martin, wallpaper-manufacturer, in black letters; an English fan of Jenny Lind's has written her name; there is also a pear, representing Louis-Philippe."

Tourism is, in general, a human activity that is neither desirable nor undesirable, merely existing in relationship with some landscape or other because people in their incessant curiosity will travel and observe and explore. Under certain circumstances, however, and usually after the passing of a long period of time, tourism becomes absolutely essential to the life of a place, becomes symbiotic, indeed so organically linked as to resemble the teeming bacterial flora that inhabits the human alimentary tract and that contributes to the body's very survival. Over the past one hundred and fifty years or so, Egypt has developed just such a relationship with its legions of visitors. The tourists who pour in season after season, year after year, comprise a critical factor in Egypt's economy; remove tourism, and the country would suffer a catastrophic blow. What makes the present situation so ironic, and so gloomy to contemplate, is that the very tourism that supplies Egypt with an essential part of its sustenance is threatening to destroy the body of the host. Aggravating as they were to Flaubert, and are to the modern visitor, the composers of graffiti are a minor annoyance compared to the larger menace. Both the proliferation of people—in multinational droves becoming more uncontrollable each year—and the sheer physical damage caused by so many millions of shoes stirring up so many tons of abrasive dust, by countless lungs exhaling huge volumes of corrosive carbon dioxide into the fragile environment of the tombs, have brought on a situation of real crisis. Expert observers believe that only immediate and drastic measures will enable Egypt to save the Nile and its treasures for future generations.

As if this were not enough, there is the matter of the dam—the High Dam at Aswan. Built in the 1960s by the Russians at the behest of Gamal Abdel Nasser, then Egypt's president, this vast edifice—now the second-largest rock-filled dam in the world—was intended to usher in the nation's new economic millennium; by the trapping of billions of tons of Nile water in a prodigious reservoir named Lake Nasser, the river would be subjugated, while judicious control and manipulation of the water would bring cheap electrical energy to the entire Nile Valley, along with the potential for millions of newly irrigated acres of fertile land. That much of this has already been accomplished seems indisputable, but, it is becoming increasingly clear, the cost may eventually cancel out the benefits. Many observers believe that the negative effects wrought upon the river by the dam will prove in the long run to be, quite simply, disastrous. I was to learn in detail about these consequences and to view at first hand some of the harbingers of the Nile's change for the worse (I had been on the river once before, in 1967) during a recent February trip down the waterway from Aswan to Cairo, when I was from time to time made uneasily aware that I, too, along with my companions on the voyage, had become yet another manifestation of the tourist pestilence. But even so, it was possible to take some comfort from the fact that the auspices under which we traveled were both dignified and felicitous. Our host on the trip, and a good friend of each of the dozen or so Americans and Europeans whom he had invited aboard the M.S. *Abu Simbel,* was Prince Sadruddin Aga Khan, son of the late Aga Khan and until recently the High Commissioner for Refugees of the United Nations. Married to an Egyptian and profoundly involved in Egypt, its culture, and its history, the prince has a house in Cairo; even more significantly, it was in large measure due to his efforts through UNESCO that the majestic colossi and temples of Abu Simbel and Philae were rescued from the encroaching waters created by the High Dam. Thus, plainly, although we were traveling in privacy and style (the comfort of a boat of one's own is something one need not apologize for), the prince's intimate connection with the Nile and his concern for its heritage and its future allowed his guests a unique perspective—without overly solemnizing what still remains, despite the foregoing auguries, one of the most mysteriously ravishing and moving journeys it is possible to make on the face of the earth.

"Handsome heads, ugly feet" is Flaubert's comment upon the Colossi of Abu Simbel, those gargantuan figures that stand guard on the shores of the Upper Nile, six hundred miles from Cairo; in 1850 the four statues were still partially buried under the sand. Flaubert's companion, Du Camp, made the first known photographs of these sandstone figures of Rameses II, after a boat trip from Cairo that lasted nearly two months. Our own trip from Cairo to Abu Simbel (which we visit before boarding our vessel in Aswan) takes a bare two hours by Egypt Air Boeing 737. In these upper reaches of the waterway, the Nile itself, of course, has become obliterated below the vast and murky expanse of Lake Nasser, which spills out across the desert in a desolate pool nearly the size of Delaware. Interspersed with jagged rock promontories and devoid of vegetation at its edges save for a rare patch of the palest green, like lichen, the lake from the air has an evil, unearthly look, resembling the kind of lake astronauts might encounter beneath the mantle of Saturn or Venus. We land on the recently built airstrip, step out into desert air, which at noon is briskly chill, and are thankful that it is winter. In the depths of summer it has sometimes become so hot that planes have been unable to land; the tarmac melts, turned to the consistency of black glue. A brief overland trip by bus brings us to the site.

Rescued from the flood and, by a marvel of engineering, hoisted above it nearly two hundred feet, the Abu Simbel colossi are appallingly big, exceeding all preconceived notions (derived from photographs, even Du Camp's flat, primitive ones) of their bigness; they are simply *immense*. And awe-inspiring, without a doubt. That these great effigies might have been allowed to sink without trace beneath the waters of Nasser's lake is unthinkable. But despite the sense of awe that they elicit—monuments to human ingenuity, human toil—they do not, for me at least, inspire that ineffable thrill of pleasure that one experiences in the presence of great heroic art. This could be partly due to that "pitiless rigidity" of which Flaubert complained in regard to Egyptian sculpture; or it might be because the colossi, with their enigmatic smiles that so often seem to possess the faintest shadow of a smirk, are simply intimidating, vainglorious, invoking the idea not of true grandeur but of pelf, influence, power. Also, to reproduce one's self four times in figures sixty-six feet high would seem to be a redundancy. The playwright Arthur Miller, one of the *Abu Simbel*'s voyagers, sits in the chill afternoon light regarding these grandiose duplications (a cast on a recently fractured ankle renders Miller less mobile than the rest of us). "Think of the poor people in those days," he muses, "who dared to come down the river to invade Egypt from the south. One look at this display and they'd be ready to run back home." One agrees. They are paradigms of a universal motif: human domination. They would not look out of place adorning the façade of the Chase Manhattan Bank. Even so, they may be more perishable than one might imagine. Farida Galassi, the eloquent French-born Egyptologist who is our guide and who has lived in Egypt for most of her seventy-four years, speaks dispiritedly of the future of the colossi, remarking that she and some of her colleagues feel that the elevation of the statues to higher ground is not only a mere reprieve but a move that in itself contains the seeds of doom. The reason for this is that the old site offered shelter to these vulnerable sandstone figures, while the new location provides exposure to frequent sandstorms, which could prove to be completely destructive in no more than an eyewink in Egyptian time—seventy-five to a hundred years. Thus the High Dam, in a perverse and unpredicted way, may claim Abu Simbel as a victim after all.

Our eponymous vessel awaits at dockside in Aswan. The son of a shipbuilder, I look over the M.S. *Abu Simbel* with thoughtful attention and am utterly pleased. Relatively small by Nile standards—one hundred and twenty feet long—she and her sister vessel, the *Aswan,* were built in 1979, the first metal boats to be constructed in Egypt. With a catamaran bottom, she is able to negotiate the shallows. She has nice clean lines, with no furbelows or waste space; yet there are ample cabins with efficient plumbing and abundant hot water (essential after each day's desert dust), a comfortable dining saloon with bar, and, perhaps most attractive of all, an open upper deck of fine proportions, allowing visual access to what for many travelers is a Nile voyage's greatest glory: the incomparable river itself and the timeless tableaux of its shores. Flaubert and Du Camp navigated the Nile by *cange,* a small sailboat also supplied with oarsmen. "Our two sails, their angles intersecting," Flaubert wrote, "swelled to their entire width, and the *cange* skimmed along, heeling, its keel cutting the water. . . . Standing on the poop that forms the roof of our cabin, the mate held the tiller, smoking his black wood *chibouk*." Flaubert and his friend traveled with a crew of twelve, a fairly high ratio for two passengers; our baker's dozen requires twenty in the crew, likewise a high ratio when one considers that none are oarsmen. A passage by sail and oar would surely have its own enchantments, and such a trip can still be managed for one or two adventurers; but this form of cruising has virtually disappeared from the river. We are enfolded, rather, in soothing decadence. The food is excellent, often superb. Fully air-conditioned, our vessel travels downstream at an almost vibrationless eight knots, powered by twin one-hundred-and-fifty-horsepower Caterpillar engines. But if our motors are modern, our helm is nearly as ancient as the river itself. There is not a single navigational aid on the Nile—not a buoy, not a marker or a beacon—and our helmsmen steer by sight, most often discerning the bars and shoals in this generally shallow river by the characteristic rippling effect on the surface (sometimes completely undetectable to the casual eye) and proceeding boldly at night as long as moonlight permits. They are incredibly gifted navigators but, alas, not perfect; once in a great while, the boat scrapes bottom.

We remain in Aswan for a day or two. The city, situated above the rapids of the river and its clumps of vivid green islands, is a beautiful one, even though its runaway growth (from fifty thousand to almost a million in twenty years) is a measure in itself of Egypt's huge population explosion. Just as the city dominates the river, the city is dominated by the High Dam. Dams, with their attendant benefits and mischief, are not new to Aswan. Around the turn of the century, the British built a dam that, though lower than the new Russian model, was considered a prodigy among dams in its day, allowing the cultivation of vast tracts of land in middle Egypt. It also caused the submergence, for most of the year, of the nearby Temple of Philae, a grand edifice of the Ptolemaic period dedicated to the goddess Isis. Sixty years later the High Dam threatened inundation of Philae forever. But thanks to the similar, almost superhuman efforts that saved Abu Simbel, Philae was rescued, lifted up stone by stone with astonishing precision and deposited in perfect rebirth of itself on a nearby island. Thus was effected over the High Dam a major cultural triumph. It is a pity that such triumphs are few, for it is becoming clear that the harm inflicted by the new dam is enormous. Just one unforeseen case in point may be demonstrated by a crucial difference between the old dam and the new. Whatever its drawbacks, the British structure, with its elaborate chain of sluiceways, did permit an unquestionably major function: it allowed most of the huge tonnage of silt to pass through. By contrast, the High Dam is badly flawed in this respect: so much silt has backed up in Lake Nasser that it has become an obstruction, making necessary a diversionary channel to deposit this life-giving soil in, of all places, the desert.

That the Americans, largely because of the politics of John Foster Dulles in the 1950s, were prevented from being the builders of the High Dam is perhaps just as well. Certainly, among other things, Americans are now spared the blame for that appalling monument to Egyptian-Russian friendship, which stands two hundred and fifty feet high at the dam site. Dazzlingly white and constructed in the shape of what may crudely be described as four symmetrically arranged winglike pylons rising toward heaven, the monument achieves an effect just the opposite of upward aspiration, resembling nothing so much as the exposed fins of a colossal concrete artillery shell that has embedded itself in the earth. As we ascend to the top in an elevator, Prince Nicholas Romanoff, a collateral descendant of the czar who can at other times speak with deep affection of things Russian, comments glumly on the traditional failure of Russian architecture, interestingly theorizing that as architects, Russians have been so uninspired because the country has always lacked in quantity that requisite material: stone. In any case, although the view from the top of the structure is spectacular—offering a bright blue vista of the waters of Lake Nasser; the surrounding desert; and also the dam itself, stretching an amazing two miles across the crest of the site—one is scarcely heartened by what one hears now about the dam's further pernicious effects on the river, to which it was supposed to bring an unmixed shower of blessings.

The greater part of the water of the Nile comes from heavy rainfall in Ethiopia. Because of seasonal vagaries, the volume of Nile water is produced with irregularity, but for thousands of years, life along the river has been governed by the annual flooding, whether little or great or just enough. Too much water in this flood and there is risk of a destructive inundation; too little water and the fields grow dry for want of irrigation. This is an oversimplified description of the hydrology of the Nile, about which there have been written many scientific volumes and about which, too, much remains a mystery. The High Dam, aside from its hydroelectric capabilities, was built to put an end to the unpredictable nature of the annual flood and, in effect, to stabilize the flow of water from Aswan to the sea. Probably the most serious consequence of such stabilization is this: while, indeed, the damage that comes from uncontrolled flooding has been eliminated, there has resulted a situation in which the great deposits of silt, so necessary to agriculture, have also been eliminated. Thus the land has suddenly and for the first time become seriously dependent on artificial fertilizer, which is extremely expensive and something few Egyptian farmers can afford. Also, at the mouth of the Nile, fish in the Mediterranean used to feed on organisms conveyed by the silt, but now that the silt is gone, fish and fisheries have been decimated. It is an ecological nightmare. The long-range effects are incalculable—and cannot be good.

Another unforeseen result of the dam is one that demonstrates in a rather weird way man's ability to alter the very normality of certain natural phenomena. It of course almost never rains in the desert, and the green richness of Egypt comes about entirely because of the Nile. But through the formation of Lake Nasser's mammoth reservoir, one of the largest of its kind anywhere, there has been created around it a microclimate in which large-scale condensation and precipitation occur from time to time, and rain falls, reportedly often in torrents. Many villages in the Upper Nile region, made of mud brick and totally unprepared for such freakish downpours, have suffered severe damage because of the High Dam. In other times, people were at least forewarned about occasional inundations.

A few miles north of the dam, at the Temple of Philae, I remember Flaubert's reflection: "The Egyptian temples bore me profoundly." This is not entirely true, for it is belied by his vigorous descriptions at other moments in his journal; often his reactions to these antique glories are deeply appreciative and recorded with excitement. Yet there is something genuine in his boredom, and his friend Du Camp wrote: "The temples seemed to him always alike. . . . At Philae he settled himself comfortably in the cool shade of one of the halls of the great Temple of Isis to read *Gerfaut*, by Charles de Bernard." Visiting Philae myself and recalling this passage, I do not quite feel disposed to sit down and read, but I can begin somehow to partake in Flaubert's dissatisfaction (or is it merely impatience?) with these places, wondrous as they are and as essential as one feels it is that they be seen and visited and strenuously preserved. There are moments of melting and exquisite beauty in Egyptian art—the friezes, the statuary, the gods and goddesses—but for me the glory lies less in the art itself than in a resonance of time and history. This is felt (or, paradoxically, almost heard) in the architecture; for, as Flaubert wrote, "everything in Egypt seems made for architecture—the planes of the fields, the vegetation, the human anatomy, the horizon lines." And here Flaubert begins to reveal what it is about the Nile that most deeply moves him and engages his passionate attention: the people and the landscape of unparalleled enchantment. I am afraid that it is a feeling that I share. Witness, for instance, his dutiful description of the Temple of Esna: "This temple is 33m. 70 long and 16m. 89 wide, the circumference of the columns is 5m. 37. There are 24 columns. . . . An Arab climbed onto the capital of a column to drop the metric tape. A yellow cow, on the left, poked her head inside." Plainly, it is the cow that interests Flaubert, not the temple. It is much the same with me.

I wish to board the *Abu Simbel* and leave Aswan on an upbeat note, wanting to feel at ease with this majestic river, but it is very hard. I think of the "sociological" concerns I would like to touch upon but cannot. By Egyptian standards Aswan is as clean as, say, Toronto, yet its backstreets smell of filth, of urine and corruption. Much of Egypt smells like this. I cannot hesitate even a second to ponder the squalor and poverty of Egypt; it would require the passion, the commitment, of an entire book. Meanwhile, my concern is with the dam and its twin goblin, tourism. Realizing the possible absurdity of my obsession with the latter when I am but a particle of the tourist mass, I find that what I see still bothers me sorely. Above Cairo, Flaubert's Nile was virtually empty, its mode of navigation primitive; certainly the river did not lack a few travelers, but when Flaubert writes about them they take on the quality of being unannounced, rare, a little strange. ("A *cange* carrying a party of Englishmen comes sailing furiously down the river, spinning in the wind.") Berthed near us at quayside are two enormous boats of the Sheraton hotel chain. Ungainly, totally utilitarian, they are painted in garish blue, white, and gold colors and are capable of accommodating one hundred and seventy-five persons.

These barges, together with their two sister vessels, are typical of the bloated floating hotels that have replaced the much smaller, humanly scaled paddle-wheelers that cruised the river as recently as 1975; those were stylish old boats, really, with the charm of Mark Twain's Mississippi. They carried a reasonable number of passengers. Unsurprisingly, the Sheraton monsters have been made possible by the High Dam, since the fluctuating depth of the water in the old days prevented vessels of such bulk and displacement. At temple sites they disgorge tourists in nearly unmanageable hordes. Also, besides carrying far too many people, these boats are of such size and power that their wake has begun to contribute to the erosion of riverbanks already eroded badly enough. In the gentle dusk they possess a truly wounding unsightliness. And I cannot decide who has produced the greatest eyesore here in lovely Aswan—Sheraton or, once again, the Russians, who during the building of the High Dam erected a hotel that unpardonably interrupts the serene, low skyline like some grandiose airport control tower. (There have been, since the departure of the Russians, serious thoughts about blowing up this structure, but like the dam, it is built for such permanence as to make the cost of demolition prohibitive.)

But during the days that follow on the *Abu Simbel,* almost all anxieties concerning the Nile's future are absorbed in contemplation of the river itself. When one is removed from the population centers like Aswan—and there are few of these—it seems impossible that anything could seriously encroach upon this timelessness. In benign hypnosis I sit on deck for hour after hour, quite simply smitten with love for this watercourse, which presents itself to the gaze in many of its aspects exactly as it did five thousand years ago. "Like the ocean," Flaubert wrote, "this river sends our thoughts back almost incalculable distances." Beyond the fertile green, unspooling endlessly on either bank, is the desert, at times glimpsed indistinctly, at other times heaving itself up in harsh incandescent cliffs and escarpments, yet always present, dramatizing the fragility but also the nearly miraculous continuousness of the river and its cycles of death and resurrection. Sometimes life teems, as at the edge of a village where men and women, children, dogs, donkeys, goats, camels, all seem arrested for an instant in a hundred different attitudes; a donkey brays, children shout and whistle at us, and the recorded voice of a muezzin from a spindly minaret follows us in a receding monotone.

At other times life is sparse, intermittent: a solitary buffalo grazing at the end of an interminable grassy promontory, seemingly stranded light-years from anything, as in outer space. A human figure on a camel, likewise appearing far from any habitation, robes flapping in the wind, staring at us until we pass out of sight. Undulant expanses of sugarcane, furiously green; groves of date palms; more cane in endless luxuriant growth; then suddenly:

a desolate and vast sandbar, taking us many minutes to pass, that could be an unmarked strand at the uttermost ends of the earth—one could rot or starve there and one's bones never be found. Now in an instant, a fabulous green peninsula with dense undergrowth, feathery Mosaic bulrushes, a flock of ducks scooting along the shore. We pass by a felucca, drifting, its sail down. One robed figure kneels in prayer; the other figure, with an oar, keeps the bow pointed toward Mecca. Then soon, as we move around a gentle bend, history evaporates before the eye, and there is an appalling apparition: a sugar refinery belching smoke. But *infernal* smoke! Black smoke such as I cannot recall having seen since childhood in the 1930s, during a trip past the terrible mills and coke ovens of western Pennsylvania. There are no smoke pollution controls along the valley—another bad sign for the beleaguered Nile.

Furthermore, lest I become too beguiled by the river's charms, I am sobered by evidence of still another kind of havoc wrought by that hulking barrage at Aswan. This threatens the very existence of the monuments themselves and can be viewed graphically at the Temple of Esna, thirty miles south of Luxor, on the west bank of the river. The harm being done is the result of the titanic volume of water behind the High Dam, the pressure of which has altered and, together with overirrigation, slowly raised the subterranean water table along the valley. In places the water contains a heavy saturation of salts, which, rising to the surface, have begun to attack not only the land but the foundations of many of the temples. Quite corrosive white streaks of this ominous residue can be plainly seen everywhere; but at the ancient Temple of Abydos (which we visit a few days later), the wonderful and mysterious underground structure known as the Oserion (aptly called "an idea in stone") has become sacrificed not to the salt but, even worse, to the water itself, and much of the great architecture is flooded forever. Thus, like an unshakable and troubling presence, the High Dam adumbrates the future of man, his heritage, and nature up and down the valley. In the gorgeous lush green fields beyond Esna, I glimpse a stunning juxtaposition that tells much about the confusion—the triumph and error, gain and miscalculation—that ensues when man attempts to modify any natural force as prodigious as the Nile: adrift in the air, a web of high-tension wires, humming, gleaming, the very emblem of newly harnessed energy; directly beneath the wires, a sickly and ravaged field not long ago cultivated in thriving vegetables, now overlaid with huge dirty-white oblongs of deadly salt.

But what is the future of the Nile? Do these alarming portents mean that the outlook for the river is inescapably somber? At the moment, one can only speculate. If it is remarkable that human beings in their recklessness and folly have, in the past hundred years or so, nearly destroyed some of their greatest and most beautiful rivers and lakes, it is equally remarkable that those very waterways have proved to be capable of survival, even health, given enough time and given the human determination to reverse the death process. The Thames, the beautiful Willamette in Oregon, and to some extent the Hudson—still in the midst of resuscitation—are just a few examples of this provisional deliverance; and it may be that even the awful felony committed upon the James in Virginia—the wanton dumping of tons of a lethal insecticide into the stream, causing a contamination of marine life that destroyed fishing and the fishing industry for years—will be alleviated by time, with the poisons eventually washed away and the natural equilibrium once again achieved. Pollution along the Nile (including much sewage and trash pollution from tourist boats) is a potential problem; more subtle and dangerous is a form of pollution by disease—and once again the culprit is the High Dam, the sins of which begin to bemuse one by the sheer monotony of their enumeration. This has to do with bilharzia (also known as schistosomiasis), the gravely debilitating, often fatal parasitic disease that is endemic in lower Egypt. Many experts in environmental medicine believe that the disease—caused by microscopic blood flukes that breed in the bodies of snails, then float about in shallow water and penetrate into the bloodstream of mammals, including human beings—was minimized in its extent by the annual flushing action of the great Nile flood, which swept up countless quantities of the snails and their larval guests and removed them from the shallows, where people were most likely to become infected. But the dam changed all this. Now the general stillness of the water means a more prolific generation of snails and parasites, more frequent infestation in the backwaters, and possibly more disease, despite strenuous public-health campaigns.

The Nile is the ancient mother-river of the Western world, and it is impossible to conceive of her failure to survive these present vicissitudes. Although what man has done in the past twenty years may appear inexplicably thoughtless, and vainglorious, too—interrupting that immemorial ebb and flow, shattering a rhythm that existed eons before man himself appeared on these seductive banks—one feels that it does not really spell the end, although much cruel injury has been done. Human beings are both resilient and ingenious in crisis—never more so than when guiltily surveying the harm that they have inflicted themselves—and one can conceive of the un-hurried pace of Egyptian time allowing men to forestall more ruin and even perhaps to rectify some (though certainly not all) of the damage that may now seem beyond repair. Finally, there might be controlled here on the Nile one of the worst of the pollutions of man: the aimless proliferation of his own peripatetic self.

Toward the end of our trip, stopping to view the Colossi of Memnon at Thebes, I recall a typical Flaubertian animadversion. "The colossi," he wrote, "are very big, but as far as being impressive is concerned, no. . . . Think of the number of bourgeois stares they have received! Each person has made his little remark and gone his way." This sour putdown inevitably causes me to think of the hordes of tourists who stream past the colossi on their way to or from the Valley of the Kings. As a fragment of one of these hordes, but momentarily detached, I stand at midday on top of the towering cliff overlooking the enormous Temple of Deir el Bahari, certainly the dom-inating man-made presence in this valley of temples and tombs. Far below on the desert floor, dozens of buses and vans are disgorging their human cargo. The visitors represent nearly every nationality in the world, and as they proceed up and down the terraces ascending to the colonnade at the temple's upper level, they seem an orderly but overwhelming mass, almost numberless; they remind me of the throngs of Disneyland or, even more claustrophobically, as I go down and move among them, of the mob of which I was a gawking young member at the New York World's Fair in 1939. It is fortunate that they—or I should say, we—have been barred permanently from many of the tombs, for it has been demonstrated that the acid exhala-tions of our breath combined with our million-footed shuffling in the dust has caused irreparable damage already. But people keep coming in ever in-creasing legions, and it may be that these very numbers, uncontrolled, will soon prove to be more injurious to Egypt than the High Dam.

This is not an alarmist view—it is based on solid evidence—but even so, the situation might change for the better through a strict and systematic program of regulation. Prince Aga Khan, who has made a study of the tour-ist crisis, believes that a rigorous policy on the part of the Egyptian govern-ment would, in not too long a time, finally restrain this runaway influx of travelers, lessening the attrition at the historic sites and making a trip to the Nile a happier event for everyone, including the Egyptians. The policy would commence not only with the limiting of permits for the building of hotels and boats but with supervision—through expert architectural advice—of the construction of these boats and hotels, so as to avoid such atrocities as the hostelry the Russians put up at Aswan or the oversize Sheraton barges. Hotels and tourist villages would be developed in conformity with local traditions and landscape and, just as importantly, be decentralized. They would be moved away from the already preposterously engorged centers of Luxor and Aswan. Such measures would benefit both the tourist and the less economically prosperous population of the backward areas. The sites themselves would undergo drastic changes and management: rotation of tourist groups according to seasonal timetables in order to avoid overlapping and overcrowding; modernization of access roads; installation of advanced systems of dust and humidity control in the tombs, along with better superintendence and better lighting. These are strenuous measures, but in the opinion of the prince, neither impossible to implement nor economically unfeasible; the vast sums of money that tourists bring to Egypt (and which now seem to benefit Egyptian antiquities in only the most marginal way) should be sufficient to pay for such a program, with much left over. But the need is immediate.

How many trips in the world does one really want to make again? For me, not many. But I could go back to the Nile over and over, as if in mysterious return homeward, or in quest for some ancestral memory that has been only partially and tantalizingly revealed to me—as at that interval when one passes from sleep to waking. On the last evening aboard the *Abu Simbel* there comes to me a moment when I know the reason why I shall always want to come back to this river. Moored to the riverbank at the edge of a small village, the boat is peaceful, all energies unwound; at dusk, alone, I go up on deck and feel in my bones the chill of the coming night. In the village I see a nondescript street, children, a camel, a minaret. Far back on the river two feluccas rest as if foundered immovably upon a sandbar; the light around them is pearl-gray, aqueous, and they seem to hover so delicately on the river that it is as if they were suspended in some nearly incorporeal substance, like gauze or mist. With their furled sails, they are utterly motionless; they are like the boats on an antique china plate of my childhood. As the light fades from the sky and the stars appear, the village is silhouetted against the faintest pink of the setting sun. I am aware of only two sounds: the clinking of a bell, perhaps on some cow or donkey, and now the voice of a muezzin from the minaret, intoning the Koran's summons in dark and monotonous gutturals. It is then, in a quick flood of recognition, that I feel certain that *I have been here before,* in some other century. But as the sensation disappears, almost as swiftly as it comes, I ponder whether this instant of déjà vu means anything at all; after all, I am a skeptic about mystical experiences. Nonetheless, the feeling persists, I cannot quite shake it off—nor do I want to. And so I remain there in the dusk, listening to the soft muttering of the muezzin and gazing at the distant feluccas miraculously afloat in the air. And then I wonder how many others—hypnotized like me by this river and the burden of its history, and by the drama of the death along its shores and waters, and eternal rebirth in all—might have known the same epiphany.

[*GEO,* September 1981.]

Literary

.

Lie Down in Darkness

When, in the autumn of 1947, I was fired from the first and only job I have ever held, I wanted one thing out of life: to become a writer. I left my position as manuscript reader at the McGraw-Hill Book Company with no regrets; the job had been onerous and boring. It did not occur to me that there would be many difficulties to impede my ambition; in fact, the job itself had been an impediment. All I knew was that I burned to write a novel and I could not have cared less that my bank account was close to zero, with no replenishment in sight. At the age of twenty-two I had such pure hopes in my ability to write not just a respectable first novel, but a novel that would be completely out of the ordinary, that when I left the McGraw-Hill Building for the last time I felt the exultancy of a man just released from slavery and ready to set the universe on fire.

I was at that time sharing a cheap apartment with a fellow graduate from Duke University, a Southerner like myself. It was a rather gloomy basement affair far up Lexington Avenue near Ninety-fourth Street. I was reading gluttonously and eclectically in those days—novels and poetry (ancient and modern), plays, works of history, anything—but I was also doing a certain amount of tentative, fledgling writing. The first novel had not yet revealed itself in my imagination, and so most of my energies were taken up with short stories. The short story possessed considerably more prestige then than now; certainly, largely because of an abundance of magazines, the short story had far greater readership, and I thought that I would make my mark in this less demanding art form while the novel-to-be germinated in my brain. This, of course, was a terrible delusion. The short story, whatever its handicaps, is one of the most demanding of all literary mediums and my early attempts proved to be pedestrian and uninspired. The rejection slips began to come back with burdensome regularity.

Yet plainly there was talent signaling its need to find a voice, and the voice was heard. An extremely gifted teacher, Hiram Haydn, was conducting a writing course at the New School for Social Research, and I enrolled. Haydn was a pedagogue in the older, nonpejorative sense of the word, which is to say a man who could establish a warm rapport with young students. He had a fine ear for language, and something about my efforts, groping and unformed as they were, caught his fancy and led him to an encouragement that both embarrassed and pleased me.

Hiram Haydn was also an editor in a book publishing house. He said that he felt my talents might be better suited to the novel and suggested that I start in right away, adding that his firm would underwrite my venture to the extent of a $100 option. While hardly a bonanza, this was not nearly as paltry as it might sound. One hundred dollars could last a frugal young bachelor quite a long time in 1947. More importantly, it was a note of confidence that spurred my hungry ambition to gain glory and, perhaps, even a fortune. The only drawback now—and it was a considerable one—was that I had no idea as to how I would go about starting a novel, which suddenly seemed as menacing a challenge as all the ranges and peaks of the Himalayas. What, I would ask myself, pacing my damp Lexington Avenue basement, just what in God's name am I going to write about? There can be nothing quite so painful as the doubts of a young writer, exquisitely aware of the disparity between his capabilities and his ambition—aware of the ghosts of Tolstoy, Melville, Hawthorne, Joyce, Flaubert, cautionary presences crowding around his writing table.

That winter, between Christmas and New Year's Day, a monumental blizzard engulfed New York City. The greatest snowfall in sixty years. During that snowbound time two things occurred that precipitated me into actual work on my novel, as opposed to dreaming. The first of these was my receipt of a letter from my father in my hometown in Virginia (after three days the mail had begun to arrive through the drifts), telling me of the suicide of a young girl, my age, who had been the source of my earliest and most aching infatuation. Beautiful, sweet, and tortured, she had grown up in a family filled with discord and strife. I was appalled and haunted by the news of her death. I had never so much as held her hand, yet the feeling I had felt for her from a distance had from time to time verged on that lunacy which only adolescent passion can produce. The knowledge of this foreshortened life was something that burdened me painfully all through those cold post-Christmas days.

Yet I continued to read in my obsessed way, and the book which I then began—and which became the turning point in my struggle to get started—was Robert Penn Warren's *All the King's Men*. I was staggered by such talent. No work since that of Faulkner had so impressed me—impressed by its sheer marvelousness of language, its vivid characters, its narrative authority, and the sense of truly felt and realized life. It was a book that thrilled me, challenged me, and filled me with hope for my own possibilities as a writer. And so it was that soon after finishing *All the King's Men,* I began to see the first imperfect outline of the novel—then untitled—which would become *Lie Down in Darkness*. I would write about a young girl of twenty-two who committed suicide. I would begin the story as the family in Virginia assembled for the funeral, awaiting the train that returned her body from the scene of her death in New York City. The locale of the book, a small city of the Virginia Tidewater, was my own birthplace, a community so familiar to me that it was like part of my bloodstream.

And so even as the book began to take shape in my brain I became excited by the story's rich possibilities—the weather and the landscape of the Tidewater, against which the characters began to define themselves: father, mother, sister, and the girl herself, all doomed by fatal hostility and misunderstanding, all helpless victims of a domestic tragedy. In writing such a story—like Flaubert in *Madame Bovary,* which I passionately admired—I would also be able to anatomize bourgeois family life of the kind that I knew so well, the WASP world of the modern urban South. It was a formidable task, I knew, for a man of my age and inexperience, but I felt up to it, and I plunged in with happy abandon, modeling my first paragraphs on—what else?—the opening chapter of *All the King's Men.* Any reader who wishes to compare the first long passage of *Lie Down in Darkness* with the rhythms and the insistent observation and the point of view of the beginning pages of

Warren's book will without difficulty see the influence, which only demonstrates that it may not always be a bad thing for a young writer to emulate a master, even in an obvious way.

Lie Down in Darkness also owes an enormous debt to William Faulkner, who is of course both the god and the demon of all Southern writers who followed him. Writers as disparate as Flannery O'Connor and Walker Percy have expressed their despair at laboring in the shadow of such a colossus, and I felt a similar measliness. Yet, although even at the outset I doubted that I could rid myself wholly of Faulkner's influence, I knew that the book could not possibly have real merit, could not accrue unto itself the lasting power and beauty I wanted it to have, unless the voice I developed in telling this story became singular, striking, somehow uniquely my own. And so then, after I had completed the first forty pages or so (all of which I was satisfied with and which remain intact in the final version), there began a wrestling match between myself and my own demon—which is to say, that part of my literary consciousness which too often has let me be indolent and imitative, false to my true vision of reality, responsive to facile echoes rather than the inner voice.

It is difficult if not impossible for a writer in his early twenties to be entirely original, to acquire a voice that is all his own, but I was plainly wise enough to know that I had to make the attempt. It was not only Faulkner. I had to deafen myself to echoes of Scott Fitzgerald, always so easy and seductive, rid my syntax of the sonorities of Conrad and Thomas Wolfe, cut out wayward moments of Hemingway attitudinizing, above all, be myself. This of course did not mean that the sounds of other writers could not and did not occasionally intrude upon the precincts of my own style—T. S. Eliot, who was also a great influence at the time, showed definitively how the resonance of other voices could be a virtue—but it did mean, nonetheless, the beginning of a quest for freshness and originality. I found the quest incredibly difficult, so completely taxing that after those forty pages I began contemplating giving up the book. There seemed no way at all that I— a man who had not even published a short story—could reconcile all the formidably complex components of my vision, all of the elements of character and prose rhythms and dialogue and revelation of character, and out of this reconciliation produce that splendid artifact called a novel. And so, after a fine start—I quit.

I went down to Durham, North Carolina, where I had gone to college, and there took a tiny backstreet apartment, which I shared with a very neurotic cocker spaniel. Here I tried to write again. I toyed with the novel but it simply would not move or grow; the dispirited letters I wrote to Hiram Haydn must have told him that his one hundred dollars had gone down the drain. But plainly he was not to be discouraged, for after a whole year had gone by he wrote me from New York suggesting that my energies might be recharged if I once again moved north. It seemed a reasonable idea, and so in the summer of 1949, after transferring ownership of my spaniel to a professor of philosophy at Duke, I came back to the metropolis, still so impecunious that I had to take a cheap room far away from Manhattan's sweet dazzle, in the heart of Flatbush. (I stayed there only a month or so but it was an invaluable experience, demonstrating the serendipitous manner in which life often works to a writer's advantage: that month's residence provided the inspiration for a novel I wrote much later, *Sophie's Choice*.) In Brooklyn, too, I was unable to write a word.

But salvation from all my dammed-up torment came soon, in the form of two loving friends I had met earlier in the city. Sigrid de Lima, a writer who had also been in Haydn's class, and her mother, Agnes, recognized my plight and invited me to live in their fine old rambling house up the Hudson in the hills behind Nyack. There, in an atmosphere of faith and affection and charity (a homelike ambience which I plainly needed and whose benison I have never been able to repay), I collected my wits and with a now-or-never spirit set forth to capture the beast which had so long eluded me.

And as I began to discipline and harness myself, began for the first time to examine as coldly and as clinically as I could the tough problems which before this I had refused to face, I had a fine revelation. I realized that what had been lacking in my novelist's vision was really a sense of architecture—a symmetry, perhaps unobtrusive but always there, without which a novel sprawls, becoming a self-indulged octopus. It was a matter of form, and up until now this was an issue that out of laziness or fear, perhaps both, I had tried to avoid. I did not have to construct a diagram or a "plot"—this I have never done. I merely had to keep aware, as I progressed with the narrative in flashback after flashback (using the funeral as the framework for the entire story), that my heroine, Peyton Loftis, would always be seen as if through the minds of the other characters; never once would I enter her consciousness.

Further, she would be observed at progressive stages of her life, from childhood to early adulthood, always with certain ceremonials as a backdrop—country-club dance, a Christmas dinner, a football game, a wedding—and each of these ceremonials would not only illuminate the tensions and conflicts between Peyton and her family but provide all the atmosphere I needed to make vivid and real the upper-middle-class Virginia milieu I had set out to describe. Only at the end of the book, toward which the entire story was building—in Peyton's Molly Bloom–like monologue—would I finally enter her mind, and I hoped this passage would be all the more powerful because it was suddenly and intensely "interior," and personal. This, at any rate, was the scheme which I evolved, and from then on the writing of the book, while never easy (what writing is?), took on a brisk, self-generating quality in which I was able to command all other aspects of the story—dialogue, description, wordplay—to my own satisfaction, at least.

I completed *Lie Down in Darkness* on a spring evening in 1951 in a room on West Eighty-eighth Street in Manhattan, where I had moved after my liberating year in Rockland County. I finished Peyton's monologue last (having already written the ultimate scenes), and if to the present-day reader the passage has an added sense of doom and desperation, this may be because, a few months before, I had been called back by the Marine Corps to serve in the Korean War. Thus I think I had, like Peyton, only meager hopes for survival. I was twenty-five years old and—like Peyton—was much too young to die. But I survived, happy beyond my craziest dreams at the generally good reviews and at the fact that *Lie Down in Darkness* even reached the best-seller list. This was on the same list as two other first novels which, said *Time* magazine later on that year, expressed like mine a depressing and negative trend in American letters: *From Here to Eternity* and *The Catcher in the Rye*.

[*Hartford Courant Magazine,* January 3, 1982.]

"I'll Have to Ask Indianapolis—"

T here was a time in my life when Indianapolis figured very large as an influence on me. About two hundred years ago—it was 1951, to be exact—I finished my first novel, *Lie Down in Darkness*. In those post–World War II years there was a reverent, I should say almost *worshipful*, aura that surrounded the writing and publishing of novels. This is not to say that even today the novel as a literary form has lost cachet or distinction (though there are critics who would argue that position), but in those days to be a young novelist was a little like being a rock star in our time. The grand figures of the previous generation—Faulkner, Hemingway, Dos Passos, Sinclair Lewis, James T. Farrell—were still very much alive, and we young hopefuls were determined to emulate these heroes and stake our claim to literary glory. The first among the newcomers to make his mark was Truman Capote, whose brilliant tales and lovely novel *Other Voices, Other Rooms* filled me, his exact contemporary, with inordinate envy. Soon after this came *The Naked and the Dead* by Norman Mailer, a writer of such obvious and prodigious gifts that it took the breath away. Following on Mailer's triumph was James Jones's monumental *From Here to Eternity*, which was quickly succeeded by that classic which forever crystallized the soul of the American adolescent, *The Catcher in the Rye* by J. D. Salinger. I don't think it was vainglory on my part, as I was writing my own novel and was watching these fine books appear one after another, to consider myself an authentic member of the same generation and to want to make *Lie Down in Darkness* a worthy companion to those works.

I wrote the first pages of *Lie Down in Darkness* while I was living in New York City in the basement of a brownstone on upper Lexington Avenue. It was the winter of 1947. I was twenty-three years old and had just been fired from my job as junior editor with the McGraw-Hill Book Company—a fiasco I described much later in another book of mine, *Sophie's Choice.* There was a blizzard raging outside—it's still memorialized in weather annals as the greatest New York blizzard of the century—and those opening pages were written in passion and in the incomparable assurance of youth, and were never later touched or revised.

After the blizzard subsided I had a stack of manuscript pages and a burning desire to see them amplified with a full-fledged novel. But I sensed that I needed guidance and, even more than guidance, encouragement. I had heard of a lively and interesting class in fiction writing at the New School for Social Research, and I enrolled in this class, conducted by an engaging, scholarly teacher named Hiram Haydn. He was the ideal preceptor for a writing course, strict and no-nonsense regarding the substance of one's text, quick to detect softness or sloppiness or sentimentality, yet eager to find and nurture those radiant beams of true talent that occasionally appear in such a class. I was enormously pleased when I realized that he liked my work and, beyond that, thrilled that through him I was able to establish a publishing connection. For, as it turned out, Haydn had just been hired as New York editor of the Indianapolis-based house of Bobbs-Merrill. It also turned out that he had been given the authority to sign up for book contracts those among his students who he felt had literary promise. I sensed in Hiram an enormous zeal and idealism, a man determined to transform Bobbs-Merrill from a rather commercial enterprise, one whose chief previous glory had been the perennially huge best-seller *The Joy of Cooking,* into a publishing house that would honor and nurture good writing. And so I was flabbergasted and filled with joy when he offered me an option on my first novel and a check for an amount that was somewhat modest in those days, even by Indiana standards—one hundred dollars.

For the next three years I struggled to complete the book, moving all over the map, to North Carolina, to Brooklyn, to a small town up the Hudson River, to a cramped apartment that I shared with a young sculptor who was as poor as I was, on the Upper West Side of Manhattan. Money was a major problem for me—I had next to none except for a tiny stipend from my generous father—and the income I could expect derived entirely from what Hiram could shake from the coffers of Bobbs-Merrill. This is where the word *Indianapolis* began to loom large in my destiny. Whenever, literally down to my last single dollar, resorting to pawning the Elgin wristwatch I had received on my fifteenth birthday, or going to a grocery store and trying to redeem, for a box of frozen Birds Eye peas, the coupon my sculptor friend had received upon complaining about a worm he had found in another box of peas—when, in these straits, I approached Haydn for an advance on my royalties, the reply would come, "I'll have to ask Indianapolis." Mercifully, the response from this city was almost always favorable, ensuring my humble survival, but in any case the name *Indianapolis* acquired the quality of an incantation, rather portentous and ominous at the same time, like *Hanoi* during the time of Vietnam or *Moscow* throughout the Cold War.

The talismanic nature of Indianapolis became even more apparent somewhat later when, exhaustedly, I finished the last chapter of the book and went off as a Marine lieutenant to Camp Lejeune, North Carolina, where I began training for combat in the Korean War. This was a dark time indeed. Firmly believing that in September, when the book was scheduled to be published, I would be fighting the Chinese in Korea, I spent the spring and summer despairingly in the Carolina swamps, at least part of the time correcting the galleys of *Lie Down in Darkness*. Where Indianapolis came in once again was through the views of Bobbs-Merrill's management over matters of literary taste and propriety.

That time—the late 1940s and early '50s—was a watershed period in our literature. Although some years earlier *Ulysses* had been approved by the federal courts for adult consumption, Joyce's masterpiece was virtually unique in being exempt from the scrutiny of the censors and the puritans. But in the years following World War II there began a profound if gradual change toward permitting writers to express themselves more freely, particularly in the use of the vulgar vernacular and in matters of sex. I emphasize the gradualness of the transition. For example, in *The Naked and the Dead*, published in 1948, Norman Mailer was forced to use, for the common vulgarism describing sexual intercourse, not the four-letter word but a foreshortened three-letter epithet, *fug*. Among other results, this prompted the raunchy old actress Tallulah Bankhead, upon meeting young Mailer for the first time, to say, "Oh, you're the writer who doesn't know how to spell *fuck*." But the times were changing. The first book in American literature to employ this and other Anglo-Saxon expletives with absolute freedom was James Jones's *From Here to Eternity;* and even *The Catcher in the Rye,* published in that same year, 1951, used the word, although in a way that was intended to demonstrate its offensiveness. It's interesting, by the way, that even today *The Catcher in the Rye* is among the books most frequently yanked off the library shelves of public schools, usually at the behest of angry parents who, ironically and certainly stupidly, seem to be unaware that in this one case the word is seen by the young hero, Holden Caulfield, as objectionable.

But what about *Lie Down in Darkness,* also published in that turning-point year of 1951? As it developed, while I was with the Marines in North Carolina, Hiram Haydn was having trouble with Indianapolis. The powers that be at Bobbs-Merrill were getting upset over a few of the situations and the dialogue in my about-to-be-published manuscript. Unlike Mailer and Jones, I was writing of a domestic fictional milieu in which the common four-letter words were not employed frequently, at least at that time, but I had retained a few of the more or less milder dirty words, as they were called then, and several erotic situations that by present-day standards would seem amusingly tame. Nonetheless, Hiram Haydn, representing the New York office, found himself in conflict with the higher-ups in the Midwest office, and down in the Carolina boondocks I was caught in the cross fire. I remember some of Hiram's messages, which in those days, particularly because of my frequent inaccessibility, reached me by telegram. Once again the name of the capital city of Indiana took on the quality of an incantation. "Indianapolis," the wire would read, "suggests page 221 drop the word ass. Would you consider *bottom*?" Or, "Indianapolis concerned phrase page 140 *felt her up* too suggestive. Would you think of alternative?" And once I got a message that read, "Indianapolis will accept *big boobs* but will you still revise bit about *the open fly.*"

Fortunately, these strictures and reservations did no permanent damage to my text; nor did I feel that my work suffered any major violation. I mostly managed to knuckle under for Indianapolis without complaint. But what I've said does show you how, at midcentury, there still existed in certain quarters in America a point of view about free expression that was severely circumscribed, still profoundly in thrall to nineteenth-century standards and to a prudery that now seems so quaint as to be almost touching. It could be said, of course, that we have gone over the edge; indeed, there have been some books published in recent years that I've found so scabrous and loathsome that I've yearned, at least for a moment, for a return to Victorian decorum and restraint. Yet my yearning is almost always short-lived. People, after all, are not *forced* to read garbage, which, even if it overwhelms us—or seems to at times—is preferable to censorship.

And this brings me to a consideration of what my chronicle of *Lie Down in Darkness* and its problems has been leading up to—and that is, in fact, freedom of expression in our time, and the importance of libraries to our culture, and the danger that exists to the written word, whether those words be dirty or clean, simple or sublime. For it goes without saying that the written word is in peril, and its enemies are not just the yahoos and the censors but those who dwell in the academic camp.

Let me relate what recently happened to me. If you write long enough you will inevitably suffer the misfortune of having your words subjected to scholarly scrutiny. This is much worse than getting bad reviews. Not long ago I received in the mail a two-hundred-page thesis from a graduate student at a California university that bore the following title—I quote verbatim: "*Sophie's Choice:* A Jungian Perspective." Beneath this was the description "Prepared for Karl Kracklauer, Ph.D., for Partial Fulfillment of the Requirement for the Course 'Therapeutic Process.'" I will now quote from the first page of the introduction: "As Styron's Sophie is a complicated character, and because her relationships are multifaceted and equally complex, I focus primarily on a single event in Sophie's life in order to gain entry into her psyche. In analyzing Sophie I rely on Greek mythology, Greek artwork and Jungian psychology." The important line: "In this paper I analyze the character Sophie from the *movie* 'Sophie's Choice.'" There was a footnote to this statement that read: "Where the movie was vague I referred to the book, *Sophie's Choice,* for clarification."

This, it seems to me, is the ultimate anti-literary story. It follows logically that I should want to say a few words about the most pro-literary of institutions, the library. After all, we're gathered here in behalf of a library. I'd like to describe how in my early life the library evolved from a forbidding place, ruled by frightening Minotaurs and guardian demons, into a refuge, the center of my soul's rescue, the friendliest place on earth.

When I was fourteen John Steinbeck's epic novel *The Grapes of Wrath* was published, to mixed reviews. While it was generally praised as a literary achievement, there were dissenters who were profoundly offended by some of the coarsely realistic language. It should be noted that this language is totally innocuous by present-day standards, containing none of the wicked four-letter vocables that have even plopped onto the pages of the new *New Yorker.* Still, the book had created enormous protest in some quarters; like many works of the period it had been threatened by a ban in—where else?—Boston. My schoolmate Knocky Floyd had somehow briefly gotten hold of a copy of *The Grapes of Wrath,* and he told me that if I, too, could obtain the book I would find on page 232 the word *condom.* Or perhaps it was in the plural—*condoms.* It was a word that was nowhere, even in the dictionaries of those pre–World War II years, nor was another Steinbeckian sizzler, that is, *whore;* the idea of seeing these words in print made me nearly sick with desire, though in fairness to myself I also wanted to read the story of the suffering Joad family. The elderly Miss Evans, God rest her soul, was the librarian who presided over the public library in my hometown in Tidewater Virginia, and it was she whom I confronted when, on a lucky day, I managed at last to find on its shelf one of five or six already smudged and dog-eared copies of this incredibly popular book. As she finished stamping the back page she handed me the book with an intense scowl and asked me my age; when I replied fourteen, she gave a kind of squeal and began to snatch the volume away. "Unfit! Unfit!" Miss Evans cried. "Unfit for your age!" There was a tugging match that both embarrassed and horrified me—she kept repeating "Unfit!" like a malediction—and I finally let her grab the book back in triumph.

The next episode in my depraved quest for sensation took place a year later, when I was fifteen, in New York City. It was my first trip to the metropolis, a vacation at Christmastime from my Virginia prep school. I had a single goal. More than the Statue of Liberty, more than Times Square, my mind was set on one thing. On my second day I trudged through the snow past the icicle-clad lions of the New York Public Library and into the catalog room, where I thumbed through the cards in search of a volume that had been spoken of at school as one of the most erotically arousing works ever printed. I don't exaggerate when I recall my heart being in a near-critical seizure when I located the card and the name of the author, Richard von Krafft-Ebing (1840–1902), and the title, almost brutal in its terrifying promise, *Psychopathia Sexualis.* Every schoolboy of that time wanted to read this Germanic compendium of sexual horrors. With the scrawled Dewey decimal number and the title in hand I made my way to the circulation desk. Miss Evans would have approved of her much younger male counterpart: his face wore a look of lordly contempt. He was tall; in those days I was short. He looked down at me as, in my changing voice, I croaked out my request; he said scathingly, "This book is for specialists. Are you a specialist in the field?"

"What field?" I replied feebly.

"Abnormal psychology. Are you a specialist?"

His tone and manner had so smothered me with humiliation that I was speechless; after a silent beat or two he said: "This book is not for young boys seeking a thrill."

The effect was catastrophic, nearly fatal; I slunk out of the New York Public Library, resolved never to enter a library again.

These countless years later I've been able to regard those incidents in the way one regards so many experiences that seem tragic at the time they happen; they were both educating and valuable. Recently, when I've pondered the issue of censorship and pornography I've remembered these moments of awful rejection and have seen that they comprise an object lesson. Of course, my own youth was a factor in having been denied, and neither of those books were pornography. Still, there's a point to be made. It was not prurience, not lust that impelled me to seek out these works but a far simpler instinct: curiosity. In a puritanical society—and America is, par excellence, a puritanical society—it is the veil of forbiddenness, as much as what lies behind the veil, that provokes the desire for penetration, if I may use the word. Had Miss Evans permitted me to read the word *condom,* or had I been able to while away a winter afternoon immersed in Krafft-Ebing, whose juiciest passages, I later learned, were obscured in a smoke screen of Latin, I might have fulfilled at least some of my curiosity and then returned to normal adolescent concerns. As it was, I remained heavy-spirited and restless with need. The present-day foes of sexually explicit writing and other depictions of sex, whether art or pornography, and those who would censor such works don't understand this underlying psychological reality and thus undermine their own cause. There is, it is true, a group, probably not very large, of super-enthusiasts for whom pornography is an obsession and a necessity. Joyce Carol Oates has likened these people to religious votaries: one might morally disagree with them even as one scorns so much seemingly displaced heat, but their requirements should be democratically tolerated and finally even respected. At the same time, the nearly universal availability of erotica has allowed most other people to take it or leave it; many find it somehow fulfilling, and there is nothing wrong with that. I suspect that the great mass of people, their curiosity blessedly satisfied, have discovered in the aftermath an excruciating monotony and have signed off for good. The censors who would reestablish the tyranny of my youth should quit at this point, accepting the fact that it's the sordid absolutism of denial—not what is made accessible—that turns people into cranks and makes them violent and mad.

After I experienced rejection, acceptance, and total immersion in reading, the United States Marine Corps introduced me to the glories of the library. During World War II, at the age of seventeen, I joined the Marines but was deemed too young to be sent right away into the Pacific combat. I was delivered for a time, instead, to the V-12 program at Duke University, which then, as now, possessed one of the great college libraries of America. I'm sure it was at least partially the Zeitgeist that led me into a virtual rampage through those library shelves. When one has intimations of a too early demise it powerfully focuses the mind. The war in the Pacific was at a boiling fury, and there were few of us young marines who didn't have a prevision of himself as being among the fallen martyrs. I was taking a splendid course in seventeenth-century English prose and I'd hoarded an incantatory line from Sir Thomas Browne: The long habit of living indisposeth us for dying. This, of course, is British understatement. I wanted desperately to live, and the books in the Duke University library were the rocks and boulders to which I clung against my onrushing sense of doom and mortality. I read everything I could lay my hands on. Even today I can recall the slightly blind and bloodshot perception I had of the vaulted Gothic reading room, overheated, the smell of glue and sweat and stale documents, winter coughs, whispers, the clock ticking toward midnight as I raised my eyes over the edge of *Crime and Punishment*. The library became my hangout, my private club, my sanctuary, the place of my salvation; during the many months I was at Duke, I felt that when I was reading in the library I was sheltered from the world and from the evil winds of the future; no harm could come to me there. It was doubtless escape of sorts but it also brought me immeasurable enrichment. God bless libraries.

It's hard for me to realize that this was exactly fifty years ago, perhaps to this very night. Truly still, the long habit of living indisposeth us for dying. I forgot to mention that among the books at the Duke library I desperately wanted to read in those days, but was unable to obtain, were *Lady Chatterley's Lover* by D. H. Lawrence and *Tropic of Cancer* by Henry Miller. I did, however, see them incarcerated, immobilized like two child molesters, behind heavy wire grillwork in the Rare Book Room. I've learned that they were finally set free some years ago with an unconditional pardon.

[*Traces* (Indiana Historical Society), Spring 1995.]

Letter to an Editor

Dear—:

The preface which you have wanted me to write, and which I wanted to write, and finally wrote, came back to me from Paris today so marvelously changed and reworded that it seemed hardly mine. Actually, you know, it shouldn't be mine. Prefaces are usually communal enterprises and they have a stern and dull quality of group effort about them—of Manifesto, Proclamation of Aims, of "Where We Stand"—of editors huddled together in the smoke-laden, red-eyed hours of early morning, pruning and balancing syntax, juggling terms and, because each editor is an individual with different ideas, often compromising away all those careless personal words that make an individualist statement exciting, or at least interesting. Prefaces, I'll admit, are a bore and consequently, more often than not, go unread. The one I sent you, so balanced and well-mannered and so dull—I could hardly read it myself when I finished it—when it came back to me with your emendations and corrections I couldn't read it at all. This, I realize, is the fault of neither or none of us; it's inevitable that what Truth I mumble to you at Lipp's over a beer, or that Ideal we are perfectly agreed upon at the casual hour of 2 A.M. becomes powerfully open to criticism as soon as it's cast in a printed form which, like a piece of sculpture, allows us to walk all around that Truth or Ideal and examine it front, side, and behind, and for minutes on end. Everyone starts hacking off an arm, a leg, an ear—

and you end up with a lump. At any rate, I'd like to go over briefly a few of the things you questioned; we'll still no doubt disagree, but that's probably for the better. There are magazines, you know, where a questioning of words amounts to dishonesty, and disagreement means defection.

First, I said, "Literally speaking, we live in what has been described as the Age of Criticism. Full of articles on Kafka and James, on Melville, or whatever writer is in momentary ascendancy; laden with terms like 'architectonic,' 'Zeitgeist,' and 'dichotomous,' the literary magazines seem today on the verge of doing away with literature, not with any philistine bludgeon but by smothering it under the weight of learned chatter." (Perfect beginning for a preface, you may note; regard the arch rhythms, the way it fairly looks down the nose at the reader.)

All right, then I said, "There is little wonder" (always a nice oblique phrase to use in a preface) "that, faced with Œdipus and Myth in Charlotte Brontë, with meter in Pope and darkness in Dante, we put aside our current quarterly with its two short poems, its one intellectualized short story, in deference to *Life*, which brings us at least *The Old Man and the Sea*." This, of course, as you remember, was only by way of getting to the first brave part of the Manifesto: that *The Paris Review* would strive to give predominant space to the fiction and poetry of both established and new writers, rather than to people who use words like "Zeitgeist." Now in rebuttal, one of you has written that it is not always editorial policy that brings such a disproportion of critical manuscripts across the editors' desks, pointing out that "in our schools and colleges all the emphasis is on analysis and organization of ideas, not creation." The result is that we have critics, not creators; and you go on to suggest that, since this is the natural state of things, we should not be too haughty in the stating of our intention of having more fiction and poetry in *The Paris Review*.

To this I can only say: *d'accord*. Let's by all means leave out the lordly tone and merely say: Dear reader, *The Paris Review hopes* to emphasize creative work—fiction and poetry—not to the exclusion of criticism, but with the aim in mind of merely removing criticism from the dominating place it holds in most literary magazines and putting it pretty much where it belongs, i.e., somewhere near the back of the book. OK? But as for "Zeitgeist," which you accuse me of denouncing unnecessarily, I still don't like it, perhaps because, complying with the traditional explanation of intolerance, I am ignorant of what it means. I hope one of you will help me out.

Among the other points I tried to make was one which involved *The Paris Review* having no axe to grind. In this we're pretty much in agreement, I believe, although one of you mentioned the fact that in the first number of *The Exile* there were "powerful blasts" by Pound, among others, which added considerably to the interest of the magazine. True, perhaps. But is it because we're sissies that we plan to beat no drum for anything; is it only because we're wan imitations of our predecessors—those who came out bravely for anything they felt deeply enough was worth coming out bravely for? I don't think so. I think that if we have no axes to grind, no drums to beat, it's because it seems to us—for the moment, at least—that the axes have all been ground, the drumheads burst with beating. This attitude does not necessarily make us the Silent Generation (the fact of *The Paris Review* belies that), or the Sacred Generation, either, content to lie around in one palsied unprotesting mass. It's not so much a matter of protest now, but of waiting; perhaps, if we have to be categorized at all, we might be called the Waiting Generation—people who feel and write and observe, and wait and wait and wait. And go on writing. I think *The Paris Review* should welcome these people into its pages—the good writers and good poets, the non-drumbeaters and non-axe-grinders. So long as they're good.

Finally, and along these lines, I was taken pretty much to task by one of you for making the perhaps too general statement that there are signs in the air that this generation can and will produce literature equal to that of any in the past. Well, I suppose that is another Ringing Assertion, but it's a writer's statement, almost necessarily, and not a critic's. A critic nowadays will set up straw men, saying that Mailer had Ahab in mind when he created Sergeant Croft, that Jim Jones thought of Hamlet when he came up with his bedevilled Private Prewitt, stating further, however, that neither of these young men have created figures worthy of Melville or Shakespeare; they do this, or they leap to the opposite pole and cry out that no one writing today even *tries* to create figures of the tragic stature of Lear. For a writer, God forbid either course. I still maintain that the times get precisely the literature that they deserve, and that if the writing of this period is gloomy the gloom is not so much inherent in the literature as in the times. The writer's duty is to keep on writing, creating memorable Pvt. Prewitts and Sgt. Crofts, and to hell with Ahab. Perhaps the critics are right: this generation may not produce literature equal to that of any past generation—who cares? The writer will be dead before anyone can judge him—but he *must* go on writing, reflecting disorder, defeat, despair, should that be all that he sees at the moment, but ever searching for the elusive love, joy, and hope—qualities which, as in the act of life itself, are best when they have to be struggled for, and are not commonly come by with much ease, either by a critic's formula or by a critic's yearning. If he does not think, one way or another, that he can create literature worthy of himself and of his place, at this particular moment in history, in his society, then he'd better pawn his Underwood, or become a critic.

Ever faithfully yours,
BILL STYRON

[*Paris Review*, inaugural issue, Spring 1953.]

The Paris Review

Memory is, of course, a traitor, and it is wise not to trust any memoir which lends the impression of total recall. The following account of the founding of *The Paris Review* comprises my *own* recollection of the event, highly colored by prejudice, and must not be considered any more the gospel than those frequent narratives of the twenties, which tell you the color of the shoes that Gertrude Stein wore at a certain hour on such and such a day. . . .

The Paris Review was born in Montparnasse in the spring of 1952. It was, as one looks back on it through nostalgia's deceptive haze, an especially warm and lovely and extravagant spring. Even in Paris, springs like that don't come too often. Everything seemed to be in premature leaf and bud, and by the middle of March there was a general great stirring. The pigeons were aloft, wheeling against a sky that stayed blue for days, tomcats prowled stealthily along rooftop balustrades, and by the first of April the girls already were sauntering on the boulevard in scanty cotton dresses, past the Dôme and the Rotonde and their vegetating loungers who, two weeks early that year, heliotrope faces turned skyward, were able to begin to shed winter's anemic cast. All sorts of things were afoot—parties, daytime excursions to Saint-Germain-en-Laye, picnics along the banks of the Marne, where, after a lunch of bread and saucissons and Brie and Evian water (the liver was a touch troubled, following a winter sourly closeted with too much wine), you could lie for hours in the grass by the quiet riverside and listen to the birds and the lazy stir and fidget of grasshoppers and understand, finally, that France could be pardoned her most snooty and magisterial pride, mistress as she was of such sweet distracting springs.

At night there was a bar called Le Chaplain, on a little dogleg street not far from the Dôme, where a lot of people used to go; you could carve your name with an outstretched forefinger in the smoke of the place, but the refreshment was not too expensive, and in its ambience—quiet enough for conversation yet lively enough to forestall boredom, gloom, self-conscious lapses—it seemed to be a fine place to sit and work up a sweat about new magazines and other such far-fetched literary causes. Even though outside there was a kind of calm madness in the air—French boys, too, were being sent to that most futile and insane of wars, Korea—and in spite of the beatific spring, there was a subdued yet tense quality around, as of a people pushed very close to the breaking point, or as of one hysteric woman who, if you so much as dropped a pin behind her, would break out in screams. "*U.S. Go Home.*" The signs are gone now, for the moment. At that time, though, our national popularity had reached *the* nadir and in Paris there have been better times for literary ventures. But all of us had been in one war; besides, the young *patron* of Le Chaplain, named Paul, by his own proclamation loved America almost as much for "*ses littérateurs*" as for "*ses dollars*" (winks, knowing laughter, toasts in beer to two great nations), and if *The Paris Review* were to celebrate a patron saint, it would possibly have to be this wiry, tough, frenetic Algerian with the beneficent smile, who could vault over the bar and stiff-arm a drunk out into the night in less time than it takes to say Edgar Poe, and return, bland as butter, to take up where he left off about Symbolist imagery. Try starting a little magazine at Toots Shor's. *Les américains en Amérique!* indeed.

Later that spring, as the idea of a new magazine grew less far-fetched (by this time someone mentioned that he actually knew where he could raise $500), we convened in an apartment on a hidden, sleepy street behind the Gare Montparnasse called the Rue Perceval. The apartment belonged to Peter Matthiessen, to whom credit is due for having originated the idea for the magazine. No one seemed to know the obscure street, not even the shrewdest of Left Bank cabdrivers, and in this seclusion three flights up, in a huge room with a sunny terrace overlooking all of Paris, the plans went forward in euphoria, in kennel snarls of bickering, in buoyant certitude, in

schism and in total despair. Though it is no doubt less complicated to organize a little magazine than to start some sort of industrial combine, it is
imponderably more difficult an enterprise, I will bet, than opening a delicatessen, and in France one must multiply one's problems—well, by France; to
learn successfully how to browbeat a Parisian printer, for instance, is rough
schooling for a Parisian, even more so for a recent graduate of Harvard or
Yale, and the bureaucratic entanglements involved in setting up a corporation known as *Société à Résponsibilité Limitée au capital de 500.000 frs.*
must be self-evident to anyone who has even so much as lost his passport.
Yet somehow the thing was accomplished.

To be young and in Paris is often a heady experience. In America a writer
not only never knows who or where he is ("Well, what I mean is, was it a best
seller?" "Is this novel of yours sort of historical, or maybe what they call
psychological?" "Well, I really meant, what do you do for a *living*?"), he gets
so he does not *want* to know. In Paris, on this level at least, it is different, as
we all know, and like that hardship case of an American writer of authenticated record whose landlady, spying his translated poem in *Les Nouvelles
Littéraires* and recognizing his name, offered him out of glowing pride a two
percent reduction in his rent—like this young writer, touched by the sentiment even if not by sheer largesse, we feel peculiarly at ease for a change,
we know where we are, and we wish to stick around. And so we persisted.

One sunny afternoon toward the end of that spring George Plimpton,
another of the founders (the others were Thomas Guinzburg, Harold
Humes, William Pène du Bois, and John Train), arrived at Matthiessen's
apartment bearing two sinister-looking green bottles of absinthe. He burst
in upon a glum gathering desultorily testing names. *Promises. Ascent. Vil-
lanelle. Tides. Weather-cock. Spume. Humes.* (I think it was Matthiessen
who later hit upon the perfectly exact and simple title that the magazine
bears.) Everyone was at low ebb, and it is quite probable that once again the
group would have broken up had it not been for Plimpton's absinthe. Here
I do not wish to suggest that there was something so fortuitously creative
about that afternoon as to lead us to discover right then, once and for all,
what we wished the magazine to "be"; by the same token, absinthe, according to the *Britannica*, "acts powerfully upon the nerve centers, and causes
delirium and hallucinations, followed in some cases by idiocy." One can
make what one will out of that; for myself, I simply believe that that afternoon was the one upon which we were destined to make a breakthrough,

and that Plimpton's absinthe, while it might not have aided us in our efforts to define our policy, did nothing to hinder us, either. At any rate, toward the end of that day we had discovered roughly what we wished to make of the magazine, and we were in surprising accord.

[From Styron's introduction to *Best Short Stories from The Paris Review*. Dutton, 1959.]

The Long March

A lthough not nearly so long nor so ambitious as my other works, *The Long March* achieved within its own scope, I think, a unity and a sense of artistic inevitability which still, ten years after the writing, I rather wistfully admire. Lest I appear immodest, I would hasten to add that I do not consider the book even remotely perfect, yet certainly every novelist must have within the body of his writing a work of which he recalls everything having gone just *right* during the composition: through some stroke of luck, form and substance fuse into a single harmonious whole and it all goes down on paper with miraculous ease. For me this was true of *The Long March,* and since otherwise the process of writing has remained exceedingly painful, I cherish the memory of this brief work, often wondering why for a large part of the time I cannot recapture the sense of compulsion and necessity that dominated its creation.

Possibly much of the urgency of the book is due to factors that are extremely personal. As the reader may eventually begin to suspect, the story is autobiographical. To be sure, all writing is to some degree autobiographical, but *The Long March* is intensely and specifically so. I do not mean that the central figures are not more or less imaginary—they are; but the mortar explosion and the forced march, which are central to the entire narrative, were actual incidents in which I was involved, just as I was bound up, for a time, in the same desolating atmosphere of a military base in the midst of a

fiercely hot American summer. If the story has a sense of truth and verisimilitude, it is because at the time of the writing all of these things—the
terrible explosion, the heat of summer, and the anguish of the march itself—
still persisted in my mind with the reality of some unshakable nightmare.

Perhaps it was an even larger nightmare which I was trying to create
in this book, and which lends to the work whatever symbolic power it has
the fortune to possess. Because for myself (as I do believe for most thoughtful people, not only Americans but the community of peaceable men everywhere) the very idea of another war—this one in remote and strange
Korea, and only five years after the most cataclysmic conflict ever to engulf
mankind—possessed a kind of murky, surrealistic, half-lunatic unreality that
we are mercifully spared while awake, but which we do occasionally confront in a horrible dream. Especially for those like myself who had shed
their uniforms only five years before—in the blissful notion that the unspeakable orgy of war was now only a memory and safely behind—the experience of putting on that uniform again and facing anew the ritualistic death
dance had an effect that can only be described as traumatic. World War II
was dreadful enough, but at least the issues involved were amenable to reasonable definition. To be suddenly plunged again into war, into a war, furthermore, where the issues were fuzzy and ambiguous, if not fraudulent, a
war that could not possibly be "won," a senseless conflict so unpopular that
even the most sanguinary politician or war lover shrank from inciting people
to a patriotic zeal, a war without slogans or ballads or heroes—to have to
endure this kind of war seemed, to most of us involved in it at the time,
more than we could bear. War was no longer simply a temporary madness
into which human beings happily lapsed from time to time. War had at last
become *the* human condition.

It was this feeling I believe I was trying to recapture when sometime
later, in the summer of 1952, I found myself in Paris still unable to shake off
the sense of having just recently awakened from a nightmare. My own ordeal and the ordeal of most of my Marine Corps friends (including one or
two who died in Korea) was over—yet the persistent image of eight boys
killed by a random mortar shell and of a long and brutal march lingered in
my mind. Senseless mass slaughter and a seemingly endless march, the participants of which were faceless zeroes, were all that in retrospect appeared
to me significant about this war without heroes, this war which lacked so
utterly a sense of human identity, and which in so sinister a fashion presaged

the faceless, soulless, pushbutton wars of the future. All right, I would write about this faceless, soulless march. Yet, all my intentions to the contrary, I began to understand, as I wrote, that even in the midst of an ultimate process of dehumanization the human spirit cannot be utterly denied or downed: against all odds, faces emerge from the faceless aggregate of ciphers, and in the middle of the march I was creating I found Captain Mannix slogging and sweating away, tortured, beaten but indomitable. A hero in spite of himself or me, he endures, and in the midst of inhumanity retains all that which makes it worthwhile to be human. I myself cannot be sure, but possibly it is the hopeful implications derived from this mystery—this kind of indefatigable man—which are all an artist can pretend to suggest, however imperfectly, in his struggle to comprehend the agony of our violent, suicidal century.

[Introduction to the Norwegian edition of *The Long March;* Cappelens, 1963.]

We Weren't in It for the Money

ost of us writers who were involved as judges at the birth of an unfortunate literary enterprise called the Turner Tomorrow Award wish we had never heard of it, for the thing was misshapen, ill-conceived in its Atlanta womb, and caused us who presided at its parturition to be cast as the venal midwives. Sponsored by the Turner Publishing Co., offshoot of Ted Turner's communications empire, the award of $500,000 (reputedly the largest of its kind ever given) was to go to a single work of fiction that would produce "creative and positive solutions to global problems." Four awards of $50,000 each would go to the runners-up.

In a diatribe written by Jonathan Yardley, *The Washington Post*'s in-house Torquemada, the judges—who included Carlos Fuentes, Peter Matthiessen, Wallace Stegner, Nadine Gordimer, and myself—were accused of being whorish sellouts who not only would comprise our literary standards, if we had any, by getting connected with such a venture but "would do just about anything" to obtain the $10,000 fee we were each given for our labors.[1] Yardley's piece is filled with silly judgmental bluster, but if, as a responsible journalist, he had bothered to discover some of the facts about our involvement in this venture he could have easily done so.

Most of us had some misgivings when the Turner organization enlisted us through Thomas Guinzburg—a respected New York literary figure who was a friend of all of us—but I think that we each felt it was possible that our participation might at least cause some of this huge amount of money to be distributed to a few writers of promise. But this was before the outlines of the woeful project became clear. Some months later, early this year, when we learned of the extraordinary dreck the first readers were encountering in the winnowing-out process (one manuscript among the 2,500 submitted worldwide contained the word "pray" repeated an estimated 150,000 times) our earlier doubts crystallized into dismay. We sent a letter to Guinzburg stating our misgivings and making it clear that we wished to resign, categorically, so that other judges might be substituted. Interestingly, the letter contains virtually the same indictment of the award that Yardley made (including the impossibility of good fiction being served up on demand) and that he implied we would never dare to express, being "blinded by the bucks."

If we had insisted on resigning, as we should have, each of us would have had to forfeit the $10,000 fee, a reward which Yardley really believes had held us in greedy expectation for nearly a year. One hates to paw over this matter in public, but it's hard to avoid Yardley's vulgar fixation on money. He is at his most sanctimonious in his insistence that the prospect of this "fortune," as he puts it, unhinged us with avarice. Few American writers make as much as a second-rate TV anchorperson or a second-rate second baseman, but some of us do quite well. Carlos Fuentes, who lectures widely, receives a minimum of $15,000 an appearance. There is scarcely one of the judges who could not with ease get $10,000 for a lecture or an appearance and spare him or herself the miseries of the Turner Tomorrow Award, which required—in my case—setting aside numerous afternoons better devoted to my work, plowing through twelve hulking manuscripts, taking three thousand words of notes, conferring with fellow judges, and traveling to the final judges' meeting with its poisonous unpleasantness. (Nadine Gordimer, a woman of stony integrity, told me in distress that she actually lost income during the grind, which included a fourteen-thousand-mile round-trip from South Africa.) On emotional grounds alone, I would not repeat the experience for twice the fee.

But we were persuaded to stay by Guinzburg and in the process were blandly deceived by the Turner organization. One of our inducements was the claim that there were many promising entries from the Third World and Eastern Europe, where money, publication, and media attention would be a significant boon to writers who had worked long in obscurity. (These never materialized.) We were also told that if we stayed we would be free to make any prize-winning decisions we chose to, even if our judgments were negative. Indeed, we could make no awards at all. Given this autonomy, we stayed. Our reading did turn up, surprisingly enough, four novels by writers we felt were deserving of encouragement, though no single one of the books, in the opinion of the majority of the judges, was exciting enough to make us want to anoint it with $500,000—a sum we thought from the beginning (and said in our letter) was cosmically inflated. We therefore decided on the more modest course of awarding each of the four winners the runner-up prize of $50,000, with *Ishmael*—an intelligent and provocative work by Daniel Quinn—being singled out for special attention.[2] This seemed a way of bringing sensible scale, at least, to a project badly afflicted by grandiosity.

At a fairly rancorous judges' meeting in New York City early in May— also attended by one Michael Reagan, a self-styled "media" person representing the Turner management—our majority decision was accepted as binding. Of the final panel of nine judges only three, including the science-fiction writer Ray Bradbury, favored the bloated half-million-dollar award and took the side of Reagan, who, though a nonvoting onlooker, was plainly seething over our refusal to give the seal of approval to Ted Turner's megalomaniacal shower of gold. (Reagan would later make whiny remarks about the dissenting judges' failure to hand our fees back, his apparent logic being that only judges favorable to the Cause deserved recompense; he also was plainly determined to overlook our authority to make any decision we pleased.) When we left the meeting it was with the understanding that our decision would be honored.

We were wrong. At the Turner Tomorrow Award ceremony early in June it was announced that *Ishmael* had received the $500,000 prize. We had been lied to and betrayed. Our public protest over the betrayal comprised a tempest that would fit comfortably into my granddaughter's half-inch-wide china teapot.[3] And even she could tell that we were badly taken. But being taken is not the same as being venal—and one trusts this puts the record straight.

[*Washington Post*, July 16, 1991.]

The Book on *Lolita*

N̲ews of the new movie version of *Lolita*, starring Jeremy Irons as Humbert Humbert and about to begin filming in North Carolina, has caused me to recall my own odd involvement with the book, in the months before Vladimir Nabokov's masterpiece was first published in the United States. Part of the myth surrounding the novel is the notion that Bennett Cerf, the co-owner of Random House, was one of the group of hapless publishers (others being Douglas Black of Doubleday; Roger Straus of Farrar, Straus & Young; and Max Schuster) who so lacked foresight, or were so timid in the face of *Lolita*'s ostensibly salacious subject matter, that they missed out on one of the great publishing coups of all times. But Cerf, at least, has to be excused from this group, since his failure to publish the book was not one of either will or vision but was due to his being hamstrung by a corporate decree of his own devising.

I first read *Lolita* in 1957, in the original Olympia Press edition, published in Paris by Maurice Girodias; the twin green volumes had been smuggled through New York customs by a friend of mine, the theatrical producer Lewis Allen. That *Lolita* was published by the firm that also brought out such incandescent titles as *White Thighs, With Open Mouth,* and *The Sexual Life of Robinson Crusoe* helped create a notoriety that Nabokov rightly deplored but which did in fact contribute to the widespread impression that the novel was unfit to be read by decent Americans. Publishers all over New York shunned the work. The book, of course, is a sidesplitting and heart-breaking triumph, and entirely filth-free; Allen and I were so smitten by Humbert Humbert's sublime obsession that we toyed with the idea of trying to persuade Nabokov to let us publish *Lolita* in a private edition, and to hell with the obscenity laws. But financial problems sent me instead to Bennett Cerf, who had recently become my publisher.

Not long before this, Bennett had named a new editor-in-chief, Hiram Haydn. A sophisticated and rather scholarly man, Haydn had brought me along from Bobbs-Merrill, where he had edited my first novel, *Lie Down in Darkness,* and where he had fought valiantly and more or less successfully against the company bluenoses, based in the Indianapolis home office, who had objected to my fairly tame sexual tableaux and occasionally crude language. Cerf greatly respected Haydn. For the first time during his presidency of Random House, Bennett had bestowed on an editor absolute autonomy, and so I was reasonably certain that, given Haydn's broadmindedness, *Lolita* would be a shoo-in for prompt and enthusiastic publication, even though I had had early qualms about Bennett. When I handed him the two volumes, he fingered them with gingerly distaste, shook his head, and murmured something like "Well, I don't know . . . dirty books."

A week or so later, warm with pleasure and anticipation, I marched into Haydn's office in the old Villard mansion, on Madison Avenue. Before I could utter a word, Hiram rose from his desk, his face actually blue with rage. "That loathsome novel will be published over my dead body!" he roared. Dumbfounded, I asked him what in God's name had caused him to react this way to such a splendid literary achievement. He ranted and shouted, and when I asked him to explain, to *please* explain, the reason for his fury he replied that I, Bill Styron, knew full well that he, Hiram Haydn, had a daughter the age of the victim of Humbert Humbert's disgusting lust, and that when my own daughter was that age perhaps I'd understand the hatred a man might feel for *Lolita*. For some reason, I was not angry with Hiram. It was an outburst that revealed the power of art's sometimes terrifying menace.

I fled to the office next door, where Bennett, his pipe propped against his cheek, was gazing desolately into the distance. "That novel is a masterpiece," he said, in a choked voice, "but I can't budge the man. He said if I overruled him he'd quit." He paused, then added, "What a *wonderful* book!" His eyes had the look of one who had divined the wretched future: *Lolita* published by some second-rate outfit like Putnam; ecstatic reviews; week after week at the top of the best-seller lists; and any new works of Vladimir Nabokov forever lost to Random House.

[*New Yorker,* September 4, 1995.]

Fessing Up

I was a member of the entirely white, predominantly male, and somewhat doddering Modern Library editorial board that compiled a list of the hundred best novels written in English in the twentieth century. I don't want to dodge my contribution to the list's notoriety. In fact, I want to cheerfully assent to the opinion expressed in these pages that the list is "weird." When I saw the final roster, I was a little shocked at what the ten of us had wrought, not only in respect to the list's glaring omissions (no Toni Morrison, no Patrick White, only eight women in the lot) but in respect to its generally oppressive stodginess. The voting process was partly at fault for this quality of desuetude. A luncheon meeting with a good wine that allowed for lively disputation would have soon eliminated such toothless pretenders as *The Magnificent Ambersons* and *Zuleika Dobson*.

As it was, we voted by mail ballot. Each judge checked off from a roll call of several hundred novels the works he (or, in the case of A. S. Byatt, she) thought worthy of making the cut. The books were then ranked by the number of the votes tallied. Those receiving, say, nine votes (like *Ulysses* and *The Great Gatsby*) were placed at the top of the list, and the others were rated downward accordingly. Such a procedure led to some odd (or weird) results. That Aldous Huxley's *Brave New World* and Samuel Butler's *The Way of All Flesh* reached the empyrean (at Nos. 5 and 12, respectively) didn't necessarily mean they deserved such an exalted rating. It meant only that eight or nine judges just happened to believe those books belonged somewhere among the anointed hundred.

People who were legitimately exasperated by the Modern Library's inventory might take heart from a rival list drawn up by the bright members of the course in publishing at Radcliffe College, and printed in *The Boston Globe* and *USA Today,* among other papers. They would be encouraged, at least at first, by the youth of those involved (most are in their twenties) and by the fact that most are female and some nonwhite. The students' choices, while often extravagant, are in many cases a bracing corrective to the Modern Library's pervasive air of superannuation. An example: *The Catcher in the Rye,* bogged down at No. 64 on our list, vaults to second place, right after *The Great Gatsby.*

In a way, the Radcliffe list is as proper and predictable as the Modern Library's. It pays appropriate homage to the great modernist authors: Joyce, Faulkner, Hemingway, Woolf, Steinbeck, James, Orwell, Nabokov. Yet it also affirms the importance of certain women writers not present on the other list, notably Toni Morrison (with three titles) and Flannery O'Connor. Sometimes the importance is exaggerated: Alice Walker's *The Color Purple* at No. 5? But most of the old fogies to whom one might rightly object have been dumped: Booth Tarkington, Arnold Bennett, James T. Farrell, Thornton Wilder, and John O'Hara. These patricides seem to be worthy ones, allowing space not only for writers whose absence was conspicuous from the Modern Library list—John Updike and Don DeLillo—but for a small yet refreshing category: children's books.

They seemed a wonderful addition. I found myself not giving a damn that *Charlotte's Web* (No. 13) and *Winnie-the-Pooh* (No. 22) were in a much loftier position than *A Passage to India* (No. 59) and *Sons and Lovers* (No. 64). But I began to be made uneasy by the realization that many significant gains were offset by inexplicable losses. Where was the matchless Graham Greene? What happened to Saul Bellow and Philip Roth? Walker Percy's *The Moviegoer* was gone, as was John Cheever's *The Wapshot Chronicle;* and who should pop up in their stead but the hectoring Ayn Rand, represented by her dismal blockbusters *The Fountainhead* and *Atlas Shrugged.*

Moreover, just as the Modern Library list had done, the Radcliffe list ignored virtually all experimental fiction and many widely read contemporaries—from Beckett to Pynchon, from Joan Didion to Robert Stone. Finally, there were the profoundly eccentric rankings. Is Douglas

Adams's *The Hitchhiker's Guide to the Galaxy* really better than anything written by Theodore Dreiser?

Somewhere in this is a lesson. Perhaps it's only that all lists are weird, but each list is weird in its own way.

[*New Yorker,* August 17, 1998.]

The MacDowell Medal

I was quite bowled over when John Updike telephoned last spring to tell me that he and the distinguished members of the committee had chosen me for the medal. I had of course heard of it and knew of its very special quality. But, in all honesty, I never thought it would come my way. I was very surprised, but gradually I cooled off and began to wonder at the reason for my intense mixed reaction. I began to feel a little troubled. I asked myself why news of such an honor—even one of the greatest prestige like the MacDowell Medal—should leave me with this sense of uneasiness. Was it because some inner voice told me that I might not really deserve it— that there were at least three or four writers whom I greatly admired whose work should have gained the accolade instead of mine? Or was it because the whole issue of medals and prizes had once more surfaced, this time beneath my nose, making me ask the question again: "Are prizes necessary, or even desirable?" Isn't satisfaction in one's work sufficient reward, and so forth? These are, of course, tiresome worries. I am a Gemini with a bifurcated ego, one branch of which delights in being stroked, while the other emits howls of dismay. I was at that moment rereading the stories of my fellow Virginian (although born in Boston), Edgar Allan Poe, and it suddenly occurred to me that some of the distress I felt may have come from the question I abruptly asked myself: "Had Edgar Allan Poe ever won a medal?" I went to the source book (an old and rather ponderous biography by one Edmund Clarence Stedman), in which I was puzzled to discover, among other things, that Poe suffered from, and may have even died in part from, a malady described as "platonic erotomania," which baffled me for a long time because Stedman offered no explanation. I put aside, however, the search for this riddle, and was able to ascertain after diligent checking that, no, Poe had never won a medal. This fact so piqued my interest that I was led to further research on medals, especially of the nineteenth century and more particularly as they affected the culture of the United States and of Europe, and I came up with some provocative data that I want to share with you very briefly. I'm concentrating on literary artists, though I'm sure similar cases could be made in music and the visual arts.

In the 1800s, Europe rewarded its writers handsomely with medals and trophies. Victor Hugo was a major collector of laurels; he had a whole room filled with bronzes and statuettes that fed a self-esteem already swollen by public idolatry scarcely equalled in the history of literature. At the same time, the behavior of Gustave Flaubert is an example of the extreme ambivalence toward medals which artists have often displayed. There is no more crushingly contemptuous line in all of world fiction than the final sentence of *Madame Bovary,* where the narrator, simultaneously summing up his feelings for his least favorite character, the odious Monsieur Homais, and expressing his hatred of such bourgeois claptrap as the Legion of Honor, writes: "He has just been awarded the Legion of Honor." It is the put-down par excellence. Yet, a few years after *Madame Bovary* appeared, the recently reviled but now redeemed Flaubert was himself offered the Legion of Honor, a medal which one biographer described the great man as accepting with "gleeful alacrity." So much for the famous cold Flaubertian detachment. But the champion acquirer of medals has to be Henrik Ibsen. So great was the demand for Ibsen's presence at medal-giving ceremonies all over Europe that the dramatist wrote his plays for half the year and went collecting medals the other half. Departing Oslo, then known as Christiania, in the spring, he would head southward to Bonn and Leipzig, pause, then mosey on to Vienna and Budapest—at all of which places there were kings and princes to hang medallion-bedecked ribbons around his neck—and then, as summer grew ripe, he would pass on down to Torino, Milano, Rome, back up to Paris and Brussels, thence to London for a whole clutch of medals and on to Amsterdam, Dublin, and Edinburgh, returning at last, when the first chill breeze of autumn roiled the North Sea, to Norway, clanking with bronze and gold, so weighted down with the ornaments that overlaid his chest that he was actually seen to list slightly to port as he trudged down the gangplank into the arms of his cheering admirers.

Contrast, if you will, this European cornucopia of honors with the situation as it existed at the same time in our country. No one cared a fig for literature. No medals for Edgar Allan Poe, no medals for Fenimore Cooper or Hawthorne, no medals for Whitman. No medals, no prizes, no annual publishers' awards, no seals of approval from a book critics circle, no fellowships, no grants, no MacDowell Colony, nothing. It may have seemed a bleak and ungenerous society when compared with Europe, if anyone bothered to make the comparison, and certainly nineteenth-century American writers were unrewarded when likened to their present-day counterparts, yet it is hard to believe that the existence of awards and honors might have improved the quality of the work of our literary ancestors. There is something about the immense and tormented loneliness of the writers at that time—an alienation far more intense, really, than the one rather facilely attributed to our own period—that makes it plausible to think that their work might have been violated, perhaps even irreparably damaged, had that loneliness been intruded upon by anxieties over winning a prize. Like all artists, they were hungry for recognition, and this a few of them got, though most failed to receive anything like renown commensurate with their genius; it may be that at least part of the splendor of their achievement derives from the very loneliness and obscurity out of which it flowered. One thinks with relief of Emily Dickinson never having had to compound her existential dread by missing out, once again, on the Bollingen, and only horror could attend contemplation of what twentieth-century book chat might have achieved back in those days, the gossip churning about Melville's stupendous, perennially doomed quest for the Pulitzer, or a MacArthur grant going to Mark Twain, who didn't need it.

The twentieth century, however, has offered no dearth of awards in America. Only France exceeds us in the bestowal of public bouquets to flatter the artistic self (in France it is often literally nothing but a bouquet). But the trouble is that the proliferation of awards has frequently debased the very concept of honor, and laurel branches descend indiscriminately upon the brows of the journeyman and the hack. If, as in my Presbyterian childhood, every boy and girl wins a Bible, there is not much feeling of distinction. More seriously, the reputedly prestigious prizes become tainted, like virtually everything else in the nation, by commercialism or, worse, by political infighting which results in cowardly compromises and the award going to individuals of stunning mediocrity. But perhaps one should not complain too strenuously about this situation and rejoice rather in the knowledge that a nation which has had so little use for aesthetic endeavor has developed sufficient maturity to honor genuine artists, no matter how imperfect their achievement. Who knows, maybe artists in America will someday gain the repute now enjoyed by health food advisors and anchorpersons.

In an election year, I do not think it vainglorious to proclaim or echo, once again, that poets are the unacknowledged legislators of the world. The recent conventions in Atlanta and New Orleans, with their bloated self-love and obscene jingoism, would convey to a man from Mars, or even from Italy, the impression that American politicians and their camp followers are drunk with power and totally insane. And the impression would be largely correct. With important and revered exceptions—and one wonders how Jefferson and Franklin D. Roosevelt ever managed to survive, much less triumph—politicians have ill-served their fellow man in our Darwinian struggle toward the light. The departed writer of whose gifts, in many ways, we most stand in need—I am thinking of H. L. Mencken—once contemplated the long list of American presidents, rolling off their names with heady delight: Harding, Fillmore, Taft, Hayes, not one but two defunct Harrisons, Taylor, Tyler, Pierce, Polk, Buchanan, Garfield, McKinley, on and on. Mencken wrote that their names had all the incantatory magic of a "roll call of mummified Sumerian kings." I have not meant to be frivolous in conjuring Mencken's list but to juxtapose it against another list, which strikes me as being its antipodean opposite, and constitutes the reason why I am standing here today. I am speaking, of course, of the roster of distinguished artists who have received the Edward MacDowell Medal before now. The name of any one of these dedicated and greatly gifted men and women could not fail to inspire admiration; taken in aggregate, the group—all twenty-eight of them—represents the brightest constellation of American talent that could be assembled in the latter half of this century. The combined power of their creation has provided, I suspect, the invisible counterforce, the equilibrium, which has helped keep our bedeviled nation from the barbarism and darkness—the political vandalism—into which, suicidally, it keeps threatening to plunge. Their work has been of supreme value to the world, and to be asked to join their company flatters me beyond measure.

I would like to close not by asking you to join me in the Pledge of Allegiance but to ask you to listen to a few lines in prose from a poet and translator whose work I greatly admired, and whom I wish I had known better—Robert Fitzgerald, who died in 1985, at the age of 74. "So hard at best is the lot of man," he wrote not long before his death, "and so great is the beauty he can apprehend, that only a religious conception of things can take in the extremes and meet the case. Our lifetimes have seen the opening of abysses before which the mind quails. But it seems to me there are a few things everyone can humbly try to hold on to: love and mercy (and humor) in everyday living; the quest for exact truth in language and affairs of the intellect; self-recollection or prayer; and the peace, the composed energy of art."

Such serenity seems appropriate to the ideals of which the Edward Mac-Dowell Medal is an embodiment, and I leave it for your contemplation.

[Speech delivered at the MacDowell Colony, Peterborough, New Hampshire, August 21, 1988.]

Antecedents

William Faulkner

He detested more than anything the invasion of his privacy. Though I am made to feel welcome in the house by Mrs. Faulkner and his daughter, Jill, and though I know that the welcome is sincere, I feel an intruder nonetheless. Grief, like few things else, is a private affair. Moreover, Faulkner hated those (and there were many) who would poke about in his private life—literary snoops and gossips yearning for the brief kick of propinquity with greatness and a mite of reflected fame. He had said himself more than once, quite rightly, that the only thing that should matter to other people about a writer is his books. Now that he is dead and helpless in the gray wooden coffin, I feel even more an interloper, prying around in a place I should not be.

But the first fact of the day, aside from that final fact of a death which has so diminished us, is the heat, and it is a heat which is like a small mean death itself, as if one were being smothered to extinction in a damp woolen overcoat. Even the newspapers in Memphis, sixty miles to the north, have commented on the ferocious weather. Oxford lies drowned in heat, and the feeling around the courthouse square on this Saturday forenoon is of a hot, sweaty languor bordering on desperation. Parked slantwise against the curb, Fords and Chevrolets and pickup trucks bake in merciless sunlight. People in Mississippi have learned to move gradually, almost timidly, in this climate. Black and white, they walk with both caution and deliberation. Beneath the portico of the First National Bank and along the scantily shaded walks around the courthouse itself, the traffic of shirtsleeved farmers and dewy-browed housewives and marketing Negroes is listless and slow-moving. Painted high up against the side of a building to the west of the courthouse and surmounted by a painted Confederate flag is a huge sign at least twenty feet long reading "Rebel Cosmetology College." Sign, flag, and wall, dominating one hot angle of the square, are caught in blazing light and seem to verge perilously close to combustion. It is a monumental heat, heat so desolating to the body and spirit as to have the quality of a half-remembered bad dream, until one realizes that it has, indeed, been encountered before, in all those novels and stories of Faulkner through which this unholy weather—and other weather more benign—moves with almost touchable reality.

In the ground-floor office of *The Oxford Eagle,* the editor and co-owner, Mrs. Nina Goolsby, bustles about under a groaning air conditioner. She is a large, cheerful, voluble woman and she reveals with great pride that the *Eagle* has recently won first place for general excellence among weekly newspapers in the annual awards of the Mississippi Press Association. She has just returned from distributing around town handbills which read:

In Memory

OF

William Faulkner

This Business Will Be

CLOSED

From 2:00 to 2:15 PM

Today, July 7, 1962

It was her idea, she says, adding, "People say that Oxford didn't care anything about Bill Faulkner, and that's just not true. We're proud of him. Look here." She displays a file of back issues of the *Eagle,* and there is the front-page headline: "Nobel Award for Literature Comes to Oxonian." There is a page from another issue, a full page paid for by, among others, the Ole Miss Dry Cleaners, Gathright-Reed Drug Company, Miller's Cafe, the A. H. Avent Gin and Warehouse Company. The emblazoned message reads: "Welcome Home, Bill Faulkner. We want to tell people everywhere—Oxford, and all of us, are very proud of William Faulkner, one of us, the

Nobel Prize winning author." The page is full of pictures of Faulkner in Stockholm: receiving the Nobel Prize from the king of Sweden, walking in the snow with his daughter, crouched beside a sled where he is seen chatting with "a little Swedish lad."

"So you can see how proud we are of him. We've always been proud of him," Mrs. Goolsby says. "Why, I've known Bill Faulkner all my life. I live not two blocks away from him. We used to stop and talk all the time when he was taking his walks. Lord, dressed in that real elegant tweed jacket with those leather patches on the elbows, and that cane curved over his arm. I've always said that when they put Bill Faulkner in the ground it just won't be right unless he has that tweed jacket on."

Back at the Faulkner house, the shade of the old cedars which arch up over the walkway and the columned portico offers only scant relief from the noonday heat. It is shirtsleeve weather, and indeed many of the men have removed their coats, around the front door where already some of the family has gathered: John Faulkner, himself a writer and almost a replica, a ghost of his brother down to the quizzical lifted eyebrows and downward-slanting mustache; John's grown sons; another brother, Murry, sad-eyed, gentle-spoken, an FBI agent in Mobile; Jill's husband, Paul Summers from Charlottesville, Virginia, a lawyer: like Jill, he refers to Faulkner as "Pappy." The conversation is general: the heat, the advantages of jet travel, the complexities of Mississippi's antediluvian liquor laws. The group steps aside to allow passage for a lady bearing an enormous cake with raspberry-colored icing; it is only one of many to arrive this day.

Inside, it is a little cooler, and here in the library to the left of the door—just opposite the cleared living room where the coffin rests—it seems easier to pass the time. It is a spacious, cluttered, comfortable room. A gold-framed portrait of Faulkner in hunting togs, looking very jaunty in his black topper, dominates one wall; next to it on a table is a wood sculpture of a gaunt Don Quixote. There are gentle, affectionate portraits of two Negro servants painted by "Miss Maud" Falkner (unlike her son, she spelled the name without the "u," as does most of the family). Around the other walls are books, books by the dozens and scores, in random juxtaposition, in jackets and without jackets, quite a few upside down: *The Golden Asse*, Vittorini's *In Sicily*, *The Brothers Karamazov*, Calder Willingham's *Geraldine Bradshaw*, the *Short Stories of Ernest Hemingway, From Here to Eternity,* Shakespeare's *Comedies, Act of Love* by Ira Wolfert, *Best of S. J. Perelman,* and many more beyond accounting.

Here in the library I meet Shelby Foote, the novelist and Civil War historian and one of Faulkner's very few literary friends. A pleasant, dark Mississippian in his mid-forties (he is dressed in seersucker and looks extremely cool), he observes that, naturally, a mere Virginian like myself cannot be expected to cope with such heat. "You've got to walk through it gently," he counsels; "don't make any superfluous moves." And he adds depressingly, "This is just beginning to build up pressure. You should be around here in August."

Foote is searching for a book, an anthology which contains one of Faulkner's early poems—a short poem written more than thirty years ago called "My Epitaph." I join in the search, which leads us to Faulkner's workroom at the rear of the house. There is more clutter here, more books: *40 Best Stories from Mademoiselle, Doctor Zhivago,* Dos Passos's *Midcentury, Judgment of Julius and Ethel Rosenberg,* H. K. Douglas's *I Rode With Stonewall* (one of the books Faulkner was reading just before his death), a hundred others jammed into a low bookcase, several shelves of which contain parcels of books sent to Faulkner for autographing: all of these remain dusty and unopened. The heavy antique typewriter which Faulkner worked on has been taken away and in its place on the table rests, somewhat inexplicably, a half-gallon bottle of Old Crow, one-fourth full. Behind this table on a mantelpiece littered with ashtrays, ornamental bottles, a leaking tobacco pouch, there stands a small comic painting of a mule, rump up high, teeth bared in manic laughter. "I think Faulkner loved mules almost as much as people," Foote reflects. "Maybe more." He has found the book and the poem.

Now several electric fans are whirring in the downstairs rooms and hallways, and a buffet lunch is being served. The food at a Southern funeral is usually good, but this food is splendid: turkey and country ham and stuffed tomatoes, loaves of delectable soft homemade bread and gallons of strong iced tea. We sit informally around the dining-room table. The hour of the service is approaching and outside through the window the afternoon light casts black shadows of trembling oak leaves and cedar branches against the rich hot grass.

———

From far off comes a mockingbird's rippling chant. Suddenly someone in the family recalls that just the night before, they had run across something which must have been one of the last things Faulkner had written, but that it was in French and they couldn't read it. It is brought forth and as a couple of us begin to puzzle it out we see that it is written in pencil on the front of a business envelope—the draft of a reply, in Faulkner's tiny, vertical, cramped, nearly illegible calligraphy, to an invitation to visit from someone in France—a note courteous, witty, and in easy French. He said he couldn't come.

Promptly at two o'clock a hush comes over the house as preparations for the service begin. We put our coats back on. There are several dozen of us—all but a handful (like his publishers, Bennett Cerf and Donald Klopfer) members of the family, gathered here from all over the South, Mississippi and Alabama and Louisiana and Virginia and Tennessee—and we stand in the two rooms, the dining room, from which the table has been removed now, and the living room, where the coffin rests. The Episcopal minister in white surplice and stole, the Reverend Duncan Gray, Jr., is bespectacled and balding, and his voice, though strong, is barely heard above the whine and chattering vibration of the electric fans:

"The Lord is my light and my salvation; whom shall I fear? the Lord is the strength of my life; of whom shall I be afraid?"

The mockingbird again sings outside, nearer now. Through the hum of the fans the minister reads Psalm 46:

"God is our refuge and strength, a very present help in trouble.

"Therefore will not we fear, though the earth be removed, and though the mountains be carried into the midst of the sea. . . ."

We repeat the Lord's Prayer aloud, and soon it is all over. There is a kind of haste to leave the house. The procession to the cemetery is up South Lamar Avenue through the center of town, past the statue of the Confederate soldier and the courthouse. As the line of cars stretches out ahead behind the black hearse and as we near the courthouse, it becomes plain that Mrs. Goolsby's campaign to close the stores has had good effect. For though it is now past two-fifteen, the stores are still shut up and the sidewalks are thronged with people. White and Negro, they stand watching the procession in the blazing heat, in rows and groups and clusters, on all sides of the courthouse and along the sidewalks in front of Grundy's Cafe and Earl

Fudge's Grocery and the Rebel Food Center. I am moved by this display and comment on it, but someone who is a native of the region is rather less impressed: "It's not that they don't respect Bill. I think most of them do, really. Even though none of them ever read a word of him. But funerals are a big thing around here. Let a Baptist deacon die and you'll *really* get a turnout."

Our car comes abreast of the courthouse, turns slowly to the right around the square. Here the statue of the Confederate soldier ("Erected 1907" is the legend beneath) stands brave and upright on his skinny calcimine-white pedestal, looking like a play soldier and seeming vaguely forlorn. Both courthouse and statue loom over so much of Faulkner's work, and now, for the first time this day, I am stricken by the realization that Faulkner is really gone. And I am deep in memory, as if summoned there by a trumpet blast. Dilsey and Benjy and Luster and all the Compsons, Hightower and Byron Bunch and Flem Snopes and the gentle Lena Grove—all of these people and a score of others come swarming back comically and villainously and tragically in my mind with a kind of mnemonic sense of utter reality, along with the tumultuous landscape and the fierce and tender weather, and the whole maddened, miraculous vision of life wrested, as all art is wrested, out of nothingness. Suddenly, as the watchful and brooding faces of the towns-people sweep across my gaze, I am filled with a bitter grief. We move past a young blue-shirted policeman, crescents of sweat beneath his arms, who stands at attention, bareheaded, his cap clapped to his breast. Up North Lamar the procession rolls, then east on Jefferson.

The old cemetery has been filled; therefore his grave lies in the "new" part, and he is one of the first occupants of this tract. There is nothing much to say about it, really. It is a rather raw field, it seems to me, overlooking a housing project; but he lies on a gentle slope between two oak trees, and they will grow larger as they shelter him. Thus he is laid to rest. The crowd disperses in the hot sunlight and is gone.

At the end of *The Wild Palms,* an early novel of Faulkner's, the con-demned hero, speculating upon the possibility of a choice between nothing and grief, says that he will choose grief. And certainly even grief must be better than nothing. As for the sorrow and loss one feels today in this hot dry field, perhaps it needs only to be expressed in Faulkner's own words, in the young poem he called "My Epitaph":

If there be grief, let it be the rain
And this but silver grief, for grieving's sake,
And these green woods be dreaming here to wake
Within my heart, if I should rouse again.
But I shall sleep, for where is any death
While in these blue hills slumbrous overhead
I'm rooted like a tree? Though I be dead
This soil that holds me fast will find me breath.

[*Life,* July 20, 1962.]

"O Lost!" Etc.

The shade of Thomas Wolfe must be acutely disturbed to find that his earthly stock has sunk so low. All artists want fame, glory, immortality, yet few were so frankly bent on these things as Wolfe was, and no writer—despite his agonizing self-doubts—seemed so confident that they lay within his grasp. The unabashed desire for perpetuity moves in a rhythmic, reappearing theme through all of his works. In a typically boisterous apostrophe to the power of booze in *Of Time and the River* he chants:

> You came to us with music, poetry, and wild joy when we were twenty, when we reeled home at night through the old moon-whitened streets of Boston and heard our friend, our comrade, and our dead companion, shout through the silence of the moonwhite square: "You are a poet and the world is yours." . . . We turned our eyes then to the moon-drunk skies of Boston, knowing only that we were young, and drunk, and twenty, and that the power of mighty poetry was within us, and the glory of the great earth lay before us—because we were young and drunk and twenty, and could never die!

But poor Tom Wolfe if not dead is currently moribund, and the matter of his resuscitation is certainly in doubt. The young, one is told, being gland- and eyeball-oriented, read very little of anything anymore, and if they do it is likely to be Burroughs or Beckett or Genet or a few of the bards of black humor or camp pornography. Of the older writers, Hemingway and Fitzgerald are still read, but Wolfe seldom. When the literary temper of a generation is occult, claustrophobic, doom-ridden, and the qualified snigger is its characteristic psychic response, no writer could be so queer as the shambling, celebratory hulk of Thomas Wolfe, with his square's tragic sense and his bedazzled young man's vision of the glory of the world. What a comedown! In Europe, with the possible exception of Germany, he is not very well known. No, the reputation of Wolfe is in very bad shape; I suppose it was inevitable that, a short time ago, when I asked a college English major what he thought of the work of Thomas (not Tom) Wolfe he actually *did* reply seriously, "You mean the Tangerine Streamlined Whatever-it's-called guy?"

Yet it would be hard to exaggerate the overwhelming effect that reading Wolfe had upon so many of us who were coming of age during or just after World War II. I think his influence may have been especially powerful upon those who, like myself, had been reared, as Wolfe had, in a small Southern town or city, and who in addition had suffered a rather mediocre secondary education, with scant reading of any kind. To a boy who had read only a bad translation of *Les Misérables* and *The Call of the Wild* and *Men Against the Sea* and *The Grapes of Wrath* (which one had read at fourteen for the racy dialogue and the "sensational" episodes), the sudden exposure to a book like *Look Homeward, Angel,* with its lyrical torrent and raw, ingenuous feeling, its precise and often exquisite rendition of place and mood, its buoyant humor and the vitality of its characters and, above all, the sense of youthful ache and promise and hunger and ecstasy which so corresponded to that of its eighteen-year-old reader—to experience such a book as this, at exactly the right moment in time and space, was for many young people like being born again into a world as fresh and wondrous as that seen through the eyes of Adam. Needless to say, youth itself was largely responsible for this feverish empathy, and there will be reservations in a moment in regard to the effect of a later rereading of Wolfe; nonetheless, a man who can elicit such reactions from a reader at whatever age is a force to be reckoned with, so I feel nothing but a kind of gratitude when I consider how I succumbed to the rough unchanneled force of Wolfe as one does to the ocean waves.

Among other things, he was the first prose writer to bring a sense of America as a glorious abstraction—a vast and brooding continent whose untold bounties were waiting every young man's discovery—and his endless catalogues and lyric invocations of the land's physical sights and sounds and splendors (a sumptuous description of the Boston waterfront, for instance, where "the delicate and subtle air of spring touches all these odors with a new and delicious vitality; it draws the tar out of the pavements also, and it draws slowly, subtly, from ancient warehouses, the compacted perfumes of eighty years: the sweet thin piney scents of packing boxes, the glutinous composts of half a century, that have thickly stained old warehouse plankings, the smells of twine, tar, turpentine and hemp, and of thick molasses, ginseng, pungent vines and roots and old piled sacking . . . and particularly the smell of meat, of frozen beeves, slick porks, and veals, of brains and livers and kidneys, of haunch, paunch and jowl . . .") seemed to me anything but prolix or tedious, far from it; rather it was as if for the first time my whole being had been thrown open to the sheer *tactile* and *sensory* vividness of the American scene through which, until then, I had been walking numb and blind, and it caused me a thrill of discovery that was quite unutterable. It mattered little to me that sometimes Wolfe went on for page after windy page about nothing, or with the most callow of emotions: I was callow myself, and was undaunted by even his most inane repetitions. It meant nothing to me that some astonishingly exact and poignant rendition of a mood or remembrance might be followed by a thick suet of nearly impenetrable digressions; I gobbled it all up, forsaking my classes, hurting my eyes, and digesting the entire large Wolfe oeuvre—the four massive novels, plus the short stories and novellas, *The Story of a Novel,* the many letters and scraps and fragments, and the several plays, even then practically unreadable—in something less than two weeks, emerging from the incredible encounter pounds lighter, and with a buoyant serenity of one whose life has been forever altered.

I think it must have been at approximately this moment that I resolved myself to become a writer. I was at college in North Carolina at the time; it was October, Wolfe's natal, favorite, most passionately remembered month, and the brisk autumnal air was now touched, for the first time in *my* life, with the very fragrance and the light that Wolfe's grand hymn to the season had evoked:

October has come again—has come again. . . . The ripe, the golden month has come again, and in Virginia the chinkapins are falling. Frost sharps the middle music of the seasons, and all things living on the earth turn home again . . . The bee bores to the belly of the yellowed grape, the fly gets old and fat and blue, he buzzes loud, crawls slow, creeps heavily to death, the sun goes down in blood and pollen across the bronzed and mown fields of old October . . . Come to us, Father, while the winds howl in the darkness, for October has come again bringing with it huge prophecies of death and life and the great cargo of the men who will return . . .

With words like this still vivid in my brain, I gazed at the transmuted tobacco-hazed streets of Durham, quite beside myself with wonder, and only the appearance of a sudden, unseasonable snowstorm frustrated my immediate departure—together with a friend, similarly smitten—for Asheville, over two hundred miles away, where we had intended to place flowers on the writer's grave.

Now thirty years after Wolfe's death, the appearance of Andrew Turnbull's biography marks an excellent occasion to try to put the man and his work in perspective. Turnbull's work is a first-rate study, and not the least of its many worthy qualities is its sense of proportion. Too many biographies—especially of literary figures—tend to be overly fleshed out and are cursed with logor-rhea, so that the illustrious subject himself becomes obliterated behind a shower of menus, train tickets, opera programs, itineraries, and dull mash notes from lovelorn girls. I could have done without so many of the last item in this present volume—from Wolfe's paramour Aline Bernstein, who, though by no means a girl, often fell to gushing at inordinate length; but this is a small complaint, since throughout the book Turnbull generally maintains a congenial pace and supplies us with just the proper amount of detail. One of the surprises of the biography is the way in which it manages to be fresh and informative about a person who was probably the most narrowly autobiographical writer who ever lived. The very idea of a life of Thomas Wolfe is enough to invoke dismay if not gentle ridicule, since our first reaction is, "But why? Everything he did and saw is in his books." Yet Turnbull, clearly with some calculation, has expertly uncovered certain facts having to do with Wolfe's life which, if not really crucial, are fascinating just *because* we realize that we did not know them before. The actual financial situation of Wolfe's family in Asheville, for example, is interesting, since the impression one gets of the deafening tribe of Gants in *Look Homeward, Angel* is that of a down-at-the-heel, lower-middle-class clan which may not have been destitute but which always had a hard time of it making ends meet. The truth of the matter, as Turnbull points out, is that by Asheville standards the Wolfes were literally affluent, belonging to the "top two percent economically." Likewise it turns out that Wolfe had a touch of the sybarite in him; as an instructor at New York University he chose to live by himself in lodgings that for the time must have been very expensive, rather than share quarters with several others as practically all of the instructors did. Such details would be of little interest, of course, were they not at variance with the portraits of Eugene Gant–George Webber, whose careers in the novels are considerably more penurious, egalitarian, and grubby.

Wolfe was an exasperating man, a warm companion with a rich sense of humor and touching generosity of spirit, and, alternately, a bastard of truly monumental dimensions, and it is a tribute to the detachment with which Mr. Turnbull has fashioned his biography that the good Wolfe and the bad Wolfe, seen upon separate occasions, begin to blend together so that what emerges (as in the best of biographies) is a man—in this case a man more complex and driven even than is usual among those of his calling: obsessively solitary yet craving companionship, proud and aloof but at the same time almost childishly dependent, open-handed yet suspicious, arrogant, sweet-hearted, hypersensitive, swinishly callous, gentle—every writer, that is, but magnified. In his mid-twenties on board a ship returning from Europe, Wolfe met and fell in love with Aline Bernstein, a rich and well-known New York stage designer who was eighteen years older than he was. In the ensuing affair, which was bizarre and tumultuous to say the least, Mrs. Bernstein quite clearly represented a mother figure, an image of the Eliza Gant from whom, in his first two novels, Tom-Eugene is constantly fleeing as from a Fury, and, with cyclic regularity, returning home to in helpless and sullen devotion. (Julia Wolfe nursed her son until he was three and a half and cut off Tom's beautiful ringlets at nine only after he had picked up lice from a neighbor. How Wolfe escaped being a homosexual is a mystery, but no one has ever made that charge.) The same ambivalent feelings he had toward his mother he expressed in his relations with Aline, who, though extremely pretentious and rather silly, did not deserve the treatment she suffered at his hands, which was largely abominable. He was of course capable of great tenderness and it is obvious that they had many happy moments together, but one cannot help feeling anything but rue for the plight of the poor woman, who had to be subjected to interminable grillings by him about her former lovers and who, when circumstances forced them apart, still was made to endure a barrage of letters in which in the most irrational and cruel terms he accused her of betrayal and unfaithfulness. He also shouted at her that she smelled like goose grease, adding the attractive observation that "all Jews smell like goose grease." It was a hopeless situation, and although it makes for grim reading, the section on Wolfe's stormy time with Aline is one of the most illuminating in the book, revealing as it does so much of the man's puerile inability to form any real attachment to anyone, especially a woman—a shallowness of emotional response, on a certain level at least, which caused him to be in perpetual flight and which may be a key to both his failings and his strengths as a writer.

There was also, naturally, his editor Maxwell Perkins—still one more relationship filled with *Sturm und Drang* and, on the part of Wolfe, impositions and demands on another's time and energy so total as to be positively hair-raising. Obviously Perkins was a very fine gentleman, but that a broad streak of masochism ran through his nature there can also be no doubt; only a man born to enjoy terrible suffering could have absorbed the pure fact of daily, committed *involvement* which Wolfe's tyrannically dependent personality imposed. It was of course untrue, as had been hinted during Wolfe's years at Scribner's, that Perkins *wrote* any part of Wolfe's books but certainly he was instrumental in putting them together—maybe not quite as instrumental as Bernard DeVoto implied in his famous review of *The Story of a Novel* but a thoroughly dominating force nonetheless.[1] There is no other way that we can interpret the hilarious statement which Turnbull—perhaps with irony, perhaps not—makes in a section on the finishing of *Of Time and the River:* "Early in December Perkins summoned Wolfe to his office and told him the book was done. Wolfe was amazed." Yet if it is true that Wolfe wrote the words of the books and if it is also true, as someone said, that the trouble with Wolfe was that he put all of his gigantic struggle into his *work* and not his *art*—a nice distinction—it does look as if DeVoto might not have been too far off the mark, after all, in asserting that Perkins caused much of the "art" that exists in the sprawling work of Thomas Wolfe. Which is to say a semblance, at least, of form. And it is the lack too often of an organic form—a form arising from the same drives and tensions that inspired the work in the beginning—which now appears to be one of Wolfe's largest failings and is the one that most seriously threatens to undermine his stature as a major writer. The awful contradiction in his books between this form-lessness and those tremendous moments which still seem so touched with grandeur as to be imperishable is unsettling beyond words.

Rereading Wolfe is like visiting again a cherished landscape or town of by-gone years where one is simultaneously moved that much could remain so appealingly the same, and wonderstruck that one could ever have thought that such-and-such a corner or this or that view had any charm at all. It is not really that Wolfe is dated (I mean the fact of being dated as having to do with basically insincere postures and attitudes: already a lot of Hemingway is dated in a way Wolfe could never be); it is rather that when we now begin to realize how unpulled-together Wolfe's work really is—that same shape-lessness that mattered so little to us when we were younger—and how this shapelessness causes or at least allows for a lack of inner dramatic tension, without which no writer, not even Proust, can engage our mature attention for long, we see that he is simply telling us, often rather badly, things we no longer care about knowing or need to know. So much that once seemed grand and authoritative now comes off as merely obtrusive, strenuously willed, and superfluous. Which of course makes it all the more disturbing that in the midst of this chaotically verbose and sprawling world there stand out here and there truly remarkable edifices of imaginative cohesion.

Wolfe's first novel, *Look Homeward, Angel,* withstands the rigors of time most successfully and remains his best book, taken as a whole. Here the powers of mind and heart most smoothly find their confluence, while a sense of place (mainly Altamont, or Asheville) and time (a boy's life between infancy and the beginning of adulthood) lend to the book a genuine unity that Wolfe never recaptured in his later works. Flaws now appear, however. A recent rereading of the book caused me to wince from time to time in a way that I cannot recall having done during my first reading at eighteen. Wolfe at that point was deeply under the power of Joyce (whom Wolfe, in-cidentally, encountered years later on a tour of Belgium, Turnbull relates in an engaging episode, but who so awed him that he was afraid to speak to the great Irishman) and if the influence of *Ulysses* can be discerned in the book's many strengths it can also be seen in its gaucheries. An otherwise vivid pas-sage like the following, for example (and there are many such in the book), is diminished rather than reinforced by the culminating Joyce-like allusion:

Colonel Pettigrew was wrapped to his waist in a heavy rug, his shoulders were covered with a gray Confederate cape. He bent forward, leaning his old weight upon a heavy polished stick, which his freckled hands gripped upon the silver knob. Muttering, his proud powerful old head turned shakily from side to side, darting fierce splintered glances at the drifting crowd. He was a very parfit gentil knight.

But *Look Homeward, Angel* can be forgiven such lapses precisely because it is a youthful book, as impressive for its sheer lyricism and hymnal celebration of youth and life as is the Mendelssohn Violin Concerto, from which we do not expect profundities, either. In addition, the novel is quite extraordinarily *alive*—alive in the vitality of its words (Wolfe wrote many bad sentences but *never* a dead one), in its splendid evocation of small-town sights and sounds and smells, and above all and most importantly, in the characters that spring out fully fleshed and breathing from the pages. The figures of W. O. and Eliza Gant are as infuriatingly garrulous and convincing now as when I first made their acquaintance, and the death of the tragic older brother Ben is fully as moving for the simple reason that Wolfe has made me believe in his existence. With all of its top-heaviness and the juvenile extravagances that occasionally mar the surface of the narrative, *Look Homeward, Angel* seems likely to stand as long as any novel will as a record of early-twentieth-century provincial American life.

It is when we run into *Of Time and the River* and its elephantine successors, *The Web and the Rock* and *You Can't Go Home Again,* that the real trouble begins. One of the crucial struggles that any writer of significance has had to endure is his involvement in the search for a meaningful theme, and Wolfe was no exception. The evidence is that Wolfe, though superbly gifted at imaginative projection, was practically incapable of extended dramatic invention, his creative process being akin to the settling into motion of some marvelous mnemonic tape recorder deep within his cerebrum, from which he unspooled reel after reel of the murmurous, living past. Such a technique served him beautifully in *Look Homeward, Angel,* unified as it was in time and space, and from both of which it derived its dramatic tension; but in the later works as Tom-Eugene-George moved into other environments—the ambience of Harvard and New York and, later, of Europe—the theme which at first had been so fresh and compelling lost its wings and the narrator became a solipsistic groundling. Certainly the last three books are still well worth reading; there is still the powerful, inexorable rush of language, a Niagara of words astonishing simply by virtue of its primal energy; many of the great set pieces hold up with their original force: old Gant's death, the *Oktoberfest* sequence in Munich, the apartment-house fire in New York, the portraits of Eugene's Uncle Bascom, Foxhall Edwards, the drunken Dr. McGuire—there are many more. These scenes and characterizations would alone guarantee Wolfe a kind of permanence, even if one must sift through a lot of detritus to find them. But there is so much now that palls and irritates. That furrow-browed, earnest sense of discovery in which the reader participates willingly in *Look Homeward, Angel* loses a great deal of its vivacity when the same protagonist has begun to pass into adulthood. In *Of Time and the River,* for example, when Eugene has become a student at Harvard, we are introduced to a young student named Francis Starwick:

> He spoke in a strange and rather disturbing tone, the pitch and timbre of which it would be almost impossible to define, but which would haunt one who had heard it forever after. His voice was neither very high nor low, it was a man's voice and yet one felt it might also have been a woman's; but there was nothing at all effeminate about it. It was simply a strange voice compared to most American voices, which are rasping, nasal, brutally coarse or metallic. Starwick's voice had a disturbing lurking resonance, an exotic, sensuous and almost voluptuous quality. Moreover, the peculiar mannered affectation of his speech was so studied that it hardly escaped extravagance. If it had not been for the dignity, grace and intelligence of his person, the affectation of his speech might have been ridiculous. As it was, the other youth felt the moment's swift resentment and hostility that is instinctive with the American when he thinks someone is speaking in an affected manner.

In the first place, his voice wouldn't "haunt one who had heard it forever after." This exaggerated sensibility, this clubfooted, gawky boy's style, becomes increasingly apparent throughout all of Wolfe's later work, in which the author-protagonist, now out in the world of Northern sophisticates, falls unconsciously into the role of the suspicious young hick from Buncombe County, North Carolina. In the passage just quoted the reader, Starwick—indeed, everyone but Eugene Gant—is aware that Starwick is a homosexual, but these labored and sophomoric observations have so begun to dominate Wolfe's point of view that much later on in the book, when Starwick's homosexuality *is* revealed, Eugene's chagrin over that belated knowledge fills the reader with murderous exasperation. The same passage illustrates another trait which crops up increasingly in the later books, and that is a tendency to generalize promiscuously about places and things which demand, if anything, narrow and delicate particularization—especially about a place as various and as chaotically complex as America. The part about voices, for instance. Most American voices, though sometimes unpleasant, are not generally "rasping, nasal, brutally coarse or metallic"; forty or fifty million soft Southern voices alone, including presumably Wolfe's, are—whatever else—the antithesis of all those careless adjectives. Nor is it at all accurate to proclaim either that "the American"—presumably meaning all Americans—feels resentment and hostility at affected speech or that the reaction is peculiarly American. Many Americans are simply tickled or amused by such speech, while at the same time it is surely true that if resentment and hostility are felt, they can be felt by the French over French affectations as well. Wolfe's writing is filled with such silly hyperbole. Similarly, a statement such as "we are so lost, so naked, and so lonely in America"—a refrain that reappears over and over again in Wolfe's work—seems to me the worst sort of empty rant, all the more so because Wolfe himself surely knew better, knew that lostness, nakedness, loneliness are not American but part of the whole human condition.

It is sad that so much disappoints on a rereading of Wolfe, sad that the "magic and the singing and the gold" which he celebrated so passionately seem now, within his multitudinous pages, to possess a lackluster quality to which the middle-aging heart can no longer respond. It is especially sad because we can now see (possibly because of the very contrast with all that is so prolix and adolescent and unfelt and labored) that at his best Wolfe was capable of those epiphanies that only writers of a very high order have ever achieved. I am thinking particularly of the death of W. O. Gant, in *Of Time and the River,* where the cancer-ridden old man lies in bed, falling in and out of a coma as he drowses over the landscape of his youth in Pennsylvania.

> Towards one o'clock that night Gant fell asleep and dreamed that he was walking down the road that led to Spangler's Run. . . .
> It was a fine morning in early May and everything was sweet and

green and as familiar as it had always been. The graveyard was carpeted with thick green grass, and all around the graveyard and the church there was the incomparable green velvet of young wheat. And the thought came back to Gant, as it had come to him a thousand times, that the wheat around the graveyard looked greener and richer than any other wheat he had ever seen. And beside him on his right were the great fields of the Schaefer farm, some richly carpeted with young wheat, and some ploughed, showing great bronze-red strips of fertile nobly swelling earth. And behind him on the great swell of the land, and commanding that sweet and casual scene with the majesty of its incomparable day was Jacob Schaefer's great red barn and to the right the neat brick house with the white trimming of its windows, the white picket fence, the green yard with its rich tapestry of flowers and lilac bushes and the massed leafy spread of its big maple trees. And behind the house the hill rose, and all its woods were just greening into May, still smoky, tender and unfledged, gold-yellow with the magic of young green. And before the woods began there was the apple orchard halfway up the hill; the trees were heavy with the blossoms and stood there in all their dense still bloom incredible.

And from the greening trees the bird-song rose, the grass was thick with the dense gold glory of the dandelions, and all about him were a thousand magic things that came and went and never could be captured.

At this point Gant in his dream encounters one of the neighbors, a half-wit named Willy Spangler, and he stops and they chat together for a moment. Gant gives Willy a plug of chewing tobacco, then he turns to continue his walk when Willy says anxiously:

"Are ye comin' back, Oll? Will ye be comin' back real soon?"

And Gant, feeling a strange and nameless sorrow, answered:

"I don't know, Willy"—for suddenly he saw that he might never come this way again.

But Willy, still happy, foolish, and contented, had turned and galloped away toward the house, flinging his arms out and shouting as he went:

"I'll be waitin' fer ye. I'll be waitin' fer ye, Oll."

And Gant went on then, down the road, and there was a nameless sorrow in him that he could not understand, and some of the brightness had gone out of the day.

When he got to the mill, he turned left along the road that went down by Spangler's Run, crossed by the bridge below, and turned from the road into the woodpath on the other side. A child was standing in the path, and turned and went on ahead of him. In the wood the sunlight made swarming moths of light across the path, and through the leafy tangle of the trees: the sunlight kept shifting and swarming on the child's gold hair, and all around him were the sudden noises of the wood, the stir, the rustle, and the bullet thrum of wings, the cool broken sound of hidden water.

The wood got denser, darker as he went on and coming to a place where the path split away into two forks, Gant stopped, and turning to the child said, "Which one shall I take?" And the child did not answer him.

But someone was there in the wood before him. He heard footsteps on the path, and saw a footprint in the earth, and turning took the path where the footprint was, and where it seemed he could hear someone walking.

And then, with the bridgeless instancy of dreams it seemed to him that all of the bright green-gold around him in the wood grew dark and somber, the path grew darker, and suddenly he was walking in a strange and gloomy forest, haunted by the brown and tragic light of dreams. The forest shapes of great trees rose around him, he could hear no bird-song now, even his own feet on the path were soundless, but he always thought he heard the sound of someone walking in the wood before him. He stopped and listened: the steps were muffled, softly thunderous, they seemed so near that he thought that he must catch up with the one he followed in another second, and then they seemed immensely far away, receding in the dark mystery of that gloomy wood. And again he stopped and listened, the footsteps faded, vanished, he shouted, no one answered. And suddenly he knew that he had taken the wrong path, that he was lost. And in his heart there was an immense and quiet sadness, and the dark light of the enormous wood was all around him; no birds sang.

After this passage Gant awakes suddenly to find himself gazing into the eyes of his wife, Eliza, who is maintaining vigil at his bedside. There follows then a long colloquy between the dying man and the woman (who has never called him anything but "Mr. Gant")—a disconnected, faltering, fragmented murmuration of words, profoundly moving, in which they reexperience all the old sorrows and failures of the tormented, bitter, yet somehow triumphant life they have lived together for forty years. At last—

He was silent again, and presently, his breath coming somewhat hoarse and labored, he cleared his throat, and put one hand up to his throat, as if to relieve himself of some impediment.

Eliza looked at him with troubled eyes and said:

"What's the matter, Mr. Gant? There's nothing hurtin' you?"

"No," he said. "Just something in my throat. Could I have some water?"

"Why, yes, sir! That's the very thing!" She got up hastily, and looking about in a somewhat confused manner, saw behind her a pitcher of water and a glass upon his old walnut bureau, and saying, "This very minute, sir!" started across the room.

And at the same moment, Gant was aware that someone had entered the house, was coming towards him through the hall, would soon be with him. Turning his head towards the door he was conscious of something approaching with the speed of light, the instancy of thought, and at that moment he was filled with a sense of inexpressible joy, a feeling of triumph and security he had never known. Something immensely bright and beautiful was converging in a flare of light, and at that instant, the whole room blurred around him, his sight was fixed upon that focal image in the door, and suddenly the child was standing there and looking towards him.

And even as he started from his pillows, and tried to call his wife he felt something thick and heavy in his throat that would not let him speak. He tried to call to her again but no sound came, then something wet and warm began to flow out of his mouth and nostrils, he lifted his hands up to his throat, the warm wet blood came pouring out across his fingers; he saw it and felt joy.

For now the child—or someone in the house—was speaking, calling to him; he heard great footsteps, soft but thunderous, imminent, yet immensely far, a voice well-known, never heard before. He called to it, and then it seemed to answer him; he called to it with faith and joy to give him rescue, strength and life, and it answered him and told him that all the error, old age, pain, and grief of life was nothing but an evil dream; that he who had been lost was found again, that his youth would be restored to him and that he would never die, and that he would find again the path he had not taken long ago in a dark wood.

And the child still smiled at him from the dark door; the great steps, soft and powerful, came ever closer, and as the instant imminent approach of the last meeting came intolerably near, he cried out through the lake of jetting blood, "Here, Father, here!" and a strong voice answered him, "My son!"

At that instant he was torn by a rending cough, something was wrenched loose in him, the death gasp rattled through his blood, and a mass of greenish matter foamed out through his lips. Then the world was blotted out, a blind black fog swam up and closed above his head, someone seized him, he was held, supported in two arms, he heard someone's voice saying in a low tone of terror and pity, "Mr. Gant! Mr. Gant! Oh, poor man, poor man! He's gone!" And his brain faded into night. Even before she lowered him back upon the pillows, she knew that he was dead.

Wolfe would have to be cherished if only for the power he exerted upon a whole generation. But even if this were not enough, the clear glimpses he had at certain moments of man as a strange, suffering animal alone beneath the blazing and indifferent stars would suffice to earn him honor, and a flawed but undeniable greatness.

[*Harper's,* April 1968.]

An Elegy for F. Scott Fitzgerald

It is perhaps inevitable that nearly all very good writers seem to be able to inspire the most vehement personal reactions. They might be quite dead but their spirits remain somehow immortally fleshed, and we are capable of talking about them as we talk about devoted friends, or about a despised neighbor who has just passed out of earshot. In certain cases it amounts to a type of bewitchment. Thus I heard only a short time ago a conservative, poetasting lawyer say that as much as he admired the work of Dylan Thomas, he would never allow the philandering rascal in his house.

Of course, the passions such writers arouse are especially strong when the writer—unlike, say, William Faulkner, who sedulously cultivated the private life—is F. Scott Fitzgerald, whose life has fallen so under the dominion of the legend that this occasionally tends to obscure the fact that he possessed, at his best, an original and beautiful talent. Nonetheless, it is the mythic aspects of a writer's life that generate all the gossip, the ugly resentment along with the tender sentiments, and Fitzgerald has by now had a disproportionate share of both. Here, for instance, is Katherine Anne Porter, in a recent *Paris Review* interview: "Even now when I think of the twenties and the legend that has grown up about them, I think it was a horrible time: shallow and trivial. . . . The remarkable thing is that anybody survived in such an atmosphere—in the place where they could call F. Scott Fitzgerald a great writer! . . . I couldn't read him then and I can't read him now. . . .

Not only didn't I like his writing, but I didn't like the people he wrote about. I thought they weren't worth thinking about." One senses a sort of gratuitous outrage here which has less to do with Fitzgerald's talent than with the Fitzgerald myth. It is hard to believe that Miss Porter, who is such an estimable writer herself, is really so down on Fitzgerald's "writing"; one feels rather that she simply doesn't want him in her house. But if the Fitzgerald myth can elicit calumny, it can also inspire quivering obeisance, such as this from Professor Arthur Mizener, a professional Fitzgeraldian, who is reduced to a kind of stammer: "Fitzgerald's greatest value for us is his almost eponymous character, the way his life and his work taken together represent what in the very depths of our nature we are—we Americans, anyhow, and—with some variations—perhaps most men of the western world." Spoken like a born undertaker.

Yet, since in Fitzgerald's case the myth and the work *are* indissolubly mingled, what is so fascinating about this large collection of letters, edited by Andrew Turnbull, is that in a sense it allows the writer to explicate his own legend. So revealing are these letters—to Zelda and his daughter, Scottie, to Edmund Wilson and Hemingway and Maxwell Perkins and his friends Gerald and Sara Murphy, among others—that one might feel that nothing further needs to be said about the writer's life. As for the book itself, one could question, as Malcolm Cowley has already done, Mr. Turnbull's arrangement—grouping the letters according to the person they are written to rather than running them chronologically and thus allowing them to tell their own story—but this is a small matter. The book remains a fascinating one.

From the very beginning there is a pervasive feeling of honesty in Fitzgerald's letters, and though some of the earliest correspondence contains a touch of collegiate fakery, of the innocuous kind, there is very little posturing. Unlike the letters of those writers who have written with a sense of posterity mooning at their elbow (Thomas Wolfe is a good example), Fitzgerald's were composed with a spontaneity that must have been one of the most fetching aspects of his charm as a person. In fact, a writer with less spontaneity and more guile would never have written words like these, in a letter of 1920, to his agent, Harold Ober: "Enclosed is a new version of 'Barbara,' called 'Bernice Bobs Her Hair,' to distinguish it from Mary Rinehart's 'Bab' stories in the *Post*. I think I've managed to inject a snappy climax into it." Such an utterance I think helps explain why these early letters are the least satisfying and least interesting of the collection. For though, to be sure, this was the decade of the matchless *Gatsby* and several of the finest stories—"Absolution," "The Rich Boy," "The Baby Party"—it was also the time of an astonishing amount of pure waste, when the hectic, frazzled, and, above all, expensive life the Fitzgeralds were leading resulted in the production of a great deal of sloppy and hastily written fiction. As a result, these early letters, strewn with such complaints as "If I don't in some way get $650.00 in the bank by Wednesday morning I'll have to pawn the furniture" are often tedious; we are, after all, witnessing not the struggle of a desperate pauper, a Mozart or a Franz Schubert, but that of a spoiled young writer living far beyond his means, and much of Fitzgerald's bellyaching is cause for legitimate exasperation. Even so, even when Fitzgerald has put us out of sorts with his clamorous preoccupation with his "standard of living," when his silly conceit and his youthful pomposity about his not-very-good early work has begun to aggravate us the most, the artist in Fitzgerald, the conscientious and coolly disciplined craftsman suddenly comes through, and we find him writing to Perkins in 1924 about the nearly finished *Gatsby:* "In my new novel I'm thrown directly on purely creative work—not trashy imaginings as in my stories but the sustained imagination of a sincere yet radiant world. So I tread slowly and carefully and at times in considerable distress. This book will be a consciously artistic achievement." Oppressively superficial as he may have appeared during the twenties—and may have been in important respects—he never abandoned, even then, this stony, saving honesty and self-awareness.

In his biography of Fitzgerald, Turnbull quotes Rebecca West as saying: "I knew Zelda was very clever but from the first moment I saw her I knew she was mad." She was speaking of the year 1923, three years after Zelda married Fitzgerald. By 1930, when Zelda was a patient in a Swiss sanitarium, the "gay parade," as Fitzgerald called the decade, was over, and the *allegro vivace* which had dominated the mood of his life dwindled and died, replaced by something at first only elusively somber, then steeped in an unutterable melancholy: it was a tone which from then on never disappeared. By 1932, living in Baltimore and slipping slowly into alcoholism (though still toiling away at *Tender Is the Night*), Fitzgerald is writing to Perkins: "Five years have rolled away from me and I can't decide exactly who I am, if anyone." Throughout these letters of the early and mid-thirties there are marvelous flashes of wit and warmth, his intense concern for books, for literature, never flags—he seems to have read everything; no writer ever had such appreciative and generous interest in his contemporaries, such an acute, unjealous response to excellence, along with a fine nose for a fraud—but the sense of melancholy, of encroaching danger, shadows over these pages like a bleak, wintry afternoon. (Again to Perkins, 1934: "The mood of terrible depression and despair is not going to become a characteristic and I am ashamed and felt very yellow about it afterward. But to deny that such moods come increasingly would be futile.") Since her apparent recovery in Switzerland, Zelda has had two breakdowns. *Tender Is the Night* appears and is a critical and financial failure. Hemingway, whom he admires almost to the point of worship, turns on him, cruelly lampooning him in *The Snows of Kilimanjaro* with the famous episode about "the very rich," calling him "poor Scott Fitzgerald." ("Dear Ernest," he replies in a letter, "please lay off me in print." Then he adds: "It's a fine story—one of your best." Fitzgerald's magnanimity was truly incalculable. Although much later, to Perkins, he writes bitterly of this betrayal, saying: "Once I believed in friendship, believed I *could* make people happy and it was more fun than anything. Now even that seems like a vaudevillian's cheap dream of heaven, a vast minstrel show in which one is the perpetual Bones.") And as Fitzgerald fights against his drinking, and frets and broods, the sense of oncoming doom grows and grows. One is reminded of the harrowing lines from Job: *I was not in safety, neither had I rest, neither was I quiet; yet trouble came.*

And so it comes. In Turnbull's biography there is a terrible chapter describing those months that must have been the abyss of Fitzgerald's career. The time is 1936 and the place is Asheville, where Fitzgerald—now nearly broke and in debt, ill of tuberculosis, a frail alcoholic masochist smothering in the warm love of his own failure—has set up residence in order to be near the sanitarium to which Zelda has been committed. Zelda is at this point desperately off; she has taken to carrying a Bible, and occasionally, garbed in the superannuated flapper's clothing of the twenties, she kneels in public to pray. When the haggard couple arrives one evening to call on neighbors, Zelda is bearing with her a bunch of water lilies she has gathered on the way, and she reminds one guest of Ophelia; later, on the terrace, Fitzgerald leads her to a stone wall and proclaims, "You're the fairy princess and I'm the prince," and for several minutes they ring changes on this sentiment—Zelda wide-eyed, still lovely, and utterly mad, Fitzgerald gazing at her transfigured with sorrow. The entire desolating passage—perhaps because of its semi-public nature (to the very end, the Fitzgeralds were always being *observed*)—reads like nothing so much as a travesty, a reverse image of one of those elaborate gay pranks of a decade or so before, when they would go to a party in a taxi, he on the roof, she on the hood, or when at the theater they would sit together silent during the funny parts and then laugh uproariously when the house was still. Yet sad as this vignette is, an incident soon occurs which drives Fitzgerald even further away from himself and reality—to the black edge of death and madness. Ever generous and trusting, he also possesses the true writer's immense vanity, and mistakenly grants an interview to the *New York Post*, whose editor sees in Fitzgerald's fortieth birthday an opportunity to make hay with the myth of the twenties and its most distinguished surviving symbol, and dispatches to Asheville an expertly ingratiating reporter named, rather aptly, Michael Mok. Taken off guard, Fitzgerald is polite and as garrulous as his combination of illnesses will allow, and Mok's front-page article—certainly as grimy a claim to immortality as ever fell to any newspaperman—begins as follows:

> The poet-prophet of the post-war neurotics observed his fortieth birthday yesterday in his bedroom in the Grove Park Inn here. He spent the day as he spends all his days—trying to come back from the other side of Paradise, the hell of despondency in which he has writhed for the last couple of years. Physically he was suffering the aftermath of an accident eight weeks ago when he broke his right shoulder in a dive from a fifteen-foot springboard. But whatever pain the fracture might still cause him, it did not account for his jittery jumping off and onto his bed, his restless pacing, his trembling hands, his twitching face with its pitiful expression of a cruelly beaten child. Nor could it be held responsible for his frequent trips to a highboy, in a drawer of which lay a bottle. Each time he poured a drink into the measuring glass behind his table, he would look appealingly at the nurse and ask, "Just one ounce?"

After reading this article, Turnbull tells us, Fitzgerald tried to kill himself, swallowing the contents of a vial of morphine, which was a sufficient overdose to make him vomit and save his life. But, "gradually anger and despair gave way to shame. He had touched bottom. The article rallied his self-respect and laid the foundation for a comeback of sorts." That "comeback" comprised the last four years of Fitzgerald's life, which were, of course, largely the Hollywood years, the time of feverish sickness and near-destitution, of eleven-dollar bank balances and seedy apartments, of humiliating hack work for the movies, and the excruciating effort to wrest from his talent ("a delicate thing—mine is so scarred and buffeted that I am amazed that at times it still runs clear") one last good book which might resurrect him from the oblivion into which he had been cast. Reading about these appalling, ugly, and very courageous years, one is again struck by that sense of ironic transposition which dominates the Fitzgerald legend. It all seems like a romantic movie based on the Artist's Life yet run off at a frantic clip backwards: the glittering success, the money and the fame all coming at the beginning, until, finally, contrary to romantic conventions, we observe the hero terminating his career quite as bleakly as a hopeful yet unpublished poet begins his own—and in the chill and hideous garret of Hollywood. One somehow looks for self-pity: it would be expected in a man who had fallen so far and so hard. And to be sure, there is the natural lament of a writer who feels that both his work and his memory have been banished forever from the public mind. "My God, I am a forgotten man," he cries, and his concern for *Gatsby*, then out of print, is the well-founded anxiety of any writer over the mortality of an offspring. "To die, so completely and unjustly after having given so much!" he protests to Perkins, and adds in that wonderfully characteristic tone of Fitzgerald's, a tone of mingled modesty and pride: "Even now there is little published in American fiction that doesn't slightly bear my stamp—in a *small* way I was an original." But although the quality of these last letters is often elegiac, rueful, and sometimes tinged with bitterness, there is very little self-pity. That this is so is part of their great dignity, and considering the mean and woeful circumstances, something of a marvel. Even the lousy films he worked on caused him anguish. A letter to Joseph Mankiewicz, for instance—wheedling, imploring, cajoling—attempting to persuade the producer to restore Fitzgerald's original touches to the script of a movie, is almost insupportable in its degradation. "Oh Joe, can't producers ever be wrong?" he demands, and the sense of futility is suddenly like a howl in a closet: "I'm a good writer—honest."

But throughout this bedraggled finale of his life, he was sustained by his intense concern for his daughter, Scottie, then at Vassar, and by his enduring devotion to Zelda; the letters included here to his wife and daughter are the best in the book, and those to Scottie, taken together, form a small master-piece. It is hard to imagine that more winning letters from a father to a child have been written by an American. They are hortatory to a degree—Fitzgerald's solicitude for her welfare, doubtless because of Zelda's continuing illness and his doubled responsibility, can only be described as ferocious—but they are also tender, allusive, witty, stern, playful, and, finally, informed by wisdom. One cannot read them without feeling a vast respect for this man who—sick and poor, feeling himself forgotten—could retain the splendid equanimity, the compassion and humor, the *love* that sounds through these pages like a heartbeat. Nor is it possible to scorn someone who in the midst of penury and raging sick fevers and neglect still had the boldness of spirit to try for "a big book." He survives what he believed to be his failure triumphantly, a loving and courageous man.

Fitzgerald was not above pettiness, and his most destructive fault was perhaps his lack of self-esteem. But a quality of abiding charity was at the root of his character, and if a collection of letters has the power to illuminate the myth by suffusing it with the sense of a dominant virtue, then this collection succeeds, for it is everywhere filled with Fitzgerald's charity. In 1937, Fitzgerald's close friends of the Riviera days, Gerald and Sara Murphy, had suffered the death within the space of two years of two of their three young children. The letter which Fitzgerald wrote them upon the death of their second child seems appropriate to quote in its entirety, if only for the reason that it may be one of the most beautiful letters of its kind that we have.

Dearest Gerald and Sara:

The telegram came today and the whole afternoon was so sad with thoughts of you and the happy times we had once. Another link binding you to life is broken and with such insensate cruelty that it is hard to say which of the two blows was conceived with more malice. I can see the silence in which you hover now after this seven years of struggle and it would take words like Lincoln's in his letter to the mother who had lost four sons in the war to write you anything fitting at the moment. The sympathy you will get will be what you have had from each other already and for a long, long time you will be inconsolable.

But I can see another generation growing up around Honoria and an eventual peace somewhere, an occasional port of call as we all sail deathward. Fate can't have any more arrows in its quiver for you that will wound like these. Who was it said that it was astounding how deepest griefs can change in time to a sort of joy? The golden bowl is broken indeed but it *was* golden; nothing can ever take those boys away from you now.

Scott

[*New York Review of Books,* November 28, 1963.]

A Second Flowering

For too long there has existed a misconception as to what comprises a literary generation. Most of the writers of the post–World War II era, linked only by the common fact that their work commenced sometime during the years after Hiroshima, have, I'm sure, wondered at one time or another why the notion of belonging to a "generation" has seemed so ill-fitting or embarrassing. Born in 1925, I have always considered Saul Bellow, born a decade earlier, as much a part of "my" generation as Philip Roth, who is eight years younger than I am. This comprises a time span of eighteen years, and I have remained uneasy with the idea—pleased enough to be associated with two writers I consider admirable but rather put off by its palpable lack of logic. It should not have bothered me (not that it has to any great degree), for as Malcolm Cowley points out, we have all been merely victims of an error of definition.

"A generation," he writes accurately, "is no more a matter of dates than it is one of ideology. A new generation does not appear every thirty years. . . . It appears when writers of the same age join in a common revolt against the fathers and when, in the process of adopting a new life style, they find their own models and spokesmen."

In this case he is speaking of that gorgeously endowed group of creative spirits, born in the charmed, abbreviated space of years between 1894 and 1900, whose collective self-discovery as literary artists was so dazzling that it remains an almost comic irony that we know them as the Lost Generation. Specifically, the representatives Cowley deals with are Hemingway, Fitzgerald, Dos Passos, Cummings, Thornton Wilder, Faulkner, Wolfe, and Hart Crane. (Edmund Wilson should have been included, and Cowley laments his absence.) Together they made up "the second flowering" of the title of Malcolm Cowley's book, which is at once a memoir, a series of biographical essays, a literary reexamination, a tribute, and a memorial to that extraordinary company of writers, about whom he wrote earlier in *Exile's Return* and elsewhere.

It is possible to approach a work like this with just a touch of resentment. We have read about the Lost Generation until our heads are waterlogged with its self-congratulation, its nostalgia. One broods over the gallons, the tuns, the tank cars of ink spilled out on the lives and work of these men— Hemingway's bibliography alone must be on its way to several volumes requiring sturdy bookends—and one thinks: Enough. Whatever the honesty, the wit, the grace, even the possible originality of the new offering, do we really want or need another account of Scott and Zelda's Riviera turn and the golden couple's tragic decline, or the way Hemingway's magnetic appeal was so often negated by his contemptible treatment of his friends, or Wolfe's hysterical self-concern and *Weltschmerz*?

These are not just thrice-told tales; they seem by now to be so numbingly familiar as to be almost personal—tedious old gossip having to do with some fondly regarded but too often outrageous kinfolk. And if the work also affects a critical stance, do we look forward to still more commentary on *The Bear* or Cummings's love lyrics? Or another desolating inventory of the metaphors in *Gatsby*? In *A Second Flowering* all of these matters are touched upon, yet it is testimony to Cowley's gifts as both a critic and a literary chronicler that the angle of vision seems new; that is, not only are his insights into these writers' works almost consistently arresting but so are his portraits of the men themselves.

Of course it helped to be present, and it was Cowley's great fortune to have often been very much on the scene; he was an exact contemporary. "I knew them all and some have been my friends over the years," he writes. A lesser commentator might have made a terrible botch of it just because of this propinquity and friendship, giving us one of those familiar works of strained observation, at once fawning and self-flattering, where the subject is really victimized as if by a distorting lens held scant inches from the nose.

Several of the writers under consideration—notably Hemingway and Fitzgerald—have already undergone such mistreatment. But Cowley's affection for these writers, his honesty and devotion to what they stood for, are too deep and inward-dwelling—this feeling pervades every page of the book—for him to sentimentalize them or falsify their image. That he admires them all needs no saying—it is a sign of his critical integrity that one can search in vain to find him in a posture of adulation; even the magnificent achievement of Faulkner, whom Cowley regards as the greatest of the group, is an achievement that he feels (perhaps in a form of antiphonal response to Faulkner's own remark that his generation would be judged upon the "splendor of our failures") falls short of the very highest level and one that cannot properly be set beside the work of such giants as Dostoevsky and Dickens.

One of the finest parts of Cowley's book, incidentally, is the now famous pioneering essay on Faulkner, published in 1945 as the introduction to the Viking *Portable Faulkner*, which is a lucid jewel of exegesis. It opened up Faulkner's world for me when I was a very young man struggling to read a difficult writer who was then out of print, little known, and less understood. Nearly a quarter of a century later, during which time Faulkner has been smothered in scholarship, the essay is still fresh and brilliant.

Cowley can be as rough and relentless as an old millwheel in his judgments, whether it be upon some odious personal quality, such as Hemingway's unregenerate and infantile competitiveness, or on a matter of literature. Either way, the critic cuts close to the bone. In college I read *U.S.A.* with the awe of a man discovering a new faith. Yet one passage in Cowley is the most succinctly stated I have ever read in explanation of the sad bankruptcy of Dos Passos's later fiction: "He broke another rule that seems to have been followed by great novelists. They can regard their characters with love or hate or anything between, but cannot regard them with tired aversion. They can treat events as tragic, comic, farcical, pathetic, or almost anything but consistently repulsive."

Cowley's criticism of *The Sun Also Rises*, while considerably more generous in its overall feeling, has the same kind of tough abrasiveness. But again, although he can be rueful about the failures and lapses of the writers—scolding Cummings for his frequent triviality, Wolfe about his "mania for bigness"—the prevailing tone is not that of a dismantler of reputations, a type often so prompt to scuttle into sight with his little toolkit at the end of an era, but one of generosity and preoccupying concern, as if Cowley knew he was an overseer—a kind of curator of some of the loveliest talents, however self-damaged and flawed, that America ever produced.

It is clear that Cowley still takes delight in having known them, and one can appreciate his delight. To recollect one's own modest familiarity with the ancestors is irresistible. Being of another time and place, I had no opportunity to know them—though on a couple of very brief occasions I saw two of the gentlemen plain. (I will not invade the privacy of Mr. Wilder, with whom I am acquainted, and who is a noble survivor.) By the time I came to the pleasure of reading, in the forties, Fitzgerald and Hart Crane and Wolfe—my earliest passion—had met untimely deaths.

Later, in New York in the early fifties, I met E. E. Cummings for a weird, bewitched hour or so. It was for tea at the tiny apartment of a pleasant old lady in Patchin Place, where Cummings also lived. Let Cowley describe him as he also appeared to me: "He had large, well-shaped features, carved rather than molded, eyes set wide apart, often with a glint of mischief in them. . . . In later years, when he had lost most of the hair and the rest was clipped off, he looked more like a bare-skulled Buddhist monk." Although the poet was considerably older than the Cummings of Cowley's reminiscence when I met him, and his tempo must have been slower, his manner more subdued, Cowley's further description corresponds nicely to my impression during that little encounter. What a talker!

"He was the most brilliant monologuist I have known," writes Cowley; "what he poured forth was a mixture of cynical remarks, puns, hyperboles, outrageous metaphors, inconsequence, and tough-guy talk spoken from the corner of his wide, expressive mouth: pure Cummings, as if he were rehearsing something that would afterward appear in print."

My only other contact with the Lost Generation was when I had lunch with Faulkner a single time, again in New York. Faulkner was then writing in an office at Random House. What I remember most vividly about this gentle, soft-speaking, somber-eyed little man with the drooping gray mustache is not his conversation, which was rambling and various (he talked lovingly and a lot about horses—one reason being that he was preparing to write an article on the Kentucky Derby for *Holiday*—and about Truman Capote, whose talent he genuinely admired but whose personality left him rather unnerved), but a beguiling item of literary marginalia. I had gotten up to go to the men's room, and when I returned Faulkner had vanished.

"He said to tell you he'd see you again," said Robert Linscott, the Random House editor who had been dining with us. "Bill sometimes gets that strange look in his eye and that means he can't sit still another minute. He's just got to go back to the office and work."

What Linscott then told me supported an observation that Cowley makes—that is, how generally unremarked or indeed unknown is the influence that certain members of the Lost Generation had upon each other. Cowley singles out the effect of Hemingway's work on Faulkner—an unlikely connection until one rereads Faulkner's short masterpiece, "Red Leaves," that grim and marvelous tale set in the autumnal light of early-nineteenth-century Mississippi, when the Indians owned black slaves and practiced human sacrifice.

Linscott related how Faulkner had once told him about the great difficulty he had in getting down the feel and atmosphere of the story to his satisfaction. It was not the story itself; the painful part had to do with the dialogue, a grappling with Anglicized Choctaw which thoroughly buffaloed Faulkner, since he had no idea how to render imaginary Indian talk into English. Finally, according to Linscott, Faulkner solved the problem while rereading a book he admired very much, *Death in the Afternoon*. The stilted, formalized Castilian-into-English which Hemingway had contrived seemed to Faulkner's ear to have just the right eccentric intonation for his Indians, and so his dialogue became a grateful though individualized borrowing—as anyone who compares the two works will readily see.

But these blurred yet memorable impressions—notes of an old-time fan—are mere filigree compared to the actuality of the books themselves, which penetrated the consciousness of so many young men of my time with the weight and poignancy of birth or death, or first love, or any other sacred and terrible event. With Wolfe alone I felt I had been captured by a demon, made absolutely a prisoner by this irresistible torrent of language. It was a revelation, for at eighteen I had no idea that words themselves—this tumbling riot of dithyrambs and yawping apostrophes and bardic cries—had the power to throw open the portals of perception, so that one could actually begin to feel and taste and smell the very texture of existence.

I realize now the naïveté of so many of Wolfe's attitudes and insights, his intellectual virginity, his parochial and boyish heart, his inability to objectivize experience and thus create a believable ambience outside the narrow range of self—all of these drastically reduce his importance as a writer with a serious claim on an adult mind. However, some passages—including the majestic death of old Gant in *Of Time and the River*—are of such heartrending power and radiant beauty that for these alone he should be read, and for them he would certainly retain a place in American literature.

Cowley makes somewhat the same point in his section on Wolfe in *A Second Flowering*, which is the most clear-headed brief analysis of Wolfe and his work that I have seen in print. If others of such passages as I just mentioned "had each been published separately," Cowley writes, "Wolfe might have gained a different reputation, not as an epic poet in prose, but as the author of short novels and portraits, little masterpieces of sympathy and penetration." But then Cowley doubts that he would have cared for that kind of fame. Mania for bigness again.

His portrait of Wolfe, while unsparing in its details about all that made the man such a trial to himself and others—his paranoia, his nearly fatal lack of self-criticism, his selfishness and grandiosity, all the appurtenances of a six-foot-seven-inch child writing in his solipsistic hell—is nonetheless enormously sympathetic and filled with respect. "He had always dreamed of becoming a hero," Cowley writes, "and that is how he impresses us now: perhaps not as a hero of the literary art on a level with Faulkner and Hemingway and Fitzgerald, but as *Homo Scribens* and *Vir Scribentissimus,* a tragic hero of the act of writing."

And so the other fathers also quickly took possession. I was soon reading *Gatsby* and *In Our Time* and *The Sound and the Fury* with the same devouring pleasure that I had read Wolfe. Perhaps I sound too idolatrous. It would be misleading to give the impression that the Lost Generation had exclusive hold on our attention—we who were coming out of college in the forties and early fifties. Recalling my own licentious eclecticism, I realize I was reading everything, from Aeschylus to John Donne to Flaubert to Proust to Raymond Chandler. Yet I think it has to be conceded that rarely has such a group of literary figures had the impact that these writers have had upon their immediate descendants and successors.

This is not to say that at least a good handful of the writers and poets who followed them have failed to be artists in their own right—several of them masterly ones—and who if they genuflect before the fathers do so with pride as well as gratitude. It is only that the influence of the older men— themselves influenced by Eliot and Joyce and Whitman and Mark Twain— has been at once broad and profound to an exceptional degree, so that while we have thankfully moved out of their shadow we have not passed out of their presence.

It is impossible to conceive, for example, that anyone born during the twenties or afterward who was crazy enough to embrace literature as a vocation was not at one time or another under the spell of Hemingway or Faulkner or Fitzgerald, to mention only the most richly endowed members of the generation. The final question is: Aside from the sharply individuated gifts that each possessed, what did they share as writers that may at least partly explain their common genius and its continuing hold on us?

Cowley's speculations are worth our attention. He starts with such considerations—superficial at first glance until one perceives their appropriateness for that epoch—as the fact that all of the members of the group except for Fitzgerald were WASPs, that most were from the Midwest or the South, and that all sprang from the middle class. "They all had a Protestant ethic drilled into them, even if they were Catholics like Fitzgerald." Cowley also notes, in a passage which is an oblique commentary on the squalor we have produced in our schools, that every one of these men was the recipient of a sound, old-fashioned early education which placed a premium on the classics, English literature, syntax, and Latin grammar while ignoring social studies, civics, baton twirling, and other depravities.

Except for Dos Passos and Hemingway, whose friendship was destroyed because of the Spanish Civil War, they were generally either unconcerned or sophomoric in regard to politics. They had all had the experience of World War I, a "nice war," in Gertrude Stein's phrase, which had left most of the men physically intact, restless and filled with reservoirs of unexpected energy. It was a war, however, that was foul and ugly enough to unite them all against "big words and noble sentiments."

Ultimately more important, it seems to me, is Cowley's somewhat paradoxical but compelling notion that although each of these writers was an individualist, committed heart and mind to solitary vision, they were all bound together subconsciously by a shared morality which viewed the husbanding of one's talent as the highest possible goal. Thus, he argues, the garish myth has been deceptive. Many of them indeed had a hunger for self-destruction and were spendthrift livers, but when it came to their talent they were passionate conservationists. Measured in terms of their refusal to allow their splendid gifts to become swallowed up in the vortex of their frenzied, foolish, alcoholic, and often desperate lives, they were brave and moral men. In this sense, aside from the varied marvels of their best work, the writers of the Lost Generation provide us with a lesson in the art of self-realization.

"The good writers regarded themselves as an elite," Cowley writes. "They were an elite not by birth or money or education, not even by acclaim—though they would have it later—but rather by such inner qualities as energy, independence, rigor, an original way of combining words (a style, a 'voice') and utter commitment to a dream." Within the persuasive context of a book so free of idealization, so detached and balanced as *A Second Flowering*, such a statement seems enviable, exemplary, and true. Only two things matter: talent and language. "Their dream," Cowley concludes, "was . . . of being the lords of language."

As for Malcolm Cowley himself, he is seventy-five this year and rightly considers himself one of the last members of a glorious team whose exploits and defeats it was his privilege to help explain. "Now most of the team is gone," he writes, "and the survivors are left with the sense of having plodded with others to the tip of a long sandspit where they stand exposed, surrounded by water, waiting for the tide to come in." It should be of consolation to him that it is unthinkable that this beautiful, honest book will not be read as an indispensable companion piece to the works of Hemingway, Fitzgerald, Faulkner, Wolfe, and all the rest as long as they are read and have bearing upon men's common experience. *Ave atque vale!*

[*New York Times Book Review*, May 6, 1973.]

A Literary Forefather

He is my most beloved literary forefather, but it's not just my affection for *Adventures of Huckleberry Finn* that makes me feel close to Mark Twain. Our other affinities continually surprise me. Although a century, minus a decade, separates our birth dates, we had curiously similar upbringings. Mark Twain's border South and my Tidewater Virginia shared the burden of a sullen racism, even though the functional slavery of Hannibal, Missouri, had been in my case replaced by the bitter pseudoslavery of Jim Crow; both left imprints on a white boy's soul. Plainly it affected Mark Twain that the Clemens family had been slaveholders; I was haunted (and am still amazed) by the reality that my grandmother, an old lady still alive in the mid-1930s, had owned slaves as a little girl. Our early surroundings possessed a surface sweetness and innocence—under which lay a turmoil we were pleased to expose—and we both grew up in villages on the banks of great rivers that dominated our lives.

The muddy James was an essential presence in my boyhood ("It was a monstrous big river down there," says Huck of the Mississippi as he and Jim drift southward, "sometimes a mile and a half wide"; my James River was *five* miles wide), and the edgy relationship I had with black children was identical to that of Mark Twain. "All the negroes were friends of ours, and with those of our own age we were in effect comrades," he wrote in his autobiography. "We were comrades, and yet not comrades; color and condition interposed a subtle line which both parties were conscious of and which rendered complete fusion impossible." This near paralysis of affection (which has such a modern resonance) remained as true for me in my Tidewater village as it had been for Mark Twain in Hannibal, and worked on both of us its psychological mischief. In our later lives Mark Twain and I chose to dwell among Connecticut Yankees (during years interrupted by sojourns as Innocents Abroad), and it was there, bedeviled by our pasts, that we wrote books about slavery called *Huckleberry Finn* and *The Confessions of Nat Turner.* Both of these novels gained indisputable success and a multitude of readers but, because they dealt with America's most profound dilemma—its racial anguish—in ways that were idiosyncratic and upsetting, and because they contained many ambiguities, they invited the wrath of critics, black and white, in controversies that have persisted to this day.

As for *Huckleberry Finn,* it's quite likely that if Mark Twain had merely used "slave" instead of the word "nigger," which appears more than two hundred times during the course of the narrative, many of those who have recently attacked the book on the grounds of racism would have been at least partially appeased. But "nigger," our most powerful secular blasphemy—now that virtually all crude sexual expressions have become part of public speech, melded into the monotonous jawing of stage, screen, and cable TV—still has a scary force. Huck Finn's use of it, especially in these touchy years, has driven some people around the bend. Although a twelve-year-old Missourian would have had scant familiarity, in the 1840s, with the word "slave"—a term that was generally confined to governmental proclamations, religious discussions, and legal documents—Huck's innocent vernacular usage appears to be one of the reasons for the panic that recently impelled the Cathedral School of Washington, D.C., of all esteemed institutions, to remove *Huckleberry Finn* from its tenth-grade curriculum. Only the nature of the school surprises; over the past decades the book has been banished from library shelves innumerable times.

Even more incoherent is the activity of a black educator from Fairfax, Virginia, named John H. Wallace. With some success, Wallace has campaigned to protect youth from the bad word by insisting that *Huckleberry Finn* be taken away from school libraries, and has published what has to be an all-time curiosity in the annals of bowdlerization: a version of the text from which every use of the word "nigger" has been expunged. The crusade of Wallace, who has described his nemesis as "the most grotesque example of racist trash ever written," might be considered merely a spectacular eccentricity if it weren't a fairly menacing example of the animus that has always coalesced around the novel. Not that the book is beyond criticism. It has been charged that *Huckleberry Finn* reveals the mind of a writer with equivocal feelings about race, and signs to that effect may certainly be found. The wonder is that his upbringing and experience (including a brief stint in the Confederate army) should have left Mark Twain so little tainted with bigotry. Although most of its millions of readers, including many black people, have found no racism in the book (Ralph Ellison wrote admiringly of the author's grasp of the tormented complexity of slavery, his awareness of Jim's essential humanity), *Huckleberry Finn* has never really struggled up out of a continuous vortex of discord, and probably never will as long as its enchanting central figures, with their confused and incalculable feelings for each other, remain symbols of our own racial confusion.

As I reflect on the kinship I have always felt with Mark Twain, I am reminded that no American rivers are so bound up with the history of slavery as are the Mississippi and the James. As a boy I had learned that our own slavery began on the James, in 1619; I sometimes had vivid fantasies in which I would see, far out in the channel, that first small clumsy Dutch galleon beating its way upriver to Jamestown, with its cargo of miserable black people in chains. For me the river meant stifling bondage. For Mark Twain, writing after the Civil War, the Mississippi, and the uproarious, extravagant voyage he launched upon it, meant freedom—not merely freedom for Jim but a nation's freedom from the primal ache that had racked its soul ever since Jamestown. It's a measure of *Huckleberry Finn*'s greatness, but also perhaps of the insufficiency of the relief it has given us from pain, that it still receives such savage attacks. The pain continues. Let the attacks continue, too. They will only prove the durability of a work that has withstood the complaints of boors and puritans, and will surely weather the blows of this grim and dogmatic time.

[*New Yorker*, June 26–July 3, 1995. The text was abbreviated by *The New Yorker*; the full version published here is taken from the surviving manuscript at Duke University.]

Friends and
Contemporaries

My Generation

L et me try to define my generation—rather narrowly, but in a way similar to Fitzgerald's—as those of us who approached our majority during World War II, and whose attitudes were shaped by the spirit of that time and by our common initiation into the world by that momentous event. For a slightly earlier generation the common initiation was the Spanish Civil War; for us it somehow simultaneously ended and began when Harry Truman announced the destruction of Hiroshima. I wish I could say that in 1945—at the end of *our* war—I did anything so blissfully adventurous as to steal a locomotive as had Scott Fitzgerald. That distant war in Europe had had its own terrible ferocity but mainly for Europeans; as Fitzgerald says, it left America and Americans generally intact. By contrast our war, despite a nervous overlay of the usual frivolity (do you recall the *Rosie the Riveter* or *Slap the Jap* or the aching erotic schmaltz that suffused those "Back Home for Keeps" ads?), was brutally businesslike and anti-romantic, a hard-boiled matter of stamping out a lot of very real and nasty totalitarianism in order to get along with the business of the American Way of Life, whatever that is. Our generation was not only not intact, it had been in many places cut to pieces. The class just ahead of me in college was virtually wiped out. Beautiful fellows who had won basketball championships and Phi Beta Kappa keys died like ants in the Normandy invasion. Others only slightly older than I—like myself young Marine Corps platoon leaders, primest cannon fodder of the Pacific war—stormed ashore at Tarawa and Iwo Jima and met ugly and horrible deaths on the hot coral sands.

I was lucky and saw no battle, but I had the wits scared out of me more times than I could count, and so by the time the bomb dropped on Hiroshima, thus circumventing my future plans (I was on my way: "You can figure that four out of five of you will get your asses shot off," I can recall some colonel telling us, as he embroidered dreamily about the coming invasion of the Japanese mainland), an enormous sense of relief stole over my spirit, along with a kind of dull weariness that others of that period have recalled and which, to a certain offshoot of my generation, later came to be characterized as "beat." I disclaim any literary link with this splinter group but certainly the "beat" sensation was all too real, and though it may have sent Kerouac off on the road in search of kicks, to others of us it was a call to quiet pursuits: study and the square rewards of family and rather gloomy stocktaking. I think most of us were in a way subtly traumatized, which is why we didn't steal any locomotives or pull off any of the wild capers that so richly strew the chronicles of Fitzgerald's Jazz Age. We were traumatized not only by what we had been through and by the almost unimaginable presence of the bomb, but by the realization that the entire mess was not finished after all: there was now the Cold War to face, and its clammy presence oozed into our nights and days. When at last the Korean War arrived, some short five years later (it was this writer's duty to serve his country in the Marines in that mean conflict, too), the cosmos seemed so unhinged as to be nearly insupportable. Surely by that time—unlike Fitzgerald's coevals, "born to power and intense nationalism"—we were the most mistrustful of power and the least nationalistic of any generation that America has produced. And just as surely, whatever its defects may have been, it has been this generation's interminable experience with ruthless power and the loony fanaticism of the military mind that has by and large caused it to lend the most passionate support to the struggle to end war everywhere. We have that at least in our favor.

I think that the best of my generation, those in their late thirties or early forties, have reversed the customary rules of the game and have grown more radical as they have gotten older—a disconcerting but healthy sign. To be sure, there are many youngish old fogies around and even the most illustrious of these, William Buckley, is blessed by a puzzling, recondite, but undeniable charm, almost as if beneath that patrician exterior an egalitarian was signaling to get out. We seem to be gradually shaking loose of our trauma (which for some of us, by the way, also includes the remembered effect of the Depression) and one has only to flourish the picture of an embattled Norman Mailer on the steps of the Pentagon to put down the claim that political activism is the purview of the very young. Perhaps the act of participating in one horrendous war, or two, has allowed most of us to sympathize with young people and be bitterly troubled by much of the shit they have to put up with. Having been pushed around by bully boys and sub-cretins, by commissioned shoe clerks and *salauds* of every stripe and gauge, we tend toward more than a twinge of empathy at the sight of youth struggling with the managerial beast, military, secular, or scholastic.

In 1944, as a Marine recruit, I was shanghaied into the "clap shack," the venereal-disease ward of the Naval Hospital at Parris Island, South Carolina. There at the age of eighteen, only barely removed from virginhood, I was led to believe that blood tests revealed I had a probably fatal case of syphilis—in those pre-penicillin days as dread a disease as cancer—and was forced to languish, suicidal, for forty days and forty nights amid the charnel-house atmosphere of draining buboes, gonorrhea, prostate massages, daily short-arm inspections, locomotor ataxia, and the howls of poor sinners in the clutch of terminal paresis, until at last, with no more ceremony than if I were being turned out of veterinary clinic, I was told I could go back to boot camp: I would not die after all, *it was all a mistake*, those blood tests had turned up a false reaction to an old case of trench mouth. I could have wept with relief and hatred. Such experiences have given our generation, I believe, both the means and the spirit to bridge the generation gap.

Literary sweepstakes are a bore, especially when this is a matter of comparing generations, and the situation is not enhanced in this case by Fitzgerald's boast, with its implication that the men of his era produced achievements in prose writing that would cause those who followed after to feel like sacred epigones. The stature of Faulkner alone would have been enough to cow any young writer, all the more if he were Southern; as Flannery O'Connor remarked so wonderfully: "No one wants to get caught on the tracks when the Dixie Special comes through." Yet it has been a rich time for writing, I think, richer than may be imagined. Certainly, whether or not as a group we shall receive posterity's sweet kiss—whether our names will date as sadly as Cyril Hume and Edward Hope Coffey—no gathering ever comprised a clutch of talents so remarkably various: Mailer, Baldwin, Jones,

Capote, Salinger, the incomparably infuriating Gore Vidal, John Barth, Terry Southern, Heller (where's that second book, Joe?), Walker Percy, Peter Matthiessen—who would survive as the finest writer on nature since John Burroughs even if he never found due recognition for his badly under-estimated fiction—William Gaddis, Richard Yates, Evan Connell, George Mandel, Herbert Gold, Jack Kerouac, Vance Bourjaily, John Clellon Holmes, Calder Willingham, Alan Harrington, John Phillips, William Gass, and, honorifically, George Ames Plimpton.

To this roll must be added, incidentally, the name of Richard Howard, the city of Cleveland's gift to France and the most elegant translator from the French tongue writing in English.°

Catalogs like the foregoing are at best an amusement, surely a trifle silly, so I won't make another quite as extensive, but a list of the poets of this generation would sparkle brightly, from Simpson to Merwin, James Dickey to Anthony Hecht, Snodgrass to Allen Ginsberg.† There are, obviously, quite a few others of equivalent stature. As John Hollander, himself a fine poet, has written about their best poems: "[They] stand as some sort of tes-tament to the continuing spiritual revolution to which poetry in English has been committed for more than a century-and-a-half, and to the ancillary struggle to redeem poetry itself, as the product of imaginative creation, from the sickness with which Literature as a realm is too often infected."[1]

So all in all a pretty good show, I would say, for a crowd that started out with the blind staggers—with the disease of McCarthy and the drug of Eisenhower—one that some ineffably fatuous critic long ago dismissed with the tag, "the Silent Generation." And let us brood for a moment on our pre-decessors. Despite the buoyancy in which Fitzgerald commences his reflec-tions on his own brothers in art, there is something dispirited, tired, elegiac about that little memoir. There is an odor of the grave about it. Faced with the sure prospect of a cataclysmic war and—who knows?—a premonition of his own imminent death, perhaps this fading tone, this pervasive mood of farewell was inevitable. Wolfe, Hemingway, Dos Passos, Faulkner, Wilder, all his peers—Fitzgerald had truly been born into noble company. But the

° Howard (b. 1929), American poet, critic, and translator of Baudelaire, Barthes, Fou-cault, Gide, Robbe-Grillet, and other French authors.—J.W.

† Chronologically, Richard Wilbur should be included here, but he started publishing very young, and might be considered an influence on, rather than a member of, this generation.—W.S. (1968)

best, the greatest work of all these men was long behind them, including Faulkner, who was the only one of them capable of a sustained level of quality until the very end. It is perhaps this knowledge, an instinctive sense of decline, that causes a mood of sadness to overlay this essay of Fitzgerald, who knew no better than the rest of us why whole groups of talents will burst into thrilling efflorescence, and then as mysteriously fade away. Writing now at roughly the same age as Fitzgerald, I can say that I feel no such a falling off, no similar sense of loss about my own generation. Revolution rends the air, the world around us shivers with the brave racket of men seeking their destiny, with the invigorating noise of history in collision with itself. This generation, once so laggardly, now confronts a scene astir with great events, such a wild dynamo of dementedly marvelous transactions that merely to be able to live through them should be cause for jubilation. *Mes amis, aux barricades!* I would not be astonished if our truly most precious flowering lay in the time to come. As for myself—reflecting on the way in which we all started out—I have never felt so young.

[*Esquire*, October 1968. Published together with essays by F. Scott Fitzgerald and Frank Conroy on their respective literary generations.]

Robert Penn Warren

I have been lucky to have known Red Warren well for quite a few years and to have been privy to certain personal matters known only between good friends. I am therefore aware of an interesting fact about Red's early life that is not generally understood by less favored mortals. This is that as a boy in his teens Red's simple but very red-blooded American ambition was to become an officer in the United States Navy. This, ladies and gentlemen, is the truth, not an idle fiction. Indeed, it was *more* than an ambition; it was a goal very close of attainment, for Red had obtained his appointment and was all but packed up and ready to leave the bluegrass of Kentucky for Annapolis when he suffered an injury to his eye which made it impossible for him ever to become a midshipman. There is irony in this, for it always has seemed to me that Red at least *looks* like a sailor. If you will glance at him now, you will see it: that seamed and craggy face which has gazed, like Melville's, into the briny abyss, that weather-wise expression and salty presence which have made him physically the very model of a sea dog; and as a consequence I have often become thoroughly bemused when speculating on Red's career if he *had* gone off to the Naval Academy. I would like to consider this prospect for a moment.

First, let no one underestimate the military mind; at the highest levels of command great brilliance is required, and for this reason Red would have been what is known as a "rising star" from the very beginning. Thus I visualize the scenario—if I may use that awful word—like this. Number one in his class at Annapolis, Red becomes the first naval Rhodes scholar at Oxford, where his record is also spectacular. He takes his degree in Oriental history, writing a thesis which is a revisionist examination of Genghis Khan, largely laudatory in tone. Later in my fantasy I see Red at the end of World War II, much decorated, at the age of forty the youngest captain in the seagoing navy, attending the Naval War College at Newport, writing learned dissertations on the nuclear capabilities of the Soviet fleet. His recommendation is: Let's press the button, *very softly,* before the Russians do. During the Korean War, a rear admiral now, he wins his fourth Navy Cross, is made commander in chief of the Pacific fleet, is on the cover of *Time* magazine, has a tempestuous though necessarily discreet affair with Ava Gardner. Through the dull and arid years between Korea and Vietnam, Red Warren plays golf with Eisenhower, rereads Thucydides and Clausewitz, hobnobs with Henry Luce, Barry Goldwater, and Mendel Rivers, and is appointed Chief of Naval Operations under Lyndon Johnson.

I don't know why my fantasy brightens and becomes happy at this point. Maybe it's because I see Red Warren miraculously turn a major corner in his life, undergoing—as it were—a sea change. He becomes a *dove*! After all, a great Marine general, ex-Commandant David Shoup, did this: why not Red in my fantasy? Now as he reverses himself, the same grand historical imagination which in his alter ego produced *All the King's Men, World Enough and Time,* and *Brother to Dragons* is suddenly seized with the folly and tragedy of our involvement in Southeast Asia, so that on one dark night in 1966 there is a confrontation, many hours long, between the admiral from Kentucky—now chairman of the Joint Chiefs of Staff—and the Texas president, two Southerners eyeball to eyeball; and in this passionate colloquy it is the *Kentuckian* who finally gains the upper hand with his forceful, humanitarian argument—founded upon the ineluctable lessons of history of which he is master—that this war can only lead to futility, disaster, and national degradation. I even see the droplets of sweat on Lyndon Johnson's forehead as, after a grave long pause, he gives in, saying, "God damn yore soft-hearted hide, Admiral Warren, you've convinced me!" And immediately I see him getting on the telephone to McNamara: "Bob, git those advisers out of Vietnam! We're going to nip this here dirty little war in the bud!"

But this kind of wish-fulfillment becomes almost unendurable, and so in my mind's eye I bring Red's naval career to a merciful close, seeing him as grim and cruel reason dictates he most likely *would* be today—not basking in well-deserved homage at the Lotos Club but retired to the Pacific seaside at Coronado, cultivating prize asparagus or roses, writing letters to the *San Diego Tribune* about stray dogs, queers, and the Commie menace, and sending monthly donations to Rabbi Korff.

So by that fateful accident years ago America lost a master mariner but gained a major novelist and poet, a superb essayist, a literary critic of great breadth and subtle discrimination, a teacher of eloquence, a sly and hilarious storyteller, and altogether one of the best human beings to break bread with, or join with in *spirituous* companionship, or just simply *be around* in this desperate or any other time. . . .

I would like to conclude with a couple of brief reminiscences having to do with Red Warren which in each case are oddly connected with—of all things for two good ole Southern boys—winter snow. The first of these events occurred a long time ago in New York City during the famous blizzard of late December 1947 (which many of you here doubtless still remember), when I—a young and aspiring and penniless writer up from the Virginia Tidewater living in a basement on upper Lexington Avenue—first read *All the King's Men*. I think it is absolute and unimpeachable testimony to a book's impact on us that we are able to associate it so keenly with the time and the surroundings and the circumstances in which we read it. Only a very great work can produce this memory; it is like love, or recollections of momentous loving. There is what psychologists call a *gestalt,* an unforgettability of interwoven emotions with which the work will ever in recollection be connected with the environment. Somehow the excitement of reading *All the King's Men* is always linked in my mind with the howling blizzard outside and the snow piling up in a solid white impacted mass outside my basement window. The book itself was a revelation and gave me a shock to brain and spine like a freshet of icy water. I had of course read many novels before, including many of the greatest, but this powerful and complex story embedded in prose of such fire and masterful imagery—this, I thought with growing wonder, this was what a novel was all about, this was *it*, the bright book of life, what writing was supposed to be. When finally the blizzard stopped and the snow lay heaped on the city streets, silent as death, I finished *All the King's Men* as in a trance, knowing once and for all that I, too, however falteringly and incompletely, must try to work such magic. I began my first novel before that snow had melted; it is a book called *Lie Down in*

Darkness, and in tone and style, as any fool can see, it is profoundly indebted to the work which so ravished my heart and mind during that long snowfall.

Many years and many snowfalls later I was walking with Red Warren one late afternoon on, of all absurd things, *snowshoes* through the white silence of a forest in Vermont—a rather clumsily comical trek which, had you told the young man on Lexington Avenue he would be making it in the future, would have caused him both awe and incredulity. Red and I were by this time fast and firm friends, bonded in a friendship long past the need of forced conversation, and as we puffed along in Indian file across the mountainous snowdrifts, each of us plunged in his own private meditation, it creepily occurred to me that we were far away from home, far away from the road, still miles away from anything or anybody—and that, worst of all, it was almost night. I had a moment of terrible panic as I thought that Red and I, having unwittingly strayed in our outlandish footgear off the beaten track, would find ourselves engulfed by darkness in this freezing wilderness, utterly lost, two nonsmokers with not a match between us, or a knife to cut shelter—only our foolhardy, vulnerable selves, floundering in the Yankee snows. After the initial panic slid away and I had succumbed to a stoic reckoning, a resignation in face of the inevitable, it occurred to me that if I had to die there was nobody on earth, aside from perhaps Raquel Welch, that I'd rather freeze to death with than Robert Penn Warren: this noble gentleman from Guthrie, Kentucky, whose humane good sense and lyric passion had so enriched us all through these many novels and poems and essays and plays, and whose celebration of the mystery and beauty and, yes, even the inexplicable anguish of life had been one of those priceless bulwarks against death in a time of too much dying. Just then I heard Red casually say, "Well, here's the road." And I was a little ashamed of my panic, but not of those thoughts, which also had included my heartfelt thanks to God that Red Warren never became an admiral.

[Speech delivered at the Lotos Club, New York City, April 1975.]

Lillian's Bosom

I'm Bill Styron, an old friend of Lillian's, like many of us here. She once told me that this would be the day that I yearned for more than anything in my life—speaking words over her remains—and she cackled in glee. "Ha, ha," she said, and I cackled back. She said, "If you don't say utterly admiring and beautiful things about me, I'm going to cut you out of my will." I said there was no possible way that I could refrain from saying a few critical things, and she said, "Well, you're cut out already."

That was the way it went with us. I think we had more fights per man-and-woman contact than probably anyone alive. We were fighting all the time, and we loved each other a great deal for sure, because the vibrations were there. But our fights were never really, oddly enough, over abstract things like politics or philosophy or social dilemmas; they were always over such things such as whether a Smithfield ham should be served hot or cold, or whether I had put too much salt in the black-eyed peas.

This anger that spilled out from the lady, almost a reservoir of anger, was really not directed at me or her other friends or even the black-eyed peas, but was directed at all the hateful things that she saw as menaces to the world. When she hated me and the ham, she was hating a pig like Roy Cohn. I think this is what motivated her; when one understood that the measure of her anger was really not personal but cosmic, then one was able to deal with her.

I was privileged, I think the word is, to take Lillian out—to be the last person to take her out to dinner. I did so a few days ago here in Chilmark at La Grange. It was quite an ordeal. We sat down (I had to get her into a chair), just the two of us, and she groped for the various things she had to grope for because, as you know, she was blind and quite radically crippled. Then we had conversation. We carved up a few mutually detested writers and one or two mediocre politicians and an elderly deceased novelist whom she specifically detested, and we got into this sort of thing; and we then started talking about her age.

I didn't tell her the snoop from *The New York Times* had called me up asking if I knew her age. I said the only biographical data I had at hand was that she was probably seventy-nine. And she said, "I don't know whether the twentieth of June was my seventy-fourth or my seventy-third." She had been doing this all of her life, not as a vanity—though that was fine too—but as a demonstration of the way that she was hanging on to life.

I realized as I was sitting there that she was painfully uncomfortable. She said that she was cursed by God with having from birth a skinny ass. So I had to go and put things under her constantly, which was fine. She said this bolstered her skepticism about the existence of God. So I told her something that she had always responded to: that the curse was made up for with an ample and seductive bosom. She smiled at that. Through all of this, she was gasping for breath and was suffering. It hit me that this woman was physically in agony. There was something enormously wrenching about being seated alone with this fragment of a human being, suffering so much, gasping for breath. Yet I had a glimpse of her almost as if she was a young girl again, in New Orleans with a beau and having a wonderful time.

As these memories came flooding back, I remember that gorgeous cackle of laughter which always erupted at moments when we were together, with other people or alone. It was usually a cackle of laughter which followed some harpooning of a fraud or a ninth-rater. It was filled with hatred, but hatred and anger which finally evolved into what I think she, like all of us, was searching for—some sort of transcendental idea, which is love. As we went out, I was in awe of this woman. I have no final reflection except that perhaps she was in the end a lover, a mother, a sister, and a friend—and in a strange way a lover of us all.

[Tribute spoken at a memorial service for Lillian Hellman, July 3, 1984, in the town of Chilmark on Martha's Vineyard.]

Irwin Shaw

Back in the 1940s, if you were an aspiring young writer—or even if you merely cared for literature—you passionately read short stories. You read novels and poetry, too, but the short story was the proving ground for your own talent, and you experienced this most demanding of literary forms in a very personal way. You read the stories of the masters with that mixture of critical alertness and abandoned devotion that is the mark of the hopeful apprentice. Of the many masters of that form whose work was part of my self-imposed curriculum, there was no one who stirred me to more open and defenseless admiration than Irwin Shaw. The passage of time, however, has eroded Shaw's reputation. His stories, appearing regularly in *The New Yorker*, were models of the form, possessing all the elements I yearned to emulate: irony, a beautifully attuned ear for the demotic speech of mid-century America, humor, controlled rage at the world's injustices, and a casually elegant lyricism which pervaded each tale and stamped it as the work of Irwin Shaw and no one else. Hemingway had this magnetic appeal for a somewhat earlier generation of readers, and J. D. Salinger would exert the same magic a bit later. One of the higher tributes one can pay to a writer is when, as in certain remembered glimpses of a passionate love affair, the reader can recall the place and time of the act of reading. I was in the Duke University library reading room when I read, in a collection of Shaw stories, that seductive gem of a tale, "The Girls in Their Summer

Dresses," and felt the little chill that attends the experience of almost perfectly realized inspiration.

A few months later I was in Marine boot camp when a *New Yorker*
somehow came my way and I read "Walking Wounded." It was a story of
military life and sexual frustration, both of which weighed on me heavily at
the time, and I responded vibrantly to the author's mordant depiction of the
erotic tensions in Cairo (where Shaw had been stationed), and the toplofty
behavior of the American women there, all of which reinforced my belief
that no one spoke more eloquently about the outrages suffered by men at
war than Irwin Shaw. During the postwar years, when I returned to Duke to
complete my studies, I had read nearly everything in prose that Shaw had
written—which is to say several collections of his stories and the novel *The
Young Lions*. There were other stories that I thought just as marvelous as
those I'd read earlier—"Sailor Off the Bremen," "Act of Faith," and that
incomparably poignant study—so deep in the American grain—of failed
ambition, "The Eighty-Yard Run." I considered myself something of an expert on Shaw, so much so, in fact, that when I briefly harbored the notion of
becoming a graduate student in English I thought it might be a fine idea to
write a thesis on his work. I was inordinately sensitive to Shaw's writing and
felt very protective toward him, becoming mildly disappointed when his
work was not quite up to snuff but never failing to recognize that what he
wrote—even slightly second-class Shaw—was written by an outstanding artist. Shaw's war novel, *The Young Lions,* was one of those mild disappointments which might have been less so had it not emerged in the shadow of
The Naked and the Dead, a work which had overwhelmed me. So sweeping
and passionate had Mailer's novel seemed to me that *The Young Lions* suffered somewhat by comparison. I was bothered by an element of contriv-
ance, especially in the character of Noah Ackerman, whose victimization in
the Army at the hands of anti-Semites—echoing a theme which had worked
well in Shaw's stories—bore the ponderous stamp of Message. Still, I
thought the book a tremendous achievement, and it helped consolidate the
hero worship I had for Irwin Shaw.

A year or so after this, having come to New York to give a try at chipping
out a niche in the pantheon where Shaw was solidly lodged, I was sitting one
night with some literary pals in a restaurant we all went to in those days.
This was the Blue Mill Tavern on Commerce Street, not far from the seven-
dollar-a-week cell I inhabited on West Eleventh Street. The Blue Mill was

smoky, crowded, and cheap, with plain but admirable cuisine. The place specialized in steaks, and $1.25 bought a portion of sirloin of the same high quality that is sold today at the Palm or Christ Cella for twenty times the price. That night my heart nearly stopped when I saw through the murk a big burly man with powerful shoulders edging his way toward a table where not one but two girls waited, fresh-faced and with adoring eyes. I was certain this was Irwin Shaw. I had been seeing Irwin from time to time on the streets of the city ever since I had arrived. Almost any heavyset, athletic young man with dark hair and radiantly good-looking Jewish features was someone I suspected of being Shaw. That night my suspicion grew into conviction simply because—I later realized—I *wanted* the person to be Shaw, and I said as much to my companions. In doing so, of course, I was made to appear foolish, for the big guy was not my idol at all, I could soon tell, and I retracted my claim with flustered embarrassment. I could not have known then that Shaw was already a high-roller and bon vivant of great magnitude and would have found the Blue Mill a most unlikely place to dine, not because he lacked the common touch but because it was far off the beaten track between places like "21" and Le Pavillon, which had become his accustomed haunts.

Several more years passed. I had written my first novel, which for a first novel had been quite successful, and had settled upon Paris as a temporary home before proceeding on my European *Wanderjahre*. It was in that war-tired but resurgent and beautiful city, where American money and American energy were helping give birth to literary projects like *The Paris Review*—with which I had become marginally associated—that I finally met Irwin Shaw. He was climbing out of, appropriately, an American car—a gleaming green Ford convertible. Paris was still swarming largely with bicycles and motorbikes and pre-war Citroëns, and Irwin's Ford looked enormous and impressive. So too was Irwin—a rugged hulk of a man in the prime of his late youth, thirty-eight or thereabouts, with one of the most immediately appealing and warm-hearted presences I had ever known or imagined. Consider what the young first novelist's natural reaction would be if, upon meeting the writer of one's fantasies, he is told after no more than a few minutes—as Irwin told me: "You really wrote one hell of a book; man, you really took off!" (His exact words, graven upon the memory.) The young first novelist coughed, or grunted, or murmured something incoherent; I was quite choked up, stupefied by the praise, the spontaneous generosity. It was the hallmark, I would come to understand, of Shaw's personality—a genuine indwelling sweetness that made it virtually impossible to dislike the man who so steadfastly possessed such a quality, even when after becoming his friend, as I did, the first sad and troublesome doubts about his writing grew into feelings I never thought I could entertain: more than slight disappointment, and then often active dislike. *Dislike!* In those days that word attached to any of the Shaw canon would have been inconceivable.

If we are honest with ourselves we will all admit to having been happily seduced, at least once in our lives, and probably twice, by the lurid glamour of Hollywood, and it was through Irwin that my seduction began. Paris was thronged by people from the movie business and Irwin knew them all—bigtime directors like John Huston and moguls like Sam Goldwyn, stars such as Gene Kelly and Ingrid Bergman and Evelyn Keyes, and all sorts of other peripheral figures of legendary glitter: Robert Capa the daredevil photographer, the wonderfully droll screenwriter Harry Kurnitz, gorgeous French models like Bettina. It was through Irwin that I met a lifelong friend, Art Buchwald. To a boy from the Virginia Tidewater it was pig heaven, a tableau from *Life* magazine come alive, and I ate it up.

I first understood wine to be something other than dago red, a nearspiritual experience, when at a party Irwin invited me to—given by Darryl Zanuck in an incredibly chic restaurant called Chez Joseph, all brocade and damask and fawning waiters—I drank a pre-war Château Margaux, sharing in the miracle with a beautiful French starlet whose hot *venez-ici* eyes had gazed down at me from dozens of Paris billboards. What impressed me the most about Irwin's connection with this heady scene was his ease with it, his blasé attitude, a sense that even though he was involved in this world, which had begun to remunerate him so well for the scripts he was writing, he could really take it or leave it. It seemed not to be a milieu whose celebrated corruptions were for him a temptation, and I admired him even more than ever for his grand air of detachment, of being slightly above it all. One night, I witnessed this sang-froid at a screening on the Champs-Élysées of an awful movie called *Hans Christian Andersen*, unredeemable despite its wonderful star, Danny Kaye. Old Sam Goldwyn, the producer of the film and our host (and who had proclaimed it his greatest effort), sat in the darkness whispering his delight while in the seat behind him, and next to me, Irwin fell sound asleep. Not only that, he began to snore, which made me queasy lest it disturb the old man's rapture. Yet in the end it affirmed more than ever Shaw's disdain for Hollywood. Like Faulkner he appeared to me a man who could feed at that banquet but duck out from it at will, feeling no need to join the party.

The next year, when I was in Rome, Irwin was there also, tooling around with his lively wife, Marian, in that huge barge of a green Ford. Once more I felt the full impact of his spacious generosity. I was about to get married and while I had arranged for the ceremony to be held in Michelangelo's splendid Campidoglio, I had made no plans for the postnuptial festivities. Irwin immediately took care of all this, arranging a huge party at his apartment in Parioli, constantly fussing over my bride and me with loving attention and making hilariously bawdy toasts as the blowout drew to a close. That spring and early summer Rose and I saw a lot of the Shaws, taking long drives to places like Ostia and Anzio, where we often dined—dangerously, as we would later learn—on raw oysters and mussels, and drank cold Frascati wine. We talked about travel in Europe, sports, politics, books. Irwin had read prodigiously, and continued his reading; I was always impressed by the breadth of his literary tastes—his love for the Romantic poets and the Victorian novelists, the European modernists—Mann and Proust, Camus and Koestler and Joyce. He was almost unqualifiedly magnanimous about those of his contemporaries whom he respected, the only real exception being Hemingway, for whom he bore a long-standing grudge dating back to wartime London. This antagonism had to do with the woman they had shared, Mary Welsh, whom Hemingway later married, but they would have loathed each other anyway, like rival buck deer. The machismo for which Hemingway was so famous was by no means absent from Shaw; one writer I knew who played tennis with Irwin described him as a "hyper-competitive pain in the ass." But I admired Shaw's exemplary kindheartedness concerning his literary colleagues, especially the promising younger ones, to whom he could be actually tender. He had certainly been that to me; in many ways the writer whom I had admired from such an impossible distance had not only become my literary older brother but for a while at least—such was my emotional commitment—a surrogate brother for the one I never had.

❊   ❊   ❊

When he died in 1984 at the age of seventy-one near his home of exile for many years—Klosters, Switzerland—Shaw was not included on most lists of illustrious American writers. Despite a large and continuous output of novels and stories, which kept him plugging valiantly away right through the painful illnesses of his last days, his work had long before been dismissed as, at best, journeyman entertainment of slightly sub-middlebrow blandness, slick and proficient, but devoid of any of the merits that would elevate his words to the realm of literature. He was regularly roasted by the critics; probably no serious writer of his time received so many go-arounds of hearty walloping as Irwin Shaw. He had been snubbed by the awarders of prizes, and for him the doors of the prestigious literary academies and societies had been firmly shut. It was said that he had exchanged the rich heritage of his humble Jewish origins in Brooklyn and a once proudly eloquent social consciousness for a world of glitzy glamour.

Probably the worst insults he received were from critics who made unflattering, and unfair, comparisons to writers who were unblushing hacks. Shaw wrote with integrity, but the sad truth about his later career is that much of the criticism leveled against him was well founded: those who were devoted to Shaw's early writing, and those devoted to the boisterously generous and captivating man, had occasion to rue the decline of his work after its grand beginnings. Lumping him in with the potboiler kings was, however, a canard. None of them were ever capable of a novel with the power and magnitude of *The Young Lions*. Nor did any of them possess a shred of the passion and musical grace that informed Shaw's early stories, which belong in the durable canon of American short fiction, along with the tales of Welty, Cheever, and Salinger.

In his fine study of Shaw's life, *Irwin Shaw: A Biography*, Michael Shnayerson has set down a vivid account of the writer's often turbulent career, taking a hard-nosed view of the easy seductions that led him into too many commercial back alleys, yet never failing to honor Shaw's immense personal charm and his substantial literary achievement. Few biographies have so well portrayed a writer torn between heeding the siren song of art and the more tempting moans of the various bitch goddesses. The tension produced by this dichotomy in Irwin Shaw helps give Shnayerson's book great dramatic impact.

In one of his letters, Joseph Conrad wrote of the frustration and hardship of writing and the chanciness of a writer's fate, observing that even the most ambitious and hopeful artist must live with the knowledge that the permanence of his work is a matter of doubt. Shaw's later work somehow reflects a lack of hardship; it suffers from an absence of real pain. It is too bad that this work appears meretricious, and that the resurgent fame which fell upon him toward the last was the result of a television miniseries based on one of his less compelling books. One must respect, however, the courage that held him to his writer's calling until he could write no more; this would inspire one's admiration even if he had not given us those stories that sprang, elegant and tender, from the splendid dawn of his career and which seemed destined, as surely as do those of any writer of his time, for the permanence they deserve. These too are traces of one's self that are worth leaving behind.

[*Vanity Fair,* August 1989. See the Editor's Note for information about the blended text published here.]

Jimmy in the House

James Baldwin was the grandson of a slave. I was the grandson of a slave owner. We were virtually the same age and both bemused by our close link to slavery, since most Americans of our vintage—if connected at all to the Old South—have had to trace that connection back several generations. But Jimmy had vivid images of slave times, passed down from his grandfather to his father, a Harlem preacher of fanatical bent who left a terrifying imprint on his son's life. Jimmy once told me that he often thought the degradation of his grandfather's life was the animating force behind his father's apocalyptic, often incoherent rage.

By contrast my impression of slavery was quaint and rather benign; in the late 1930s, at the bedside of my grandmother, who was then close to ninety, I heard tales of the two little slave girls she had owned. Not much older than the girls themselves at the outset of the Civil War, she knitted stockings for them, tried to take care of them through the privations of the conflict, and, at the war's end, was as wrenched with sorrow as they were by the enforced leave-taking. When I told this classic story to Jimmy he didn't flinch. We both were writing about the tangled relations of blacks and whites in America, and because he was wise Jimmy understood the necessity of dealing with the preposterous paradoxes that had dwelled at the heart of the racial tragedy—the unrequited loves as well as the murderous furies. The dichotomy amounted to an obsession in much of his work; it was certainly a part of my own, and I think our common preoccupation helped make us good friends.

Jimmy moved into my studio in Connecticut in the late fall of 1960 and stayed there more or less continuously until the beginning of the following summer. A mutual friend had asked my wife and me to give Jimmy a place to stay, and since he was having financial problems it seemed a splendid idea. Baldwin was not very well known then—except perhaps in literary circles, where his first novel, *Go Tell It on the Mountain,* was gradually gaining momentum—and he divided his time between writing in the cottage and trips out to the nearby lecture circuit, where he made some money for himself and where, with his ferocious oratory, he began to scare his predominately well-to-do, well-meaning audiences out of their pants.

Without being in the slightest comforted as a Southerner, or let off the hook, I understood through him that black people regarded *all* Americans as irredeemably racist, the most sinful of them being not the Georgia redneck (who was in part the victim of his heritage) but any citizen whatever whose de jure equality was a façade for de facto enmity and injustice.

Jimmy was writing his novel *Another Country* and making notes for the essay *The Fire Next Time.* I was consolidating material, gathered over more than a decade, for a novel I was planning to write on the slave revolutionary Nat Turner. It was a frightfully cold winter, a good time for the Southern writer, who had never known a black man on intimate terms, and the Harlem-born writer, who had known few Southerners (black or white), to learn something about each other. I was by far the greater beneficiary. Struggling still to loosen myself from the prejudices and suspicions that a Southern upbringing engenders, I still possessed a residual skepticism: could a Negro *really* own a mind as subtle, as richly informed, as broadly inquiring and embracing as that of a white man?

My God, what appalling arrogance and vanity! Night after night Jimmy and I talked, drinking whiskey through the hours until the chill dawn, and I understood that I was in the company of as marvelous an intelligence as I was ever likely to encounter. His voice, lilting and silky, became husky as he chain-smoked Marlboros. He was spellbinding, and he told me more about the frustrations and anguish of being a black man in America than I had known until then, or perhaps wanted to know. He told me exactly what it was like to be denied service, to be spat at, to be called "nigger" and "boy."

What he explained gained immediacy because it was all so new to me.

This chronicle of an urban life, his own life, was unself-pityingly but with quiet rage spun out to me like a secret divulged, as if he were disgorging in private all the pent-up fury and gorgeous passion that a few years later, in *The Fire Next Time*, would shake the conscience of the nation as few literary documents have ever done. We may have had occasional disputes, but they were usually culinary rather than literary; a common conviction dominated our attitude toward the writing of fiction, and this was that in the creation of novels and stories the writer should be free to demolish the barrier of color, to cross the forbidden line and write from the point of view of someone with a different skin. Jimmy had made this leap already, and he had done it with considerable success. I was reluctant to try to enter the mind of a slave in my book on Nat Turner, but I felt the necessity and I told Jimmy this. I am certain that it was his encouragement—so strong that it was as if he were daring me not to—that caused me finally to impersonate a black man.

Sometimes friends would join us. The conversation would turn more abstract and political. I am surprised when I recall how certain of these people—well-intentioned, tolerant, "liberal," all the postures Jimmy so intuitively mistrusted—would listen patiently while Jimmy spoke, visibly fretting then growing indignant at some pronouncement of his, some scathing aperçu they considered too ludicrous for words, too extreme, and launch a polite counterattack. "You can't mean anything like that!" I can hear the words now. "You mean—*burn* . . ." And in the troubled silence, Jimmy's face would become a mask of imperturbable certitude. "Baby," he would say softly and glare back with vast glowering eyes, "yes, baby. I mean *burn. We will burn your cities down.*"

Lest I give the impression that that winter was all grim, let me say that this was not so. Jimmy was a social animal of nearly manic gusto and there were some loud and festive times. When summer came and he departed for good, heading for his apotheosis—the flamboyant celebrity that the 1960s brought him—he left a silence that to this day somehow resonates through the house.

In 1967, when *The Confessions of Nat Turner* was published, I began to learn with great discomfort the consequences of my audacity in acquiring the persona of a black man. With a few distinguished exceptions (the historian John Hope Franklin for one), black intellectuals and writers expressed their outrage at both the historical imposture I had created and my presumption. But Jimmy Baldwin remained steadfast to those convictions we had expressed to each other during our nighttime sessions six years before. In the turmoil of such a controversy I am sure that it was impossible for him not to have experienced conflicting loyalties, but when one day I read a public statement he made about the book—"He has begun the common history—ours"—I felt great personal support but, more importantly, the re-affirmation of some essential integrity. After those days in Connecticut I never saw him as often as I would have liked, but our paths crossed many times and we always fell on each other with an uncomplicated sense of joy-ous reunion.

Much has been written about Baldwin's effect on the consciousness of the world. Let me speak for myself. Even if I had not valued much of his work—which was flawed, like all writing, but which at its best had a bur-nished eloquence and devastating impact—I would have deemed his friend-ship inestimable. At his peak he had the beautiful fervor of Camus or Kafka. Like them he revealed to me the core of his soul's savage distress and thus helped me shape and define my own work and its moral contours. This would be the most appropriate gift imaginable to the grandson of a slave owner from a slave's grandson.

[*New York Times Book Review,* December 20, 1987.]

Celebrating Capote

Truman and I were approximately the same age, although when I got to know him he always insisted that I was six weeks older. This was not accurate—it turned out that *I* was several *months* younger than he was—but it doesn't matter. I make this point only to underline the appalling chagrin I felt, in my tenderest years as an aspiring, unpublished writer, when I read some of Truman's earliest work. The first story of his that I read was, I believe, published in *Mademoiselle*. After I finished it, I remember feeling stupefied by the talent in those pages. I thought myself a pretty good hand with words for a young fellow, but here was a writer whose gifts took my breath away. Here was an artist of my age who could make words dance and sing, change color mysteriously, perform feats of magic, provoke laughter, send a chill up the back, touch the heart—a full-fledged master of the language before he was old enough to vote.

I had read many splendid writers by that time, but in Truman I discovered a brand-new and unique presence, a storyteller whose distinctive selfhood was embedded in every sentence on the page. I was of course nearly sick with envy, and like all envious artists I turned to the critics for some corroboration of that mean little voice telling me that he wasn't all that good. *Ornamental* and *mannered* were the words I was looking for, and naturally I found them, for there are always critics driven wild by the manifestation of talent in its pure, energetic exuberance. But basically I knew better, as did the more discerning critics, who must have seen—as I saw, in my secret reckoning—that such gemlike tales as "Miriam" and "The Headless Hawk" had to rank among the best stories written in English. If they were ornamental or mannered, they corresponded to those adjectives in the same way that the finest tales of Henry James or Hawthorne or Edgar Allan Poe do, creating the same troubling resonance.

Needless to say, it is only the most gifted stylists who inspire imitation, and I confess to having imitated Truman in those days of my infancy as a writer. There is a wonderful story of his called "Shut a Final Door," which details the neurotic anguish of a young man living near Gramercy Park, that still captures the atmosphere of Manhattan during a summer heat wave better than almost any work I know. Not too long ago, I unearthed from among some old papers of mine a short story I wrote during that period, and it seems to be written in a manner almost plagiaristically emulative of Truman's story, containing nearly everything in "Shut a Final Door," including the heat wave and the neurotic young man—everything, that is, except Truman's remarkable sensibility and vision. When his first novel, *Other Voices, Other Rooms,* appeared and I read it, flabbergasted anew by this wizard's fresh display of his narrative powers, his faultless ear—the luxuriant but supple prose, everywhere under control—my discomfort was monumental. If you will forgive the somewhat topical reference, let me say that, although my admiration was nearly unbounded, the sense I felt of being inadequate would have made the torment of Antonio Salieri appear to be dull and resigned equanimity.

A few years later, my own first novel, *Lie Down in Darkness,* was published. Among the early reviews I read was one by Lewis Gannett in the *Herald Tribune*—a mildly favorable appreciation that noted my indebtedness to the following: William Faulkner, F. Scott Fitzgerald, and Truman Capote. I was a little crestfallen. I thought I had become my own man, you see, but Truman's voice was a hard one to banish entirely.

Shortly after this, I met Truman for the first time, during a Roman soirée. I was left with three separate, distinct memories of the evening: he was accompanied by a mistrustful-looking black mynah bird, whom he called Lola and who perched gabbling on his shoulder; he told me that I should definitely marry the young lady I was with, which, as a matter of fact, I did; and he informed me with perfect aplomb that he had been written up in all twelve departments of *Time* magazine, with the exception of "Sport" and

"Medicine." We became friends after that. Although we were not close, I always looked forward with pleasure to seeing him, and I think the feeling was reciprocal. I somehow managed to avoid those sharp fangs he sank into some of his fellow writers, and I took it as a professional compliment of a very high order when, on several occasions, something I had written that he liked elicited a warm letter of praise. Generally speaking, writers are somewhat less considerate of each other than that.

A certain amount of Truman's work might have been a little fey, some of it insubstantial, but the bulk of the journalism he wrote during the following decades was, at its best, of masterly distinction. His innovative achievement, *In Cold Blood*, not only was a landmark in terms of its concept but possesses both spaciousness and profundity—a rare mingling—and the terrible tale it tells could only be told by a writer who had dared to go in deep and brush flesh with the demons that torment the American soul. Shrewd, fiercely unsentimental, yet filled with a mighty compassion, it brought out all that was the best in Truman's talent: the grave, restrained lyricism, the uncanny insights into character, and that quality which has never been perceived as the animating force in most of his work—a tragic sense of life.

Truman's work is now solidly embedded in American literature. Certainly it is possible to mourn the fact that the latter part of his too early ended life seemed relatively unproductive, but even this judgment is presumptuous, since I doubt that few of us have ever had to wrestle with the terrors that hastened his end. Meanwhile, let us celebrate the excellence of the work he gave us. Like all of us writers, he had his deficiencies and he made his mistakes, but I believe it to be beyond question that he never wrote a line that was not wrested from a true writer's anguished quest for the best that he can bring forth. In this he was an artist—I think even at times a great one—from the top down to the toes of his diminutive, somehow heroic self.

[*Vanity Fair,* December 1984.]

James Jones

From *Here to Eternity* was published in 1951 at a time when I was in the process of completing my own first novel. I remember reading *Eternity* while I was living and writing in a country house in Rockland County, not far from New York City, and as has so often been the case with books that have made a large impression on me, I can recall the actual reading—the mood, the excitement, the surroundings. I remember the couch I lay on while reading, the room and the wallpaper, white curtains stirring and flowing in an indolent breeze, and cars that passed on the road outside. I think that perhaps I read portions of the book in other parts of the house but it is that couch I chiefly recollect, and myself sprawled on it, holding the hefty volume aloft in front of my eyes as I remained more or less transfixed through most of the waking hours of several days, in thrall to the story's power, its immediate narrative authority, its vigorously peopled barracks and barrooms, its gutsy humor, and its immense, harrowing sadness. The book was about the unknown world of the peacetime army. Even if I hadn't myself suffered some of the outrages of military life, I'm sure I would have recognized the book's stunning authenticity, its burly artistry, its sheer richness as life. A sense of permanence attached itself to the pages. This remarkable quality did not arise from Jones's language, for it was quickly apparent that the author was not a stylist, certainly not the stylist of refinement and nuance that we former students of creative writing classes had been led to emulate.

The genial rhythms and carefully wrought sentences that English majors had been encouraged to admire were not on display in *Eternity,* nor was the writing even vaguely experimental; it was so conventional as to be premodern. This was doubtless a blessing. For here was a writer whose urgent, blunt language with its off-key tonalities and hulking emphasis on adverbs wholly matched his subject matter. Jones's wretched outcasts and the narrative voice he had summoned to tell their tale had achieved a near-perfect synthesis. What also made the book a triumph was the characters Jones had fashioned—Prewitt, Warden, Maggio, the officers and their wives, the Honolulu whores, the brig rats, and all the rest. There were none of the wan, tentative effigies that had begun to populate the pages of postwar fiction during its brief span, but human beings of real size and arresting presence, believable and hard to forget. The language may have been coarse-grained but it had Dreiserian force; the people were as alive as those of Dostoevsky. One other item, somewhat less significant but historic nonetheless, caught my attention, and this was how it had fallen to Jones to make the final breakthrough in terms of vernacular speech which writers—and readers—had been awaiting for hundreds of years. The dread *f*-word, among several others, so sedulously proscribed by the guardians of decency that even Norman Mailer in his admirable *The Naked and the Dead,* only three years before, had had to fudge the issue with an absurd pseudospelling, was now inscribed on the printed page in the speech pattern of those who normally spoke it. This alone was cause to celebrate, totally aside from the book's incandescent strengths.

It has been said that writers are fiercely jealous of each other. Kurt Vonnegut has observed that most writers display toward one another the edgy mistrust of bears. This may be true, but I do recall that in those years directly following World War II there seemed to be a moratorium on envy, and most of the young writers who were heirs to the Lost Generation developed, for a time at least, a camaraderie, or a reasonable compatibility, as if there were glory enough to go around for all the novelists about to try to fit themselves into Apollonian niches alongside those of the earlier masters. Many of us felt lucky to have survived the war, and the end of the war itself was a convenient point of reckoning, a moment to attempt comparisons. If the Armistice of 1918 had permitted prodigies such as Hemingway, Faulkner, and Fitzgerald to create their collective myth, wouldn't our own war produce a constellation just as passionately committed, as gifted and illustrious? It was a dumb notion (though it often cropped up in book chat), since we had overlooked the inevitable duplicity of history, which would never allow reassembly of those sovereign talents; we would have to settle for the elegant goal of becoming ourselves. But there was tremendous excitement about being a young writer in those days, and of taking part in a shared destiny. When I finished reading *From Here to Eternity* I felt no jealousy at all, only a desire to meet this man, just four years older than myself, who had inflicted on me such emotional turmoil in the act of telling me authentic truths about an underside of American life I barely knew existed. I wanted to talk to the writer who had dealt so eloquently with those lumpen warriors, and who had created scenes that tore at the guts. And then there was that face on the dust jacket, the same face that had glowered at me from bookstore displays and magazine covers and newspaper articles. Was there ever such a face, with its Beethovenesque brow and lantern jaw and stepped-upon-looking nose—a forbidding face until one realized that it only *seemed* to glower, since the eyes really projected a skeptical humor that softened the initial impression of rage. Although, as I later discovered, Jim Jones contained plenty of good clean American rage.

When I first met Jim, during the fall of that year, *Lie Down in Darkness* had recently been published, and we were both subjected to a considerable amount of not unpleasant lionization. Jim was a superlion; his book, after these many months, was still riding high on the best-seller lists. He had achieved that Nirvana which, if I may tell a secret, all writers privately cherish—critical acclaim *and* popular success. My book, on a much more modest level, had also done well critically and commercially, and in fact there was a period of several months during 1951 when still another first novel destined for some durability shared the best-seller list with Jim's and mine—*The Catcher in the Rye*. But Jim's celebrity status was extraordinary, and the nimbus of stardom that attended his presence as we tripped together from party to party around Manhattan was testimony to the appeal of those unforgettable looks but also to something deeper: the work itself, the power of a novel to stir the imagination of countless people as few books had in years. Moving about at night with Jim was like keeping company with a Roman emperor. Indeed I may have been a little envious, but the man had such raw magnetism and took such uncomplicated pleasure in his role as the Midwestern hick who was now the cynosure of Big Town attention that I couldn't help being tickled by the commotion he caused, and his glory; he'd certainly earned it. It was a period when whiskey—great quantities of it—was the substance of choice. We did a prodigious amount of drinking, and there were always flocks of girls around, but I soon noticed that the hedonistic whirl had a way of winding down, usually late at night, when Jim, who had seemingly depthless stamina, would head for a secluded corner of a bar and begin speaking about books, about writers and writing. And we'd often talk long after the booze had been shut off and the morning light seeped through the windows.

Jim was serious about fiction in a way that now seems a little old-fashioned and ingenuous, with the novel for him in magisterial reign. He saw it as sacred mission, as icon, as Grail. Like so many American writers of distinction, Jim had not been granted the benison of a formal education, but like these dropouts he had done a vast amount of impassioned and eclectic reading; thus while there were gaps in his literary background that college boys like me had filled (the whole long curriculum of English and American poetry, for instance), he had absorbed an impressive amount of writing for a man whose schoolhouse had been at home or in a barracks. He had been, and still was, a hungry reader, and it was fascinating in those dawn sessions to hear this fellow built like a welterweight boxer (which he had occasionally been) speak in his gravelly drill sergeant's voice about a few of his more recherché loves—Virginia Woolf was one, I recall, Edith Wharton another. I didn't agree with Jim much of the time but I usually found that his tastes and his judgments were, on their own terms, gracefully discriminating and astute. He had stubborn prejudices, though—a blind spot, I thought, about Hemingway. He grudgingly allowed that Hemingway had possessed lyric power in his early stories, but most of his later work he deemed phony to the core. It filled him with that rage I mentioned, and I would watch in wonder as his face darkened with a scowl as grim as Caliban's, and he'd denounce Papa for a despicable fraud and poseur.

It sounded like overkill. Was this some irrational competitive obsession, I wondered, the insecure epigone putting down the master? But I soon realized that in analyzing his judgments about Hemingway I had to set purely literary considerations aside and understand that a fierce and by no means aimless, or envy-inspired, indignation energized Jim's view. Basically, it had to do with men at war. For Jim had been to war, he had been wounded on Guadalcanal, had seen men die, had been sickened and traumatized by the experience. Hemingway had been to war too, and had been wounded, but despite the gloss of misery and disenchantment that overlaid his work, Jim maintained, he was at heart a war lover, a macho contriver of romantic effects, and to all but the gullible and wishful the lie showed glaringly through the fabric of his books and in his life. He therefore had committed the artist's chief sin by betraying the truth. Jim's opinion of Hemingway, justifiable in its harshness or not, was less significant than what it revealed about his own view of existence, which at its most penetrating—as in *From Here to Eternity* and later in *The Pistol* and *The Thin Red Line*—was always seen through the soldier's eye, in a hallucination where the circumstances of military life cause men to behave mostly like beasts and where human dignity, while welcome and often redemptive, is not the general rule. Jones was among the best anatomists of warfare in our time, and in his bleak, extremely professional vision he continued to insist that war was a congenital and chronic illness from which we would never be fully delivered. War rarely ennobled men and usually degraded them; cowardice and heroism were both celluloid figments, generally interchangeable, and such grandeur as could be salvaged from the mess lay at best in pathos: in the haplessness of men's mental and physical suffering. Living or dying in war had nothing to do with valor, it had to do with luck. Jim had endured very nearly the worst; he had seen death face-to-face. At least partially as a result of this he was quite secure in his masculinity and better able than anyone else I've known to detect musclebound pretense, empty bravado. It's fortunate that he did not live to witness Rambo, or our high-level infatuation with military violence. It would have brought out the assassin in him.

I went to Europe soon after this and was married, and Jim and I were not in close contact for several years. When we got together again, in New York during the waning 1950s, he too was married, and it was his turn to shove off for Europe, where he settled in Paris, and where he and Gloria remained for the better part of the rest of his life. We saw each other on his frequent trips to the United States, but my visits to Paris were even more frequent during the next fifteen years or so, and it is Paris, nearly always Paris, where I locate Jim when I conjure him up in memory. Year in and year out—sometimes with my wife, Rose, sometimes alone—I came to roost in the Joneses' marvelous lodgings overlooking the Seine, often freeloading (*à l'anglaise,* observed Gloria, who took a dim view of the British) so long that I acquired the status of a semipermanent guest. My clearest and still most splendid image is that of the huge vaulted living room and the ceiling-high doors that gave out onto the river with its hypnotic, incessant flow of barge traffic moving eastward past the stately ecclesiastic rump of Notre Dame. The room was lined with books, and an entire wall was dominated by the nearly one hundred thickly hulking, drably bound volumes of the official United States government history of the Civil War. The very thought of shipping that library across the Atlantic was numbing. What Jim sometimes called Our Great Fraternal Massacre was his enduring preoccupation, and he had an immense store of knowledge about its politics, strategies, and battles. Somehow in the lofty room the dour Victorian tomes didn't really obtrude, yet they were a vaguely spectral presence and always reminded me how exquisitely *American* Jim was destined to remain during years in Paris. War and its surreal lunacy would be his central obsession to the end, and would also be that aspect of human experience he wrote best about.

Into this beautiful room with its flood of pastel Parisian light, with its sound of Dave Brubeck or Brahms, there would come during the sixties and early seventies a throng of admirable and infamous characters, ordinary and glamorous and weird people—writers and painters and movie stars, starving Algerian poets, drug addicts, Ivy League scholars, junketing United States senators, thieves, jockeys, restaurateurs, big names from the American media (fidgety and morose in their sudden vacuum of anonymity), tycoons and paupers. It was said that even a couple of Japanese tourists made their confused way there, en route to the Louvre. No domicile ever attracted such a steady stream of visitors, no hosts ever extended uncomplainingly so much largesse to the deserving and the worthless alike. It was not a rowdy place— Jim was too soldierly to fail to maintain reasonable decorum—but like the Abbey of Thélème of Rabelais, in which visitors were politely bidden to do what they liked, guests in the house at 10, Quai d'Orléans were phenomenally relaxed, sometimes to the extent of causing the Joneses to be victimized by the very waifs they had befriended. A great deal of antique silver disappeared over the years, and someone quite close to Jim once told me they reckoned he had lost tens of thousands of dollars in bad debts to smooth white-collar panhandlers. If generosity can be a benign form of pathology, Jim and Gloria were afflicted by it, and their trustingness extended to their most disreputable servants, who were constantly ripping them off. One, an insolent Pakistani houseman whom Gloria had longed to fire but had hesitated to do so out of tenderheartedness, brought her finally to her senses when she glimpsed him one evening across the floor of a tony nightclub, bewigged and stunningly garbed in one of her newly bought Dior gowns. Episodes like that were commonplace *chez* Jones in the tumultuous sixties.

There were literary journalists of that period who enjoyed pointing to a certain decadence in the Joneses' lifestyle and wrote reproachful monographs about the way that Jim and Gloria (now parents of two children) comported themselves: dinners at Maxime's, after-dinner with the fat squabs at hangouts like Castel's, vacations in Deauville and Biarritz, yachting in Greece, the races at Longchamps, the oiled and pampered sloth of Americans in moneyed exile. Much the same had been written about Fitzgerald and Hemingway. The tortured puritanism that causes Americans to mistrust their serious artists and writers, and regards it as appropriate when they are underpaid, evokes even greater mistrust when they are paid rather well and, to boot, hobnob with the Europeans. Material success is still not easily forgiven in a country that ignored Poe and abandoned Melville. There was also the complaint that in moving to France for such a long sojourn Jim Jones had cut off his roots, thus depriving himself of the rich fodder of American experience necessary to produce worthwhile work. But this would seem to be a hollow objection, quite aside from the kind of judgmental chauvinism it expresses. Most writers have stored up, by their mid-twenties, the emotional and intellectual baggage that will supply the needs of their future work, and the various environments into which they settle, while obviously not negligible as sources of material and stimulation, don't really count for all that much. Jim wrote some exceedingly inferior work during his Paris years. *Go to the Widow-Maker*, which dealt mainly with underwater adventure—a chaotic novel of immeasurable length, filled with plywood characters, implausible dialogue, and thick wedges of plain atrocious writing—spun me into despondency when I read it. There were, to be sure, some spectacular underwater scenes and moments of descriptive power almost like the Jones of *Eternity*. But in general the work was a disappointment, lacking both grace and cohesion.

Among the distressing things about it was its coming in the wake of *The Thin Red Line*, a novel of major dimensions whose rigorous integrity and disciplined art allowed Jim once again to exploit the military world he knew so well. Telling the story of GIs in combat in the Pacific, it is squarely in the gritty, no-holds-barred tradition of American realism, a genre that even in 1962, when the book was published, would have seemed oafishly out-of-date had it not been for Jim's mastery of the narrative and his grasp of the sun-baked milieu of bloody island warfare, which exerted such a compelling hold on the reader that he seemed to breathe new life into the form. Romain Gary had commented about the book: "It is essentially an epic love poem about the human predicament and like all great books it leaves one with a feeling of wonder and hope." The rhapsodic note is really not all that overblown; upon rereading, *The Thin Red Line* stands up remarkably well, one of the best novels written about American fighting men in combat. Comparing it, however, with *Go to the Widow-Maker* produced a depressing sense of retrogression and loss. It was like watching a superb diver who, after producing a triple somersault of championship caliber, leaps from the board again and splatters himself all over an empty pool. Jim's nettled response to my hesitantly negative criticism makes me glad that I never expressed my real feelings or my actual chagrin; he might have wanted to strangle me.

But it is important to point out that although *Go to the Widow-Maker* was written in Paris, so was *The Thin Red Line*. This would strongly suggest that the iniquitous life that Jim Jones had reputedly led in Paris, the years of complacent and unengaged exile, bore little relation to his work, and that if he had stayed at home, the motivations that impelled him in a particular literary direction, and that shaped his creative commitments, would probably have remained much the same. Jim loved the good life. He would have richly enjoyed himself anywhere and would have, as always, worked like hell. But a common failing of many writers is that they often choose their themes and address their subject matter as poorly as they often choose wives or houses. What is really significant is that while a book like *Go to the Widow-Maker* represents one of those misshapen artifacts that virtually every good writer, in the sad and lonely misguidedness of his calling, comes up with sooner or later, *The Thin Red Line* is a brilliant example of what happens when a novelist summons strength from the deepest wellsprings of his inspiration. In this book, along with *From Here to Eternity* and *Whistle*—a work of many powerful scenes that suffered from the fact that he was dying as he tried, unsuccessfully, to finish it—Jim obeyed his better instincts by attending to that forlorn figure whom in all the world he cared for most and understood better than any other writer alive: the common foot soldier, the grungy enlisted man.

Romain Gary wasn't too far off. There was a certain grandeur in Jones's vision of the soldier. Other writers had written of outcasts in a way that had rendered one godforsaken group or another into archetypes of suffering—Dickens's underworld, Zola's whores, Jean Genet's thieves, Steinbeck's migrant workers, Agee's white Southern sharecroppers, Richard Wright's black Southern immigrants, on and on—the list is honorable and long. Jones's soldiers were at the end of an ancestral line of fictional characters who are misfits, the misbegotten who always get the short end of the stick. But they never dissolved into a social or political blur. The individuality that he gave to his people, and the stature he endowed them with, came, I believe, from a clear-eyed view of their humanness, which included their ugliness or meanness. Sympathetic as he was to his enlisted men, he never lowered himself to the temptations of an agitprop that would limn them as mere victims. Many of his soldiers were creeps, others were outright swine, and there were enough good guys among the officers to be consonant with reality. At least part of the reason he was able to pull all this off so successfully, without illusions or sentimentality, was his sense of history, along with his familiarity with the chronicles of war that were embedded in world literature. He had read Thucydides early, and he once commented to me that no one could write well about warfare without him. He'd also linked his own emotions with those of Tolstoy's peasant soldiers, and could recite a substantial amount of *Henry V*, whose yeoman-warriors were right up his alley. But the shades of the departed with whom he most closely identified were the martyrs of the American Civil War. That pitiless and aching slaughter, which included some of his forebears, haunted him throughout his life and provided one of the chief goads to his imagination. To be a Civil War buff was not to be an admirer of the technology of battle, although campaign strategy fascinated him; it was to try to plumb the mystery and the folly of war itself.

In 1962, during one of his visits to America, I traveled with Jim to Washington. Among other things, an influential official with whom I was friendly and who was on President Kennedy's staff had invited the two of us to take a special tour of the White House. Oddly, for such a well-traveled person, Jim had never been to Washington, and the trip offered him a chance to visit the nearby battlefields. He had never seen any of the Civil War encampments. Jim went out to Antietam, in Maryland, after which we planned to go to the Lincoln Memorial before driving over to the White House. When he met me at our hotel, just after the Antietam visit, Jim was exceptionally somber. Something at the battlefield had resonated in a special troubling way within him; he seemed abstracted and out-of-sorts. It had been, he told me finally, a part of the battleground called the Bloody Lane that had so affected him when he'd seen it. He'd read so much about the sector and the engagement and had always wondered how the terrain would appear when he viewed it firsthand. A rather innocuous-looking place now, he said, a mere declivity in the landscape, sheltered by a few trees. But there, almost exactly a century before, some of the most horrible carnage in the history of warfare had taken place, thousands of men on both sides dead within a few hours. The awful shambles was serene now, but the ghosts were still there, swarming; it had shaken him up.

Soon after this, at the Lincoln Memorial, I realized that the cavernous vault with its hushed and austere shadows, its soft footfalls and requiem whispers, might not have been the best place to take a man in such a delicate mood. Jim's face was set like a slab, his expression murky and aggrieved, as we stood on the marble reading the Gettysburg Address engraved against one lofty wall, slowly scanning those words of supreme magnanimity and conciliation and brotherhood dreamed by the fellow Illinoisan whom Jim had venerated, as almost everyone does, for transcendental reasons that needed not to be analyzed or explained in such a sacred hall. I suppose I was expecting the conventional response from Jim, the pious hum. But his reaction, soft-spoken, was loaded with savage bitterness, and for an instant it was hard to absorb. "It's just beautiful bullshit," he blurted. "They all died in vain. They all died in vain. And they always will!" His eyes were moist with fury and grief; we left abruptly, and it required some minutes of emotional readjustment before the storm had blown over and he regained his composure, apologizing quickly, then returning with good cheer and jokes to more normal concerns.

Many years went by before I happened to reflect on that day, and to consider this: that in the secret cellars of the White House, in whose corridors we were soon being shepherded around pleasantly, the ancient mischief was newly germinating. There were doubtless all sorts of precursory activities taking place which someday would confirm Jim's fierce prophecy: heavy cable traffic to Saigon, directives beefing up advisory and support groups, ominous memos on Diem and the Nhus, orders to units of the Green Berets. The shadow of Antietam, and of all those other blind upheavals, was falling on our own times. James Jones would be the last to be surprised.

[Introduction to *To Reach Eternity: The Letters of James Jones;* Random House, Inc., 1989.]

Transcontinental with Tex

One of my oddest trips in a lifetime of odd trips was the one I took with Terry Southern across the U.S.A. in 1964. At that time I'd known Terry (whom I also called, depending on mood and circumstance, "Tex" or "T") ever since 1952 during a long sojourn in Paris. Like a patient in lengthy convalescence, the city was still war weary, with its beauty a little drab around the edges. Bicycles and motorbikes clogged the streets. *The Paris Review* was then in its period of gestation, and the principals involved in its development, including George Plimpton and Peter Matthiessen, often spent their late evening hours in a dingy nightspot called Le Chaplain, tucked away on a back street in Montparnasse. In the sanatorium of our present smoke-free society it is hard to conceive of the smokiness of that place; the smoke was ice-blue, and almost like a semisolid. You could practically take your finger and carve your initials in it. It was smoke with a searing, promiscuous smell, part Gauloises and Gitanes, part Lucky Strikes, part the rank bittersweet odor of pot. I was new to pot, and the first time I ever met Terry he offered me a roach.

I was quite squeamish. Marijuana was in its early dawn as a cultural and spiritual force, and the idea of inhaling some alarmed me. I connected the weed with evil and depravity. We were sitting at a table with Terry's friends, the late film director Aram ("Al") Avakian and a self-exiled ex–New York state trooper and aspiring poet whose name I've forgotten but who looked very much like Avakian, that is to say mustachioed and alternately fierce and dreamy-eyed. Also present was a *Paris Review* cofounder, the late Harold L. ("Doc") Humes, who had befriended me when I first arrived in Paris and was no stranger to pot. The joint Terry proffered disagreed with me, causing me immediate nausea; I recall Terry putting down this reaction to the large amount of straight brandy I'd been drinking, cognac being the *boisson de choix* in those days before Scotch became a Parisian commonplace. Terry responded quite humanely, I thought, to my absence of cool. He was tolerant when, on another occasion, I had the same queasy response. In our get-togethers, therefore, I continued to abuse my familiar substance, and Terry his, though he could also put away considerable booze.

I was living then in a room that Doc Humes had found for me, at a hotel called the Libéria that had been his home for a year or so. The hotel was on the little rue de la Grande Chaumière, famous for its painters' ateliers; my Spartan room cost the equivalent of eight dollars a week, or eight dollars and a half if you paid extra to get the henna-dyed Gorgon who ran the place to change the sheets weekly. The room had a bidet, but you had to walk half a mile to the toilet. You could stroll from the hotel in less than two minutes to La Coupole or to the terrace of Le Dôme, Hemingway's old hangout, which also reeked of pot or hash and featured many young American men sitting at tables with manuscripts while affecting the leonine look of Hemingway, right down to the mustache and hirsute chest. I even overheard one of those guys address his girl companion as "Daughter." Terry and I would sit after lunch on the terrace, drinking coffee and smirking at these poseurs.

Terry was really hard up for money in those days, even in a Paris where a franc went a long way. I wasn't rich myself but I was, after all, a recently published bestselling author, and I could occasionally buy him a meal. We ate a couple of times in a cramped but excellent bistro on the avenue du Maine and had such luncheons as the following, which I recorded in a notebook: *entrecôte, pommes frites, haricots verts, carafe de vin, tarte tatin, café filtre.* Price for *two:* $3.60. The U.S. dollar was, of course, in a state of loony ascendancy, for which the French have been punishing us ever since; if, in addition, you exchanged your traveler's checks for the fat rate given by Maurice Loeb, the cheerful *cambiste* who hung out on the rue Vieille du Temple, in the Jewish Quarter, you could really become a high roller in 1952. It was one of the reasons the Communists plastered *U.S. Go Home* signs on every available wall.

That June I was busy in my room each afternoon, writing on a manuscript that would eventually become my short novel *The Long March*. One afternoon, unannounced, Terry showed up with his own manuscript and asked me if I would read it. His manner was awkward and apologetic. I knew he was working on a novel; during our sessions on the terrace of Le Dôme he had spoken of his serious literary ambitions. I had met a lot of Texans in the Marines, most of whom lived up to their advance reputation for being yahoos and blowhards, and I never thought I'd encounter a Texan who was a novelist. Or a Texan who was really rather shy and unboastful. The manuscript he brought me made up the beginning chapters of *Flash and Filigree,* and I was amazed by the quality of the prose, which was intricately mannered though evocative and unfailingly alive. The writing plainly owed a debt to Terry's literary idol, the British novelist Henry Green, one of those sui generis writers you imitated upon pain of death, but nonetheless what I read of *Flash and Filigree* was fresh and exciting, and later I told him so. Even then he had adopted that mock-pompous style that was to become his trademark, yet I sensed a need for real encouragement when he said: "I trust then, Bill, that you think this will put me in the quality lit game?" I said that I had no doubt that it would (and it did, when it was finally published), but as usual his talk turned to the need to make some money. "De luxe porn" was an avenue that seemed the most inviting—lots of Americans in Paris were cranking out their engorged prose—and of course it was one of the routes he eventually took, culminating a few years later in the delectable *Candy*. For Tex, success was on the way.

I didn't see a great deal more of Terry in Paris. That summer I went off to the south of France and, later, to live in Rome. But back in the States Terry was very much a part of the quality lit scene in New York during the next twenty years, frequenting places like George Plimpton's and, later, Elaine's, where I too hung out from time to time. He had great nighttime stamina, and we closed up many bars together. He bought a house in the remote village of East Canaan, not very far from my own place in Connecticut. And it was either at this house or mine that we decided to make a transcontinental trip together. I had been invited to give a talk at a California university, while Terry, having collaborated on the screenplay of Stanley Kubrick's *Dr. Strangelove,* a great hit, had been asked to come out to the coast to write the script for a film version of Evelyn Waugh's *The Loved One.* It was a perfect vehicle, I thought, to hone his gift for the merrily macabre.

But the catalytic force for the whole trip was Nelson Algren. Nelson had written me, asking me to visit him in Chicago. The two of us had become friends and drinking companions during several of his trips to New York from Chicago, a city with which he had become identified as closely as had such other Windy City bards as Saul Bellow and Carl Sandburg and Studs Terkel. In his letter he said that he'd show me the best of Chicago. I had for some reason never been to Chicago, and so Terry suggested that we go west together and stop by and make a joint visit to Nelson, with whom he had also become pals. He had the notion of doing the Chicago–Los Angeles leg by train since soon, as he astutely predicted, no one would be traveling on the rails except the near destitute and those terrified by airplanes. By taking the fabled Super Chief of the Santa Fe, he pointed out, we'd be able to get a last glimpse of the great open spaces and also of the sumptuous club cars upon whose banquettes the movie bigwigs and sexy starlets had cavorted while the prairies whizzed by. It would be a precious slice of Americana soon to be foreclosed to travelers in a hurry, and I thought it was a fine idea.

Nelson was in his mid-fifties, one of the original hipsters. He had been telling stories about junkies and pimps and whores and other outcasts while Kerouac and Ferlinghetti were still adolescents, and had nailed down as his private literary property the entire grim world of the Chicago underclass. After years of writing, including a stint with the WPA Federal Writers' Project during the Depression and another one hammering out venereal-disease reports for the Chicago Board of Health, he hit it big with *The Man with the Golden Arm,* a vigorous novel about drug addiction that won the first National Book Award in 1950 and was made into a successful movie starring Frank Sinatra. Money and fame were unable to go to Nelson's resolutely nonconformist head; "down-at-the-heel" would have been the politest term for the neighborhood he still lived in, where he took the three of us (my wife, Rose, having signed on at the last minute) after meeting our plane at O'Hare. It was a predominantly Polish faubourg, hemmed in by mammoth gas-storage tanks, and the odor of fatty sausage and cabbage began at the curb, becoming more ripe and pronounced as we labored up the five flights to what Nelson called his "penthouse"—an incredibly cramped and cluttered apartment with only two small bedrooms, a tiny kitchenette, and an old-fashioned bathroom with water-stained wallpaper.

The boxy living room was dark and jammed with books. It was fairly clean amid the disorder, but the pad was the lair of a totally undomesticated animal. I do recall a framed photograph of Simone de Beauvoir, with whom Nelson had had a torrid affair, and whom he still referred to as "the Beaver." That night we partook of Polish cuisine, mystery stew and memorably awful, in a nearby restaurant, where Nelson titillated us with secret hints about the Chicago he was going to show us the next day. With the exception of Rose we all got pie-eyed. I was very fond of Nelson but I always thought he was half crazy. When he got enthusiastic or excited his eyes took on a manic gleam, and he would go off on a riff of giggles that was not unlike Richard Widmark's in *Kiss of Death*. Terry and I exchanged bewildered glances. I frankly had no idea what we would experience, thinking of such wonders as Michigan Avenue, the Art Institute, lunch at the Pump Room, the great Museum of Science and Industry, the Merchandise Mart, even the celebrated stockyards. That night, we three visitors slept in the same room, Rose and I locked immobile in a narrow, sagging single bed and Terry on a cot only a foot away, where he drifted off to sleep with a glass of bourbon still in his hand, heaving with laughter over Nelson and our accommodations.

Early the next morning, still behaving like a man withholding knowledge of a delightful mystery, Nelson took us by taxi on a meandering route through the city and deposited us at the entrance of the Cook County Jail. He then revealed that he had arranged to have us given a guided tour. This would be our most authentic taste of Chicago. We were all stunned—Terry, wearing his shades, said, "Well, Nelse old man, you shouldn't have gone to all the bother"—but in a way it was something I might have anticipated. Despite the merciless realism that he brought to his subject, Nelson was basically an underworld groupie; he loved all aspects of outlaw life, and his obsession with crime and criminals, though romantic, was eclectic to the extent that it also embraced the good guys. He counted among his many cronies a number of law enforcement officers, and one of these was the warden of the Cook County Jail. Despite the drab municipal sound of its name, the Cook County Jail was then, as now, a huge heavy-duty penitentiary, with harsh appurtenances such as a maximum-security unit, industrial areas, facilities for solitary confinement, and a thriving—if the term may be used—Death Row. All this was explained to us in his office by the warden, a thin man with a disarmingly scholarly look, whom Nelson introduced us to before vanishing—to our intense discomfort—saying he'd pick us up later. Clearly none of us could comprehend this sudden abandonment. While the warden fiddled with the buttons of his intercom, Terry wondered in a whisper if I was as hungover as he was; beneath his dark glasses his cheeks were sickly pale and I heard him murmur, "Man, I think this is turning into some kind of weird nightmare." Rose tried to appear happy and self-contained. We heard the warden summon Captain Boggs.

Captain Boggs had a round, cheerful, fudge-colored face and could not have weighed an ounce less than 250 pounds. His title was associate captain of the guards, and he would be our guide through the institution. As we trailed him down the corridor I couldn't help being struck by his extreme girth, which caused his arms to swing at wide angles from his body and made his body itself, beneath the slate-gray uniform jacket, appear somehow inflatable; he looked like a Negro version of the Michelin tire man. I was also fetched by his accent, with its rich loamy sound of the Deep South. I thought of Richard Wright's native son, Bigger Thomas, also an émigré from the cotton fields to Chicago, only to become the doomed murderer of a white girl; plainly Captain Boggs, in all of his heftiness, had made a prodigious leap for a onetime black boy. He had a rather deliberate and ornate manner of speaking, possibly the result of many trips with what he called "VIP honorees," and the tour itself dragged on through the prison's depressing immensity, seeming to continue hour after hour. "Dis yere is de inmates' dinin' facilities," he said as we stood on a balcony overlooking an empty mess hall. "Dis yere," he yelled at us at the doorway to a deafening machine shop, "is where de inmates pays off they debts to society." We went down into a cavernous basement, chilly and echoing with a distant dripping sound. "Dis yere is what is called de Hole. Solitary confinement. You gits too smart, dis yere where you pays fo' it." We would not be able to go on the tiers of the cell blocks, Captain Boggs explained, Rose being a distracting presence. "Dem suckers go wild aroun' a woman," he declared.

We did end up, finally, on Death Row. After going through a series of doors, we immediately entered a small, windowless room, where we had a most disconcerting encounter. Seated at a table was a white inmate in orange prison coveralls being given an intravenous injection by a black male nurse. Captain Boggs introduced us to the prisoner, whose name was Witherspoon, a mountaineer transplant up from Kentucky (and known in the press as "the Hillbilly from Hell") who had committed a couple of particularly troglodytic murders in Chicago, and whose date with the executioner was right around the corner. Witherspoon and his gruesome crimes were of national interest, his case having made the New York papers.

"Howya doin', Witherspoon?" said Captain Boggs in a hearty voice. "Dese is two writer gentlemen. Doin' de VIP tour."

"Howdy," said Witherspoon, as he flashed a smile and in so doing displayed a mouth full of blackened teeth in a beetle-browed skeletal face that had doubtless inspired many bad dreams. "I've got diabeet-ees," he went on to say, as if to explain the needle in his arm, and then, without missing a beat, added: "They done railroaded me. Before Almighty God, I'm an innocent man." Terry and I later recalled, while ensconced in the lounge car of the Super Chief, the almost hallucinatory sensations we both experienced when, most likely at the same time, we glimpsed the tattoos graven on Witherspoon's hands: LOVE on the fingers of the right hand, HATE on those of the left. They were exactly the mottoes that decorated the knuckles of Robert Mitchum's demented backwoods preacher in *The Night of the Hunter.* Witherspoon himself had a preacher's style. "I hope you two good writers will proclaim to the world the abominable injustice they done to me. God bless you both."

"Mr. Witherspoon," Terry deadpanned, "be assured of our constant concern for your welfare."

I had undergone a recent conversion about capital punishment, transformed from a believer—albeit a lukewarm believer—into an ardent opponent; hence my chagrin, after we bade good-bye to Witherspoon, when Captain Boggs walked us down a narrow corridor and acquainted us with the vehicle that would soon speed the Hillbilly from Hell back whence he came. We trooped into a sort of alcove where the captain motioned us to stand, while he went to one wall and yanked back a curtain. In glaring light there was suddenly revealed the electric chair, a huge hulking throne of wood and leather, out of which unraveled a thicket of wires. I heard Rose give a small soprano yelp of distress. In the lurid incandescence I noted on the far wall two signs. One read: SILENCE. The other: NO SMOKING. I felt Terry's paw on my shoulder, as from somewhere behind me he whispered: "Did you ever dig anything so fucking *surreal*?"

Captain Boggs said: "De supreme penalty." His voice slipped into the rhythmic rote-like monotone with which I was sure he had addressed countless VIP honorees. "De procedure is quick and painless. First is administered two thousand volts for thirty seconds. Stop de juice to let de body cool off. Den five hundred volts for thirty seconds. Stop de juice again. Den two thousand mo' volts. Doctor makes a final check. Ten minutes from beginnin' to end."

"Let me out of here," I heard Rose murmur.

"I always likes to ax de visitors if they'd care to set down in de chair," the captain said, his cheerful grin broadening. "How 'bout you, Mr. Starling?" he went on, using the name he'd called me by all morning.

I said that I'd pass on the offer, but I didn't want the opportunity lost on Terry. "What do you think, Tex?" I said.

"Captain Boggs," said Terry, "I've always wanted to experience the hot squat—vicariously, that is. But I think that today I'll decline your very tempting invitation."

I've recently discovered that the quite accurate notes I kept about our trip, which allow the foregoing account to possess verisimilitude, become rather sketchy after we leave the Cook County Jail. This is probably because our trip farther westward on the elegant Super Chief was largely a warm blur of booze and overeating, causing me to discontinue my notes except for a few random jottings, themselves nearly incoherent. (I want to mention, however, while the fact is fresh in mind, that some months after our trip I read that Witherspoon never had to receive that voltage; his death sentence was commuted, through a legal technicality, to life imprisonment.) I thought of Terry recently when I read, in an interview, the words of a British punk-rock star, plainly a young jerk, nasty and callow but able to express a tart intuitive insight: "You Americans still believe in God and all that shit, don't you? The whole fucking lot of you fraught with the fear of death."

Terry would have given his little cackle of approval at the remark, for it went to the core of his perception of American culture. Like me, Terry was an apostate Southern Protestant, and I think that one of the reasons we hit it off well together was that we both viewed the Christian religion—at least insofar as we had experienced its puritanical rigors—as a conspiracy to deny its adherents their fulfillment as human beings. It magnified not the glories of life but the consciousness of death, exploiting humanity's innate terror of the timeless void. High among its prohibitions was sexual pleasure. In contemplating Americans stretched on the rack of their hypocrisy as they tried to reconcile their furtive adulteries with their churchgoing pieties, Terry laid the groundwork for some of his most biting and funniest satire. Christianity bugged him, even getting into his titles—think of *The Magic Christian*.

Nor was it by chance that the surname of the endearing heroine of *Candy* was—what else?—Christian. His finest comic efforts often come from his juxtaposing a sweetly religious soul—or at least a bourgeois-conventional one—with a figure of depravity or corruption. *Candy* was surely the first novel in which the frenzied sexual congress between a well-bred, exquisitely proportioned young American girl and an elderly, insane hunchback could elicit nothing but helpless laughter. ("Give me your *hump!*" she squeals at the moment of climax, in a *jeu de mots* so obvious it compounds the hilarity.) One clear memory I have is of Terry in the lounge car, musing over his Old Grand-Dad as he considered the imminent demise of the Super Chief and, with it, a venerable tradition. His voice grew elegiac speaking of the number of "darling Baptist virgins aspiring to be starlets" who, at the hands of "panting Jewish agents with their swollen members," had been ever so satisfactorily deflowered on these plush, softly undulating banquettes.

In fact, he had a fixation on the idea of "starlets," and it was plain that in Hollywood he would be looking forward to making out with a gorgeous ingénue from MGM and embarking on a halcyon erotic adventure. Toward the end of the trip we stayed up all night and drank most of the way through Arizona and Southern California, watching the pale moonscape of the desert slip by until morning dawned and we were in Los Angeles. Rose and I had to catch a late-morning plane to San Francisco but we all had time, it suddenly occurred to me, to visit the place that was the reason for Terry's trip. This was Forest Lawn Memorial Park, the "Whispering Glades" of Waugh's scathing send-up of America's funerary customs; how could Rose and I leave Los Angeles without viewing the hangout of Mr. Joyboy and his associate morticians? Terry agreed that we should all see it together. It was inevitable, I suppose, that the studio had arranged to put Terry up at that decaying relic the Chateau Marmont; for me it was an unexpected bonus to catch a glimpse of the mythic Hollywood landmark before heading out to Whispering Glades.

Terry and I were both in that sleepless state of jangled nerves and giggly mania, still half blotto and relying heavily on Rose and her sober patience to get us headed in the right direction. At Forest Lawn, in the blinding sunlight, our fellow tourists were out in droves. They were lined up in front of the mausoleum where the movie gods and goddesses had been laid to rest, stacked up in their crypts, Terry observed, "like pies in the Automat." Marilyn Monroe had passed into her estate of cosmic Loved One only two years before, and the queue of gawkers filing past her final abode seemed to stretch for hundreds of yards. Cameras clicked, bubble gum popped, babies shrieked. One sensed an awkward effort at reverence, but it was a strain; the spectacular graveyard was another outpost of Tinseltown. As we ambled over the greensward, vast as a golf course, we moved past a particularly repellent statuary grouping, a tableau of mourning marble children and a clutch of small marble animals. A woman onlooker was gushing feverishly, and Terry said he felt a little ill. We all agreed to be on our separate ways. "A bit of shut-eye and I'll soon be in tip-top shape," he assured us as we embraced. We left him standing at the taxi stop. He had his hands thrust deep in his pockets, and he was scowling through his shades, looking fierce and, as always, a little confused and lost but, in any case, with the mammoth American necropolis as a backdrop, like a man already dreaming up wicked ideas.

[*Paris Review*, Spring 1996.]

Peter Matthiessen

When I first met Peter Matthiessen I was in my mid-twenties, feeling rather nervous and unhappy and very much out of my element on my initial visit to Paris. I had published a first novel to considerable acclaim in New York, but small word of the book's existence, and nothing of its success, had reached France during that balmy and beautiful spring of 1952, and I suppose I was a little disappointed that Peter did not display the deference I thought fitting to the situation. Thus at first glance I thought Peter a trifle cold, when in reality his perfectly decent manners were really all one should have expected in view of the fact that I was merely another of the dozens of visiting American firemen who, at the behest of well-meaning friends back in the States, came knocking at the Matthiessen door that year. Peter and his wife, Patsy, lived in a modest but lovely apartment on a Utrillo-like backstreet in Montparnasse; spacious, airy, its one big room filled with light, the Matthiessen pad (the word was just coming into use about then) became the hangout for many of the mob of Americans who had hurried to Paris to partake of its perennial delights, to drink in the pleasures of a city beginning to surge with energy after the miseries of the recent war. "*U.S. Go Home*" was painted by the Communists on every wall—it was possibly the most ignored injunction in recent history. For the Americans happily established there, Paris *was* home, and no place was more homelike than the Matthiessen establishment on the rue Perceval. To this day I recollect with awe the sense of an almost constant open house, in which it was possible at practically any time to obtain music and food and drink (Peter was unfailingly generous with what seemed to be a nearly inexhaustible supply of Scotch) or, if need be, a spot to sleep off a hangover and—of course always—conversation. George Plimpton and Harold Humes were among the many visitors, and much of the conversation had to do with a literary magazine which the three friends were then in the process of bringing into hesitant life and which now, seemingly deathless, is known as *The Paris Review*. I am rather proud of the fact that the interview with me, done by Peter and George Plimpton, was the first of the celebrated *Paris Review* series (although not the first published)—first undoubtedly because at the time I was the only published novelist any of us knew.

We also talked a great deal about books and writing. We were swept up in the very midst of a postwar literary fever. Peter had not yet written a book (his fledgling effort, the affecting story "Sadie," had been published in *The Atlantic*) but he was, after all, barely twenty-five; he had time to burn and I remember telling him so, from the senior and authoritative vantage point of a writer who was two years older. So it is not to belittle Peter's capacity for work—and he is one of the most industrious writers alive—to say that much of our time during that spring and summer was spent at play. My French was rudimentary, while both Peter and Patsy had an excellent command of the language, and this helped bring me in contact with French people I might not have met; my linguistic ability slowly improved. That same savoir-faire of Peter's enabled me (a gastronomic idiot) to become acquainted with the native cuisine, and one of the remembered joys of that long-ago season, when a solitary dollar could buy considerable French joy, is our single-minded cultivation of the restaurants of Montparnasse and Saint-Germain-des-Prés. We had become good friends and I saw a lot of Peter during the following year in Europe—in Saint-Jean-de-Luz, where Peter and Patsy rented a house for the summer; in Rome, where to my enormous and happy surprise Peter turned up with a group of *Paris Review* cronies at my wedding the next spring; and finally during a splendid sojourn at Ravello, on the Amalfi Drive, where for several weeks Peter and Patsy (along with their newborn son, Lucas) shared a house with Rose and me and played tennis and interminable word games, talked for long hours about writers and writing, and swam in the then pellucid and unpolluted Mediterranean.

In 1954, when we all moved back to America, Peter set up housekeeping on Long Island and began to write seriously (though spending much of his time in good weather plying a trade as commercial fisherman), while Rose and I began to plant domestic roots in the hills of western Connecticut. During this period we kept close contact, visiting back and forth with considerable regularity, and it was at that time that I read Peter's first novel, *Race Rock,* in manuscript, beginning a tradition that has lasted to this day; amiably critical of each other's output, Peter and I have read (I think it is safe to say) nearly every word of each other's work—at least of a major nature—and I like to think that the habit has been mutually beneficial. Later I read *Partisans* and *Raditzer* with the same careful eye that I had *Race Rock;* as talented and sensitive as each appeared to be, the statement of a writer at the outset of his career, they were, I felt, merely forerunners of something more ambitious, more complex and substantial—and I was right. When *At Play in the Fields of the Lord* was published in 1965 there was revealed in stunning outline the fully realized work of a novelist writing at white heat and at the peak of his powers; a dense, rich, musical book, filled with tragic and comic resonances, it is fiction of genuine stature, with a staying power that makes it as remarkable to read now as when it first appeared.

But before *At Play* was published Peter had to begin that wandering yet consecrated phase of his career which has taken him to every corner of the globe, and which, reflected in a remarkable series of chronicles, has placed him at the forefront of the naturalists of his time. I saw Peter off in 1959 on the first of these trips—bidding him a boozy bon voyage athwart the Brooklyn docks, on a freighter that was to carry him up to the remotest reaches of the Amazon. Seemingly unperturbed, his spectacles planted with scholarly precision on his long angular face, he might have been going no farther than Staten Island, so composed did he seem, rather than to uttermost jungle fastnesses where God knows what beasts and dark happenings would imperil his hide. Weeks later I received a jaunty postcard from a distant and unheard-of Peruvian outpost, and I marveled at the sang-froid and the self-sufficiency but also at the quiet excitement the few words conveyed; in later years I would receive other droll, understated communiqués from Alaska, New Guinea, and the blackest part of Africa.

From what sprang this amazing obsession to plant one's feet upon the most exotic quarters of the earth, to traverse festering swamps and to scale the aching heights of implausible mountains? The wanderlust and feeling for adventure that is in many men, I suppose, but mercifully Peter has been more than a mere adventurer: he is a poet and a scientist, and the mingling of these two personae has given us such carefully observed, unsentimental, yet lyrically echoing works as *The Cloud Forest, Under the Mountain Wall, The Tree Where Man Was Born,* and *The Snow Leopard.* In the books themselves the reader will find at least part of the answer to the reason for Peter's quest. In these books, with their infusion of the ecological and the anthropological, with their unshrinking vision of man in mysterious and uneasy interplay with nature—books at once descriptive and analytical, scrupulous and vivid in detail, sometimes amusing, often meditative and mystical— Peter Matthiessen has created a unique body of work. It is the work of a man in ecstatic contemplation of our beautiful and inexplicable planet. To this body of natural history, add a novel like *At Play in the Fields of the Lord* and that brooding, briny, stormswept tone poem, *Far Tortuga,* and we behold a writer of phenomenal scope and versatility.

[Introduction to *Peter Matthiessen, A Bibliography: 1951–1979,* compiled by D. Nichols; Canoga Park, Calif.: Orirana Press, 1979.]

Bennett Cerf

ennett might have appreciated the fact that several years ago two of his Random House writers, Philip Roth and myself, walked along a beach in East Hampton loftily pigeonholing people into three categories: the well poisoners, the lawn mowers (these are most of the people), and the life-enhancers. Needless to say, Bennett belonged to that rare and precious species called the life-enhancers, of which humankind has so much need. Being a life-enhancer, he invigorated and replenished the world he lived in, leaving the people with whom he came in touch exhilarated by his presence. The vital force in Bennett was so powerful, so seemingly indomitable, that he appeared virtually deathless, and perhaps that is one of the reasons that his passing causes us this dismay we feel. I recall one night some years ago flying on a plane with Bennett through a dark, lovely, star-crowded sky over Pennsylvania. The clear light of the cities below seemed to merge with the glittering stars, creating a wonderful radiant effect that touched us both deeply. Suddenly Bennett turned to me and said something which in another man might seem odd or even slightly bizarre but which in Bennett expressed his own quintessence. "Ah, Bill," he exclaimed, "I love being alive so much!" Perhaps this explains why he was both so rare and so valuable. Loving life with that unquenchable love of his, he imparted the very spirit of life to others—that buoyant, generous, inimitably vivacious spirit that became apparent the instant he entered a room and that no one who knew him will ever forget. He adored jokes, of course, and I think he might have appreciated it had I tried to make one up for this occasion. At the moment my own sense of loss is too keen, although I am consoled by the thought that there will come a time when memory will permit us all to reexperience, without grief, the warmth and the good cheer that were bestowed upon us by this immeasurably loving, life-enhancing man.

[Speech delivered at a memorial service, St. Paul's Chapel, Columbia University, August 1971.]

Bob Loomis

I met Bob in 1946—the year after the invention of the printing press. I'd gone back to Duke University after being in the Marines, and Bob had come to Duke after service in the Army Air Force, and he looked about sixteen years old. We met in a tobacco-fragrant part of West Durham, in a sort of seedy salon presided over by an editor of the Duke Press named Ashbel Brice.

Brice called me Junior, and he called Bob—a year or so younger than me—Junior Junior. Brice introduced Bob and me to our first glorious dry martinis and also, bless him, to Joyce and Faulkner and Yeats. Bob's and my friendship was cemented by our passion for books and writing, which at that age is such a touchingly committed, exquisitely focused matter, like religion. We were also united, in that painfully repressed era, by our unrequited longing for girls. I recall walking on the Duke campus with Bob and glimpsing an especially gorgeous coed sauntering by. I said wryly, "Well, Bob, you can't have everything." To which he replied, in despair, "You can't have *anything*!"

When he married, I was his best man. I've never seen anyone in such ghastly throes of prenuptial nervousness. To allay his anguish, I walked him up Fifth Avenue to the Central Park Zoo, where I tried to distract him by showing him the lions and tigers. We were late getting back to St. Patrick's. His bride, Gloria, was frantic. "Where have you been?" she shouted. Bob replied, accurately in fact: "To a cathouse."

With the exception of my first novel, Bob has been the overseer of all the thousands of words I've written for publication at Random House. What a splendid overseer he has been. Bob's reputation has of course preceded him, and people have often asked me what it is that has made him such a great editor. I can't explain the source of his genius—the why of it—but I can briefly describe the mysterious and baffling process whereby his amazing intuition has taken hold and gone to the heart of a problem.

I've learned to dread the tiny, nearly invisible pencil marks Bob will make in the margins of a manuscript. I dread and welcome them. I dread them because, as we go over the text together, they are almost invariably ego-damaging, uncannily catching me out in some little nasty self-indulgence I thought I could get away with. But with Bob you can't get by with these moments of laziness or failure of clarity or self-flattering turgidity; he pounces like a cobra, shakes the wretched phrase or sentence into good sense or meaning, and soon all is well. How sweet-mannered and gentle Bob is—but how ruthless, how uncompromising. That's why the better part of me has learned to welcome those faint little pencil marks: They signal perception and wisdom.

But there is something beyond this devastating technical brilliance that has made Bob Loomis so important to me. It goes beyond the pleasure I take in seeing his happy life with his second wife, Hilary, and his son, Miles. It has to do with the faith and loyalty and the friendship of—I can scarcely believe it, saying these words—half a century. Had it been mere editorial wizardry, that would have been wonderful, but, even so, scarcely enough. What has sustained me for so many years as a writer is the knowledge that possibly the oldest friend I have is always there and, without necessarily speaking the words, patiently urging me on, helping me in spirit to continue striving to be the artist I hope to be.

[*At Random,* no. 17, Spring/Summer 1997.]

Philip Rahv

I first met Philip in the mid-1950s at a dinner party in rural Connecticut, only a few years after my first novel had been published. Mine was a book which, for a first novel, had received considerable acclaim in the popular press; although in terms of what I conceived to be the New York literary establishment—most notably *Partisan Review*—my Southern gothic tragedy may as well have been printed on water. That evening, therefore, I felt myself dining, if not precisely among the enemy, then with a species of intellectual so high-powered and demanding that I could not help but feel intimidated, and a little resentful. I had of course read much of Philip's admirable and brilliant criticism, which made it all the more painful to feel something of a nonentity in his presence. And what a presence it was! There Philip sat across the table, heavy-lidded, glowering, talking in nearly unfathomable polysyllables—not so unfathomable, however, that I might fail to understand that he was cutting some poor incompetent wretch of a writer to shreds. But how devastating and deserved was that demolition job, how pitiless was his judgment upon that star-crossed nincompoop so misguided as to ever have taken pen in hand! I think I shivered a little, and after dinner sidled away. Later, though, when goodbyes were being said, I was dumbstruck when Philip approached me and took my hand, saying in that voice which was such a strange amalgam of fog and frog, "Hope to see you again. I liked your book." And then, as if to endorse this stunning statement, he added with a negligent flap of his arm, "It was a good book." When he was gone, the enormous astonishment lingered, along with an unabashed and immodest satisfaction. Even then, before I knew him, I was powerfully aware that you had passed a crucial muster if, in the eyes of Philip Rahv, you had written "a good book."

In retrospect, I can understand that my initial discomfort in Philip's presence had to do in part with a mistaken prejudice. At a time when the urban Jewish sensibility was coming to the forefront of American literature, and the writing of Southerners was no longer the dominant mode, I shared some of the resentment of my fellow WASPs over what we construed as the self-conscious chauvinism often displayed by the literary establishment. Thus, in an awful momentary lapse, I had confused Philip with somebody like Leslie Fiedler. Certainly, I should have known better—should have known that among the things that characterized Philip's approach to literature were his utter lack of parochialism, his refusal to be bamboozled by trends or fashionable currents, and, most importantly, his ability to appreciate a work in terms of difficult and complex values which he had laid down for himself and which had nothing to do with anything so meretricious as race or region or competing vogues. If one knew this—as I had after college and postcollege years during which *Partisan Review* was required reading—then to have earned the respect of Philip Rahv was exhilarating. I shudder to think what it must have been to experience Philip's disfavor.

Some years later I got to know Philip very well. Strangers often found it hard to understand how one could become a good friend of this brusque, scowling, saturnine, sometimes impolite man with his crotchets and fixations, his occasional savage outbursts and all the other idiosyncrasies he shared with Dr. Johnson. But I found it easy to be Philip's friend. For one thing, I was able almost constantly to relish his rage, which was a well-earned rage inasmuch as he was an erudite person—learned in the broadest sense of the word, with a far-ranging knowledge that transcended the strictly literary—and thus was supremely competent to sniff out fools. I discovered it to be a cleansing rage, this low, guttural roar directed at the frauds and poseurs of literature. He had, besides, an unerring eye for the opportunists in his own critical profession, where he vented his contempt in equal measure on the "trendy"—a word he virtually coined—and those who were merely windy and inadequate, the pretentious academics who might have had a simple-minded taste for novels but lacked utterly the acquaintance with politics, philosophy, and history which was essential to the critical faculty and a civilized perception of things. If any critic had the right to be magisterial, it was Philip Rahv.

But if Philip was angry much of the time, there was beneath it all an affecting and abiding gentleness, a real if biting sense of humor, and throughout, a strange vulnerability. One felt that his arduous grappling with the world of men and ideas had caused him anguish, and that a sense of the disparity between the scrupulous demands of his conscience and vision—whether reflected in literature or life—and the excesses and lunacies of modern society had laid actual hands on him, wrenching him with a discomfort that was nearly intolerable. At the same time, I delighted in his ease and pleasure in preparing good food, in being a host for the men and women he respected and chose to charm. He was often a difficult and prickly soul, at once outgoing yet so secretive as to be almost unknowable. I was proud to be a friend, if only because he was a man who, steadfast to the end, held to those principles and ideas that he felt to be liberating, humane, and—Philip, I can almost see you flinch at the word—eternal.

[Speech delivered at a memorial service, Brandeis University, January 1974.]

Remembering Ralph

I first got to know Ralph Ellison back in the early 1960s, when he and Fanny often came up to Connecticut for weekend visits. We had wonderful, rather liquid evenings. Our Virginia and Alabama by way of Oklahoma origins gave us a common ground of interest, and we talked about Southern matters—such things as bird dogs and cars and whiskey and the native cuisine. This is not to say that we shied away from intellectual or social concerns, far from it, but though the civil rights movement was on the horizon we rarely spoke of race and the racial conflict. Neither, for some reason, did we dwell much on literary things. A mutual reticence, I suppose, kept us from talking about our own novels. Which, as I reflect on it, was a great pity, for I really yearned to have the courage to tell him how passionately I admired *Invisible Man.*

Recently I received a set of the volumes in the new and beautiful Modern Library. I was especially pleased to see that *Invisible Man* was one of the few novels by a contemporary writer included in this collection. *Invisible Man* surely deserves its place among the modern classics. It appeared in 1952, a year after my own first novel was published, and I recall that when I first read it I had none of the envy first novelists have for each other, because I realized I was in the presence of one of those amazing books that one can call *transforming.* A transforming work is one that breaks all the rules and causes you to rearrange your understanding of the world so radically that an important part of you, at least—your conscience or your sensibility, proba-bly both—is never really the same again. *Invisible Man* is, of course, essen-tially about the anguish of being black in America, but countless books have been written about that experience, and while many of these have been ex-cellent only a very few have been transforming. The difference between *Invisible Man* and these others, and what makes it a masterpiece, is that it is a great fable which, though it never loses the particularity of its negritude, is really about the half-madness of the human condition.

Ralph was an artist of the first rank and his artistry is the secret ingredi-ent of the book, really, and the reason why its naked bleakness and manic glee continue so to haunt white people as well as black people and to com-mand our respect and attention. As only a few writers have done—Gogol is one, Mark Twain in *Huckleberry Finn* is another—Ralph, with his musi-cian's sense of tonality, struck the perfect eternal pitch between hilarity and excruciating pain, and the reverberations have been immense and lasting. He will be with us as long as the written word has meaning.

[*Sewanee Review,* January–March 2009.]

C. Vann Woodward

One of my great strokes of luck was to have known Vann Woodward for a very long time. Forty-six years ago—1954, to be exact—Rose and I had a lunch of crab cakes with Vann in Baltimore, where he was teaching at Johns Hopkins, and for me it was love at first sight. Needless to say, I was not alone in my intense admiration. It was not difficult for anyone with normal human responses to fall under the spell of this beguilingly soft-spoken man, who understood so much about so many matters, and imparted his generous wisdom with so little pretense and such good humor. I say *good humor* guardedly; while geniality was certainly his dominant mood, he was not put here on earth to spread sweetness and light, as can be demonstrated by virtually every one of his distinguished works. I always awaited with keen pleasure, when I was with him, the withering diatribes that so accurately skewered their target, usually some wretched and worthless politician who posed a momentary danger to the Republic.

Role model is a term of which I'm not particularly fond but I'll use it anyway. Consider, if you will, Vann's amazing physical self, living to the age of ninety-one with such undiminished energy, the mind capable of turning out powerfully discerning and imaginative books and essays that appeared for well over two decades after most of his contemporaries had vanished into the coffins of their Barcaloungers. Who wouldn't want to emulate a man in whom such a mysterious life force seemed to mock triumphantly all our notions about age and aging? Once, not long ago, I tried to fathom the secret, or secrets, of Vann's tireless vitality so humiliating to those of us in our sixties and seventies. For many summers, Vann came up for brief visits on Martha's Vineyard. He and I always scheduled a single long walk together. A couple of summers ago we slogged along the beach in the hot sun for over an hour. As usual he kept up with my pretty steady pace, and at the end of the hike he was scarcely winded despite his eloquent, nearly nonstop analysis of the odious tactics of Kenneth Starr, whom he called, I remember, "a Christian terrorist," and "a demonstrable moral imbecile." Back at the house, we had noontime drinks and I then plunged into my inquiry.

"Vann," I said, "how do you do it? This vigor."

"Part of it may be this," he replied, indicating his vodka martini.

"No, seriously," I continued, "is it your diet? Are you really careful about what you eat?"

"Not particularly," he said, ". . . a certain amount of animal fat every day."

"Then surely," I persisted, "it's exercise. Do you exercise regularly?"

"Yes," he said, "regularly every summer I take this walk with you."

His fellow historians and his students are better equipped than I am to describe and celebrate Vann's contribution to the study of history and to our culture, a gift which is clearly monumental. As for myself, I could not have written much of my work without Vann Woodward's books as guideposts to my own historical awareness. Although Southerners of different generations, or nearly so, we both grew up in states, Arkansas and Virginia, where segregation was a grinding and sinister reality; both of us were from families in which the ownership of slaves had left the stain of remorse. This shared background provided each of us with a reason to try to divine the origins of an appalling dilemma that burdened the society where we were reared. When I first read *The Strange Career of Jim Crow*, I experienced what some call an epiphany; at last I could discern the provenance of that demented structure of laws which throughout my lifetime had kept a race of people in a virtual replica of bondage. Vann's book was in effect the essential missing link that bound the present to the past. His vision clarified for all time the moral and political breakdown that made a mockery of emancipation and the principle of liberty and justice for all. For one who, like myself, was trying to decipher the conundrum of race and the cruel bequest of slavery, it was a revelation.

Vann's spaciousness of mind—he was, of course, the epitome of the liberated Southerner—allowed him to chastise the citizens of his native region, but he was ever mindful of its sometimes nearly unbearable contradictions. He knew better than almost anyone the power of the traditions that shaped the souls of Southerners, the load of panic, fear, and mistrust that history itself had imposed on Southern minds. Nothing better demonstrated his understanding of this tortured ambiguity than the reflection he made to me soon after he returned from the famous march on Selma in 1965, when he'd joined with other historians to express solidarity with the growing civil rights movement. Toward the end of the procession, the marchers had been set upon by a huge mob of Alabama rednecks, screaming and jeering, their harm and vicious intent forestalled only by the presence of the National Guard. "I was shaken up badly," Vann said. "But you know something? I looked into those raging white trash faces and I saw myself there, if things had gone another way for me. Part of my heart went out to those people."

It was a remark I've never forgotten, and I'm still not sure whether Vann was aware of how those few wrenching words captured the essence of his own tragic and majestic view of the Southern experience.

I'm only sorry that during his last days I failed to visit him more often in the rather dismal place where he lodged. I say this with the deepest regret if only because, if I had done so, I would have been able to pay back Vann in kind for all the attention he paid to me years ago, in New Haven, when I was locked away on a mental ward. Except for Rose, no one visited me more faithfully or often during those many weeks, and I would await his presence eagerly, looking forward to the hour or so when he would sit in my room, chatting in his soft voice about books and politics and the desperate mediocrity of certain public figures and other poignant topics. Vann did most of the talking; indeed, he was forced into a monologue for I was virtually mute, and I'll always recall how his gentle murmurous voice was a growing consolation, reaching out to me through the fog of my madness. There was such reason there, such calm wisdom, such humor, such sanity. And now, reflecting on those therapeutic hours, I think I can understand how his being there may have worked upon me an effect not dissimilar from that which his noble body of work has had upon the world at large. That is, a voice sane and logical, eloquent, balancing despair with hope, bringing order to the madness of history, teaching us how to live at peace with great events.

[This tribute to Woodward was read at the Academy Dinner Meeting, April 4, 2000.]

It Cannot Be Long

Willie Morris left us much too soon. It seems inconceivable to me that now, after our friendship of nearly thirty-five years, I won't be hearing that soft voice calling me from Jackson, Mississippi, on the telephone. For many years he'd addressed me by the name of the narrator of one of my novels. "Stingo," I'd hear him say, "this is Willie. Are you in good spirits?" When I'd tell him I was or wasn't, or was somewhere in between, he'd then ask the next most urgent question. For Willie the creatures in God's scheme of things that ranked right next to people in importance were dogs, and he would ask about my golden retriever and black Lab. "How is Tashmoo? And how is Dinah? Give them all my love." Now that impish and tender voice is gone forever.

In 1965, before I ever met him, Willie extracted from me a long article for the issue of *Harper's* commemorating the end of the Civil War. Shortly after this I first laid eyes on Willie in the office at Yale University of the South's greatest historian, C. Vann Woodward, from whom Willie had also enticed an essay for that issue. That afternoon I drove Willie into New York City and we got so passionately engrossed in conversation, as Southerners often do when they first meet, about places and historical events and ancestral connections—in particular, our stumbling upon the realization that my North Carolina–born great-great-uncle had been state treasurer of Mississippi when Willie's great-great-grandfather was governor—we got so hypnotically involved in such talk that I missed the correct toll booth at the Triborough Bridge and drove far into Long Island before the error dawned.

I can't imagine a more glorious time for writers and journalists than the frenzied last years of the '60s when Willie, a mere kid, was guiding *Harper's Magazine* with such consummate skill and imagination, summoning the finest writing talents in America to describe and interpret an unprecedented scene of social upheaval, with the war in Vietnam and racial strife threatening to blow the country apart. In the pages of his magazine Willie orchestrated these themes—and sub-themes like the sexual revolution—with the wise aplomb of an editorial master, and for several golden years his creation was the preeminent journal in the nation, not only its keenest observer of political and social affairs but its most attractive literary showcase.

I was a night person in those days, and Willie too was nocturnal, and I think it was partly our mutual restlessness—two excited Southern nightowls on the prowl in the Big Cave, as he called New York City—that cemented our friendship. We also spent countless evenings together in one or another of our homes in the country north of the city. Needless to say, we shared a great deal of strong drink, which helped us know each other better. What I came to know about Willie, among other things, was that an innate and profound Southernness was the energizing force in his life and what made him tick. Not that he was a professional Southerner—he despised the obvious Dixieland clichés—and he got along well with Yankees; he had a richly and often humorously symbiotic relationship with New York Jewish intellectuals, many of whom admired him as much as he did them. It was just that he felt more at home with Southerners, with whom he could share tall tales and indigenous jokes and family anecdotes and hilarious yarns that only the South can provide, and that perhaps only expatriate Southerners can enjoy in their cloying and sometimes desperate homesickness. Even then I had very little doubt that someday Willie would return home to Mississippi.

As I got to know Willie and became a close and devoted friend, I learned certain immutable things about him. I learned that he was unshakably loyal, that he was amazingly punctual about birthdays and commemorations and anniversaries of all sorts, that he drank past healthy limits and that booze sometimes made him maudlin but never mean, that he was wickedly funny, that his country-boy openheartedness and candor masked an encyclopedic knowledge and an elegantly furnished mind, that he was moody and had a streak of dark paranoia that usually evaporated on a comic note, that he was an inveterate trickster and anecdotalist of practical jokes, that his furiously driven literary imagination allowed him to produce several unostentatious masterworks; that in him, finally, there was an essential nobility of spirit—no one ever possessed such a ready and ungrudging heart.

One of Willie's obsessions, aside from dogs, was graveyards. We went to many a burial ground together, from Appomattox to Shiloh. Once, on one of the many visits to Mississippi, he drove me out to a country cemetery some miles from Oxford. We had a few drinks and after a while he took me for a stroll among the headstones. Then, lo and behold, we spied an open book, a novel, propped against a grave marker. It took me a minute to realize that Willie had planted there my first novel, open to its epigraph from Sir Thomas Browne:

> And since death must be the *Lucina* of life . . . since the brother of death daily haunts us with dying mementos . . . since our longest sun sets at right descencions, and makes but winter arches, and therefore it cannot be long before we lie down in darkness and have our light in ashes. . . .

He was obviously delighted at my surprise. For Willie, a son of the South and from the town of Yazoo, death was as fitting, in its place and season, as life—the life in which he achieved so much and gained such glory.

[*Oxford American,* September/October 1999. The title is an allusion to St. Augustine, *Confessions*, 11.15.20—a meditation on the brevity of our memories of the departed.]

My Neighbor Arthur

Americans, including writers and artists, are supposed to be compulsively sociable, but I lived for six years as a close neighbor of Arthur Miller's in Roxbury—a rural village then populated with but six hundred souls—before we ever laid eyes on each other. Even then we met in, of all places, the lobby of the Hotel Vier Jahreszeiten in Munich, where we had converged on separate literary missions. Arthur was aware, as I was, of the oddness of our not having met, for in Munich his first words to me were those which Stanley might have wished he had actually used upon encountering Livingstone, i.e., "At Last!" This was in 1961, a short while after he had married Inge Morath, who was accompanying him and who helped make our brief sojourn in Bavaria such a pleasure. Like Eckermann on his first visit to Goethe,* I think I was prepared to find something about Arthur that was fairly Olympian. I am regrettably susceptible to unsubstantiated opinion, and in New York several years before this an academic gentleman of forlorn mien told me, after I said I was an unfulfilled neighbor of Arthur's, that when I finally met him I would be encountering a man of "sadness and incredible dignity, like Abraham Lincoln."

This asinine impression derived more, of course, from the general grav-

---

* Johann Peter Eckermann (1792–1854), best known for his *Conversations with Goethe*, published between 1836 and 1848.—J.W.

ity of the Miller oeuvre than from the man. Arthur, I discovered, has as much dignity as the next person but the primary characteristic he shares with Lincoln is that of great height; as for sadness, Arthur manages to conceal his with deftness. The salient feature of Arthur's personality is, as a matter of fact, humor, and his comedic gift is the quality that makes him such buoyant company.

It is a sense of humor born out of the memory of neediness and hard times, and is one that haunts his otherwise intense and rather somber view of life. In the past thirty years I've spent many hours listening to Arthur, at each other's houses in Connecticut or on certain peculiarly conceived trips that have taken us to the globe's far corners—Chile, for example, or Egypt. When I remember Arthur settling back in a deck chair on a luxurious boat cruising the Nile—exclaiming expansively, "What is it that the working class is complaining about?"—I realize that the laughter induced in me by the mock-plutocratic tone has an ambiguous quality owing to my knowledge of his working-class experience and allegiance. Likewise, an exquisitely American perception of the dynamics of class and power overlaid his response to the colossal Pharonic effigies sculpted into the cliffs of Abu-Simbel. They were created, Arthur observed, in precisely the same spirit as that which caused to be erected the various facades of the National City Bank Building and bore the identical intimidating message for their beholders: "We're in charge here. Keep the hell out." Traveling with Arthur as I have over so many thousands of terrestrial miles has not been like traveling with your run-of-the-mill CEO, say, or a politician. His curiosity is unquenchable, his ability to make associative connections is formidable, and it is all held in equipoise by a marvelous sense of the absurd. However, his pleasure in travel seems provisional. One feels his longing to get back to the Connecticut countryside and to his fine but sensibly proportioned house, where he can look at the woods and fields which he has been looking at serenely for over forty years.

Critics have adduced many subtle reasons (and will continue their analyses for generations) to explain Arthur's mastery as a dramatist, but few are likely to come up with the crucially simple truth that he is a consummate storyteller. Having watched him on numerous occasions, clad in his gentleman farmer's rumpledness, sidling into my crowded living room, I have etched on my mind his expression of richly amused dejection, that of a man experiencing both pleasure and anguish, one deathly afraid of bores and of being bored yet warily hopeful for that blessed moment of communion that sometimes happens. And after a while it usually does happen. Arthur has found an audience—or, more significantly, they have found him, which is the rarest tribute of all since only a great storyteller can exert such magnetism without a trace of self-devotion. As the yarn unwinds, Arthur's eyes sparkle and his voice becomes sly, conspiratorial, reflective, studded with small abrupt astonishments, the denouement craftily dangled and delayed: he is also an actor of intuitive panache. Is it a performance? Perhaps. But whatever it is unfolds with eloquence, and his listeners are lost in it, and it is then that I am able to perceive, simultaneously, the inspired vision of the playwright and the energizing charm of the man.

[From *Arthur Miller and Company,* ed. Christopher Bigsby. Methuen, 1990.]

Big Jim

One of the most beautiful tributes ever made by one writer to another was the one that Jim Dickey wrote upon the death of Truman Capote.[1] It could only have been written by a man who, like Jim, knew firsthand of the hard work, the anguish, but also of the final exaltation of the artist's calling. I wish I had the time, and also the gift, to be able to pay such homage to my friend Jim, but I hope these few hasty words will in some way express my admiration for the poet who was the laureate of his generation. I come from the same generation—the generation of World War II—and Jim and I were both born in the South; our Southern upbringing in the years of the Great Depression and our experience in uniform during the war helped weld our companionship.

Jim was Southern to his fingertips but he was of that category, richly endowed with humanity and learning, that always confounds Northerners. Willie Morris is fond of telling the story of a taxi ride he made, with Jim and another Southerner, from LaGuardia Airport into Manhattan. The taxi was driven by a beetlebrowed type who thought the Dixie accents from the backseat gave him the license to erupt in a tirade against black people. For a long while the three riders listened to this racist diatribe, until at last Jim, exasperated beyond endurance, leaned forward and said: "Shut up! We don't need advice from an amateur bigot."

What Jim had seen and suffered during the war was, like his Southernness, a determining element in much of what he wrote, and I began to understand this part of him back in the early 1970s, when he lived near me for part of a summer on Martha's Vineyard. It was the summer just before the release of that very fine movie *Deliverance,* and Jim was on a perpetual high, quite aware that he was on the verge of a rare happening, that of an author of an exceptional novel seeing an exceptional movie made of it. As everyone in the world knows, Jim loved the bottle—and so did I in those days—and we would hit the tennis court at ten in the morning, falsely emboldened by (I shudder at the recollection) a pitcher of dry martinis. After these disastrous games we'd sit on my front porch, and it was there that he told me something about his life in the Air Force. He spoke of fear, and of the exquisite fragility and vulnerability of the men who flew those planes, and as he told me of those things I began to see how *Deliverance,* which I had so admired as a novel, was in a sense an allegory of fear and survival: of innocent and well-meaning men, set upon by forces of inexplicable evil, who nonetheless come through by the skin of their teeth. An awareness of life's sweetness, which we cling to despite preposterous hazards, is at the heart of Jim's writing.

Jim was rambunctiously and vigorously alive to a degree I've rarely known in anyone. His energy carried over into his prose and, perhaps most significantly, into the best of his poetry, which will surely live as long as that of any poet of his time. His personal excesses and abuses upon himself were the result of journeying to dark places that others have shunned, and having the need to find the solace of oblivion. What one must remember about James Dickey are his words, words that will forever sing:

> My green, graceful bones fill the air
> With sleeping birds. Alone, alone
> And with them I move gently.
> I move at the heart of the world.

[Tribute read at a memorial service for Dickey at the University of South Carolina, February 14, 1997. Previously unpublished.]

The Contumacious Mr. Roth

In the interest of full disclosure I want to say that I have long been a friend of Philip Roth's. Therefore it may seem odd to you that I accepted being not only today's speaker but also the chairmanship of the selection committee, and that I did not recuse myself (I think that's the term) from a situation in which there was an obvious conflict of interest. But I figured, what the hell, if the Supreme Court, from which we are supposed to draw many of our moral examples, could so flagrantly and so often demonstrate partiality to the point of actually electing a president, why shouldn't I merely indulge myself in some high-powered literary logrolling and get my old pal a nice medal? So I had no hesitation in agreeing to the chairmanship, determined to muscle my way into a position of force that would brook no opposition to the choice of Philip Roth. Fortunately, my task became sublimely simple. While the committee members did put forth other names—and there were some immensely worthy names, I might add—the presence of Philip Roth so truly dominated our gathering that he became a shoo-in. Thus, whatever guilt I anticipated over being a shameless, even ruthless, partisan was mercifully allayed.

I've been closely connected with the present recipient of the MacDowell Medal since a year far back in the 1950s when my wife, Rose, served as midwife to one of Philip Roth's firstborn literary offspring. *The Paris Review*, which I had helped found, had been in existence for only four or five years, and Rose had signed on as an editorial assistant, which meant that she worked pro bono as manuscript reader. This was an especially thankless job since the magazine had yet to achieve the lofty reputation it now has and the submissions, mainly short stories, were accordingly of fairly humble quality. Rose and I were living then in a cottage in Connecticut. While she felt that she was laboring in a noble cause, her exposure to so many works of feeble inspiration and haphazard syntax left her pretty enervated. Few literary agents had learned of the *Review*'s existence, so most of the entries arrived "over the transom," as they said in those days, unsolicited. I can still remember the sighs of delight, modulating almost into wonder, that came from Rose as she finished an entry from a writer named Philip Roth. Here finally was the genuine article, a story with bite and originality, zestfully written, obviously from someone young, but marked by the confident authority of a guy who knew exactly what he wanted to say and how to say it.

In his autobiographical writings, Philip has said of his undergraduate stories that he had "managed to extract from Salinger a very cloying come-on and from the young Capote his gossamer vulnerability, and to imitate badly my titan, Thomas Wolfe, at the extremes of self-pitying self-importance." What was evident from this story, called "Epstein," written a scant few years after his days at Bucknell University, was that its author had immediately rid himself of all vestiges of self-pity or self-importance and composed a first-rate narrative marked with the poise of early maturity. The story was eagerly accepted by the *Paris Review*'s editor, George Plimpton; he soon published other Roth stories which were included in the collection *Goodbye, Columbus*, an exciting volume that appeared when the author was only twenty-six and made him, like Byron, famous overnight. I first met Philip in 1960, in Rome, just as his fame was cresting. We had only known each other for a short time when he got word that *Goodbye, Columbus* had won the National Book Award. He was obviously pleased, though a little flabbergasted, and flew back to New York to receive the prize. Later on, when he returned, and we sat up late in trattorias, talking about books and American politics (it was the last gasp of the Eisenhower days) and other matters, I could sense through what he said that his pleasure over the success of *Goodbye, Columbus* was not unalloyed; there were responses to the work that bothered him, though I couldn't tell at the time how truly bothered he was.

But I'll come back to this. The young fellow I knew in Rome was marvelous company. The Jewish comic strain that imbued the tales in *Goodbye, Columbus* with their essential flavor was part of Philip's appeal. We had rollicking Roman dinners and other mildly manic get-togethers. On the spur of the moment we flew off to the British Isles, Rose and me, Philip and his then wife Maggie, in an escapade which might have ended in disaster—so soggy was the weather in London and Dublin and so dismal, after Italy, was the food in both places—had we not been buoyed by a kind of insouciant determination to enjoy ourselves and by Philip's running commentary on the prevailing horrors, a take that was hilariously scathing and cathartic. During our travels together we inevitably exchanged details about our respective and profoundly disparate upbringings—mine in Tidewater Virginia, his in New Jersey—and I began to see how the all-Jewish world of Philip's Newark neighborhood and Weequahic High School so decisively formed the spirit and marrow of the creatures inhabiting *Goodbye, Columbus*. In a later memoir touching on this period he wrote: "Discussions about Jewishness and being Jewish, which I was to hear so often among intellectual Jews once I was an adult in Chicago and New York, were altogether unknown; we talked about being misunderstood by our families, about movies and radio programs and sex and sports. . . . About being Jewish there was nothing more to say than there was about having two arms and two legs. It would have seemed to us strange *not* to be Jewish—stranger still, to hear someone announce that he wished he weren't a Jew or that he intended not to be in the future."

Everyone by now knows of the hazards of being a writer of fiction in a multicultural society. As I found out years ago, to attempt to interpret the experience of an ethnic group other than one's own, grounded in the notion that a common humanity gives out the license to do so, is like walking into a minefield. But Philip's ugly awakening came from a crueler irony: even writing about one's own group can elicit rage, if the truths one tells cut too close to the bone. During a symposium at Yeshiva University not too long after the appearance of *Goodbye, Columbus*, Philip was asked: "Mr. Roth, would you write the same stories you've written if you were living in Nazi Germany?" Philip goes on to say: "Thirty minutes later, I was still being grilled. No response I gave was satisfactory and, when the audience was allowed to take up the challenge, I realized that I was not just opposed but hated. I've never forgotten my addled reaction: an undertow of bodily fatigue took hold and began sweeping me away from that auditorium even as I tried to reply coherently to one denunciation after another. . . . I had actually to suppress a desire to close my eyes and, in my chair at the panelists' table . . . drift into unconsciousness." Later at a restaurant, still infuriated, he says to his companions, over a pastrami sandwich no less: "I'll never write about Jews again." Well, fat chance.

Over the years Philip and I have been drawn together by various mutual concerns but never have I felt so sympathetic, never did my heart beat with such a sense of brotherly accord, as during those times in the past when he was warding off assaults from crazed and vindictive rabbis. Or from Hadassah matrons bent on redeeming places like Asbury Park from Philip's brand of moral pollution. By the late 1960s there had appeared—or I should say, exploded—*Portnoy's Complaint*, which was all about Jews, and not just Jews but mainly one young Jew, the Assistant Human Opportunity Commissioner of New York City and, more specifically, his lascivious juxtaposition with any number of randy girlfriends, particularly a West Virginia shiksa, known as The Monkey. All in all a breakthrough novel, feverish, a sensation, a wildly scabrous book which once and for all established a norm of sexual candor from which there could be no turning back. If nothing else, *Portnoy* made life forever safe for masturbation. *Portnoy* did not, however, escape the pursuit of self-appointed watchdogs and pecksniffs, a large portion of them Jewish, who were bent upon inflicting vengeance for its author's inexcusable slander. Philip and I had become rural Connecticut neighbors by then. I had been through my own crucible, having published a novel dealing with American slavery which was quite successful in many ways but which incurred the wrath of numerous black intellectuals who pounced upon me with the same *ad hominem* fury that Philip had experienced with rabbis.

Like Philip, who should have stayed away, I foolishly allowed myself to be grilled in public: in my case the foe were seething black inquisitors who caused me to realize, like Philip, that I was not just opposed but hated. I too had felt the need to close my eyes and drift into unconsciousness. The experience we both shared had helped anneal our already strong friendship. And in Philip's case I have the feeling that such brainless enmity may have had the salubrious effect of making him increasingly alert to some of the more insidious threats looming on the national horizon. We had little inkling, during the anarchic, freedom-loving last years of the 1960s, when a book like *Portnoy's Complaint* happily flourished, of a not-so-far-off time when the equality and dignity so justly sought by disenfranchised groups would be provisionally achieved, or at least enormously ameliorated, only to be confounded by dogma and fanaticism. This poisonous new conformism would be most immediately apparent on college campuses, but in government too, and in subtle ways it would permeate society. It would also become one of Philip's preoccupations, in his later work, as he both soberly and gleefully exposed the raw face of Jewish bigotry, black bigotry, Arab bigotry, feminist bigotry, left-wing bigotry, right-wing bigotry, and all the other large and small tyrannies that bedevil us and lessen us as a people.

In one of his memoirs Philip has his alter ego, Nathan Zuckerman, speak to him, Philip, as follows: "If there's one thing that can put the kibosh on a literary career, it's the loving forgiveness of one's natural enemies." He then goes on to say: "The whole point about your fiction (and in America, not only yours) is that the imagination is always in transit between the good boy *and* the bad boy—that's the tension that leads to revelation" (*The Facts,* p. 167). Here in brief, Zuckerman gets to the core of much of the magnetic appeal of Philip's books, reminding us that the cute high school lad portrayed in his 1950 yearbook (described as "a boy of real intelligence, combined with wit and common sense") has come a long way on that journey in which, seeking to find his Americanness, seeking it with an urgency only possible in the grandson of Yiddish-speaking immigrants, he found it, and with it found both a lot of good and a great deal of wickedness. Because he couldn't take his Americanness for granted—as say, a Virginia-born WASP might do—there has been a hard-won quality in Philip's work, which has added depth to his achievement. Like that of nearly all good authors one should care about, Philip's writing has powerful elements of the transgressive, the shocking, the contumacious; he wants to root out evil wherever he can find it, but since the good boy and the bad boy are in perpetual conflict, and there is a constant quarrel going on, and mistrust and doubt, the result— as in such superb recent novels as *American Pastoral* and *The Human Stain*—is a kind of majestic equipoise. Here the wreckage of the American dream, its sad miscalculations and fatal errors—sometimes viciously initiated but as often the product of decent people smothered by circumstance— is fully glimpsed by an artist of rare tragic vision.

Throughout his career Philip has worked with the focused energy of the committed writer, turning out a shimmering body of work. It's been an often exhilarating experience to have come to know him as well as I do, to be a good friend and neighbor, and to be able to enjoy as frequently as I have the company of one so mercurially alive, whether in a somber mood or explosively, peerlessly funny. Like his alternate persona, the descriptively named writer E. I. Lonoff, Philip has labored away without stint in the Connecticut woods, isolated, converting the vicissitudes of a seemingly uneventful existence into imaginative edifices rich with fully limned characters acting out their compelling dramas, written in what can only be called the Rothian style, exclusively his own, and resolutely, though unaffectedly, nonpostmodern.

There has of course been some domestic turbulence, caustically described. It has also been a life not unhaunted by the darkest of shadows, and these too have been transformed into powerful elements of this fiction. Occasionally, a life-threatening event has paralleled my own and further drawn us together. In the early 1990s Philip was besieged by a monstrous black cloud bank of clinical depression, one which, though fueled by some vile medication, was doubtless chiefly the result of that mysterious constellation of causes that even now, universally, makes the treatment and understanding of this terrifying illness so problematical. Anxiety-ridden, racked by dreams of self-destruction, and in excruciating pain, Philip finally put himself behind institutional walls where he eventually recovered as, thankfully, most people do. His ultimate triumph, however (or perhaps revenge), was that of the resourceful artist. This was an exquisitely detailed and harrowing account of his own ordeal that takes place at the beginning of *Operation Shylock;* it is one of the clearest portraits of clinical depression to be found in fiction.

That we are near the end of an era, that the novel is moribund or irrelevant, that writing itself is in peril, that the creation of fiction is a marginal occupation, that literature is due to be vaporized in a cosmic swarm of delights—these reports keep up their tedious buzz. Not too long ago I heard Philip himself utter a chillingly bleak pronouncement about the future of the Word, and I thought: well, maybe he's got a point. Later, though, I had second thoughts, and backtracked in the realization that I may be far more of an optimist than I care to admit. My provisional cheer is based largely on a subjective view of imaginative writing but I think it might be shared by some of you today who truly value reading and the immeasurable rewards of great fiction. Of course we prize the novel for many good reasons: for the special authority of the writer's voice; for its style, whether low-keyed or rambunctious or seductively lyrical; for its philosophical challenge or subtlety; for its uncanny rendition of a sense of place; for the authenticity of its dialogue—the list goes on; usually our pleasure comes from an amalgam of all these things. But one feature of great fiction seems to me so central, so essential that it reduces all the others to secondary roles. I'm thinking of the astounding invention of human beings. That a mob of vital creatures could spring from the synapses of the brain of a sleepless, overcaffeinated Balzac strikes me as one of the great and beautiful mysteries. Ever since the beginning of the novel we have embraced with passion these flesh-and-blood offspring of their creators' fantasies, reacting to the most memorable among them with the same relish and admiration, disappointment and suspicion, perplexity and chagrin—and ultimate awe—that we feel for grand historical figures. These people ("characters" if you will) have also been essential in establishing our own identity as members of the human race. Whether commonplace or noble, shady or godly, princes or putzes, whether they are named Emma Bovary or Raskolnikov, Huck Finn or Jay Gatsby, Molly Bloom or Rabbit Angstrom, they have made claims on our allegiance, and even our capacity for love, which we would honor only a touch less readily than those of cherished family members. Why great fiction will never die, I feel certain, is because the inhabitants of fiction's pages—and often sublime figments we've come to know as Dilsey and Ahab and Sancho Panza—are profoundly mortal even in their immortality; they are perishable just as we are perishable. We shall ever refuse even to think of consigning these creatures, and the books in which they dwell, to oblivion. To do so would be to signal our own deaths.

Philip Roth in his long and productive career has written book after book in which his scrupulous artistry has allowed us a unique vision of the times—the nearly half century—we've lived in. He has been one of the most penetrating witnesses to the flagrant disasters and precious conquests of our boisterous era. He has conveyed his vision in ever-shifting modes of hectic comedy and somber tragedy, delighting countless readers even as he mercilessly rattled their bones, and they've deserved both. But at last, more importantly, he has caused to be lodged in our collective consciousness a small, select company of human beings who are as arrestingly alive and as fully realized as any in modern fiction. Among their names are Swede Levov and his daughter Merry, Coleman Silk, Brenda Patimkin, Eli the Fanatic. And still there are more: a special group named Peter Tarnopol, David Kepesh, Alexander Portnoy, and Nathan Zuckerman. It is the author's triumph that he has placed these figures firmly among the world's fictional immortals, and this despite our knowledge that they are merely models of their creator's greatest character, Philip Roth.

[Read by Styron at the Awards Ceremony, MacDowell Colony, Peterborough, New Hampshire, August 19, 2001.]

Crusades,
Complaints, Gripes

If You Write for Television . . .

SIRS:

As one who has felt the hand of television upon his own work, I would like to endorse Frank R. Pierson's lucid analysis of television censorship.[1]

Last fall CBS bought my short novel *The Long March* for production on *Playhouse 90*. Somewhat like the draftee protagonist of Robert Dozier's *A Real Fine Cutting Edge**—a "daring" work, perhaps, but one which, as Mr. Pierson ruefully points out, was finally broadcast only because the network censor mistakenly believed that it *had* the approval of the Army—my story's hero is also a rebellious soul, a young Marine reserve officer whose mutinous rage against authority in general, and his commanding officer in particular, leads to his own downfall. Unlike the hero of *Cutting Edge,* however, my captain loses. He resists the System and it is his ruin. You cannot buck the System—I think that is what I was trying to say, for if you do you will pull disaster down upon your head. . . . At the end of my story the captain (who is not without his foolish, impulsive moments), having faced down his commanding officer at the conclusion of a senseless and brutal hike ordered by the same CO, stands ready to receive a court-martial. The tragedy is implicit here. At the same time, however, the commanding officer is treated with

---

* Dozier's drama was presented on *The Kaiser Aluminum Hour,* January 15, 1957. The cast included George Peppard, Jack Warden, and Dick York.—J.W.

sympathy and, all things considered, the Marine Corps gets off probably with more grace than it deserves. You might think that even Procter & Gamble and the manufacturers of Prestone (this was October, remember, and anti-freeze was getting the hard sell), would have been satisfied with some honest and straightforward treatment of this story, which attempts to demonstrate the truth known perhaps, far down, even to Union Carbide vice presidents: that military life corrupts and we would be a lot better off without it.

But how naïve. I shall leave out the esthetic side of the televised version—the script, the acting, the direction—which was catastrophically bad even for television (my grocer, who ordinarily admits to watching everything, turned the program off mid-way and asked me indignantly the next day if I was planning to sue). Just as importantly, or even more so, the show simply suggested that Mr. Pierson knows what he is talking about when he maintains that television is "in fact officially censored and colored to show authority in a favorable light." Because the script was submitted to the Marine Corps. Naturally, it had to be, not only because, as Mr. Pierson points out, all scripts that touch on government matters are submitted to authority but also because the story calls for masses of marching men, which the brass—after approving the script with what I suppose amounted to some glee—handily provided. One can imagine what was left of my hero after this collusion of Public Information Office second lieutenants, ad men, and soap peddlers had done with him. My bedeviled, desperate captain had become a self-pitying zero who, far from eliciting the viewer's sympathies, really deserved all the punishment that the Marine Corps could heap upon him. Further, rather than end the show upon the same note that my story ended (a very simple note of defeat, really, with the captain in ruin and promised a court-martial), the powers that arranged the TV version saw fit to stage an actual military trial in which it was safely pointed out that the Marine Corps is still pretty much tops any way you look at it.

I understand that in making these comments I am in that position known to anyone who has trafficked with TV or Hollywood, which is somewhat like that of a woman who cries rape when in fact she acquiesced freely and received good money for the undertaking. In reality, however, my heart was *not* greatly troubled by this travesty of my work; a book remains a book. Also several thousand dollars remain several thousand dollars. But one or two disturbing questions haunted my mind, and Mr. Pierson's article sheds considerable light upon the mystery of why it is that any attempt to grapple on TV with problems dealing with the military is doomed to failure from the start.

My most bothersome question, of course, was the ancient one: why did they do it at all? *The Long March* is not (unfortunately) a celebrated work, bound to attract millions of viewers by its very name. Divorced of its philosophical content, the narrative becomes utterly routine, so routine indeed that it is difficult to see why, instead of "adapting" my story, the producer did not just hire some accomplished hack to compose a nice slick original script glorifying the Marine Corps. The producer himself is an intelligent, decent, well-intentioned man, with many worthwhile things in television to his credit; honestly caring for my story as much as he did, it is difficult to believe that it was any such simple matter as a final lapse of taste on his part which caused the disaster. (Actually I must confess that I was so dazzled by his sincerity and good intentions that, reading the script just prior to the broadcast—cold with horror, yet still somehow unable to believe that what I beheld on the printed page could be transmitted in all of its sordidness to the tiny screen—I wired the producer a demented, "Well done.")

But then who or what was the real culprit? The sponsors? The network watchdogs? Military censors? A combination of these? I do not know. Nor do I know whether the downright badness of the script with its military yea-saying made approval by authority a foregone conclusion; nor whether a perfectly adequate script became perverted as it went through the labyrinths of sponsor approval and then through the Pentagon mill: either way, what happened to the story in its transformation from an artistic insight to a shoddy lie makes me realize that Mr. Pierson's concern with TV censorship is rather more than academic and that in the instance of *The Long March* something more dangerous was in operation than a mere failure of talent. Someone somewhere along the line messed it up because someone was afraid. . . . In the end the real culprit in television is not *just* sponsor approval or official censorship but an ignorant fear of the truth which permeates all other aspects of our society too, and which poisons art at its roots. It is almost as ignoble a censorship as censorship itself.

[*New Republic,* April 6, 1959.]

Fie on Bliss

My good friend and fellow writer John Marquand, son of the eminent novelist, retains a blinding image of his childhood and of Christmas. This is the memory of his father, groaning with rage and his face flushed to an alarming crimson, bearing the family Christmas tree—still loaded with its pretty ornaments—to the front door and hurling it out into the snows of Boston. The younger Marquand tells me that he can no longer remember his father's words as he committed this ritual murder. John Jr. was a tiny child at the time and was transfixed with horror at the sight. He only recalls the look of triumph on his father's face.

The elder Marquand has been a cultural hero to me ever since I heard this reminiscence. Oh how I have longed to do the same to our yule tree, Christmas after Christmas, but have been prevented by cowardice from achieving such a satisfying catharsis. For the fact is that although I loathe Christmas to the nethermost part of me I have never been brave enough either to perform such a soul-satisfying act or to do something even more obvious—and that is simply to get out of there, split, leave home, take flight, abandon Christmas once and for all.

One more true anecdote will illustrate this latter impulse. Another cherished friend of mine—a distinguished professor of literature, a man of spaciously humane instincts—was faced some fifteen years ago with his first

Christmas as a married man. Like me, he had suffered an ever-deepening disenchantment with Christmas as he had grown older but resolved that year to put on a happy face, so to speak, if only to indulge his bride. A person of substantial independent means, he had bought her a bewitching, recklessly expensive watercolor by Paul Klee, and on Christmas Eve he had set it under the tree in a place that would stun her eye. His young wife in turn had bought him a beautifully groomed French poodle, with which she joyously burst in upon him that same night. He admired the poodle, she swooned at the Klee. While they were embracing, giddy with the spirit of the moment, the poodle pranced across the room to the tree and urinated torrentially over the Klee, virtually emulsifying the painting before their horrified gaze. The marriage, however, survived. My friend did not kill the dog. He remembers exclaiming: "All right, that's it! NO MORE CHRISTMAS!" By which he meant that the poodle's act had effectively wiped out Christmas from their lives. He resolved, with his wife's acquiescence, never to celebrate Christmas again. And so each year since then during the holiday season they have stolen away to hideaways devoid of wreaths, tinsel, snow—places like Antigua, Mexico, Curaçao. I might add that their offspring, a charming lad in excellent mental health, clearly has never minded this sort of Christmas a bit.

A comfortable bank account, you might argue, permits my professor friend his easy escape—an escape which is blessed, or a craven cop-out, depending upon your point of view. But what of those of us who have chosen to man the fort? What of a trapped Christmas-hater like myself, one who through inertia or a sense of tradition or weak-minded familial loyalty allows himself year in and year out to be engulfed by the Yuletide nightmare? What masochism in me lets this dreadful season annually perform its ruinous handiwork on my spirit when perhaps with only a little connivance, a touch of ingenuity, or the manly exercise of my self-respect, I too might escape? Are both my loathing of the holiday and the supine way in which I allow it to overwhelm me the signs of an illness which might be called the "Christmas psychosis"? The terrible thing is that the mood haunts me at certain times *all year long,* not only in December, when naturally the feeling is at its darkest, but even in the summer. More than once, sunning myself peaceably on a beach in July, I have happened upon an odious little notice in a magazine advertising bargain prices for early mail orders of Christmas cards, and have suddenly felt my skin crawl and sensed the summer sky darkening and my soul filling up with despair.

Or there have been other ghastly harbingers. The sight of those Christmas tree lights in late October, strung up with indecent haste even before the Halloween pumpkins have vanished, casts over me the funereal gloom of certain lines from Emily Dickinson. I dread the coming of Christmas just as I dread the stygian nights and brief days of that solstice season itself, with its sense of things passing away. Those twinkling lights and brave little candles avail nothing against the cosmic darkness. Even booze, I know, will produce no ease, will fail as an anodyne.

I have searched my innermost depths for an answer to the reason for my phobia, but to no avail. Perhaps the closest to an answer I have is buried between the lines of the following fragmentary transcript of a tape recording—made covertly last Christmas Eve by my teenage son—of a colloquy between myself and my wife, who here is in the process of wrapping presents. She is a good and generous person for whom Christmas provides great draughts of mysterious, uncomplicated bliss.

SHE: Don't make me cry. I thought we were going to get through it this year without my crying.

HE: I thought so too. But I'm getting this feeling that I can't stand it. It's stealing over me, that awful creepy feeling.

SHE: *Please,* you've been so good up until now. I haven't cried since last Christmas. Don't make me cry now.

HE: I've tried. But the feeling—it's getting at me. [*Pauses.*] There are all the boxes again.

SHE: What boxes?

HE [*voice rising*]: What do you mean, *what boxes*? There are all these *boxes,* all over the house! By actual count I've counted *one hundred and twelve boxes*! They're everywhere! They're all over our *bed*! I can't *sleep* in that bed!

SHE: I asked you tonight to sleep in the attic, don't you remember—

HE [*furiously*]: I won't be cast out of my own bed, do you hear—

SHE: Don't raise your voice so! *Please!* Why oh *why* do you hate Christmas like this?

HE: Because of the boxes! These presents! The materialism of it all, that's why! The *materialism*! I can't stand the commercialized orgy of Christmas, the gross, sordid materialism! You and your wretched *catalogues*! Ever since Thanksgiving! Saks, Altman's, F. A. O. Schwarz—

S H E [*voice rising*]: It's practically *all* for the *children*! And don't talk about materialism! What about *your* materialism? The Mercedes you bought in October, that thermostatically controlled wine vault, the depth finder for the boat—and you've got *three* digital watches for Christ's sake! At least Christmas isn't *that* kind of materialism! It's for the *children*! Oh, I'm going to cry—

H E [*voice edged with rage and despair*]: Speaking of Christ, our Lord and Savior whose birth we celebrate this day, wouldn't He go absolutely crackers, sweet buddy, over this display of useless material *things*—one hundred and twelve boxes, F. A. O. Schwarz crud and junk, all over the goddamned bed—He who preached moderation, poverty, simplicity—

S H E [*her voice a wail*]: And giving! Preached that! *Giving!* Something you've *forgotten*! Oh, you insufferable, sanctimonious ass! You—You—well-poisoner! You detestable—You—Oh! Oh! [*She bursts into tears.*]

So much for one Christmas Eve. I have a troubled suspicion that this year, in a somewhat modified version, the dialogue will be repeated. Yet there is a more tranquil ending than the foregoing embroilment might suggest. For if Christmases past are any indication of the one impending, our hero—chastened as always by his wife's tears—will wobble quietly to bed. He will sleep in the attic, far away and high over the morning pandemonium, until past noon, when he will make his way downstairs and into the benign chaos of 112 eviscerated boxes. His children, who were briefly awakened by that unseemly squabble, will glare at their father with mean reproach and perhaps a touch of pity, but soon he will allow his rumpled and sourly hungover presence to become absorbed into the day's manic joy. His wife will be amazingly fresh-faced and forgiving. He will be showered with thanks for presents he did not know he was the bestower of, and his ogreish heart will start to glow.

There will be a few friends in to share a fine Christmas dinner at some lackadaisical hour. Toward twilight he will finally open his own many gifts, several of which will give him a secret thrill of pleasure. With languid limbs he will settle back, letting most of his rancor flow away from his mind and— like some fumbling, sluggish Abraham—he will gather his sleepy children to his bosom. From a far source a tenor voice—year in and year out so familiar, so freighted with prophecy and hope—will be heard singing: "Comfort ye, my people . . ." He will at last lift a glass and toast the Season. He will not say: "God bless us everyone!" For he has not sold out to the dark forces of Christmas. But he will be free to admit to himself that he is most mysteriously touched with contentment. And grace. There will be other Christmases to hate.

[*Potomac*, December 19, 1976.]

The Habit

The lamentable history of the cigarette is that of a mortally corrupting addiction having been embraced by millions of people in the spirit of childlike innocence. It is a history which is also strikingly brief. Cigarettes began to be manufactured extensively around the turn of the century, but it was not until as recently as 1921 that cigarettes overtook chewing tobacco, as well as pipes and cigars, in per capita consumption, and the 1930s were well along before cigarette smoking became the accepted thing for ladies.

The popularity of cigarettes was inevitable and overwhelming. They were not offensive in close quarters, nor messy like pipes and cigars. They were easily portable. They did not look gross and unseemly in a lady's mouth. They were cheap to manufacture, and they were inhalable. Unlike the great majority of pipe and cigar smokers, whose pleasure is predominantly oral and contemplative, most cigarette smokers inhale deep into their lungs with bladelike, rhythmic savagery, inflicting upon themselves in miniature a particularly abrasive form of air pollution. Further, the very fact of inhalation seems to enhance the cigarette's addictive power. Unhappily, few suspected the consequences in terms of health until long after cigarette smoking had gained its colossal momentum. That this type of auto-contamination is a major cause of lung cancer—that it is also a prime causative factor in deaths from coronary artery disease, bronchitis, asthma, emphysema, among other afflictions—was established, and for the first time well publicized, only a decade ago. The effect this knowledge has had upon the public consciousness may be suggested by the fact that sales this year reached the galactic sum of one-half trillion cigarettes—one hundred billion more than in 1953. There is something historically intimidating in the idea that cigarette smoking as a mass diversion and a raging increase in lung cancer have both come about during the lifetime of those who are now no more than fifty years old. It is the very *recentness* of the phenomenon which helps make it so shocking. The hard truth is that human beings have never in such a brief space of time, and in so grand and guileless a multitude, embraced a habit whose unwholesome effects not only would totally outweigh the meager satisfactions but would hasten the deaths of a large proportion of the people who indulged in it. Certainly (and there seems little doubt that the Surgeon General's report will make this clear) only nuclear fallout exceeds cigarette smoking in gravity as a public health problem.

For its lucid presentation of the medical evidence alone, *The Consumers Union Report on Smoking* would be a valuable document. "The conclusion is inescapable," the *Report* begins, "and even spokesmen for the cigarette industry rarely seek to escape it: we are living in the midst of a major lung cancer epidemic. This epidemic hit men first and hardest, but has affected women as well. It cannot be explained away by such factors as improved diagnosis. And there is reason to believe that the worst is yet to come." Yet despite this minatory beginning the tone throughout is one of caution and reasonableness, and the authors—who manage an accomplished prose style rare in such collective undertakings—marshal their facts with such efficiency and persuasion that it is hard to imagine anyone but a fool or a tobacco lobbyist denying the close association between smoking and lung cancer. Yet, of course, not only lung cancer. The *Report* quotes, for instance, data based on an extensive study of smokers and nonsmokers among English physicians, where the death rate *from all causes* was found to be doubled among heavy cigarette smokers in the group of men past 65, and quadrupled in the group 35 to 44. And the *Report* adds, with the modest and constructive irony that makes the book, if not exactly a joy, then agreeable to read: "These death rates among smokers are perhaps the least controversial of all the findings to date. For with respect to any particular disease there is always the possibility, however remote, that mistaken diagnosis and other conceivable errors may cast doubt on the statistics. But death is easily diagnosed."

In the end, however, what makes the *Report's* message supportable to those distracted souls among the millions of American smokers who may wish to kick the habit—or who, having kicked the habit, may wonder if it is not too late—is a kind of muted optimism. For all present evidence seems to indicate that the common cocktail party rationalization ("I've smoked too long to stop now, the damage is done") has no real basis in fact. In research carried out by the American Cancer Society, microscopic studies of the lung tissues of ex-smokers have shown a process in which precancerous cells are dying out instead of flourishing and reproducing as in the tissues of continuing smokers. Here the *Report* states, in regard to a carefully matched group composed in equal numbers of nonsmokers, ex-smokers and smokers: "Metaplastic cells with altered nuclei [i.e., precancerous cells] were found in 1.2 percent of the slides from the lungs of nonsmokers, as compared with 6.0 for ex-smokers—and *93.2 percent* for current smokers."

Certainly such evidence, combined with the fact that ex-smokers have a lung cancer death rate which ranges down to one-fifth of that of smokers who continue to smoke, should be of the greatest practical interest to anyone who ponders whether it may be worthwhile abandoning what is, after all, a cheerless, grubby, fumbling addiction. (Only the passion of a convert could provoke these last words. The *Report* was an aid to my stopping a two-pack-a-day habit, which commenced in early infancy. Of course, stopping smoking may be in itself a major problem, one of psychological complexity. For myself, after two or three days of great flaccidity of spirit, an aimless oral yearning, aching moments of hunger at the pit of the stomach, and an awful intermittent urge to burst into tears, the problem resolved itself, and in less than a week all craving vanished. Curiously, for the first time in my life, I developed a racking cough, but this, too, disappeared. A sense of smugness, a kind of fatness of soul, is the reward for such a struggle. The intensity of the addiction varies, however, and some people find the ordeal fearfully difficult, if not next to impossible. I do have an urgent suspicion, though, that the greatest barrier to a termination of the habit is the dread of some Faustian upheaval, when in fact that deprivation, while momentarily oppressive, is apt to prove not really cruel at all.)

But if the *Report* is splendidly effective as a caveat, it may be read for its sociological insights as well. Certainly the history of commerce has few instances of such shameful abdication of responsibility as that displayed by the cigarette industry when in 1952 the "health scare," as it is so winsomely known in the trade, brought about the crisis which will reach a head in this month's report by the Surgeon General. It seems clear that the industry, instead of trying to forestall the inevitable with its lies and evasions, might have acquitted itself with some honor had it made what the *Report* calls the only feasible choices: to have urged caution on smokers, to have given money to independent research organizations, to have avoided propaganda and controversy in favor of unbiased inquiry. At the very least the industry might have soft-pedaled or, indeed, silenced its pitch to young people. But panic and greed dominated the reaction, and during the decade since the smoking–lung cancer link was made public, the official position of the industry has been that, in the matter of lung cancer, the villain is any and everything *but* the cigarette. Even the American Cancer Society is in on the evil plot and, in the words of one industry spokesman, "relies almost wholly upon health scare propaganda to raise millions of dollars from a gullible public."

Meanwhile, $200 million was spent last year on cigarette ballyhoo, and during these last crucial ten years the annual advertising expenditure has increased 134 percent—a vast amount of it, of course, going to entice the very young. One million of these young people, according to the American Public Health Association, will die of smoking-induced lung cancer before they reach the age of seventy years. "Between the time a kid is eighteen and twenty-one, he's going to make the basic decision to smoke or not to smoke," says L. W. Bruff, advertising director of Liggett & Myers. "If he does decide to smoke, we want to get him." I have never met Mr. Bruff, but in my mind's eye I see him, poised like a cormorant above those doomed minnows, and I am amused by the refinement, the weight of conscience, the delicate interplay of intellectual and moral alternatives which go into the making of such a prodigious thought. As the report demonstrates, however, Mr. Bruff is only typical of the leaders of an industry which last year received a bounty of $7 billion from 63 million American smokers. Perhaps the tragic reality is that neither this estimable report nor that of the Surgeon General can measurably affect, much less really change, such awesome figures.

[*New York Review of Books*, December 26, 1963.]

This piece about smoking had a singular effect on a number of people of my acquaintance. Almost more than anything I have written, it demonstrated the immediate way in which an opinion, if strongly enough expressed, can have practical results. As soon as they had read the piece, a large group of my friends, plainly gripped by anxiety, quickly stopped smoking. This included—aside from my three-pack-a-day brother-in-law—Robert Brustein, John Hollander, Peter Matthiessen, Jason Epstein, and Norman Podhoretz—representative members of the country's intellectual community who are still nonsmokers and, at this writing, alive and well.
—W.S. (1982)

Cigarette Ads and the Press

I was born and reared in a major tobacco-growing and manufacturing state, Virginia, and was educated and lived for a long time in an even more important tobacco state, North Carolina. In that environment it was difficult not to be seduced at an early age into making cigarettes part of one's way of life. Back in the 1940s, salesmen from such nearby cigarette-producing citadels as Richmond, Durham, and Winston-Salem used to swarm like grasshoppers all over the campuses of the upper South, hustling their wares. Usually dressed in seersucker suits and wearing evangelical smiles, they'd accost you between classes and press into your palm little complimentary packs of four Lucky Strikes or Chesterfields, give you a pep talk, and try to sell you their brand. If you were not a smoker, which was rare at a time when cigarettes were not only in vogue but the norm, you would soon become one, made helpless by the unremitting largesse. I was hooked at age fourteen, initially succumbing because my role in a school play—that of frenetic Chicago gangster—called for me to be a chain smoker. It was a delightful rationale for commencing my addiction, although I'm certain that, given the intensity of peer pressure, I would have started smoking any-way, especially since I had acquired a whole laundry bag full of those little packs and was looking forward not only to an exciting habit but to one that for some time would be absolutely free.

Like renegade Catholics and alcoholics who have sworn off, ex-smokers are often tediously zealous about the addiction they have left behind. I confess to being a member of that group and in fact feel so strongly about the dangers of cigarettes that the subject has frequently turned me into a bleak moralist. But I have my reasons. In my mid-twenties, after I had been smoking for a decade, persistent attacks of bronchitis drove me to a very good New York doctor who examined me with a fluoroscope (no longer in general use) and told me that he had detected what looked like scar tissue on my bronchial tree. He advised me to stop smoking, which was fairly advanced advice for a physician of the early 1950s, who could only have deduced empirically what the later reports of the Surgeon General demonstrated scientifically: cigarettes are a direct cause of chronic bronchitis. The Surgeon General's reports also point out another sinister fact: the earlier one begins smoking, the greater the risk is of permanent damage to the lungs, especially the bronchial tubes.

I ignored the doctor and continued to smoke for the next fifteen years. I stopped cold turkey after a winter of bronchial attacks that came one after another and left me weak and, I might add, rather scared. I have never had a moment's doubt that my decision to stop salvaged me from dire illness, and I only wish that the cure had been more nearly complete. I have abstained from cigarettes for twenty-three years, more than double the time one should stop in order to achieve the mortality rate of lifelong nonsmokers, and therefore I have reason to believe, or hope, that in terms of lung cancer and heart disease I bailed out in time. Yet although the attacks of bronchitis are not nearly so virulent and debilitating as they were when I was still a smoker, they do come back with chronic, often exhausting persistence, casting a somber cloud over all my winters. I trace their origin to that first long and thrilling drag I took from a Philip Morris at the age of fourteen.

I have dwelt in this clinical and, I'm afraid, somewhat testimonial way on my own experience only to lend credence to the all but blind rage I feel I must express when confronted with the cigarette companies and the Tobacco Institute and their stupefying lies. It is intolerable to be told by their mouthpieces that no causal link can be shown between smoking and any serious illness, when after ceasing to smoke I experienced immediate and long-lasting relief from the acute manifestations of a disease. Plainly the Tobacco Institute proceeds on the assumption that most lay people are too stupid, or too supine, to care to take a look at either of the Surgeon General's major reports, which, for bureaucratic documents, are written in surprisingly lucid prose.[1] The reports show that the lungs of a young person who began smoking at fourteen or earlier will often show damage, while those of a young nonsmoker will most likely show none. It is intolerable to accept the bland claims of the cigarette industry that such a finding has no bearing on health. Of the quartet of major diseases caused by smoking—lung cancer, heart disease, emphysema, chronic bronchitis—bronchitis is the least deadly, yet it is a wretched ailment and a possible precursor of emphysema. The fact that the havoc it causes is often the result of smoking at an early age should justify outrage at anyone who would promote or tolerate cigarette advertising, which even in a television culture is read by the very young.

But the advertising of cigarettes in the print media is a troublesome matter because it presents ethical issues that a zealot like myself would initially like to see sidestepped. It is necessary to adopt the politic view. That cigarettes might be phased out of existence through education and by way of antismoking laws currently being enacted everywhere is a bright hope in lieu of making them illegal, which would likely be impossible if not undesirable, given the memory of Prohibition. Although the warnings attached to media ads possess good sense, if limited efficacy, an outright ban on advertising does not seem to square with our accepted principles of freedom of the press as long as cigarettes remain legal. That leaves the moral option in the hands of the newspaper and magazine publishers, who have not shown themselves willing to make honorable decisions.

In defending their right to help seduce the young through cigarette ads, newspaper publishers like to protect themselves by some blurred doctrine of fair play, pointing to the inconsistency of eliminating cigarette advertising while retaining ads for numerous products that might in some way harm the flesh or addle the brain. Chief among those, of course, is alcohol. But to equate in this way the harm, actual or potential, of liquor, wine, and beer with that of cigarettes seems to me a cop-out—for reasons I will mention— and also brings into focus two factors concerning cigarettes that are generally overlooked: their aberrant nature as articles of pleasure and their uselessness.

No possible claim can be made for cigarettes as enhancers of life on any level. The solace they provide is a spurious one, since they merely quell the pangs of an insatiable addiction created by one of their pharmacological components, nicotine. Also it should be remembered how recently cigarettes have appeared on the scene. In the chronicle of human pleasure, cigarette smoking is a gruesomely freakish phenomenon. In any universal sense cigarettes have existed for scarcely a couple of generations, and their toxicity and carcinogenic nature have been scientifically validated only in the past twenty-five years. They should be regarded, then, as the vile little marauders that they are, possessing no merit and vast lethal capacity, needing to be banished with the passion that we banish any other product that we innocently adopt only to discover that it endangers our lives. (How many truly conscientious publishers would have continued advertising products containing DDT or an item like the Dalkon Shield after learning of their deadly nature?)

With alcohol, by contrast, we have lived in a state of mixed grace and distemper since the dawn of the species. It has been an integral part of our experience, rooted in virtually all cultures as deeply as food and fire. It has been far from an unqualified blessing. Its destructive potential has been recognized ever since the first crocked Cro-Magnon slid into a gully, and measures have always been taken to restrict its use. Most of the current limitations placed on the advertising of various forms of alcohol are judicious enough, especially those that help curtail their use by minors; still, it would seem intensely desirable to reduce the flamboyance of much alcohol advertising to a tone commensurate with moderate tippling, enjoyment of wine and beer as an adjunct to meals, and safe driving. But unless one is a prohibitionist one could not discover an ethical need for the eradication of ads for liquor, wine, and beer, since it would be tantamount to calling for an end to those beverages themselves. It is difficult to find any persuasiveness in the publishers' view that so long as they are allowed to advertise alcohol the banishment of cigarette ads would be a form of discrimination. Throughout history there has been bountiful pleasure and a calculated risk in drinking; in its own short and nasty history, cigarette smoking has produced merely bogus pleasure and incalculable harm. The publisher who cannot accept this simple distinction might be able to cover himself with honor if, in forgoing a small slice of what are often enormous profits, he would consign those malign solicitations to the oblivion they deserve.

But I suspect that this is a vain hope. Whenever I think of the self-concern and intransigence that prevent certain people from facing up to this plague, I recall the tobacco manufacturer I encountered some years ago. I am an alumnus of a so-called prestigious Southern university, and I met the gentleman on a spring morning when we sat in our robes waiting for the commencement exercises to begin. The university has been endowed principally through fortunes made in cigarettes, so it was not unfitting that he, a member of the board of trustees, was also chief executive officer of one of the largest tobacco companies in America. Although he lived in New York, he was a Southerner (you could tell from his down-home accent and a kind of countrified friendliness that he was a good ole boy), and as we sat in the heat, shooting the breeze, I gradually perceived that he was in something less than robust health. His complexion was sallow—no, waxen—bags hung haggardly beneath his eyes; his lips had a violet, cyanotic hue. His end of the conversation was interrupted by thick, croupy coughs. Unfiltered cigarettes of the brand he manufactured never left his lips except when he removed a butt to light a fresh one. He was a caricature of a chain smoker, but then I asked myself, What did I expect? Certainly not abstinence in a tobacco tycoon—but even moderation?

Finally his voice grew serious. He said he was in a long, drawn-out fight with the Surgeon General, whom he called a son of a bitch. He expressed his belief that the Surgeon General's report on smoking was a plot, although he didn't say whose. I listened patiently for a while, and I suppose I should have been more circumspect, but I wasn't. I told him, in as delicate a fashion as possible, that I had quit cigarettes some years before due to chronic bronchitis and that, begging to differ with him, I felt that the Surgeon General's report had made a good case for smoking as the cause of my trouble. At that point I sensed a veil coming down between us, and his eyes narrowed, reflecting betrayal. "There's not an iota of truth in that entire book," he said sharply, "and you are very gullible if you buy any of its cheap line of garbage." Those were his exact words, and they are imprinted on my memory as clearly as the terrible convulsion that seized him at that instant, turning his face crimson and causing him to lose his voice in a fit of strangulation. Both embarrassed and concerned, I rose to fetch a glass of water, but when I returned I saw that he had wheeled about and his back was implacably set against me. I was the enemy. We never spoke again. Thus always yawns the chasm between the apostate and the true believer.

[*Nation,* March 7, 1987.]

Too Late for Conversion or Prayer

I must speak of my favorite pill in the perspective of Christian theology. In order to explain this connection I shall have to include some intimate personal details that I hope will not offend sensitive readers.

A number of years ago I got into a friendly but spirited argument with the Episcopal bishop of New York, whom I encountered at a party on Martha's Vineyard. We were discussing the existence of God. I declared to the bishop that the nonexistence of God could be proved by the existence of the prostate gland. The bishop, a liberal, had been describing Darwinian evolution as the product of "God's divine wisdom." No wise God, I countered, could have let evolve a biological species, such as *Homo sapiens,* in which any organ so stupid, so faulty, so prone to disease and dysfunction as the prostate gland had been allowed to exist. Ergo: if God did exist, he certainly was not wise. The assembled guests, who were listening to our discussion, applauded me—at least the men did—but the argument went unresolved.

Some years after this meeting, when I began to experience prostate trouble, I wondered if I might not have courted the wrath of God through my contemptuous skepticism. Maybe the bishop was right. It could be that God did exist, after all, and it was disbelievers like me whom he punished most exultantly by wreaking havoc on their prostate glands. I thought about expressing contrition, but the seriousness of my symptoms convinced me that it was too late for conversion or prayer.

When a man begins to have prostate trouble he experiences difficulties with his plumbing. The problem is often idiosyncratic, varying from man to man, but it almost always involves aberrant behavior of the bladder. Sometimes a man will feel the urgent need to urinate many times a day, discovering that each time he goes to the bathroom he passes only a small amount of urine. Sometimes the flow is not steady, sometimes it is weak; often one has to push or strain to begin urination. All of these difficulties are the result of a usually benign condition in which the enlarged prostate encroaches on the urethra.

In my own case the most serious manifestations occurred at night, when the call to urinate forced me to get up almost every hour. Such an irregular sleeping pattern began to create in me severe exhaustion. More seriously, however, I discovered that my flow was beginning to shut down almost completely. One morning at dawn I realized to my horror that I couldn't urinate at all. I had to be driven to the emergency room of the hospital, where I was relieved of my distress by a catheter inserted into my bladder. It was my birthday. You may imagine the revolting self-pity I felt at celebrating that day as I shuffled around hesitantly with a tube stuck up my penis and a plastic bag attached to my leg.

Of course, I went to a urologist immediately. The doctor examined me carefully and determined that I didn't have cancer. This was a great relief, but then he said that I might have to submit to a surgical procedure to relieve the symptoms. I asked him to describe the operation. He told me jovially that, because the procedure resembled the technique used to ream out sewer pipes, it was often called the "Roto-Rooter." A long instrument with a blade at the end was inserted up through the penis, and portions of the prostate gland were shaved off; this allowed the return of the urine flow, and the patient began to function normally. Well, almost normally, the doctor said after a pause. I asked him to explain.

There were side effects to be expected, he went on. The most common complication had to do with sexual function. The capacity for orgasm was usually retained, although, he added, a bit hesitantly, some men felt diminished pleasure. More significant, however, was the nature of the ejaculation. He then described a process so bizarre that I scarcely believed it, but it happens to be true. In the majority of cases, the semen was propelled not forward in the usual fashion but backward into the bladder, where it was eliminated through urination. Would this cause one's partner, I wondered, to whisper not "Have you come, darling?" but "Have you gone?" At any rate, as he described this process, known as "retrograde ejaculation," I began to feel faint. Although the majority of the operations had no seriously negative aftermath, he continued, he felt it was his duty to tell me that, in a few cases, there were complications. I again asked him to elaborate. Some men were left impotent, he said, with no erectile function. What else? I inquired. A small number of patients suffered permanent urinary incontinence, requiring the daily use of diapers.

By this time I was sobbing uncontrollably, but inside, so the doctor couldn't see.

Then his expression brightened. Surgery should of course be avoided if possible, and he wanted me to try a new pill that had just been made available to urologists. Although it was not yet approved by the Food and Drug Administration, many urologists had achieved great success in preliminary tests. Originally intended as a medication to lower blood pressure, it was discovered to have the property of relaxing the muscles at the bladder outlet. The doctor urged me to take the pills home and see if they worked.

Dear reader, to make a long story short, a miracle happened. The pill worked magnificently. For the past five years I have been taking one small five-milligram dose nightly, and my flow has been like Niagara. There have been no side effects. I did not have to have that Roto-Rooter. I do not have to wear diapers. I am not impotent. My semen does not go backward but still spurts out merrily in the direction Nature intended. I am at peace with my genitourinary system and with the world. The pill is a true wonder drug, which demonstrates for me that if the bishop of New York was right and God exists, and that if he is trying to punish men by way of their prostate glands, we have triumphantly outwitted him.

[*Egoïst* 7 (1985).]

Bagatelles

The Big Love

It usually requires a certain arrogance to say of a new book that it is a masterpiece. For one thing, the risks are large; in his runaway enthusiasms, the person who is rash enough to proclaim a new book "great," "a staggering achievement," "a work of art of the highest order" (these are the phrases most commonly employed) is likely to be proved wrong, even long before time and posterity have had a chance to assay his judgment. Recall, for example, *By Love Possessed*. A masterpiece? The reviewers seemed to think so, yet now it seems apparent that it wasn't that at all—at least not proven; opposed to what was originally claimed for it, too many people have considered it an unfair struggle and a thick-headed bore. At certain rare moments, however, there will appear a work of such unusual and revealing luminosity of vision, of such striking originality, that its stature is almost indisputable; one feels that one may declare it a masterpiece without hesitation, or fear that the passing of time might in any way alter one's conviction. Such a book is *The Big Love*, a biography of Beverly Aadland by her mother, Mrs. Florence Aadland. To Mrs. Aadland and her collaborator, Tedd Thomey, we owe a debt of gratitude; both of them must feel a sense of pride and relief at having delivered themselves, after God alone knows how much labor, of a work of such wild comic genius.

I would like to make it plain, however, that—as in most high comic art—there is a sense of moral urgency in *The Big Love* which quite removes it from the specious and, more often than not, sensational claptrap we have become accustomed to in popular biography. Witness the first line of the book—a first line that is as direct and in its own way as reverberant as any first line since "Call me Ishmael."

> There's one thing I want to make clear right off [Mrs. Aadland begins], my baby was a virgin the day she met Errol Flynn.
> [Continuing, she says:] Nothing makes me sicker than those dried-up old biddies who don't know the facts and spend all their time making snide remarks about my daughter Beverly, saying she was a bad girl before she met Errol. . . . I'm her mother and she told me everything. She never lied to me. Never.

Already it is obvious that we are in contact with a moral tone entirely different from, let us say, the lubricity of Errol Flynn's own biography, *My Wicked, Wicked Ways,* or the self-exploitation and narcissism so prevalent in those boring memoirs, which appear almost monthly, of yet another international lollipop. In striking this note of rectitude, Mrs. Aadland makes it clear that furthest from her desires is a wish to titillate, or in any way to make sensational an affair which, after all, ended in such tragedy and heartbreak for all concerned. Indeed, if it were not for the sense of decency and high principles which informs every page of *The Big Love,* we would be in the presence not of a comic masterwork at all, but only one more piece of topical trash, hardly distinguishable from the life of a Gabor sister.

The stunning blonde who was to become "Bev" to her mother and, at the age of fifteen, "Woodsie" (because of her resemblance to a wood nymph) to Errol Flynn, was conceived, so Flo Aadland tells us, in an apartment on Mariposa Avenue in Hollywood on December 7, 1941. The date, of course, was ominous, contributing much to further Flo's lasting suspicion that her own life, and now Bev's, was "preordained." Tragedy had dogged much of Flo's life. She possessed, for one thing, an artificial foot, the result of a traffic accident, and this misfortune—usually referred to as "the tragedy of my leg"—coupled with a previous miscarriage, had made it seem to her that life had hardly been worth living until Bev came along. Bev—who was a precocious child, walking at ten months, singing "all the radio commercials" at a year—altered the complexion of Flo's life entirely. "She was such a different baby, different in intelligence as well as beauty. I wondered . . . if she had been given to me . . . to make up for the tragedy of my leg." Shortly after this her speculation was confirmed when, riding with little Bev on a Hermosa Beach bus, she met a female Rosicrucian "who had made a deep study of the inner ways of life."

Discussing Bev, the Rosicrucian told Flo: " 'This baby has an old soul. . . . She is very mature. . . . Were the babies you lost before both girls?'

" 'Yes,' I said.

"The Rosicrucian lady nodded and then held both of Beverly's hands tightly in her own. 'Twice before, this baby tried to be born. . . . She has always known she was to fill the emptiness that entered your life when you lost your leg. . . . And you must realize this also. . . . This child has been born for untold fame and fortune.' "

Bev's early life was the normal one for a Hollywood youngster. So gifted that she was able to sing, in immaculate pitch, a popular song called "Symphony" at seventeen months, she was also almost overwhelmingly beautiful, and at the age of three, impersonating Bette Davis, won the costume beauty contest at the Episcopal Sunday School (an Episcopal activity peculiarly Californian in flavor). Later she was chosen mascot for the Hermosa Beach Aquaplane Race Association, cut the ceremonial tape for a $200,000 aquarium, and, not yet six, played in her first movie, a Technicolor epic called *The Story of Nylon*. As young as Bev was, she already exerted upon men a stupefying enchantment. A Hollywood doctor—"a very learned man, an authority on Eastern religions who had lectured all over the world and written many books"—was the first to pronounce the somber warning. "He held her hands the way that Rosicrucian lady had done. . . . 'Mrs. Aadland,' he said seriously, 'wherever did you get this little girl?' . . . Then he sat down in his chair and did a very strange thing. He closed his eyes and passed his hand back and forth just above Beverly's bright blonde curls. 'I think I see sort of a halo on this girl,' he said." Shortly Flo hears the gloomy, admonitory words: " 'I think men will be terribly affected by this girl. . . . Be very careful with your daughter. . . . I think men are going to kill over this girl. I have the feeling in my heart that she has the scent of musk on her.' " Her religious training enables Flo to comprehend: "I knew what he meant [about musk]. It wasn't the first time I had run into that phrase. I had read it in the Bible."

When Flynn began seeing Bev—then aged fifteen, and dancing in the movie version of *Marjorie Morningstar*—Flo sensed no impropriety. Thrilled that her daughter should be dating such a famous man, "overwhelmed by the fact that my baby called this man Errol," she confesses that she nearly fainted dead away when first led into his presence. To be sure, she says, "I'd read about his trials for the statutory rape of those two teenagers in 1942. And I'd seen the headlines in 1951 when he was charged with the rape of a fifteen-year-old French girl." As for Bev, however, "I still didn't believe he would take advantage of her." Against this gullibility may be measured Flo's near-insane outrage, some months later, when, during the course of a plane ride to join Errol in New York, Bev reveals not only that she was no longer chaste, but that Errol—on their very first night together—had done what the cynical reader knew he had done all along: he had, indeed, ravished her, tearing her seventy-five-dollar bolero dress, muttering "Woodsie, Woodsie" over and over, and "growling in his throat." Flo's indignation, however, is short-lived; despite this traumatic event, Bev seems deeply in love with Errol and Errol with Bev. On sober second thought, in fact, the future looks pretty rosy for Flo.

> While [Bev] talked, the love bloom was all over her—in her eyes, making her cheeks pink. "Mama," she said, "can't you imagine what it's going to be like with Errol from now on? Can't you imagine the lovely clothes, the spending, the famous people we'll meet? . . . Mama . . . he's told me how good I am for him. He's told me that we're going to write the Arabian Nights all over again."

And so the incredible joy ride commences, and the sedulous Florence is rarely absent from the scene, or at least its periphery. There are drinking bouts, yachting trips, dances, and other social events, including a well-publicized nude swimming party at a country estate near New York which Flo, with characteristic delicacy, assures us was *not* an orgy. "Beverly later told me all about it. [The people] *weren't* riotously drunk or mad with passion. It was an unconventional but casual swim. Afterwards they got out, dressed, and enjoyed some pork chops and apple sauce together. Beverly helped serve the food and was complimented by the others on her clothes and manners." The East Coast holds Flo—L.A. born and bred—in its thrall; her description of the Connecticut countryside, "the homes with their unusual gabled roofs," has a quality both eerie and exotic, as if it were the Norwegian troll country. At one club function, a handsomely swank place, also in Connecticut, Bev has her first encounter with snow. "We sat down at a table . . ." Flo says, and describes a boring situation.

> I looked around for a movie magazine or something interesting to read, but could find only copies of *Time* and *Fortune*. . . . Pretty soon we noticed it was snowing outside. Without saying a word to me or anyone else, Beverly got up and went outside. It was the first time Bev had ever seen snow falling and, being a native Californian, she was thrilled. I watched her through the large picture window. . . . She held up her arms gracefully and whirled them through the air, touching the falling snowflakes. She never looked lovelier. Her cheeks were flushed to a healthy pink and she wore one of her nicest outfits, a gorgeous peach-colored cashmere sweater and matching skirt. . . . As the big white snowflakes came down thicker and thicker, she did a very crazy thing. She took off her shoes and began dancing and skipping around on the golf greens. . . . She looked like an absolutely mad fairy princess, whirling and cavorting, holding her arms out so beautifully. . . . When she came in, she said: "Oh, Mother, it was so beautiful!" Her nose was red as a raspberry and when I touched it with my finger tip it felt like a cold puppy's nose.

The note of pathos here, fugitive but intensely real, as it is in all comic art of a high order, is the mysterious ingredient which pervades every page of *The Big Love* and compels the book, in a grotesque fashion that surpasses all aesthetic laws, to become a kind of authentic literary creation in spite of itself. It was along about the passage just quoted that I was persuaded that Tedd Thomey, Mrs. Aadland's ghost, was in reality Evelyn Waugh, come back after a long silence to have another crack at the bizarre creatures who inhabit the littoral of Southern California. In truth, however, from this point on the book more reasonably brings to mind Nathanael West's *The Day of the Locust,* if for no other reason than the fact that, as in that fine and funny book, in which horror and laughter are commingled like the beginning of a scream, the climax of *The Big Love* swiftly plunges toward nightmare and hallucination in a fashion that all but overwhelms the comedy. Errol Flynn dies of a heart attack in Vancouver, and Beverly goes to pieces. She becomes the unwilling object of the attentions of a young madman who, one night in Hollywood, rapes her at pistol point, and then in her presence blows out his brains—a tragedy which, Flo concludes, like the multiple tragedy of Errol Flynn and Beverly and Florence Aadland, must have been "preordained." Flo is charged with five counts of contributing to the delinquency of a minor; Beverly, in turn, is remanded into the custody of a movie-colony divine, the Reverend Leonard Eilers, whose wife, Frances, in an admirable spirit of Christian guardianship, is now chaperoning Bev during her appearances on the Midwest nightclub circuit.

But at last the true comic spark returns, jewel-bright, in the ultimate scene of this terrifying, flabbergastingly vulgar, and, at times, inexplicably touching book. It takes place, appropriately enough, in the celebrated Forest Lawn Memorial Park, whither Flo, out on bail, and Bev and a friend have gone one morning at dawn to deposit flowers on Errol's grave, near a spot called the Garden of Everlasting Peace.

> "My God," I said to Bev. "Can you imagine an unpeaceful man like the Swashbuckler in here?"
>
> We took the flowers from the car and placed them on the grave. . . . Then, although Errol's grave now had more flowers than any of the others, Beverly and our friend decided he deserved even more.
>
> So they went to the other graves and took only a few of the fresh flowers that had been left the day before. They took a bit of larkspur from one, a daisy from one and a lily from another. Then, frisking around like wood nymphs, the two of them leaped gracefully over Errol's grave, dropping the flowers at his head and feet.
>
> I watched them dance . . . for a few more moments and then I said to Beverly: "You didn't kiss him yet, did you?"
>
> "No, Mama," she said.
>
> Then she knelt down very carefully and touched her lips to the grass near Errol's headstone.
>
> "Mama!" she said suddenly.
>
> "What's the matter?" I said.
>
> "Mama!" she said. "I just heard a big belly laugh down there!"
>
> After that we left. . . . As we drove away, we waved and called out gaily: "Good-by, Errol!"

It had been, Flo muses, "a tremendously swanky graveyard."

[*Esquire,* November 1961.]

The article on Flo and Beverly Aadland was primarily responsible for converting *The Big Love* into something of a cult book, with a large and loyal following. One of the chronicle's greatest admirers was W. H. Auden, who told me he had given numerous copies to friends, and who quoted Flo Aadland in his incomparable miscellany *A Certain World*. (Auden had a great feeling for the bizarre; he also quoted at length from the autobiography of Rudolf Höss, *Commandant of Auschwitz*.) It is an immeasurable loss to American literature that *The Big Love* is out of print.
—W.S. (1982)

Candy

Assuming that we are to use the word in a derogatory sense, any honest definition of pornography must be subjective. For me it reduces itself to that which causes me disgust. (There is also a good kind of pornography, like *Fanny Hill,* which may give pleasure.) In order to appreciate the satire on "bad" pornography in Terry Southern and Mason Hoffenberg's *Candy,* it is helpful to dip into some of the aids to erotic enjoyment which are currently filling the bookstores. One of the most notable of these works is *Sex and the Single Man* by Dr. Albert Ellis, author of an impressive number of studies, including the well-known *Sex Without Guilt, The American Sexual Tragedy,* and *A Guide to Rational Living.* Dr. Ellis's most recent work is an elaborate, detailed training manual which pits the bachelor trainee ("you") against a hypothetical foe known as "your girlfriend." Most of the tactics in seduction are elementary, and the physiological terrain described by Dr. Ellis is old and trampled ground. The book's real distinction lies in its style; and since the style, among sexologists as among poets and novelists, is the measure of the man, let Dr. Ellis speak for himself: "Coitus itself can in some instances be unusually exciting and arousing. If your girlfriend is not too excitable at a certain time, but is willing to engage in intercourse, she may become aroused through doing so, and may wind up by becoming intensely involved sexually, even though she was relatively passive when you first started to copulate."

It is this kind of mechanical how-to-ism, with its clubfooted prose and its desolating veterinary odor, that constitutes the really prurient writing of our time. It is pornographic and disgusting, and it is one of the major targets of *Candy* in its satirical foray against sickbed sex, both scientific and literary. *Candy* was first published in 1957 in Paris by the Olympia Press, which concealed the authors' names under the swank *nom de plume* "Maxwell Kenton." Although *Candy* is by no stretch of the imagination an obscene novel, a bizarre feature of the book's history is that it became—along with a number of others of the Olympia list—one of the few works in English ever to be banned by the French government on the grounds of indecency. This is a circumstance which might make the book appear positively satanic were it not for the fact that *Candy* is really a droll little sugarplum of a tale and a spoof on pornography itself. Actually, considering its reputation, it may be surprising to discover that much of the book is not about sex at all. At any rate, there was no official reaction in France when, in an evasive maneuver, *Candy*'s publisher continued to issue it under the name *Lollipop*. Now it comes to us in the United States from Putnam, unexpurgated, and with the real names of the authors revealed. Let us hope that Candy, the adorable college-girl heroine of the book, is not hounded into court after the fashion of Lady Chatterley—and this for a couple of reasons. First, since this book, too, is not a supreme masterpiece, we shall be spared the spectacle of eminent critics arguing from the witness stand that it is. But more importantly, *Candy* in its best scenes is wickedly funny to read and morally bracing as only good satire can be. The impure alone could object to it, and we should not risk letting ourselves be deprived of such excellent fun even when a certain wobbly and haphazard quality, which may be due to the problems created by collaboration, causes the book to creak and sag more often than it should.

Candy Christian—for such is her beautiful name—is a delectable, neo-Victorian American sophomore on the verge of emancipation: that is to say, she is a girl who has been freed of all unreasonable puritanical restraints, yet who dwells in a limbo where up-to-date young females are expected to give sexual pleasure without, however, experiencing pleasure themselves. To this extent, she vaguely resembles Dr. Ellis's endlessly besieged "girlfriend"—a nightmare in the mind of a *Playboy* reader—trembling maddeningly at the brink of desire. Yet Candy is not just neo-Victorian but post-1950; for where her college counterpart of half a generation ago was a furtive virgin who did something with boys called (the phrase is almost unprintable) "petting to climax," Candy is not much improvement, having replaced her virginity with a greedy narcissism based on fantasies of "need." Such fantasies compel a kind of idiot generosity, and the phrase *"Oh you do need me so!"* is Candy's constant secret thought about men.

The need-principle, we learn early in the story, has been engendered in Candy through the influence of her Ethical Philosophy teacher, Professor Mephesto. This ass, full of devious altruism ("To give of one's self fully . . . is a beautiful and thrilling privilege," he mutters to Candy, a fat hand on her knee), is a wonderful caricature of the academic seducer, with his cozy little office and his afternoon sherry, his snuffling importunities ("'It's an "A" paper . . . Absolutely top-drawer . . . Comfort those whose needs are greatest, my dear,' he implored her"); and although Candy evades the gross fellow she is not without immediate remorse:

> Selfish! Selfish! she was thinking of herself. To be needed by this great man! And to be only concerned with my material self! She was horribly ashamed. How he needs me! And I deny him! I deny *him*! Oh how did I *dare*!

Thus simultaneously chastened and enlightened, Candy resolves to leave college, and it is her wide-eyed, warm-hearted journey through the great world which occupies the rest of the book. Part fantasy, part picaresque extravaganza (the resemblance between the names Candy and Candide is anything but coincidental), the story often suffers from the fact that its larger design is formless and episodic; a number of the sequences, unfortunately, seem to be dreamed-up, spur-of-the-moment notions in which the comic impact is vitiated by obvious haste and a sense of something forced. But in many of its single scenes the book is extremely funny: it is surely the first novel in which frenzied sexual congress between an exquisite young American girl and an insane, sadistic hunchback can elicit nothing but helpless laughter. And at its very best—as with Professor Mephesto—when we perceive that the comic irony is a result of the juxtaposition of Candy's innocent sexual generosity with duplicitous sexual greed, the book produces its triumphs. For none of Candy's seducers seems to realize that he needs only to ask in the most direct and human way in order bountifully to receive. Like Dr. Ellis, they are technocrats and experts, possessing a lust to bury this most fundamental of human impulses beneath the rockpile of scientific paraphernalia and doctrine and professional jabber. Swindlers by nature, they end up only swindling themselves. It is part of our heroine's unflagging charm and goodness that she confronts each of these monsters with blessed equanimity. They include Dr. Irving Krankeit (*né* Irving Semite), a messianic psychotherapist crazed with the belief that a cure for the world's ills lies in masturbation; another medical wretch named Dunlap; Dr. Johns, an unorthodox gynecologist who submits Candy to an examination in the ladies' room of a Greenwich Village bar; and finally a really superb creation in the form of a character named Great Grindle. Grindle, an egg-bald guru with a luxuriant black mustache and a thick accent, is the spiritual leader of a group of male and female youths who call themselves Crackers—a sort of demented Peace Corps which labors in the national interest deep in the bowels of a Minnesota mine. In Grindle is the gathering together of a number of miscellaneous practices and faiths—Zen and yoga and Reichian orgone theory—and while his interest in Candy is ostensibly spiritual, it is clear from the outset that Grindle, no less than the other quacks she has encountered, is conceiving labyrinthine designs upon "the darling girl's precious little honeypot." And so, deep within a grotto the preposterous ogre sets his trap:

"Good!" said Grindle. "Now then, lace your fingers together, in the yoga manner, and place them behind your head. Yes, just so. Now then, lie back on the mossy bed."

"Oh gosh," said Candy, feeling apprehensive, and as she obediently lay back, she raised one of her handsome thighs, slightly turning it inward, pressed against the other, in a charming coy effort to conceal her marvelous little spice-box.

"No, no," said Grindle, coming forward to make adjustments, "legs well apart."

At his touch, the darling girl started to fright, but Grindle was quick to reassure her. "I am a doctor of the soul," he said coldly: "I am certainly not interested in that silly little body of yours . . ."

"Now this is a so-called 'erogenous zone,'" explained Grindle, gingerly taking one of the perfect little nipples which did so seem to be begging for attention . . .

"*I'll* say," the girl agreed, squirming despite her efforts to be serious . . .

"*This is* another of these so-called 'erogenous zones,'" announced Grindle contemptuously, addressing the perfect thing with his finger . . . "Tell me, how does it feel now?"

The lovely girl's great eyelids were fluttering.

"Oh, it's all tingling and everything," she admitted despairingly . . .

This is not pornography, but the stuff of heartbreak. It is hard to conceive that even Orville Prescott will not somehow be touched by such a portrait of beleaguered goodness.

[*New York Review of Books*, May 14, 1964.]

Amours

Virginia Durr for President

My fellow Americans: Four score and five years ago, in the great state of Alabama, on the sacred soil of "The Cotton State," in the heart of Dixie, the state that is still among the preeminent producers of the fleecy white blooms that clothe mankind with such unparalleled comfort and fitness, but a state that's an outstanding provider of peanuts, too, being second only to Georgia in output of the versatile legume, and a leader in timber products, textiles, and bituminous coal . . . Alabama, home of the original capital of the Confederacy, scene of the great Indian wars of Andrew Jackson and of the great naval battle of Mobile, birthplace of illustrious Americans—Hugo Black, Truman Capote, Bill Connor, and Governor Kissin' Jim Folsom not to speak of other raunchy inhabitants of the Governor's Mansion such as George Wallace and his wife, Cornelia, known privately behind poor George's back as the Montgomery Man Eater . . . Alabama, home of other celebrities like the great nineteenth-century slavery enthusiast W. L. Yancey and the internationally acclaimed poetess of the same period, the seventy-seven-pound Mabel Vanlandingham Potts, known as the Little Song Sparrow of the Tombigbee . . . My fellow Americans, it was eighty-five years ago in Alabama's greatest metropolis, the great city of Birmingham, the Pittsburgh of the South, world-ranking producer of steel and pig iron, major consumer of coal and supplier of coke—in the old-fashioned sense of the word—to the world, thriving railroad center, being the hub of the L.&N., the G.M.&O., the A.C.K., the S.A.L., the S.L. & S.F., the C. of G. and the Southern . . . Birmingham—chief operating center for the Southern region of both J. C. Penney and Burger King, city of verdant peaks and mountain vistas, home of higher institutions of learning such as Birmingham-Southern University, proudly and affectionately known as the Southern Rutgers . . . Fellow Democrats, beloved brothers and caring Americans, it was in the great city of Birmingham in the great state of Alabama in the golden year of 1903 that there first saw the light of day the great lady whose nomination for President of the United States I proudly second this evening, Virginia Foster Durr!

Virginia Durr was the granddaughter of a slave owner, born to comfort and privilege, with all the advantages accruing to a young white maiden of her class. Such a young woman might have been expected to succumb to all the easy shibboleths of her time and place—to become a snob and a suburban dilettante, a frequenter of high-society galas and country-club blowouts, to fall into the indolent pose of the trifler, the parlor reactionary, and kitchen racist. This type is endemic in the South, as fixed in legend as Scarlett O'Hara. You see them everywhere in Dixie, from Fredericksburg, Virginia, to Fredericksburg, Texas. Married or unmarried, they have chaste bodies and even chaste minds, unsullied by so much as a flyspeck of rational cognition. They have believed in the preservation of social and racial purity, the preservation of the maidenhead, and the preservation of the human spirit against all invasion by Beauty and Truth. They have besmirched God's glorious footstool—and the beautiful Southland—by their vain and silly hypocrisy. They have glorified the vice of flibbertigibbety.

But, my fellow Americans, what a splendid thing it was when Virginia Durr—almost uniquely among her contemporaries—broke out of this constricting mold which would have so bound her to the conventional pieties. Almost single-handedly and with great bravery, during a period of hatred and reaction, she demonstrated that a Southern belle—and a beautiful one at that—need not obey those rules that dictated that a young girl be blind to poverty and ignorance, to racial inequality and the savagery of vested power. She showed that the flower of Southern womanhood need not be symbolized by a pale and damp camellia, languishing in hothouse desuetude, but by a triumphant rose vigorously ablush with moral courage and ready to put forth wrathful thorns in the pursuit of decency and justice. My friends and fellow Americans, the noble example of Virginia Durr, her intense probity and the passionate zeal she has displayed in her lifelong quest for liberty and a fair shake for all of God's creatures here on earth—this example supremely qualifies her for the highest office in the land, and I therefore proudly and humbly second her nomination for President of the United States of America!

[Delivered at a celebration of Virginia Durr's eighty-fifth birthday, August 6, 1988, Vineyard Haven. Previously unpublished.]

My Daughters

The relationship of fathers and daughters has been a significant theme in world literature. Consider the stage alone. The theme has arrested the attention of playgoers at least since the time of Sophocles and Euripides, who wrote of the intertwined fates of Oedipus and Antigone, and of Agamemnon and Electra. In a companion play Euripides told of how the tormented Agamemnon was forced to appease the wrath of the goddess Artemis by sacrificing another daughter, Iphigenia. One of the most anguished cries in an ancient theater renowned for its anguished cries is that of Iphigenia in Tauris: "My life hath known no father; any road to any end may run!" Shakespeare's world teems with father-daughter groupings, of which King Lear and his confounding bevy of girls make up only the most famous. Think of *Hamlet*'s Polonius and Ophelia, the Duke and his Rosalind in *As You Like It*, the great Athenian and his Marina in the eponymous *Pericles*. Shylock and Jessica of *The Merchant of Venice*, *The Tempest*'s lyrically linked Prospero and Miranda.

In modern times one has only to remember Ezra and Lavinia in O'Neill's *Mourning Becomes Electra* or Boss Finley and his daughter in *Sweet Bird of Youth* by Tennessee Williams or Shaw's *Major Barbara*, whose title character is the offspring of the unforgettable Undershaft. The connection is there in much European and American fiction: Hardy's *Far From the Madding Crowd*, Victor Hugo's *Les Misérables* (Jean Valjean and Cosette, his surrogate daughter, were among the first fictional characters I encountered), Faulkner's Will Varner and Eula. In modern poetry two instances of the kinship come quickly to mind: John Crowe Ransom's poignant "Bells for John Whiteside's Daughter," in which a father's grief for his dead daughter is expressed by the poet's voice and, somewhat perversely perhaps, the later poems of Sylvia Plath, which articulate a discomforting daughterly rage against daddy.

In brooding over this remarkable portfolio of photographs by Mariana Cook, which includes my own familial cluster, I was reminded more than once of how the theme of fathers and daughters gained a prominent place in my work over the years. In the early 1950s, quite some time before I had a daughter myself, I finished a first novel, *Lie Down in Darkness,* which is in large part the story of a father's obsessive love for his firstborn girl, a love which may have (according to some critics) incestuous overtones but which in any case helped precipitate her early death by suicide. I was quite young— twenty-five—when I completed this book and, as I say, had no experience in parenting; still, putting aside the incest motif (which was always problematical anyway), it was the emotional interplay between father and daughter which I believe was among the most successfully rendered parts of the book. I like to think that such imaginative empathy helped prepare me for the real role of being father to three daughters.

Whatever, the theme never really left my consciousness and in fact reappeared, somewhat menacingly, in my later novel *Sophie's Choice.* There I attempted to create a relationship in which the father's attitude toward his daughter—harsh, judgmental, and authoritarian—could be seen as part of a complex metaphor for Polish anti-Semitism, through which, at Auschwitz, Sophie and her children became the unintended but certain victims of that vicious oppression of Jews her father so passionately espoused. Thus, though her doom and that of her children had its origin in other causes, it was truly sealed by the absence of that affection and decency that binds father to daughter, daughter to father, and both to the natural world.

American fathers possess a peculiarly bifurcated attitude when it comes to the matters of gender in their offspring. Fathers, in other words, are supposed to be loving and supportive toward their daughters, but both the joys and burdens of parenthood fall chiefly upon the mother. This concept springs from a culture in which masculinity and femininity are polarized to a rather intense degree; a father may be profoundly fond of his daughter, but to immerse himself too thoroughly in his daughter's concerns is to risk emasculation, or at least a form of sissification. Better that he focus his interest on a son, or sons. Many cultures have practiced infanticide of daughters (it is still shockingly prevalent in parts of India), and while our own overall view of the worth of a child's gender is, largely speaking, free of prejudice, it is still a matter of jocular folklore that a son is to be preferred. The celebratory cigars and the joyous announcement, "It's a boy!" composed a ceremony that spoke volumes, at least until recently, when our changing mores would make it appear appallingly sexist.

Traditionally, fathers preferred to beget sons rather than daughters. The chief reasons for this desirability are embedded in the generally patriarchal nature of human society stretching back to pre-antiquity: sons carry on the family trade or craft, continue to make the money, are the entrepreneurs and explorers, the movers and shakers. Daughters, necessary for procreation, nurturing, and housekeeping, fulfill a lesser role; to all but the most intransigently hidebound fathers, girls are welcome all the same, and are even greatly beloved. This is monumental condescension but it is also a measure of history's cruelty that for most of its course such has been the prevailing view.

What a pleasure it was for me to step outside history and greet my three daughters when they arrived during the decade between the mid-1950s and the mid-1960s. First, there was Susanna. In her prenatal months (this was before amniocentesis might have permitted me to divine her sex), I lived in a state of happy ignorance as to what I might expect on the day of genesis. I was also honestly indifferent as to whether I might be presented with a boy or girl. Insofar as the baby's sex was concerned I must admit, however, to a small prickling of self-concern, so that when the doctor announced, "It's a girl!" I knew I'd be relieved of certain obligations. I knew I would not be expected to go hunting or to play softball or involve myself companionably at any deafening spectator sport, especially professional football, which I despise.

Susanna is the young lady in the top right of Mariana Cook's vivid photograph. I'm astonished when I think that this immensely poised and accomplished person is the same human being, *in extenso*, as the squirming pink and squalling bundle of flesh I beheld for the first time, my heart pounding with apprehension and wonder, in the days of my hopeful youth. I have no favorites among my delightful daughters but one's firstborn commands a special place in memory, if only because the very novelty of her presence provoked an exquisite concern. What was she crying about? What about that cough? I was always worried about her health, and was in constant consultation with the era's guru, Dr. Spock. I needn't have worried. She was as spunky and resilient in those days as she now triumphantly appears.

If I were to write a verse about Polly, daughter number two (seated at my knee), it would be to rhyme her name with *melancholy*. She has a dark streak of this mood, inherited from me, and has fought at least one tough battle against it, but lest one think it might have been a ruinous burden to her, or afflicted her in some unyielding way, these confident and humorous eyes should put the idea to rest. Again, those early years are hard to reconcile with the present image but I keep remembering a droll fact of her babyhood: she produced the loudest sounds ever heard in a small human being. These shrieks were not a product of her melancholy but of her lung power and healthy rage, lusty fishmonger's cries totally at odds with the image of the grown young woman, soft of speech, a slim dancer of remarkably supple grace.

Alexandra, the youngest (top left), is a young lady of saucy wit, pleasantly rambunctious, one whose adhesive good humor (though she, too, has a dark side) has kept the family sanely united at moments of stress. She is an actress, and Mariana Cook has captured the gleams of expressiveness that help make her a very good one. Al came late to the family and therein lies an instructive tale. We must remember, while we're on the subject of daughters, that there are also sons. Tom, my only boy, was born shortly after Polly, and became odd man out in a family which, except for the paterfamilias, was exclusively female, including dogs, cats, birds, and even boa constrictors. Gentlemen do not have an entirely carefree time in such an environment.

Tom pined during most of his first seven years for a baby brother, and I'll never forget the note of piping grief and anguish in his voice when, calling him from the hospital after Alexandra's birth, I told him he had yet another sister. ("Daddy! *Daddy,* no!") I rather feared for his sanity when the next day, en route to his little workshop in the cellar, he asked me for the following items: rope, nails, a piece of lead, a sharp blade. I was certain he was building a torture device for his baby sister. But in fact, after a long and sinister silence, he emerged with a wondrous artifact: a wooden bird with metal wings, a gift for Alexandra, and tribute to the fact that even he, after all his isolated maleness, wished to celebrate the arrival of another sister, my new daughter. He does not, of course, belong in these pictures but I can't help seeing his ghostly outline here, smiling as he fills out the family portrait of a kind of obverse King Lear, composed and untormented, in the company of his joyous and (one hopes) grateful daughters.

Mariana Cook has, in this portfolio of pictures encompassing so many fathers and daughters, achieved a substantial miracle of photography. There is not only a remarkable clarity of technique and vision, but an ability to capture the nuances of relationship: one can assume that these moments, electric and vivid, are created out of that intuitive grasp of the revealing instant possessed only by the most accomplished artists. There is nothing lax or dilatory in any of these pictures; each has both precision and luminosity, and in each of them one can perceive the nearly visible energy that flows from the intimacy of kinship. That all of these images and arrangements are not entirely harmonious, not without emotional tension, adds to their appeal, and to their honesty. What matters is the poetic grace with which the artist has arrested for a moment the humor, the tenderness and, most often, the love that underlie one of the best of all human connections.

[Originally written as an introduction to a book of portraits by Mariana Cook called *Fathers and Daughters* (Chronicle Books, 1994).]

Our Model Marriage

Speaking on behalf of me and the missus, I want to thank you all for this demonstration of affection. I'm grateful first to Bill and Wendy for conceiving this beautiful dinner—it was their generous idea—but also to every one of the rest of you, whom Rose and I know and love. Forty years ago on this date, in Rome, I somehow knew that Rose and I would be celebrating, in 1993, the fruits of our model marriage. I know that while in other marriages the partners would, inevitably, be at each other's throats, Rose and I would be throughout the years steadfastly at each other's sides, a constant reproach to those less patient, tolerant, and faithful.

Philoprogenitive, and sharing a passion for books and pets, we have spent scarcely a night apart, and I hope our example of an almost insanely obsessive monogamy will prove to be an example to the rising generation for whom words like *devotion* and *caring* are but cheap coinage. Rose has endured much at the hands of her demanding husband, and for this I bless her. God bless all of *you* for having been so much a part of our interminable partnership experiences. God bless our noble marriage and, while we're at it, God bless America!

[Speech on the occasion of the Styrons' fortieth wedding anniversary—at a dinner hosted by their friends William and Wendy Luers, May 4, 1993. Previously unpublished.]

In Closing

Walking with Aquinnah

For the last four or five years, whenever I am home—which has been most of the time—I have been accustomed to taking long daily walks with my dog, Aquinnah. Our walks are for business and pleasure, and also for survival—interlocking motives that have somehow acquired nearly equal importance in my mind. From the professional point of view, there is nothing better than walking at a brisk pace to force oneself into a contemplative mood. I say force because there is, I'm sorry to relate, an early resistance. I am not by nature a very active person and it's a little embarrassing to confess that after many years of walking, with all sorts of dogs that preceded Aquinnah, it still takes at least a mild act of will to get started on my daily journey. For unlike most purely athletic activities, there is at the outset an element of joylessness in the walking process.

Strange that this is so. It requires absolutely no skill save the natural one that we all acquire at infancy. Why should the mere act of consecutively putting one foot ahead of the other for mile after mile be in itself so unpleasant an idea as to inspire a reluctance still difficult for me to surmount? But once I get myself going there always comes a breakthrough, after the boredom that usually envelops me like a dank mist during the first quarter of a mile or so of my hike. At the start it is like a faint palpable ache, not in the feet or legs but somewhere around the rim of the cranium. I wonder why, once again, I am engaging in this ponderous movement. My mind is cluttered by a series of the most dismally mundane preoccupations: my bank balance, a dental appointment, the electrician's failure to come and repair a critical outlet. Invariably the first five or ten minutes are filled with sour musings—a splendid time to recollect old slights and disappointments and grudges, all flitting in and out of my consciousness like evil little goblins. They are the grimy bits and pieces of the initial boredom.

Yet almost without fail there comes a transitional moment—somewhat blurred, like that drowsy junction between wakefulness and sleep—when I begin to think of my work, when the tiny worries and injustices that have besieged me start to evaporate, replaced by a delicious, isolated contemplation of whatever is in the offing, later that day, at the table at which I write. Ideas, conceits, characters, even whole sentences and parts of paragraphs come pouring in on me in a happy flood until I am in a state close to hypnosis, quite oblivious of the woods or the fields or the beach where I am trudging, and finally as heedless of the rhythmic motion of my feet as if I were paddling through air like some great liberated goose or swan.

This, you see, is the delight and the value of walking for a writer. The writer lounging—trying to think, to sort out his thoughts—cannot really think, being the prey of endless distractions. He gets up to fix himself a sandwich, tinkers with the phonograph, succumbs weak-mindedly to the pages of a magazine, drifts off into an erotic reverie. But a walk, besides preventing such intrusions, unlocks the subconscious in such a way as to allow the writer to feel his mind spilling over with ideas. He is able to carry on the essential dialogue with himself in an atmosphere as intimate as a confessional, though his body hurries onward at three miles an hour. Without a daily walk and the transactions it stimulates in my head, I would face that first page of cold blank paper with pitiful anxiety.

I am lucky to have, in the colder part of the year, a house in the New England countryside, and in the summer a place by the sea. Thus on my walks I am exposed to manifestations of Nature in several of its most seductive moods; the aspects of pleasure and survival I mentioned are connected with being able to walk through serene, lovely, unpolluted landscapes while at the same time feeling throughout my body a diurnal blessing. As any knowledgeable doctor will testify, walking three to six miles or more at a steady pace—fast, energetic, taxing one's self but not to the point of exhaustion—is a motor activity of the most beneficial sort; privately, it is my view that any more arduous form of perambulation (for the middle-aged nonathlete, at least) must be a danger.

A case in point—perhaps more meaningful because this narrative is about warfare, and specifically the Marines—would be my recollection of Major General Brenton Forbes, United States Marine Corps, whose poignantly familiar countenance peered out at me from the top of the obituary page of *The New York Times* one summer morning in the mid-1970s. The face of General Forbes, then in his early fifties and recently photographed (one could see the two stars on his epaulet), was the same face, only slightly larded over by the flesh of maturity, of Private "Brent" Forbes, who had shared with me a double-decker bunk at the Parris Island boot camp in 1944. The magisterially handsome man with the heavy eyebrows and humorous eyes and dimpled chin was the grown-up boy who had been the star recruit and superjock in our college-bred platoon, crack rifle shot and natural leader, inevitably destined to make the Marine Corps his career. It is striking how, if one is at all attentive, one rarely loses sight of the trajectory of the brilliant friends of one's youth, and later I had seen Forbes's name celebrated more than once: during the Korean War, in which as a captain he had won the Medal of Honor, and as a regimental commander in Vietnam, where by way of television one evening I saw, to my exquisite surprise, good old Brent standing beneath the whirling blades of a helicopter, pointing out something on a map to Henry Kissinger. The obituary stunned me—so young, so soon! Now the gorgeous ascent had been arrested close to its zenith, and the commanding general of the First Marine Division, Camp Pendleton, California, had dropped dead, found sprawled on the back lawn of his house in his *jogging clothes*!

I don't mean to mock the dead—a residual part of me admires such a man—but I can't help thinking that a program of walking, not jogging, would have allowed him to be alive today. Besides, there is something about jogging that is too trendy, verging on the effete; certainly it is *un-Marine*. It is inconceivable that an old-time Marine general—Smedley Butler, for instance, that salty old warrior of the early decades of the century—would have ever donned the uniform of a jogger. Walking, yes. Butler was as tough an egg as was ever hatched and—so the chronicles have it—an inveterate walker. Thus one does not visualize him jogging or, God forbid, running; one fancies him, rather, striding purposefully through some Coolidge-era dawn at Quantico or San Diego, thinking important thoughts about the destiny of the Corps, or of Caribbean skirmishes in bygone days, and the tidy machine-gun emplacements, and the bodies of Haitians and Nicaraguans mingled with those of his own beloved marines. Jogging would have appeared to Butler an absurdity, not only because the added exertion is unseemly and unnecessary (and, as we have just seen, sometimes lethal) but because it precludes thinking. Many of history's original and most versatile intellects have been impassioned walkers who, had speedier locomotion appeared to be a desirable adjunct to the idea of *mens sana in corpore sano,* would surely have adopted it, and so it is grotesque to think of Immanuel Kant, Walt Whitman, Einstein, Lincoln, Amiel, Thoreau, Vladimir Nabokov, Emerson, Tolstoy, Matthew Arnold, Wordsworth, Oliver Wendell Holmes, George Gissing, John Burroughs, Samuel Johnson, or Thomas Mann ajog. "Intellectual activity," wrote Nathaniel Hawthorne, "is incompatible with any *large amount* of bodily exercise." The italics are mine, but they could as well have been supplied by Hawthorne, who was a notorious devotee of walking.

But enough of that. Because it may be already apparent, I have not mentioned an aspect of walking that for me, at least, is absolutely essential: one must be alone. There are communal walks that are fun, but I am not referring to these, only to the ones where some sort of creativity can take place. Here a dog may be a welcome exception to the rule of solitude; one's dog—whose physiology prevents it from being a chatterbox—can be a wonderful companion, making no conversational demands while providing an animated connection with one's surroundings. On a walk the writer doesn't want to get so totally absorbed in his thoughts that he loses sight of the countryside; despite the rewarding trancelike periods I have mentioned, one must also enjoy the scenery—otherwise an indoor treadmill would suffice. This is where Aquinnah becomes important to me—important as I am to her, I might add, since her enthusiasm for walking is persistent and obvious, verging on the frantic as she waits for the stroll. The offspring of a black Labrador sire and an incredibly sweet-tempered golden retriever, she acquired her mother's tawny hue plus a large measure of her gentle saintliness, while the paternal genes gave her pluck and boisterousness. At the risk of an absurd anthropomorphism, I must say that the result is a bit like an amalgam of Mother Teresa and Muhammad Ali: moral grandeur and fierce tomfoolery in one beast, with just a touch of the lunacy of each model.

Aquinnah—the name is Wampanoag Indian from Martha's Vineyard—

has been surgically deprived of her capacity for motherhood, and the transformation has made her neither less feminine nor rudely masculine but somehow pleasantly androgynous, mixing all the maddening and beguiling singularities of both sexes: timorousness and reckless courage; an almost feline fastidiousness combined with the gross corruption of a creature whose greatest joy is to dive, sleazily grinning, from a hayloft into a towering pile of cow manure; a docile homebody one day and a swaggering wanderer the next—and so on. I delight in the remarkable variety of Aquinnah's many natures—never more so than on our hundreds of walks together, whether she be trotting ladylike by my side or streaking out across a field for some prey that her nose detects far more quickly and surely than my vision. At that instant, with her caramel hair abristle and her white muzzle glued to the spoor, she appears to my somewhat nearsighted eyes as fierce and as fleet as a lioness of the Serengeti, although I must confess that not once, not a single time, has she tracked down so much as a chipmunk.

[From a manuscript in Styron's papers at Duke University. Composed ca. 1985.]

"In Vineyard Haven"

Once at a summer cocktail party in Menemsha I was asked by a lady: "Where on the island do you live?"

"In Vineyard Haven," I replied.

She suddenly gave me a look that made me feel as if I harbored a communicable disease. "My God," she said, "I didn't think anyone *lived* there."

Well, people do live there, and the moment of the year that I look forward to with unsurpassed anticipation is when I roll the car off the ferry, negotiate the fuss and confusion of the dock area, wheel my way past the homely façade of the A&P, twist around down Main Street with its (let's face it) unprepossessing ranks of mercantile emporiums, and drive northward to the beloved house on the water. On an island celebrated for its scenic glories, Vineyard Haven will never win a contest for beauty or charm; perhaps that's partly why I love it. The ugly duckling gains its place in one's heart by way of an appeal that is not immediately demonstrable. The business district is a little tacky, but why should it be otherwise? It is neither more nor less inspiring than other similar enclaves all across the land. People often think they yearn for quaintness, for stylishness, for architectural harmony; none of these would be appropriate to Vineyard Haven, which thrives on a kind of forthright frowziness. A few years ago, an overly eager land developer—now mercifully departed from the island—was heard proclaiming his desire to transform downtown Vineyard Haven into a "historical" site, similar to the metamorphosis effected by Mr. Beinecke on Nantucket. It is good that this plan came to naught. How silly and dishonest Cronig's Market and Leslie's Drug Store would look wearing the fake trappings of Colonial Williamsburg.

As for residential handsomeness, the good town of Tisbury cannot compete with Edgartown—that stuffy place; even so, had the lady from Menemsha walked along William Street or viewed more closely some of the dwellings lining the harbor, she would have discovered houses of splendid symmetry and grace. She would have also found some of the noblest trees lining the streets of any town its size on the eastern seaboard. It is this loose, amorphous "small townness" that so deeply appeals to me. A large part of the year, I live in a rural area of New England where one must drive for miles to buy a newspaper. The moors of Chilmark and the lush fens of Middle Road then, despite their immense loveliness, do not lure me the way Vineyard Haven does. I like the small-town sidewalks and the kids on bikes and the trespassing gangs of dogs and the morning walk to the post office past the Café du Port, with its warm smell of pastry and coffee. I like the whole barefoot, chattering mêlée of Main Street—even, God help me, the gawping tourists with their Instamatics and their avoirdupois. I like the preposterous gingerbread bank and the local lady shoppers with the Down East accents, discussing bahgins.

Mostly I love the soft collision here of harbor and shore, the subtly haunting briny quality that all small towns have when they are situated on the sea. It is often manifested simply in the *sounds* of the place—sounds unknown to forlorn inland municipalities, even West Tisbury. To the stranger, these sounds might appear distracting, but as a fussy, easily distracted person who has written three large books within earshot of these sounds, I can affirm that they do not annoy at all. Indeed, they lull the mind and soul, these vagrant noises: the blast of the ferry horn—distant, melancholy—and the gentle thrumming of the ferry itself outward bound past the breakwater; the sizzling sound of sailboat hulls as they shear the waves; the luffing of sails and the muffled boom of the yacht club's gun; the eerie wail of the breakwater siren in dense fog; the squabble and cry of gulls. And at night to fall gently asleep to the far-off moaning of the West Chop foghorn. And deep silence save for the faint chink-chinking of halyards against a single mast somewhere in the harbor's darkness.

Vineyard Haven. Sleep. Bliss.

[*New York Times Magazine,* June 15, 1990.]

Acknowledgments

I am grateful to Rose Styron for permission to assemble this collection and to Robert Loomis and Noah Eaker for suggestions about its form and arrangement. Michael V. Carlisle provided valuable assistance and advice throughout.

I thank the curators at the David M. Rubenstein Rare Book & Manuscript Library, Duke University; the Manuscript Division of the Library of Congress; and the Irwin Department of Rare Books and Special Collections, University of South Carolina, for their expertise and courteous service.

Bryant Mangum located an important reference to *The New Yorker*. Ethan Mannon and Bethany Ober Mannon, my research assistants, were most helpful with transcriptions, annotations, and other editorial labors.

J.L.W.W. III

William Styron's Nonfiction:
A Checklist

A: BOOKS

First American editions:

This Quiet Dust and Other Writings. New York: Random House, 1982. xii, 308 pp. Expanded edition, New York: Vintage, 1993. xiv, 354 pp. The expanded edition adds six items and substitutes a later memoir of James Jones for the memoir that appears in the 1982 edition. See Section C below.

Darkness Visible: A Memoir of Madness. New York: Random House, 1990. x, 86 pp.

Havanas in Camelot: Personal Essays. New York: Random House, 2008. x, 166 pp.

B: FIRST-APPEARANCE CONTRIBUTIONS TO BOOKS

Best Short Stories from The Paris Review. New York: E. P. Dutton, 1959. Introduction by Styron. Collected in *This Quiet Dust* (1982), but cited there incorrectly as the article *"The Paris Review"* from the August 1953 issue of *Harper's Bazaar,* the fourth item in Section C below.

The Artists' and Writers' Cookbook, ed. Beryl Barr and Barbara Turner Sachs. Sausalito, Calif.: Contact Editions, 1961. Styron's recipe "Southern Fried Chicken (with Giblet Gravy)."

Under Twenty-five: Duke Narrative and Verse, 1945–1962, ed. William Blackburn. Durham, N.C.: Duke University Press, 1963. Introduction by Styron.

The Four Seasons. University Park: Pennsylvania State University Press, 1965. Boxed set of four etchings by Harold Altman. Introduction by Styron.

Double Exposure. New York: Delacorte, 1966. Photographs by Roddy McDowall. Styron's prose sketch "Lillian Hellman."

Authors Take Sides on Vietnam, ed. Cecil Woolf and John Bagguley. London: Peter Owen, 1967. A statement by Styron appears on p. 70.

Encyclopaedia Britannica. Chicago: William Benton, 1972. Vol. 22 contains Styron's entry for Nat Turner, p. 413.

A Death in Canaan, by Joan Barthel. New York: E. P. Dutton, 1976. Introduction by Styron. Collected in *This Quiet Dust* (1982) as "*A Death in Canaan.*"

William Styron: A Descriptive Bibliography, by James L. W. West III. Boston: G. K. Hall, 1977. Preface by Styron.

Duke Encounters, ed. Elizabeth H. Locke. Durham: Duke University Office of Publications, 1977. Styron's untitled memoir of William Blackburn, pp. 77–80. Collected in *This Quiet Dust* (1982) as "William Blackburn."

Peter Matthiessen: A Bibliography, 1951–1979. Compiled by D. Nicholas. Canoga Park, Calif.: Orirana Press, 1979. Introduction by Styron. Collected in *This Quiet Dust* (1982) as "Peter Matthiessen."

The Wheat and the Chaff, by François Mitterrand. New York: Seaver Books, 1982. Introduction by Styron. Collected in the expanded edition of *This Quiet Dust* (1993) as "François Mitterrand."

Conversations with William Styron. Compiled by James L. W. West III and W. Pierre Jacoebee. Jackson: University Press of Mississippi, 1985. Foreword by Styron.

Donald S. Klopfer: An Appreciation. New York: Random House, 1987. Styron's memoir of Klopfer. Privately printed.

The View from Space: American Astronaut Photography, 1962–1972, by Ron Schick and Julia Van Haaften. New York: C. N. Potter, 1988. Foreword by Styron.

The Human Experience: Contemporary American and Soviet Fiction and Poetry. New York: Knopf, 1989. Foreword by Styron.

William Styron's Sophie's Choice: Crime and Self-Punishment, by Rhoda Sirlin. Ann Arbor: UMI Research Press, 1990. Foreword by Styron.

To Reach Eternity: The Letters of James Jones, ed. George Hendrick. New York: Random House, 1989. Foreword by Styron. Collected in the expanded edition of *This Quiet Dust* (1993), where it replaces an earlier memoir of Jones from *New York,* June 6, 1977, which is listed in Section C below.

Doing Justice: A Trial Judge at Work, by Robert Satter. New York: Simon & Schuster, 1990. Introduction by Styron.

Arthur Miller and Company, ed. Christopher Bigsby. Norwich, England: Arthur Miller Centre for American Studies, 1990. Styron's sketch of Miller. Collected in *My Generation* (2015) as "My Neighbor Arthur."

Writers at Work: The Paris Review Interviews, Ninth Series, ed. George Plimpton. New York: Viking Press, 1992. Introduction by Styron.

Writers Dreaming: 25 Writers Talk About Their Dreams and the Creative Process, ed. Naomi Epel. New York: Carol Southern Books, 1993. Styron's contribution is on pp. 270–79.

No Beast So Fierce, by Edward Bunker. New York: Vintage Crime/Black Lizard Books, 1993. Introduction by Styron.

The Face of Mercy: A Photographic History of Medicine at War, by Matthew Naythons. New York: Random House, 1993. Prologue by Styron.

Fathers and Daughters, by Mariana Cook. Photographs. San Francisco: Chronicle Books, 1994. Introduction by Styron. Collected in *My Generation* (2015) as "My Daughters."

Dying Without God: François Mitterrand's Meditations on Living and Dying, by Franz-Olivier Giesbert. New York: Arcade, 1998. Introduction by Styron.

Dead Run: The Untold Story of Dennis Stockton and America's Only Mass Escape from Death Row, by Joe Jackson and William F. Burke, Jr. New York: Times Books, 1999. Introduction by Styron.

The Education of a Felon: A Memoir, by Edward Bunker. New York: St. Martin's Press, 2000. Introduction by Styron.

Novel History: Historians and Novelists Confront America's Past (and Each Other), ed. Marc C. Carnes. New York: Simon & Schuster, 2001. Includes an exchange between Styron and Eugene D. Genovese. Styron's contribution is titled "More Confessions."

Farewell, Godspeed: The Greatest Eulogies of Our Time, ed. Cyrus M. Copeland. New York: Harmony Books, 2003. Includes Styron's eulogy for Lillian Hellman. Collected in *My Generation* (2015) as "Lillian's Bosom."

C: NONFICTION IN PERIODICALS AND NEWSPAPERS

"William Styron," *New York Herald Tribune Book Review,* October 7, 1951, p. 26. Autobiographical sketch. Collected in *My Generation* (2015) as "Autobiographical."

"Letter to an Editor," *Paris Review* 1 (Spring 1953), 9–13. Statement of purpose for the journal. Collected in *My Generation* (2015).

"The Prevalence of Wonders," *Nation,* May 2, 1953, pp. 370–71. Contribution to a symposium on creativity. Collected in *My Generation* (2015).

"*The Paris Review,*" *Harper's Bazaar* 87 (August 1953), 122–23, 173. On the founding of the journal.

"Novel, Far From Dead, Is Very Much Alive," *Richmond Times-Dispatch,* November 29, 1953, p. 14. On the future of novel-writing.

"If You Write for Television . . . ," *New Republic* 140 (April 6, 1959), 16. On the TV version of *The Long March.* Collected in *My Generation* (2015).

"Mrs. Aadland's Little Girl, Beverly," *Esquire,* November 1961, pp. 142, 189–91. On Florence Aadland and Tedd Thomey, *The Big Love.* Collected in *This Quiet Dust* (1982) as "*The Big Love.*"

"The Death-in-Life of Benjamin Reid," *Esquire,* February 1962, pp. 114, 141–45. Collected in *This Quiet Dust* (1982).

"As He Lay Dead, a Bitter Grief," *Life,* July 20, 1962, pp. 39–42. On William Faulkner's funeral. Collected in *This Quiet Dust* (1982) as "William Faulkner."

"The Aftermath of Benjamin Reid," *Esquire,* November 1962, p. 79 ff. On capital punishment. Collected in *This Quiet Dust* (1982) as "Benjamin Reid: Aftermath."

"New Editions," *New York Review of Books,* Inaugural Issue, February 1963, p. 43. Review of Frank Tannenbaum, *Slave and Citizen: The Negro in the Americas.* Collected in *This Quiet Dust* (1982) as "*Slave and Citizen.*"

"Overcome," *New York Review of Books,* September 26, 1963, pp. 18–19. Review of Herbert Aptheker, *American Negro Slave Revolts.* Collected in *My Generation* (2015).

"An Elegy for F. Scott Fitzgerald," *New York Review of Books,* November 28, 1963, pp. 1–3. Review of Andrew Turnbull, ed., *The Letters of F. Scott Fitzgerald.* Collected in *This Quiet Dust* (1982).

"The Habit," *New York Review of Books,* December 26, 1963, pp. 13–14. Review of *The Consumers Union Report on Smoking and the Public Interest.* Collected in *This Quiet Dust* (1982).

"A Southern Conscience," *New York Review of Books* 2 (April 2, 1964), p. 3. Book review of Lewis H. Blair, *A Southern Prophecy.* Collected in *This Quiet Dust* (1982).

"MacArthur," *New York Review of Books,* October 8, 1964, p. 305. Review of Douglas MacArthur, *Reminiscences.* Collected in *This Quiet Dust* (1982).

"Tootsie Rolls," *New York Review of Books,* May 14, 1964, pp. 8–9. Review of Terry

Southern and Mason Hoffenberg, *Candy.* Collected in *This Quiet Dust* (1982) as "*Candy.*"

"This Quiet Dust," *Harper's Magazine* 230 (April 1965), 135–46. On the Nat Turner Rebellion. Collected in *This Quiet Dust* (1982).

"'John Fitzgerald Kennedy . . . As We Remember Him,'" *High Fidelity* 16 (January 1966), 38, 40. Review of a book/record set, *John Fitzgerald Kennedy . . . As We Remember Him,* Columbia L2L 1017.

"The Vice That Has No Name," *Harper's Magazine* 236 (February 1968), 97–100. Review of B. G. Jefferis and J. L. Nichols, *Light on Dark Corners.*

"The Shade of Thomas Wolfe," *Harper's Magazine* 236 (April 1968), 96, 98–104. Review of Andrew Turnbull, *Thomas Wolfe.* Collected in *This Quiet Dust* (1982) as "'O Lost!' Etc."

"William Styron Replies," *Nation* 206 (April 22, 1968), 544–47. Essay-length letter replying to charges by Herbert Aptheker relating to Nat Turner.

"The Oldest America," *McCall's* 95 (July 1968), 94, 123. On the Virginia Tidewater region. Collected in *This Quiet Dust* (1982).

"In the Jungle," *New York Review of Books,* September 26, 1968, pp. 11–13. On the 1968 Democratic National Convention, Chicago. Collected in *This Quiet Dust* (1982) as "Chicago: 1968."

"My Generation," *Esquire,* October 1968, pp. 123–24. On writers of his generation. Collected in *My Generation* (2015).

"On Creativity," *Playboy* 15 (December 1968), 136–39. Symposium. Styron's contribution is on p. 138.

"Acceptance by Mr. Styron," *Proceedings of the American Academy of Arts and Letters and the National Institute of Arts and Letters,* 2nd series, no. 21 (1971), pp. 30–32. Styron's acceptance speech for the Howells Medal for Fiction, awarded May 26, 1970, for *The Confessions of Nat Turner.* Collected in *My Generation* (2015) as "Acceptance."

Untitled review of James Blake, *The Joint, New York Times Book Review,* April 25, 1971, pp. 1, 10, 12. Collected in *This Quiet Dust* (1982) as "*The Joint.*"

Untitled review of two books: Richard Hammer, *The Court-Martial of Lt. Calley,* and John Sack, *Lieutenant Calley: His Own Story, New York Times Book Review,* September 12, 1971, pp. 1 ff. Collected in *This Quiet Dust* (1982) as "Calley."

"The Red Badge of Literature," *Washington Monthly* 4 (March 1972), 32–34. Review of Ronald J. Glasser, *365 Days.* Collected in *This Quiet Dust* (1982).

Untitled review of Neil Sheehan, *The Arnheiter Affair, American Scholar* 41 (Summer 1972), 487–90. Collected in *This Quiet Dust* (1982) as "Arnheiter."

Untitled review of Malcolm Cowley, *A Second Flowering: Works and Days of the Lost Generation, New York Times Book Review,* May 6, 1973, pp. 8 ff. Collected in *This Quiet Dust* (1982) as "*A Second Flowering.*"

"The End of the World, in 20 Words or Less," *Yale Daily News Magazine,* April 17, 1974, pp. 18–21. Facsimile of a Styron letter.

"Auschwitz's Message," *New York Times,* June 25, 1974, p. 37. Op-ed. Collected in *This Quiet Dust* (1982) as "Auschwitz."

"William Styron's Afterword to *The Long March,*" *Mississippi Quarterly* 28 (Spring 1975), 185–89. Afterword to the Norwegian edition of *The Long March.* Collected in *This Quiet Dust* (1982) as "*The Long March.*"

"Presentation to Thomas Pynchon of the Howells Medal for Fiction of the Academy," *Proceedings of the American Academy of Arts and Letters and the National Institute*

of Arts and Letters, 2nd series, no. 26 (1976), pp. 43–46. Styron's speech on presenting the medal to Pynchon for *Gravity's Rainbow.*

"Fie on Bliss, and You Too, F.A.O. Schwarz," *Potomac,* December 19, 1976, pp. 13,
44–45. On Christmas celebrations. Collected in *My Generation* (2015) as "Fie on
Bliss."

"A Friend's Farewell to James Jones," *New York,* June 6, 1977, pp. 40-41. Memoir of
Jones. Collected in the 1982 edition of *This Quiet Dust* as "James Jones." Replaced
with a different reminiscence of Jones in the 1993 expanded edition.

"A Farewell to Arms," *New York Review of Books,* June 23, 1977, pp. 3–6. Review of
Philip Caputo, *A Rumor of War.* Collected in *This Quiet Dust* (1982).

"Hell Reconsidered," *New York Review of Books,* June 29, 1978, pp. 10–14. Review of
Richard Rubenstein, *The Cunning of History.* Collected in *This Quiet Dust* (1982).

"Almost a Rhodes Scholar," *South Atlantic Bulletin* 45 (May 1980), 1–7. Memoir. Collected in *This Quiet Dust* (1982).

"Perennial Fear," *New York Times,* June 7, 1981, p. 21. On warfare.

"Honored Virginian Honors Virginia," *Newport News Times-Herald,* July 18, 1981, p. 7.
Acceptance speech for the Virginian of the Year award.

"A Leader Who Prefers Writers to Politicians," *Boston Globe,* July 26, 1981, pp. A21, 24.
On the inauguration of Mitterrand. Collected in *Havanas in Camelot* (2008) as "*Les
Amis du Président.*"

"In the Southern Camp," *New York Review of Books,* August 13, 1981, pp. 24–26. Review of C. Vann Woodward, ed., *Mary Chesnut's Civil War.* Collected in *This Quiet
Dust* (1982).

"William Styron's Nile Diary," *Geo* 3 (September 1981), 10–24. Travel. Collected in *This
Quiet Dust* (1982) as "Down the Nile."

"Recollections," *Hartford Courant Magazine,* January 3, 1982, pp. 4–9. On the composition of *Lie Down in Darkness.* Collected in *This Quiet Dust* (1982) as "*Lie Down in
Darkness.*"

"The Short Classy Voyage of JFK," *Esquire,* December 1983, pp. 124 ff. Memoir.

"Children of a Brief Sunshine," *Architectural Digest,* March 1984, pp. 32 ff. Reflections
on Shirley, the antebellum Virginia mansion on the James River. Collected in *My
Generation* (2015).

"Historic Houses: Thomas Wolfe Remembered," *Architectural Digest,* October 1984,
pp. 194–200. On Wolfe's childhood home in Asheville, N.C.

"In Celebration of Capote," *Vanity Fair,* December 1984, pp. 120–22. Memoir. Collected in *Havanas in Camelot* (2008) as "Celebrating Capote."

"Cigarette Ads and the Press," *Nation,* March 7, 1987, pp. 283 ff. On advertisements for
tobacco products. Collected in *My Generation* (2015).

"Death Row," *New York Times,* May 10, 1987, p. 25E. Op-ed, on Shabaka Sundiata
Waglini. Reprinted *New York Times,* September 30, 1990, sect. 4A, p. 2. Collected
in the expanded edition of *This Quiet Dust* (1993).

"Virginia Foster Durr," *Esquire,* June 1987, p. 161. Appreciation.

"Jimmy in the House," *New York Times Book Review,* December 20, 1987, p. 30. Memoir. Collected in *Havanas in Camelot* (2008).

"Family Album," *Paris Review,* Spring 1988, pp. 269–87. Photographs with commentary.

"Farbar: The Crime and the Punishment," *Esquire,* September 1988, p. 154. Article
about Buzz Farbar.

"International Books of the Year," *Times Literary Supplement,* December 2–8, 1988, p.
1342. Praise for Roy Gutman, *Banana Diplomacy.*

"Why Primo Levi Need Not Have Died," *New York Times,* December 19, 1988, p. A17. Op-ed. Collected in the expanded edition of *This Quiet Dust* (1993).

"A Literary Friendship," *Esquire,* April 1989, pp. 154 ff. Memoir of James Jones. Reprinted as the foreword to *To Reach Eternity* (1989). See Section B. Collected in the 1993 expanded edition of *This Quiet Dust* as "James Jones," where it replaces a 1977 memoir of Jones listed above.

"The Distant Shaw," *Vanity Fair,* August 1989, pp. 48 ff. Memoir of Irwin Shaw. Collected in *My Generation* (2015); a shortened version of the *Vanity Fair* text follows Styron's original beginning, published for the first time.

"A Voice from the South," *Sewanee Review* 97 (Fall 1989), 512–24. Memoir of Styron's paternal grandmother. Collected in the expanded edition of *This Quiet Dust* (1993).

"Darkness Visible," *Vanity Fair,* December 1989, pp. 212 ff. The initial version of Styron's memoir of depression, later expanded for book publication.

"In Praise of Vineyard Haven," *New York Times Magazine,* June 15, 1990, p. 30. On Styron's summer home. Collected in *Havanas in Camelot* (2008) as " 'In Vineyard Haven.' "

"Presentation to E. L. Doctorow of the Howells Medal," *Proceedings of the American Academy and National Institute of Arts and Letters,* 2nd series, no. 41 (1990). Styron's speech on presenting the medal to Doctorow for *Billy Bathgate.*

"Dear Dirty Dublin: My Joycean Trek with Philip Roth," *New York Times Book Review,* June 9, 1991, p. 9. Remarks on presenting the National Arts Club Medal of Honor for Literature to Roth.

"We Weren't in It for the Money," *Washington Post,* July 16, 1991, p. A19. Styron's account of his service as a judge for the Turner Tomorrow Award. Collected in *My Generation* (2015).

"The Wreckage of an American War," *New York Times Book Review,* July 16, 1991, p. 71. Review of Lewis B. Puller, *Fortunate Son.* Collected in the expanded edition of *This Quiet Dust* (1993).

"On William Blackburn and Creative Imagination," *Duke Dialogue,* September 13, 1991. On his college mentor.

"The Little Pills That Depress," *Newsday,* July 31, 1991. Adapted from a speech on depression.

"Nat Turner Revisited," *American Heritage* 42 (October 1992), 64–73. On the controversy over *The Confessions of Nat Turner.* Collected in *My Generation* (2015).

"Prozac Days, Halcion Nights," *Nation* 256 (January 4/11,1993), pp. 1 ff. On the Upjohn company. Collected in *My Generation* (2015).

"The Enduring Metaphors of Auschwitz and Hiroshima," *Newsweek,* January 11, 1993, pp. 28–29. On the aftermath of World War II. A longer version, from the surviving typescript, collected in *My Generation* (2015) as "Auschwitz and Hiroshima."

" 'An Interior Pain That Is All but Indescribable,' " *Newsweek,* April 18, 1994, pp. 52–53. On depression. Collected in *My Generation* (2015) as "Interior Pain."

"Slavery's Pain, Disney's Gain," *New York Times,* August 4, 1994, p. A23. Op-ed on Disney's plans for a Civil War theme park. Collected in *Havanas in Camelot* (2008).

"Too Big for Disney," *Washington Post,* August 16, 1994, p. A19. On the proposed Disney theme park.

Untitled statement by Styron about *Brown v. Board of Education, American Heritage* 45 (December 1994), 84.

" 'I'll Have to Ask Indianapolis—' " *Traces* (Indiana Historical Society) 7 (Spring 1995),

5–12. On the expurgation of *Lie Down in Darkness* in 1951. Collected in *Havanas in Camelot* (2008).

Untitled statement about *Adventures of Huckleberry Finn, New Yorker,* June 26–July 3, 1995, pp. 132–33. A longer version, from the surviving typescript, is collected in *Havanas in Camelot* (2008) as "A Literary Forefather."

"The Writer in a Mean and Dogmatic Time," *Confrontation: A Literary Journal of Long Island University* 56/57 (Summer/Fall 1995), 15–20. Acceptance speech for the 27th Annual Literary Award of the National Arts Club, New York City, delivered February 1, 1995.

"Last-Minute Pleas," *New Yorker,* August 14, 1995, p. 26. Statement on Mumia Abu-Jamal.

"The Book on *Lolita*," *New Yorker,* September 4, 1995, p. 33. On the rejection of *Lolita* at Random House. Collected in *My Generation* (2015).

"A Case of the Great Pox," *New Yorker,* September 18, 1995, pp. 62–75. Memoir. Collected in *Havanas in Camelot* (2008).

"A Horrid Little Racist," *New York Times Magazine,* October 8, 1995, pp. 80–81. Memoir. Styron's title in the surviving MS is "A Youthful Transgression."

"Transcontinental with Tex," *Paris Review,* Spring 1996, pp. 215–26. Memoir of Terry Southern. Collected in *Havanas in Camelot* (2008).

"Havanas in Camelot," *Vanity Fair,* July 1996, pp. 32–41. Memoir of John F. Kennedy. Collected in *Havanas in Camelot* (2008).

"Nat Turner Turns 30," *Boston Globe,* April 13, 1997, p. D1. On the novel and its history of controversy.

"Fifty Years of Literary Friendship," *At Random,* no. 17 (Spring/Summer 1997), 3. Memoir of his friendship with Robert Loomis, his editor at Random House. Collected in *My Generation* (2015) as "Bob Loomis."

"A Wheel of Evil Come Full Circle: The Making of *Sophie's Choice*," *Sewanee Review* 105 (Summer 1997), 395–400. Account of a friendship with Hannah Arendt and of the composition of the novel. Collected in *My Generation* (2015).

"A Modern Library Juror Fesses Up," *New Yorker,* August 17, 1998, pp. 29–30. On an end-of-the-century literary contest. Collected in *Havanas in Camelot* (2008) as "Fessing Up."

"American Dreamers," *George,* August 1998, p. 76. Introduction by Styron: statements by others about various American citizens.

Untitled comment on the Bill Clinton/Monica Lewinsky scandal, *New Yorker,* October 12, 1998, p. 10. Collected in *My Generation* (2015) in a longer version, from the manuscript, titled "Clinton and the Puritans."

"It Cannot Be Long: Remembering a Friend," *Oxford American,* September/October 1999, p. 111. Memoir of Willie Morris. Collected in *My Generation* (2015).

"C. Vann Woodward: 1908–1999," *Proceedings of the American Academy of Arts and Letters* 51 (2000), 92–95. Memoir. Collected in *My Generation* (2015).

"Why Great Fiction Will Never Die," *MacDowell Colony Newsletter* 30 (Winter/Spring 2002), 3–7. Speech on the occasion of presenting the MacDowell Medal to Philip Roth. Collected in *My Generation* (2015) as "The Contumacious Mr. Roth."

Notes

APPRENTICESHIP

The Prevalence of Wonders

1. The essay appears in Bell's *Art* (London: Chatto & Windus, 1914).
2. T. S. Eliot, "Burbank with a Baedeker: Bleistein with a Cigar" (1920).

RACE AND SLAVERY

A Southern Conscience

1. Whitney Balliett, "Books: Finis," *New Yorker*, March 30, 1963, pp. 174–77.

Overcome

1. The essay by Baldwin is "Letter from a Region in My Mind," published in *The New Yorker* for November 17, 1962; collected as "Down at the Cross" in Baldwin's *The Fire Next Time*.
2. Ulrich B. Phillips, *Life and Labor in the Old South* (1929); Gunnar Myrdal, *An American Dilemma: The Negro Problem and Modern Democracy* (1944).

Our Common History

1. Quoted in Raymond A. Sokolov, "Into the Mind of Nat Turner," *Newsweek*, October 16, 1967, p. 69.

In the Southern Camp

1. Kenneth S. Lynn, "The Masterpiece That Became a Hoax," *New York Times Book Review*, April 26, 1981, p. 9.

Nat Turner Revisited

1. C. Vann Woodward, "Confessions of a Rebel: 1831," *New Republic,* October 7, 1967, pp. 25–28.
2. *American Quarterly* 23 (October 1971), 486–518.
3. *New York Times Book Review,* June 3, 1984, sec. 7, p. 47.
4. Martin Duberman, "Historical Fictions, *New York Times Book Review,* August 11, 1968, pp. 1, 26–27. Eliot Fremont-Smith, "Nat Turner I: The Controversy," and "Nat Turner II: What Myth Will Serve?" *New York Times,* August 1 and 2, 1968, pp. 29, 31.
5. Genovese, "The Nat Turner Case," *New York Review of Books,* September 12, 1968, pp. 34–37.
6. *Ascension Day,* play by Michael Henry Brown, reviewed by Mel Gussow in *New York Times,* March 4, 1992, p. C19.
7. Baldwin, from "Here Be Dragons" (1985), in *The Price of the Ticket: Collected Nonfiction, 1948–1985* (New York: St. Martin's Press, 1985), p. 690.

FINAL SOLUTIONS

Auschwitz

1. The symposium was held on June 3–6, 1974, with much coverage in newspapers and other media. The proceedings, edited by Eva Fleischner, were later published by Ktav Publishing House as *Auschwitz: Beginning of a New Era? Reflections on the Holocaust* (1977).

Auschwitz and Hiroshima

1. *Judgment at the Smithsonian,* ed. Philip Nobile, afterword by Barton J. Bernstein (New York: Marlowe, n.d.).
2. "Hiroshima: Why the Bomb Was Dropped," ABC broadcast, July 27, 1995.
3. McGeorge Bundy, *Danger and Survival: Choices About the Bomb in the First Fifty Years* (New York: Random House, 1988), p. 64.
4. Buruma's essay is collected in *The Missionary and the Libertine: Love and War in East and West* (New York: Random House, 2000).
5. Gavan Daws, *Prisoners of the Japanese: POWs of World War II in the Pacific* (New York: William Morrow, 1994).

A Wheel of Evil Come Full Circle

1. "Trivializing Memory," in Elie Wiesel, *From the Kingdom of Memory: Reminiscences* (New York: Summit, 1990), 166.

DISORDERS OF THE MIND

Why Primo Levi Need Not Have Died

1. Stewart Kellerman, "Shadow of Auschwitz on Primo Levi's Life," *New York Times,* November 26, 1988, pp. 1–4.
2. *New Yorker,* May 11, 1987, p. 2.

Prozac Days, Halcion Nights

1. "Jury Partly Blames Sleeping Pill in a Murder," *New York Times,* November 13, 1992, p. A20.
2. See Roth's "Roth on the Record" (letter to the editor), *Atlantic,* June 2012, p. 14.

PRISONERS

The Death-in-Life of Benjamin Reid

1. Chessman (b. 1921) was convicted of robbery, kidnapping, and rape in 1948 and was sentenced to death. Acting as his own attorney, he avoided eight execution deadlines; in published letters, essays, and books he argued for his innocence and sparked a national debate about capital punishment. He died in the gas chamber at San Quentin on May 2, 1960.

A Death in Canaan

1. Joan Barthel, "Did Peter Reilly Murder His Mother?" *New Times,* February 8, 1974, p. 20.
2. John Corry, "Arthur Miller Turns Detective in Murder," *New York Times,* December 15, 1975, p. 46.

PRESIDENTIAL

Havanas in Camelot

1. Alfred Kazin, "The President and Other Intellectuals," *American Scholar* 30 (Autumn 1961), 498–516.

Clinton and the Puritans

1. *Wall Street Journal,* September 14, 1998.

LITERARY

We Weren't in It for the Money

1. Jonathan Yardley, "Literary Lions and the Tame Turner Award," *Washington Post* (Style section), June 17, 1991.
2. Daniel Quinn, *Ishmael* (New York: Bantam/Turner, 1992).
3. See Edwin McDowell, "Judges in Turner Award Dispute Merits of Novel Given a $500,000 Prize," *New York Times,* June 5, 1991.

ANTECEDENTS

"O Lost!" Etc.

1. Bernard DeVoto, "Genius Is Not Enough," *Saturday Review of Literature,* April 25, 1936, pp. 3–4, 14–15.

FRIENDS AND CONTEMPORARIES

My Generation

1. Hollander, *Poems of Our Moment* (New York: Pegasus, 1968), p. 20.

Big Jim

1. Dickey's eulogy for Capote was published in the *Proceedings of the American Academy and Institute of Arts and Letters,* 2nd series, no. 35 (May 16, 1984).

CRUSADES, COMPLAINTS, GRIPES

If You Write for Television . . .

1. Pierson, "The Censorship of Television," 2 parts, *New Republic,* March 23 and 30, 1959.

Cigarette Ads and the Press

1. *Smoking and Health* (1964), and *The Health Consequences of Smoking* (1967).

Index

WILLIAM STYRON (1925–2006), a native of the Virginia Tidewater, was a graduate of Duke University and a veteran of the U.S. Marine Corps. His books include *Lie Down in Darkness, The Long March, Set This House on Fire, The Confessions of Nat Turner, Sophie's Choice, This Quiet Dust, Darkness Visible, A Tidewater Morning,* and *Havanas in Camelot.* He was awarded the Pulitzer Prize for Fiction, the Howells Medal, the American Book Award, and the Légion d'Honneur. With his wife, the poet and activist Rose Styron, he lived for most of his life in Roxbury, Connecticut, and Vineyard Haven, Massachusetts, where he is buried.

JAMES L. W. WEST III is an Edwin Erle Sparks Professor of English at Pennsylvania State University. He is the author of *William Styron: A Life* (1998) and the editor of Styron's *Letters to My Father* (2009). West is the general editor of the ongoing Cambridge Edition of the Works of F. Scott Fitzgerald.

ABOUT THE TYPE

This book was set in Caledonia, a typeface designed in 1939 by W. A. Dwiggins (1880–1956) for the Merganthaler Linotype Company. Its name is the ancient Roman term for Scotland, because the face was intended to have a Scottish-Roman flavor. Caledonia is considered to be a well-proportioned, businesslike face with little contrast between its thick and thin lines.